Web-Based Training

Web-Based Training

Badrul H. Khan
EDITOR

Educational Technology Publications
Englewood Cliffs, New Jersey 07632

Note: All Website addresses in this volume appear without: http://www.

Library of Congress Cataloging-in-Publication Data

Web-based training / Badrul H. Khan, editor.
  p. cm.
  Includes bibliographical references and indexes.
  ISBN 0–87778–302–0 (clothbound)—ISBN 0–87778–303–9 (softcover)
  1. Employees—Training of—Computer-assisted instruction.
2. Web sites—Design. 3. World Wide Web. I. Khan, Badrul Huda.
HF5549.5.T7 W384   2001
658.3′124′02854678—dc21   00–051384
                                                              CIP

Printed in the United States of America.

Library of Congress Catalog Card Number:
00–051384.

International Standard Book Numbers:
0–87778–302–0 (hardcover).
0–87778–303–9 (softcover).

First Printing: January, 2001.

This book is dedicated to my late parents:

Mr. Lokman Khan Sherwani &
Mrs. Shabnom Khanam Sherwani
of
Khan Manzil, Pathantooly, Chittagong, Bangladesh

Acknowledgments

I wish to express my appreciation to the authors of the chapters included in this volume. I would like to thank Lawrence Lipsitz and the staff of Educational Technology Publications for their editorial assistance. Finally, I would like to thank my wife, Komar Khan, and my sons, Intisar Khan and Inshat Khan; my brothers, Kamrul H. Khan, Manzurul H. Khan, and Nazrul H. Khan; and my sisters, Nasima Zaman and Akhtar Janhan Khanam, and my cousin, Dr. Mahmudul Alam, for their continued support and encouragement. I would like to thank all my nieces and nephews for their support as well.

Preface

Advances in information technology, coupled with changes in society, are creating new paradigms for education and training. These massive changes have tremendous impact on our educational and training systems. Participants, from the perspective of this educational and training paradigm, require rich learning environments supported by well-designed resources. They expect on-demand, anytime/anywhere high-quality instruction with good support services. To stay viable in this global, competitive market, providers of education and training must develop efficient and effective learning systems to meet society's needs. Therefore, there is a tremendous demand for affordable, efficient, easily accessible, open, flexible, well-designed, learner-centered, distributed, and facilitated learning environments. Corporations, government agencies, educational institutions, and other organizations worldwide are increasingly using the Web to deliver instruction and training. Web-based training (WBT) is becoming an increasingly prevalent method for delivering training. At all levels of these institutions, employees and students are being encouraged to participate in online learning activities.

Web-Based Training (WBT) systems deal with open, flexible, and distributed learning environments. Design, development, implementation, and evaluation of open, flexible learning systems is a new experience to many trainers and educators. Design, development, implementation, and evaluation of open, flexible learning systems require thoughtful analysis and investigation of how to use the Web's potential in concert with instructional design principles and issues important to various dimensions of online learning environments. Therefore, WBT is a very challenging task. Considering the newness of the WBT field, no one author can give a total perspective of Web-based training. This book is a compendium of original thought and issues concerning various dimensions of Web-based training by renowned researchers and practitioners from around the globe.

The purpose of this book is to provide readers with information related to design, development, delivery, management, implementation, and evaluation aspects of WBT. The book is divided into three main Sections—Section I: Web-Based Training: Introduction; Section II: Web-Based Training: Design and Development Perspectives; and Section III: Web-Based Training: Implementation and Evaluation Perspectives. The book, containing 63 chapters, contributed by more than one hundred authors from throughout the world, explains how to use the Internet's World Wide Web for training in corporations, government agencies, and educational institutions.

Please note that this is an edited book, and the insights presented reflect both richness and diversity. The contributors offer a variety of points of view on various aspects of Web-based training. Each perspective is unique. Therefore, opinions expressed by authors in their chapters may differ from one another on the same issues. As an editor, I have tried to foster this diversity of opinions so that readers could get multiple perspectives. It is not a cookbook. This book covers various ideas, concepts, and philosophies about Web-based training which I believe will help us to create our own customized cookbooks by reflecting on both the breadth of Web-based training issues and the depth of challenges in designing meaningful WBT.

Finally, I hope that chapters included in this book will help readers to understand all aspects of Web-based training. We have provided authors' e-mail addresses and Websites at the end of each chapter. Readers are encouraged to contact authors to inquire about any changes in URLs or any other chapter-relevant information. We maintain a Website (BooksTo Read.com/wbt/update.htm) which will update any change of addresses for chapter-related Websites and other corrections. I would appreciate hearing your comments regarding this book.

Badrul H. Khan
BadrulKhan@BadrulKhan.com

Table of Contents

SECTION III
WEB-BASED TRAINING:
IMPLEMENTATION AND EVALUATION PERSPECTIVES

Web-Based Training

SECTION I
Web-Based Training: Introduction

1

Web-Based Training: An Introduction

Badrul H. Khan

Advances in information technology, coupled with the changes in society, have created a new paradigm for training. Participants, from the perspective of this new training paradigm, require rich learning environments supported by well-designed resources (Reigeluth & Khan, 1994). New developments in learning science and technology provide opportunities to create well-designed, learner-centered, engaging, interactive, affordable, efficient, easily accessible, flexible, meaningful, distributed, and facilitated learning environments. To meet the needs of distributed learning environments, corporations, government agencies, and universities worldwide are increasingly using the Web to deliver instruction and training. At all levels of these institutions, employees and learners are being encouraged to participate in on-line learning activities.

Designing and delivering instruction on the Web requires thoughtful analysis and investigation of how to use the Web's potential in concert with instructional design principles (Ritchie & Hoffman, 1997) and issues critical to various dimensions of Web-based learning environments, including pedagogical, technological, interface design, evaluation, management, resource support, ethical, and institutional (Khan, 2001). Therefore, *Web-based training (WBT) can be viewed as an innovative approach for delivering hypermedia-based instructional programs to a remote audience by utilizing the attributes and resources of the Web to create well-designed, learner-centered, interactive, engaging, and facilitated learning environments.*

In designing training on the Web, we should explore various issues encompassing the eight dimensions of the Web-based learning environment (for detailed discussion, see Chapter 8) that can help us think about various learning features appropriate for our target audience. The capabilities of various attributes and resources of the Web must be examined to see how they can be best utilized to create WBT learning features.

In this chapter, a WBT program is discussed in terms of components and features that can be conducive to learning environments. *Components* are integral parts of a WBT system. *Features* are characteristics of a WBT program contributed by those components. Components, individually and jointly, can contribute to one or more features (Khan, 1997). For example, *e-mail* (component) in a WBT program can provide *asynchronous communication* (feature) to students and the instructor. Likewise *e-mail, listservs, newsgroups, conferencing tools, etc.* (components) can jointly contribute to the creation of a virtual community (feature) on the Web.

WBT Components ⟶ WBT Features

WBT Components

WBT components are clustered into eight general categories. Please note that within the scope of this chapter, it was not possible to discuss the functions of all the various components that might constitute a WBT program. However, several chapters in this book and my edited book entitled *Web-Based Instruction* (1997) address many of these components (please use the book index to locate them). Within the scope of this chapter, WBT components are listed in the following eight categories. As the technology evolves, however, new components may become available to be added to this list.

1. *Content Development*
   - (a) Learning and instructional theories
   - (b) Instructional design (ID)
   - (c) Curriculum development

2. *Multimedia Component*
   - (a) Text and graphics
   - (b) Audio Streaming (e.g., RealAudio)
   - (c) Video Streaming (e.g., QuickTime)
   - (d) Graphical User Interface (GUI)-uses icons, graphics, windows and a pointing device instead of a purely character-mode interface (Tittel & Gaither, 1995) Microsoft Windows and MacOS are examples of GUIs
   - (e) Compression technology (e.g., Shockwave)

3. *Internet Tools*
   - (a) Communications Tools
     - i) Asynchronous: E-mail, Listservs, Newsgroups, etc.
     - ii) Synchronous: Text-based (e.g., Chat, IRC, MUDs, etc.) and audio-video (e.g., Internet Phone, CuSeeMe, etc.) conferencing tools
   - (b) Remote Access Tools (Log in to and transferring files from remote computers)
     - i) Telnet, File Transfer Protocol (ftp), etc.
   - (c) Internet Navigation Tools (Access to databases and Web documents)
     - i) Gopher, Lynx, etc.
   - (d) Search and Other Tools
     - i) Search Engines
     - ii) Counter Tool

4. *Computers and Storage Devices*
   - (a) Computer platforms running Unix, DOS, Windows, and Macintosh operating systems.
   - (b) Servers, hard drives, CD-ROMs, etc.

5. *Connections and Service Providers*
   - (a) Modems

(b) Dial-in (e.g., standard telephone line, ISDN, etc.) and dedicated (e.g., 56kbps, DSL, digital cable modem, T1, E1 lines, etc.) services (whatis.com/dsl.htm)

(c) Gateway Service Provider, Internet Service Provider, etc.

6. *Authoring Programs*

(a) Programming languages (e.g., HTML—Hypertext Markup Language, VRML—Virtual Reality Modeling Language, Java, Java scripting, etc.)

(b) HTML Converters and Editors, etc.

(c) Authoring Tools and Systems (easier to use than programming languages)

7. *Servers*

(a) HTTP servers, HTTPD software, Website, URL—Uniform Resource Locator, etc.

(b) Common Gateway Interface (CGI)—a way of interacting with the http or Web servers; CGI enables such things as imagemaps and fill-out forms to be run

8. *Browsers and Other Applications*

(a) Text-based browser, Graphical browser, VRML browser, etc.

(b) Links (e.g., Hypertext links, Hypermedia links, 3-D links, imagemaps, etc.)

(c) Applications that can be added to Web browsers such as plug-ins

WBT Features

A WBT program can provide numerous features conducive to learning. These features can encompass various dimensions of Web-based learning environment, including: pedagogical, technological, interface design, evaluation, management, resource support, ethical, and institutional (Khan, 2000). For an example, *ease of use* is a WBT feature, and it encompasses critical issues in all eight dimensions of the framework, such as "does the course provide clear directions of what learners should do at every stage of the course?" *(pedagogical);* "do users receive any guidance on how to print within Webpage frames?" *(technological);* "how quickly can users find answers to the most frequently asked questions on the course site?" *(interface design);* "does the course use an instant feedback button on most screens/pages in order to receive learners' feedback for improvement of the course?" *(evaluation);* "does the course notify students about any changes in due dates or other course relevant matters such as server down?" *(management);* "does the course provide clear guidelines to the learners on what support can and cannot be expected from a help line?" *(resource support);* "does the course make an effort to reduce or avoid the use of jargon, idioms, ambiguous or cute humor, and acronyms?" *(ethical);* and "are instructor/tutor and technical staff available during online orientation?" *(institutional).* I believe learners will find a WBT program *easy to use* if it addresses such issues as mentioned. Therefore, WBT designers should explore as many issues within the eight dimensions of the Web-based learning environment in order for each learning feature to be effective.

There are many features that can be included in WBT. Some of these features are: ease of use, interactivity, cross-cultural interaction, multiple expertise, industry supported, learner-controlled, convenient, self contained, online support, authentic, course security, environmentally friendly, non-discriminatory, cost-effective, collaborative, formal and informal environments, online evaluation, virtual cultures, etc. Within the scope of this chapter, several WBT learning features (encompassing various dimensions of Web-based learning environment) that are contributed by WBT components are presented in Table 1. For further exploration of other features, read Khan (1997).

Table 1. Features and components associated with WBT learning environments.

WBT Features	Web-Based Learning Dimensions								WBT Components	Relationship to WBT
	Pedagogical	Technological	Interface Design	Evaluation	Management	Resource Support	Ethical	Institutional		
Interactive	✓	✓	✓	✓	✓	✓	✓		Internet tools, hyperlinks, browsers, servers, authoring programs, instructional design, etc.	Interactivity in WBT is one of the most important instructional activities. Engagement theory based on online learning emphasizes that students must be meaningfully engaged in learning activities through interaction with others and worthwhile tasks (Kearsley & Shneiderman, 1999). WBT students can interact with each other, with instructors, and online resources. Instructors and experts may act as facilitators. They can provide support, feedback, and guidance via both synchronous and asynchronous communications. Asynchronous communication (i.e., e-mail, listservs, etc.) allows for time-independent interaction, whereas synchronous communication (i.e., conferencing tools) allows for live interaction (Khan, 1997).
Ease of Use	✓	✓	✓	✓	✓	✓	✓	✓	A standard point and click navigation system. Common user interface, search engines, browsers, hyperlinks, etc.	A well-designed WBT course with intuitive interfaces can anticipate learners' needs and satisfy the learners' natural curiosity to explore the unknown. This capability can greatly reduce students' frustration levels and facilitate a user-friendly learning environment. However, delays between a learner's mouse click and the response of the system can contribute to the frustration level of users. The hypermedia environment in a WBT course allows learners to explore and discover resources which best suit their individual needs. While this type of environment facilitates learning, it should be noted that learners may lose focus on a topic due to the wide variety of sources that may be available in a WBT course. Also, information may not always be accessed because of common problems related to servers, such as connection refusal, no DNS entry, etc. (Khan, 1997).

Table 1. Features and components *(continued).*

WBT Features	Web-Based Learning Dimensions								WBT Components	Relationship to WBT
	Pedagogical	Technological	Interface Design	Evaluation	Management	Resource Support	Ethical	Institutional		
Learner-Controlled	✓	✓	✓	✓	✓	✓	✓		Internet tools, authoring programs, hyperlinks, instructional design, etc.	The filtered environment of the Web allows students the choice to actively participate in discussion or simply observe in the background. WBT puts students in control so they have a choice of content, time, feedback, and a wide range of media for expressing their understandings (Relan & Gillani, 1997). This facilitates student responsibility and initiative by promoting ownership of learning. The learner-control offered by WBT is beneficial for the inquisitive student, but the risk of becoming lost in the Web and not fulfilling learner expectations can be a problem and will require strong instructional support (Duchastel, 1996).
Collaborative Learning	✓	✓	✓	✓	✓	✓	✓	✓	Internet tools, instructional design, etc.	WBT creates a medium of collaboration, conversation, discussions, exchange, and communication of ideas (Relan & Gillani, 1997). *Collaboration* allows learners to work and learn together to accomplish a common learning goal. In a collaborative environment, learners develop social, communication, critical thinking, leadership, negotiation, interpersonal, and cooperative skills by experiencing multiple perspectives of members of collaborative groups on any problems or issues.
Authentic	✓	✓	✓	✓	✓	✓	✓	✓	Internet and the Web	The conferencing and collaboration technologies of the Web bring learners into contact with authentic learning and apprenticing situations (Bonk & Reynolds, 1997). WBT courses can be designed to promote authentic learning environments by addressing real-world problems and issues relevant to the learner. The most significant aspect of the Web for education at all levels is that it dissolves the artificial wall between the classroom and the 'real world' (Kearsley, 1996).
Multiple Expertise	✓	✓	✓	✓	✓	✓	✓	✓	Internet and the Web	WBT courses can use outside experts to guest lecturers from various fields from all over the world. Experiences and instruction that come directly from the sources and experts represented on the Web can tremendously benefit learners.

Conclusion

WBT design requires exploration of issues critical to various dimensions of Web-based leaning environments, and careful consideration of the Web's potential in relation to instructional design principles. An understanding of capabilities of WBT components and features can facilitate the design of meaningful Web-based learning environments. A well-designed WBT, therefore, has the ability to provide learner-centered, engaging, interactive, affordable, efficient, easily accessible, flexible, meaningful, distributed, and facilitated learning environments.

References and Suggested Readings

Andrews, D. H., & Goodson, L. K. (1980). A comparative analysis of models of instructional design. *Journal of Instructional Development, 3*(4), 2–16.

Bannan, B., & Milheim, W. D. (1997). Existing Web-based instruction courses and their design. In B. H. Khan (Ed.), *Web-based instruction* (pp. 381–387). Englewood Cliffs: Educational Technology Publications.

Banathy, B. H. (1991). *Systems designs of education: A journey to create the future.* Englewood Cliffs: Educational Technology Publications.

Banathy, B. H. (1992). *A systems view of education: Concepts and principles for effective practice.* Englewood Cliffs: Educational Technology Publications.

Berge, Z. L., & Collins, M. P. (Eds.). (1995). *Computer-mediated communication and the online classroom* (Vols. 1–3). Cresskill, NJ: Hampton Press.

Bonk, C. J., & Reynolds, T. H. (1997). Learner-centered Web instruction for higher-order thinking, teamwork, and apprenticeship. In B. H. Khan (Ed.), *Web-based instruction.* Englewood Cliffs: Educational Technology Publications.

Butler, B. S. (1997). Using the World Wide Web to support classroom-based education: Conclusions from a multiple-case study. In B. H. Khan (Ed.), *Web-based instruction* (pp. 417–423). Englewood Cliffs: Educational Technology Publications.

Dede, C. (1996). The evolution of constructivist learning environments: Immersion in distributed, virtual worlds. In B. G. Wilson (Ed.), *Constructivist learning environments: Case studies in instructional design* (pp. 165–175). Englewood Cliffs: Educational Technology Publications.

Dick, W., & Carey, L. (1996). *The systematic design of instruction* (4th ed.). New York: HarperCollins.

Duchastel (1996). Design for Web-based learning. *Proceedings of the WebNet-96 World Conference of the Web Society,* San Francisco.

Duffy, T. M., & Jonassen, D. H. (Eds.). (1992). *Constructivism and the technology of instruction: A conversation.* Hillsdale, NJ: Lawrence Erlbaum Associates.

Gagné, R., Briggs, L., & Wager, W. (1992). *Principles of instructional design* (4th ed.). New York: Harcourt, Brace, Jovanovich.

Harasim, L., Calvert, T., & Groenboer, C. (1997). Virtual-U: A Web-based system to support collaborative learning. In B. H. Khan (Ed.), *Web-based instruction* (pp. 149–158). Englewood Cliffs: Educational Technology Publications.

Harasim, L., Hiltz, S. R., Teles, L., & Turoff, M. (1995). *Learning networks: A field guide to teaching and learning online.* Cambridge, MA: MIT Press.

Hill, J. R. (1997). Distance learning environments via the World Wide Web. In B. H. Khan (Ed.), *Web-based instruction* (pp. 75–81). Englewood Cliffs: Educational Technology Publications.

Hiltz, S. R. (1994). *The virtual classroom: Learning without limits via computer networks.* Norwood, NJ: Ablex Publishing.

Hughes, K. (1994). Entering the World Wide Web: A guide to cyberspace; eit.com/web/www.guide/

Jonassen, D. H. (1996). *Computers in the classrooms: Mindtools for critical thinking.* Englewood Cliffs: Prentice-Hall.

Kearsley, G. (1996, winter). The World Wide Web: Global access to education. *Educational Technology Review, 5*, 26–30.

Kearsley, G., & Shneiderman, B. (1999). Engagement theory: A framework for technology-based teaching and learning; home.sprynet.com/~gkearsley/engage.htm

Kemp, J. E., Morrison, G. R., & Ross, S. M. (1994). *Designing effective instruction.* New York: Merrill.

Khan, B. H. (1997). Web-based instruction: What is it and why is it? In B. H. Khan (Ed.), *Web-based instruction.* Englewood Cliffs: Educational Technology Publications.

Khan, B. H. (2001). A framework for Web-based learning. In B. H. Khan (Ed.), *Web-based training.* Englewood Cliffs: Educational Technology Publications.

Khan, B. H., Murphy, K., & Lopez, C. (1996, March). Models for collaborative teaching/learning at a distance. In R. Robin, J. D. Price, J. Willis, & D. A, Willis (Eds.), *Technology and Teacher Education Annual, 1996* (pp. 524–527). Charlottesville, VA: Association for the Advancement of Computing in Education.

Kinzie, M. B. (1996). Frog dissection via the World Wide Web: Implications for widespread delivery of instruction. *Educational Technology Research and Development, 44*(2), 59–69.

Leshin, C. B., Pollock, J., & Reigeluth, C.M. (1992) *Instructional design strategies and tactics.* Englewood Cliffs: Educational Technology Publications.

Lin, X. D., Bransford, J. D., Hmelo, C. E., Kantor, R. J., Hickey, D. T., Secules, T., Petrosino, A. J., Goldman, R., & The Cognition and Technology Group at Vanderbilt (1995). Instructional design and development of learning communities: An invitation to a dialogue. *Educational Technology, 35*(5), 53–63.

McGreal, R. (1996). Roy's list of a dozen things that can go wrong in a World Wide Web course or even worse." *The Distance Educator, 2*(2), 6.

McLellan, H. (1997). Creating virtual communities via the Web. In B. H. Khan (Ed.), *Web-based instruction* (pp. 185–190). Englewood Cliffs: Educational Technology Publications.

Murphy, K., Khan, B., Knupfer, N., & Cifuentes, L. (1997, February). Implementing online student-to-student distance dialogue: Adding depth to local course offerings. Paper presented at the Annual Meeting of the Association for Educational Communications and Technology (AECT), Albuquerque, NM.

Reigeluth, C. M. (1983). *Instructional-design theories and models: An overview of their current status.* Hillsdale, NJ: Lawrence Erlbaum Associates.

Reigeluth, C. M., & Khan, B. H. (1994, February). Do instructional systems design (ISD) and educational systems design (ESD) really need each other? Paper presented at the annual meeting of the Association for Educational Communications and Technology (AECT), Nashville, TN.

Reigeluth, C. M. (1995). Educational systems development and its relationship to ISD. In G. J. Anglin (Ed.), *Instructional technology* (pp. 84–93). Englewood, CO: Libraries Unlimited.

Relan, A., & Gillani, B. B. (1997). Web-based instruction and the traditional classroom: Similarities and differences. In B. H. Khan (Ed.), *Web-based instruction* (pp. 41–46). Englewood Cliffs: Educational Technology Publications.

Rheingold, H. (1993). *The virtual community.* Reading, MA: Addison-Wesley.

Ritchie, D. C., & Hoffman, B. (1997). Incorporating instructional design principles with the World Wide Web. In B. H. Khan (Ed.), *Web-based instruction* (pp. 135–138). Englewood Cliffs: Educational Technology Publications.

Romiszowski, A. J. (1981). *Designing instructional systems.* East Brunswick, NJ: Nichols.

Schwier, R. A., & Misanchuk, E. R. (1993). *Interactive multimedia instruction.* Englewood Cliffs: Educational Technology Publications.

Sherry, L., & Wilson, B. (1997). Transformative communication as a stimulus to Web innovations. In B. H. Khan (Ed.), *Web-based instruction* (pp. 67–73). Englewood Cliffs: Educational Technology Publications.

Shotsberger, P. G. (1996). Instructional uses of the World Wide Web: Exemplars and precautions. *Educational Technology, 36*(2), 47–50.

Smith, P. L., & Ragan, T. J. (1993). *Instructional design.* New York: Macmillan Publishing Company.

Spiro, R. J., Feltovich, P. J., Jacobson, M. J., & Coulson, R. L. (1992). Cognitive flexibility, constructivism, and hypertext: Random access instruction for advanced knowledge acquisition in ill-structured domains. In T. M. Duffy & D. H. Jonassen (Eds.), *Constructivism and the technology of instruction: A conversation* (pp. 57–75). Hillsdale, NJ: Lawrence Erlbaum Associates.

Stancil, D. D. (1995). The virtual lab: Engineering the future; ece.cmu.edu/afs/ece/class/projects/badelt/www/virtual-lab.html

Sherry, L. (1996). Raising the prestige of online articles. *Intercom, 43*(7), 24–25, 43.

Tittel, E., & Gaither, M. (1995). *60-minute guide to Java.* Foster City, CA: IDG Books.

Wiggins, R. (1995). Growth of the Internet: An overview of a complicated subject; msu.edu //staff/rww/netgrow.html

Willis, B., & Dickinson, J. (1997). Distance education and the World Wide Web. In B. H. Khan (Ed.), *Web-based instruction* (pp. 159–165). Englewood Cliffs: Educational Technology Publications.

Willis, J. (1995). A recursive, reflective, instructional design model based on constructivist-interpretivist theory. *Educational Technology, 35*(6), 5–23.

Wilson, B. G. (1995). Metaphors of instruction: Why we talk about learning environments. *Educational Technology, 35*(5), 25–30.

Wilson, B.G. (Ed.). (1996). *Constructivist learning environments: Case studies in instructional design.* Englewood Cliffs: Educational Technology Publications.

For additional readings in Web-based learning and distance education, please visit Recommended Books Site *(BooksToRead.com/de.htm).*

The Author

Badrul H. Khan (e-mail: khanb@gwu.edu, or **khanb@BooksToRead.com; Web homepage: BooksTo Read.com/khan)** is Associate Professor and Director, Educational Technology Leadership cohort graduate program, George Washington University, Washington, DC. He is the founder of BooksToRead.com, a recommended readings site on the Internet.

2

Web-Based Training: Advantages and Limitations

Wallace Hannum

Web-based training (WBT) refers to training delivered in whole or in part over the Internet's World Wide Web. Many organizations see advantages to WBT when compared to traditional instructor-led training or to computer-based training (CBT). While WBT is still a fairly recent phenomenon, there has been enough experience with WBT to identify a set of advantages emerging from WBT use. Likewise, the limitations of WBT are becoming apparent. This chapter describes the advantages and limitations of Web-based training.

Advantages of WBT

The advantages of WBT are grouped into three major categories: logistical, instructional, and economic. Logistical advantages refer to those advantages of WBT that have to do with ease of distribution and use. Instructional advantages refer to those advantages that directly impact the quality and potency of instruction delivered via WBT. Economic advantages refer to cost advantages of WBT.

Logistical Advantages

WBT offers several logistical advantages when compared with other forms of training (Hall, 1998; Khan, 1997; Saltzberg & Polyson, 1995). Perhaps the greatest logistical advantage of WBT is its flexible, distributed delivery that allows the learner to learn any time and any place. The flexibility of WBT provides for training at the learner's location and on the learner's schedule. No longer do people have to come to a training facility or room to take a class scheduled at a specific time on a specific day. Training content is delivered to the learner's desktop or laptop at the worksite, at home, or while in transit. Those taking a course can be scattered across the globe and still participate in a class. By taking the training content directly to the learners, WBT eliminates travel and time away from the job required by traditional training.

Another logistical advantage of WBT is the cross-platform compatibility of the software. A training organization does not have to maintain multiple versions of courses for different computer platforms and operating systems. A training organization has to develop and maintain only one version of a course when using WBT. Because WBT courses are Internet-based, they will work with different computer platforms, operating systems, and browsers. WBT also simplifies technical support issues. The initial learning curve is shorter, and supporting users requires less time and effort.

The distribution system for WBT is much simpler than for other forms of training. Traditional training requires considerable scheduling to arrange for the course, the instructor, and the learners to be at the same location at the same time. Training rooms must be scheduled; training material must be ordered and distributed in advance. Even a CBT course delivered via CD-ROM to learners at their site requires considerable logistical effort. The learners must register for the course, the correct CD-ROM must be sent to the learners, any accompanying printed materials must be forwarded, and information about the learners' progress must be sent back to the training organization for recordkeeping. In many instances, the learners must take a separate certification examination upon course completion to demonstrate that they finished the course and learned from it. In a WBT course, most of these activities happen online automatically. A learner can register for a WBT course at any time via e-mail or a telephone call. All the training content for that course is available online, and certification examinations can be completed online, also. Access to any proprietary or sensitive material in WBT is controlled through course registration. Thus, WBT offers easy distribution of training while maintaining security.

Another logistical advantage is the easy access to any information available on other sites on the World Wide Web. A wonderful array of reference material for any WBT course resides on the Web. WBT courses may incorporate this existing material in a seamless fashion rather than duplicate it.

Because the training content resides on a central server, WBT content can be updated very easily. It is very easy to update a WBT lesson and deliver it to all learners almost instantaneously. It is much easier to update WBT content than to revise and reprint training manuals or to reproduce and distribute CD-ROMs or videotapes.

Instructional Advantages

When carefully planned and designed, WBT provides a powerful instructional environment (Starr, 1997). An obvious instructional advantage of WBT is the ability to provide for the delivery of rich multimedia to the learners (McManus, 1996). The stimulus for learning may include video segments, audio, graphics, animation, and text. The choice of how to orchestrate these multimedia possibilities depends on the specific learning objectives. Certainly, it is neither necessary nor desirable to have all multimedia elements in all lessons, but when used appropriately, the multimedia possibilities of WBT enhance instruction and learning (Bagui, 1998).

Another important instructional advantage of WBT is the ability of the learners to control aspects of the lessons. This is seen most often in control of pacing or advancement through lessons. In WBT, learners advance at their own rate, going quickly through more familiar material and slowing down for newer, less familiar material. Learners in WBT lessons can also be given control over other aspects of lessons. For example, WBT can allow the learners to choose among different instructional events within a lesson. A learner may ask for a definition or an example of a new concept being taught. Any time in a lesson, a learner may ask to see the objectives, review the prerequisites, see an overview, attempt a practice problem and get feedback, or take a mastery test. The learners have control over the training and can dynamically select those options that will best aid in their learning.

Another instructional advantage of WBT has to do with the freshness of the training content. Any revisions or changes made in the training content are available immediately to all learners.

The ability to include many forms of collaboration is another instructional advantage of WBT. Learners in WBT courses can use the Internet, or intranets, to communicate with other learners or instructors via e-mail, discussion forums, or chats. Learners at different sites can work as members of virtual groups to complete case studies or assignments. Learners can participate in discussions about lessons even though they are at remote locations. The ability to collaborate with persons at other sites is a very significant advantage of WBT.

When compared to training sessions conducted by different instructors, WBT offers a needed training consistency. Even when the same instructor conducts different training sessions, consistency of presentation is not assured; different learners may hear different training messages. When consistency of training is necessary, WBT has an advantage over traditional training.

Another advantage of WBT is that it is delivered on demand to the workstation and can be integrated with electronic performance support systems (EPSS). By integrating WBT with EPSS, organizations can provide a rich, supportive environment for employees to enhance their performance. This environment can furnish both longer term training needs and more immediate performance support needs for employees.

Economic Advantages

WBT offers organizations several important economic advantages (Dyer, 1997; Kilby, 1998). Primary among these economic advantages are the lower costs of WBT when compared to traditional training, even CBT. WBT offers a clear cost advantage over traditional training because WBT eliminates the need for travel and time away from the job. The costs of sending employees to training classes include transportation costs, per diem costs, and the opportunity costs of having employees not performing their work. Traditional training costs also include the costs for training facilities, instructors, and materials. With WBT, the transportation costs, per diem costs, facility costs, and instructor costs disappear. Opportunity costs are greatly reduced and development costs are less than CBT. Costs for WBT course maintenance are much less than for CBT maintenance. Overall, WBT is a very attractive training option from the standpoint of cost.

Because WBT development and distribution are centralized, WBT reduces expensive duplication of training effort. If organizations rely on WBT for training, they are less likely to have decentralized duplication of equivalent courses or training lessons. An inventory of WBT resources can easily be made available on an enterprise-wide basis so that any unit requiring training can access and employ any available WBT courses or lessons meeting their training needs. This helps hold training costs down without sacrificing training quality. The compatibility of WBT delivery across computer platforms and operating systems contributes to this capability to "develop once" and reuse WBT training content. Duplication of training effort is very common in traditional training because different instructors at different locations are developing and offering very similar courses. Even in training delivered by CBT, duplication can occur because many CBT lessons are delivered on stand alone CD-ROMs. Persons at different training locations may not be aware of the CBT lessons developed elsewhere, or the CBT lessons developed elsewhere may not be compatible with their computer platforms or operating systems.

WBT is based on familiar open standards, and many excellent development tools exist; therefore, creating WBT does not require the expensive programming common in creation of CBT. The programming language of the Web, HTML, is straightforward and simple to learn. Many excellent software packages allow the user to work in a word processor fashion with what-you-see-is-what-you-get screens and create HTML. In addition, many word processors and presentation packages allow the user to save documents in Web-ready HTML format. Expensive custom programming is not required when creating WBT. Thus, the development costs of WBT are constrained, especially when compared to custom CBT development.

Because WBT runs on familiar browsers, using WBT does not require much training or technical support. The ease of operation of WBT is much greater than CBT because WBT is

Table 1. Advantages of WBT.

Logistical	Instructional	Economic
• flexible delivery of training	• delivery of multimedia	• less costly than traditional training
• learn any time, any place	• learner control	• reduces duplication of effort
• delivery to learners' desktop or notebook computer	• immediate delivery of updated programming	• doesn't require expensive facilities
• cross platform compatibility	• variety of instructional events	• requires less technical support
• no scheduling problems	• collaboration	• can bill per use
• easy distribution	• consistency	• inexpensive, widespread distribution of materials
• security through registration	• supports EPSS	
• links to other sites		
• ease of content update		

based on the Internet and runs under the browsers people already use. WBT adds no special technical support requirements; an organization using the Internet or intranets should expect no additional technical support requirements from implementing WBT.

The economics of course distribution also favor the use of WBT. World-wide distribution of a WBT course is achieved by the one-time placing of the course on an organization's Web server. This allows instant access to the training material by people scattered anywhere in the world. There is no other training method as easy or inexpensive to distribute. Traditional training requires advanced printing and mailing of training manuals to each participant. Mediated forms of training, such as video-based training or CBT, require expensive creation, duplication, and distribution of videotapes or CD-ROMs. This adds to both the time and expense of distributing training materials.

WBT can be billed on a per use basis so that organizations purchasing WBT pay only for training they receive. Through per use billing, organizations providing WBT can be compensated for the training they provide each time a lesson is used.

Summary of Advantages

Web-based training offers many advantages to a training organization. The advantages of WBT are summarized in Table 1. Obviously, organizations should seriously consider WBT as a primary training method. WBT is a very attractive alternative when compared to other training options, like traditional leader-led training, CBT, or video-based training.

Limitations of WBT

While WBT may offer advantages to help organizations meet their training needs, this is coupled with some limitations (Filipczak, 1996). The limitations of WBT are grouped into the same three major categories as the advantages: logistical, instructional, and economic.

Logistical Limitations

WBT is currently limited by several logistical factors (Hall, 1998). Perhaps the most serious limitation to widespread WBT use is available bandwidth. Organizations with slow connections have a bottleneck that limits WBT use. When WBT uses graphically intensive pages, the downloading time can become excessive. Regardless of the connection speed, multimedia is slow in downloading. This limitation imposed by available bandwidth restricts the use of interactive multimedia in WBT. Since multimedia enhances WBT, the fact that it is much slower in loading somewhat limits this advantage of WBT. WBT in organizations using dial-up connections over modems is especially restricted. Slow connections may cause learners' attention to wander from the lesson as the long wait distracts and annoys them.

The Web sites specified by links in a WBT lesson are maintained by persons other than the WBT developers. These sites may be changed or eliminated without knowledge of the WBT developers. A learner using a particular WBT lesson may encounter links that no longer work or links that no longer contain the information the WBT developer expected them to contain. In essence, some parts of the training can be altered or eliminated any time without the WBT developers' knowledge.

When WBT includes any testing or analysis of learners' work for the purpose of grading or certification, the issue of authenticity of learners' work arises. How can you certify that the examinations or work submitted were the sole effort of the learner seeking course credit or certification? Unfortunately, in some situations when pressures may be on people to pass a course, get a certain grade on an examination, or become certified through course completion, they may be less than truthful regarding who did the work or who took the examination. Since this is occurring online, you are not there to monitor the work or the examination. In high stakes situations, you may establish a testing center at the learners' locations to authenticate that they were in fact the ones completing the examinations.

Instructional Limitations

In WBT, the training is delivered to individual learners at different locations, so there is limited interaction between instructor and learner or among other learners. Since these human interactions can facilitate learning, this is a limitation of WBT. Of course, WBT can be designed to incorporate e-mail, computer conferencing, and desktop videoconferencing to add more interaction. Still, this is not identical to the face-to-face interactions that happen in classrooms.

WBT is self-paced, allowing learners to advance at will, entering and exiting as they choose. However, some learners may not have sufficient initiative and motivation to complete the training or to do so in an orderly manner. WBT may not be appropriate for all learners, especially those requiring the structure of scheduled classes and the external pacing provided by an instructor. With current WBT, it is difficult to monitor the learners' progress. This could further exacerbate orderly progression through the training for some learners who are not being monitored and receiving regular progress reports. While learners may enter and exit WBT at any point, it is often difficult for a learner to leave a lesson at one point and then later return and continue at that same point. This may lead to parts of a lesson being inappropriately skipped or repeated.

While Web browsers offer a familiar interface to many people, not all learners may have used the World Wide Web and thus they must learn how to use some Web-based tools. If the WBT makes use of many features, such as e-mail, conferencing, FTP, and chat, a naive user must first learn how to use these features before beginning the WBT course. This adds additional training time and may require some face-to-face training.

The formatting in WBT courses cannot go beyond the capabilities offered by browsers. While the browsers add cross-platform compatibility, different learners' screens may be formatted in a different fashion. Thus, while the WBT lessons do get to everybody, these lessons may appear differently on different systems. This variance may compromise the instructional quality of the lessons, as what was a good design on one screen becomes a poor design on another screen.

WBT also imposes some design constraints because tools for Web authoring are still not as sophisticated as CBT authoring systems. This is changing as Web authoring tools gain sophistication and as plug-ins become available to support Web delivery of interactive multimedia developed with CBT authoring systems. However, we are not yet at the point that authoring for the Web is as powerful as authoring for CD-ROM-based CBT.

Many WBT lessons are repurposed print lessons. This compromises the effectiveness of WBT by limiting the technology to presenting pages of information. Just as much CBT, especially early CBT, was little more than a page-turner, a lot of WBT also falls in the category of a page-turner. This is a limitation imposed by WBT developers, not the technology itself. Appropriate WBT requires instructional designers who understand and appreciate the features of WBT, not people who simply put printed training materials on the Web. The designers must also be familiar with non-linear design of training. Designers accustomed to developing printed materials or video may have difficulty designing hypertext for WBT.

Undoubtedly, much training content may be delivered very effectively by WBT, but *all* training content might not be compatible with WBT. Learning complex motor skills is best accomplished when a skilled instructor provides specific, detailed feedback to a learner attempting to execute the motor skill. Evaluating a learner's motor skill and providing appropriate feedback is beyond the capability of most WBT. Thus, WBT may not be the appropriate training approach for all subjects.

Perhaps the greatest instructional limitation of WBT is a misplaced emphasis on the technology itself by some people (Alexander, 1996). As has been pointed out by considerable research, it is rarely the technology that improves the training. Technology improves training when the designers of the training use the technology to provide important instructional elements. Technology by itself does not improve poorly designed lessons; there is no magic in the chips and wires. Poorly designed WBT remains poor training. WBT is limited by the zeal of some proponents who believe WBT is *the* answer to all training needs.

Economic Limitations

WBT can produce cost savings for organizations in many cases. However, WBT does require a longer development time than traditional training. The development costs are likewise higher than traditional training, although delivery costs are lower.

Other economic factors limit may WBT use. Like CBT, WBT requires considerable funding during development before any delivery of training can occur. Traditional training does not require such up-front funding. WBT is not as cost effective when a small number of people will be using the training. It is not cost-effective to develop WBT for 12 people. In such situations, traditional training may be a better solution because it does not have high development costs and the delivery costs would be small for such a low number of learners. Likewise, if the training is to be used once then discarded, WBT is not as cost effective because you will not have the opportunity to offset the development costs with repeated use over time. WBT is appropriate for training larger numbers of people and when the training has a longer shelf life.

Table 2. Limitations of current WBT.

Logistical	Instructional	Economic
• limited bandwidth	• no face-to-face interaction	• longer developmental time
• multimedia slow in loading	• requires more learner initiative	• up-front funding
• changed or eliminated links	• limited formatting in current browsers	• costly for small numbers
• dial-up connections too slow, especially for multimedia	• difficult to monitor learners' progress	• costly for single-shot training
• difficult to authenticate learners' work and examinations	• hard to pick up where learners left off	
	• learners must know or learn Web-based tools	
	• WBT authoring systems not as sophisticated as CBT authoring systems	
	• not for all subjects	
	• much WBT is re-purposed printed pages	
	• instructors must use non-linear design	
	• misplaced emphasis on the technology itself	

Summary of Limitations

Web-based training has some limitations training organizations should consider. The limitations of WBT are summarized in Table 2. WBT is a valuable training method that can be used effectively in training organizations. However, organizations must consider the limitations of WBT, just as they should consider the limitations of any training method when making decisions about how to provide training.

Conclusion

Web-based training has emerged as a powerful training technology. WBT offers many advantages to training organizations. Certainly organizations that build on these WBT advantages should improve their training programs. However, the rush to implement WBT should be tempered with a consideration of the current limitations of WBT. Appropriate use of WBT requires an examination of both the advantages and limitations of WBT before making the decision to use WBT to meet a particular training need.

References

Alexander, S. (1996). Teaching and learning on the World Wide Web; scu.edu.au/sponsored/ausWeb/ausWeb95/papers/education2/alexander/

Bagui, S. (1998). Reasons for increased learning using multimedia. *Journal of Educational Multimedia and Hypermedia, 7*(1), 3–18.

Dyer, B. (1997). Web-based training: Pros and cons; dyroWeb.com/wbt/page1.html

Filipczak, B. (1996). Training on intranets: The hope and the hype. *Training, 33*(9), 24–32.

Hall, B. (1998). FAQ for Web-based training; brandon-hall.com/faq.html

Khan, B. H. (1997). Web-based instruction (WBI): What is it and why is it? In B. H. Khan (Ed.) *Web-based instruction*. Englewood Cliffs: Educational Technology Publications.

Kilby, T. (1998). WBT advantages and disadvantages; filename.com/wbt/_private/advdis.htm

McManus, T. F. (1996). Delivering instruction on the World Wide Web; ccwf.cc.utexas.edu/~mcmanus/wbi.html

Saltzberg, S., & Polyson, S. (1995). Distributed learning on the World Wide Web; umuc.edu/iuc/cmc96/papers/poly-p.html

Starr, R. M. (1997). Delivering instruction on the World Wide Web: Overview and basic design principles. *Educational Technology, 37*(3), 7–15.

The Author

Wallace Hannum (e-mail: whannum@mindspring.com; Web homepage: soe.unc.edu/hannum) is Associate Professor of Educational Psychology at the University of North Carolina at Chapel Hill.

3

Web-Based Training: Benefits and Obstacles to Success

Zane L. Berge, Mauri Collins,
and Tim Fitzsimmons

The explosive growth in technology and the expanding access to and use of the World Wide Web (the Web) has resulted in the increasing use of the Web for the delivery of education and training. Delivering training via the Web is attractive to corporate trainers in companies with intranets and/or access to the Internet, since every computer in the company has the potential to become a "just-in-time" training station, delivering training to the trainee's own desktop in modules that are quick and easy to update. This chapter will explore the potential benefits of and obstacles to success in Web-based training from the point of view of the corporation, the training professional, and the trainee.

Online Learning

The growth in training online in a Web-based environment can be attributed to several factors. Based on both academic research and on first-hand, online training experience, there are several good reasons for using the Web for training. The asynchronous mode of Web-based learning provides tremendous flexibility. The training module sits on a server so a learner can participate whenever and wherever the time for doing so is available. The move to just-in-time and just-in-place training can more easily be satisfied, as training is no longer offered in the rigid environment of the traditional university or college (Updegrove, 1995) or by bringing employees together in corporate training rooms.

The number and variety of pre-packaged, basic office and literacy skills training modules already available via the Web dwarf the output possible for any single training department, however large, and can meet the need for basic skills and software-specific training. Institutions and corporations around the world are offering a tremendous variety of certification programs that may allow the trainer or the learner to select the right training at the proper time.

The availability of Web-based training resources often allows the learner to rapidly follow any path of interest. The amount of reference material available online provides an almost unlimited wealth of information. Granted, useful and reliable material is not always easily located; but there is hope on the horizon. Search engines are becoming better and more specialized, and archives of information are becoming better organized. As more learners use the net and as

21

more demand is placed on rapid, organized retrieval of data, the technology will be developed to more easily retrieve data.

Benefits of Web-Based and Web-Enhanced Training

Training is delivered over an existing corporate infrastructure. Most corporate intranets running at least 486 PC machines and Windows software (or PowerMacs) can deliver training effectively. Although some machines may need to be upgraded, the upgrades can primarily be limited to audio and graphics capabilities. Even these upgrades can be minimized, based on the design of the training modules. Training modules can be modified so all components can be viewed and heard on all machines.

The technology is cross-platform. Regardless of the platform on which a trainee is working, Web-based training materials can be retrieved by users. The materials are authored once and then can be delivered to any machine that can run a browser on the Internet or the corporate intranet. IBM-compatible PCs and Macs, as well as UNIX based platforms, like Sun and SGI, can all run the same Web-based materials without changes. Depending upon the software used to create existing computer-based training, conversion to Web-delivery can be rapid. Conversion to HTML, the primary software for Web-based delivery, usually requires only minor formatting changes. There exists a number of applications that can convert existing applications with little external help.

Access to an intranet or the Internet is widely available. Most corporate computer users are already connected to an intranet and often there is corporate access to the Internet. Training can be installed on a single corporate server and accessed from any location within the corporation. Even users outside of the corporate headquarters can easily access the training by either dialing into the corporate server or using an ISP and connecting via the corporate Web page. It is no longer necessary to spend money or lose production time in sending people to a central training location. Training can be readily available at the trainee's desk.

Browsers provide a standard interface to multiple-media presentations. Browsers provide a consistent user interface that remains the same regardless of the content being delivered. This can provide the trainee with some built-in familiarity and reduces the cognitive load of having to learn a new application at the same time as acquiring new content. The trainee can concentrate fully on the content material. This will also reduce trainee anxiety at having to learn new applications.

The Web allows the training designer to use a much greater variety of media than is ordinarily available. E-mail, synchronous (i.e., real-time) and asynchronous communication, real-time video and audio feeds, online conferencing, graphics, and more are available via the Web, without the trainee having to learn multiple applications. The trainer now has a much wider opportunity to enhance the learning process and to provide training that matches multiple learning styles. This is an important consideration in designing training modules applicable across an organization(s). Trainees will be more willing to learn and learn more if material is presented in a familiar and desired style. The goal is to adapt the content to the learner, not the learner to the content.

Asynchronous communication: training that is flexible and convenient. The asynchronous nature of most Web-based classes will allow trainees to attend at times most convenient to them—a significant factor, considering the trend toward continuous learning. Training can also be accessed from a desktop at work, by salespersons or field service engineers on the road, or telecommuters from home. The more adaptable a program is to the varied lifestyles of today's trainees, the more willing and able the trainees will be to take courses.

These features also benefit the corporation. Training does not have to be conducted during a predetermined timeframe or even during normal business hours. Training can take place anytime during the day and the duration of the training can be varied, depending on the workload. Training can also be provided to employees stationed anywhere, regardless of geographical location or time zone restrictions.

Cost savings and time savings over traditional training methods. Training materials, once developed and stored on a Web-server, can be accessed from the trainee's location and viewed on screen. If the trainee wants a hard copy of specific training materials, it can be generated on a printer at the employee's work station. This saves printing, warehousing, and shipping costs for bulky paper training materials. With training delivered just-in-time to the desktop, a considerable savings can be realized in travel and housing costs, and trainees are not absent from their regular workstations during training. The cost of maintaining a separate training area to which trainees must travel can be recouped many times over, after the initial expenditure to provide all potential trainees with technology sufficient to receive workplace training.

Training materials can be prepared once and loaded onto a server, to be accessed from any computer attached to the corporate intranet, and via the Internet, from computers worldwide. Materials that may have been distributed on paper in the past—at significant cost in time, labor, materials, and shipping—can now be viewed onscreen and downloaded at the trainee's discretion.

Ease of update and revision. Corporations like UPS use Web pages on their corporate intranet to disseminate such volatile information as weather and road conditions nationwide (Wreden, 1997), illustrating the speed at which information can be revised and updated within prepared templates. A training document can be downloaded from a server for revision, and then uploaded back to the server in a matter of seconds. Of course, the revising may take significantly longer. As soon as a training document is loaded onto the server, the new or revised information is then instantaneously available to all learners regardless of their physical distance from the server. Additionally, keeping the training materials in soft copy form virtually eliminates the trainee from having to integrate the changes into existing printed material, thus ensuring that the most current material is always available.

Benefits to instructors and to instructional designers. Training room benefits might be a bit more intangible, at least at the beginning. Web-based programs can significantly increase both the number and the diversity of the trainees, since trainees can take courses from anywhere in the world. The resulting increase in enrollments may result in economies-of-scale, and will probably outpace the initial costs of developing additional online courses (Peraya, n.d.). However, this may also increase the support and diversity issues with which trainers must deal.

The Web is an extensive warehouse of knowledge, containing more information than any other single library. Instructors can more easily make use of this reservoir of information in an online class than in a traditional class by making additional resources just a "click" away. Trainees may be more willing to spend the necessary search time on the Web to find materials specific to their interests if they are already using it for training.

Obstacles to Success in
Online Teaching and Learning

The corporate culture. How a corporation regards access to information in general will have an impact on how using the Web for training is implemented. If a corporate culture values openness and accessibility to information within the corporation, then the use of Web for open access to training is more likely to find ready acceptance. However, if corporate culture views access to information as a matter of individual and departmental empowerment and wishes to maintain centralized control, then it may be more difficult for trainers to persuade management to allow open access to any portion of the corporate intranet.

The corporate infrastructure. To take advantage of the opportunity to make every corporate workstation a training station, time and resources must be invested in building and maintaining the corporate intranet (Feretic, 1997). The Web has often been adopted piecemeal by departments who have had the hardware and network resources to do so, whereas other departments have continued to use older technologies that, while adequate to access text-based mainframe applications, do not have the power on each desktop to access the Web, download and play video and sound clips, etc.

Lack of online learning skills. Both trainers and trainees must become comfortable and confident enough with the required technology that enables Web learning. For the instructor, it may be a matter of rethinking the traditional training room group approach and adapting material to individual Web delivery. The instructor must be able to anticipate potential areas of trainee concern and incorporate answers into the content material. For the trainees, greater responsibility must be assumed in the learning process and sometimes the initial acquisition of basic computer use skills—like typing. The trainee must become more proactive in assimilating the requisite information and translating it into everyday use.

Bandwidth is limited. Bandwidth refers to the number of simultaneous transmissions that can be carried through a network at any one time, or the size of the files that can be transmitted. The speed at which data can be transferred from a network to a personal computer is usually a function of the codec (coder-decoder) or modem used. Slow transfer speeds result in the user waiting while large files like graphic images, movie or sound clips are downloaded before they are played. Limited bandwidth means slower performance for sound, video, and graphics. This can impact both the learning process and place constraints on how the learning materials are designed.

Lack of "human contact." Most trainees have become conditioned to receiving instruction in a face-to-face mode, either in training rooms or on-the-job. While some will adapt more easily than others, it will take some time for all to become accustomed to an individualized distributed learning environment. Sometimes access to a trainer who can answer trainee questions is problematical, especially if the trainee chooses to access materials during non-business hours. Trainees can miss the support of a group or cohort of fellow learners. This can be a critical concern for the less-motivated trainee. Without an instructor present, this trainee may not be diligent in reaping the benefits of the training.

Corporate lack of expertise. All too often, what is called "Web-based training" amounts to little more than static Web pages full of text, and the "interactive" part is merely the clicking of a button to go to the next page. Often manuals are the first "training" that is converted to Web-based delivery, because conversion of existing word-processor files to HTML is relatively easy. Face-to-face training techniques like group exercises or discussions are impossible to implement in some Web-based training environments, especially when they are designed for individualized, asynchronous, just-in-time learning.

Development can be costly and time-consuming. Not only are costs measured in dollars higher, but also the time it takes for up-front design and development often increases. Trainers often have to rethink their approach and adapt their style of teaching to this new medium. Additional time is spent in learning HTML and related applications used to develop the course, rather than polishing in-person delivery techniques. However, once this up-front time is spent; maintenance of the course is often relatively fast and easy.

Whether converting an existing class or creating a course from scratch, a Web-based course costs money for the infrastructure, required software and support hardware, and development time for designing the course. The infrastructure cost is primarily a one-time expense. Once the software and related equipment is purchased, there is limited additional cost over the life of the course. The only exception would be to upgrade the technology involved with the class and revise the materials as new information becomes available.

Trainers have to learn to think through all aspects of the training and to anticipate where trainees may have questions or become confused, as they may not be present, or available in person, to deal with them when the training module accessed.

Not all training should be delivered by computer. Some topics, such as team-building activities, or emotional issues, such as the control of information in organizations, might best be delivered face-to-face. Sometimes online training serves best as an adjunct to face-to-face training. When the material to be covered can be read and talked about via some form of computer-mediated communication in advance, trainees can come better prepared to hands-on training. But where tactile or kinesthetic skills that are not computer-related must be developed, then working with computer simulations cannot be entirely substituted for working with the actual machine, equipment, or real people. Pilots can go far in their training in a simulator, but must actually fly a real plane before they can be licensed.

Conclusion

While there are significant benefits to be realized from Web-based training, there are also obstacles to effective usage that must be considered. Embarking on the delivery of Web-enhanced or Web-based training is not a decision to be made capriciously, nor just because "everyone else is doing it." Knowing well the strengths and liabilities of Web-based training technologies and methods is the best guide to making appropriate choices based on corporate goals, available technologies, and the needs of the trainees.

References

Alexander, S. (1995). *Teaching and learning on the World Wide Web.* Paper presented at the AusWeb95-Education-Learning-Teaching and Learning on the World; scu.edu.au/ausWeb95/papers/education2/alexander/

Feretic, E. (1997). The corporate looking glass. *Beyond Computing,* 6(2), p. 6.

Laws, R. (Ed.). (n.d.). *The official alt.education.distance FAQ;* pages.prodigy.com/PAUM88A

Peraya, D. (n.d.). *Distance education and the Web;* tecfa.unige.ch/edu-comp/edu-ws94/contrib/peraya.fm.html

Updegrove, K. H. (1995, August). *Teaching on the Internet.* Paper submitted in partial fulfillment of the requirements of N900, Nurse Midwifery Program, School of Nursing, University of Pennsylvania; pobox.upenn.edu/~kimu/teaching.html

Wreden, N. (1997). Corporate reflections. *Beyond Computing, 6*(2), 20–29.

The Authors

Zane L. Berge (e-mail: berge@umbc.edu; Web homepage: jan.ucc.nau.edu/~mpc3/berge/zane.html) is Director of the Graduate Program in Training Systems at the University of Maryland, Baltimore County. **Mauri P. Collins** (e-mail: mauri.collins@odu.edu; Web homepage: jan.ucc.nau.edu/~mpc3/mauri.html) is an instructional designer at Old Dominion University, Norfolk, Virginia. **Timothy J. Fitzsimmons** (e-mail: tjfitzs@erols.com) currently works as a training analyst for a government contractor, where he is involved in designing and developing a Web-delivered, interactive electronic performance support system (EPSS).

4

Infostructures: Technology, Learning, and Organizations

Greg Kearsley and
Michael J. Marquardt

The impact of technology, particularly networks (i.e., the Internet/Web, intranets, LANs), is dramatically altering the nature of organizations and the workplace, and radically changing our ideas about learning and knowledge. The old ways of hierarchical structures and clear boundaries are no longer effective (or even important in many cases!). The new building blocks of organizations are their "infostructures"—organizational structures built on information, learning, and technology.

In this chapter, we examine some of these trends with a focus on the new infostructures that are emerging. We begin by examining the current use of the Web for training and then go on to discuss the more general impact of networks on learning and organizations.

Use of the Web in Training Today: Some Examples

The use of the Web for learning has been somewhat slower to develop in the corporate world than in higher education. This is partly because, unlike in academic settings, there is no tradition of Internet access, while there is more limited availability of personal computers and a concern about the confidential/proprietary nature of training materials. On the other hand, almost every large business entity has a Website now—used primarily for marketing and product information. The percentage of employees with access to a computer in their workplace (not to mention at home) increases each year. Internal versions of the Web (intranets) as well as external links to the Internet are present or being developed in most organizations (Cronin, 1996; Gascoyne & Ozcubucku, 1996). So, there is every reason to expect that the explosive growth of the Web that has occurred in the educational domain will be duplicated in the corporate world in the next few years.

The Web is being used as a delivery mechanism for text-based learning materials by many professional societies, particularly those in technical/technological fields, such as engineering or telecommunications, which have been fairly quick to put their publications and conference proceedings up on the Web. To the extent that a significant amount of continuing education takes place through these organizations, we can say that the professional sector is taking advantage of the Web for personal learning activities. In addition, many adults are involved in taking courses from post-secondary institutions which use the Web extensively. While the Web may not be in formal use by many training departments at present, a large percentage of working individuals may already be engaged in Web-based learning.

One of the most popular uses of the Web is to provide customer education, either in the form of formal courses or more informal means, such as newsletters and conference/chat areas. For example, the Microsoft Online Institute [moli.microsoft.com] provides a catalog of online classes related to its products, as well as a newsletter, conference, and career center. This site also serves as a showcase for Internet Explorer (a Web browser offered by Microsoft) in terms of the features used in the newsletter and conference facilities. The IBM Global Education site [ibm.com] also provides listing of courses relevant to its product offerings and services, as well as a directory of conferences/trade shows featuring IBM involvement, and listing of its consulting and certification programs. Visitors to the IBM site can select the country or region of the world about which they are interested in seeing information. Motorola University, the internal training component of Motorola Corporation, provides information about course offerings, career opportunities, and technical publications (print or electronic) at its Website [mot.com/MU].

In addition to corporate sites offering information related to their products or services, a number of virtual training providers have appeared that are providing Web-based courses, especially in the computer and technology domain. Given the worldwide nature of the audience, and the minimum delivery costs involved, this is a very attractive marketplace. However, its growth will be constrained by the high costs of developing good multimedia courses and the availability of suitable hardware and high-speed network connections at the customer locations. Developing a course that takes advantages of the latest multimedia features of the Web but also can run successfully on a wide range of different customer systems is a difficult challenge.

An interesting example of a virtual training program is the CyberTravel Specialist program developed by New Media Strategies and supported by the Institute of Certified Travel Agents and Hyatt Hotels [cybertravelspecialist.com]. The program, which describes itself as the "Internet School for the Travel Professional," provides a full training course on how to use the Internet for travel-related activities. It consists of two components: a half-day lab session of supervised CBT conducted at CompUSA stores and a Web-based course that can be taken anywhere. There is also an online certification test intended to verify that the student has achieved the competencies taught in the CBT component of the course. This type of program could well be a model for future online training courses intended for independent professionals, featuring a certification test and a supervised lab session for those lacking computer background or when hands-on skills need to be taught.

While the current and emerging applications of the Web for training are exciting, they represent the beginning of much broader changes that technology and networks portend. Let's consider the full scope of these changes.

Technology Is Transforming Organizations

Technology is dramatically transforming the world of work and the workplace. Workers no longer need to work in an office. Corporations can collaborate and compete with one another at the same time. Customers can provide supervision as well as dictate services. Fellow employees now are able to work closely with each other while never even having met one another. Companies have temporary CEOs and part-time strategic planners. Corporate headquarters staff may consist of less than one percent of the company's workforce—if there is a headquarters in the normal sense. The Gross Domestic Product is more and more bytes of information and cyberspace and less and less manufacturing and products. Organizations are not even "organized." "Chaos" reigns, which is the energy that can propel and energize organizations. And this fundamental transformation of business and work caused by technology has only begun!

Technology enables the re-creation and redefinition of the organizations as we know them. It permits the redistribution of power, function, and control to wherever they are most effective, and depending on the mission, objectives, and culture of the organization. Because of this technology, corporations will become cluster organizations or *adhocracies,* groups of geographically dispersed people—typically working at home—that come together electronically for a particular project and then disband, having completed their work.

The technology-driven networks and databases will replace the depth of knowledge that a multitiered hierarchy offers with a wider breadth and even deeper depth of knowledge that is the sum of employees' collective experience. The new organizational architecture will evolve around autonomous work teams and strategic alliances.

As more companies realize that the key resource of business is not capital, personnel, or facilities, but rather knowledge, information, and ideas, many new ways of viewing the organization begin to emerge. Everywhere companies are restructuring, creating integrated organizations, global networks, and leaner corporate centers. Organizations are becoming more fluid, ever shifting in size, shape, and arrangements.

Technology makes it easy to form virtual organizations. Virtual organizations, a form of restructuring that is rapidly gaining popularity, are temporary networks of independent companies, suppliers, customers, even rivals, linked by information technology to share skills, costs, and access to one another's markets. In its purest form, a company decides to focus on the thing it does best. Then it links with other companies, each bringing to the combination its own special ability. The virtual corporation has neither central office nor organization chart, and no hierarchy or vertical integration. Teams of people in different companies routinely work together. After the business is done, the virtual organization disbands.

Infostructure and the Learning Organization

To obtain and sustain competitive advantage in this new technology-based environment, organizations will have to learn better and faster from their successes and failures. They will need to continuously transform themselves into learning organizations with new infostructures in order to become places where groups and individuals continuously engage in new learning processes. A learning organization has the powerful capacity to collect, store, and transfer knowledge, and thereby continuously transform itself for corporate success. It empowers people within and outside the company to learn as they work. A most critical component is the utilization of technology to optimize both learning and productivity (Marquardt, 1996).

Organizational learning represents the enhanced intellectual and productive capability gained through corporate-wide commitment to continuous improvement. It differs from individual and group/team learning in two basic respects. First, organizational learning occurs through the shared insights, knowledge, and mental models of members of the organization. Second, organizational learning builds on past knowledge and experience—that is, on organizational memory, which depends on institutional mechanisms (e.g., policies, strategies, and explicit models) used to retain knowledge.

There is no way an organization can adapt to the rapid change in the environment without a sound and solid use of technology; therefore, learning organizations can only be created and succeed with the intelligent application of technology. Technology is necessary to create the appropriate learning organization "info-structure" to enhance the speed and quality of needed learning, and to adequately manage the information and knowledge of the organization.

Technology not only serves as a foundation, but also as the key integrating system, including the supporting technological networks and information tools that allow access to and exchange of information and learning. It includes technical processes, systems, and structure for collaboration, coaching, coordination, and other knowledge skills. It encompasses electronic tools and advanced methods for learning, such as computer conferencing, Internets and intranets, electronic publishing, and multimedia learning, all of which work to create knowledge freeways.

In traditional hierarchical organizations with multiple layers of management, accountability, and bureaucracy, information flow was vertical. Host-based islands of technology corresponded to the old structures. But through Internetworked workgroup computing tools, the corporate pyramid can be replaced with Internetworked teams. The focus shifts from the individual who was accountable to the manager to teams that function as service units of servers and clients. Teams are both clients and servers to other teams, which are both internal and external to the organization. Technology enables designers to collaborate around workstations to engineer a new design concurrently rather than in a serial fashion. Many functions can happen simultaneously; individuals are not waiting for someone else to complete a task before they add their input.

Infostructure includes the departments, levels, and configurations of the company. A learning organization is a streamlined, flat, boundaryless structure that maximizes contact, information flow, local responsibility, and collaboration within and outside the organization. The structure in a learning organization is much different, thanks to the power of technology. The network and database replace the depth of knowledge a multitiered hierarchy offers with the breadth of knowledge that is the sum of employees' collective experience.

Technology enables an organization to move beyond the old hierarchy because layers of management are not required when information is instantly available electronically. An infostructure can enable the enterprise to function as a cohesive organization by providing corporate-wide information for decision-making and new competitive enterprise applications that transcend autonomous business units or teams.

Knowledge Management Systems

The knowledge subsystem of a learning organization is the heart of the new infostructure. This subsystem refers to the management of acquired and generated knowledge of the organization. It includes the acquisition, creation, storage, transfer, and utilization of knowledge. Specific technologies for managing knowledge include electronic performance support systems and all types of networks (i.e., Internet, intranet, Web, and LAN/WANs). Knowledge management systems are redefining the nature of modern organizations (e.g., Myers, 1996).

The knowledge elements of organizational learning are ongoing and interactive instead of sequential and independent. The collection and distribution of information occurs through multiple channels, each having different time frames. An example is an online newsletter which systematically gathers, organizes, and disseminates the collective knowledge of the organization's members.

A knowledge storage system enables an organization to contain and retain knowledge, so that it becomes company property and doesn't go home at night or leave the organization when the employee leaves. Unfortunately, knowledge (also referred to as "intellectual capital"), though far more important than physical material, is usually scattered, hard to find, and liable to disappear without a trace because it is not stored. Storage is obviously important, but what knowledge should be stored?

Knowledge is only clumsy data unless it is coded and stored in a way that makes sense to individuals and the organization. Too many organizations remain overwhelmed and inundated with vast amounts of data that clutter up the information highway. An organization cannot learn from the information if it is irretrievable, distorted, fragmented, or inaccurate. To determine what data can be used, the organization must decide what is of value, and then code the data based on learning needs as well as on organizational operations.

The knowledge stored should be easily accessible across functional boundaries. It should be structured and organized so the users can find concise information in a quick fashion. Store the knowledge not only by topical categories, but also based on learning needs of staff, organizational goals for continuous improvement, and user expertise. Finally, the knowledge stored should be continually updated so it remains accurate and valid.

It is important to remember that knowledge storage involves technical (records, databases, etc.) and human processes (collective and individual memory, consensus). As organizations become physically and geographically more spread out, as well as more specialized and decentralized, the organization's storage system and memory can become fragmented, and corporate benefits of the knowledge can be lost (Marquardt, 1996). And as work becomes more computer oriented, the information needs of different organizational specialties become potentially available across functional boundaries. Networked information technology must be utilized so that fragmented information can be reinterpreted and readily exchanged internally and externally.

A comprehensive, wide-scale transfer of knowledge, however, can occur only through the intelligent use of technology, so that the knowledge can be available anywhere, anytime, and in any form. Information communications software, including electronic mail, bulletin boards, and conferencing, allows for interactions among members both person-to-person and among dispersed groups. It also provides an electronic learning environment in which all members have equal access to data and are able to communicate freely.

Learning in the Networked Organization

We have outlined how technology is transforming organizations. This transformation affects learning in a very broad fashion. For one thing, it places a lot of attention on sharing of resources and expertise. Since it is now much easier (or should be!) to share ideas, experiences, and information, networks encourage collaboration and cooperation among employees. So the new form of learning in the networked organization is heavily dependent upon electronic interaction via e-mail, conferencing, Websites, etc. Such interaction tends to be more informal and unstructured relative to traditional means of training courses and materials. However, Web-based training can be, and is, increasingly become more formal and structured (e.g., Electronic Performance Support Systems—EPSS).

Knowing what and where information is available and how to access it becomes a very important skill in the networked organization. Part of this skill involves competence with a wide range of computer tools (i.e., computer literacy). This requires constant re-training, since both hardware and software are continually changing. Another aspect of the skills needed are information-handling techniques, i.e., being able to weed through enormous amounts of data to find something useful. Use of search facilities and detailed knowledge of different information databases is important here. Finally, people need very good communication and interpersonal skills because much of the time they will be interacting with other human beings in search of information (albeit via electronic means).

But the implications of networking for learning are even broader. Interacting with other people via electronic networks tends to break down all boundaries: geography, time, socioeconomic, cultural, age, and organizational. Individuals will seek out others with shared interests or common goals regardless of factors that would traditionally keep them apart or out-of-touch. This is the profound power of "cyberspace" or the "virtual community" that networks make possible (Jones, 1995; Rheingold, 1993). This means that employees can and will interact electronically with anyone in their organization as well as other organizations (perhaps even competitors). School kids communicate directly with university professors and scientists . . . who talk to people in corporations and government agencies . . . who can interact directly with consumers and their clientele.

So networks mean that learning is no longer encapsulated by artificial limitations, such as classrooms, curricula, and organizational/institutional delimitations. Individuals will use networks to find other people and information sources that address their specific needs and interests. All organizations need to recognize this new circumstance and do what they can to enable their staff, students or members to be as proficient as possible in the use of the networks.

The way in which organizations use technology to build the infostructure and to manage knowledge is quickly emerging as the single most important discriminator between success and failure in this intensely competitive global economy. Nonaka and Takeuchi (1995) confidently predict that a company's ability to create, store, and disseminate knowledge will become absolutely crucial for staying ahead of the competition in quality, speed, innovation, and price. Only by developing and implementing systems and mechanisms to assemble, package, promote and distribute the fruits of its thinking will a company be able to transform knowledge into corporate power.

References

Cronin, M. J. (1996). *The Internet strategy handbook*. New York: McGraw-Hill.

Gascoyne, R. J., & Ozcubucku, K. (1996). *The corporate Internet planning guide*. New York: Van Nostrand Reinhold.

Jones, S. G. (1995). *Cybersociety*. Newbury Park, CA: Sage.

Marquardt, M. (1996). *Building the learning organization*. New York: McGraw-Hill.

Myers, P. (1996). *Knowledge management and organizational design*. New York: Butterworth-Heinemann.

Nonaka, I., & Takeuchi, H. (1995). *The knowledge-creating company*. New York: Oxford University Press.

Rheingold, H. (1993). *The virtual community*. Reading, MA: Addison-Wesley.

The Authors

Greg Kearsley (e-mail: gkearsley@sprynet.com; Web homepage: gwu.edu/~lto), is Adjunct Professor of Educational Technology at the George Washington University, Washington, DC. **Michael J. Marquardt** (e-mail: mjmq@aol.com; Web homepagae: gwis2.circ.gwu.edu/~marquard/) is Associate Professor and Program Director, Human Resource Development, the George Washington University.

Portions of this chapter are adapted from *Technology-based learning: Maximizing human performance and corporate success* (1999). Boca Raton: St. Lucie Press.

5

Emerging Learning Trends and the World Wide Web

Ellen D. Wagner

Introduction

There is broad recognition that the Web-based teaching and learning methodologies currently in vogue only scratch the surface of the array of variables that designers, instructors, and learners must be able to accommodate in the future. This chapter describes e-learning as the conceptual base from which "next generation" Web-based learning designs are beginning to emerge. Particular attention is paid to issues that must be addressed when systems employing reusable learning objects* are a part of the e-learning design equation.

E-Learning

Among the wide variety of ways in which organizations use information technologies, electronic learning is emerging as the foundation upon which organizations effectively use their technology infrastructure. Electronic learning—increasingly called "e-learning" (Trondsen, 1999)—refers to the wide range of technology applications, strategies, and tools that offer learners the means to increase their knowledge and improve their skills. Earlier trends in the e-learning space included computer-based training (CBT) and computer-managed instruction (CMI), distance learning (especially programs using broadband video distribution via broadcast, coaxial cable, or satellite), computer-mediated conferencing, and distributed (online) learning. While constituting the biggest share of the e-learning space in the early 1990s, CD-ROM multimedia programs have been outpaced by interactive online learning programs available via the World Wide Web. Today, the combination of Web-based interaction functionality (particularly as related to collaborative environments) and e-commerce transactional capabilities are the foundation for today's e-learning designs and materials development.

Trends in several distinct arenas have influenced and shaped e-learning's growth. The first trend deals with issues of technology infrastructure. The ubiquitous availability, scalability, and

---

*A learning object is the smallest element of stand-alone information (including but not limited to online instruction or a performance support tool) required for an individual to achieve an enabling performance objective or outcome. This description is meant to be illustrative rather than definitive; it is an amalgam of descriptions and definitions currently being used in professional discussions, presentations, and publications dealing with learning and technology.

33

interoperability of information technologies has made e-learning a viable alternative for even small, geographically remote organizations. Secondly, increasingly complex, competitive workplace needs for information, learning, and performance support are resulting in increased demands for better management of an organization's intellectual assets: its knowledge, its history, its shared experiences, its discoveries, its record of successes and failures, its innovations—when and where these resources are needed most. Knowledge management's focus on the accessibility and reusability of an organization's intellectual assets, combined with the re-emergence of competency-based learning (CBL) that connects professional development resources to that organization's core competencies represents a third trend in e-learning circles. CBL offers a strategy for implementing e-learning solutions that employ competency models as the pattern template for compiling and assembling learning objects in meaningful, relevant ways. Very important work addressing learning architecture and learning object standards is taking place to ensure the interoperability of learning objects in a variety of learning management systems and settings. One of the outcomes of the convergence of these trends is the emergence of Knowledge Commerce (Derryberry & Anderson, in press), a term used to describe the specialized subset of the Internet Economy where knowledge is achieved through the judicious assembly and use of learning objects.

Information Technologies: Infrastructure for E-Learning

One of the most obvious attributes of e-learning is its dependence upon technology. The infrastructure needed to distribute electronic learning resources has reached a sufficient number of users to create a burgeoning market for programs and services.

Specific developments leading to the widespread availability of technology include a variety of factors (Wagner, 1999). Thanks to constantly improving browser technology, platform-independent transmission protocols, and media-capable features such as Java-enabled client-server interactivity, readily accessible "new media" such as online multimedia and hypermedia offer computer users of all levels of proficiency gateways to an array of full-motion, fully animated, interactive, responsive information resources. Among the most important outcomes of browser robustness and platform interoperability is the ability to index, store, and retrieve data files in multiple formats, and to modify and even create new data by means of system interactions.

Burgeoning developments related to learning objects and knowledge content distributors (Masie, 1998) have had significant influences on e-learning. A learning object (known more generically as a content object, or as a knowledge object, or a reusable information object) is a modular data unit that encapsulates information to describe and present a concept, skill operation, or procedure. A categorization schema called a meta-data structure defines an object's descriptive attributes (e.g., whether it is text, animation, audio or video information; the size and type of file; the topic being presented in the object, the performance that the object is intended to elicit, and so on). The meta-data structure makes it possible to combine powerful database capabilities with online search and file retrieval capabilities so that specific content objects can be identified, located and retrieved. Initially referred to as *Knowledge Content Distributors* or *KCDs* and more recently called *Learning Management systems* or *Knowledge Management systems,* these content object/metadata applications operate as "wholesalers" of online and digital learning content from vendors and authors, providing user organizations with the ability to mix and match learning products. In practical terms, this means that users can select and compile the precise content objects that they want.

Combined with the browser and KCD features noted above, programs employing full-scale database backends make it possible for even small businesses to leverage the power of real-time online transactional processing. They also make it possible to offer adaptive, fully individualized professional development resources that respond to a user's profiled needs and interests by establishing search and sort protocols that access only the information that is relevant according to that user's profile. Use of meta-data allow systems and users to store and retrieve and reuse information objects across external databases. Meta-files and pattern templates provide opportunities to assemble information objects into meaningful, personalized and contextualized structures that can be used on terms defined by users.

The ubiquitous availability of commercial Internet Service Providers (ISPs), Application Service Providers (ASPs), and Hosting Services Providers (HSPs) has also strongly influenced e-learning growth and development. The number of commercial Internet Service Providers and the appearance of companies dedicated to providing the support and services that allow companies to effectively leverage their Internet connectivity have increased exponentially in the past two years. The scalability and performance of Web-enabled databases now allow for a range of capabilities, ranging from "single instance" database use for housing enterprise-specific data objects to the convergence of a variety of database applications that offer data warehousing capabilities. Such converged databases can be "mined" for a wide range of resource planning and knowledge management uses (Harris, 1999). The competition among providers has dramatically affected the access to service, types of service, costs for service and provision of user support that Internet users have come to expect.

Demands for Workplace Performance Improvement

Success in today's economy requires an organization to develop core competencies in responding to and, ultimately, in thriving on change. These competencies are based on employees' ability to think critically, to solve problems and to anticipate new possibilities (Rothwell, 1996). Growing workplace demands for information, instruction, and training resources that are available when and where they are needed are driven by individuals' requirements for "just-in-time, just for me" learning and performance support tools, both as they perform their current jobs and as they prepare for new challenges. The presence of a growing online learning and performance support marketplace marks this shift in the balance of power away from providers to the individual learner. It is easy to understand why there is growing impatience with traditional methods of designing, delivering, and managing learning experiences that are increasingly out of touch in a "wired world."

While training is an important tool for improving employee knowledge and skills, training—whether it is instructor-led in a classroom, instructor-led online, or self-paced workbooks or self-paced online—is insufficient for providing a full range of continuous, individualized performance-improvement interventions. Training has traditionally been something which is "done to" learners, implemented to react to a performance deficiency (Ellis, Wagner, & Longmire, 1999). Specific performance-completion outcomes (e.g., graduation or certification of time-on-task) need to be achieved, so learners are expected to conform to a path dictated by either the designer of the learning experience, the instructor for the learning experience or both. Typically, it has not been a goal of training to meet the individual needs of the learner. In this paradigm, it is been easy to focus on the process of training rather than on the results of learning. Training designs typically do not address the need for flexibility required to meet an individual's learning needs, nor do training delivery mechanisms make training accessible at times when it may be needed by any given individual.

E-learning solutions typically combine the functionality of "just-in-time" access to digital, Web-delivered content with profiling functionality to assist in content filtering/selection. Further, it actively leverages online collaboration opportunities, and offers "e-commerce" transactional functionality to facilitate subscription, purchase, or "pay-per-view/hit" options. Ironically, the addition of e-commerce transactional functionality to distance and distributed learning design paradigms (Wagner, 1999) has resulted in focusing significant business-to-business and business-to-consumer attention on e-learning. This combination of features provides learners the means to proactively pursue information and performance support resources unconstrained by conventional training design or delivery mechanisms. E-learning tools can offer individualized, personalized learning by means of profiling such variables as interests, learning styles, presentation preferences and performance requirements. They can diagnose skill gaps and prescribe professional development activities ensuring the link between learning events and on-the-job practice. Individuals can monitor their own progress and determine what the next step in their professional development should be. Learning resources, ranging from individual objects to online communities of professional practice to professional advisors and mentors become available when and where those resources are needed by the learner.

Knowledge Management and E-Learning

According to current reports in strategic business planning and information technology publications (Dempsey, 1999) the knowledge management movement will continue to exert significant influence on e-learning programs in the next few years (Violino, 1999). Knowledge management refers to the way that organizations generate, communicate, and leverage their intellectual assets. The Delphi Group defines knowledge management as "all leveraging of collective wisdom to increase responsiveness and innovation," while the Gartner Group notes that knowledge management is a discipline that promotes an integrated approach to identifying, capturing, evaluating, retrieving, and sharing all of an organization's information assets (Jennings, 1999). Regardless of how it is implemented in individual organizations, knowledge management provides organizations with an essential source of competitive advantage in the information economy by capturing, storing, and making accessible its full array of intellectual assets.

While organizational size and complexity have accelerated the need to consciously manage knowledge across time and space, relatively little has been done to increase an individual's personal capacity to absorb information and create new knowledge. The central challenge is to better manage the flow of information through and around the "bottlenecks" of personal attention and learning capacity. Sieloff (1999) suggests a number of strategies for facilitating attention management to deal with "information overflow":

- **"Know what you don't need to know."** Organizations need to provide personalized solutions for addressing the knowledge needs of individuals without forcing everyone else in the organization to master the same body of information.

- **"Just-in-time, just enough" delivery of knowledge resources reduces the required inventory that an individual must hold in store.** It is no longer necessary to expose individuals to the full array of information resources that may be available. Instead, it is increasingly important to profile the knowledge needs of individuals and to link individuals to the resources they need to quickly build specific capabilities or to respond to specific performance challenges.

- **Use of trusted intermediaries.** Universal access to content—whether represented as objects, links, or frames—literally destroys the context from which content is drawn. This, in turn, compromises an individual's ability to assign meaning, create associations, and link new information with already held knowledge (Ormrod, 1998). It also makes it difficult to filter content for importance (Jonassen & Grabowski, 1993). Technology mediated intermediaries (such as online advisors, intelligent search tools, adaptive profiling tools, pattern templates, literature summary services, and learning management systems) help establish, maintain, and monitor frameworks that can define (situational) context. Even so, online communities of practice, knowledge advisors, and learning mentors are playing increasingly important roles in helping individuals to filter and to assign meaning to the array of elements that may be contained in a "content object library."

- **Precision distribution provides individuals with content objects and context for interpretation.** The degree of precision for accessing content objects is a function of the quality and robustness of schemas used to organize and arrange data files and define access and retrieval strategies. Significant work has been undertaken by such groups as the Aviation Industry Computer-Based-Training Committee (AICC), the IEEE Learning Technology Standards Committee, the IMS (Instructional Management Systems) Global Consortium, and the World Wide Web Consortium (W3C) to address the notion of system-level interoperability (Richards, 1998).

E-Commerce, Knowledge Management, and E-Learning

There is no question that the impact of the World Wide Web on business practice, particularly in the United States, has been profound. Ledbetter (1999) has noted that "dot-com" companies are now firmly entrenched in popular culture; U.S. leaders from Wall Street to the White House have endorsed the Internet as America's financial engine. In a recent article published in *The Industry Standard,* Ledbetter describes two major studies that attempted to quantify the Internet economy. One study, published by the University of Texas with funding from Cisco Systems, described it as an industry that generated $300 billion annually, while a follow-up study from the same investigators described a 68% annual growth rate, claiming that the Internet economy now employs more than 2.3 million people. A second report, published by the U.S. Department of Commerce, found that the so-called digital economy accounted for approximately 8% of the U.S. gross domestic product, outpacing such industries as housing construction and motor vehicle manufacturing.

The education and training industries have been as susceptible to the seduction of the Internet economy as any other economic sector currently in operation. Of particular relevance for education and training entities interested in leveraging the Internet's economic opportunities are activities associated with the creation of new content, repurposing of existing content, the aggregation of content resources from a wide variety of content holders such as publishers, universities, and subject matter experts, and the provision of content in a variety of reusable, digital forms.

According to Derryberry and Anderson (in press), the core competencies required to be an e-learning solutions provider are very similar to the core competencies required to be an e-commerce solutions provider. In many respects, an e-learning solution is a very specialized subset of an e-commerce solution; instead of selling a book or running an auction, individuals purchase a content object or array of objects. When assembled in a meaningful way, the compilation of content objects can serve as a learning solution, as long as the outcomes of the learning experience have been clearly articulated as part of the compilation and assembly process.

In its broadest sense, the product to be purchased in an e-learning solution framework *is* knowledge. However, since knowledge tends to function as a social construct—that is, it is an outcome that emerges through interaction and interpretation (Empson, 1999)—the knowledge product itself typically consists of content objects, assembled in a meaningful way, so that a learning solution can emerge. The learning solution must ensure the judicious compilation and assembly of content. The resulting "personalized learning plan" that is generated to guide content assembly improves learning outcomes in measurable, observable ways. The ultimate end result of this process is an improved process for attaining knowledge (see Figure 1).

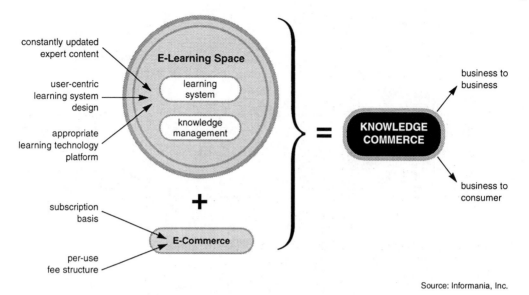

Source: Informania, Inc.

Figure 1. Knowledge commerce: The convergence of e-learning, e-commerce, and knowledge management.

Realizing the Power of E-Learning Systems: Learning Objects, Metadata, and Pattern Templates

Hodgins (1999a) has noted that, for e-learning systems to realize their full power, three essential system components must be in place. These elements include learning objects, metadata, and pattern templates.

Learning Objects. Learning objects offer access to content at a granular level that typically maps to a single learning objective. Learning objects (also known by other names, including but not limited to *content objects, knowledge objects, reusable information objects,* and *reusable learning objects*) are stand-alone pieces of information that are reusable in multiple contexts, depending on the needs of the individual user.

Longmire (2000) has asserted that most electronic learning content is currently developed for a specific purpose, such as a course or a situational performance intervention, rather than being developed for use in an *objectbase* (a collection of learning objects, typically contained or referenced in a relational database). However, he suggests that as object-oriented "knowledge content" becomes a valuable commodity, content will be developed and configured for deployment as learning objects in multiple settings. This shift comes from the recognition that digitized content that can be repurposed for use in a variety of setting will pay off many times over in terms of costs, development time, and learning effectiveness. The object approach can satisfy both immediate learning needs—such as a knowledge-based or skills-based course—and current and future learning needs that are not course-based. Longmire notes that the benefits of designing and developing material to be reused as learning objects in other contexts include:

- **Flexibility.** If content is designed for used in multiple contexts, it can be reused much more easily than if it must be has to be rewritten—or reconfigured—for each new setting in which it is to be used. It is much harder to uncouple an object from the context of its parent course and then re-contextualize it, than it is to contextualize as part of design and development.

- **Ease of updates, searches, and content management.** Metadata tags* facilitate rapid updating, searching, and management of content by filtering and selecting only the relevant content for a given purpose.

- **Customization.** When individual or organizational learning and performance support needs require customization of content, the learning object approach facilitates a "just-in-time" avenue to customization. Modular learning objects maximize the potential of software that personalizes content by permitting the delivery and recombination of material at the level of granularity desired.

- **Situational specifications that interoperate with industry standards.** The object approach allows organizations to set specifications regarding the design, development, and presentation of learning objects based on organizational needs, while retaining interoperability with other learning systems and contexts.

- **Facilitation of competency-based learning.** Competency-based approaches to learning focus on the intersection of skills, knowledge, and attitudes within the rubric of core competency models rather than the course model. While this approach has gained a great deal of interest among employers and educators, a perennial challenge in implementing competency-based learning is the lack of appropriate content that is sufficiently modular to be truly adaptive. The tagging of granular learning objects allow for an adaptive competency-based approach by matching object metadata with individual competency gaps.

- **Increased value of content.** From a business standpoint, the value of content is increased every time it is reused. This is reflected not only in the costs saved by avoiding new design and development time, but also in the possibility of selling content objects or providing them to partners in more than one context.

Metadata. Metadata are descriptive indexing labels, or "tags," that articulate attributes defining a variety of characteristics about each object of content. Metadata facilitates searching, management, and linking of granules of content. Metadata enables users and authors of content to search and retrieve and assemble content objects according to parameters defined by users.

As was noted earlier in this chapter, significant work has been undertaken by such groups as the Aviation Industry Computer-Based Training Committee (AICC), the IEEE Learning Technology Standards Committee, the Educause Instructional Management Systems (IMS) Project, and the World Wide Web Consortium (W3C) to address the notion of system-level interoperability (Richards, 1998). At this time, no single, official standard for learning object standards has been established. Vendors, academics, government agencies and industry consortia are collaborating to ensure that Web-enabled learning technology products can interoperate with one another, although uncoupling learning objects from the context of its "parent" course continues to present course player problems. Drivers for maintaining the need for working together to establish interoperability standards include uncertainty (e.g., what standard is likely to emerge as the *lingua franca* of online learning object deployment?), and the inability of any

---

*Metadata tags are descriptors of attributes attached to a learning object. These descriptors, or values, can indicate any number of attributes for the object.

one initiative to be able to solve the problem alone. There is a shared expectation that the various initiatives involved in defining learning technology standards will negotiate a convergent solution rather than adhering to a single organization's "proprietary" approach.

However, having noted that there currently is no single standard for defining metadata attributes, it is important to consider that work in this arena is currently being conducted at a furious pace, with every indication of accelerating. To give an example of how quickly organizations are moving to get their "stake in the ground" to define standards for learning objects, the following three press releases from three separate organizations working in this arena may be of interest:

- On February 3, 2000, the World Wide Web Consortium (W3C) announced the release of the "Authoring Tool Accessibility Guidelines 1.0" (ATAG 1.0) specification, providing guidance to developers on how to design accessible authoring tools that produce accessible Web content.

- On February 8, 2000, Microsoft Corp. and leaders of the e-learning community announced support for Learning Resource Interchange (LRN), the first commercial implementation of the Instructional Management Systems (IMS) Content and Management Systems Specification developed by the eLearning industry and the IMS Global Learning Consortium. LRN is an XML-based schema that defines course content, allowing organizations and e-learning providers to easily create and manage compatible online learning content. LRN helps customers maximize their investment in e-learning by enabling a wider range of interoperable content and applications.

- On Feb. 25, 2000, the Technical Board of the IMS Global Learning Consortium unanimously approved two new XML-based open standards for building online training and education applications. The specifications, the IMS Content Packaging Specification and the IMS Question and Test Interoperability Specification, enable "advanced online training and education technologies, as well as learning system interoperability."

This enumeration of press releases is not meant to be a comprehensive summary of activities related to learning object standards development. However, it does present a picture of an arena of activity that, after years of relegation to discussions among engineers, is now making itself widely known to such diverse groups as technology specialists, content aggregators, learning designers, business strategists, and consumers.

Pattern Templates. In spite of the significant progress being made in the metadata arena, current arrays of metadata tags may not offer learning designers and developers sufficient robustness for addressing format, concept, and context delimiters needed to organize objects into meaningful arrays. The selection and compilation of metadata attributes into stand-alone "metafiles" contextualizes learning objects according to variables defined by users. Pattern templates enhance the flexibility of a reusable information object much in the same way that words assemble individual letters in agreed-upon order to transmit specific meaning. Pattern templates enhance the meaningfulness of reusable learning objects much in the same way that sentences offer a structure for assembling words to extend and expand meaning at a higher order of thinking.

Competency Models:
Conceptual and Contextual Pattern Templates

Competency models may offer a solution for constructing pattern templates based upon "best practices" in on-the-job or performance-improvement settings. A competency model is a collection of related descriptions of the knowledge, skills, abilities, and behaviors of an excellent performer. Each competency statement describes a set of interrelated knowledge, skills, attitudes, and behaviors that characterize the excellent performer (Lucia & Lepsinger, 1999). While competency models have offered a useful means of defining employee attributes for organizations for the past 30 years, competency models may extend well beyond their original recruitment and selection applications as knowledge-management methods and tools become increasingly commonplace. By identifying the attributes of outstanding employees in given job roles, competency-based criteria can be selected that establish performance standards for reviewing the performance and capacity of existing employees. Such competency-based criteria can also establish hiring standards (or expectations or guidelines—the term used to describe the attributes varies, as does the degree of rigor used to identify or define attributes associated with specific job roles.) Competency models also provide a "best practices" template to assist in assembling reusable information and learning objects that support both individualized learning needs and cost-effective, *targeted* professional development needs of the organization. As reusable information objects (RIOs) (Wieseler, 1999) and reusable learning objects (RLOs) becomes increasingly widespread as the building blocks for constructing highly personalized learning resources, competency models can serve as the basis for establishing the framework upon which RIOs and RLOs can be contexualized and repurposed.

As has been noted, standards/expectations/guidelines expressed in a competency model for a particular job or performance category can be used in a variety of ways, including employee selection and job-performance evaluation. They can also provide employees with a mechanism for converting the description of attributes to expressions of essential skill areas. On this basis, employees are able to compare their skills with those expected of the outstanding performer. Thus, competency models support the employees' efforts to develop professional development strategies so that on an organizational level, the overall level of industry skills and competencies can be raised.

In summary, competency models benefit organizations and employees because they:

- ❑ Help organizations drive strategic change by modeling the organizations' success competency profile.

- ❑ Allow organizations to set training, hiring, and policy goals to meet the human resources requirements of the strategic vision.

- ❑ Help organizations manage to strategic plan by allowing managers to monitor the essential performance requirements of a given job at any given time.

- ❑ Align employee behaviors with organizational strategies and values.

- ❑ Help clarify job and work expectations for employees and their managers.

- ❑ Support self-improvement by giving employees benchmarks against which to see how he or she measures up to company expectations.

- ❑ Allow for the development of strategic plans that are based upon an organization's core competencies.

- ❑ Provide a "pattern template" for assembling reusable information and learning objects that respond to specific learning needs of individuals and organizations.

Competency-Based Learning

Sieloff's personal knowledge management heuristics (Dempsey, 1999) support the notion of helping individuals target their personalized learning and performance support needs. Competency-based learning (CBL) offers a strategy for achieving the ends of constructing personal-

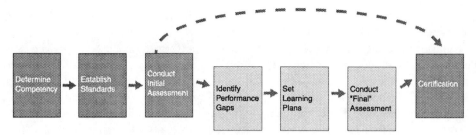

Figure 2. A competency-based learning model.

ized learning plans. CBL links competency assessments with an articulated competency model of the excellent performer. CBL thereby provides the means to benchmark an individual's competencies against specific standards of competency demonstration. When used in combination with a knowledge content distributor, individual learners can then also be linked to learning objects in the form of courses, modules and lessons that will help build capacity in empirically targeted areas (see Figure 2).

Competency-based learning has emerged from research and best practices dealing with motivation and achievement (McCombs, 1992). It is predicated on the practice of using competency models to articulate performance expectations associated with specific categories of jobs. It works by linking skills and competencies (as described in a competency model) to those learning resources that will help the individual build targeted skills and competencies (e.g., traditional classes, white papers, URL links, videos, CD-ROM/multimedia training, and Web-based training). In addition to providing employees the means of determining where (deficient) skills can be strengthened, CBL also provides a means of securing recognition of skill mastery that has been achieved but not formally acknowledged through formal training or education.

Competency-based learning is a strategy that maximizes the effectiveness of training and performance support programs and resources. Where competency models define the scope of skills expected of a high performing employee, competency-based learning provides the means of linking employees with the essential learning resources they need to build targeted skills.

Two Competency-Based E-Learning Case Studies

The following two case studies illustrate how competency-based learning strategies are being applied in practice using online systems. One case study examines the designs underlying a virtual competency-based university based in the United States, while the other case study looks at a national technology-based professional development initiative in Norway.

Western Governors University

The Western Governors University (a U.S.-based virtual university) uses objective, reflective, and portfolio-based assessments of competency as the basis for granting degrees and certifications of program completion. Courses and courseware from partner institutions are among the many means at a student's disposal for preparing for competency assessments. However, courses completed as part of a student's "academic action plan" are used only as a means of helping students master the knowledge, skills, and attitudes represented among the battery of degree/program assessments. WGU degrees do not make use of academic credit as a measure of program completion. At WGU, degrees and certificates are awarded on the basis of successfully completing a battery of objective, critical thinking, and portfolio-based competency assessments across the array of topic domains that have been identified for each specific degree and/or certification program.

The vision of a virtual university based upon documenting student achievement of competency was first articulated in June, 1995 at a meeting of the Western Governors Association. At that meeting, the Governors of 15 Western states posited that collaboration among institutions of higher learning, industry, and government could produce a new model of higher education. This new model would combine advances in technology (e.g., virtual private networks; the World Wide Web), technology-mediated teaching and learning (e.g., distance learning; distributed learning; online communities), and research in the arena of competency-based learning to create an alternative to traditional "brick and mortar," credit-based institutions. This new model was proposed as a solution for achieving sufficient flexibility needed for responding to the needs of society in a rapidly changing economy.

While reaffirming their commitment to traditional colleges and universities, the Governors were concerned that traditional institutions were increasingly unable to meet the growing demands for well-qualified, competent job candidates. According to some estimates (e.g., the American Society for Training and Development, the Kellogg Foundation, the Western Interstate Commission on Higher Education, the Gartner Group), half the jobs to be in existence 15 years from now have not yet been invented. There is, and will continue to be, a tremendous need for lifelong learning and job training that focuses on developing competencies in high-demand fields.

The Governors were also interested in providing alternatives for working adults and non-traditional students who were interested in improving their knowledge and skills in newly emerging disciplines. The Governors understood the value of making technology-mediated education alternatives available for working adults and non-traditional students that minimize disruption on work and personal obligations.

At the core of the Governors' vision was the philosophy that learning occurs throughout life; it is not limited to what is learned in the traditional classroom. Consequently, WGU degrees and certificates were designed as a reflection of what learners actually know and can demonstrate, rather than on course requirements and credits. In WGU's competency-based learning design, students earn their degrees and certifications by demonstrating knowledge, skills, attitudes, and behaviors expected of excellent performances in a given discipline of study and practice. This is accomplished by means of successfully completing a battery of domain-specific assessments that reflect the full range of knowledge, skills, and attitudes expected from high-performing practitioners of the degree-specific discipline. These assessments (along with portfolios and research projects, as appropriate for the specific degree or certification program) are the evaluation criteria used for granting a degree or a certificate—no course grades or credit hours are used in meeting WGU degree requirements. With this approach, life and work experience can count as much as coursework. Students can apply skills and knowledge gained on the job or through self-directed study toward a WGU degree, as well as through traditional or nontraditional courses.

WGU Advisor/Mentors work with students to review their areas of strength and weakness and to recommend strategies for building competency in the domains of that student's degree or certification program that need development. Pre-assessments and self-reflection guide students to appropriate learning experiences, including courses offered by the institutions that are part of the WGU partner network.

WGU articulates competencies for each program with the assistance of recognized leaders in education and industry. While not represented in a competency model, per se, the articulation of essential learning areas forms a domain structure within which specific performance expectations of program graduates are articulated on a per-domain basis. Essential domain-specific competencies identified by diverse groups of subject matter experts are validated by comparing them with standards of performance set by professional organizations for members of the targeted profession. A Program Council of respected practitioners from academe and from business and industry is then established for each degree or certificate program. Program Councils function as the "virtual faculty" for each of WGU's degree and certification programs. As faculty members, Program Council members must review and approve the articulated competency statements within each domain that is defined for a degree or certification program. Program Council members periodically reviews competencies to ensure they are up-to-date and appropriate. They also collaborate with WGU's Assessment Council on the construction of program specific assessment experiences, review the results of student assessments, and, in some programs, participate in conducting field observations, oversee bench tests, and conduct face-to-face oral examinations of candidates for degrees.

Kompetansenettet: A National Competency-Based Professional Development Network

Kompetansenettet* is an online learning management system implemented in Norway under contract with Næringslivets Hovedorganisasjon (NHO), the Confederation of Norwegian Business and Industry. Its intent is to help users improve their job performance by focusing training and education activities on building essential, job-specific knowledge, skills and attitudes rather than emphasizing mastery of a body of knowledge that may or may not be applied on the job.

The genesis for implementing Kompetansenettet was the demand for the provision of professional development opportunities for up to 10% of a worker's time on-the-job. As part of the strategy for responding to this charge, businesses looked to technology-mediated training as a solution for meeting the professional development needs of workers while minimizing the impact of workers' time away from the workplace during the pursuit of training opportunities. NHO has indicated its interest in using Kompetansenettet to document *realkompetanse*—the professional knowledge, skills, and attitudes developed over time that are not otherwise sanctioned or acknowledged by official learning credentials or certifications.

Kompetansenettet was designed to make active use of competency models that define the scope and focus of knowledge, skills, and attitudes attributed to excellent performers in a given job category or learning area (Klemp, 1980). In the initial pilot implementation of Kompetansenettet, existing Web-enabled courseware available from multiple vendors was reviewed, analyzed, and mapped to relevant elements of appropriate competency models. Wherever possible, competency models were validated using third-party data sources (e.g., professional certification guidelines, "best practices" data from professional associations) to enhance their validity and their generalizability.

Kompetansenettet compares an employee's job-specific knowledge, skills, and attitudes with standards of performance established by excellent performers in those same job-specific knowledge, skill, and attitude arenas represented in the competency models registered in Kompetansenettet. Kompetansenettet users complete assessment exercises in relevant learning areas to see how they compare to standards of performance defined in the Kompetansenettet competency models. Assessment results give a user a metric for comparing his or her competencies for his or her job with those competencies as expressed in the Kompetansenettet competency models. Assessment results diagnosed a user's strengths and greatest opportunities for improving his or her job-related knowledge skills and attitudes. Kompetansenettet uses the results of assessments to prescribe an individualized learning plan. The learning plan consists of modified content objects—typically topically-oriented modules contained within existing Web-based

---

*Kompetansenettet is a customized implementation of Informania, Inc.'s WebLearn Plus learning management system.

courseware—that correlate with competencies expected of a high performing employee in specific job classifications.

While Kompetansenettet was conceptualized to apply competency-based learning strategies and tactics to improve workplace performance, Kompetansenettet needed to accommodate robust search and retrieval capabilities to effective manage various forms of Web-enabled learning content, including intact courses and modules contained within an extant course. This was a response to two real-world contingencies: the first was the relative lack of Norwegian language Web-enabled content available in 1999; the second was that, of Web-based instructional content that was available, the vast majority was knowledge-based content rather than competency-based content.* Kompetansenettet's search and retrieval functionality was enabled by means of meta-data tags that index all data elements in the system. Meta-data tags for content mapped to competencies registered in Kompetansenettet used several categories of meta-data tags, including those that specify format attributes, subject attributes, and competency attributes. Content that is not correlated to a specific competency contained in a registered model typically only display format and subject meta-data tags. Whether or not content correlates directly to a registered competency model, use of the format and subject meta-data tags increases the number of content index terms/access points, making it easier for users to locate relevant content resources.

Case Study Observations

The outcomes of these two competency-based learning implementations have brought to the surface a number of issues that underscore the challenges of implementing competency-based learning programs using Web-enabled learning technologies. These include:

- **Knowledge-based learning designs versus competency-based learning designs.** The competency-based learning designs featured in the Western Governors University and in Kompetansenettet have attempted to establish a direct, positive correlation among:

  ❑ The competency standards for a degree certification or professional development programs.

  ❑ The assessments developed to benchmark an individual's competencies against standards of excellent performance for a targeted program of professional performance improvement.

  ❑ The modularized learning resources—"learning objects"—linked to assessment results that can build learning capacity in the arena identified by the assessment tests. Learners have empirical evidence to help discern the specific areas within a specific competency model where performance improvement is warranted.

  The vast majority of content materials currently available from universities, publishers, and commercial course providers are still based on the "knowledge model" as constructed by subject matter experts. In a "knowledge model," content is organized around topic or subject attributes rather than discrete performances expected of excellent performers. While this shift from the "Subject Matter Expert" approach to the "Expert Performer" approach will ultimately result in greater availability of reusable learning objects, content providers accustomed to producing fully integrated courses may very well question the value of changing the way that they organize learning

---

*In a knowledge-based learning model, content is organized around topic or subject attributes rather than around discrete performances expected of excellent performers as described in a competency model.

content. While Jennings (1999) and others have already predicted the "death of the online course," content providers have not yet broadly embraced the creation of digital content objects as courseware building blocks. Until such objects are more readily available, the ability to construct fully personalized competency-based learning plans may be compromised by the relative lack of availability of competency-specific content object resources. Recent developments in the Kompetansenettet project suggest that the sponsoring organizations are not leveraging the correlation among performance expectations, diagnostic assessments, and the assembly of objects into meaningful competency-based learning plans. This may be due in some measure to the resistance toward making competency assessments an integral component of the Kompetansenettet feature set. The end result appears to be a retreat to the more familiar knowledge-based learning design found in most conventional contemporary online courses.

- **Online courses vs. learning objects.** Currently there is a strong, emerging trend that calls for using learning objects as the building blocks for constructing learning interventions that meet specific interests, needs, and styles of individuals. Nevertheless, the most typical way in which individuals complete online learning experiences is by means of online courses. There appear to be two causes for this phenomenon. The first is that the idea of constructing a personalized learning program by selecting and assembling the array of learning objects that best correlate with learning interests, performance gaps, learning style, and presentation preferences is still relatively new. Courses represent the most familiar way to offer learning content to students, whether the course be a classroom-based, instructor-led course or a Web-based, instructor-led course from a virtual institution. This familiarity goes a long way in establishing the trust between the learner and the e-learning solutions provider that is necessary for building brand loyalty. Nevertheless, comfort with the familiar in an unfamiliar, virtual space will increasingly find itself balanced against improved productivity and competitiveness enabled by leveraging organizational knowledge and personalizing e-learning programs. Secondly, there is the issue of learning object interoperability. Most commercially available online providers purport that their software meets AICC, IMS, or IEEE interoperability standards. However, these courses come bundled with proprietary CGI, user tracking, and course player code that compromises interoperability. Even though individual units or lessons of an online course can be indexed using metadata tags, launching and displaying only a part of a course, users cannot typically enter and exit an extant course without compromising navigation and user tracking functions. Until such a time when reusable learning objects are readily available within organizations, from commercial content publishers or from content aggregators, online learning designs will continue to emphasize presenting content in the ready-to-use, familiar form of the course.

- **Competency articulation for knowledge-oriented programs.** The articulation of competency standards for the excellent performer works well in vocational education, practice-based performance improvement, and professional educational and development programs. How well can a competency-based learning model be used to define the expectations for a general educational program or a professional development program based entirely upon "soft skills" (e.g., leadership) that are hard to quantify?

- **Standards for Learning Architecture Learning Objects** (Hodgins, 1999b). Unlike LAN or CD-ROM development environments in which closed proprietary protocols tended to guide the design, development, and deployment of digital learning resources, developers producing Web-enabled content must ensure that open, non-proprietary standards form the foundation of the learning resources development process. The establishment of standards for learning architecture and learning objects is, therefore, based upon the goal of defining interoperability protocols so that all learning objects can be used on all varieties of learning management and content retrieval systems. Learning Architecture Learning Objects standards are either learning-focused or technology-focused. Learning-focused standards address issues related to content, metadata and the establishment of a learning management system data model. Standards typically address issues associated with the interoperability of HTML, HTTP, XML, Java, and JavaScript. They will also need to be developed to address issues related to contextualization, learning-specific utility and achievement of designated learning outcomes.

- **Dealing with "Coopetition"** (a term that combines the terms "cooperation" and "competition"). This refers to the uneasy alliance of organizational partners who have decided to collaborate on a specific venture, even though they may be direct competitors in different settings. An example of coopetition can be found by considering the challenges faced by courseware vendors accustomed to developing their products for sale using the standard knowledge-based approach to course design. What happens if a course-based content provider chooses NOT to create modularized content that can be deployed in a CBL application? Will their competitors (who do accommodate modularization) be better prepared to repurpose similar content for multiple uses? Considering the WGU example, will traditional universities be willing to configure their current courses into modular objects, for use by another institution of higher education? Even though WGU and its partner institutions purport not to compete for the same kinds of students, traditional institutions are keenly interested in leveraging their own institutional capital in establishing new student market share.

- **Valid, Reliable, and Predictive Assessments.** How can an individual (or an organization) be assured that the assessments used to predict an individual's ability to perform his or her job effectively are statistically valid, reliable, and predictive? What variety of assessment experiences (e.g., objective tests vs. reflective tests; multiple choice vs. "point and click" graphical response items) is the best measure of the learning gained? If the selection of learning resources is to be based upon profile criteria selected by and for an individual learner, then the validity, reliability, and predictability of the instruments that quantify profile attributes must be empirically supported. Knowledge-based and competency-based assessment "instruments" may range from objective multiple choice items to online case-based simulation, to skill demonstrations, to the preparation of a professional portfolio, depending upon the learning to be assessed. The challenge of implementing valid reliable and predictive assessments is exacerbated when dealing with entities that maintain strict online privacy standards, restricting the maintenance of profile data on individuals.

Summary

This chapter has described just a few of the trends that are having significant impact on how the world at large views the World Wide Web as a vehicle for supporting and enabling teaching and learning. The brief overview of issues encountered when implementing emerging e-learning, knowledge management, and knowledge commerce initiatives underscores the importance of ensuring that Web-based learning designs focus on providing individual learners with the tools, resources, and tactics for achieving specific learning outcomes. It also underscores the importance for learning designers working in the Web-based learning space to expand their thinking.

The current trends that emphasize the reconfiguration of traditional, classroom-oriented teaching and training experiences to digital, online versions of the same have been a useful intermediary step in helping learning designers get started. To be successful in the emerging e-learning space, designers will need to shift their thinking from designing relatively static distance learning solutions (that is, classroom extended, course-based experiences) and reconfiguring existing courses and content resources to digital forms. The challenge will call for learning designers to create highly personalized learning solutions that give learners the tools and resources to construct learning solutions that respond to needs defined by the individual and allow them to manage their learning experiences on terms they themselves define.

References

Dempsey, M. (1999, Nov. 10). Viewpoint. *Financial Times*.

Derryberry, A., & Anderson, J. (In press). *Projecting ROI for e-learning: Predicting the value, making the case*. Alexandria, VA: American Society for Training and Development.

Ellis, A. L., Wagner, E. D., & Longmire, W. (1999). *Managing Web-based training*. Alexandria, VA: American Society for Training and Development.

Empson, L. (1999, Oct. 4). The challenge of managing knowledge. *Financial Times*, Mastering Strategy, Part 2, 8–10.

Harris, R. (1999, Sept. 26). Personal communication.

Hodgins, W. (1999a). Learning objects: Status and direction. A presentation at the Stanford Research Institute: Learning on Demand Conference; learnativity.com/speaking.html

Hodgins, W. (1999b). Learning standards; learnativity.com/standards.html

Jennings, C. (1999, Nov. 26). Where does online learning end and knowledge management begin? A paper presented at Online Educa Berlin, the Fifth International Conference on Technology-Supported Learning, Berlin, Germany.

Jonassen, D. H., & Grabowski, B. L. (1993). *Handbook of individual differences, learning, and instruction*. Hillsdale, NJ: Lawrence Erlbaum Associates.

Klemp, G. O. (1980). (Ed.). *The assessment of occupational competence*. Washington, DC: National Institute of Education.

Ledbetter, J. (1999). The Internet economy gets real. *The Industry Standard*, 2(39), 96–106.

Longmire, W. R. (2000). Content and context: Designing and developing learning objects. In D. Brightman (Ed.). *Learning without limits, volume 3: Emerging strategies for e-learning solutions*. San Francisco: Informania, Inc.

Lucia, A. D., & Lepsinger, R. (1999). *The art and science of competency models: Pinpointing critical success factors in organizations*. San Francisco: Jossey-Bass/Pfeiffer.

Masie, E. (1998, April). Emerging acronyms spell market change. *Computer Reseller News*, 27, p. 59.

McCombs, B. L. (1992). *Learner centered psychological principles*. Washington, DC: American Psychological Association, in collaboration with the Mid-continent Regional Educational Laboratory.

Ormrod, J. E. (1998). *Educational psychology: Developing learners* (2nd ed.). New York: Merrill Prentice-Hall.

Richards, T. (1998). *The emergence of open standards for learning technology*. San Francisco: Macromedia, Inc.; learnativity.com/standards.html

Rothwell, W. J. (1996). *Beyond training and development: State of the art strategies for enhancing human performance.* New York: American Management Association.

Sieloff, C. (1999, July/August). The Sorcerer's apprentice. *Knowledge Management, 2*(10), 9–14.

Trondsen, E. (1999, Sept. 14). Learning on demand, a presentation at the Stanford Research Institute: Learning on demand conference, Palo Alto.

Violino, B. (1999, Sept. 27). IT Excellence. *Information Week,* p. 52.

Wagner, E. D. (1998). Are you ready for electronic learning? In E. D. Wagner (Ed.), *Learning without limits* (2nd ed.). San Francisco: Informania, Inc.

Wagner, E. D. (1999). Beyond distance learning: Distributed learning systems. In H. Stolovich & E. Keeps (Eds.), *Handbook of human performance technology* (2nd ed.). San Francisco: Jossey-Bass.

Wieseler, W. (1999). *RIO: A standards based approach for reusable information objects.* San Jose, CA: Cisco Systems.

The Author

Ellen D. Wagner (e-mail: edwagner@informania.com; **Web homepage: informania.com)** is Chief Learning Officer, Informania, Inc., San Francisco, California, and co-author, with A. L. Ellis and W. Longmire, of *Managing Web-Based Training,* published by the American Society for Training and Development.

6

Glossary of Terms in Web-Based Training

Rick Hall

Alpha Test. This level of testing is the first testing that a site or program goes through in the development stage.

Applet. Applets are small software applications. Java programs are usually called Java applets because they are relatively small in size, but they can be any small application that has a limited purpose.

Archie. A pre-Web file searcher, a program that searches files for documents and information that you want, a derivative of the word "archive." It is still alive and well, and has a nice Web interface these days—Archieplex. It may be used to search anonymous FTPs.

Audio-Conferencing (Teleconferencing). Audio-conferencing is used by many institutions. It uses a tele-convenor (a device that allows the instructor and the trainees to interactively talk in real time) for two-way audio (voice). It needs one phone line between two sites and a teleconferencing bridge for multi-point interaction (more than two sites). This audio-conferencing capability is becoming more and more usable over the Web.

Audio-Graphics. Audio-graphics refers to two-way communications consisting of both audio (voice) and graphics (sent, seen, and manipulated on a computer screen). It uses a PC and a tele-convenor, makes use of two-way voice and interactive computer graphics, requires two phone lines between two sites, needs a teleconferencing bridge for multi-point interaction (more than two sites), is done in real-time, and requires preparation of slides (computer displayed overheads of text, graphics, etc.). This, too, is becoming more usable over the Web.

Bandwidth. Think of this as the size of the "pipe" that the information travels through. A small bandwidth would be represented by a garden hose, a larger bandwidth by a culvert.

Beta Test. As the beta version of a site or a program is the final version before the public release, a beta test is the final round of testing before the public release.

Beta Version. When new software, hardware, or other things are being developed, they often go through a number of formal stages. Typically, the version that is ONLY being looked at and tested in-house—not by any outside agency—is called the Alpha version. Once many of the bugs are out of it, and the developer wants it tested by others, it is often called

51

a Beta version. This version is NOT for commercial release. It contains bugs (if it didn't, it would be the release version), and is often free to the tester in return for feedback and error reporting.

Browsers. Browsers are computer programs that allow HTML to be read on your computer. HTML is pretty much machine independent. A browser allows your machine to read and display HTML from other sources. Netscape, Internet Explorer, and Mosaic are some examples of browsers.

Bulletin Board. A service on the Web where people can connect and read or "post" messages. This is just an electronic Web-based version of a *cork* bulletin board on your wall.

CD-ROMs. Small plastic discs that have the capacity to hold lots of information, around 450 megabytes—and that is quite a bit! Because of this capacity, CD-ROMs (Compact Disc-Read Only Memory) are often used in connection with multimedia productions which require large amounts of storage for digital audio and digital video. CD-ROMs are NOT multimedia; they are just storage devices, a means of storing information which is quite often loaded to the hard drive of the computer or computer system where it will be used.

Chat. Chat (IRC—Internet Relay Chat) is a real-time text-based conference between two or more people. The software allows two or more people to type messages to each other (or the group) and respond to each other's messages. The chat is accomplished by typing on the computer keyboard, not by speaking to each other.

Client Server Architecture. A way of setting up a distributed network so that the Client (or workstation) performs the computations while the Server (central computer) handles other functions and takes care of file management.

CGI (Common Gateway Interface). CGI lets you use server-based programs and databases. This interface is much like an automatic translation machine. It understands everything and permits the smooth flow of specific information. For heavy duty CGI, work with a system's administrator or with someone from Computing Services. For VERY simple CGI scripts, look at the Web; there are lots of scripts that you can use and easily modify.

Compression. A method of making a file smaller. There are number of software products that will compress and decompress files to make them smaller, and as such, quicker to send over the Internet.

Conferencing Online. Online conferencing refers to interactive dialog over the Web. This is often text based and asynchronous. For example, a course instructor could post a question or discussion topic to a conference. Students would then check the course Web pages and add to the discussion and or answer the questions. They could take part as many times as the instructor allowed, and could do it any time of the day or night. This requires conferencing software. Many institutions develop their own, while others purchase commercial packages.

Cookie. Cookies are packages of data that get sent to you by a server and are stored on your computer. They can contain various different sets of information, and this information can get automatically sent back to the server when it recognizes its URL in the cookie on your browser. You can have your browser warn you before accepting a cookie; you can also have your browser not accept cookies.

Coordinates. A set of measurements (X,Y coordinates) are used to define locations on a Web page. Using a set of four coordinates, a very specific clickable area may be defined on a Web page.

Cyberspace. This is a term that was coined by William Gibson in his novel *Neuromancer.* He used it to describe the complete total of computer-accessible information in the world.

Distance Education and Distance Learning. There are as many definitions of this as there are people out there using it. My definition (and it is evolving) is "education that in some way bridges the distance between students and their ability to access educational offerings." Sometimes that distance is time, sometimes it is kilometers (miles), sometimes it is oceans. Often (and always, in some people's minds), distance education involves technology. Telephones, computers, CD-ROMs, Internet, satellites, and other things constitute some of the technologies that may be involved.

Download. When you download a file, you receive it over the Internet. The opposite is to send a file over the Internet, and is called an upload.

Dynamic HTML. Dynamic HTML (DHTML) is HTML that "dynamically" changes based on which browser is accessing it. It works using the Document Object Model (DOM) interface that allows HTML tags to be dynamically changed via a scripting language (e.g., JavaScript).

E-Commerce. Electronic commerce.

E-mail. E-mail (or electronic mail) uses the Internet to send and receive text, graphics, sounds, and other attachments on a personal basis. Many Web browsers have a built-in e-mail facility. Many commercial e-mail packages also exist.

E-Zine. An electronic magazine. Some are free, some have subscription rates.

Electronic Performance Support System (EPSS). Electronic Performance Support System is a computer system that gives you fast and easy assistance at the job desktop. It may use different multimedia delivery methods and it may use artificial intelligence (AI).

Ethernet. This is a high-speed coaxial cable system used in local area networks (LANs). It can give very fast Web connectivity.

Extranet. A private network for the secure transfer of information. It makes use of Internet protocols.

FAQ (Frequently Asked Questions). Websites often contain FAQs. This is because often many visitors to a site ask the same questions. A list of these frequently asked questions may be provided with the frequently given responses. Another alternative could be to make the Website more user friendly in the first place—and thus avoid all of those questions.

FTP (File Transfer Protocol). A protocol (set of rules) used to transfer files over a TCP/IP network. This protocol allows a user to log onto the network, see the directories, and copy files.

Firewall. Some kind of electronic or coded wall or protection that is intended to keep a network secure from outside or non-authorized users.

Frames. An HTML way of dividing a Web page into two or more parts, vertically, horizontally, or a combination of both.

.GIF (Graphic Interchange Format). This is one of the standard ways of storing graphical information for use on the Web. It is most ideal for line art or graphics that do not require a great deal of detail. These files can be very small and tend to load much faster than other, larger formats.

Gopher. A pre-Web, text-based way of moving around the Internet. It was good for those with limited computer capabilities—or with slow computer link capabilities (slow modems).

Groupware. Groupware is software that allows multiple users to access, share, and work on the same documents and files. Often, when one person makes a change to a document using groupware, the other members of the team receive notification via e-mail.

Home Page. This is the first page that is normally accessed at a Web site. It is often named "index.htm," "index.html," "default.htm," or "default.html."

HTML. HyperText Markup Language (HTML) is the language that is used for writing the directions that allow links within and without the Web. It is a universally understood language that consistently formats text and graphics for multi-platform use.

HTTP (HyperText Transfer Protocol). This is the protocol that allows servers to connect to the World Wide Web. Using HTTP, connection is non-machine dependent.

HyperLink. A connection between hypermedia documents. Clicking on a text might take you to a picture, or to a virtual reality site, or might allow you to e-mail someone.

Hypermedia. The integration of graphics, text, audio, and video which makes Websites interesting to visit.

HyperText. The text of the World Wide Web. Clicking on an "anchored" word will link you to another Website or to another place within the current Website.

Image Map. Image Map is an HTML way of taking an image and using the xy coordinates to link to different places. For example, an image of a dog could be set up so that clicking on the dog's head took you to a different place than clicking on the dog's foot.

Images online. Images can be stored on servers for viewing in conjunction with Websites in a number of formats. The most common two tend to be JPEGs and GIFs. These are best used for different reasons in different places. Most good "How To" books on HTML will tell you which to use and when to use it.

Information Highway. Popular term for the single system of modem-connected computers capable of transporting text, voice, graphics, video, and all manner of other interesting things.

Internet. This is a network of networks that enables computer communications. These communications can be in the form of text, graphics, sounds, video, and almost any other form conceivable (or yet to be conceived) by techie types. With the plethora of goodies available, it is an excellent medium for interactive instruction (see World Wide Web).

Internet Explorer. Internet Explorer is a Web browser.

Intranet. An intranet is, in essence, your own private World Wide Web technology for your own employee-only network. This could be a corporate intranet or one for your university or other institution. Intranets are private networks that look and feel the same as the Web. And, yes, they may combine text, graphics, and all the other features of the regular Internet.

IP address. An Internet machine's address expressed in numbers instead of a host name.

IRC (Internet Relay Chat). IRC is a text-based "network" that uses the Internet to allow people to type messages (chat) to each other. To access it, you will need a client program that can handle IRC. Once you log onto an IRC server, you then join the IRC stream (channel) of your choice.

ISDN (Integrated Services Digital Network). This is an international telecommunications standard for transmitting voice, video and data over digital lines. Special connectors are needed to connect your PC to an ISDN.

ISP. Internet Service Provider.

.JPEG/.JPG (Joint Photographic Experts Group). JPEG (jay peg) is a standard for compressing still images that is becoming very popular due to its high-compression capability.

Java. A Sun Microsystems team created Java, a software programming language. This programming language can be used to produce little programs (called applets) that can "run" over the Web and are machine independent. That means that these applets can be created on a PC, and run on a Mac or a Silicon Graphics machine.

JavaScript. JavaScript is a script language. It is easier to use than Java, but you cannot do as much. JavaScript works with the existing HTML page. Java, however, can generate a completely custom interface.

LAN (Local Area Network). This represents a group of computers and their peripherals that are all linked to be shared in a restricted area. Universities, businesses, and others often use LANs. Theses can in turn be connected at various places to the Internet.

Listservs. These are computer-managed mailing lists. E-mail sent to a listserv automatically goes to the e-mail of everyone subscribed to the list. Subscription may be external or may be handled completely by the listserv owner.

Lynx. A Web browser developed by the University of Kansas. It is excellent for text-only Internet connections.

Mailing Lists. These are lists of e-mail addresses that allow for easy sending of a single message to many addresses. This can be done by using a self made list and copying it into the address on the e-mail, it can be done using "nicknames" as part of an e-mail program, or it can be done using a Listserv. Mailing lists are a form of asynchronous communication and are mostly text based (most have the capability of sending files as attachments—and these files may be graphics or other multimedia files).

Modem. An electronic device (internal or external to your computer) that takes computer signals and modulates them so that they can be passed over phone lines. Incoming signals are demodulated so that the computer can understand them, hence modem (modulate/demodulate).

MOOs. A MOO, Multi-user Object Oriented environment, is a variety of MUD (see below). Most MUDs are multiplayer adventure games. MOOs open the virtual world to those either "playing a game" or exploring a theme or course. MOOs deal in a multimedia realm, whereas MUDs are text based.

Mosaic. Mosaic is the Web browser that caused the explosion of use of the Web. It was created by the University of Illinois National Center for Supercomputing Applications (NCSA) and released on the Internet in early 1993.

.MPEG. Motion Pictures Experts Group standard format for the compression and the storage of digital media files. This technology and its applications are evolving.

MUDs. MUD stands for Multiple User Dungeon or Multiple User Dimension. Multiple User Dungeon is the more traditional term and, as such, a MUD is a complete virtual world in which you become the body of a character you adopt to navigate that world. You explore in real time and usually at the same time as a number of other characters controlled by other people to whom you can talk and even team up with if you wish. MUDs differ hugely in their theme, content, and style. MUDs are being used to explore and work in a collaborative mode in educational settings as well.

Multimedia Presentation. Technically, any presentation using more than one form of media, from print and tape, voice and overheads, to virtual reality. Most people think of multi-media as using computers, CD-ROMs, or generally some combination of technologies that could be said to be heavily into the bells and whistles.

Netiquette. The Internet etiquette. Includes rules like: Be brief, and use both upper and lower case. If you use all upper case, you could be accused of SHOUTING.

Netscape. This is a browser that allows you to move easily around the Web.

Newsgroups. Text-based asynchronous "conferencing" via the Web. There are thousands of different newsgroups available, and these consist of ongoing discussions. To participate in a newsgroup, you must go and look and see what is new. It is much like going to the bulletin board and seeing who has posted a new item. Your imagination probably cannot even come close to the range of topics available!

On-Demand (Just-in-Time) Distance Education. Any form of Distance education that allows the participants their choice of when they are involved (and often where as well). Examples can include student driven/student interactive CD-ROMs, Internet delivered courses, Open Access Learning Programs, and many others.

Online Help. Help that is accessed via the Web. You must be online to access it. It usually resides on the Web pages of the company providing the product.

Open Access Learning Program. These may contain print, audio, video, and graphic components. They can also incorporate forms of interactivity such as fax communications, phone communications, computer e-mail, and Web communications or interactive CD-ROMs. The Open Access refers to the fact that students can enter these courses at any time. They are not bound by real-time attendance. They are also not bound by location.

Open University. An Open University is usually one that admits students at any time, from anywhere, giving them a set amount of time to finish a set amount of work. Admission requirements vary, as do fees and accreditation.

PC. Personal computer—a generic term, but often the user of the term implies an IBM-type PC. That is a computer capable of running Windows from Microsoft.

.PDF (Portable Document Format). .PDF is a format developed by the Adobe people that produces a word-processed document that appears the same on various platforms. If students are submitting assignments over the Web to an instructor, .PDF files tend to be the most likely to work across computers.

PERL (Practical Extraction and Report Language). This is a computer language that works very well for CGI tasks.

Plug-Ins. Small programs that are installed on your computer and aid your Web browser to do special things.

Real-Time Distance Education. Any distance education that requires participants to be logged on or tuned in at a specific time. Examples can include audio-conferencing, video-conferencing, face-to-face off campus, audio graphics, some satellite delivered offerings, synchronous Internet conferencing, and many others.

RealAudio. RealAudio is an example of sound that plays as it comes over the browser. It is continuous audio (see Streaming Technologies). RealAudio requires a player or client program that works alongside your browser. It may be a regular part of your browser or it may have to be downloaded to your computer via the Web. At the other end, the server sourcing the streaming audio must have a RealAudio server.

RealVideo. RealVideo is an example of video that plays as it comes over the browser. It is continuous video (see Streaming Technologies). RealVideo requires a player or client program that works alongside your browser. It may be a regular part of your browser or it may have to be downloaded to your computer via the Web. At the other end, the server sourcing the streaming video must have a RealVideo server.

Search engines. Search engines look like Websites that let you type in "key words," and then the Website returns "hits" (occurrences of those key words). In reality, the Website is just a front for a very sophisticated data base that uses software robots that travel the Web, looking at Websites. A person may search for a word, a phrase, a URL, or any combination of these options, plus many more.

Server. A piece of software that sits on the host computer, allowing you to use your client software to surf the net.

Streaming Technologies. Streaming technologies allow either sound or video to start playing by way of your browser as soon as a sufficient amount of data has arrived. An example of the opposite would be a sound file that loads in its entirety on your computer and then plays.

Synchronous/Asynchronous. In its simplest terms—when something is synchronous, we are all there at the same time (a typical classroom is synchronous), and when something is asynchronous, we work on our own time (a Web conference is often asynchronous)—that is, we read what has been posted—post our thoughts—and maybe come online later and post other thoughts.

T1, T3, T10, etc. A carrier system that supports internet transmission of data. The transmission rate of T1 (1.544 Mbps) is quite common. The T3 rate is 44.736 Mbps. The larger the "T" number, the faster the transmission rate.

TCP/IP (Transmission Control Protocol/Internet Protocol). TCP/IP is a communications protocol developed under contract from the U.S. Department of Defense and is the protocol that allows dissimilar systems to talk to each other.

Telnet. This is an emulation protocol used on the Internet that allows a person to log onto and run a program from a remote site. I can log on to a computer at my university and then telnet to a computer at a university in Florida and run a program down there.

Testing Online. Online testing may be accomplished using a variety of different software packages or by using scripts in CGI. Testbanks are prepared and the scripting is set up to specify the number of questions, the question bank from which to draw the questions, the time limit of the exam etc. With the case of T/F and multiple choice questions, the software can often mark the test and send the results to both the instructor and the student, if that is your wish.

.TIFF (Tagged Image File Format). This is a standard format for storing bitmapped image files. This is a very high quality way of storing, and as such, these files can also be very large. Most Web-based learning people would use the less bandwidth-intensive .GIF format.

Thread. The term thread or "common thread" is often used in computer discussions or conferences. A thread is a series of responses to an initial posting with a common theme or idea.

Upload. When you send a file over the Internet, you are uploading it. The opposite is to receive a file over the Internet and is called a download.

URL. Stands for Uniform Resource Locator. This is the address that gets you to a specific spot on the Web. Each home page of every group (company, university, agency etc.) has its own specific URL.

Video-Conferencing. Gaining use by many institutions. Uses a video-conferencing unit (PictureTel is an example) to allow students and instructors to see each other. It needs two special data lines between two sites and needs a video-conferencing bridge for multi-point (more than two sites). It is more expensive than audio-conferencing, but allows two-way picture as well as two-way voice, but is not conducive for really large groups.

Virtual Reality. A simulation of an environment that can be experienced using a computer. Usually this refers to high-end simulations such as flight simulators, but can be much more simple.

VRML. Virtual Reality Modeling Language is a 3-D graphics language used on the Web. After downloading a VRML page, you can then "virtually" manipulate it. Downloading the VRML Web page for the newest automobile will allow you to rotate the car, zoom in, and look at various parts and explore the image.

Web-Based Courses. This is a generic term for any course that uses the Web for content delivery. This can include courses that are entirely delivered over the Web, or used to enhance courses that are taught via other means. In some cases, this term has been used (incorrectly, I feel) for courses that have Websites that students refer to in order to get notes, assignments, or other parts of their learning.

Webmaster. The person within an organization that is in charge of the Web for that organization. Many attempts have been made to make the term gender non-specific, but not all have been very good.

Wide Area Network (WAN). An area network that covers a wide geographic area, as opposed to a local area network (LAN).

World Wide Web (the Web, WWW). A database of information located all around the world, accessed via the Internet. This Web is all linked together and can include text, sound, video, graphics, pictures, and much more to come.

The Author

Rick Hall (e-mail: hall@unb.ca; Web homepage: unb.ca/naweb) is Program Director, Distance Education and Off-Campus Services, University of New Brunswick, Canada.

7

Web-Based Training Resources

Manal A. El-Tigi and
Badrul H. Khan

Chapter Table of Contents

Introduction

This chapter catalogs resources related to Web-based training (WBT) that may prove useful to designers, developers, evaluators, trainers, students, faculty, administrators, and educational/information technologists interested in utilizing the World Wide Web as a learning environment. Web-based training is a new and emerging field. Abundant resources covering a wide spectrum of WBT already exist online and in print. Categories of resources listed in this chapter encompass various dimensions of the Web-Based Learning (WBL) Framework developed by Khan (2001). The WBL Framework consists of the following eight dimensions: pedagogical, technological, interface design, evaluation, management, resource support, ethical, and institutional. Each dimension of the framework encompasses various critical issues concerning open, flexible, and distributed learning environments (see Chapter 8).

A. Purpose and Scope

The number of Web-based training and instructional resources is increasing. Various categories of online and non-electronic resources include textbooks, journals, magazines, conferences, mailing lists, related articles, FAQs, jobs, examples of WBI/WBT, professional organizations and associations, authoring tools/systems, development companies, and WBI/WBT online.

This resource chapter is limited to research related to the categories above. Highlights include Web-based training applications and teaching strategies. The majority of resources are U.S.-based, but a global flavor has also been taken into consideration.

This chapter includes current literature at the time of publication. We are well aware that this topic is in its infancy, however, and we expect that many more resources will be available shortly. We intend to update these resources at the supplemental Web page for this chapter (BooksToRead.com/wbt/resources.htm).

B. Categories of Resources

1. Databases and Directories

The following directories cover a wide range of resources, including journal articles, books, online courses, graduate schools, dissertations in educational technology, and Web-based tools and catalogs. The ERIC database is the largest education database in the world, containing more than one million records of journal articles, research papers, curriculum and teaching guides, conference papers, and books. Each year, approximately 30,000 new records are added. The Web-Based Training Information Center provides a comprehensive guide and directories for many aspects of Web-based training.

- The ERIC Database
  askeric.org/Eric/

- Asynchronous Learning Network's Online Course Directory
  aln.org/coursedirectory/

- Web-Based Training Information Center—Online Course Directory
  filename.com/wbt/pages/wbtonline.htm

- Web-Based Training Information Center—Web-Based Tools Directory
  filename.com/wbt/pages/wbttools.htm

- A Hub for Excellence in E-Learning
  BadrulKhan.com

- Gradschools.com
  gradschools.com/listings/menus/edu_tech_menu.html

- Doctoral Research in Educational Technology: A Directory of Dissertations,
    1977–1997
  edtech.univnorthco.edu/disswww/dissdir.htm

2. Magazines and Journals (Print and Electronic)

The following journals address current aspects of WBT.

- AACE's *Journal of Educational Multimedia and Hypermedia*
  aace.org/pubs/jemh/Default.htm

- *CyberPsychology and Behavior*
  liebertpub.com/cpb/

- *Educational Technology*
  BooksToRead.com/etp

- *E-learning*
  elearningmag.com

- *Inside Training Technology*
  ittrain.com

- *Learning Technologies Report*
  thenode.org/ltreport/

- *New Corporate University Review*
  traininguniversity.com

- *Technical Training Magazine*
  astd.org/virtual_community/tt_magazine/

- *The Technology Source*
  horizon.unc.edu/ts

- *Training & Development Magazine*
  astd.org/virtual_community/td_magazine

- *Training Media Review*
  tmreview.com

- *Virtual University Journal*
  openhouse.org.uk/virtual-university-press/vuj/welcome.htm

- *WebNet Journal*
  webnetjrl.com/

3. Books

While this is not an exhaustive list, the books cited are among the works relevant to Web-based training. The ERIC database provides detailed online citations and abstracts for each book listed (see also: BooksToRead.com/de, for a listing of titles on distance education and online learning).

- Ellis, A. L., Longmire, W. R., & Wagner, E. D. (1999). *Managing Web-based training.* Alexandria, VA: American Society for Training & Development.

- Hall, B. (1997). *Web-based training cookbook.* New York: Wiley.

- Harrison, N. (1998). *How to design self-directed and distance learning: A guide for creators of Web-based training, computer-based training, and self-study materials.* New York: McGraw-Hill.

- Khan, B. H. (1997). (Ed.). *Web-based instruction.* Englewood Cliffs: Educational Technology Publications.

- Steed, C. (1999). *Web-based training.* London: Gower.

4. Online Book Stores

Several search engines with online shopping capabilities have emerged. Amazon.com specializes in books, videos, and CDs, among various other products. Bookfinder has a search engine that searches Amazon.com and out-of-print booksellers. Barnes & Noble's site is the online presence for the Barnes & Noble book store chain. BooksToRead.com provides recommended reading by experts in the field of educational technology, distance education, training, and Web-based learning.

- Amazon.com
  Amazon.com

- Bookfinder.com
  Bookfinder.com

- Barnes & Noble
  bn.com

- BooksToRead.com
  BooksToRead.com/e/et

5. Conferences, Workshops, and Seminars

The following list is a sampling of topic related conferences, workshops, and seminars.

- AECT International Convention
  aect.org/Convention/Default.htm

- ASTD TechKnowledge
  astd.org/virtualcommunity/astdtk

- Asynchronous Learning Networks Conference
  aln.org

- ED-MEDIA—World Conference on Educational Multimedia, Hypermedia, and Telecommunications
  aace.org/conf/edmedia/default.htm

- Designing Instruction for Web-Based Training Workshops
  dsink.com

- ICCE/ICCAI—International Conference on Computers in Education/International Conference on Computer-Assisted Instruction
  icce2000.nthu.edu.tw/

- New Media Instructional Design Symposium
  Influent.com/newmedia99/index.html

- Training 2000 Conference & Expo
  Training2000.com

- WebNet World Conference on the Internet and the WWW
  aace.org/conf/webnet/default.htm

6. Online Mailing Lists

This section contains a list of the most popular online educational technology mailing lists covering WBT. Topics include research areas, design and development, software, management, and distance education. To subscribe, send e-mail to the address listed below and in body of text type in *subscribe listserv name* exactly as provided below in parenthesis followed by *your first and last name.* Leave the subject line blank.

- Association for Educational Communications and Technology (AECT-L)
  listserv@wvnvm.wvnet.edu

- Distance Education Online Symposium (DEOS-L)
  listserv@lists.psu.edu

- Educational Technology (EDTECH)
  listserv@h-net.msu.edu

- Web Based Training/Online Learning (WBTOLL-L)
  listserv@hermes.circ.gwu.edu

- World Wide Web Courseware Developers (WWWDEV)
  listserv@unb.ca

- World Wide Web in Education (WWWEDU)
  listproc@listproc.listproc.net

- WEBTALK (WEBTALK)
  majordomo@teachers.net

- Instructional Technology Forum (ITFORUM)
  listserv@uga.cc.uga.edu

7. Articles

The following articles were selected based upon their relevancy. Key search words include instruction, learning, design, implementation, evaluation, management, and development. These recent articles reflect the current literature in the field, the rapid advancement of technology, and the exponential growth in Web-based training.

- Ashenfelter, J. P. (1997). Strategies for introducing faculty with limited computer skills to Web-based instructional projects: Case studies in drama and the classics. *Journal of Instruction Delivery Systems, 11*(4), 14–18.

- Barker, P. (1999). Using intranets to support teaching and learning. *Innovations in Education and Training International, 36*(1), 3–10.

- Barron, A. (1998). Designing Web-based training. *British Journal of Educational Technology, 29*(4), 355–370.

- Cheung, K. (1998). Educating teachers for the information age. *Educational Media International, 35*(4), 275–77.

- Davis, P., Finlay, C., Cosgrave, T., & McDonald, P. (1998). Cornell University Library Distance Learning White Paper (ERIC Document Reproduction Service No. ED 418 705).

- Dorner, R., Schafer, A., Elcacho, C., & Luckas, V. (1998). Using VRML for teaching and training in industry (ERIC Document Reproduction Service No. ED 427 699).

- Driscoll, M. (1997). Defining Internet-based and Web-based training. *Performance Improvement, 36*(4), 5–9.

- Gayeski, D. (1997). Predicting the success of new media for organizational learning: How can we avoid costly mistakes? *Educational Technology, 37*(6), 5–13.

- Geibert, R. C. (1998). *Integration of Web-based instruction to support collaboration in a graduate nursing program taught via multipoint interactive videoconferencing.* (Practicum Report). Nova Southeastern University (ERIC Document Reproduction Service No. IR 019 410).

- Graziadei, W. *et al.* (1997). Building asynchronous & synchronous teaching-learning environments: Exploring a course/classroom management system solution (ERIC Document Reproduction Service No. ED 405 842).

- Hawkins, C., Jr., Gustafson, K., & Nielsen, T. (1998). Return on investment (ROI) for electronic performance support systems: A Web-based system. *Educational Technology, 38*(4), 15–21.

- Imel, S. (1997). *Web-based training: Trends and issues alert* (ERIC Document Reproduction Service No. ED 414 446).

- Ingram, A. L. (2000). The four levels of Website development expertise. *Educational Technology, 40*(3), 20–28.

- Liang, C. C., & Schwen, T. (1997). A framework for instructional development in corporate education. *Educational Technology, 37*(4), 42–45.

- Maddux, C. (1998). The World Wide Web: Some simple solutions to common design problems. *Educational Technology, 38*(5), 24–28.

- Marshall, D. (1999). Developing interactive courseware on the World Wide Web. *Innovations in Education and Training International, 36*(1), 34–43.

- Moonen, J. (2000). A three-space design strategy for digital learning material. *Educational Technology, 40*(2), 26–32.

- Pankey, R. (1998). Piloting exercise physiology in the Web-based environment. *T.H.E. Journal, 26*(5), 62–64.

- Phelps, J., & Reynolds, R. (1999). Formative evaluation of a Web-based course in meteorology. *Computers & Education, 32*(2), 181–193.

- Pisik, G. B. (1997). Is this course instructionally sound? A guide to evaluating online training courses. *Educational Technology, 37*(4), 50–59.

- Powell, G. C. (2000). Are you ready for Web-based training? *Educational Technology, 40*(3), 52–55.

- Rankin, W. (2000). A survey of course Websites and online syllabi. *Educational Technology, 40*(2), 38–42.

- Reiss, D., Selfe, D., & Young, A. (Ed.). (1998). Electronic communication across the curriculum. National Council of Teachers of English (ERIC Document Reproduction Service No. ED 416 561).

- Ryan, W. (1997). Delivery systems reviewed. *Journal of Interactive Instruction Development, 10*(1), 18–24.

- Schweber, C., Kelley, K., & Orr, G. (1998). Training, and retaining, faculty for online courses: Challenges and strategies (ERIC Document Reproduction Service No. ED 422 874).

- Simonson, N. (1998). Design considerations in converting a stand-up training class to Web-based training: Some guidelines from cognitive flexibility theory. *Journal of Interactive Instruction Development, 10*(3), 3–9.

- Stone, D. E., & Bishop, C. A. (1997). Web-based training: How to really do it. *Journal of Instruction Delivery Systems, 11*(4), 3–9.

- Teles, L., & Rylands, J. (1998). The infoshare module: Using collaborative asynchronous training to improve Web search skills. *Educational Media International, 35*(3), 169–172.

- Tannenbaum, R. S. (1999). Education or training: Reflections of a life in computing. *Educom Review, 34*(1), 10–12, 14–15.

- Watson, J. B., & Rossett, A. (1999). Guiding the independent learner in Web-based training. *Educational Technology, 39*(3), 27–36.

- Whalen, T., & Wright, D. (1999). Methodology for cost-benefit analysis of Web-based tele-learning: Case study of the Bell Online Institute. *American Journal of Distance Education, 13*(1), 24–44.

8. FAQS (Online Courses)

This section provides pointers to several Websites that specialize in online learning. Each Website focuses on WBT and WBI issues from a particular discipline including training and education, computer science, and others. Topics range from queries on how to use the Web, meanings of various terminology, and educational application of various Web attributes, functions, and features.

- Center for Computing Systems and Mathematics
  ccism.pc.athabascau.ca/html/courses/global/cover/faqmain.htm

- Web-based Training Information Center
  filename.com/wbt/pages/faq.htm

- Learning and Training FAQs
  learnativity.com/training_FAQs/

- FAQs about Web-based Training
  multimediatraining.com/faq.html

- Joint Board of Teacher Education (JBTE)—Institute of Education Faculty of Arts & Education, University of the West Indies, Jamaica
  jbte.edu.jm:1104/faq_wbt.htm

9. Related Jobs

While there are lots of job-hunting sites on the Web, these sites are unique. They compare salaries for professionals engaged in online training activities.

- Web-based Training Information Center (WBTIC) Salary Survey
  filename.com/wbt/pages/survey_salary_results.htm

- Data Masters Computer Industry Salary Survey
  datamasters.com/dm/survey.html

- Inside Technology Training—Salary Survey
  ittrain.com/

10. Examples of WBT/WBI Courses

Many of the companies and Website sponsoring institutions cited below engage in the designing, developing, and implementation of online learning solutions. The Free Web-based Training Site, for example offers links to a wide range of online courses free of charge. The World Lecture Hall provides an avenue for faculty from various disciplines to share their Web-based courses.

- Free Web-Based Training
  freeskills.com/

- HIV Virus Life Cycle
  roche-hiv.com/lifecycle/flash/main.html

- RKG Interactive Gallery On-line Training
  rkgi.com/main/html/gallery/gallery_onln_trn.html#

- World Lecture Hall—The University of Texas at Austin
  utexas.edu/world/lecture/

11. Professional Organizations and Associations

The following professional organizations and associations conduct WBT research in the fields of Educational Technology and Electronic Media. In addition to the organizations listed below, a new Special Interest Group of the American Educational Research Association—the EdWeb/SIG—has been formed to promote the discussion, dissemination, and critical examination of a broad range of issues that relate to the use of the World Wide Web in education and training (umr.edu/~edweb).

- **American Association for Higher Education**
  aahe.org/
    1 Dupont Circle, Suite 360
    Washington, DC 20036
    Phone: (202) 293-6440
    Fax: (202) 293-0073
    E-mail: info@aahe.org

- **American Educational Research Association**
  aera.net/
    1230 Seventeenth Street NW
    Washington D.C. 20036-3078
    Phone: (202) 223-9485
    Fax: (202) 775-1824
    E-mail: webmaster@aera.net

- American Society for Training and Development
  astd.org/virtual_community/
  > Box 1443
  > 1640 King Street
  > Alexandria, VA 22313
  > Phone: (703) 683-8100
  > Fax: (703) 683-1523
  > E-mail: csc4@astd.org

- Association for the Advancement of Computing in Education
  aace.org/
  > Box 2966
  > Charlottesville, VA 22902
  > Phone: (804) 973-3987
  > Fax: (804) 978-7449
  > E-mail: info@aace.org

- Association for Educational Communications and Technology
  aect.org/
  > 1800 N. Stonelake Dr., Suite 2
  > Bloomington, IN 47404
  > Phone: (812) 335-7675
  > Fax: (812) 335-7678
  > E-mail: aect@aect.org

- The Australian Society for Educational Technology
  cleo.murdoch.edu.au/gen/aset/index.html
  > Australian Catholic University
  > 179 Albert Road, Strathfield NSW 2135
  > Australia
  > Phone: (+02) 9739-2142
  > Fax: (+02) 9739-2281
  > E-mail: asetnat@cleo.murdoch.edu.au

- Broadcast Education Association
  beaweb.org/
  > 1771 N Street, N.W.
  > Washington, DC 20036-2891
  > Phone: (202) 429-5354
  > Fax: (202) 775-2981
  > E-mail: fweaver@nab.org

- EDUCAUSE
  educause.edu/
  > 1112 16th Street N.W. Suite 600
  > Washington, DC 20036-4822
  > Phone: (202) 872-4200
  > Fax: (202) 872-4318
  > E-mail: info@educause.edu

4772 Walnut Street, Suite 206
Boulder, CO 80301-2538
Phone: (303) 449-4430
Fax: (303) 440-0461
E-mail: info@educause.edu

- **International Society for Performance Improvement**
  ispi.org/
  1300 L Street, N.W., #1250
  Washington, DC 20005
  Phone: (202) 408-7969
  Fax: (202) 408-7972
  E-mail: info@ispi.org

- **International Society for Technology in Education**
  iste.org/
  480 Charnelton Street
  Eugene, OR 97401-2626
  Phone: (541) 302-3777
  Fax: (541) 302-3778
  E-mail: cust_svc@iste.org

- **International Technology Education Association**
  iteawww.org/
  1914 Association Drive
  Reston, VA 20191-1539
  Phone: (703) 860-2100
  Fax: (703) 860-0353
  E-mail: itea@iris.org

12. Authoring Tools and Systems

The following authoring tools and systems are among the Web-based products currently on the market.

- Web-based Training Information Center—Web Tools
  filename.com/wbt/pages/wbttools.htm

- Front Page
  microsoft.com/products/

- HotDog Pro
  sausage.com/

- Hot Metal Pro
  softquad.com/products/

- Cold Fusion
  allaire.com

- Net It
  net-it.com

- Corel Web Designer
  corel.com/

- SocratEase
  eutectics.com

13. Web-Based Development Companies

The following companies engage in development of online learning solutions, or develop software for testing and development. Bobby is an example of a Web-based tool that analyzes Web pages for their accessibility to people with disabilities.

- Alaska Health Online
  health.asd.k12.ak.us/cfdocs/akonlineclone/decision.cfm
- Blackboard
  blackboard.com
- Bobby
  cast.org/bobby/
- Click2learn
  Click2learn.com
- Convene.com
  convene.com
- Corpedia, L.L.C.
  corpedia.com
- Digital Think
  Digitalthink.com
- Eduprise
  eduprise.com
- FlexTraining
  flextraining.com/
- FLSoft, Inc.
  Flfsoft.com/bobby/
- GeoLearning.com
  geolearning.com
- Geteducated
  Geteducated.com
- Hibbitts Design
  Hibbittsdesign.com/
- Knowledge Window
  KnowledgeWindow.com
- LogicBay
  logicbay.com
- NetMechanic
  Netmechanic.com/index.htm
- Perseus Development Corporation
  perseus.com/
- Software Testing Online Resources/MTSU (STORM)
  mtsu.edu/~storm
- TeraByte Alaska
  chugach.net/~terabyte/
- Web Metrics NIST
  zing.ncsl.nist.gov/webmet/

- W3C HTML Validation Service
  validator.w3.org/

- Website Garage
  Websitegarage.com/

- WIDS
  wtcsf.tec.wi.us/wids/

14. Web-Based Course Development and
Management Software

This list includes many of the commonly known and used Web course management software applications for developing Web-based courses.

- Allen Communication (Quest, Designer's Edge, Manager's Edge, Quest Net)
  allencomm.com

- Center for Complex Systems Research (CyberProf)
  howhy.com/home/

- Dazzler Max5
  dazzler.net/dazzler/

- HyperCourseware
  hypercourseware.com/

- IncWell DMG, Ltd.—SuperCard
  incwell.com/SuperCard/Roadster.html

- Lotus Development Corporation (Lotus Notes)
  www3.lotus.com/home.nsf

- Macromedia
  macromedia.com/index.html

- PerfectMatch
  biomedia.bio.purdue.edu/PerfectMatch/

- Rafael Scapin's Web page for Course Server Softwares for Online Teaching
  if.sc.usp.br/~rafael/wbt.htm

- University of British Columbia (WebCT)
  webct.com/webct/intro/new.html

- WBT Systems (TopClass)
  wbtsystems.com

- WWWAssign Documentation
  northpark.edu/~martin/WWWAssign/

15. Glossary

Online encyclopedias and glossaries are included in this section. A glossary is also included in this book.

- Glossary of Terms in Web-Based Training (see Chapter 6)
  Hall, R. (2001). In B. H. Khan (Ed.), *Web-based training*. Englewood Cliffs:
      Educational Technology Publications.

- Sun Microsystem's Glossary
  sun.com/glossary/glossary.html

- Web-Based Training Information Center Glossary
  filename.com/wbt/pages/glossary.htm

- Webopedia
  Webopedia.com

- WhatIs.com
  whatis.com

16. Other

This section contains other valuable resources that are not included in any specific category listed above. Conference calendars and events, Web Quests, and Websites on specific topics are included. The online supplement to this chapter will include an expanded list of similar resources.

- AskERIC InfoGuides—Web-based Instruction
  ericir.syr.edu/Virtual/InfoGuides/Web-instruct08-98.html

- Manal El-Tigi's Access Page to Online and Print Educational Technology Journals
  web.syr.edu/~maeltigi/webpage/journals.html

- The WebQuest Page
  edweb.sdsu.edu/webquest/webquest.html

- WebQuests
  biopoint.com/WebQuests/

- MiniQuests
  biopoint.com/wq2/Welcome.html

- Internet Conference Calendar Search
  conferences.calendar.com

- Index of Conference Calendars
  www-mtl.mit.edu/semisubway/calendars.html

- Yahoo Internet Conferences and Events
  dir.yahoo.com/Computers_and_Internet/Internet/Conferences_and_Events//Past_Events/

References

El-Tigi, M. (2000). *Web-based instruction: An AskERIC infoguide;* ericir.syr.edu/Virtual/InfoGuides/

Khan, B. H. (Ed.). (1997). *Web-based instruction.* Englewood Cliffs: Educational Technology Publications.

Khan, B. H. (Ed.). (2001). A framework for Web-based learning. In B. H. Khan (Ed.), *Web-based training.* Englewood Cliffs: Educational Technology Publications.

Schwartz, C. A., & Turner, R. L. (Eds.). (1994). *Encyclopedia of associations* (29th ed., Vol. 1). Detroit: Gale Research.

Web-Based Training Information Center. (2000); filename.com/wbt

Acknowledgments

The authors would like to thank Susann L. Wurster, Publications Specialist, Information Institute of Syracuse, Syracuse, New York, for her editorial review and suggestions. We would also like to thank Greg Ketcham, Webhosting Designer/Coordinator, Applied Theory Corporation, Syracuse, New York, for his review of the chapter.

The Authors

Manal A. El-Tigi (e-mail: maeltigi@syr.edu; Web homepage: web.syr.edu/~maeltigi) recently earned her doctorate in Instructional Design, Development, and Evaluation from Syracuse University, and is ERIC Clearinghouse Web Assistant; USA and Independent Consultant for the Office of Professional Development at Syracuse University; and TitusAustin, Egypt. **Badrul H. Khan (e-mail: khanb@gwu.edu, or khanb@ BooksToRead.com; Web homepage: BooksToRead.com/khan)** is Associate Professor and Director, Educational Technology Leadership cohort graduate program, George Washington University, Washington, D.C. He is the founder of BooksToRead.com, a recommended readings site on the Internet.

SECTION II
Web-Based Training: Design and Development Perspectives

8

A Framework for
Web-Based Learning

Badrul H. Khan

Introduction

Advances in information technology, coupled with changes in society, are creating new paradigms for education and training. These massive changes have tremendous impact on our educational and training systems. Participants, from the perspective of these educational and training paradigms, require rich learning environments supported by well-designed resources (Khan, 1997c; Reigeluth & Khan, 1994). They expect on-demand, any-time/anywhere high-quality instruction with good support services. To stay viable in this global, competitive market, providers of education and training must develop efficient and effective learning systems to meet society's needs. Therefore, there is a tremendous demand *for affordable, efficient, easily accessible, open, flexible, well-designed, learner-centered, distributed, and facilitated learning environments.* Universities, corporations, and government agencies worldwide are increasingly using the Web to deliver instruction and training. At all levels of these institutions, students and employees are being encouraged to participate in on-line learning activities (Khan, 2000a, 2000b, in press).

Open, Flexible, and Distributed Learning Environments

According to Calder and McCollum (1998), "The common definition of open learning is learning at your own time, pace and place" (p. 13). Ellington (1995) noted that open and flexible learning allows learners to have some say in how, where, and when learning takes place. Saltzberg and Polyson (1995) noted that distributed learning is not just a new term to replace that other "DL," distance learning:

> Distributed learning is an instructional model that allows instructor, students, and content to be located in different, non-centralized locations so that instruction and learning occur independent of time and place. . . . The distributed learning model can be used in combination with traditional classroom-based courses, with traditional distance learning courses, or it can be used to create wholly virtual classrooms. (p. 1)

The Web supports open learning because it is *device* (or hardware or platform), *distance* (anyplace), and *time* (anytime) independent (Khan, 1997b). It is used best by designers who take advantage of the openness of the Web to create learning environments that are flexible for

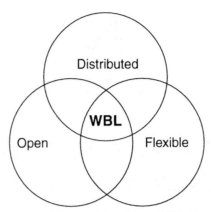

Figure 1. Open, flexible, and distributed Web-based learning.

learners. The Web, by its very nature, distributes resources and information, making it the tool of choice for those interested in delivering instruction using the distributed learning model (Saltzberg & Polyson, 1995). Thus, the Web is well-suited for open, flexible, and distributed learning. Figure 1 shows the open, flexible and distributed nature of the Web-based learning (WBL) environment. Please note that the scope of openness and flexibility is dependent on how designers design and develop the WBL activities.

The design and format of open, flexible, and distributed learning on the Web can be fundamentally different from traditional classroom instruction. Traditional classrooms are space bound. Traditional instruction treats learning pretty much as a *closed system,* taking place within the confines of a given classroom, school, textbook, field trip, etc. (Greg Kearsley, personal communication, January 27, 2000). But WBL extends the boundaries of learning, so that learning can occur in the classroom, from home, and in the work place (Relan & Gillani, 1997). It is a flexible form of education because it creates options for learners in terms of where and when they can learn (Krauth, 1998). It fosters a learner-centered approach. It enables learners to become more actively involved in their learning processes.

"While having an open system has its appeal, it can make designing for it extremely difficult, because in an open system, the designer agrees to give up a certain amount of control to the user" (Jones & Farquhar, 1997, p. 240). The more open the learning environment, the more complex the planning, management, and evaluation of it (Land & Hannafin, 1997). Designing and delivering instruction and training on the Web requires thoughtful analysis and investigation, combined with an understanding of both the Web's attributes and resources (Khan, 1997a) and the ways in which instructional design principles can be applied to tap the Web's potential (Ritchie & Hoffman, 1997, cited in Khan, 1997a). Designing Web-based courses for open, flexible, and distributed learning environments is new to many of us. To date, there is no comprehensive framework that can provide guidance in planning, designing, developing, implementing, and evaluating instructional and training materials on the Web.

A Framework for Web-Based Learning

A leading theorist of educational systems, B. H. Banathy (1991), makes a strong case for learning-focused educational and training systems where "the learner is the key entity and occupies the nucleus of the systems complex of education" (p. 96). For Banathy, "*when learning is in focus,* arrangements are made in the environment of the learner that communicate the learning task, and learning resources are made available to learners so that they can explore and master learning tasks" (p. 101). A distributed learning environment that can effectively support learning-on-demand must be designed by placing the learners at the center. In support of learner-centered learning approach, Moore (1998) states:

> Our aim as faculty should be to focus our attention on making courses and other learning experiences that will best empower our students to learn, to learn fully, effectively, efficiently, and with rewarding satisfaction. It is the responsibility of our profession to study ways of maximizing the potential of our environments to support their learning and to minimize those elements in their environments that may impede it. (p. 4).

With the Internet's rapid growth, the Web has become a powerful, global, interactive, dynamic, economic, and democratic medium of learning and teaching at a distance (Khan, 1997a). The Web provides an opportunity to develop learning-on-demand and learner-centered instruction and training. There are numerous names for Web-based learning (WBL) activities, including Web-Based Instruction (WBI), Internet-Based Training (IBT), Web-Based Training (WBT), Distributed Learning (DL), Advanced Distributed Learning (ADL), Online Learning (OL), e-Learning, etc. After reflecting on the factors that must be weighed in creating effective distributed learning environments, I developed a Framework for Web-based Learning (Khan, 1997b). The seeds for the WBL Framework (see Figure 2) began germinating with the question "What does it take to provide the best and most meaningful flexible learning environments for learners worldwide?"

Numerous factors help to create a meaningful learning environment, and many of these factors are systemically interrelated and interdependent. A systemic understanding of these factors can help designers create meaningful distributed learning environments. However, these factors, in some instances, need not be formally interrelated, but may indeed be independent and even contradictory, as postmodernists would argue. The WBL framework, dealing with an open and flexible environment, is thus well supported from a postmodernist perspective (Hlynka, 1996; personal communication, Feburary 18, 2000). I clustered these factors into eight dimensions: pedagogical, technological, interface design, evaluation, management, resource support, ethical, and institutional. Each dimension has several subdimensions (see Table 1), each consisting of items focused on a specific aspect of a Web-based learning (WBL) environment (Dabbagh, Bannan-Ritland, & Silc, 2001). This chapter will describe the dimen-

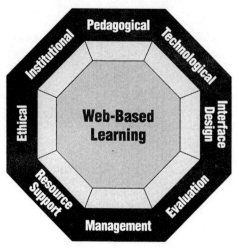

Figure 2. The WBL Framework.

Table 1. Dimensions and subdimensions of the WBL Framework.

1. Pedagogical 1.1 Goals/Objectives 1.2 Design approach 1.3 Organization 1.4 Methods and strategies 1.5 Medium	**5. Management** 5.1 Maintenance of learning environment 5.2 Distribution of information
2. Technological 2.1 Infrastructure planning 2.2 Hardware 2.3 Software	**6. Resource Support** 6.1 Online support 6.2 Resources
3. Interface Design 3.1 Page and site design 3.2 Content design 3.3 Navigation 3.4 Usability testing	**7. Ethical** 7.1 Social and cultural diversity 7.2 Geographical diversity 7.3 Learner diversity 7.4 Information accessibility 7.5 Etiquette 7.6 Legal issues
4. Evaluation 4.1 Assessment of learners 4.2 Evaluation of instruction and learning environment	**8. Institutional** 8.1 Academic affairs 8.2 Student services

sions and sub-dimensions of the framework, providing example items and Website addresses where appropriate. With so many items* within each subdimension, this chapter can examine only few of those that are most critical to planning, designing, developing, implementing, and evaluating a WBL environment. The items for the subdimensions are presented in this chapter as questions that course designers can ask themselves when planning or designing for a WBL system.

The WBL framework has been designed to apply to Web-based instruction and training of any scope. This "scope" refers to a continuum defined by the extent to which instruction is delivered on the Web and hence must be planned for. The weight placed on any WBL dimension or sub-dimension, or on any set of WBL items, will vary with the scope of the instruction (David Peal, personal communication, February 26, 2000). This continuum is described below, with examples, to show the type and scope of Web-based learning activities and how their design relates to various dimensions (discussed later in the chapter) of the WBL framework.

- At the "micro" end of the continuum, Web-based learning activities and information resources can be designed for face-to-face instruction in various educational and training settings. In the high-school physics classroom, for example, a teacher can use Shockwave simulations to support the cognitive work of analyzing data, visualizing concepts, and manipulating models. See, for example, the simulations available at Explore Science (explorescience.com.) The teacher would have to design activities that

---

*Please note that I am currently working on a new book focusing on online learning strategies *(BooksToRead.com/elearning),* which will include numerous factors relevant to WBL. Also, my forthcoming book entitled "Web-Based Learning" *(BooksToRead.com/WBL)* will include case studies, design models, strategies, and critical issues related to one or more dimensions of the WBL framework.

provide context for and elaboration of this highly visual, Web-mediated simulation. In a traditional course such as this one, WBL's institutional and management dimensions will matter much less than the instructional methods of the pedagogical dimension (see Section *1.4 Methods and Strategies*), which provide guidelines for integrating the simulation fully into the curriculum.

- Further along the continuum, more comprehensive design is required for the complete training or academic course, where content, activities, interaction, tutorials, project work, and assessment must all be delivered on the Web. Petersons.com provides links to a large number of such courses that are exclusively or primarily distanced-based (the Petersons database can be searched at lifelonglearning.com). Additional dimensions of the WBL Framework will be useful in designing such courses.

- Finally, at the "macro" end of the continuum, the WBL Framework can serve the design of complete distance-learning programs and virtual universities (Khan, 2001), without a face-to-face component, such as continuing education programs for accountants or network engineers. Petersons.com, again, provides links to dozens of such programs, as well as to institutions based on such programs. For example, designers of Web-based continuing education for accountants dispersed all around the world would have to plan for every dimension of the WBL Framework in considerable detail. They would have to work with computer programmers, testing specialists, security professionals, subject-matter experts, and accountants' professional organizations. These designers would have to do everything from planning a secure registration system to considering cultural and language differences among accountants seeking continuing education credit.

As the scope of Web-based instruction design expands, design projects change from one-person operations to complex team efforts. The WBL Framework can be used to ensure that no important factor is omitted from the design of WBL, whatever its scope or complexity.

1. Pedagogical

The pedagogical dimension of Web-based learning refers to teaching and learning. This dimension addresses issues concerning *goals/objectives, design approach, organization, methods and strategies, and instructional media* of Web-based learning environments.

1.1 Goals/Objectives

For meaningful Web-based learning environments, it is important for learners to have clear goals/objectives, and ways to achieve them. This section reviews the presence and clarity of those goals and objectives.

Does the course provide clear instructional goals (or are clear learning outcomes specified)?

If appropriate, are objectives for each section of the course clearly specified?

1.2 Design Approach

The design approach for Web-based learning activities is dependent on the type of domain of knowledge (i.e., well-defined or ill-defined) of the course content. Jonassen (1997) stated that real-world problems are *ill-structured* (e.g., figuring out whether or not to trade in your ten-year-old car, losing weight) and they have multiple solutions or methods for solving them, whereas *well-structured* problems (e.g., solving a quadratic equation, providing balanced lighting for a stage set) require the application of a limited number of rules and principles within well-defined parameters. He distinguished *well-structured* from *ill-structured* problems and recommended different design models because they call on different kinds of skills. The pedagogical philosophy of the overall design of the course is influenced by well-structured and ill-structured nature of the content. The *instructivist* philosophy espouses an objectivist episte-mology, whereas the constructivist approach emphasizes the primacy of the learners' intentions, experiences, and cognitive strategies (Reeves & Reeves, 1997). In discussing problem solving on the Web, Jonassen, Prevish, Christy, and Stavrulaki (1997) stated:

> . . . The fundamental difference between constructivist learning environment and objectivist instruction is that here the problem drives the learning. In objectivist instruction, problems function as examples or applications of the concept and principles previously taught. Stu-dents learn domain content in order to solve the problem, rather than solving the problem in order to apply the learning. (p. 51)

What is the instructor's role?
- *more facilitative than didactic*
- *more didactic than facilitative*
- *a combination of both*

If the course design allows the instructor to serve as facilitator, how/where does facilitation occur? Can it occur in any or all of the following Internet components? (Note: Student-centered learning activities allow students to become independent distance learners wherein learning is supported and facilitated.)
- *e-mail*
- *mailing list*
- *online discussion forum*
- *audio conference*
- *video conference*

1.3 Organization

Web-based learning content should be organized with proper sequencing strategies (ordering of content) to help learners achieve their goals and objectives. In the presentation of content, Web-based courses should always strive for clarity, style, readability, and the usage of content-relevant graphics (e.g., icons, buttons, pictures, images, etc.) and multimedia com-ponents (e.g., sound, audio, video, etc.). Grammar and effective usage contribute to clarity and style. To enhance readability, we should use standard writing conventions, such as grammar, capitalization, punctuation, usage, spelling, paragraphing, etc., effectively. The writing style should be simple, clear and direct, and must be appropriate for the reading level of the target audience.

> *Does the course provide clear directions of what learners should do at every stage of the course?*

> *Does the course provide a sense of continuity for the learners (i.e., each unit of the lesson builds on the previous unit where appropriate)?*

1.4 Methods and Strategies

Instructional methods/approaches and strategies can be used in WBL to facilitate learning or help students achieve their learning goals and objectives. The methods used in a Web-based course will be based in part on the philosophical approach of the course. A variety of instructional activities can be incorporated into Web-based instruction (WBI) and Web-based training (WBT) to facilitate learning, and the technical and structural attributes of the Web can be used to support these activities.

In this section, I discuss various instructional methods and strategies in terms of their usefulness in Web-based learning activities. I also look at the Web technologies that can support these activities. Please note that I maintain an up-to-date Website at *BooksToRead.com/wbt/fmktable1.htm,* which provides relevant Websites for various methods and strategies included in this section. The instructional methods and strategies included here are applicable to WBL. Their use, however, may depend on the types of learning domains (well-defined or ill-defined) and goal/objectives of the course and philosophical orientation of the designers.

Presentation relates to techniques for presenting facts, concepts, procedures and principles. A Web-based presentation can be done using only one or combination of several online delivery modes such as text, slideshows, audio clips, video clips, and video-conferencing. Supplemental (offline) materials such as print, audio, videotapes, etc., can be mailed to learners.

Demonstration is an approach of showing how something works. The demonstration approach can be used in Web-based learning in areas such as teaching procedures and equipment operation, illustrating principles, demonstrating interpersonal skills, etc.

Drill and Practice is a learning activity that helps learners master basic skills or memorize facts through repetitive practice. It is most commonly used in teaching math facts, foreign languages, vocabulary (Heinich, Molenda, & Russell, 1993), reading comprehension, basic science, history, and geography (Newby, Russell, Stepich, & Lehman, 1996). A Web-based drill-and-practice program can provide immediate feedback for learners' responses to various problems presented to them. HTML, javascript and other programming languages can be used to create Web-based drill and practice.

Tutorials use a presentation-response-feedback format. Web-based tutorials can be designed by presenting content, posing questions or problems after each content block is displayed, asking learners to respond, and finally providing appropriate feedback.

Games are highly motivational instructional approaches that can be used in Web-based courses to help learners improve various skills such as decision-making, problem-solving, interpersonal leadership, teamwork, etc. (Newby, Russell, Stepich, & Lehman, 1996). In a game, learners follow prescribed rules to attain a challenging goal. Thiagarajan and Thiagarajan (2001) describe how e-mail, chat-rooms, and listservs can be used in Web-based games.

Simulations are artificial recreations of real-life situations (Gordon, 1994; Newby *et al.,* 1996). In a simulated environment, learners can practice and make realistic decisions and explore the consequences of their decisions. Web-based courses can use simulations to improve learners' cognitive, affective, decision-making and interpersonal skills. Pappo (2001) examines various design aspects of Web-based simulations.

Role-playing can be used to represent real situations that provide learners the opportunity to practice situations they face in the real world (Rothwell & Kazanas, 1992). Learners can imagine that they are other people in different situations, then make decisions as situations change (Heinich, Molenda & Russell, 1993). Role-playing allows learners to learn social skills such as communication, interpersonal skills, etc. In Web-based learning, simulated role portrayal can be facilitated through Multi-User Dialogue (MUD) environments, in which instructors create a multi-user space with a central theme, characters and artifacts (Bannan & Milheim, 1997).

Discussion allows learners to share information, ideas, and feelings among themselves and their instructors. They can establish communication on the basis of shared interest, not merely shared geography (Harasim, 1993). Web-based discussions can be divided into two categories: asynchronous (time-independent communication) and synchronous (real-time communication). In a Web-based course, learners can be engaged in asynchronous discussions in three different formats: moderated discussion forums, unmoderated discussion forums, and subject-related outside professional discussion forums. Asynchronous text communications tools are e-mail, mailing lists, and newsgroups. Synchronous discussions can range from text-based to audio-video conferencing. Synchronous communications tools include messaging tools and audio- and videoconferencing tools.

Interaction in Web-based learning is one of the most important instructional activities. Engagement theory based on online learning emphasizes that students must be meaningfully engaged in learning activities through interaction with others and worthwhile tasks (Kearsley & Shneiderman, 1999). Students can interact with each other, with instructors, and with online resources. Instructors and experts may act as facilitators. They can provide support, feedback, and guidance via asynchronous tools (e.g., e-mail and mailing lists) and synchronous communications tools (e.g., conferencing and messaging tools). Asynchronous communication allows for time-independent interaction, whereas synchronous communication tools allows for live interaction (Khan, 1997a, 1998, in press a,b).

Depending on pedagogical philosophy of the course design, both asynchronous and synchronous communication methods can be employed. However, course designers should consider the advantage and disadvantages of both (see Berge, Collins, & Fitzsimmons, 2001; Hannum, 2001). Instructors should develop skills on how to promote online discussion, devise learning activities that work at a distance, and encourage interaction among the participants (Romiszowski & Chang, 2001). For both asynchronous and synchronous discussions, the instructor or moderator should enforce rules and decorum of discussion forum, and let students engage in vigorous discussion on their own.

Modeling is an instructional method in which learners improve their skills by observing a role model. Various modeled performances can be used for Web-based learning activities. They can range from modeling behavior in electronic communication environments to providing samples of relevant coursework. In a Web-based course, posting of sample interactions, assignments, and projects on the Web can provide the necessary modeling for expectations of course requirements (Bannan & Milheim, 1997).

Facilitation gives mentors a chance to guide students, direct discussion, suggest possible resources, and field questions (Bannan & Milheim, 1997). In a Web-based course, facilitation can be provided using various tools, such as e-mail, mailing lists, discussion forums, and conferencing tools.

Collaboration allows learners to work and learn together to accomplish a common learning goal. In a collaborative environment, learners develop social, communication, critical thinking, leadership, negotiation, interpersonal, and cooperative skills by experiencing multiple perspectives of members of collaborative groups on any problems or issues. Online learning environments such as the Web offer extensive opportunities for collaborative learning (Harasim, 1990). Two types of collaboration can be implemented on the Web: *inside collaboration* and *outside collaboration*. Inside collaboration provides a supportive environment for asking questions, clarifying directions, suggesting or contributing resources, and working on joint projects with class members. Outside collaboration is a provision for utilizing external personnel and resources (e.g., speakers, guest lecturers, Websites, etc.) to participate in course activities (Bannan & Milheim, 1997). E-mail, listservs, and conferencing tools can be used to facilitate collaboration.

Field trips allow learners to explore existing places or things to which they would otherwise not have access (Khan, 1997a). In Web-based learning environment, field trip activity allows the instructor to provide students with a guided tour to city, park, or business Websites as if the instructor were taking students on a field trip (Badger, 2000). In WBL, students should be provided with themes and objectives for the field trips so that they can visit relevant Websites and gather appropriate information as part of their assigned tasks.

Apprenticeships offer learners the chance to observe, model, and interact with mentors or experts for particular learning tasks. The conferencing and collaboration technologies of the Web bring students into contact with authentic learning and apprenticing situations (Bonk & Reynolds, 1997).

Case studies of either real or hypothetical situations can be used in a Web-based course to engage learners in the problem-solving tasks in which they can be asked to identify and solve problems. Cases can be based on the actual situations that learners are likely to encounter when they become practitioners (Brown, Collins, & Duguid, 1989). These cases should also be aligned with the learning goal(s) of the course in order for learners to benefit from such activities.

Generative development deals with assimilation, interaction, and synthesis of information through the creation, organization, or reorganization of specific content. Web-based learning activities for generating content include the development of original Web pages and the analysis of existing texts (Bannan & Milheim, 1997). Through the generative development process, learners make connections between what they already know and the new information.

Motivation in Web-based learning environments is critical. WBL courses should be designed to motivate students so that they can enjoy their learning experience on the Web and complete their assignments on time. Cornell & Martin (1997) advise course designers to pay attention to the following: how to provide variety and stimulate curiosity, make the course relevant and challenging, and provide positive outcomes. The WBL environment should be designed to create a positive first impression, be readable, use graphics and pictures that are relevant and useful, provide cues to the learners, and stimulate early interest so that students will be more likely to complete the course.

1.5 Instructional Medium

In Web-based learning, the Web is the medium through which the message is communicated. The capabilities of the Web as a medium must be examined to see how its attributes and resources can be used effectively to facilitate learning (Khan, 1997a).

> *Does this course utilize a mixture of media to create a rich environment for active learning?*

> *Does the course exploit the flexibility of the hypertext/hypermedia environment of the Web?*

2. Technological

The technological dimension of the WBL Framework examines issues of technology infrastructure in Web-based learning environments. This includes *infrastructure planning, hardware,* and *software.*

2.1. Infrastructure Planning

Infrastructure planning for WBL may include stanards, policies, and guidelines related to hardware, software, and other relevant technologies.

> *Does the course have personnel who can assist learners to set up for starting the course?*

> *(Or does the course have orientation programs that provide technical training prior to a course?)*

> *Is the cost of required hardware, software, and Internet service a deterrent to taking this course?*

2.2. Hardware

Hardware for Web-based learning may include the computer, server, modem, networking devices, printer, scanner, camera, storage devices (e.g., hard drives, CD-ROM, etc.), and other equipment.

> *Do students receive any guidance on how to set up hardware equipment for desktop video conferencing (if needed for the course)?*
>
> *Are the hardware requirements for the course clearly stated?*

2.3 Software

Software for Web-based learning may include word processor, e-mail packages, presentation program, spreadsheet, database, authoring tools, plug-ins and browsers, etc.

> *Are the software requirements for the course clearly stated?*
>
> *Do students receive any guidance on how to do the following?*
> - *send e-mail attachments*
> - *install required software*
> - *scan a picture*
> - *print within Web page frames*
> - *create online presentation using presentation software*
> - *other*

3. Interface Design

Interface design refers to the overall look and feel of a Web-based training program (Hall, 1997). Interface design dimension encompasses *page and site design, content design, navigation,* and *usability testing.* User interface design is the creation of a seamless integration of content and its organization, together with the navigational and interactive controls that learners use to work with the content (Jones & Farquhar, 1997). The design of a WBL interface is critical because it determines how learners interact with the presented information (Brown, Milner, & Ford, 2001).

3.1 Page and Site Design

Page design relates to the physical appearance and functionality of the screen. Web-based learning environments should be designed to accommodate all learners, including people with disabilities. Images and videos without text alternatives are inaccessible to learners who are visually impaired for any reason. Two design consequences are the creation of multimedia elements only when they are essential and the creation of alternate text for all non-text elements so that they can be read aloud by software for synthesizing speech. The World Wide Web Consortium's new disability guidelines for Web design is a good reference (w3.org/WAI/GL). The Center for Applied Special Technology (cast.org/bobby) provides a Web-based tool that analyzes Web pages for their accessibility to people with disabilities.

> *Do Web pages look good in a variety of Web browsers and devices—in text-based browsers, all recent versions of Internet Explorer and Netscape, and so on?*
>
> *Does the course use a standard font type so that text appears same in different computer platforms and browsers? (For example, Times Roman and Helvetica fonts appear the same in different platforms.)*

3.2 Content Design

The content has to do with a course's subject matter. Quality content is one of the most important determinants of Web usability (Nielsen, 2000). Nielsen provides guidelines for designing quality content. His guidelines encompass text density (i.e., keeping text short), copy editing (i.e., spelling and grammar checking and proofreading), scannability (i.e, scannable text layout), etc.

Does the course follow "one idea per paragraph" rule?

Is the text chunked and presented in a way that enables scanning and comprehension?

3.3 Navigation

Navigation in a Web-based course should focus on how learners can move through the site with ease and reasonable speed. Clarity and consistent use of textual, graphic, and other organizational markers throughout the site can contribute to the ease of use and speed (Simich-Dudgeon, 1998).

Does the course provide structural aids or site map to guide the learner's navigation?

To avoid bandwidth bottlenecks, does the course ask students to download large audio, video and graphic files to their hard drives before the instructional events?

3.4 Usability Testing

Usability testing is a method of testing WBL to improve its interface design. It involves users to evaluate a WBL program to make sure it is usable. Reeves and Carter (2001) categorie usability testing as follows: efficiency (i.e., cost and time saving), user satisfaction (i.e., ease of use, intuitiveness, visual appeal, etc.), and effectiveness (i.e., user retention over time). Guidelines for designing usable graphical user interfaces and Web pages can be found at: useit.com. Since the WBL programs are globally available to remote learners, it is important to conduct international user testing on the Web. Nielsen (2000) recommends that Web-based programs undergo international usability testing with users from countries in different parts of the world.

How quickly can users find answers to the most frequently asked questions on the course site?

Does the course use easy-to-understand terminology?

4. Evaluation

Online evaluation for WBL includes both *assessment of learners* and *evaluation of instruction and learning environment* (Khan, 1997a). A variety of evaluation and assessment tools can be incorporated into a Web-based course. Individual testing, participation in group discussions, questions, and portfolio development can all be used to evaluate students' progress. A Web-based course can have a facility that allows students to submit instructor evaluations to the appropriate departments in an institution. Students can also submit comments about the design and delivery of the course to the instructional designer or the instructor.

4.1 Assessment of Learners

Assessment pertains to authenticity, reliability, formats (e.g., multiple choice, case studies, etc.) and test characteristics (e.g., adaptive and randomized). Assessment should be congruent with the pedagogical approach of the course. Assessment of learners at a distance can be a challenge. Issues of cheating are a major concern (Wheeler, 1999). "Are students actually doing the work?" (Hudspeth, 1997) and "How do we know we are assessing fairly and accurately?" (Wheeler, 1999)—such questions will always be of concern for online learning environment. Assessing learners' learning from their participation in online discussion can be very difficult, especially when some students "lurk." Romiszowski and Chang (2001) note that a lurker may be benefiting just as much as the silent students in class who learn from the comments and questions of other students.

> *How is the learner's assessment on various parts of the course administered? Check all that apply:*
> - *multiple choice*
> - *true/false*
> - *fill-in-the blanks*
> - *essay questions*
> - *papers*
> - *projects*
> - *assignments*
> - *proctored tests*
> - *portfolio development*
> - *case studies*
> - *lab report*
> - *journal*
> - *other*

> *Does the assessment provide students with the opportunity to demonstrate what they have learned in the course?*

4.2 Evaluation of Instruction and Learning Environment

The design of the course greatly influences the roles the instructors and students play in the Web-based learning environment. This section deals with the performance of the instructor and the review of the learning environment (also discussed in *Section 5.1 Maintenance of Learning Environment*).

> *Does the course have a system to accept students' online evaluation of the following?*
> - *content*
> - *instructor*
> - *learning environment*
> - *learning resources*
> - *course design*
> - *technical support*
> - *other*

> *Does the course provide an instant feedback button on most screens/pages in order to receive learners' feedback for improvement of the course?*

5. Management

Management of WBL refers to the administration, maintenance, and operation of Web-based learning environments. Management of WBL courses involves various individuals who are responsible for doing specific tasks and training. These individuals may include instructors, tutors, subject matter experts, project managers, instructional designers, editors, interface designers, course developers, graphic artists, media production specialists, programmers, consultants, Webmaster, etc. A coordinated and cooperative effort by these individuals will result in the effective management of a WBL course. Issues in this dimension are clustered into two categories: *maintenance of learning environment* and *distribution of information*.

5.1 Maintenance of Learning Environment

Maintenance of the learning environment covers staffing, budgeting, management of course content and learning resources, mechanisms for evaluation, security measures, etc.

What content exists and what content must be created? Of existing content, what content requires "reprint" permission?

Does the course acquire permission to use copyrighted information and materials?

Does the course provide students with designated and secure (e.g., password protected) online spaces to store their notes and resources?

Does the course have a system of keeping track of student submissions, online quizzes, etc.?

5.2 Distribution of Information

Information distribution covers the delivery of both online and offline Web-based learning materials including schedule, syllabus, announcements, course relevant contact information, learning and testing materials, and students' grades from quizzes, assignments, exams, and projects. Students can have access to testing materials and their grades by entering their password.

Does the course notify students about any changes in due dates or other course relevant matters (e.g., server down) via the following means?
- *e-mail*
- *announcement page*
- *alert boxes*
- *running footer added to a page*
- *phone call*
- *mail*

Does the course provide back-up materials or alternative activities for students (i.e., what students will do) if any of the following is either not operating properly or unavailable during a scheduled lesson period?
- *access to the courseware*
- *discussion forum*
- *chat room*
- *e-mail and mailing list*
- *books*

- *online resources*
- *library materials*
- *study guide*
- *instructor*
- *tutor*
- *technical support*

6. Resource Support

The resource support dimension of the WBL framework examines the *online support* and *resources* required to foster meaningful learning environments.

6.1 Online Support

Both technological and human-based support throughout a Web-based course can help a course maintain momentum and become successful (Hill, 1997). This dimension deals with how a Web-based course can provide both *online instructional/counseling* support and all-purpose *technical* support and troubleshooting.

Instructional/Counseling Support. Individuals who are inexperienced as learners in distance education courses may have a particularly high degree of anxiety at the beginning of the course (Moore & Kearsley, 1996). Guidance on study skills, time management, and stress management are important components for WBL. Students should receive guidance on how to organize for online learning. Hart (1999) provides several tips on how to become effective learners in distance education environments. Web-based learning methods can be stressful for some students. Campbell (1999) provides guidance on how to overcome the personal barriers to success in distance learning. Palloff & Pratt (1999) provide guidance on time management. Learners should be advised on how they can divide their time into various course-related tasks such as assigned readings, online discussions, individual/group projects, and other assignments.

Does the course provide guidance on how to organize for online learning?

Does the course provide information or ideas about how many hours (approximately) per week students are expected to spend on course assignments?

Technical Support. Online technical support is one of the most important support services for Web-based learning environments. Technical support services must be available to help students log on, upload and download files, etc.

Does the course provide toll-free telephone numbers for online support services? (Note: If toll-free does not work for students outside the U.S. and Canada, alternatives must be considered.)

Does the course provide clear guidelines to the learners on what support can and cannot be expected from a help line? (For example, things the student is responsible for, and things that the student can expect the help line to solve.)

6.2 Resources

The WBL resources include original documents, public domain books, summaries of or discussions about books in print, reference works (such as foreign-language dictionaries), scholarly papers, new concepts, notification of both face-to-face and online conferences, job information, internship information, etc.

Online Resources. Online resource can include multimedia archives, mailing lists and their archives, newsgroups and their FAQs, dictionaries, Webliographies, recommended reading lists (e.g., BooksToRead.com), databases, online libraries, computer tutorials, experts online, electronic books, journals, magazines, newsletters, newspapers, documents, etc. All online resources should be limited to what learners need for specific tasks in the course. Learners should be provided with some guidelines on how to assess the quality and utility of information available online. All resources should be relevant and essential. An overwhelming volume of information and irrelevant resources may frustrate the learners.

> *Does the course provide examples of previous students' work on the Web? If yes, select all that apply and circle whether searchable and browsable:*
> - *projects (searchable/browsable)*
> - *papers (searchable/browsable)*
> - *text dialogue from discussion forums (searchable/browsable)*
> - *text dialogue from online conferencing exchanges (searchable/browsable)*

> *Does the institution's library have library resources online? If yes, do students have access to its databases via the Internet or other networks?*

Offline Resources. Offline resources can include books, journals, magazines, newsletters, newspapers, documents, reference works, experts, etc. Institutions offering Web-based courses to geographically dispersed remote learners should provide suggestions or information about where to find library resources, since many cannot use the host institution's library. Also, the host institution should consider joining a consortium of libraries worldwide so that their Web-based students can visit and borrow books.

> *Does the host institution's library have a system of getting books and other materials for students via interlibrary loan?*

> *Does the library fax documents to students?*

7. Ethical

Ethical considerations of Web-based learning relate to *social and cultural diversity, geographical diversity, learner diversity, information accessibility, etiquette,* and the *legal issues.*

7.1 Social and Cultural Diversity

As a result of recent advances in distributed learning technologies, Web-based courses can be accessible to anyone in any part of the world. It is wonderful to be able to offer Web-based courses to global learners with different social, cultural, economic, linguistic, and religious backgrounds. In designing Web-based learning environments, we should recognize the diversity of culture and learning styles in order to enable diverse learners to enhance their learning (Sanchez & Gunawardena, 1998).

One of the most critical issues in WBL is cross-cultural communication. Cross-cultural communication encounters problems when at least one of the parties trying to exchange information is unaware of, or chooses to disregard, a significant difference in expectations concerning the relationships between communicators (Walls, 1993). Collis and Remmers (1997) remind us that we must be alert to the fact that there are substantial cross-cultural differences in interaction and communication beyond the actual words being said. "In Bangladesh, we use the thumbs-up sign to challenge people, but to other cultures, that means you did well" (Khan,

1999, *PCWEEK* interview). Designing courses on the Web for global learners is a challenging task. Web-based course designers should try their best to be sensitive to various cross-cultural communication issues. During the design process they can ask individuals from various cultures to visit the course Website and provide feedback. They can also post messages about cross-cultural issues on mailing lists whose members might be willing to share their experiences and point to appropriate resources. Several authors provide guidance for cross-cultural issues related to Web-based education (Collis & Remmers, 1997; Rice *et al.*, 2001).

> *To improve cross-cultural verbal communication and avoid misunderstanding, does the course make an effort to reduce or avoid the use of jargon, idioms, ambiguous or cute humor, and acronyms?*

> *To improve visual communication, is the course sensitive to the use of navigational icons or images? For example, a pointing hand icon to indicate direction would violate a cultural taboo in certain African cultures by representing a dismembered body part (Reeves & Reeves, 1997).*

7.2 Geographical Diversity

Web-based courses can be offered to students from various geographical locations. In designing WBL, we should be sensitive to where students live. The use of appropriate date and time conventions in a Web-based course provides orientation for a widely distributed group of students. I recommend the use of the full-text dating convention (e.g., March 1, 2000 instead of 01-03-2000) and GMT, especially when arranging conference calls, online conferences, and other collaborative activities.

> *Is the course offered to geographically diverse population? If yes, is the course sensitive about students from different time zones (e.g., synchronous communications are scheduled at reasonable times for all time zones represented)?*

7.3 Learner Diversity

A Web-based learning system should be designed to accommodate different learning styles and the needs of individuals with disabilities, including senior citizens whose hearing is impaired; in the U.S. alone, it has been estimated that there are more than 30 million people with disabilities—inborn, acquired, and temporary. Also, a Web-based course offered to global learners should consider using relevant, diverse examples familiar to the varied audience.

> *Is the course designed to have tolerance for learners who adapt to individualized distributed learning environment more slowly than others?*

> *Does the course allow students to remain anonymous during online discussions?*

7.4 Information Accessibility

In the information society, information accessibility is a critical issue which must be discussed in terms of the gap between the digital "haves" and "have nots," a gap expressed in the term "digital divide." In designing Web-based learning activities, digital divide issues should be considered to include the learners who are affected by this division. Discussion of diverse issues around the digital divide can be found at (DigitalDivideNetwork.org). In designing WBL materials, designers need to respect differences in bandwidth and make sure any multimedia elements are (1) essential to content and (2) accompanied by text equivalents.

7.5 Etiquette

A Web-based learning environment should have the guidelines for etiquette when students post messages on discussion forums and newsgroups. Etiquette provides rules for maintaining civility in interactions and covers issues associated with considerate behavior. The etiquette promotes mutually respectful behavior in an online learning community. The use of special language such as emoticons (e.g., :-V for *shout*), abbreviations (e.g., IMHO for *in my humble opinion*), and technical terms (e.g., logon) during online communications is not uncommon. However, both instructor and learners should be knowledgeable about the meaning and appropriate usage of them.

> *Does the course provide any guidance to learners on how to behave and post messages in online discussions so that their postings do not hurt others' feelings?*

> *If a student fails to follow the etiquette of the course, how does instructor work with students to promote compliance?*

7.6 Legal Issues

This section deals with legal matters such as privacy, plagiarism, and copyright.

Privacy. In a typical Web-based course, there can be numerous text dialogs generated from mailing lists or computer conferencing exchanges. These exchanges may contain participants' personal views and biases which they may not want the outside world to know. Considering the openness of the Web, it is not difficult for search engines to find these exchanges. Palloff and Pratt (1999) suggest that participants must know that their communications are not secure and that they must use good judgment about what they share. At the beginning of the course, students should be informed about the openness of the Web and privacy guidelines. Even during the online discussions, instructor/tutor/facilitator should remind students about the privacy issues.

> *Does the course provide privacy guidelines on online postings?*

Plagiarism. Web-based courses should provide clear information regarding plagiarism policies. With a search engine or specialized directory, anyone can find reliable (and unreliable) content on any subject on the Web. Students should be cautioned about presenting someone else's work as their own. Tips for preventing plagiarism are available (plagiarism.org).

> *Does the course provide policies regarding fraudulent activities in course-related testing, assignments and projects?*

Copyright. Instructors, tutors, facilitators, guest speakers, and students should be knowledgeable about copyright issues pertaining to WBL and obtain copyright permissions when appropriate. If an instructor decides to make a journal article available to students on the Web, he or she should get permission from the journal. As far as the ownership of the course is concerned, institutions should provide very clear guidelines as to who owns the course. What happens when the faculty who developed a course leaves the institution; can he/she take the course with him/her? Likewise, does the institution have complete freedom to package, license, and sell instructors' work?

> *Does the course get students' permission to post any of the following on the Web?*
> - *Students' photographs*
> - *Students' projects*

8. Institutional

It is vital for institutions of higher education to have clear strategies for online learning. These strategies must be supported by the institutions' missions. Online learning initiatives require orchestration of personnel with diverse skills sets (Belanger & Jordan, 2000). Political factors often have significant impact upon the success of an online program (Berge, 2001). Institutional funding and resources for maintaining and delivering online courses are critical. Return on investment (ROI) evaluation should be considered before, during, and after the implementation of Web-based courses (Gustafson & Schrum, 2001; Reeves & Carter, 2001). Institutions offering Web-based courses should consider online students as the consumers of education in a competitive market. In such a market, students as consumers would compare quality, services, price and convenience of education providers. They would ask more questions and demand far more services than local campus-based students. Therefore, institutions should be ready to provide high quality education with the best learning resources and support services. The institutional dimension is concerned with issues of *academic affairs* and *student services* related to Web-based learning.

8.1 Academic Affairs

Academic affairs can encompass faculty and staff support, instructional affairs, admissions, registration and payment (e-commerce), information technology services, graduation, and alumni affairs.

Faculty and Staff Support. Faculty and staff involved in Web-based courses should receive proper training and resources to be effective in teaching and supporting student's learning. Price (1999) notes that faculty training typically focuses on technical matters such as using authoring software rather than instructional design. He thinks this insufficient training leads to the production of mediocre courses. Institutions should provide adequate support, compensation, and incentives to teach Web-based courses. These supports should also include financial resources for faculty to conduct research, attend conferences, and present papers in professional meetings. Romiszowski and Chang (2001) report that courses delivered by computer-mediated communication (CMC) almost always involve significantly more instructor time than conventionally delivered courses. Institutions should establish a system of rewarding faculty for undertaking such challenging tasks (e.g., the development of a Web-based course equals a publication in a journal or magazine).

Do faculty receive training on how to moderate and/or maintain a listserv?

Does technical and other staff receive training on how to communicate with remote learners in difficult situations?

Instructional Affairs. Instructional aspects of Web-based leaning include information about instructor and tutor, instructional quality, advising, etc.

Does the course limit the number of students per faculty member?

Does the course provide academic quality such as one would expect in a traditional course?

Admissions, Registration, and Payment. Institutions offering Web-based courses should have a secure and reliable system to accept students' applications and handle all financial transactions. As the Internet and e-commerce technology continue to improve, procedures for automated admission, registration, and online financial transactions are becoming an integral part of Web-based course offerings.

Does the site provide any information regarding whether the course is transferable to other accredited institutions?

Is the course offered at a lower fee than on-campus courses? It is not uncommon for students to expect lower fees for online courses.

Would student information submitted online to the registrar's office be kept secure and confidential to the extent possible?

Information Technology Services. Information technology services deal with the technology support infrastructure for students, faculty and staff. These support services may include managing application software and servers for courses, providing e-mail accounts, disk space for Web pages, and general technical support for students, faculty, and staff (also discussed in *Section 2. Technological*).

8.2 Student Services

Students taking Web-based courses should enjoy equal academic and student services as those taking face-to-face courses. According to Connick (1999), "Students often assume that an institution offering courses or programs at a distance will also provide all of the essential services at a distance" (p. 26). These services include orientation, bookstore, library support, financial aid, counseling and other student support services. For Web-based learners, institutions should consider providing toll-free numbers for all of these services.

Orientation. All students should be required to participate in online orientation at least a week prior to the first day of classes. Orientation should provide introduction to procedures for learning at a distance, including roles and responsibilities of instructors, learners, tutors, facilitators, guest speakers, and all other individuals involved in the process. Students, instructors, and technical staff should be encouraged to post brief biographies, as this helps to create a virtual learning community (Khan, 1997a).

Are instructor/tutor and technical staff available during online orientation?

Bookstore. Bookstore services for Web-based students may be more demanding. Bookstores should consider having an online catalog where students can order books online. Or, students should be directed to online bookstores so that they can become familiar with how to take advantage of all online resources.

Can students purchase packages of course-related supplemental reading materials online from the campus bookstore?

Library Support. Students should receive both offline and online library support (also discussion in *Section 6.2 Resources*).

Financial Aid. Students should be provided with information about financial aid, student loans, and scholarships on the Web. Institutions can provide online financial aid workshops and assist students with financial aid forms and other scholarship applications.

Can students apply for the financial aids/loans online?

Counseling. Like on-campus students, Web-based students should receive academic, career, and other counseling services. Guidance on study skills, time management, and stress management is an important component for WBL (detailed discussion is in *Section 6.1 online support*).

Using the Framework

The WBL Framework has the potential to provide guidance in planning and designing Web-based learning materials, organizing resources for Web-based learning, evaluating Web-based instruction and training courses (e.g., *WebCourseReview.com* or *BooksToRead.com/wcr*), evaluating Web-based authoring, designing comprehensive authoring systems, designing distributed learning systems, virtual universities and cyberschools. In this book, the framework is used as guiding mechanism for the following chapters:

- *Case studies of Web-based training sites* by Khan, Waddill, and McDonald (see Chapter 40).

- *Pedagogy and Web-based course authoring tools: Issues and implications* by Dabbagh, Bannan-Ritland, and Silc (see Chapter 38).

- *A framework for a comprehensive Web-based authoring system* by Khan and Ealy (see Chapter 39).

- *Web-based training resources* by El-Tigi & Khan (see Chapter 7).

- *Virtual U: A hub for excellence in education, training, and learning resources* by Khan (see Chapter 57).

Conclusion

My goal in this chapter has been to identify and clarify critical issues and the complexities of Web-based learning environment, and provide some guidance on addressing these issues for creating meaningful learning environments. I hope, by describing various dimensions of the framework, I have provided a sketch of what it takes to create meaningful distributed learning environments. I believe various issues discussed in the eight dimensions of the framework can provide guidance in the planning, design, development, delivery, and evaluation of distributed learning environments. Various sub-dimensions and issues discussed within the eight dimensions of the framework are by no means complete. I welcome comments and suggestions for improvement *(BooksToRead.com/framework)*.

This framework has been used as a guiding mechanism to (1) evaluate Web-based courses by graduate students at four U.S. universities as part of their coursework; (2) review existing WBT courses (Khan, Waddill, & McDonald, 2001); (3) review Web-based authoring tools (Dabbagh, Bannan-Ritland, & Silc, 2001); (4) design a comprehensive Web-based authoring system (Khan & Ealy, 2001); (5) design virtual universities (Khan, 2001); and (6) organize WBT resources (El-Tigi & Khan, 2001). It has *not* been used to design WBI and WBT courses. Therefore, its utility in designing effective Web-based learning activities cannot yet be judged. Further studies are needed to establish the framework's validity. The following are my recommendations for further research to improve the WBL framework:

- Examine the factors bearing on the success and failure of courses that have and/or have not adopted the framework.

- Examine the success and failure of factors bearing on each dimension of the framework for the following tasks:

— Planning of courses that have or have not adopted the framework.

— Design and development of courses that have or have not adopted the framework.

— Implementation of courses that have or have not adopted the framework.

— Organization of WBT and/or WBI resources that have or have not adopted the framework.

— Design of Web-based authoring systems that have or have not adopted the framework.

— Design of virtual universities that that have or have not adopted the framework.

By examining these research questions, I believe we can further develop our knowledge base in Web-based learning. Within the scope of this chapter, only few critical items (or questions) related to each subdimension of the framework are presented as examples. However, there are a myriad of critical items (or questions) encompassing the various dimensions of the framework that need to be explored. My research will continue to identify and discuss various critical factors related to WBL *(BooksToRead.com/elearning).*

References

Badger, A. (2000). Keeping it fun and relevant: Using active online learning. In K. W. White & B. H. Weight (Eds.), *The online teaching guide*. Boston: Allyn & Bacon.

Banathy, B. H. (1991). *Systems designs of education: A journey to create the future*. Englewood Cliffs: Educational Technology Publications.

Bannan, B., & Milheim, W. D. (1997). Existing Web-based courses and their design. In B. H. Khan (Ed.), *Web-based instruction*. Englewood Cliffs: Educational Technology Publications.

Belanger, F., & Jordan, D. H. (2000). *Evaluation and implementation of distance learning: Technologies, tools, and techniques*. Hershey, PA: Idea Group Publishing.

Berge, Z. L. (2001). Evaluating Web-based training programs. In B. H. Khan (Ed.), *Web-based training*. Englewood Cliffs: Educational Technology Publications.

Berge, Z. L., Collins, M., & Fitzsimmons, T. (2001). Web-based training: Benefits and obstacles to success. In B. H. Khan (Ed.), *Web-based training*. Englewood Cliffs: Educational Technology Publications.

Bonk, C. J., & Reynolds, T. H. (1997). Learner-centered Web instruction for higher-order thinking, teamwork, and apprenticeship. In B. H. Khan (Ed.), *Web-based instruction*. Englewood Cliffs: Educational Technology Publications.

Brown, K. G., Milner, K. R., & Ford, J. K. (2001). Repurposing instructor-led training into Web-based training: A case study and lessons learned. In B. H. Khan (Ed.), *Web-based training*. Englewood Cliffs: Educational Technology Publications.

Brown, J. S., Collins, A., & Duguid, P. (1989). Situated cognition and the culture of learning. *Educational Researcher, 18*(1), 32–42.

Calder, J., & McCollum, A. (1998). *Open and flexible learning in vocational education and training*. London: Kogan Page.

Campbell, S. M. (1999). Understanding your needs: Overcoming the personal barriers to success in distance learning. In G. P. Connick (Ed.), *The distance learner's guide*. Upper Saddle River, NJ: Prentice-Hall.

Collis, B., & Remmers, E. (1997). The WWW in education: Issues related to cross-cultural communication and interaction. In B. H. Khan (Ed.), *Web-based instruction*. Englewood Cliffs: Educational Technology Publications.

Connick, G. P. (1999). Choosing a distance education provider: Asking the right questions. In G. P. Connick (Ed.). *The distance learner's guide*. Upper Saddle River, NJ: Prentice-Hall.

Cornell, R., & Martin, B. L. (1997). The role of motivation in Web-based instruction. In B. H. Khan (Ed.), *Web-based instruction*. Englewood Cliffs: Educational Technology Publications.

Dabbagh, N. H., Bannan-Ritland, B., & Silc, K. (2000). Pedagogy and Web-based course authoring tools: Issues and implications. In B. H. Khan (Ed.), *Web-based training*. Englewood Cliffs: Educational Technology Publications.

El-Tigi, M. A., & Khan, B. H. (2001). Web-based learning resources. In B. H. Khan (Ed.), *Web-based training*. Englewood Cliffs: Educational Technology Publications.

Ellington, H. (1995). Flexible learning, your flexible friend. In C. Bell, M. Bowden, & A. Trott (Eds.), *Implementing flexible learning*. London: Kogan Page.

Gibson, C. C. (1998). In retrospect. In C. C. Gibson (Ed.), *Distance learners in higher education*. Madison, Wisconsin: Atwood Publishing.

Gordon, S. E. (1994). *Systematic training program design: Maximizing effectiveness and minimizing liability*. Englewood Cliffs: Prentice-Hall.

Gustafson, K. L., & Schrum, L. (2001). Cost analysis and return on investment (ROI) for distance education. In B. H. Khan (Ed.), *Web-based training*. Englewood Cliffs: Educational Technology Publications.

Hall, B. (1997). *Web-based training cookbook*. New York: Wiley.

Hannum, W. (2001). Web-based training: Advantages and limitations. In B. H. Khan (Ed.), *Web-based training*. Englewood Cliffs: Educational Technology Publications.

Harasim, L. (1990). Online education: An environment for collaboration and intellectual amplification. In L. Harasim (Ed.), *Online education: Perspectives on a new environment*. New York: Praeger Publishers.

Harasim, L. (1993). (Ed.). *Global networks: Computers and international communication*. Cambridge, MA: MIT Press.

Hart, J. (1999). Improving distance learning performance. In G. P. Connick (Ed.), *The distance learner's guide*. Upper Saddle River, NJ: Prentice-Hall.

Heinich, R., Molenda, M., & Russell, J. (1993). *Instructional media and technologies for learning*. Upper Saddle River, NJ: Prentice-Hall.

Hill, J. R. (1997). Distance learning environments via the World Wide Web. In B. H. Khan (Ed.), *Web-based instruction*. Englewood Cliffs: Educational Technology Publications.

Hlynka, D. (1996). Postmodernism. In D. H. Jonassen (Ed.), *Handbook of research on educational communications and technology*. New York: Macmillan.

Hudspeth, D. (1997). Testing learner outcomes in Web-based instruction. In B. H. Khan (Ed.), *Web-based instruction*. Englewood Cliffs: Educational Technology Publications.

Jones, M. G., & Farquhar, J. D. (1997). User interface design for Web-based instruction. In B. H. Khan (Ed.), *Web-based instruction*. Englewood Cliffs: Educational Technology Publications.

Jonassen, D. H. (1997). Instructional design models for well-structured and ill-structured problem solving. *Educational Technology Research and Development, 45*(1), 25–.

Jonassen, D. H., Prevish, T., Christy, D., & Stavrulaki, E. (1997). Learning to solve problems on the Web: Aggregate planning in a business management course. *Distance Education, 20*(1), 49–62.

Kearsley, G., & Shneiderman, B. (1999). Engagement theory: A framework for technology-based teaching and learning; home.sprynet.com/~gkearsley/engage.htm

Khan, B. H. (1997a). Web-based instruction: What is it and why is it? In B. H. Khan (Ed.), *Web-based instruction*. Englewood Cliffs: Educational Technology Publications.

Khan, B. H. (1997b). A framework for Web-based learning. Paper presented at the Instructional Technology Department, Utah State University, Logan, UT.

Khan, B. H. (1997c). The designing matrix: A systemic tool for understanding the visions and images of new educational system. *Performance Improvement, 36*(2), 32–36.

Khan, B. H. (1998, June). Web-based instruction: An introduction. *Educational Media International, 35*(2), 63–71.

Khan, B. H. (1999). Interviewed by Debra Donston for an article entitled "From the trenches: Distributed learning is high priority," *PCWEEK, 16*(46), p. 134.

Khan, B. H. (2000a). A framework for Web-based learning. Annual Meeting of American Educational Research Association (AERA). Invited keynote presentation at the business meeting of AERA special interest group, titled "Education and the World Wide Web," New Orleans.

Khan, B. H. (2000b, July–August). How do you train for B2B Success? "Ask the Experts" Column. *The New Corporate University Review, 8*(4), p. 19.

Khan, B. H. (2001). Virtual U: A hub for excellence in education, training, and learning resources. In B. H. Khan (Ed.), *Web-based training.* Englewood Cliffs: Educational Technology Publications.

Khan, B. H. (in press a). Discussion of resources and attributes of the Web for the creation of meaningful learning environments. *Cyber Psychology and Behavior Journal.*

Khan, B. H. (in press b). Web-based training: A discussion. In M. Marquardt (Ed.), *UNESCO encyclopedia on human development.* London: EOLSS Publishers.

Khan, B. H., & Ealy, D. (2001). A framework for Web-based authoring systems. In B. H. Khan (Ed.), *Web-based training.* Englewood Cliffs: Educational Technology Publications.

Khan, B. H., Waddill, D., & McDonald, J. (2001). Review of Web-based training sites. In B. H. Khan (Ed.), *Web-based training.* Englewood Cliffs: Educational Technology Publications.

Krauth, B. (1998). Distance learning: The instructional strategy of the decade. In G. P. Connick (Ed.), *The distance learner's guide.* Upper Saddle River, NJ: Prentice-Hall.

Land, S. M., & Hannafin, M. J. (1997). Patterns of understanding with open-ended learning environments: A qualitative study. *Educational Technology Research and Development, 45*(2), 47–73.

Moore, M. G. (1998). Introduction. In C. C. Gibson (Ed.), *Distance learners in higher education.* Madison, WI: Atwood Publishing.

Moore, M., & Kearsley, G. (1996). *Distance education: A systems view.* Belmont, CA: Wadsworth.

Newby, T. J., Russell, J. D., Stepich, D. A., & Lehman, J. D. (1996). *Instructional technology for teaching and learning: Designing instruction, integrating computers, and using media.* Upper Saddle River, NJ: Prentice-Hall.

Nielsen, J. (2000). *The design of Web usability: The practice of simplicity.* Indianapolis: New Riders Publishing.

Palloff, R. M., & Pratt, K. (1999). *Building learning communities in cyberspace.* San Francisco: Jossey-Bass.

Pappo, H. A. (2001). Simulations for Web-based training. In B. H. Khan (Ed.), *Web-based training.* Englewood Cliffs: Educational Technology Publications.

Price, R. V. (1999). Designing a college Web-based course using a modified Personalized System of Instruction (PSI) model. *TechTrends, 43*(5). 23–28.

Reeves, T. C., & Carter, B. J. (2001). Usability testing and return-on-investment studies: Key evaluation strategies for Web-based training. In B. H. Khan (Ed.), *Web-based training.* Englewood Cliffs: Educational Technology Publications.

Reeves, T. C., & Reeves, P. M. (1997). Effective dimensions of interactive learning on the World Wide Web. In B. H. Khan (Ed.), *Web-based instruction.* Englewood Cliffs: Educational Technology Publications.

Reigeluth, C. M., & Khan, B. H. (1994, February). Do instructional systems design (ISD) and educational systems design (ESD) really need each other? Paper presented at the Annual Meeting of the Association for Educational Communications and Technology (AECT), Nashville, TN.

Relan, A., & Gillani, B. B. (1997). Web-based instruction and the traditional classroom: Similarities and differences. In B. H. Khan (Ed.), *Web-based instruction.* Englewood Cliffs: Educational Technology Publications.

Rice, J., Coleman, M. D., Shrader, V. E., Hall, J. P., Gibb, S. A., & McBride, R. H. (2000). Developing Web-based training for a global corporate community. In B. H. Khan (Ed.), *Web-based training.* Englewood Cliffs: Educational Technology Publications.

Romiszowski, A. J., & Chang, E. (2001). A practical model for conversational Web-based training: A response from the past to the needs of the future. In B. H. Khan (Ed.), *Web-based training.* Englewood Cliffs: Educational Technology Publications.

Rothwell, W., & Kazanas, H.C. (1992). *Mastering the instructional design process.* San Francisco: Jossey-Bass Publishers.

Saltzberg, S., & Polyson, S. (1995, Sept.). Distributed learning on the World Wide Web. *Syllabus;* syllabus. com/archive/Syll95/07_sept95/DistrLrngWWWeb.txt

Sanchez, I., & Gunawardena, C. N. (1998). Understanding and supporting the culturally diverse distance learner. In C. C. Gibson (Ed.), *Distance learners in higher education.* Madison, WI: Atwood Publishing.

Schmitz, J. (2001), Needed: Digital libraries for Web-based training. In B. H. Khan (Ed.), *Web-based training.* Englewood Cliffs: Educational Technology Publications.

Simich-Dudgeon, C. (1998). Developing a college Web-based course: Lesson learned. *Distance Education,* 19(2), 337–357.

Thiagarajan, S., & Thiagarajan, R. (2001). Playing interactive training games on the Web. In B. H. Khan (Ed.), *Web-based training.* Englewood Cliffs: Educational Technology Publications.

Walls, J. (1993). Global networking for local development: Task force and relationship focus in cross-cultural communication. In L. Harasim (Ed.), *Global networks: Computers and international communication.* Cambridge, MA: MIT Press.

Wheeler, S. (1999). Convergent technologies in distance learning delivery. *TechTrends, 43*(5). 19–22.

For additional readings in Web-based learning and distance education, please visit our Recommended Books Site *(BooksToRead.com/de).*

Acknowledgments

When I presented the WBL Framework at Utah State University (USU) in 1997, David Merrill of USU encouraged me by saying he would definitely use the WBL Framework for designing Web-based instruction. I wish to thank Prof. Merrill for his encouragement and early endorsement. I would also like to thank students at the University of Texas at Brownsville, George Washington University, George Mason University, and Towson University, who used the WBL Framework as part of their coursework to review existing Web-based instruction and training programs. Their comments and suggestions were very useful. I would also like to thank participants in my various keynote and invited addresses for their insightful comments and suggestions about the framework. Finally, I would like to thank the following for their critical review of this chapter: Greg Kearsley, consultant; Betty Collis, University of Twente, Netherlands; Som Naidu, University of Melbourne, Australia; Robin Mason, The Open University, England; Reynold Macpherson, The University of Auckland, New Zealand; Herman Van Der Merwe, South Africa; Jeroen van Merriënboer, Open University of the Netherlands; Charlotte N. (Lani) Gunawardena, University of New Mexico; Walter Wager, Florida State University; Amy Holloway, World Bank; Thomas Reeves and Janette Hill, University of Georgia; Philip Doughty, Syracuse University; Nada Dabbagh, George Mason University; Joanne Williams, University of Texas; Zane Berge, University of Maryland; David Peal, consultant. Within the scope of the chapter, I hope that I was able to adequately address all reviewers' concerns.

The Author

Badrul H. Khan (e-mail: khanb@gwu.edu, or khanb@BooksToRead.com; Web homepage: BooksTo Read.com/Khan) is Associate Professor and Program Director, Educational Technology Leadership cohort graduate program, George Washington University, Washington, D.C. He is the founder of BooksTo Read.com, a recommended readings site on the Internet.

9

Designing Instructional Templates for Web-Based Training

Robert J. Mills,

Kimberly A. Lawless, and

M. David Merrill

The World Wide Web (the Web) has emerged as a technology with an extraordinary impact in the training world. The Internet has been called the best opportunity for improving education and training since the printing press started putting books in the hands of millions (Price, 1996). The promise of the Web offers vast training opportunities, allowing instruction to take place throughout the world to anyone with a computer, modem, telephone line, and Internet service provider. Advancements in authoring and programming technologies have even afforded the opportunity to provide interactive, multimedia training over the Internet. Yet despite the many positive possibilities for Internet training, some individuals would argue that sound instructional design—including interaction, learner control, and feedback—are often missing from Websites dedicated to instruction (El-Tigi & Branch, 1997). Many of these "educational" Websites are nothing more than information containers with hot-words embedded into the information, coupled with the latest collection of technological bells and whistles.

Why would designers not utilize the full potential of the Web? There are both logistical and practical answers to this question. First, while the Web is capable of supporting interactive multimedia learning environments, its bandwidth is often incapable of delivering them. Bandwidth refers to the amount of data that can pass through a digital line at a given time. Bandwidth problems occur when backbones and servers become overloaded. High data traffic causes information overload, congesting the Internet and slowing transfer rates. Interactive multimedia training tools that include visual and auditory information often require an enormous amount of memory and space to run efficiently. Hence, although authoring and Web development tools are very effective at creating these environments for the Internet, development so that the Web can implement them is a problem.

The second major problem in designing sound instruction based on theory for the Web is tool-based. Although authoring and Web development tools empower the developer to create and deliver media-rich instruction, they offer very little support or guidance with regard to determining the desired learning outcome and appropriate instructional strategies required to help the learner obtain these outcomes (Gros, Elen, Kerres, Merriënboer, & Spector, 1997). In fact, most authoring programs deliberately do not endorse theories of instructional design in an effort to keep the purchase market as neutral and as large as possible (Anderson, 1998). Designers, then, must become responsible for establishing conditions that encourage or require learners to interact with and process instruction at a level deep enough for them to learn it well and remember it (Price, 1996). By implementing sound instructional strategies into the Web, the Web delivery medium will be transformed from an information container to a highly interactive facilitator of the learning process.

Finally, innately tied to the issue of designing learning environments based on sound instructional theory is the issue of cost. This type of instruction, which incorporates sound design principles, is often so expensive to develop that it is out of reach for many designers and learners. The need for developing effective Internet-based instruction within a reasonable budget and time constraint is a worthy goal of many training departments.

All combined, the issues of bandwidth, theory implementation, and cost have prohibited many companies from engaging in meaningful learning over the Web. The purpose of this chapter is to offer a solution to these problems. The chapter will describe how creating instructional design templates which incorporate sound instructional design increases the efficiency and effectiveness of Web-based training, while drastically reducing the strain of implementation and exorbitant development costs.

Instructional Templates

An instructional template is a content-independent program which is developed to teach a particular kind of knowledge or skill. Since knowledge and skills can be broken into distinct categories of learning outcomes (i.e., factual knowledge, procedures, concepts), developing a generic template to teach each category of learning outcome becomes the central focus. Essentially, instructional strategies and transactions for each learning outcome are identified and programmed into individual template shells. The content of a template is then interchangeable without affecting the built-in instructional strategies of the program. These transactions can be used to teach a similar kind of knowledge or skill without reprogramming the transaction shell (Merrill, Li, & Jones, 1991).

There are a number of advantages to the reusable template approach. Perhaps the most obvious is that reusable templates are developed once, rather than building a new set of transactions each time a lesson is needed. Because a template will be reused over and over, more time can be spent fine tuning the programming code, graphics sizes, and file structure to efficiently run on the Internet. As a result, a few instructionally sound, Internet efficient programs are created, saving the company time and precious resources, and reducing the bandwidth problem. Reducing the amount of data being transferred from one machine to another is a primary method currently available to increase the performance of a Website. For example, reducing the color palette and size of images and increasing the use of text when appropriate are simple strategies to increase Web-based performance. Instructional templates can be optimized to contain only the necessary amount of resources required for a particular learning outcome while eliminating superfluous material. As a result, the learner is capable of obtaining the Web-based instruction more quickly and efficiently.

Another advantage of using instructional templates is that meaningful interactions can be carefully planned out for a particular learning outcome by incorporating all of the necessary exchanges between the user and the environment. Building effective instruction to be delivered via the Internet requires engaging interaction between the environment and the learner. However, this interaction must go beyond page linking by creating a meaningful exchange between the user and the environment (Starr, 1997). Computer-based instruction has been found to be more effective if the learner takes an active role in the learning environment rather than passive observation (Lawless, Mills, & Drake, 1997).

A natural byproduct of using an instructional template is considerable cost savings. Once a template has been developed, there is little need for additional programming. Programming often consumes a large percentage of a Web-based course budget. When using templates, replacing media resources is all that is necessary to develop a new instructional lesson. As more and more templates are developed to teach various kinds of knowledge, the instructional designer can select the appropriate template for the desired learning outcome and supply the appropriate resources without requiring expensive programming.

A Design Prescription

When developing a set of prescriptive instructional templates for the Web, the designer must select an instructional theory to serve as a foundation to build upon. Since the premise of an instructional template hinges on the identification of learning outcomes and the selection of parallel instructional activities, the instructional performance theory chosen must specifically address these issues. While a number of theories have been developed to address these basic premises of instruction (e.g., Elaboration Theory, Anchored Instruction . . .), few theories contain both descriptive and prescriptive properties that designers can implement when creating instruction. One such theory, Component Display Theory (CDT), delineates not only a macro level picture of the instructional environment, but also breaks down learning outcomes and conditions into a series of best-practices designs. As such, CDT is a natural choice for the development of a set of instructional templates (other theories may be equally well suited, but space limits the discussion to one for illustration).

In order to discuss the development for a template based on CDT, it is necessary for the readers to have a precursory understanding of CDT (individuals wishing a more in-depth explanation of CDT are referred to Merrill, 1983, 1994). At the heart of CDT is the Performance-Content Matrix (see Figure 1). This matrix describes how instructional outcomes, represented either by objects or test items, can be classified on two dimensions: student performance and subject matter content (Merrill, 1994).

Student performance outcomes include remember, use, and find. The *remember* performance requires the student to recall information previously stored in memory. The *use* performance requires the learner to "apply some abstraction to a specific case" (Merrill, 1994). In other words, rather than simply recalling information, the student must perform a higher learning outcome such as cause and effect. Finally, the *find* performance requires the student to "derive or invent a new abstraction" (Merrill, 1994). For this performance, the learner must invent, derive, or discover new ideas or relationships.

According to CDT, subject matter content is divided into *facts, concepts, procedures,* and *principles. Facts* include pieces of information such as names, dates, symbols, parts, and events.

Subject Matter Content

Remember					
Use					
Find					
	Facts	Concepts	Procedures	Principles	

(Student Performance on vertical axis; Subject Matter Content on horizontal axis)

Figure 1. The Performance-Content Matrix.

Concepts are groups of objects that share some common characteristics (i.e., what characteristics distinguish a planet from a star). Ultimately, the learner will learn to discriminate among various objects that share common characteristics. Procedures are simply steps necessary to complete a given objective. For instance, what are the steps required to set up a telescope to view the moon? Finally, principles are "explanations or predictions" of why things happen in the world. Explaining how the various phases of the moon occur is an example of a principle.

This descriptive set of relationships can be used to organize and design learning activities (Merrill, 1983). Once the designer has classified a given learning outcome on the performance-content matrix, CDT provides a practical prescription for teaching these outcomes.

The prescriptive element of CDT includes the necessary strategies to help facilitate a particular learning outcome. These strategies include when and where to incorporate items such as definitions, activities, examples, relationships, and problems (primary presentation forms). Other instructional techniques are also included to enhance learning such as attention focusing help, mnemonics, feedback, and sequencing. Depending on the learning outcomes, a different set of prescriptions is suggested.

Creating Web Templates

Designing instructional templates for the Internet requires careful planning, consideration, and integration of sound instructional theory. Once you have determined an instructional learning outcome and selected a instructional strategy, it is important to select the appropriate tool for the job. Choosing an appropriate tool for developing a template is dependent upon time, resources, and programming skill available for the project. Templates can be built in a range of products from Java to a Web-based authoring program. Authoring languages typically incorporate plug-ins such as Neuron or Shockwave. A plug-in is downloaded to the user's computer once, which provides these authoring templates the ability to load and run via the Internet. Each authoring program offers unique advantages and challenges to develop the templates depending upon the complexity desired.

For an example, we have used Toolbook II as the authoring program to design and develop a concept lesson (see Figure 2).

The empty concept template (Figure 2) contains five content slots (labeled slot #1–slot #5). A slot is a location or placeholder in the template where interchangeable resources can be inserted. In this template, each of these slots can be filled with text, graphics, audio, or video resources, dependent on lesson needs and bandwidth limitations.

Resources for our sample template are contained within the "Clips" technology that Toolbook II provides for storing and retrieving interchangeable resources. "Clips" media sources can be changed or edited very easily because clips are contained in a database-like structure separate from the program. By using the clips editor, new lessons can be created by selecting different resources for each slot. A concept lesson to teach the key characteristics for an analytical style personality may appear in a form as shown in Figure 3.

A new concept lesson could easily be created to teach another concept such as the amiable personality style rather than the analytical personality style by replacing resources in the clip editor. For example, slot #3 would replace the analytical personality style graphic and audio with new resources. Hence, a new concept lesson can be created without requiring additional programming.

The student interacts with this particular program by examining examples and non-examples of the analytical style. The examples clearly illustrate the critical characteristics while the non-examples include common situations which may confuse the learner (Pratt, 1997). The

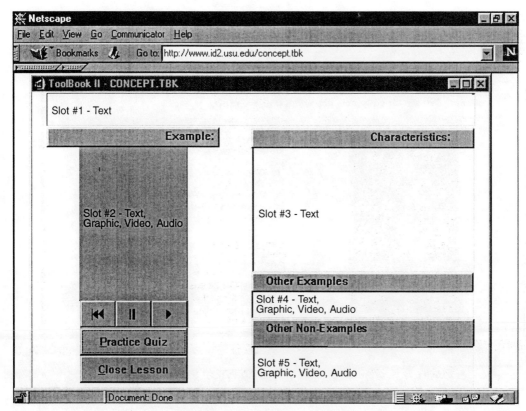

Figure 2. A concept template.

student then selects the classifying quiz where he/she judges the quiz items as either examples or non-examples of the analytical style personality.

The concept lesson previously described is a relatively simple template design. The template started by determining the desired learning outcome. An instructional strategy was then selected to teach the desired learning outcome. The interface was created, including navigation, buttons, and appropriate slots for the instructional interaction, and was optimized to efficiently run on the Internet. Finally, interchangeable resources were added using clips. Instructional templates can be as simple or complex as necessary to provide the desired learning outcome.

The technology you select for storing and retrieving resources will vary depending upon the development program being used and the complexity of the template. More advanced templates often utilize databases to store and link data into the template. Once a database of resources is properly created, simply exchanging resources to reflect the new content can create other lessons.

There are some limitations, however, to creating instructional templates. Initially, there is often an increase in design and programming required to create the organized clip system or database to hold the resources independent of the program. Also, templates are often perceived to be inflexible to some designers, who prefer to create and entirely new product each time new software products are developed. Finally, more abstract concepts and higher level skills can be difficult to design and develop using a reusable template.

The ID$_2$ Research Group at Utah State University has developed a number of instructional templates that are designed to teach a variety of learning outcomes, including facts, parts, con-

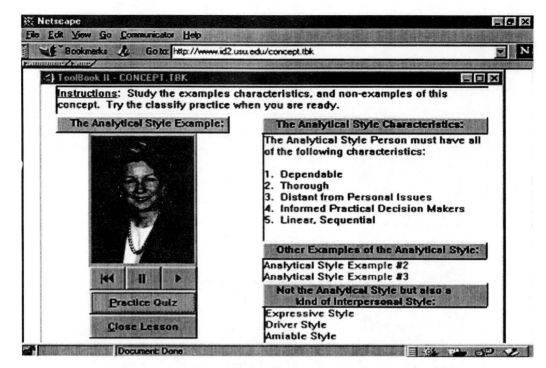

Figure 3. A concept lesson on the Analytical Style (with content).

cepts, and procedures. Tools developed by the ID$_2$ Research Group are currently being distributed by Mindware Creative, Inc. Former ID$_2$ personnel at LetterPress Software and Allen Communication have also continued to develop such templates. Examples of these instructional templates that have been designed for delivery on the Internet are available on the Web (knowva.com, lpsoftware.com, and allencomm.com).

The design and development of instructional materials is a difficult, time consuming, and expensive process. The process for the creation of training products over the Web is no exception. Added complications of off-site instructors and student anonymity may even make Web-based training more difficult than traditional methods. However, as instructional designers, if we utilize resources and design specifications wisely, we not only have the ability to decrease production time and cost, but also to increase learning effectiveness. Instructional templates based on sound instructional strategies and theory offer one solution to the problem. As technology and instructional theory continue to evolve, instructional designers and corporate trainers will need to continue seeking innovative approaches to satisfy their training needs.

References

Anderson, T. A. (1998). *Rethinking authoring tools: A design for standards-based instructional components.* Unpublished dissertation.

El-Tigi, M., & Branch, R. M. (1997). Designing for interaction, learner control, and feedback during Web-based learning. *Educational Technology, 37*(3), 23–29.

Gros, B., Elen, J., Kerres, M., Merriënboer, J., & Spector, M. (1997). Instructional design and the authoring of multimedia and hypermedia. *Educational Technology, 37*(1), 48–56.

Lawless, K. A., Mills, R. J., & Drake, L. (1997, October). *The role of scaffolding in learning environments.* Paper presented at the annual meeting of the Northern Rocky Mountain Educational Research Association, Jackson, Wyoming.

Lippert, R. C. (1989). Expert systems: Tutors, tools, and tutees. *Journal of Computer Based Instruction, 16*(1), 11–19.

Merrill, M. D. (1983). Component display theory. In C. M. Reigeluth (Ed.), *Instructional-design theories and models.* Hillsdale, NJ: Lawrence Erlbaum Associates.

Merrill, M. D. (1994). D. G. Twitchell (Ed.) *Instructional design theory.* Englewood Cliffs: Educational Technology Publications.

Merrill, M. D. (1996). Instructional transaction theory: An instructional design model based on knowledge objects. *Educational Technology, 36*(3), 30–37.

Merrill, M. D., Li, Z., & Jones, M. K. (1991). Instructional transaction theory: An introduction. *Educational Technology, 31*(6), 7-12.

Pratt, J. A. (1997) *Electronic trainer 3.5 quick start.* Unpublished manuscript.

Price, R. V. (1996). Technology doesn't teach. People do. *Tech Trends, 41*(6), 17–18.

Smith, P. L., & Ragan, T. J. (1993). *Instructional design.* New York: Macmillan.

Starr, R. M. (1997). Delivering instruction on the World Wide Web: Overview and basic design principles. *Educational Technology, 37*(3), 7–11.

The Authors

Robert J. Mills (e-mail: mills@cc.usu.edu) is a faculty member, Department of Business Information Systems and Education, Utah State University, Logan, Utah. **Kimberly A. Lawless** (e-mail: klawless@uic.edu) is Assistant Professor, Curriculum and Instruction, University of Illinois at Chicago. **M. David Merrill** (e-mail: merrill@cc.usu.edu; Web homepage: id2.usu.edu) is Professor, Department of Instructional Technology, Utah State University, Logan, Utah.

10

A Practical Model for Conversational Web-Based Training: A Response from the Past to the Needs of the Future

Alexander J. Romiszowski

and Echeol Chang

The Dimensions of WBT

WBT: the latest bandwagon? In the few years since the appearance of the World Wide Web, its use as a training delivery medium—Web-based training—seems to have already become firmly established, especially in the corporate world. Indeed, recent survey statistics indicate that WBT is the largest and fastest growing variety of technology-based training, already accounting for over twice the number of training hours of conventional CBT and CD-ROM-based multimedia training packages (Bernstein & Auerbach, 1999).

The reasons for this are practical and economic. Most of the major companies today maintain their own data and personal communication networks, so all departments can communicate effectively and efficiently by electronic means. One aspect of increasing importance of these systems is the use of electronic mail, computer conferencing, and, increasingly, computer supported collaborative work between individuals or groups who may be scattered in different regions of a country or even different continents. The emerging global communication platform is the Internet and especially the World Wide Web.

Individual companies are investing in their own private intranets that maintain privacy and security of access to company information while offering the *look and feel* of the Web hypermedia environment to internal electronic communications. These company-owned intranets can, if so desired, also give access to the public Internet resources in an apparently seamless communication process. Company employees may, at one moment, be accessing confidential information and interacting with others in their closed community and, at another moment, be accessing publicly available information from any Website in the world and interacting with total outsiders who share a common interest in this information.

This "globalization" of business communications has become a necessary condition for staying competitive. In today's rapidly changing business environment, the new breed of *knowledge workers,* who use existing (both private and public) knowledge to create new company-critical knowledge (and thus creates a business edge), is the organization's most valuable resource. The tendency to this "whole world" business view, coupled with recent developments in telecommunications and computing that offer the possibility of digitizing and storing messages for transmission at more convenient or more economical times, is transforming the nature of business communications. This *telematics* revolution is also beginning to impact the training and development world. It is natural that, given the emerging infrastructure for global digital communications, companies should consider it both effective and economical to use the same infrastructure for training purposes that they are already using for other business-related communications. The questions remain, however, whether this *natural* conclusion is indeed always correct and, even if correct in principle, how to ensure that potential benefits are indeed achieved in practice.

But What Exactly Is WBT?

Basically, WBT is a technology that delivers *anytime, anywhere training,* across the organization, on demand. Trainees can access course materials whether they are in the office, at home, or on the road. They may also interact in both large and small groups by means of electronic communication tools such as e-mail and discussion lists. WBT may in principle lead to reduced training overheads, centralized training management, learner defined training paths, and increased levels of accountability. However, within this broad definition, many different methodologies are emerging. It may be of value to commence by establishing a schema for categorizing WBT projects.

There are many possible approaches to the classification of the varieties and *flavors* of WBT. Driscoll (1997) illustrates three possible approaches. She describes two broad categories of Internet-based training: text-only and multimedia (a media-based classification). She also discusses a range of different Internet-based communication tools, including e-mail, bulletin boards, and software downloading (a tools-based classification). And she also identifies four basic types of Web-based training (see Driscoll's chapter in this present volume): Web/computer-based training, Web/electronic performance support systems, and both asynchronous and synchronous virtual classrooms (a process-based classification).

Imel (1997) differentiates between WBT and traditional computer-based training (CBT), and also between real-time WBT (in which instructors use the Web to extend the reach of the classroom) and nonreal-time WBT (which is created in a traditional CBT authoring system and simply downloaded from the Web so that students take the instruction at their leisure). She emphasizes that for WBT to be effective, it must be like CBT, but better.

However, not all is necessarily for the better. Tucker (1997), for example, in a survey of typical corporate usage of technology-based training, found that, *compared with earlier computer-based training, existing examples of Web-based training are generally of much lower quality.* It appeared certain, however, from his study, that WBT *will become increasingly prevalent because of the need for just-in-time training, the ease of updating intranet-based training easily, and intranets' distinct cost advantage.* We seem to have a paradoxical problem here.

The mainstream of WBT is, indeed, not all that different from conventional CBT. Stone and Bishop (1997) make the point that most WBT systems and materials are developed by the same set of procedures as other forms of interactive instruction. They describe the following phases of courseware production: (1) needs assessment; (2) content design; (3) rapid prototyping; (4) storyboarding; (5) developing the courseware; (6) usability testing (validation/alpha-testing); and (7) quality assurance and testing (formative evaluation/beta-testing). However, due to bandwidth and speed constraints that still exist on most electronic networks, especially on the public Internet, much of the resultant training software being currently implemented via the Web is reminiscent of the stand-alone CBT packages of ten or more years ago. The

Table 1. CBT-WBT and CMC-WBT.

	Individual Study Mode (CBT-WBT)	Group Study Mode (CMC-WBT)
Online Use or Synchronous Communication	Browsing the Web, accessing Websites for information or for online CBT modules.	Internet relay chat (IRC) or Web-based videoconference sessions.
Offline Use or Asynchronous Communication	Downloading courseware from the Web for later study on local computers.	Asynchronous CMC tools such such as e-mail, discussion lists, and groupware environments.

superior presentation and interaction capabilities of well-designed interactive multimedia, stored and delivered via CD-ROM technologies, cannot yet be matched by online access to lessons stored on distant Websites.

There are, however, practical methods for circumventing these limitations. One example is the *Learning Object Download* system of the National Education Training Group—NETg (netg.com/). NETg's Learning Object Download (LOD) format enables learners to work off-line, whether at work, at home, or while traveling. Learners download only the courses, or portions of courses, they wish to work with at that particular time. This approach conserves disk space and avoids long downloads. Local PC execution eliminates slow page displays and poor response time. Local PC execution also means workers can use the instruction even when they are not connected to the network. LOD allows learners to begin instruction as soon as their first requested topic has downloaded. Additional requested topics continue to download in the background while learners study initial topics. Using this approach, NETg can distribute the same multimedia CBT training materials that are already available in CD-ROM for stand-alone computer usage by means of the Web to authorized users anywhere in the world.

We may integrate the ideas expressed above into a meaningful schema, presented in Table 1.

We are here using the term Web-based training (WBT) in its broad, generic sense of any form of training (including educational and developmental interpretations of training) that utilizes the Web in any way whatsoever. We then differentiate between individual-study and group-study modes. This generates the rather unusual, but we believe useful subsets of *CBT-based WBT* and *CMC-based WBT* (Computer-Mediated Communication). We also differentiate between real-time and asynchronous communication patterns, thus creating four basic categories of the WBT concept.

Which Variety of WBT Is for Me?

Critics of behaviorist learning are concerned by the apparent tendency for so-called *conventional* CBT to be replicated in WBT. The idea of using cognitive-based theories as the basis for designing WBT is emerging in the literature. For example, Simonson (1998) describes a project that converted a stand-up training class to an interactive Website posted on an intranet for access by all employees. She explains the theoretical basis for this conversion process as grounded in cognitive flexibility theory. There are many different theoretical bases and instructional paradigms out there vying for our attention. In a recent publication, Dills and Romiszowski (1997) identify over 40. Let us review just some of the current *hot* debates.

One notable current debate that may impact on the role of CMC-based vs. CBT-based WBT is the "constructivism vs. objectivism" issue. The constructivist viewpoint is often aligned with CMC and opposed to CBT, which is seen as an objectivist approach to teaching and learning (Cunningham, Duffy, & Knuth, 1993; Kaye, 1992). Another not-so-recent debate which has been revived in relation to the use of WBT is the "humanism vs. mechanism" issue. The humanists see the personal interaction between people that CMC allows as an important element in the appropriate uses of computers in education and training. A similar debate on the "cognitive vs. behaviorist" psychology platform may lead to positions being taken either for or against the use of CMC or CBT approaches in the design of WBT systems.

Other groups of theorists argue for CMC-based approaches from the standpoint of learning as "conversation." In this viewpoint, the teaching/learning process is seen as a form of conversation, whether real or in the mind of the learner, which leads to an "agreement" on the meaning of specific content. It is argued that CMC, through the provision of real opportunities for conversation, may be a more appropriate approach than conventional CBT, especially for the development of higher order learning associated with problem solving and critical thinking skills (Romiszowski & Corso, 1990).

It is for such reasons that this chapter will concentrate mainly on CMC-based WBT. As we develop our discussion, it will become apparent why the focus is also on the *asynchronous communication varieties of CMC*. We shall, thus, concentrate our attention on the bottom-right hand cell of our classification schema in Table 1. This is not to criticize or to reduce the importance of the other varieties of WBT. All four basic categories of WBT have their respective roles to play in modern education and training systems. Other chapters in this book deal extensively with aspects of these categories. However, the category selected is of special interest to the present authors for three main reasons. It is, arguably, the category of WBT that has most to offer for the future improvement of corporate education and training. Furthermore, maybe for this reason, it is the area on which much of our recent research activity has been concentrated. And, as a result of this research, it is the area in which we feel most competent to make some concrete suggestions for the improvement of current practices.

Issues in CMC

We shall therefore next address some of the issues that have come up in recent research on and practice of CMC for education and training. Then, based on our analysis of these issues, we shall identify some of the problems and limitations of current CMC practices. Finally, we shall progress to a presentation of one specific form of WBT that is a fusion of some aspects of CBT-based systems with some aspects of CMC-based systems that, in our opinion, addresses some of the problems.

Changing Technologies

One important trend already mentioned is the explosive rate at which new technologies for communication are being disseminated. Current multimedia and hypermedia developments have already been absorbed into WBT environments, producing systems that, at least in principle, have the potential for vastly improving the rather unstructured and text-based modes of communication that were characteristic of earlier CMC systems. The incorporation of graphics, audio, video, and in the future perhaps even simulations of a virtual reality nature, which may all be transmitted across the digital information superhighways, is opening the potential for a much richer form of WBT. Most of the research completed so far is related to the earlier forms of text-based CBT. Some of these results may be equally valid within the context of multimedia distance education/training systems. However, we may expect many new issues and questions to emerge as these broadband, multimedia, multimodal communication systems link both people and remote databases into one seamless information and communication environment. The recurrent problem, though, is that we hop from one recently-emerged technology to another currently-emerging technology that promises ever new potential, without ever learning to fully exploit the potential of the old. It is a sobering thought that in all the centuries since the Gutenberg print technology facilitated the mass dissemination of text, we are still struggling with the issues of mediocre textbooks, instruction manuals that fail to instruct, and all manner of print communications that just do not communicate.

Replicate or Innovate?

Another issue which is increasingly facing researchers and practitioners in the area of WBT is whether this medium should be considered as an alternative way of implementing previously well-tried teaching/learning strategies, or whether the medium itself may lead to the implementation of novel strategies that previously were not used. Among the research and development work that has followed the line of replication of the past, a notable trend is illustrated by the "Virtual Classroom" methodologies (Hiltz, 1986, 1990). This work has focused on the replication of well-tried classroom-based teaching/learning strategies in a networked environment. Variations on the virtual classroom might include the virtual conference room (that is, computer conferencing), the virtual seminar room, and the virtual case study discussion room, each implying a specific set of teaching/learning strategies (Romiszowski, 1993).

An example of a somewhat novel approach is the trend toward the implementation of learner controlled environments that may combine the use of information resources stored remotely as a hypermedia network of information, together with computer supported collaborative project work between groups of individuals utilizing the asynchronous CMC capabilities of the network. A non-conventional example of a popular use of CMC is to supplement conventional classroom-based instruction with group exercises or projects that participants "take home" but continue to interact with both teacher and colleagues through the medium of CMC while working on their projects. This approach, although not new with respect to its project work details, is novel in that it extends the possibilities for group interaction (Grabowski, Suciati, & Pusch, 1990). At least in this sector of endeavor, we seem to be on the path of innovation in order to justify our use of new technologies through the achievement of some significant added value to the teaching-learning process.

Technological Synergy

The third issue is the synergetic interaction between computer sciences, cognitive sciences, and telecommunications sciences, which is offering a host of new possibilities, such as, for example, artificial intelligence software that may act as an intelligent interface between remote databases in libraries and students, or may in other ways facilitate the learning process. One area of current technological development that has yet to show its promise in practice is virtual reality. This is the simulation in computer software of personal closeness and involvement in a particular environment. It is possible to imagine WBT systems of the future that will not be open to the criticism of the loss of non-verbal communication elements, such as facial expressions, gestures, or even touch. Systems are under development that allow a group of people to meet, some of them really physically present and others apparently so but actually at a distance. The current catch-phrase in this area is *telepresence*. The applications of these new technological possibilities are yet largely unresearched, although much development work is going on and even more is written about their potential benefits. However, what about the old technologies that we have not yet fully mastered? How about giving equal attention to the *soft* (design) technologies as we do to the *hard*?

Learner Control and System Control

Some proponents of WBT see the principal value of the medium as residing in its being under the control of the users. The aspects of *just-in-time* and *anytime-anywhere* learning are emphasized as the driving reasons for adopting WBT. Self-direction manifests itself when students voluntarily elect to take a WBT course, determine how, when, and where they will study, and negotiate the learning activities and content focus they will pursue during the course. This is not without its problems and difficulties. Eastmond (1993) found that distance students taking CMC courses exhibited varying patterns of self-direction. They were confident about their abilities to manage their schedule and the study process to produce necessary learning results, but they wanted the assignments clearly set forth for them by the instructor.

There are also problems that need to be addressed when using WBT modules as an integral part of a larger course. Some of these spring from the asynchronous qualities of the communication process. Unlike face-to-face instruction, or real-time teleconferencing, in which the participants communicate during one fixed period of time, asynchronous CMC allows one to choose when to respond to another participant's comments. This offers the benefit of allowing one to think out a more structured, more complex response, and the benefit of being able to participate at times that are personally convenient. This same factor can also generate communication difficulties. One problem is that it may promote procrastination, leaving the response for later, and perhaps in some cases, failing to respond altogether. This adds to the complexity of the developing structure in that students may, at any time, be inputting new comments related to different stages of the development of the topic. Not only is the discourse "multi-level" in that several different topics may be in simultaneous discussion, but it is also "multi-speed" (Romiszowski & DeHaas, 1989).

Another problem originates from the distance communication aspect of CMC-based WBT. Although distance communication allows one to participate in a discourse that may otherwise be impossible, it also introduces some difficulties of control of the discourse. The instructor loses some of the benefits offered by a face-to-face group situation. When the discussion drifts off the topic, it often takes longer, and is more difficult, to bring the group back on task. There is also the problem of knowing who is/is not participating. There is only knowledge of who is contributing. How can we know who is "lurking" on the system and, maybe, benefiting just as much as the silent student in class who learns from the comments and questions of other colleagues? And, if we do not know who is absent and who is present but just *silent*, how do we proceed in order to try to draw everyone into the discourse?

Instructors and Teaching

The role of the CMC-based instructor is quite different from that of the traditional classroom instructor. Course design becomes more important and preparation entails the careful structuring of content into self-study units available online and the design of both individual learning activities and small-group work. During a computer-delivered course, the teacher must adopt the role of facilitator, not content provider. While the instructor's role is particularly time-consuming in the initial phase of a CMC-based course, it usually lessens as students take over the discussions. Nevertheless, some reports indicate that instructors spend up to twice as long, overall, to deliver a course via CMC methodologies as they do to give the same course by traditional means.

Staff Training and Preparation

Teaching in a WBT environment requires a high degree of familiarity with the system's features and architecture. The training and support of instructors and students is a critical aspect of any program using this medium. While it is relatively easy to train instructors and students to use a computer network system, it is much more difficult to teach the skills of moderating computer conferences, for example. Instructors must learn how to promote on-line discussion, devise learning activities that work at a distance, and encourage interaction among the participants.

The current trends in WBT systems (especially *groupware*) design are hard-technology-driven, seeking to offer ever more sophisticated electronic intercommunication environments, but largely ignoring the questions of the skills, preferences, habits, and practical constraints of the intended users. The design of practical and sustainable WBT systems should take such factors into consideration. Whereas in the area of CBT-based systems, the instructor role is much reduced as the software takes over the teaching and the evaluation and control functions are well-supported by tracking, testing, and course management software, the situation in the area of CMC-based systems is just the opposite. The instructor's role becomes more complex and new duties are added to the job description.

The approach presented in this chapter seeks, among other things, to redress this situation by offering software support for the instructor. By partially automating the process of moderating an online discussion, we reduce the amount of extra time and effort spent on keeping a CMC-WBT course running smoothly. By partially pre-programming the study materials and related exercises, we reduce the need for generating often-repetitive surface-level feedback messages, thus allowing instructors to engage in a deeper level of discussion with students.

A Look to the Future

Electronic Networks and Future Education and Training

The development of telecommunications and digital data transmission is revolutionizing the ways in which business is performed. People are working and communicating more and more by means of computer-based work stations that support databases, electronic mail, and a host of other information tools. As electronic communication networks become more ubiquitous, easier to use, and more powerful, the trend towards electronic, networked, business communications grow rapidly. As a result, people spend an increasing proportion of their time at workstations and proportionately less in live meetings (Zuboff, 1988).

This trend has also spread to meetings with educational or human-resource development aims. Of course, the rapid expansion in use of electronic teletraining is being driven, as always, not so much by effectiveness, but rather by economic factors. For example, AT&T, since adopting mass teletraining, has reported an overall reduction of over 50% in the costs per student hour of training. This cost saving comes almost entirely from savings in travel and subsistence costs when employees participate in centrally organized "place-based" courses, as well as from reduced loss of productivity, due to a reduction in the time that employees are away from their jobs (Chute, 1990).

New Forms of Education and Training

There are also other pressures, both organizational and philosophical, that are increasing the amount of autonomy, self-directedness, and responsibility that learners have in respect of their own education and development. From the philosophical side, there is the viewpoint that people should have more control over what they learn and how they learn it. These viewpoints are embodied in the principles of modern adult education, or *andragogy*. They also reflect earlier humanist traditions. They are further strengthened by the modern concepts of continuing or "permanent education," which spring from the realization that change in society, and particularly in the workplace, is now so fast that everyone is of necessity involved in a process of lifelong learning.

The need for constant updating of professional education and training programs is driven by the rapid technology-driven rate of change in the workplace and may therefore in many respects be very specific and personal for each individual. Hence the growing popularity of the "Open Learning" concept. This is a modular approach to the design of education and training systems that can take anyone from wherever they are at present in a given domain to wherever they need/want to be, relatively independently of the needs/wants of other people (Paine, 1988).

Given the increasingly competitive nature of business in the international marketplace and the critical importance that access to and use of up-to-date information and methods plays in a company's competitiveness, it is not surprising that the concept of human resources development as "self-development" is taking root. This concept sees keeping up-to-date and employable as the responsibility of every employee. The employer's responsibility is to make this possible, by helping to identify the needs of the individual and by facilitating access to the resources necessary to satisfy those needs. This will ever less frequently call for lengthy courses organized either within the company or by outside providers, but will instead make much more use of networking, access to external databases and electronic libraries, small specialist group tele-training, and self-instruction in all its forms (Eurich, 1990).

The R&D focus should be on the effective implementation of group discussion, or "conversational" methodologies on electronic telecommunications networks. This focus is particularly important, as we know much less about how to converse effectively on electronic networks than we do about electronic self-instruction. There is a long history and fairly developed technology of the design, development, and delivery-at-a-distance of self-study materials. There is much less known about the running of effective group-discussion sessions at a distance.

Such teaching methods as seminars or case studies are traditionally implemented in small or medium sized groups, led by skilled and experienced "facilitators." The success of these methods depends much on the facilitators and the skill with which they focus discussion, guide the approaches adopted by the participants, use the natural group dynamics to stimulate interest, participation, and deep involvement, and pull together what has been learned in the final debriefing discussion. Can such participatory discussion methods be effectively orchestrated at a distance? How might this be done? And, most importantly, how might we do it so as to create practical and sustainable WBT systems that will survive the test of time as the initial enthusiastic *early adopters* move on to other projects and their place is taken by the rank and file of the HRD profession?

Two Paradigms Compared

In order to answer these questions, let us review a little theory and also some of the research that is already available on this topic. It may help to compare and contrast two alternative paradigms, or maybe philosophies. We may call them the "instructional" and the "conversational" paradigms. They are summarized in Table 2.

The instructional paradigm is the one that has driven much (though by no means all) of the research and development of the past 30 years that has been performed under the label of educational (or instructional) technology. The conversational paradigm may be seen as the basis of much of the work done on small-group study, group dynamics, experiential learning, and so on.

In relation to distance teaching specifically, one may notice at the bottom of Table 2 that the more conventional "study module" or typical correspondence course model may serve as a

Table 2. Two teaching paradigms.

PARADIGM	INSTRUCTION	/ CONVERSATION
Objectives (why?)	specific pre-defined products standard	general negotiable processes variable
Messages (what?) (when?) (who?)	designed pre-prepared instructor one-to-many	created online participants many-to-many
Interaction (focus) (analysis) (feedback) (complexity)	behaviors criterion-referenced corrective one-layer-thick	ideas content/structure constructive interwoven layers
Distance Education	Correspondence Courses	Teleconferencing Videoconferencing
	Computer Mediated Communication	

good example of the instructional paradigm. Synchronous teleconferencing, both audio and video based, is (if appropriately planned and implemented) a good example of the conversational paradigm in action. CMC, however, is seen as being able to support both conversational and instructional procedures.

For example, joint cooperation on the analysis and development of a hypertext document satisfies all the basic requirements of a conversation between the participants. The study of an online version of a maintenance manual for an airplane in order to learn a particular set of troubleshooting procedures satisfies the requirements of instruction. This versatility of CMC systems and their potential integration with online information sources such as hypertext makes them particularly interesting systems to study with a view to their rational adoption in education and training (Horn, 1989; Romiszowski, 1990).

Constructivism Revisited

Dewey (1900) emphasized the necessity of a "special linking science" between the behavioral and cognitive sciences and instructional practice. However, many learning principles from the laboratory have failed to be correctly understood and applied to complex real-life instructional problems. Gagné (1962) also expressed dissatisfaction with his attempts to apply laboratory-based learning principles in military and industrial training situations. One of the reasons for the failure is that those principles were developed without sufficiently taking into consideration the context to which they were to be applied. In addition, the principles are too general to apply to subject- and context-specific situations.

Duffy and Jonassen (1992), in arguing that there has been a lack of interchange of ideas between learning theory and instructional practices, believe that constructivism must play an important role for building this relationship. According to them, "two changes in our society—

the volume of information we must manage and the new opportunities provided through technology—have caused us to revisit constructivism" (preface, p. ix). These two fundamental changes, according to them, have caused us to reconceptualize the learning process and to design new instructional approaches. Cunningham, Duffy, and Knuth (1993) identify seven pedagogical goals for constructivist learning environments: (1) Provide learners with experience in the knowledge construction process. (2) Provide learners with experience in and appreciation for multiple perspectives. (3) Embed learning in realistic and relevant contexts. (4) Encourage ownership and voice in the learning process. (5) Embed learning in social experience. (6) Encourage the use of multiple modes of representation. (7) Encourage self-awareness of the knowledge construction process.

Based on these goals, McMahon, Carr, and Fishman (1993) suggest three major principles for designing instruction. First, learners should be placed in authentic learning environments. Second, modeling, coaching, and scaffolding as instructional strategies should be stressed. Third, collaboration and multiple perspectives should be encouraged and supported.

Structural Communication

General Description

Structural Communication is an instructional approach that provides a simulated dialogue between an author of instructional materials and the students. It has been called "an interactive technique for communicating understanding" (Egan, 1976). Understanding is "inferred if a student shows the ability to use knowledge appropriately in different contexts, and to organize knowledge elements in accordance with specified organizing principles" (Egan, 1972, p. 66).

The original developmental work was performed in the late 1960s and early 1970s, by Bennett and Hodgson (Hodgson, 1972) at the Institute for the Comparative Study of History, Philosophy, and the Sciences, in London, U.K. The primary purpose of this Institute was to conduct research into methods of analyzing and organizing knowledge, aiming to develop practical techniques which can lead to more effective thinking and more insightful understanding (Egan, 1976, p. ix). The technique was designed to encourage creative thinking in learners, allowing them to develop an understanding of a topic, not simply to memorize facts.

Structural Communication was developed and implemented in the same historical period as Programmed Instruction and was viewed by its inventors as a cognitive psychologist's version of Programmed Instruction. However, the similarity is in the delivery of the exercise as self-instructional text. The structure and authoring style of the materials are very different. Whereas Programmed Instruction may be viewed as a text version of a rigidly controlled training session or tutorial, Structural Communication is open-ended, loosely controlled, and incorporates many of the characteristics of Socratic Dialogue as exemplified by Plato in his writings. Egan (1976) compares and contrasts Structural Communication to Programmed Instruction in three areas: individualizing, efficiency, and control. Table 3 summarizes this comparison.

Structural Communication combines the best of Programmed Instruction (the ability to individualize instruction) with the ability to account for different learning styles and increased learner control. Furthermore, while behaviorism rejects the concept of mind and refuses to discuss cognition, the Structural Communication model incorporates these elements in its basic formulation. It does this in a way that both constructivists and cognitive theorists (some of them) can (maybe) accept.

Table 3. Structural Communication and Programmed Instruction.

	In Common	**Contrast**
Individualizing	Programmed Instruction makes it possible to include strategies, pacing, and feedback that is tailored to the needs of individual learners.	Linear programming allows for self-paced instruction, but does not account for differences in learning style. Branched programs do increase the possibility of accounting for learning styles, but this is still limited. Structural Communication was designed so it may be possible that no two learners take the same path through the instruction.
Efficiency	Programmed Instruction allows for increase in efficiency when compared to teacher led instruction.	While both linear and branched programs increase the efficiency in certain types of subject matter, they tend to be limited to reproductive or low levels of thinking. Structural Communication was designed to encourage creative thinking, so it can be adapted to a greater variety of subject matter.
Control	Programmed Instruction allows for greater control over the learning process.	Traditional linear and branched programs allow the program's author to maintain control over what the student learns. Structural Communication, since it encourages creative thinking, increases the control that the learner has on what is learned.

Structural Communication was designed to promote learning for social action. Bennett and Hodgson, in line with many current constructivists, viewed the social contexts of the learning activity to be critical for the transfer of learning to practical situations (Egan, 1976). The distinctions between the learning of knowledge and the learning for social action are evident in the actual components Bennett and Hodgson designed into the Structural Communication technique. The typical components of a Structural Communication unit are described below (see Figure 1).

Intention: The opening statement, which defines what is to be studied, provides an overview, possibly an "advance organizer," and sometimes a rationale. It is used to provide a context for the content of the study unit.

Presentation: The material, experience, exercise, case study, etc., which supplies the essential facts and concepts of the domain being studied. This may be an existing text, a video, a case study, a simulation, or real-life experience, depending on the overall strategy of the exercise. This could also be any sort of computer-based instruction, including simulations.

Investigation: A set of problems for solution, which are designed to present the "intellectual challenge" that is an essential part of the Structural Communication methodology.

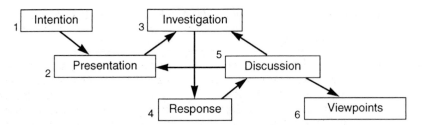

Figure 1. Main pathway through a Structural Communication study unit.

These problems are interrelated and are open-ended to allow multiple responses and viewpoints. The purpose of the investigation section is for the learner to interact with the subject matter.

Response: A randomized array or matrix of items which summarize key parts, concepts or principles from the knowledge base that is being used and studied in the exercise. Often it resembles a "key point summary" of the Presentation. The student composes a response (outlines an essay) by selecting any number of these items as a "best" response to a given problem.

Discussion: The Discussion has two parts: a Discussion Guide and a set of Discussion Comments. The Guide is a set of if–then rules, which test the student's response for omission or inclusion of certain significant items, or combinations of items. The Comments are constructive statements which discuss in depth the rationale for including or excluding certain items.

Viewpoints: An outline of the author's, and other alternative viewpoints; this may review some aspects stated in the Intention, make explicit some biases or standpoints held dear by the author, draw attention to other views in the literature, etc. Ideally, the viewpoint section plays a final, interactive role between author and learner.

An additional aspect of the Structural Communication study unit is the assessment of the learner's responses to the questions posed by the study unit. Bennett and Hodgson (Egan, 1976) developed a numerical measure called the coherence index. To obtain student's coherence index, each item on the response matrix is weighted for each of the questions. Thus, each item has as many weights as there are questions, and each question has as many weighted items assigned to it as there are response items. The weights usually range from +2 to –2. A student's coherence index is equal to the sum of weighted values for the response items he or she has chosen. A separate coherence index value is obtained by each student for each question.

According to Egan (1976), Hodgson and Bennett interpret the coherence index as an objective measure of how well the student organizes knowledge about the specific topic in the study unit. However, the constructivist may reject this interpretation, since it implies a correct set of responses based upon the ideal organization and analysis of the presented data. The constructivist is more likely to agree with the alternative interpretation of the coherence index as an objective measure of the degree of agreement of the student with the author of the Structural Communication unit. Measures of divergence of viewpoints rather than convergence on a uniform, or coherent, viewpoint on the issues being discussed in the study unit may be of greater interest to the constructivist.

Applications of Structural Communication in Management Training

During the late 1960s and early 1970s, there were a number of articles that described the use of the Structural Communication methodology in schools. Structural Communication was also used to provide supplemental materials for lectures or to deliver the lecture itself at the higher education level. Of more relevance to WBT, Hodgson and Dill (1970a, b, 1971) described a business management case study formatted as a Structural Communication unit. The unit was published in the *Harvard Business Review,* and readers were invited to mail in their responses to the questions at the end of the case. A significant response was received, which the authors analyzed. They found that the coherence index increased from question one to question four, suggesting that whatever skills were involved in using this technique improved with experience. Hodgson (1971), in another article, concludes that if combined with a computerized delivery system, Structural Communication could be used effectively as the basis for a computer-managed correspondence course system in a variety of teaching areas suitable for the use of the case study method.

Subsequently, both Romiszowski (1976) and Mitchell and Meilluer-Baccanale (1982) published experimental studies attempting to determine the effectiveness of Structural Communication. Romiszowski compared a Structural Communication unit on set theory, previously developed by Fyfe and Woodrow (1969) to existing, traditional materials for teaching set theory. He concluded that, although the students had difficulties with the reading level of the units, the Structural Communication unit taught concepts and principles to a greater depth of understanding than did the traditional materials. Likewise, Mitchell and Meilluer-Baccanale (1982) found that their experimental group studying a Structural Communication unit on systems analysis outperformed their control group by 58% on an immediate test and by 51% on the delayed test.

The wide availability of computers since the 1985–1990 period stimulated interest in a computer-based version of Structural Communication. Romiszowski, Grabowski, and Damadaran (1988) examined the ability of Structural Communication to increase the scores of students using a business decision simulation-game, *Decision Point: A Living Case Study,* delivered by means of an interactive video package that enjoyed outstanding commercial success at the time. The study showed that students failed to improve their management decision-making skills over successive trials when using the simulation as a business case. When given a Structural Communication unit that "debriefed" the students after the simulation case, their scores on the next trial on the case did improve most significantly. This suggests that the Structural Communication debriefing aided learners to analyze the case study information better and improved their use of this information in making decisions during the case analysis, as compared to the effects of the simulation alone.

The Harvard business case materials used earlier by Hodgson and Dill (1970a, b), and published in the *Harvard Business Review,* served as the basis for a Structural Communication unit investigated by Mitchell and Emmott (1990). They used two versions, a print-based and a computer-based version. They found that the coherence index was greater for subjects using the computer version than those using the print version.

The seminal research study of Hodgson and Dill, described earlier, also reported a serious limitation in terms of follow-up interaction between readers and experts. Readers couldn't get any further information if they had a different opinion or question on the expert's comments. Learners could read the comments that were relevant to their initial viewpoint, but no further interaction was possible to verify if and how that viewpoint then changed.

A new version of the methodology, developed by Romiszowski and Chang, overcame this weakness by fusing the open-ended CBT characteristics of the original version with a follow-up CMC facility.

Chang developed a HyperCard structure for the purpose of presenting and controlling a Structural Communication exercise. The shell enables the selection of a variety of study units to be presented automatically to the student. The shell also tracks exactly how the learner utilized these units. A characteristic of this shell is that it allows for student-generated comments and insights to be added to the already-prepared materials to be shared between students and tutors as a form of an in-depth, student-generated seminar. This fusion of pre-designed study exercises (a form of CBT) with collaborative group discussion by e-mail (a form of CMC) was then applied to the computer delivery of case studies in a variety of contexts (Romiszowski & Chang, 1992).

One early context was a series of case studies developed for use in the training of educational technologists, instructional designers, and human resources development personnel. These cases were used on university campus networks equipped with Macintosh computers (a necessary condition since the SC exercise shell was developed in HyperCard). The course participants were able to engage in asynchronous collaborative discussion of the cases from any cluster or dormitory (or indeed from home over a modem connection). Research focussed on the effectiveness of the SC methodology as a means of promoting and developing creative problem-solving skills. The online discussion logs were compared to the transcripts of face-to-face group discussion sessions of the same case study materials. The measure used for evaluation of the efficiency, or productivity, of the method was a count of the rate of contribution of different ideas to the discussion (mean number of new ideas contributed per student-hour of participation in the discussion). The measure used for evaluating effectiveness was the classic approach of rating the ideas contributed for originality and creativity by an expert panel. The SC groups scored significantly higher on both measures.

A later application used existing and well-tried *Harvard Business* cases adapted to a Structural Communication study format. These included the case materials previously used in earlier studies of the SC method (described above) so that current results could be placed in the context of earlier findings. These online case study exercises were used during a full academic year by a large cohort of several hundred Business Management students. The research agenda of this project investigated the effectiveness of alternative approaches to the structure and organization of online collaborative learning environments and exercises. One should remember that this study preceded the implementation of the Internet and the Web as we know it today. However, it was conducted in order to simulate and test out such an environment, in which, it could be expected, online case materials would be available for study by groups of interested participants who would form a virtual study group almost accidentally, as they happen to log into a particular Website and *get involved* in discussing a particular case.

The large group of voluntary users of our on-campus simulation of the Internet was automatically sub-divided by the software we developed into a number of collaborative learning groups of "ideal" size. As students logged into the case study environment, the software would monitor the size of the group and, if the group size exceeded predetermined numbers, would divide the students into two sub-groups, like an amoeba splitting into two during its reproduction process. Similarly, if groups dwindled to below ideal numbers, the management software would combine two small groups into a bigger one. What exactly is an ideal group size for collaborative online discussion was one of the research questions investigated, as were several other organizational and practical aspects of effective and manageable online group discussion environments. Practical experience suggested that maintaining the study group size between ten and twenty participants tended to supply the critical mass required to keep an online discussion going, without excessive information overload for the participants.

Design for Collaborative Learning in WBT Systems

A Revised Structural Communication Shell

The main research agenda of the above mentioned study focussed, however, on issues related to the pedagogical design of collaborative learning environments. In this section, we describe how we redesigned the original SC methodology in order to overcome some of its limitations and also our investigations into the creation of a somewhat more *constructivist* collaborative learning environment. Further details may be found in Chang (1994). Some of the most important features of the SC method, for example, individualized learning of basic content and access to expert opinions, were maintained. However, the revised form of the *shell* (into which any SC exercise may be inserted as content) provided open-ended discussion environments for students to share, argue, persuade, and negotiate their perspectives on the expert's feedback comments as well as on their own opinions.

The methodology was revised taking into account several learning principles taken from the constructivist point of view. First, the new *shell* allows students to construct their own responses by selecting from the response matrix as many items as they wish. This is the same procedure that the conventional Structural Communication method uses. Second, the shell asks students to write the justifications for their selection of certain items. This procedure is one of the new features that the revised Structural Communication shell contains. Third, the shell allows students to access an expert's feedback comments as often as they want. Again, this procedure is the same as in the old version.

Up to this point, all activity is individualized and self-paced. In the old Structural Communication method, the planned learning activity ends here with reading the expert's comments. Since the revised method is designed for small-group collaborative learning, from this point on, further learning activity needs to occur collaboratively with group members. After completing their work individually, students browse what each group member did. A summary table tells the group members who selected certain items in the response matrix during individual study. With the summary table, group members can access any item, and read different justifications of other group members. They are asked to react to each other's justifications stating whether they agree or disagree with each others' opinions. As the process continues, the pool of the students' discussion log grows. The shell is designed to save every justification and discussion statement that students make, and to enable students to browse those reactions and opinions in a cumulative mode as the process continues. While they are performing these activities, they may access expert's feedback comments any time if they wish to refresh their memory on what the expert says.

Four different versions of the revised Structural Communication shell were developed for experimental purposes. One version does not include the expert's feedback comments. This means that students select their responses and justify their selection, without expert's feedback and then they discuss the justifications. This version is most in line with our interpretation of constructivist learning principles applied to a structured online learning environment. The second version contains every procedure mentioned above plus the expert's feedback comments. In the third version, students are not asked to justify what they selected as their responses. They do receive the expert's feedback comments and are expected to discuss these comments among themselves. This version is similar to the one used in our earlier research studies described above.

In the last type of the shell, students are neither asked to justify their selections nor to discuss anything. They just select items from the response matrix and then read expert's feedback comments on their selections. Therefore, the last type of shell is designed exclusively for individualized learning. It is closest in design to the original Structural Communication methodology and least influenced in its design by principles of learning drawn from constructivism. However, it should be remembered that the expert's feedback in all of the versions is never *corrective* but always in the form of constructive and challenging *Socratic Dialogue* types of comments.

Findings and Their Implications

The main objective of this study was to investigate whether the four different combinations of *neo-constructivist* learning strategies—justify-discuss, justify-feedback-discuss, feedback-discuss, or just feedback—would have different outcomes in terms of the scores on a coherence index or indeed some other measure of convergence/divergence of viewpoints. Although some qualitative differences between the study patterns of students using the different shells were noted, no significant differences were found in the quantitative measures of convergence or divergence of ideas expressed about the case material studied. On the basis of the coherence index, it is not clear which, if any, of the combinations of learning strategies is "better."

One of the arguments of a constructivist learning viewpoint is that participation in hypothesis building by students themselves, with interaction between each other, should be conducive to the development of more powerful and personal constructs in a given knowledge domain and therefore more powerful problem analysis and problem solving strategies. It is suggested that in theory, the mix of learning activities used in the more complex treatments could be more favorable to the learning of complex problem-analysis skills. These theoretical claims have not been substantiated. Indeed, in this study, although there is a slight advantage in terms of the coherence index shift for these groups, this did not prove to be sufficiently large to be statistically significant. The only significant quantitative measure was the time-on-task. Those treatments that required students to write justifications for their choices of response required more than twice the study time of those treatments that did not.

Even though there were no statistically significant differences among them, the most complicated learning strategies group (i.e., justify-feedback-discuss) yielded the highest scores on the coherence index. A coherence index represents convergence on a given set of opinions. In this treatment, quantitative analysis of the viewpoints expressed in discussion was expected to show convergence towards the expert's opinions prompted or implied by the pre-prepared feedback comments. The one group that studied without access to the expert's feedback comments was expected to register a lower coherence index. This was the case, but the differences were not statistically significant. Qualitative analysis of the students' discussion log was expected to show that the convergence registered between the different students' viewpoints in this treatment group would be less in line with the viewpoints implied by the experts' feedback. However, the differences between groups were very small and did not support this hypothesis.

It is indeed a moot point whether such differences, if they did exist, should be considered a *good thing* or a *bad thing*. One could hypothesize that those treatment groups that had access and exposure to the author's viewpoints would move closer to that author's position in their post-test solution of the case study, than groups who were not exposed to the author's views. However, this hypothesis was not supported. This lack of significant differences may, however, be construed as being a positive rather than a negative outcome of this study. After all, had a significant difference in favor of the groups exposed to author viewpoints been registered, then the interpretation of these results would be that these treatments had led to a convergence of viewpoints among the students toward a particular pre-determined externally imposed viewpoint. This is quite the opposite of what a constructivist learning philosophy would value and seek to achieve. Therefore, the lack of significant difference between groups in this respect could be taken as good news in the sense that the simpler to implement and less time-consuming (though more *objectivist*) strategies are found not to *brainwash* students into a particular predetermined viewpoint.

Practical Conclusions and Their
Implications for Conversational WBT

Several conclusions may be drawn from this study. In addition to the theoretical interest of the findings, one practical conclusion is that the use of simpler and less time-consuming discussion environments, even if these seem to be less in line with currently popular philosophical positions, may offer the requisite environment for intensive small group conversational interaction via CMC networks, without the supposed perils of limiting the creative and critical thinking of the discussion participants or imposing an externally generated *expert* viewpoint. It seems to us that such perils are much more a consequence of the nature of the instructor's interventions in the learning process, whether as materials designer/developer or discussion leader/facilitator. However, the environments must support the discussion process in an effective and efficient manner. This implies, among other things, ensuring that the discussion process is motivating and not over-taxing in terms of workload.

In regard to student motivation, there is little doubt in our minds that exercises organized in the form of Structural Communication are most effective. The several hundred students who participated in the above-mentioned four-treatment study worked voluntarily and without recompense in the form of grade points throughout a whole semester with very low drop-out rates. The students in our earlier studies showed similar levels of motivation. For example, in the study that investigated the effects of a SC debriefing exercise added to an otherwise rather ineffective multimedia-delivered interactive case study, students studied the same case followed by different versions of the exercises four or more times during a semester, voluntarily, without extrinsic rewards and with very low dropout rates. Perhaps most relevant in the present context was the original SC business case application in the *Harvard Business Review*. Hodgson and Dill (1970b) reported that well over 2000 readers of the *Review* voluntarily participated in the Dashman Case (the misfired missive) when this was published in the form of a Structural Communication exercise, whereas the baseline experience of the *Review* was that previously (and subsequently) published Harvard business cases (with requests inviting comments) seldom result in even 200 letters from readers. This finding is important in the context of conversational CMC-type WBT in that the study materials placed in a publicly *open* WBT environment will survive and prosper, or alternatively wither and die, as a function of their ability to attract voluntary participation from a significant number of Web navigators.

It may well be that the reasons for the high levels of motivation encountered in these various studies are not entirely and uniquely a consequence of the SC format. As mentioned before, the quality of design of the exercises themselves is probably a most critical factor. In Khan's earlier collection of essays on *Web-Based Instruction* (Khan, 1997), two chapters are devoted to issues of motivation in WBI (Cornell & Martin, 1997; Duchastel, 1997). Both of these discuss a range of issues related to student motivation and review the well known approaches and models, such as ARCS (Keller, 1983), for the design of motivational materials. However, we believe that the unique mechanism of the response matrix, which allows for easy and rapid multiple-choice responding while allowing one to explore one's own and each others' conceptual schemata and cognitive structures in some detail, contributes much to the inherent attractiveness of the methodology to the interested and reflective student.

We should not leave the question of motivation without also considering the motivation of the instructor or discussion facilitator. Of the two chapters mentioned above, only one

(Cornell & Martin, 1997) addresses the question of instructor motivation for WBI. The authors mention seven reasons for lack of instructor motivation (as compared to twelve for student motivation) and, interestingly, this list of seven reasons does not include the avoidance of extra workload. In the light of research findings quoted earlier in this chapter, that CMC-delivered courses almost always involve significantly more instructor time than conventionally delivered courses, we feel that we must add this eighth reason to the list. Furthermore, we believe that our work with Structural Communication offers, at least in part, a solution to this eighth reason. The solution is, of course, to plan the CMC environment is such a way as to reduce or even eliminate the extra workload.

We start from the axiomatic acceptance of the principle that if a student makes a comment or asks a question, he or she deserves to receive an appropriately structured response. In conventional instruction, this is handled by the teacher *live* as questions are asked or comments are made by students. The workload for the teacher is automatically controlled by the fact that (unless anarchy reigns in the classroom) only one question can be asked and answered at one time and the session has a predetermined duration that limits the total number of interactions. The instructor is *saved by the bell* from excessive workload. In CMC (asynchronous) learning environments, time is not a limiting factor. If the topic is interesting, important, and motivational for the students, the flow of questions and comments can represent a daunting and indeed impossible workload for the conscientious instructor. The decision to avoid getting involved in conversational WBT may be an instructor's rational assessment that probable workload and available time will make it impossible to give students the levels of attention they request and deserve.

In discussions organized within a SC-based CMC environment, the problem of instructor overload is much reduced. The automatic generation of extensive and constructive feedback messages to students on the basis of the pattern of responses they select from the response matrix acts like a first-round response from the instructor to specific aspects of the student's overall response. In practice, well over 70% of these automatically generated feedback messages satisfy the students' needs for clarification or orientation. The remaining 20% to 30% generate second-round student responses in the form of electronic messages that pose supplementary questions or comments, but always at a deeper and more specific level of discourse. The results of this, from the viewpoint of the motivation of the instructor/facilitator, are twofold. First, the overall workload of responding to students (measured in terms of the number of messages to compose) is reduced by some 70%. Second, the messages to be responded are on issues that are often more interesting and always relatively original and non-repetitive. If, in practice, the first-round automatic feedback interactions result in the same second-round interactions occurring with high frequency, it is a sign to rewrite the first-round feedback to better handle these oft-repeating aspects of the discussion.

Having touched on the issue of workload as it relates to the instructor/facilitator, we may mention our experience with the SC response-matrix mechanism as a device for the reduction of student workload. In selecting a subset of response elements from the universe represented by the items in the response-matrix, the student is in effect composing a complex, structured response to the problem under analysis. This is analogous to the preparation of an outline for an essay or live seminar presentation. The intellectual effort necessary to evaluate the relevance of each item of the matrix to the problem being studied is equal to that required to plan the essay/presentation. However, the time and effort involved in writing an essay or preparing and delivering a seminar presentation are saved. Students spend more time, more productively, in the intellectual restructuring of ideas and the creation of their own knowledge structures than is often the case in conventional instruction. And, in our view, the relatively unstructured discussion lists that abound in current WBT environments are even more wasteful of student time, in that every contribution must be produced as an original typed message.

It is not our argument to eliminate written communication from the ideal WBT environment. There are strong learning benefits to *putting pen to paper* (or fingers to keyboard). As Albert Einstein is purported to have replied when asked what he thought of a novel scientific issue: *I don't know what I think until I have written it down.* However, as in real-life situations, time is always limited, why not use it most efficiently? In the SC-based form of WBT environment, the composing, in writing, of *what I think* occurs in the second-round interactions at a deeper and more challenging level. The student is saved the effort of writing out surface-level arguments that serve to *get the ball rolling* by acting as stimuli for comments from instructor/facilitators or peers.

Conclusion: The Design of WBT Environments

In another chapter of this book, Villalba and Romiszowki review several of the currently most-used WBI/WBT learning environments and compare the *mainstream* to some recently emerging *innovative* environments that claim to be more up-to-date in certain respects. That chapter makes the point that the innovations appearing in recently released products and tools are not really that innovative and, although extending the richness of communication tools available to the WBT system designer and user, still do not meet some of the expectations of instructional designers, instructors, and students. In one sense, that chapter echoes the viewpoints expressed by Collis (1997) that the effectiveness of collaborative learning on the Web *may get disturbed by the loss of efficiency due to the number of telematic-based facilities that are difficult to control.* In another sense, it argues that some communication facilities that are desirable or even essential for small-group collaborative learning are not available at all. In summary, the development of collaborative group WBT learning environments is following too closely the route of replicating the conventional classroom environment and is too little concerned with innovating to overcome the limitations or weaknesses of that environment.

The present chapter has argued the case for one such innovation, based on the revival of a largely forgotten *good idea* of the past and its insertion within the context of up-to-date Web-based training technology, currently prevalent educational philosophy and practice, sound instructional/learning design principles, and an overarching concern for the overall effectiveness and efficiency of the resultant system. The *good idea* (Structural Communication) was itself in its time the revival of earlier *good ideas,* as expressed by educators since the time of Socrates and Plato, who were particularly concerned with the structure of knowledge and meaning and the insertion of these ideas into the prevalent technologies, philosophies, and educational/training realities of the day.

Is the idea all that good? The research and development of its application over several decades, summarized in this chapter, is our attempt to answer this question. Readers may seek other routes to an answer. Here is one suggested route, based on models for the design and development of Web-based instructional environments that appeared in Khan's earlier collection of essays on WBI (Khan, 1997). Reeves and Reeves (1997) present a ten-dimensional model for the analysis and evaluation of WBI systems (or indeed of any educational or training system that purports to be innovative and relevant to today's world). They present the profiles of two examples of actual WBI courses, one a chemistry course based on an instructional design that *includes direct tutoring and drill-and-practice, using principles of behavioral psychology to stimulate and reinforce learning* and the other a constructivist program about HIV/AIDS in which *there are no right answers to solving the problems presented . . . teachers are collaborators in the intrinsically motivating quest to solve real problems . . . with high levels of learner control and collaborative learning.* We used this model to analyze and evaluate our own Structural Communication-based conversational WBI environments. The profile we sketched matched neither of these two examples perfectly. However, on key dimensions, such as motivation, teacher role, metacognitive support, collaboration, and flexibility, it tended towards the constructivist end of the continuum. On the other five dimensions—philosophy, learning theory, goal orientation, task orientation, and cultural sensitivity—the SC exercises we have used and developed over the years *cover the map,* including examples at both ends of the continuum for each of these dimensions. Maybe that is what flexibility is all about.

References

Bernstein, S., & Auerbach, S. (1999, June). 1999 state of the industry report. *Training* Magazine.

Chang, E. (1994). *Investigation of constructivist principles applied to collaborative study of business cases in computer-mediated communication.* Ph.D. dissertation, Syracuse University.

Chute, A. G. (1990). Strategies for implementing teletraining systems. *Educational and Training Technology International, 27*(3), 264–70.

Collis, B. (1997). Supporting project-based collaborative learning via a World Wide Web environment. In B. Khan (Ed.), *Web-based instruction.* Englewood Cliffs: Educational Technology Publications.

Cornell, R., & Martin, B. L. (1997). The role of motivation in Web-based instruction. In B. Khan (Ed.), *Web-based instruction.* Englewood Cliffs: Educational Technology Publications.

Cunningham, D. J., Duffy, T. M., & Knuth, R. A. (1993). The textbook of the future. In C. McKnight (Ed.), *Hypertext: A psychological perspective.* London: Horwood.

Dewey, J. (1900). Psychology and social practice. *The Psychological Review, 7,* 105–24.

Dills, C., & Romiszowski, A. J. (Eds.). (1997). *Instructional development paradigms.* Englewood Cliffs: Educational Technology Publications.

Driscoll, M. (1997). Defining Internet-based and Web-based training. *Performance Improvement, 36*(4), 5–9.

Duchastel, P. (1997). A motivational framework for Web-based instruction. In B. Khan (Ed.), *Web-based instruction.* Englewood Cliffs: Educational Technology Publications.

Duffy, T., & Jonassen, D. (1992). Constructivism: New implications for instructional technology. In T. Duffy & D. Jonassen (Eds.), *Constructivism and the technology of instruction: A conversation.* Hillsdale, NJ: Lawrence Erlbaum Associates.

Eastmond, D. V. (1993). *Adult learning of distance students through computer conferencing.* Ph.D. dissertation, Syracuse University.

Egan, K. (1972). Structural Communication: A new contribution to pedagogy. *Programmed Learning and Educational Technology, 9*(2), 63–78.

Egan, K. (1976). *Structural Communication.* Belmont, CA: Fearon Publishers.

Eurich, A. P. (1990). *The learning industry: Education for adult workers.* Princeton, NJ: Carnegie Foundation for the Advancement of Teaching.

Fyfe, R. M., & Woodrow, D. (1969). *Basic ideas of abstract mathematics.* London: University of London Press.

Gagné, R. M. (1962). Military training and principles of learning. *American Psychologist, 17,* 83–91.

Grabowski, B., Suciati, A., & Pusch, W. (1990). Social and intellectual value of computer-mediated communications in a graduate community. *Educational and Training Technology International, 27*(3), 276–83.

Hiltz, S. R. (1986). The *virtual classroom:* Using computer-mediated communication for university teaching. *Journal of Communication, 36*(2), 95–104.

Hiltz, S. R. (1990). Evaluating the virtual classroom. In L. M. Harasim (Ed.), *Online education: Perspectives on a new environment.* New York: Praeger.

Hodgson, A. M. (1971). An experiment in computer-guided correspondence seminars for management. In D. Dackman, A. Cleary, & T. Mayes (Eds.), *Aspects of educational technology, Volume 5* (pp. 82–89). London: Kogan Page.

Hodgson, A. M. (1972). Structural learning in social settings: Some notes on work in progress. *Programmed Learning and Educational Technology, 9*(2), 79–86.

Hodgson, A. M., & Dill, W. R. (1970a, Sept./Oct.). Programmed case: The misfired missive. *Harvard Business Review,* 140–46.

Hodgson, A. M., & Dill, W. R. (1970b, Nov./Dec.). Programmed case: Sequel to the misfired missive. *Harvard Business Review,* 105–110.

Hodgson, A. M., & Dill, W. R. (1971, Jan./Feb.). Programmed case: Reprise of the misfired missive. *Harvard Business Review,* 140–45.

Horn, R. E. (1989). *Mapping hypertext.* Lexington, MA: The Lexington Institute.

Imel, S. (1997). Web-based training: Trends and issues alerts. ERIC No. ED414446.

Kaye, A. R. (Ed.). (1992). *Collaborative learning through computer conferencing: The Najadan papers.* New York: Springer.

Keller, J. (1983). Motivational design of instruction. In C. Reigeluth (Ed.), *Instructional-design theories and models: An overview of their current status.* Hillsdale, NJ: Lawrence Erlbaum Associates.

Khan, B. H. (1997). (Ed.). *Web-based instruction.* Englewood Cliffs: Educational Technology Publications.

McMahon, T. A., Carr, A. A., & Fishman, B. J. (1993). Hypermedia and constructivism: Three approaches to enhanced learning. *Journal of Hypermedia and Multimedia Studies, 2*(2), 5–10.

Mitchell, P. D., & Emmott, L. (1990). Eliminating differences in comprehension due to cognitive style through computer-based instructional systems. Paper presented at the ADCIS conference, San Diego, CA.

Mitchell, P. D., & Meilleur-Baccanale, D. (1982). Differential effects of wholist and serialist learning style on learning with structural communication. In *Progress in cybernetics and systems research.* New York: Halsted Press; Washington: Hemisphere Publishing Corporation.

Paine, N. (1988). *Open learning in transition: An agenda for action.* London: Kogan Page.

Reeves, T. C., & Reeves, P. M. (1997). Effective dimensions of interactive learning on the World Wide Web. In B. Khan (Ed.), *Web-based instruction.* Englewood Cliffs: Educational Technology Publications.

Romiszowski, A. J. (1976). *A study of individualized systems for mathematics instruction at the post-secondary levels.* Ph.D. dissertation, University of Loughborough, UK.

Romiszowski, A. J. (1990). Computer-mediated communication and hypertext: The instructional use of two converging technologies. *Interactive Learning International, 6,* 5–29.

Romiszowski, A. J. (1993). Telecommunications in training. In G.M. Piskurich (Ed.), *The ASTD handbook of training technology.* Alexandria, VA: American Society for Training and Development.

Romiszowski, A. J., & Chang, E. (1992). Hypertext's contribution to computer-mediated communication: In search of an instructional model. In M. Giardina (Ed.), *Interactive multimedia environments* (pp. 111–130). Heidelberg: Springer-Verlag.

Romiszowski, A. J., & Corso, M. (1990). Computer mediated seminars and case studies. Paper presented at the 15th World Conference on Distance Education, Caracas, Venezuela.

Romiszowski, A. J., & DeHaas, J. (1989). Computer-mediated communication for instruction: Using e-mail as a seminar. *Educational Technology, 24*(10).

Romiszowski, A. J., Grabowski, B.L., & Damadaran, B. (1988). Structural Communication, expert systems, and interactive video: A powerful combination for a nontraditional CAI approach. Paper presented at the AECT conference, New Orleans, LA.

Simonson, N. (1998). Considerations in converting a stand-up training class to Web-based learning. Some guidelines from Cognitive Flexibility Theory. *Journal of Interactive Instruction Development, 10*(3), 3–9.

Stone, D., & Bishop, C. A. (1997). *Web-based training: How to really do it.* ERIC No. ED421660.

Tucker, B. (1997). Research into the use of intranets for training. *Journal of Instruction Delivery Systems, 11*(4), 3–9.

Zuboff, S. (1988). *In the age of the smart machine: The future of work and power.* New York: Basic Books.

The Authors

Alexander J. Romiszowski (e-mail: alexromi@sued.syr.edu; Web homepage: tts-global.com) is Director, Technology-Based Training Systems, Rio de Janeiro, Brazil, and Adjunct Professor, Instructional Design, Development, and Evaluation at Syracuse University. He serves as Coordinator of the Syracuse University IDD&E distance-education program for students in Latin America. **Echeol Chang (e-mail: echang@kyungpook.ac.kr)** is Professor, Department of Education, Kyung Pook University, Taegu, South Korea.

11

Web Architectures for Learning

Peter G. Fairweather,
Richard B. Lam, and Lei Kuang

The huge array of architectures marshalled to support different kinds of computer-based learning can only be evaluated within the shifting set of purposes they serve. Obviously, the architectures themselves are useful only if they accomplish the goals set for them. Less obvious is how the appearance of successive architectures shapes our ideas of purpose for computer-based learning. The interplay between architectural form and instructional purpose, especially the way architectures shape what practitioners think they are trying to do, is the focus of this chapter (see Figure 1).

Certainly the forms of computer-based learning considered legitimate or most appropriate change over time. Some forms take center stage while others lurk at the margins, exchanging places as instructional philosophies and technologies evolve. Consider, for example, the last half-dozen years' proliferation of tools for knowledge generation, transformation, and demonstration in the K–12 arena, such as Belvedere (Paolucci, Suthers, & Weiner, 1996), CSILE (Scardamalia & Bereiter, 1992), or CaMILE (Guzdial et al., 1995), accompanied by the somewhat tendentious condemnation of practice-oriented learning software (see Anderson, Reder, & Simon, 1996).[1]

Currently favored pedagogical directions contrast knowledge construction (Harel & Papert, 1991) against the notion of the transmission of information from a source and its absorption by the learner. It recognizes that such construction builds upon learners' variable previous knowledge (Gibbons & Fairweather, 1998), instead of having them absorb packages of self-contained instructional content. Moreover, it insists on situating learning appropriately (Lave & Wenger, 1991), presenting problems in purposefully relevant contexts to enhance motivation, transfer, utility, and accessibility of that which is learned.

It would seem that purposes of computer-based learning should drive the establishment of architectural features, not the other way around. However, consider authoring and delivery

---

[1]There seem to be stark differences in what is considered legitimate computer-based learning across different cultures as well. Almost twenty years ago, while most in the US were enmired in a drill-and-practice-dominated culture in schools, many in the UK were pursuing notions of computer-based learning reflecting self-directed, constructivist, and distributed pedagogy, exemplified by the *Domesday* project. It was almost as if they had skipped the protracted tutorial period that reigned in the US from the early seventies to the late eighties.

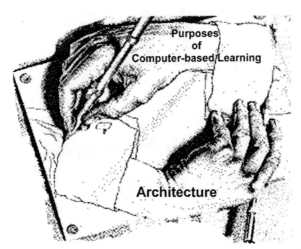

Figure 1. Mutual influence of purposes of computer-based learning and architecture.

systems of the 1970s and 1980s, such as TUTOR (Sherwood, 1972), DAL (Digital Equipment Corporation, 1980), or WISE (WICAT Systems, 1986), with their exquisitely refined constructed-response judging capabilities. With these tools, authors could exploit special vocabularies, synonyms, measurement unit translation, ignorable words, or rudimentary concept-based judgment. But in the ensuing years, enriched GUI architectures enabling direct manipulation interfaces came on the scene and simply banished judged constructed-responses from developers' repertoires. Present day systems, instead of boasting advances on those rich technologies of the eighties, have dispensed with them entirely.

Shifting our gaze to the Web, we might ask if its architectures that we appropriate for learning bias us toward developing certain kinds of interactions and away from others. Moreover, does the Web offer the right kinds of architectures to support the kinds of learning purposes considered legitimate today?

The Promise and Limits of Conventional Web Architectures

Tim Berners-Lee (1996a,b) spawned the Web in part as a means for scientists to access one another's work, as a communication system whose architecture aimed at efficiently moving document contents across the Internet. In his own words:

> The goal of the Web was to be a shared information space through which people (and machines) could communicate.

> The intent was that this space should span from a private information system to a public information, from high value carefully checked and designed material, to off-the-cuff ideas which make sense only to a few people and may never be read again. (Berners-Lee, 1996b)

The stated goal for the Web—and, as we shall see, its fundamental architecture—aligns itself with a few of the currently legitimate aims of computer-assisted learning:

- Its shared information space explicitly recognizes that cognition—and therefore, learning—is fundamentally a social affair.

- Critical evaluation of one's own and others' contributions can engender reflection and metacognition as sources of learning.

- Learner-created Web material offers the possibility of explicit knowledge construction and transformation.

The tentative language is intentional. Although arguably a rich medium for learning, the Web has been used as a tool of that impoverished metaphor whereby information moves from a source into learners' heads (see Carroll, 1990, 1998). Although by itself instructionally thin, this approach can be scaffolded with such things as problems presented in realistic contexts, motivated co-learners with whom to fashion solutions, or a communication framework within which to incubate and test those solutions.

The design of the Web presents the widest potential range of instructional metaphors of all multimedia, from the "information transmission" model mentioned above to rich, problem-centered, multi-person solution spaces. This quirky potential is built into the technology standards that undergird the Web, in particular, the HyperText Markup Language (HTML) and the HyperText Transport Protocol (HTTP). Both define how the Web works and, through their adoption, propel its exponential growth. However, because their structure reflects more concern with issues such as the format of documents or how they are moved about, basic Web architecture, unless augmented, supports only a small sub-spectrum of teaching and learning interaction types.

Cleaving appearance from behavior with HTML and HTTP: The universal Web client, the browser, provides a consistent interface and set of functions, whether the user is reviewing a course syllabus, signing up for a test, or collaborating on a circuit design. Browsers share a set of common, almost standard functions, including the abilities to:

- communicate over a TCP/IP connection using HTTP to any reachable Web server;

- render a document written in HTML;

- execute scripting functions embedded in the document, using moderately standardized languages such as JavaScript or display formats such as animated gif;

- execute applications referenced in the document using fairly standardized languages such as Java;

- spawn "plug-in" programs that execute within the browser to perform specific functions, such as media handling or operations using special protocols; and

- perform an expanding set of universal Internet functions using specialized protocols such as file transfer (FTP), news receipt (NNTP), etc.

Practically speaking, the document-centric posture of unadorned HTML limits it to representing the surface messages of instruction and organizing them into some sort of navigable structure. Static Web pages created with HTML cannot support the kind of adaptive interaction required by, for example, intelligent tutoring or immersive simulation.

HTML richly describes documents, and can even describe interactions with such documents to some extent. However, although it can describe how the document should *appear,* neither the Web client nor the server change in any way as a result of the rendering of the HTML[2] (see Figure 2).

---

[2]We must keep in mind that we are speaking of simple HTML, unaugmented by scripting, applets, CGI, or any other means of simulating state and accumulating history.

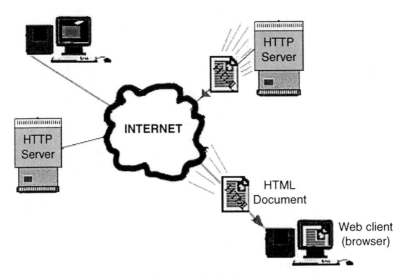

Figure 2. Simplest Web document serving.

To restrict matters further, HTML documents are served up using the HTTP protocol whose efficiency is derived in part from the fact that it is *stateless*. In other words, each time the server responds to the browser, the server knows nothing of previous contacts, so adaptation can only be accomplished by routing the browser through different sequences of documents, by somehow passing information back and forth between client and server, or, if permitted, by stashing some historical information about the interaction on the client device, in the form of a "cookie."

Immediately, the Web spawned a compensatory architectural extension, Common Gateway Interface (CGI) that permits the attachment of server behavior to the HTML documents. CGI programs or scripts can be crafted in almost any computer language, but are most frequently assembled in Perl, Visual Basic, C, or C++ more often than others, because of either their support for database access or the ease with which programs can be built.

A document representation scheme like HTML cannot be expected to supply strong features for such things as numerical or string processing or dynamic graphics. CGI scripts can provide this and, albeit awkwardly, provide a means for getting around the statelessness of the HTTP server. The learner's state—all those things that might be used to make instructional decisions—can be passed back and forth between the learner's browser and the CGI programs running on the server (see Figure 3).

From the point of view of instructional development, CGI poses several difficulties. CGI scripts require programming, making difficult the use of available authoring systems and narrowing the pool of developers. Development of computer-based learning materials almost always requires some sort of authoring platform to remain cost-effective because programming is too expensive for other than mission-critical training. Because HTML has become to simple to produce, it is becoming a technology of choice—whether appropriate or not—for many dabbling with distributed training. In practice, CGI programs have been limited to back-end database operations to route students to appropriate points in the curriculum and store their responses to online questions or threaded discussions.

CGI programs fail to scale to heavy use well, as a new copy of the program must be loaded and executed with each user request. The HTTP server starts up a copy of the CGI program with information collected through an HTML page. If the server must deal with many requests

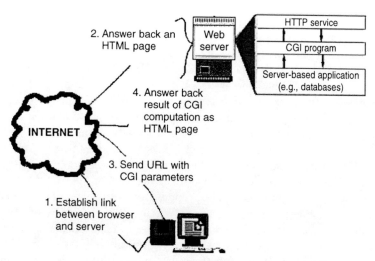

Figure 3. CGI augmented architecture.

simultaneously or even in close succession, it can fall behind or worse. Cases like this often benefit from a multi-threaded architecture that permits one copy of a program to run and deal with all requests itself, obviating the overhead of loading or the danger of blocking while waiting for I/O operations to complete. For example, the Java Servlet application programming interface (API) is being widely favored over CGI because servlets avoid the overhead of starting a new process with each HTTP request.

Finally, the requirement of having to link the user interface through a constrained parametric interface to CGI programs or servlets makes the rich execution environment required of simulations or intelligent tutoring, for example, altogether too difficult to create. True, server-side programs can perform any operation needed in an instructional system. True, HTML can provide a rich user interface. However, the narrow pipe between them cannot carry much, so each side fails to take advantage of the full potential of the other. More insidiously, however, this stateless architecture forces developers to ignore most of what the learner does because it is so difficult to get information back from the browser. This yields instruction that can only poorly adapt to a learner's characteristics or behavior.

The semantic gap: At a different level of abstraction, a pure HTML or HTML + CGI/ servlet strategy widens the semantic gap between instructional construct and implementation that computer-based learning has struggled with since its beginnings. Consider, for example, a computer-based learning module to tutor a pilot on the procedure to enter waypoints into an inertial navigation system. A procedure that requires developers to deal with constructs such as pixels or radians, when all they are trying to do is convey the motion of a detente knob, will choke off development quickly. When the language of the instructional domain and that of the implementation differ too much, development remains expensive and slow. Successful authoring systems had taken us beyond that, but HTML and CGI have knocked us back again.

Carving specialized clients out of universal ones: When commercial applications underwent large-scale migration to client-server architectures, computer-based training applications followed only insofar as they might take advantage of central information collection. Although some multi-person crew training applications required tight, synchronous network integration (Alluisi, 1991; Fishwick *et al.,* 1994), specialized clients could rarely be justified on the basis of cost. The offer of a completely general client in the form of a Web browser enables training and education to reap some of the benefits of client-server architecture, but, as suggested above, sorely limits the kinds of applications that can be built.

Browsers flexibly respond to this challenge by extending themselves through pluggable components, enabling much tighter integration between the client and server, or at least providing the opportunity for some sort of shared persistent state. The client and server communicate by sending data back and forth, but in a proprietary manner so that, for example, information directing the client to update an altimeter can only be understood by a pluggable component designed to receive it. Besides enriching the capabilities of the learner's client application, plug-ins often dramatically reduce the amount of information that must be sent from the server, enabling operations in lower bandwidth environments.

In effect, the pluggable component interpreting data streams from the host creates a specialized client within the general purpose browser. With it, a rich repertoire of behavior needed to support complex tutorials or simple simulations can be made available, as long as the basic functions are present in the plug-in. Plug-ins are not constrained in terms of what they are allowed to do by such considerations as security models, a powerful development advantage that cannot be underestimated, especially when computing resources remain challenged. For example, a plug-in crafted to handle streaming video might take advantage of local disk resources to cache the stream either to enhance performance or to enable rapid re-display.

However, commitment to a plug-in means circumscribing development needs, and the capabilities the vendor provides for plug-ins are not usually extensible. For example, one group of developers found themselves with the need to create a "waterfall" signal processing display that could not be effectively rendered with the plug-in they had chosen. Their only alternative was to re-create the entire simulation by programming a custom applet at considerable cost.

A modular architecture for learning: Development and delivery platforms such as Java offer a means to create software components that operate over the Internet or intranets. Component technologies such as Java Beans enable objects to be aggregated into instructionally useful chunks, such as inference engines, calculators, or outlining tools, for example. Java in particular affords interfaces to permit programmatic disclosure of the methods supported by a Bean so that it can be interrogated by other components to determine how it should be used. Technologies such as InfoBus permit Beans not originally designed to work with one another to interoperate effectively (see Figure 4).

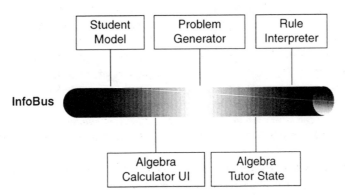

Figure 4. Component objects of an algebra tutor communicating state through dataflows over an "InfoBus").

The availability of a generally available communication mechanism cannot be underestimated. Other component technologies have depended on a computer language to provide the connective tissue among components. Java goes one step further by standardizing inter-component communication and component documentation. By doing so, Java restores the promise of reuse to components used in building up software.

Spohrer (1998) has organized the construction of a truly remarkable repository of Java components on the Web so the network can be used not only to implement learning tools, but to identify and locate their constituent parts as well. These repositories attack problems which may be the most serious real threats to reuse, such as locating components, aggregating a critical mass of repository contents, identifying cost of use, or evaluating the quality of the components themselves. His and others' efforts, under the name "Educational Object Economy," have tried to identify and overcome the marketplace barriers to the dissemination of components useful for learning that so often prevent technical innovation from escaping out of the lab.

This architecture maintains a significant advantage over other object-oriented languages because its platform has been built for operation on the Internet (or on an intranet), enabling "distributive distributed learning" applications that emphasize inter-user interaction. Special components have evolved, such as Lotus' SameTime technology, that streamline implementations of software built for collaboration by providing services such as server-side object locking and event reflection. For example, in a collaborative design effort, a learner proposing a particular modification might drag a visual component onto his or her screen. SameTime provides the low-level mechanisms that prevent other users from disrupting the object being dragged, and to show the object's course across all users' screens simultaneously. This server-side component takes a good portion of the sting out of developing the complex conversational protocols that accompany multi-user interactions.

Other architectures? Most Web learning discussions focus on collaborative discussions as a basis for reflection, elaboration, and metacognition. The basic architecture of the Web can support these well, and specialized "knowledge management" systems such as LotusDomino and Web application suites built upon it (e.g., LearningSpace) put such power within the reach of practically anyone. These systems dominate discussions because the prevalent Web architectures permit these systems to be the most readily implemented. While we are learning much about collaborative learning (Koschmann, 1996) through experimentation with them, the deployment of more sophisticated architectures in the near future promises much more.

Indeed, the febrile pace of architectural advance will expand the definition of the Web and blur training with intelligent performance support. For example, JINI (Sun Microsystems, 1998) promises to quickly extend the concept of the Web beyond desktops, laptops, and personal digital assistants to automobiles, vending machines, copiers, and toll-booths, enabling embedded training and testing in ways that would have made good science fiction only a few years ago. Emergent Web learning architectures will extend our notions of what makes for good instructional strategy by defining new types of interactions yielding types of teaching and learning based on expanded definitions of the computing environment itself.

References

Alluisi, E. A. (1991). The development of technology for collective training: SIMNET, a case history. *Human Factors, 33*(3), 343–362.

Alpert, S. (1998). *Personal communication on an intelligent tutoring project.* Yorktown Heights, NY: IBM T. J. Watson Research Center.

Anderson, J. R., Reder, L. M., & Simon, H. A. (1996). Situated learning and education. *Educational Researcher, 25*(4), 5–11.

Berners-Lee, T. (1996a). geo.web.ru/Mirrors/www.w3.org/People/Berners-Lee/1996/EUUS.html

Berners-Lee, T. (1996b). geo.web.ru/Mirrors/www.w3.org/People/Berners-Lee/1996/ppf.html

Carroll, J. M. (1990). *The Nurnberg Funnel: Designing minimalist instructions for practical computer skill.* Cambridge, MA: MIT Press.

Carroll, J. M. (1998). *Minimalism beyond the Nurnberg Funnel.* Cambridge, MA: MIT Press.

Digital Equipment Corporation. (1980). *Digital authoring language manual.* Maynard, MA: Digital Equipment Corporation.

Fishwick, P., Glisky, E. L., Gullapali, V., Herrmann, D., & Shafto, M. G. (1994). Modulated cognition. In V. L. Shalin (Ed.), *Human performance in the complex workplace: Implications for basic research in cognitive science.* Washington, DC: National Science Foundation.

Gibbons, A. S., & Fairweather, P. G. (1998). *Computer-based instruction: Design and development.* Englewood Cliffs: Educational Technology Publications.

Guzdial, M., Rappin, N., & Carlson, D. (1995). Collaborative and multimedia interactive learning environment for engineering education. In *Proceedings of the ACM Symposium on Applied Computing* (pp. 5–9). Nashville, TN: ACM Press.

Harel, I., & Papert, S. (1991). *Constructionism.* Norwood, NJ: Ablex Publishing Corp.

Lave, J., & Wenger, E. (1991). *Situated learning: Legitimate peripheral participation.* Cambridge, UK: Cambridge University Press.

Koschmann, T. (Ed.). (1996). *CSCL: Theory and practice of an emerging paradigm.* Mahwah, NJ: Lawrence Erlbaum Associates.

Paolucci, M., Suthers, D., & Weiner, A. (1996). Automated advice-giving strategies for scientific inquiry. In C. Frasson, G. Gauthier, & A. Lesgold (Eds.), *Intelligent tutoring systems* (pp. 372–381). Berlin: Springer-Verlag.

Scardamalia, M., & Bereiter, C. (1992). An architecture for collaborative knowledge-building. In E. De Corte, M. Linn, H. Mandl, & L. Verschaffel (Eds.), *Computer-based learning environments and problem solving* (pp. 41–46). Berlin: Springer-Verlag.

Sherwood, B. A. (1972). *The TUTOR language.* Urbana, IL: CERL.

Spohrer, J. C. (1998). eoe.org

Sun Microsystems. (1998). java.sun.com/products/jini/

WICAT Systems. (1986). *WISE author's guide.* Provo, UT: WICAT Systems.

The Authors

Peter G. Fairweather (e-mail: peterf@watson.ibm.com), Richard B. Lam (e-mail: rblam@watson.ibm.com), and Lei Kuang (e-mail: kuang@watson.ibm.com) are with the IBM T. J. Watson Research Center, Yorktown Heights, New York.

12

The Web and Model-Centered Instruction

Andrew S. Gibbons,

Kimberly A. Lawless,

Thor A. Anderson,

and Joel Duffin

Information and Instruction

Both economy and effectiveness will determine the future success of the Web as an instructional distribution channel. The instruction the commercial Web delivers will have to be powerful, but it will also have to be affordable. Consider the effectiveness issue. The Web is today without dispute the world's premier *information* system. But what will it take to make it the premier *instructional* system? That answer has to take into account the difference between instructing and informing. For our present purposes, we will define instruction as the engagement of two or more individuals' wills or plans in a cooperative effort to first establish and then verify new personal meaning and performance capacity.

Verification—the search for evidence that learning goals have been attained—distinguishes *instructing* from just *informing*. You are never tested to see if you learned what the newspaper informed you about, but you must demonstrate performance ability and the attainment of certain knowledge before you can be certified in an area of professional practice. During instruction, two individual wills negotiate learning and performance goals and then work in concert to achieve them. Sometimes the goals are unspoken and sometimes they are explicit, but they always exist, if it is instruction.

What makes instruction effective? That question has been the center of a great debate, and some useful new answers are emerging. One thing certain is that instructional techniques that have been used regularly for years are being joined by new ones. Perhaps a better way to put it is that instructional methods that have been given low priority in the past are now being rediscovered and given much higher priority; at the same time, some of the old standbys are being given lower priority. The standard forms of the past 30 years are only a small subset of the possibilities that can be generated by considering new instructional roles, activities, formats, and relationships made possible by these newly-emphasized methods.

Recent developments to remove some of the old assumptions of instruction emphasize the importance of the social context of learning (Collins, Brown, & Newman, 1989; Rogoff, 1990), learning by problem solving (Barrows, 1985, 1992), and the situation of learning in realistic contexts (Lave & Wenger, 1991). These trends are closely related to an evolving instructional viewpoint called *model-centered instruction* (Gibbons, 1998; Gibbons & Anderson, 1994; Gibbons & Fairweather, 1998).

Model-centered instruction, which is described below, involves an instructional relationship consisting of a learner and a companion-in-learning who together observe and interact with one or more real or modeled environments, cause-effect systems, and/or samples of expert behavior. The companion supplies instructional support in a variety of forms and through a variety of roles as the learner solves a series of problems of escalating difficulty defined with respect to a set of models or systems of escalating complexity. The work of White and Frederiksen (1990) summarizes principles for defining externalized instructional models, from which learners can construct corresponding internalized mental models. The import of model-centering is that it assumes *experiencing a model or a system in some form as a primary instructional means*. Model-centering also assumes that a secondary, companion function accompanies that experience in ways that guide and support learning.

How can the Web make the transition from offering almost exclusively informational services to accommodating a greater share of truly instructional ones? This will entail considerable change: (1) a new Web designer mindset, changed from traditional instructional views to ones that incorporate model-centering, and (2) tools of new kinds not widely used yet, even for the development of stand-alone (non-Web-based) computer-based instruction. As new instructional viewpoints such as model-centered instruction emerge to bring out the unique strengths of the computer as an instructional tool, they will broaden the computer's traditional role to include new uses as a multi-purpose tool (Lajoie & Derry, 1993).

To tease out the implications of the instructional Web, let's look at computer-based instruction in terms of its internal structures.

Instructional Considerations:
Convergence of Instructional and Logical Constructs

An instructional designer, through the act of designing, builds abstract event structures that embody strategic plans. An event structure may consist of a presentation of information, a quiz, a practice exercise, a problem to solve, a demonstration of performance, or one of numerous other options. The designer designs these event structures so that a learner can have goal-relevant experiences. In order to move from design to product, designers must match these *event structures* with the *expressive* and *interactive structures* supplied by—and unique to—the medium they are using for instruction. Books supply page structures; computer-based authoring tools supply programming structures like control or decision points, icons or frames, branching, graphic objects, and text objects.

The most important issue for computer-based instruction of all kinds—including Web-based instruction—is the *convergence zone* shown in Figure 1. This is the place where the designer's abstract instructional constructs and the concrete logic constructs supplied by the development tool come together to produce an actual product. At this point, the abstract event constructs are given expression—if possible—by the constructs supplied by the development tool.

This zone is especially critical for computer-based instruction because CBI demands explicit and detailed specification of logical structures to a degree required by no other medium.

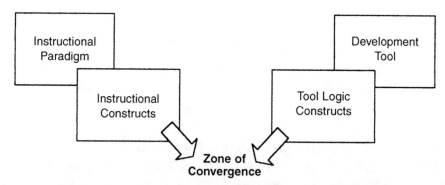

Figure 1. Factors that define a convergence zone where abstract instructional constructs and logic tool constructs meet in computer-based and Web-based instruction.

Other media depend heavily on pre-sequenced blocks of content, message, and representation. The computer is capable of computing a sequence of events for individual learners.

Attention to the convergence zone by CBI designers is crucial because the zone moderates: (1) the exactness with which the designer's strategic plans are implemented, and (2) the time and effort required for developing the instruction. The convergence zone is where the effectiveness and the cost of the instruction are mostly determined.

Figure 1 shows that computer logic constructs are supplied by specific development tools and tool families. For instance, a frame-based tool supplies different types of frame (subroutine) logic. An object tool supplies generic objects that can be customized by the user to perform specific functions.

Here is what happens at the convergence zone: The theoretic or paradigmatic orientation of the individual designer causes certain kinds of instructional construct to appear in his or her designs. The development tool chosen determines the logic constructs that will be available for use. The match or mismatch between the designer's instructional abstractions and the tool's logic structures at this point either supports or constrains the degree of implementation of the design. Since even software tools are maximized for certain uses and minimized for others, it is almost unavoidable that a given development tool will either express or restrict a given instructional event plan. This phenomenon has led in the past to a restriction in the designs themselves and encourages a kind of conformity to the tool rather than an expression of more powerful and effective designs. This pattern from the past needs to be reversed, and the instructional Web may be an opportunity to do so.

In terms of abstract design constructs, the Web's current metaphor is the network of hyperlinked documents and resources. Web tools provide logic constructs that match this metaphor perfectly. With a Web tool, you can construct Web *pages* (of the document) with special *formats* provided by HTML. Pages are populated with various textual and graphic information *resources,* and can provide special effects and interactivity using *applets* and *controls,* which are simply types of resources. *Links* or *hotwords* are the paths that tie pages together.

The design constructs used for Web pages for the most part correspond directly with the tool constructs provided by Web development tools, and if the informational metaphor of the Web was also a suitable instructional metaphor, then the transition to the instructional Web using existing tools would be smooth and uneventful. But informing is not instructing, and so a significant shift toward instructional development tools for the Web can be expected, and that may pose some difficulties to the mindset of designers and to the formation of development tools. The shift will involve not just Web page construction tools, but also the *informa-*

tion-linking design constructs now firmly implanted in the minds of tens of thousands of Web designers. These patterns of thinking and designing may in the short term hinder the use of the Web for highly interactive instruction, because they conflict with the *instructional constructs* that must come to share the Web. Let's examine two prevailing views of instruction in more detail and the tool requirements they entail.

Two Instructional Paradigms

Hannafin and his associates (Hannafin, Hannafin, Land, & Oliver, 1997) provide an excellent description of two major views of instruction in their discussion of *instructivist* versus *constructivist* instructional approaches as foundations for instructional designs. These two major views of instruction lead a designer to apply much different abstract instructional constructs in their designs. The task of expressing these two families of constructs in the form of computer logic brings the designer face to face with two different families of logic structures.

Gibbons and Fairweather (1998), for instance, define multiple, nested levels of construct that are involved in *direct,* or *tutorial,* instructional designs (see especially pp. 171–180 and 421–462). They define *four levels* of design construct: a strategic level, a content level, a message level, and a representation level.

At each of these four successive levels, abstract design constructs from the previous level unfold to create a complete and detailed design, *whose structures at the lowest level must in some way be made to correspond with the logic structures supplied by some authoring tools.* This is the convergence zone. (Keep in mind that for the present moment we are focusing on *direct, tutorial, strategy-centered* instruction. What we are saying does not apply to the second type of instruction defined by Hannafin, which we will treat in a moment.)

At the highest level of design construct (the strategic), the structure consists of a strategic plan divided into functional sub-constructs (for instance, "present information," "provide an appropriate demonstration," "provide practice"). Each of these strategic sub-constructs splits along the lines of content structure to produce smaller constructs ("present one example of a concept class" or "practice of one step of a procedure"). These content-tempered sub-constructs break down further to produce message sub-constructs ("present the definition of the concept," "present one example," "present one paired non-example"). Message-tempered constructs unfold one more step to produce representational sub-constructs ("provide the text portion of the definition at the appropriate screen position and at the right timing," "accept the learner's response to the non-example and check it"). It is at this lowest level of detail, the representational, that the structures, which to this point have been only conceptual and involve an abstract design, are made to correspond with the reality of some set of logic structures supplied by an authoring tool.

Displaying the text for the concept definition may involve presenting a text string, a bitmap, or a fixed string in some typeface at some size, and at a particular place on the display. Accepting the learner's response involves specifying several items of information: location of the response, type of response, disposition of the response (stored or not stored), appearance of the response on the display, and so forth. The authoring tool may or may not provide the type of service the author envisions. If it provides it, it may be easy (inexpensive, modest skill) or hard (expensive, high skill) to arrange. At this convergence zone and in this way, the authoring tool influences the cost and effectiveness of designs.

Hannafin and his associates identify a second type of *indirect* instruction that relies more heavily on direct experience supplemented by coaching and other forms of learning augmentation activity. The constructs required to create this type of instructional experience differ considerably from those for direct instruction. They include: environments in which a problem can be posed and solved; the data and representations related to the problems themselves; interactive cause-effect systems (computer models) that can be manipulated during problem solving; systems of expert behavior that can supply models of performance for learners to observe; resources that supply content for problem solving; dramatic overlays that situate problems in realistic contexts; recording and analysis tools for the collection and manipulation of data; communication tools; and auxiliary instructional features that supply the functionality of a learning companion.

These abstract design constructs can be subdivided and eventually matched with the logic constructs of the tool that will give them life, just like direct instruction constructs, but the indirect design constructs break down in different ways. For instance, environments for problem solving normally divide into individual locations (real or metaphorical) that can be "visited" to obtain information that is available there; pathways connect these locations, implying the need for movement controls. The representations used to display locations and their information ranges from simple textual presentation at one end of the spectrum to virtual experiences at the other, and the range of options between these extremes includes every form of representation available to computers and all combinations of them.

The other high-level constructs listed earlier for indirect instruction break in similar fashion into sub-constructs in their own ways, but the goal of the reduction process is the same, whatever the structure, and whether for direct or indirect instruction: to produce a set of abstract design structures that can be matched with the logic structures offered by the development tool of choice. Since the constructs for indirect instruction differ from those of direct instruction, it turns out in many cases that the logic structures supplied by authoring tools designed primarily for direct forms of instruction match poorly with the abstractions created for indirect forms of instruction. This will prove to be the greatest challenge for the instructional Web.

Tool Implications

The benefit obtained from specialized Web authoring tools is not just functionality but *productive* functionality. Increased productivity is the primary reason for building such tools. If no authoring tools existed, the designer would be required to use a high-level programming language like "C."

In fact, some organizations do use high-level languages despite their higher development price tag because they have had a chance (paid for by volume production) to design their own set of specialized routines (logic structures) that can be strung together according to need to match a set of standardized design constructs. In effect, they have constructed their own special purpose authoring tool. Many large training software vendors are positioning themselves and their products to be Web-compatible in this way. Likewise, virtually all major commercial authoring tool vendors, seeing the potential (can we say inevitability?) of the Web as an instructional channel, are migrating their products toward Web compatibility and Web friendliness. Instructional designers now face difficult tool choices and wonder if there is a best choice that will not require future adjustments and re-programming of their products. Even more important, many are wondering how they will be able to implement a newer instructional paradigm (indirect instruction) in a medium that is not yet fully compatible (in terms of productivity) with the high interactive demands of the old paradigm (direct instruction).

Examining the Web's Underlying Metaphor More Closely

During the coming period of transition, when the Web will try to embrace interactive instruction in addition to information access, it will be a good time to reconsider the basic structural metaphors of instruction and to compare them with the structural metaphor of the Web and its tools. We should ask, "Can we see a clear path for the creation of Web development tools that will implement today's instructional metaphors and allow for their future growth in feature and function?"

We believe that the answer to this question begins with a closer inspection of the language metaphors currently available for Web development. We should begin an inquiry by examining the basis of the most common, popular, user-friendly, and productive Web language, HTML, to see if it supplies the necessary logic constructs to implement the kinds of direct and indirect instructional designs we have described.

HTML is the *lingua franca* of the Web for the average designer. It is the tool most friendly to the average Web page designer, and it is the tool taught to most beginning designers. It is designed specifically to allow page authors to prepare *documents* containing a range of resources and linkages once for interpretation and display on many properly configured computers. It allows designers to ignore differences in computer hardware, operating systems, display size, and local software preference settings.

This alone is a spectacular achievement, especially appreciated by those who have worked in earlier environments where cross-platform compatibility was in most cases unobtainable. But much of HTML's compatibility is a result of its membership in a larger group of markup languages (ML), all of which have similar cross-platform compatibilities. These markup languages are all descendants of a parent language called SGML (Standard Generalized Markup Language). Each markup language in the SGML family has the capacity for communicating a specific type of document, with its formatting, to a distant browser.

The important point to be made is that markup languages derived from SGML are all based on the document metaphor, with a document, somewhat like a data base, having a certain standard structure (Leventhal, Lewis, & Fuchs, 1998). A markup language is simply a way of tagging the individual elements of a particular type of document (having a specific internal document structure) before sending the document's elements for display.

HTML documents have display elements such as "body," "title," and "list." They also have reader-reactive elements such as form fields, click-sensitive graphic areas, and buttons. They also have relational links that permit the elements of the document to be accessed in various orders. But the range of structures and interactivity using this set of elements and resource types—as impressive as they are—is limited, especially when the processing of a learner response is taken into account. Moreover, markup languages are not sensitive to the context or meaning of a reader's response, so a programmer has to supply it in the form of answer processing logic, which is not within the range of HTML user-friendliness. To handle these additional requirements, new tools like Java, and Perl are called into use and interfaced with HTML, and the user-friendliness and productivity of Web authoring plummets.

To escape some of the limitations of HTML, groups of users with specialized document types have created their own markup languages—derived from SGML and usually created in a tool language called XML—for the authoring, transmission, and display of documents that contain specialized structures. Mathematicians have constructed a Mathematical Markup Language (MathML). Its structures include formatting tags that allow the mathematician to specify to a browser how the individual elements are linked in terms of meaning (semantic or content tags) and how they are to be displayed.

The benefit of MathML is that equations that would otherwise be difficult to display in readable form come to the reader looking just like equations on a printed page, with spacing and placement of symbols just as they were intended by the author, regardless of the computer they are displayed on.

Musicians have a Music Markup Language (MML). The benefits of Music ML are the same: Musicians can send otherwise unreadable musical documents in a form that allows the receiver to read and interact with them.

These and other markup languages, however, skirt the issue addressed in this chapter and do not deal with the implementation of highly interactive and sometimes adaptive instruction over the Web. The central question we must ask is whether the document metaphor and its implied logic constructs that lie at the base of the markup languages can also be used as the base for implementing the conceptual structures we have described—for both the direct and indirect instructional paradigms. We do not believe that the document metaphor alone can suffice, unless the definition of "document" is a data base of retrievable resources changes. The specialized markup languages are designed for the display of static document content. In contrast, the content of instruction, especially for indirect instruction which relies heavily on learner interaction with models and expert systems capable of making instructional decisions and exhibiting dynamic performance, is not easily contained within the boundaries of a collection of static, categorized structures that store and fit neatly within a data base. Indirect instruction often requires the construction of displays based on computed responses to learner actions.

Tool Solutions

How can tools be made easier to use, even when the forms of instruction created seem to be demanding more sophisticated logical structures and interactions between independent logical agents? What patterns of tool use and logic processing will minimize traffic over the instructional Web, yet permit power, speed, flexibility, and individual learner attention in products?

Some solutions present themselves that are within the immediate grasp of the designer, while longer-term solutions continue to evolve: (1) the construction of reusable logic templates for direct instruction, (2) the construction of reusable components for indirect instruction, and (3) migration toward tools with more flexible and broadly applicable logic constructs for both types of instruction.

Reusable templates for direct instruction. For many years, computer-based instruction developers have relied on template logic structures made of frames or hand-made logic routines as an economy measure. Financial success for most CBI product companies is possible only by adopting a template approach. The economics of the Web will demand the same thing. Low-cost development will continue to be a requisite. Reusable templates are the most direct way to this goal for some types of instruction, especially the direct type.

Reusable components for indirect instruction. Indirect instruction logics employ components that permit free play within an environment, as well as system models and tools for use within a problem solving environment. Just as templates can be used to capture direct instruction logic for message delivery and practice interaction, reusable components can be manufactured that create environments, simulate cause-effect systems (models), and perform expert system functionalities. Many of these components can be created as empty logic shells that are provided with usable data at the time of use.

Template components of this type have been used to create instruction for the training of aviators (Gibbons, 1993; Gibbons & Rogers, 1991a, 1991b), and for the training of library skills (Lacy & Gibbons, 1994; Wolcott, Gibbons, Lacy, & Sharp, 1994). These applications involve free-play environmental simulations followed by intelligent, real-time, performance-referenced feedback.

These products involve the creation of independent, reusable components: a shell simulation engine, and a separate shell expert system for feedback. These efficient and compact instructional components are capable of generating instructional messaging from problem data files and live response records of the learner. Duffin and Gibbons (1997) and others (Gibbons, Duffin, Robertson, & Thompson, 1997) have also reported using object systems to create simple, parameterized, and switch-controllable expert systems capable of both coaching and feedback in either delayed or instantaneous mode. These expert systems operate on selectable comparison sources—either the expert's or the learner's own performance. These designs are well-suited to the Web because of their parsimony.

Migration to more flexible tools. Many designers find object-oriented development systems more economical and more flexible for building structures typical of indirect instruction. Not only can one-of-a-kind object suites be created, but templated object structures have been used to create efficient but instructionally effective object families (Gibbons & Thompson, 1997). Traditional authoring tool frames themselves can be created using object tools, suggesting that object systems represent a superset of tool constructs. In terms of Web-focused object tools, Java appears to be preeminent, and authoring interfaces are emerging that provide non-programmers access to Java functionality. These facilitate designer creation of both direct and indirect instructional products and allow a larger number of authors to access the power of the programming language.

Object tools are uniquely suited for the construction of models of both natural and manufactured systems. The object-oriented approach to programming has its roots in creating simulations (Shasha & Lazere, 1995). However, simulation models alone do not constitute an instructional product. The experience of the model through problem solving normally requires support in the form of instructional augmentations (coaching, hinting, directing, explaining, giving feedback, etc.) that support the learner's extraction of information from experience, construction of knowledge, and formation of performance patterns. These instructional augmentations often imply that two programs need to run simultaneously or in close coordination. The independence of these functionalities is essential for their portability and reuse.

Conclusion

We have tried to outline issues at the heart of Web-based instructional design and production. We have invoked one old and one recent instructional paradigm to show the instructional implications for a medium hitherto purposed for information exchange. If the Web is to supply both direct and indirect instructional forms, new tools for Web-based design and production must evolve.

Several decades of experience that have already accumulated in computer-based instruction have shown that when the *instructional constructs* of a design correspond well with *tool constructs* provided by a specific tool being used, and when reusable logic patterns can be constructed and applied, the result is a product whose instructional plan is preserved intact and whose cost is reduced. However, when there is a mismatch between instructional and tool constructs, or when template logic cannot be used, instructional designs are compromised, or costs soar, and there are less frequently exportable and reusable elements of program code produced.

The task of creating economical development tools that implement a new metaphor will be an especially difficult but critical challenge. Throughout the history of computer-based instruction, there has been a tendency for logic tool constructs to initially facilitate but later restrict the implementation of the designer's strategic ideas due to the relatively rapid advance of theoretic ideas compared with the relatively slow advance of tools. Currently, conventional computer-based instruction faces these same challenges. The advent of the instructional Web will accelerate progress—hopefully in both Web-based and stand-alone CBI. We therefore look forward with anticipation to the creation of the truly instructional Web and more powerful CBI development tools than ever before.

References

Barrows, H. S. (1985). *How to design a problem-based curriculum.* New York: Springer.

Barrows, H. S. (1992). *The tutorial process.* Springfield, IL: Southern Illinois University School of Medicine.

Collins, A., Brown, J. S., & Newman, S. E. (1989). Cognitive apprenticeship: Teaching the craft of reading, writing, and mathematics. In L. B. Resnick (Ed.), *Knowing, learning, and instruction: Essays in honor of Robert Glaser.* Hillsdale, NJ: Lawrence Erlbaum Associates.

Duffin, J. R., & Gibbons, A. S. (1997). Intelligent interactive math testing shells. Presented at the Ninth Annual Summer Institute, Utah State University, Department of Instructional Technology, Logan, Utah.

Gibbons, A. S. (1993). New tools for creating instruction and simulations. Technical Paper No. 932600, Education, Training, and Human Engineering in Aerospace (SP-992), SAE International, Costa Mesa, CA.

Gibbons, A. S. (1998). Model-centered instruction. Paper presented at the Annual Meeting of the American Educational Research Association, San Diego.

Gibbons, A. S., & Anderson, T. A. (1994). Model-centered instruction. Paper presented at the Sixth Annual Summer Institute, Utah State University, Department of Instructional Technology, Logan, Utah.

Gibbons, A. S., Duffin, J. R., Robertson, D. J., & Thompson, B. (1997). Instructional feedback and simulation: A model-centered approach. Paper presented at the Annual Meeting of the Northern Rocky Mountain Educational Research Association, Jackson, Wyoming.

Gibbons, A. S., & Fairweather, P. G. (1998). *Computer-based instruction: Design and development.* Englewood Cliffs: Educational Technology Publications.

Gibbons, A.S., & Rogers, D. H. (1991a). The maintenance evaluator: Feedback for extended simulation problems. Paper presented at the Ninth Conference on Interactive Instruction Delivery, Society for Applied Learning Technology, Orlando.

Gibbons, A. S., & Rogers, D. H. (1991b). Use of an expert critic to improve aviation training. Paper presented at the Ohio State Symposium on Aviation Psychology. Sponsored by Ohio State University, Columbus.

Gibbons, A. S., & Thompson, B. (1997). Pseudosimulation: An example of low-cost authoring. Paper presented at the Ninth Annual Summer Institute, Utah State University, Department of Instructional Technology, Logan, Utah.

Hannafin, M. J., Hannafin, K. M., Land, S. M., & Oliver, K. (1997). Grounded practice and the design of constructivist learning environments. *Educational Technology Research and Development, 45*(3), 101–117.

Lacy, M., & Gibbons, A. (1994). The library location simulation at USU. Paper presented at the Annual Meeting of the Association for Educational Communications Technology—Region 8, Park City, Utah.

Lajoie, S. P., & Derry, S. J. (1993). *Computers as cognitive tools.* Hillsdale, NJ: Lawrence Erlbaum Associates.

Lave, J., & Wenger, E. (1991). *Situated learning: Legitimate peripheral participation.* Cambridge, MA: Cambridge University Press.

Leventhal, M., Lewis, D., & Fuchs, M. (1998). *Designing XML Internet applications*. Upper Saddle River, NJ: Prentice-Hall.

Rogoff, B. (1990). *Apprenticeship in thinking: Cognitive development in social context*. New York: Oxford University Press.

Shasha, D., & Lazere, C. (1995). *Out of their minds: The lives and discoveries of 15 great computer scientists*. New York: Copernicus/Springer-Verlag.

White, B. Y., & Frederiksen, J. (1990). Causal model progressions as a model foundation for intelligent learning environments. *Artificial intelligence, 24*, 99–157.

Wolcott, L., Gibbons, A. S., Lacy, M., & Sharp, J. (1994) Navigating the information environment: An instructional simulation of information retrieval processes for university students. Paper presented at the Annual Meeting of the Association for Educational Communications and Technology.

The Authors

Andrew S. Gibbons (e-mail: gibbons@cc.usu.edu) is Professor, Instructional Technology Department, Utah State University, Logan, Utah. **Kimberly A. Lawless** (e-mail: klawless@uic.edu) is Assistant Professor, Curriculum and Instruction, University of Illinois at Chicago. **Thor A. Anderson** (e-mail: thor@ learningcomponents.com; Web homepage: learningcomponents.com) is President, Learning Components.com, San Jose, California. **Joel Duffin** (e-mail: Joel.Duffin@NextPage.com; Web homepage: cc.usu.edu/~sllcd/) is a doctoral student, Department of Instructional Technology, Utah State University, Logan, Utah.

13

Activity Theory and
Web-Based Training

D a v i d   P e a l   a n d
B r e n t   G .   W i l s o n

How is it that children in some cultures learn to do complex mental calculations, identify dozens of plant types, and use star patterns to pilot canoes over long distances, all without the benefit of formal schooling? Activity theory seeks to account, among other things, for the effectiveness of everyday learning environments. Researchers are beginning to identify how activity theory can inform the *design* of learning environments as well (Jonassen & Murphy, 1998). In this chapter, we introduce activity theory as a framework for creating one particular type of designed environment: Web-based training (WBT). We also suggest ways in which designers can address the difficulties inherent in implementing realistic learning environments on the Web.

Activity Theory Essentials

Activity theory starts not with the individual learner, but with the *activity system,* a larger and more realistic unit of analysis. An activity system consists of a group, of any size, pursuing a specific goal in a purposeful way. For example, doctors practicing preventive medicine in a health-maintenance organization make up an activity system (Cole & Engestrom, 1993). Students in different countries collaborating on a project to build a Website about the Himalayas make up another activity system. A telephone sales unit of a precision-parts distributor provides another example (Laufer & Glick, 1996). Even seemingly isolated activities are usually embedded in a larger system, as in the case of collaborating researchers who must negotiate differing approaches, align schedules, agree on a division of labor, and coordinate their actions with colleagues, editors, and others.

These examples can be analyzed into the elements shown in Figure 1, adapted from a diagram created by Finnish researcher Yrjo Engestrom (Cole & Engestrom, 1993, p. 8). The central relationship is between the individual *participant* (or subject) and the activity system's *purpose* (or object); this relationship is not direct, but is mediated by artifacts *(tools).* Participants are usually part of communities, a relationship mediated by *rules* for acceptable interactions. Communities in turn help accomplish system purposes and outcomes through a *division of labor.* The model depicted in the figure has the advantage over other situated-learning approaches of allowing for the identification of an activity system's elements and for the com-

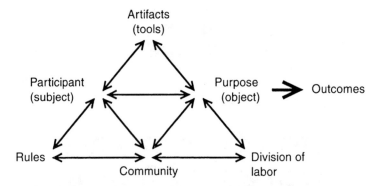

Figure 1. The structure of an activity system.

parison of dynamic systems over time (Nardi, 1996). Activity systems are, in fact, in constant flux, always subject to change through the intrusion of new participants, purposes, and tools.

The Centrality of Tools

By bridging the worlds of participant and purpose, tools (depicted at the apex of the figure above) make activity possible in the first place. Tools can be both physical (notebooks, books, software) and cognitive (concepts, language, notational systems). Physical tools shape what people can and cannot do, as Norman (1988) shows in his critique of poorly designed doors and countless other everyday things. Cognitive tools likewise enable (mediate) and constrain activity. Instructional design procedures in the training world, for example, prescribe a way of doing (and not doing) design, thereby shaping associated ways of thinking (and not thinking) about learning. Cognitive tools are of special importance because they free us from immediate stimuli, providing access to the past, to situations not physically present, and to imaginary worlds (Cole, 1996, pp. 121–122). Consider, for example, the centrality of tools for engineers, who could not function without tables, regulatory guides, design software, and a vast conceptual apparatus shared with other engineers (Perkins, 1993). For the engineer, conceptual tools can serve as "functional organs," experienced almost as personal properties (Kaptelinin, 1996, p. 51).

An *activity,* then, is simply what the activity system does: people using tools for more or less well-defined purposes. Any activity consists of deliberate *actions,* which can be further decomposed into automatic *operations* (Leont'ev, 1974). In the case of telephone sales, for example, order-processing constitutes an activity carried out through deliberate calculations (actions) and automatic order-writing (operations). These three levels (activity, action, operation) are situationally defined and subject to change. For management, order-processing is but a lower-level action in a larger corporate activity system. And we've all experienced how otherwise-ignored operations can become disrupted. When software crashes (ceasing to be a tool and forcing itself into consciousness as a troublesome object), automatic operations are halted as one tries to figure out which actions are required to resume work (Nardi, 1996, p. 75).

Everyday Learning in Activity Systems

To account for the relation between learning and human development, Lev Vygotsky, the Soviet psychologist who laid the groundwork for activity theory, developed the concept of *zone of proximal development* (ZPD) in 1934; the term has been popularized in the U.S. since the translation of his *Mind and Society* in 1978. Vygotsky defined the ZPD as the distance between a child's current development (as measured by independent problem solving) and that child's potential development (as measured by what can be accomplished "under adult guidance or in collaboration with more capable peers"; Vygotsky, 1978, p. 86). Implicit in this definition is a prescription for adults (and teachers of every kind) to engage learners one at a time, at the limit of their potential. Under guidance, with practice, novices "gradually increase their relative responsibility until they can manage" on their own (Cole, 1985, p. 155). Skills, rules, knowledge, and tools are thereby internalized, forming the basis of the cognitive tools used in problem-solving and self-directed learning.*

Vygotsky's concept has helped anthropologists explain how, in non-Western cultures, complex skills such as weaving and midwifery pass between generations (Lave & Wenger, 1991; Rogoff, 1990). In North American classrooms, educators have attempted to design ZPDs (e.g., Campione *et al.,* 1984; Newman, Griffin, & Cole, 1989). Such designs have at least four elements:

(1) learning activities that are part of real or simulated activity systems, with close attention to the tools and interactions characteristic of actual situations;

(2) structured interaction among participants;

(3) guidance by an expert; and

(4) eventual surrender of learning control to increasingly competent learners.

"Guidance by an expert" requires a more active role than suggested by "guide on the side," today's jargon for the teacher who no longer merely purveys information in a didactic fashion. To be effective, instructors must be sufficiently expert in their domain to judge individual learning needs, sufficiently experienced as instructors to adjust dynamically as needs change, and sufficiently sensitive as people to continuously juggle the novice's and expert's perspectives, with the steady goal of pulling the novice toward mastery (Newman, 1997; Wells, 1996; Wertsch, 1984). In the ZPD, learning takes place not "in the head," through a one-way process of knowledge transmission. Some theorists discount individual cognition altogether, arguing that thought and intelligence are embedded in and "stretched across" the larger structures of activity (Lave & Wenger, 1991; Pea, 1993; Salomon & Perkins, 1998).

A final general point: activity systems are not normative, and the "natural" way of learning is not necessarily the best. Instead, the activity system model helps the designer see current systems over time and as a whole. Such systems can be rife with contradictions—differences, for example, among participants about purpose, division of labor, and tool selection and use. By analyzing the troubles of current activity systems, designers can help emerging ones develop successfully.

Implications for WBT

WBT can focus at any level of an activity system—activity, action, or operation. The lower the level, the looser the ties to a specific activity system and more transferable the skill, since activities are unique to systems while operations can be applied in many systems. WBT itself can be seen as both a tool and a simulated activity system within which participants are introduced

---

*The apprenticeship process presented schematically here, and only characterized at a high level by Vygotsky himself, has been closely analyzed by Barbara Rogoff (1990) in her cross-cultural study of child development—a more readable account of apprenticeship than Lave and Wenger's popular theoretical study of situated learning (1991). Though dealing with children, Rogoff's work bears close reading by designers of training for adults. Gordon Wells (1996) provides many insights into teacher-student dynamics in the classroom ZPD. Kieran Egan (1997) has developed Vygotsky's hints about the genesis of cognitive tools into a highly imaginative theory of human development and education, with many implications for trainers.

to and refine their use of actions and operations. Purposive, coordinated learning can be organized and led by an instructor, automated by a computer-based tutorial, or created by the learners themselves, depending on the WBT design. In this respect, the Web, like any other medium, affords a variety of interactions in support of activity, depending on the use to which it is put.

Using WBT merely to teach routine behaviors (operations and actions) fails to do much more than automate current practice or lower costs, thereby shoehorning what is often procedural knowledge into a hypertext format. The novel contribution of activity theory is to focus attention on the ways in which WBT can support higher-level activity by enabling reflection on current business processes and facilitation of new teams, rules, and divisions of labor. WBT in support of activity can be delivered as a course, but perhaps more effectively as part of everyday activity systems. Further, what Kuutti (1996) says of information technologies applies to WBT as well. WBT can make new, distributed activities possible and allow organizations to take on new purposes (pp. 35ff).

Regardless of the level of training, activity theory (see Table 1) can inform the design of the key aspects of WBT: what is being learned, how training takes place, and what is expected of the learner.

What Is Being Learned

For activity theorists, community knowledge lies in activities and tools, not syllabi and performance objectives. WBT designers should arguably spend more time designing activities that use the resources of activity systems and less time worrying about whether some sort of purified expertise has been "captured" from a subject-matter expert. One could safely assume that it hasn't, since the needed expertise will likely emerge from activity itself. Ideally, assessment should include a way of tracking students' day-to-day activities and judging the adequacy of their participation.

WBT makes the most sense when activities are already on the Web, such as learning HTML, designing e-commerce sites, and programming in JavaScript. Also, it makes sense when activities are easily represented in virtual environments, such as collaborative research and writing. With mature learners and independent professionals, conveyance of discrete information (as in continuing medical education) also lends itself well to WBT, especially when an instructor is not required.

In other cases, WBT should arguably be integrated with real-world training. A WBT course on data-entry skills could pair novices with experienced colleagues who know the tricks and shortcuts as well as the rule-based techniques. A WBT course on coaching for managers could include Web-based tutorials on rules and skills, but significant time should also be spent in actual performance settings, with learners working alongside experienced practitioners. Here they can learn the ways in which experts recognize and grapple with the messier problems that emerge in everyday situations.

How Training Takes Place

American educators prefer the term *scaffolding* to *zone of proximal development,* but both terms denote the guidance learners need as they acquire new skills. In traditional activity systems, the community and especially the adult guide provide much of the scaffolding for novices. The same can be true in WBT environments, which have the benefit of providing access to distributed expertise (Brown *et al.,* 1993). However, because the Web medium is presently limited to text, sound, pictures, and to some extent video, fewer cues and far less everyday information can be shared than in face-to-face encounters; "live" communications usually take place using text alone. This inherent deficit can leave learners feeling isolated and adrift, lacking in cues and immediacy.

Table 1. Design guidelines.

Activity Theory and WBT: Some Design Guidelines

Cultivate the social. Communities are central to normal training practices and should also be central to WBT. Even individualized modules need to be conceived as part of a broader network of interacting people.

Get people talking. Learning happens when people get practice using the community's tools, with all the associated jargon and tricks of the trade.

Provide continued scaffolding. Learners benefit most when they stay engaged at that "stretching" level, with support from multiple experts, including experienced peers.

Tap inherent intentionality. Every activity system has its purposes, which inform all underlying actions and operations. WBT environments will be successful to the extent that they tie learners' goals to these larger purposes.

Build around meaningful activity. The power of WBT lies in the cases, projects, and problems— not in objectives and content outlines. Activity-based WBT draws on the power of authentic collaborative activity to convey what needs to be taught.

Work with the available tools. Some WBT tools will be richly simulated; others will be lower fidelity, text-only case studies. Learners and trainers need to improvise and adapt as they accustom themselves to the online environment. Even so, impressive learning can result through creative use of online tools and resources.

Use collaboration to allow different levels of participation, support, and learning. Not every learner has to engage in the same activity in the same way; such standardization can kill a creative activity system. Learners need to be encouraged to find a place where they can learn— at the center, periphery, or somewhere in between. In collaborative activities directed at challenging, complex problems, room can be made for everybody.

With some ingenuity in implementation, WBT can compensate for media limitations. Instructors will themselves need guidance in the art of scaffolding as they learn to use e-mail, chat, and message boards to engage students regularly, substantively, and supportively as required. An effective WBT environment will also include a variety of directly useful performance supports such as job aids and reference sheets. Above all, realistically presented activity will allow participants to master tools thoroughly and in context—not just as skills, but as "personal properties."

Virtual learning communities can hold some advantages over the face-to-face variety. Because WBT interactions can be archived, students can consult previous work samples. A searchable and browsable library of such samples (as in a Lotus Notes discussion database) can make a workgroup's history readily retrievable. By making a community's knowledge tangible, collaborative visualization technologies can help participants resolve differences and build joint understandings (Edelson, Pea, & Gomez, 1996). Even in the text-only world of Usenet newsgroups, compilations of frequently asked questions (FAQs) have successfully met this need for years by representing shared knowledge in a compact format, efficiently bringing novices up to speed and reducing the burdens placed on the community's most experienced members. Such digital archives do not, of course, encapsulate human interactions in quite the way Vygotsky might have envisioned. Even so, networked storage, retrieval, collaboration, and visualization capabilities can help compensate for WBT's inherent limitations.

What Is Expected of the Learner

Traditional and virtual communities differ in the expected roles of students. In WBT environments, instructors cannot micro-monitor students' progress, or even be aware of learning needs on a daily basis—a real obstacle to implementing ZPDs on the Web. Students must be encouraged to take the initiative and seek out needed resources. Because WBT constrains opportunities for the direct observation and modeling of expert participants, designers should expect failures—not so much in content transmission as in learners' inadequate adaptation to new roles.

For WBT to be effective, students need to see learning goals in terms of problems to be solved. The metacognitive skills of self-monitoring, question-asking, decision-making, and self-evaluation must be constantly in play. A key task for instructors in this environment is to cultivate such skills and also to encourage students to model experienced peers. Since many students do not arrive well-prepared in these areas, WBT environments must include support for high-level skills. Scaffolding thus supports not just technical skills, but also reflection, troubleshooting, and self-guided learning.

References

Brown, A., *et al.* (1993). Distributed expertise in the classroom. In G. Salomon (Ed.), *Distributed cognitions: Psychological and educational considerations* (pp. 188–228). Cambridge, UK: Cambridge University Press.

Campione, J., *et al.* (1984). The Zone of Proximal Development: Implications for individual differences and learning. In B. Rogoff & J. Wertsch (Eds.), *Children's learning in the Zone of Proximal Development* (pp. 77–91). San Francisco: Jossey-Bass.

Cole, M. (1985). The Zone of Proximal Development: Where culture and cognition create each other. In J. Wertsch (Ed.), *Culture, communication, and cognition: Vygotskian perspectives* (pp. 146–161). Cambridge, UK: Cambridge University Press.

Cole, M. (1996). Cultural psychology: *A once and future discipline.* Cambridge, MA: Belknap Press of Harvard University Press.

Cole, M., & Engestrom, Y. (1993). A cultural-historical approach to distributed cognition. In G. Salomon (Ed.), *Distributed cognitions: Psychological and educational considerations* (pp. 1–46). Cambridge, UK: Cambridge University Press.

Cole, M., & Wertsch, J. V. (1996). Beyond the individual-social antinomy in discussions of Piaget and Vygotsky. *Human Development, 39,* 250–256

Edelson, D., Pea, R., & Gomez, L. (1996). Constructivism in the collaboratory. In B. G. Wilson (Ed.), *Constructivist learning environments: Case studies in instructional design* (pp. 151–164). Englewood Cliffs: Educational Technology Publications.

Egan, K. (1997). *The educated mind: How cognitive tools shape our understanding.* Chicago: University of Chicago Press.

Engestrom, Y. (1996). *The activity system;* helsinki.fi/~jengestr/activity/6b0.htm

Jonassen, D. H., & Murphy, M. (1998, February). *Activity theory as a framework for designing constructivist learning environments.* Paper presented at the meeting of the Association for Educational Communications and Technology.

Kaptelinin, V. (1996). Computer-mediated activity: Functional organs in social and developmental contexts. In B. Nardi (Ed.), *Context and consciousness: Activity theory and human-computer interaction* (pp. 45–68). Cambridge, MA: MIT Press.

Kuutti, K. (1996). Activity theory as a potential framework for human-computer interaction research. In B. Nardi (Ed.), *Context and consciousness: Activity theory and human-computer interaction* (pp. 17–44). Cambridge, MA: MIT Press.

Lave, J., & Wenger, E. (1991). *Situated learning: Legitimate peripheral participation.* Cambridge, UK: Cambridge University Press.

Laufer, E., & Glick, J. (1996). In Y. Engestrom & D. Middleton (Eds.), *Cognition and communication at work* (177–96). Cambridge, UK: Cambridge University Press.

Leont'ev, A. (1974). The problem of activity in psychology. *Soviet Psychology, 13*(2), 4–33.

Nardi, B. (1996). Studying context: A comparison of activity theory, situated action, and distributed cognition. In B. Nardi (Ed.), *Context and consciousness: Activity theory and human-computer interaction* (pp. 69–102). Cambridge, MA: MIT Press.

Newman, D. (1997). Functional environments for microcomputers in education. In M. Cole, Y. Engestrom, & O. Vasquez, (Eds.), *Mind, culture, and activity: Seminal papers from the Laboratory of Comparative Human Cognition* (pp. 279–291). Cambridge, UK: Cambridge University Press.

Newman, D., Griffin, P., & Cole, M. (1989). *The construction zone: Working for cognitive change in school.* Cambridge, UK: Cambridge University Press.

Norman, D. (1988). *The design of everyday things.* New York: Doubleday/Currency.

Pea, R. D. (1993). Practices of distributed intelligence and designs for education. In G. Salomon (Ed.), *Distributed cognitions: Psychological and educational considerations* (pp. 47–87). Cambridge, UK: Cambridge University Press.

Perkins, D. N. (1993). Person plus: A distributed view of thinking and learning. In G. Salomon (Ed.), *Distributed cognitions: Psychological and educational considerations* (pp. 88–110). Cambridge, UK: Cambridge University Press.

Rogoff, B. (1990). *Apprenticeship in thinking: Cognitive development in social context.* Oxford, UK: Oxford University Press.

Salomon, G., & Perkins, D. N. (1998). Individual and social aspects of learning. In P. D. Pearson & A. Iran-Nejad (Eds.), *Review of Research in Education, 23,* 1–24.

Vygotsky, L. S. (1978). *Mind and society.* Cambridge, MA: Harvard University Press.

Wells, G. (1996) *The Zone of Proximal Development and its implications for learning and teaching.* Presented at the 2nd Conference for Sociocultural Research, Geneva.

Wertsch, J. (1984). The Zone of Proximal Development: Some conceptual issues. In B. Rogoff & J. Wertsch (Eds.), *Children's learning in the "Zone of Proximal Development"* (pp. 7–18). San Francisco: Jossey-Bass.

For more information: Martin Ryder has collected a large set of Web links relating to Activity Theory (cudenver.edu/~mryder/itc_data/activity.html).

The Authors

David Peal (e-mail: davidpeal@aol.com) writes and edits computer books for Sybex, Osborne/McGraw-Hill, Lycos Press/Macmillan, and AOL Press. **Brent G. Wilson (e-mail: brent.wilson@cudenver.edu)** is Associate Professor, Information and Learning Technologies, School of Education, University of Colorado at Denver.

14

Design and Development Issues in Web-Based Training

Wallace Hannum

Organizations are increasingly turning to Web-based training (WBT) for their training needs. As other chapters in this book argue, WBT can be a powerful training delivery technology. However, as many studies of technology applications to instruction indicate, it is not the technology itself that improves the instruction (Clark, 1994; Gagné & Medsker, 1996; Russell, 1997). Rather, it is careful attention to the design that impacts learning (Duchastel & Spahn, 1996). Thus, for WBT to be effective, developers must use powerful instructional design principles. A primary aspect of effective design for WBT is attention to those critical issues that influence WBT's effectiveness. The purpose of this chapter is to identify the critical issues that affect WBT and provide guidance in dealing with those issues.

The critical design and development issues for WBT can be organized into three main areas. The first area relates to issues associated with the type of model to use as a basis for the WBT. The second relates to issues associated with the flow, or logic, for individual WBT lessons. The third area relates to issues associated with screen design and navigation. By addressing these critical issues, WBT developers can create training content that has instructional value. Simply putting information on the Web does not constitute WBT.

WBT Models

A variety of models can form the basis for WBT content. These models are derived from one of two main approaches to using the Web for training. One approach views the Web as a means of **publishing**. Those adhering to the publishing approach see WBT as a way to distribute training content any time, anywhere, to any person. The function of the Web is to assist with publishing the training materials. The other approach views the Web as a means of **communicating**. Those adhering to the communications approach see WBT as a way to facilitate instructional communications with any person, any time, anywhere. Both the publishing and communication approaches of the Web are appropriate for WBT. Each view leads, however, to different WBT models (Welsh, 1997).

Library Model

One WBT model based on the publishing approach is the library model. In the library model, the WBT consists mainly of links to instructional resources, such as online encyclopedias, online journals, online books, and other Web sites that have relevant content. In a library model, the links to other sites can be organized by topic to facilitate the learners' location of desired information. Additionally, some WBT using the library model includes brief descriptions along with the URL for each link. This allows the learners to review information about a site before deciding to visit that site. The library WBT model is best used for providing links to resources as a supplement to a course. The library WBT model can be used to supplement a regular leader-led course or for an online course.

Textbook Model

Another WBT model based on the publishing approach is the textbook model. The textbook model provides learners with online access to instructional materials, such as course syllabi, lecture notes, slides, and video or graphics used in class. An online textbook or training manual is an example of the textbook model. The textbook WBT model is appropriate as the main way to deliver content in a WBT course. This model can also be used as a supplement to a regular class.

Interactive Instruction Model

A third WBT model based on the publishing approach is the interactive instruction model. The interactive instruction WBT model provides CBT or interactive multimedia online to learners via the Internet or intranets. This WBT model is considerably more interactive than either the library or textbook model. The interactive instruction model can be very rich instructionally, extending considerably beyond drill and practice CBT models. The interactive instruction WBT model is appropriate for stand-alone instruction when an instructor is not available. This can also be used as a supplement to a regular class when assignments require learners to acquire some content on their own.

Computer Mediated Communications Model

While the other WBT models are based on a publishing approach, the computer mediated communications model is based on the communications approach for the Web. The purpose of the computer mediated communications (CMC) model is to facilitate communications between instructor and students or among students (Berge, 1995). There are a variety of levels of computer mediated communications (Trentin & Benigno, 1997). At its simplest level, the computer mediated communications WBT model consists of e-mail between instructor and student. This is point-to-point communications. Another option is to use a listserv, an Internet mailing list that automatically sends a message to everybody on the list. By using a listserv, the computer mediated communications WBT model could incorporate point-to-multipoint communications, allowing any participant to post a message to all other participants. By using discussion forums, the computer mediated communications WBT model could allow a "class" of learners to carry on an asynchronous discussion about topics in a course. The instructor could pose a question or raise an issue and any class participant could contribute to the discussion. At a higher level of sophistication, the computer mediated communications WBT model could include synchronous computer conferencing using desktop video or chats. The computer mediated communications WBT model is appropriate when learners are scattered geographically but participating in the same class. This model is likewise appropriate as a way to compensate for time barriers. The asynchronous nature of most computer mediated communications allows learners to participate when they have time available.

Hybrid WBT Model

WBT developers can combine features of the publishing models and the computer mediated communications WBT model to form a hybrid WBT model. For example, you could create a WBT course that used both the textbook model and the computer mediated communications model. This particular hybrid WBT model could have online training materials and a discussion forum. By combining features of several WBT models, the hybrid model can offer a rich WBT experience. The hybrid WBT model is the most widespread in actual use.

Virtual Classroom Model

The final WBT model is a combination of all the features of the other WBT models to create a virtual classroom (Saltzberg & Polyson, 1995). This virtual classroom WBT model uses technology to create an online classroom that comes very close to duplicating what is possible when instructors and learners are physically in the same training room. Instructors and learners communicate in real time by desktop video conferencing, assignments and class notes are distributed on a Web site, interactive multimedia materials are shown as lecture supplements, and learners can discuss issues in real time chats or in asynchronous discussion forums. The virtual classroom WBT model leverages the Web for providing distance education. This model represents a stand-alone alternative to traditional training.

Selecting WBT Models

The type of model to use when creating WBT is one of the issues faced by WBT developers. When selecting from among these WBT models, developers should consider several factors. Four of the main factors to consider are development time, the audience of learners, the instructional intent, and the availability of instructors.

Development Time

If time available for development is short, then the library model and perhaps the textbook model are appropriate. The interactive instruction model and virtual classroom model are not appropriate, as these models require considerably more development time. Likewise, the library model is inexpensive to develop, while the interactive instruction model is very expensive.

Audience

The audience for the WBT also influences the decision about which model to use. If the audience has high prior knowledge about the topic and is fairly well motivated, the library model would be fine. If they were mere novices with regard to the content or were not well motivated, the library model would be less appropriate. In this case, the learners would require more "hand holding" as they completed the instruction. The interactive instruction model would be a better choice. If you desire the audience to interact as a group or complete activities as a team, a computer mediated communications model or hybrid model would be appropriate (Hedberg, Brown, & Arrighi, 1997). In this situation, the library model or textbook model would be inappropriate.

Instructional Intent

The intent of the instruction influences one's choice of WBT model. Is the instruction to convey some information, or to teach certain intellectual skills, like problem solving? The textbook model is fine for teaching information but is less appropriate for teaching problem solving. The interactive instruction model or a hybrid model are better choices for teaching problem solving. Another aspect to instructional intent is whether the WBT model will stand alone to provide all the training, or be used as a supplement to other forms of training, such as leader-led training. The interactive instructional model can function as stand-alone training, while the library model is more appropriately used as a training supplement. Depending on the completeness of content, the textbook model and hybrid model may stand alone or be used as a supplement. The virtual classroom model would suffice as stand-alone training. The CMC model is normally used as a supplement combined with another WBT model, such as the textbook model, or with printed materials.

Instructor Availability

Finally, we must consider the availability of instructors. In some models, instructors must be available for learners to interact with. For example, in the computer mediated communications model, instructors are essential. Unless instructors are available, this model canot be used.

Lesson Logic for WBT

The second major design issue a WBT developer faces is what types of content to include in the WBT and how this content should be organized. This is a key decision, for it affects how the WBT lesson will look and work. One must identify the components to include in the WBT lesson to make it instructionally sound. This is an essential difference between WBT sites and other Web sites. All Web sites provide information; WBT sites must provide instruction or training (Ritchie & Hoffman, 1997).

WBT developers must determine what components to add to their sites to ensure instructional effectiveness. In short, they develop a template for WBT lessons. This template is a "placeholder" for all the information they will include in their WBT lessons. We refer to this as the "lesson logic," for it specifies the logic, or organization and flow, within a lesson.

Creating a template for lesson logic is similar to creating a database of contacts for personal or business use. First, you design the layout, or template, of the database. This identifies what information is to be included. For example, your contacts template may include such entities as last name, first name, street address, town, telephone number, e-mail address, business affiliation, etc. Once you have the template, you can start creating the contacts by entering the necessary information. Likewise, once you have a template for your WBT lesson logic, you can begin creating the lesson content according to the template specifications.

Because the WBT models differ in how they approach instruction, the templates you develop for WBT lesson logic must be a function of the specific model selected. Obviously, the lesson logic for a library WBT model will differ considerably from that for an interactive instruction WBT model.

The lesson logic for the library model is very simple. These models include lists of links to relevant sites. The lists can be categorized and may be annotated. The textbook model can include a variety of elements: course syllabus, lecture notes, slide presentations, class comments, assignments, graphics, video clips, and practice examinations. If the textbook model includes an online training manual, the lesson logic could be the parts of each chapter in the manual. For example, the lesson could have an overview, objectives, exposition of new material, examples, summary, and related references for each major section or chapter.

The interactive instruction model has the most complex lesson logic. This could include all types of CBT software, such as drill and practice, tutorials, and simulations. There are options for elaborations on these traditional CBT categories. For example, in a simple CBT drill, the trainer presents a question, accepts the learner's response, evaluates the response, and provides feedback. A variation for drill and practice is to incorporate stronger hints after each incorrect response to assist learners. Another option is to create adaptive drills that vary the level of difficulty according to a learner's responses. This adaptive drill ensures that the learners are working at the appropriate level of difficulty and challenge.

Many lesson logics are available for tutorials. The most common form of a tutorial is to present a statement of a rule or concept, followed by an example and then a drill using the example. This is based on older behavioral ideas about learning. Cognitively based tutorials feature more flexibility and more learner control. Smith and Ragan (1993) offer cognitively based instructional strategies that could form the basis for lesson logic. They include several components, as shown in Table 1.

Gagné's instructional event model (Gagné & Medsker, 1996) or Merrill's component display theory (Merrill, 1983; Merrill, Li, & Jones, 1992) could be the basis for WBT lesson logic. Likewise, Kemp, Morrison, and Ross (1994) identify a variety of instructional events that could be the basis for lesson logic. Table 2 shows how Gagné's instructional event model could be used as the basis for WBT.

Suggestions for lesson logic can be found in military documents. In a technical report for designing an instructional design advisor, Gagné, Tennyson, and Gettman (1991) identify three

Table 1. Lesson logic components (from Smith & Ragan).

Component	Specifics
1. Activate attention	• Use graphics. • Use animation. • Use sounds.
2. Establish purpose	• State purpose. • Describe objectives in general terms.
3. Arouse interest	• Describe importance of lesson. • Describe relevance of lesson. • Show how lesson relates to their jobs.
4. Preview lesson	• Summarize the lesson. • Provide lesson outline. • Provide lesson overview.
5. Recall prior knowledge	• Provide advance organizer. • Point out what learners already know. • Review prior knowledge.
6. Process information and examples	• Define new content. • Describe new content. • Give examples. • Show graphic representations of content.
7. Focus attention	• Highlight key content. • Ask leading questions. • Point out important aspects.

Table 2. Lesson logic components (from Gagné).

Component	Specifics
1. Gain the learner's attention	• Show an image related to the lesson. • Play a sound related to the lesson. • Show short animation segment.
2. Inform the learner of the objective	• Tell learners what they will be able to do after the lesson. • Show someone demonstrating the performance.
3. Stimulate recall of prerequisite knowledge	• Remind learners of prerequisites; tell them. • Review the prerequisites; show them.
4. Present stimulus for learning	• Show images to gain attention. • Explain lesson topic. • Introduce each new content item separately by showing and describing it. • Show examples of each content item. • Show charts comparing each content item.
5. Provide guidance and prompts	• Highlight differences among content items. • Point out common features. • Focus on organization and purpose of content items.
6. Provide for practice	• Provide exercises to complete. • Have learners summarize information. • Ask questions about aspects of content items.
7. Provide feedback	• Confirm correct responses to the exercises. • Point out any errors and correct them. • Provide a sample summary to learners for comparison.
8. Assess the performance	• Score learner responses to exercises. • Score learner responses to questions. • Have learners fill out an incomplete chart and note any errors.
9. Promote transfer and retention	• Use content items as examples. • Show how basic information about a content item applies to a variety of other content items. • Review information about content items in subsequent sessions.

stages to an instructional strategy: the setup stage, the initial presentation stage, and the practice stage. The **setup stage** could include some grabber, a scenario, a verbal reminder of previously acquired knowledge, or examples of prerequisite concepts or procedures. The **initial presentation stage** could include statements of the rules or procedures to be learned, examples, a mnemonic to aid remembering the new content, discourse explaining the new content, analogies, or elaborations of the new content. The **practice stage** could include practice examples with feedback, assessment items, and opportunities for learners to apply the new content in different situations.

A common approach could allow learners to select from advance organizers, overviews, objectives, definitions of terms, descriptions of concepts, elaborations of content, examples, exercises with feedback, summaries, and criterion tests. This represents a learner control lesson logic.

While simulations are very complex to create, the underlying lesson logic is simple (Choi, 1997). Simulations present a situation to the learner, such as being the manager of a small firm that produces some product. Then the simulation describes the initial status to the learner. This includes information about number of employees, available cash, amount of the product produced, etc. The learner makes certain decisions and inputs the results. This could include how much to produce, whether to hire or fire employees, how much to spend advertising, and what price to charge for the product. The simulation then calculates the impact of these decisions and displays the results. WBT simulations can be very engaging to learners and appropriate for teaching complex skills.

Deciding which lesson logic to select is fundamentally a matter of determining what lesson components the instructor thinks will have the greatest impact on instruction. Rather than selecting a pre-existing model, the WBT developer may choose to create a new WBT lesson logic model by selecting from components of several models. When creating a lesson logic model, the emphasis must be on what components will facilitate learning.

Screen Design and Navigation

The third major design and development issue a WBT developer faces is how to design individual screens and enable navigation among screens (Henke, 1997; Jones & Okey, 1995). This involves the creation of a set of standards for screen design and for navigation. This is especially critical in WBT instruction because it is based on hypermedia principles (Yang & Moore, 1995). Without consistent screen designs and navigation, learners easily become lost, confused, and frustrated. Their attention turns away from the instructional content to trying to figure out how to move around in the Website or how to get back to where they were. In short, you have lost them as learners. With appropriate attention to design, learning can be enhanced (El-Tigi & Branch, 1997).

Because WBT is delivered over the Web, guidelines for designing Web pages usually apply as well to designing WBT. Many organizations have established standards for design of Web pages and all interface components. Several of these guidelines are very well done and can provide excellent guidance to WBT developers as they specify the design for individual screens and for navigation. See especially the guidelines published by Apple (1996), IBM (1997), Sun Microsystems (1995), and Lynch and Horton (1997).

While these guidelines offer far more specific advice than can be included here, we can draw some general rules for screen design and navigation.

Screen Design

The design of individual screens must follow a general pattern. It is neither esthetically pleasant nor instructionally helpful for each screen to have different fonts, different backgrounds, different color combinations, and different layouts. Rather, each screen should be similar in look and feel to all the other screens to form a consistent whole. To achieve this, the WBT developer must specify screen design standards before beginning to develop the WBT lessons. These standards identify the overall layout of screens; the choice, color, and sizes of fonts; the background image or color; and the navigation scheme. Each screen created for the WBT lesson will follow these standards.

Some suggestions for screen design are shown in Table 3.

Table 3. Screen design for WBT.

Category	Suggestion
Window Elements (supplied by browser)	• Menu bar (save, print, go) • Toolbar (back, forward, stop) • Location (URL of current page) • Resizable windows
Organizing Elements	• Use headers (screen title) • Have separate place for content (actual instruction) • Include navigation controls (move to specific section, page)
Text Elements	• Limit text to decrease scrolling • Use consistent fonts (one for headings, another for body) • Limit text style (few bold words, underline only links, no flashing text, little or no animated text, italics for emphasis) • Select appropriate colors to have contrast between foreground and background
Graphic Elements	• Use for conveying instruction, not just to adorn • Consider size so loading time isn't too long • Avoid unnecessary clutter of graphics

Navigation

Without careful attention to the issue of navigation in WBT, learners can easily become lost and give up. Because WBT is built on hypertext principles, learners can move around freely. With this comes the problem of learners knowing where they are, where they have been, and how to get elsewhere. Navigation must be carefully planned from the start so it becomes natural to the learners.

Navigation is more than having a button to move forward one page or back one page in a WBT lesson. This type of navigation is appropriate only for the most simple "page turner," a type of lesson we expect to avoid. Navigation should allow learners to move among major sections of the WBT lesson, selecting from among content topics and lesson logic components. Learners should be able to enter and exit at will. They should be able to see an overview, or course map, which indicates the parts of the WBT lesson.

Taken together, screen design and navigation form the look and feel of the WBT lesson. They are the important components to the human-computer interface that affect the usability of the WBT lessons (Jones & Farquhar, 1997).

Summary

Web-based training extends beyond just putting some information up on the Web. To be instructionally sound and to add training value, WBT must attend to critical WBT issues. Three critical design and development issues for WBT are: (1) which WBT model to use, (2) how to create appropriate lesson flow or logic, and (3) what guidelines for screen design and navigation to use. This chapter has examined these critical issues from the perspective of a WBT developer.

References

Apple Computer Inc. (1996). Macintosh human interface guidelines; developer.apple.com/techpubs/mac/HIGuidelines/HIGuidelines-2.html#avail1-0

Berge, Z. (1995). Facilitating computer conferencing: Recommendations from the field. *Educational Technology, 35*(6), 22–30.

Choi, W. (1997). Designing effective scenarios for computer-based instructional simulations: Classification of essential factors. *Educational Technology, 37*(5), 13–21.

Clark, R. E. (1994). Media and method. *Educational Technology Research and Development, 42*(3), 7–10.

Duchastel, P., & Spahn, S. (1996). Designs for Web-based learning; nova.edu/~duchaste/design.html

El-Tigi, M., & Branch, R. M. (1997). Designing for interaction, learner control, and feedback during Web-based learning. *Educational Technology, 37*(3), 23–29.

Gagné, R. M., & Medsker, K. L. (1996). *The conditions of learning: Training applications.* Ft. Worth, TX: Harcourt Brace & Company.

Gagné, R. M., Tennyson, R. D., & Gettman, D. J. (1991). *Designing an advanced instructional design advisor: Conceptual frameworks.* Brooks Air Force Base, TX.

Hedberg, J., Brown, C., & Arrighi, M. (1997). Interactive multimedia and Web-based learning: Similarities and differences. In B. H. Khan (Ed.) *Web-based instruction.* Englewood Cliffs: Educational Technology Publications.

Henke, H. (1997). Evaluating Web-based instructional design; scis.nova.edu/~henkeh/story1.htm

IBM (1997). Human computer interaction; ibm.com/ibm/hci/guidelines/design/principles.html

Jones, M. G., & Farquhar, J. D. (1997). User interface design for Web-based instruction. In B. H. Khan (Ed.), *Web-based instruction.* Englewood Cliffs: Educational Technology Publications.

Jones, M. G., & Okey, J. R. (1995). Interface design for computer-based learning environments; hbg.psu.edu/bsed/intro/docs/idguide/

Kemp, J. E., Morrison, G. R., & Ross, S.M. (1994). *Designing effective instruction.* New York: Macmillan.

Lynch, P., & Horton, S. (1997). Yale C/AIM Web style guide; info.med.yale.edu/caim/manual/index.html

Merrill, M. D. (1983). Component display theory. In C. M. Reigeluth (Ed.), *Instructional-design theories and models: An overview of their current status.* Hillsdale, NJ: Lawrence Erlbaum Associates.

Merrill, M. D., Li, Z., & Jones, M. K. (1992). Instructional transaction shells: Responsibilities, methods, and parameters. *Educational Technology, 32*(2), 5–26.

Richie, D. C., & Hoffman, B. (1997). Incorporating instructional design principles with the World Wide Web. In B. H. Khan (Ed.) *Web-based instruction.* Englewood Cliffs: Educational Technology Publications.

Russell, T. (1997). The "no significant difference" phenomenon; tenb.mta.ca/phenom/phenom1.html

Saltzberg, S., & Polyson, S. (1995). Distributed learning on the World Wide Web; umuc.edu/iuc/cmc96/papers/poly-p.html

Smith, P. L., & Ragan, T. J. (1993). *Instructional design.* New York: Merrill.

Sun Microsystems. (1995). Guide to Web style; sun.com/styleguide/tables/Welcome.html

Trentin, G., & Benigno, V. (1997). Multimedia conferencing in education: Methodological and organizational considerations. *Educational Technology, 37*(5), 32–38.

Welsh, T. M. (1997). An event-oriented design model for Web-based instruction. In B. H. Khan (Ed.) *Web-based instruction.* Englewood Cliffs: Educational Technology Publications.

Yang, C. S., & Moore, D. M. (1995). Designing hypermedia systems for instruction. *Journal of Educational Technology Systems, 24*(1), 3–30.

The Author

Wallace Hannum (e-mail: whannum@mindspring.com; Web homepage: soe.unc.edu/hannum) is Associate Professor of Educational Psychology at the University of North Carolina at Chapel Hill.

15

Web-Based Training Site Design Principles: A Literature Review and Synthesis

Richard H. Hall

Introduction

The purpose of this chapter is to review the existing literature relevant to Web-based training site design, with the aim of deriving general principles and specific applications useful to the Web-based training site designer. This review was specifically carried out to derive generic principles for site design, as opposed to presenting multiple models based on various learner, content, and outcome variables. It is my view that such a focus can serve an important function as a foundation and starting point. However, I certainly recognize the fact that no one set of design principles will be satisfactory for all conditions (Smith, Newman, & Parks, 1997). Further, it is important to emphasize that the World Wide Web, like all instructional and training media, is simply a means for providing effective instruction (Reeves & Reeves, 1997)

Organizational Framework

This review and the principles which emerged will be couched within the framework displayed in Figure 1. As the figure shows, the basic starting point of Website design is the page, which is fundamentally a textual and imagic display. Links make up the other basic component of the page, and it is these associative links which make the Website fundamentally different from traditional text. Further, the links are the beginning point for determining the overall structure of the Website. We must also differentiate between the self-contained site controlled and created by a given designer and the external Web, as represented by the area outside the dashed line.

Text

The most consistent single-page-text principle which emerges from the present literature is that the text presented on a given page should be limited (Cotrell & Eisenberg, 1997; DeBra, 1996; Jones & Farquhar, 1997), and that scrolling should be avoided (Shotsberger, 1996). This position is supported by most designers, and there is also evidence from traditional instruction that breaking instructional units into smaller parts can enhance learning and increase motivation (Cornell & Martin, 1997; Keller & Burkman, 1993). Breaking the text into individual pages should not consist of simply taking a large, linear page of text and breaking it into a se-

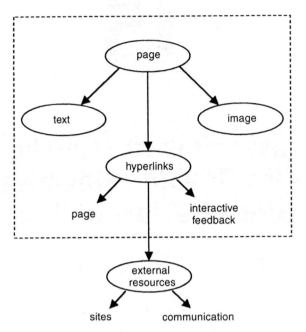

Figure 1. The basic framework.

quential series of pages (DeBra, 1996; Nielson, 1997); rather, the linking should be used to allow the learner to have more control in reading than would be the case with traditional text, although, as is discussed below, learner control can be a two-edged sword.

Not only should the text segments be small, but also, the author should write less, in general, than would be the case with traditional text (DeBra, 1996; Nielson, 1997). Reading information from a computer screen can be as much as 30 percent slower than reading from paper (DeBra, 1996; Wright & Lickorish, 1983). Although this problem can be largely overcome with greater screen resolution (DeBra, 1996), learners still report frustration with reading text from a screen (Bostock, 1997). For this reason, those presenting training materials via text should make a concerted effort to be succinct. Nielson (1997) suggests that instructional text on the computer should be about 50% as long as would be the case if the same text were presented as hard copy.

One aspect of traditional text, which should be imitated on the computer, is the shape of the traditional text page, which is taller than it is wide. For example, newspapers create multiple columns to exaggerate the short line length. Unfortunately, most computer screens are designed in the exact opposite fashion. This creates more strain on the users in the effort required to move their eyes back across long lines to the next line, and can be confusing, especially if some of the lines begin with the same words. There is research which indicates that learning is more effective with more shorter lines than with fewer long lines (Hansen & Haas, 1988). For this reason, DeBra (1996) suggests that the designer use multiple columns on the screen and/or break up the text with graphics to make the line length more manageable.

Images

The inclusion of graphics in combination with text is common practice in Web displays. There is much theoretical and research support for the notion that combining text with graphical representations can enhance learning (e.g., "contiguity theory," Mayer, 1997; Mayer & Anderson, 1991). However, there is also evidence that this potential effectiveness can be circumvented by the long download time associated with graphics in a hypermedia environment (Dennison, Seyedmonir, & Meadows, 1998). In general, Web developers are in agreement that graphics, and multimedia in general should be used only when they directly support the materials (Cotrell & Eisenberg, 1997; DeBra, 1996), when they serve a "clear instructional purpose" (Everhart, 1997). In addition to increasing download time, including too much graphical information is inconsistent with the theme developed above, that the site should consist of small instructional units.

Hyperlinks/Site Organization

Hyperlinks are the basic building blocks and determinants of the overall structure of the training Website.

Links on the Page. Just as was the case with images and other multimedia, designers are in agreement that links should be included on a page only if they serve a clear purpose (DeBra, 1996; Schneiderman & Kearsley, 1989). In one experiment, a negative correlation was found between the number of links on a page and learners' comprehension of the information contained in a site (User Interface Engineering, 1998). A second consistent suggestion is that links should be clearly labeled (Berners-Lee, 1995; DeBra, 1996; Jones & Farquhar, 1997; User Interface Engineering, 1998). This not only lets the learners make a more informed decision as to whether or not they should click on the link, but it also gives the learner more clear information about the overall organization of the site, which is an issue I will develop further below. For the same reason, the over-all layout of links on the page should have some definite organizational/structural meaning (Jones & Farquhar, 1997; Nielson, 1997).

Organizational Structure. One of the fundamental advantages of hypertext is the potential for representing complex knowledge via multiple associative links (Frick, Corry, & Bray, 1997; Reeves & Reeves, 1997). The World Wide Web certainly represents such a complex structure, in fact, an infinitely large, complex, ill-structured domain. Unfortunately, such a structure is ideal for facilitating browsing and exploring, but is not well suited for searching (Smith, Newman, & Parks, 1997). More importantly, the large amount of freedom and control that this allows the learner may be particularly detrimental for the novice learner (Large, 1996; Niemiec, Sikorski, & Walberg, 1996). In fact, there is a surprising amount of research with hypertext systems that indicates that including too much learner control can, contrary to expectations, decrease learning effectiveness (Large, 1996; Niemiec, Sikorski, & Walberg, 1996). This is not so surprising when one considers how complex—and novel—hyperspace is for the average learner. This phenomena has lead to the term "lost in hyperspace" (Burbules & Callister, 1996; Hill, 1997; Nielson & Lyngbaek, 1990). For this reason, one of the most important design principles, which is supported both by Web designer published experiences, and by research on hypertext learning environments, is that the learner should be provided with some degree of guidance (Smith, Newman, & Parks, 1997).

There are a number of ways that the Web-based-training designer can combat the "lost in hyperspace" problem and provide the learner with some guidance. The first method is to create a clear and systematic organization scheme for the learning site (DeBra, 1996; Shneiderman & Kearsley, 1989). For example, Everhart (1997) suggests that the site should be "sensible, clear, and clutter free." Such a clear organizational scheme can increase learner motivation in addition to enhancing learning (Cornell & Martin, 1997; Keller & Burkman, 1993). The usual/prototypical path through the pages should be obvious (Goldberg, 1997), and the information should be in a modular fashion within a well-structured hierarchy (Smith, Newman, & Parks, 1997; Young & Watkins, 1997).

In this same vein, the main points should be obvious to the learner (Shotsberger, 1996). In fact, a consistent theme in the literature is that some sort of advance organizer should be included in the site design so that the learner can easily get an overview of the site organization (Burbules & Callister, 1996; Cornell & Martin, 1997; Cotrell & Eisenberg, 1997; Dodge, 1995; Everhart, 1997). A clear organization also includes consistency in design across all the pages of a site (Cotrell & Eisenberg, 1997; Everhart, 1997; Shotsberger, 1996; Young & Watkins, 1997).

Although the importance of providing clear organization and learner guidance is of fundamental importance, it is also important to take advantage of the flexibility of hypertext. For this reason, Web designers—and learning theorists—have also emphasized the need for creating a flexible site design, which accommodates the more inquisitive or expert learner whose goal is to explore (Goldberg, 1997; Reeves & Reeves, 1997; Siegel & Kirkley, 1997). While this may seem to be inconsistent with the organization and guidance themes presented above, hypertext environments are flexible enough to provide guidance and flexibility simultaneously. In order to do this, the organizational structure should provide a clear route back to the starting point (Goldberg, 1997; Hardman, 1989), to allow the site "explorer" to find his or her way back. For this reason, designers emphasize that a site should not include dead ends (Young & Watkins, 1997; Shotsberger, 1996).

Internal Links. The most basic type of link is from one page in a site to another page within the same site, analogous to a self-contained hypertext environment. Such links are subject to the discussion above about site structure principles, and the pages are subject to the discussion about page design. In addition, these within-site links can include interactive activities, created using program techniques such as CGI scripts or Java Script. Such activities require that the learner respond to some type of question or exercise provided by the instructor. The learner's response can be sent to some external location (see discussion below), or the program can provide some sort of instant feedback for the learner.

Such an interactive activity constitutes one of the most powerful learning tools that Web-based-training designers have at their disposal. Such a system can be used to provide the learner with information about his or her comprehension of the material (Nichols, 1997). Such activities act to enhance metacognitive awareness and active learning, two of the most important factors in learning of all kinds (Reeves & Reeves, 1997). It is not surprising, then, that Web designers emphasize the importance of such activities (Gillani & Relan, 1997; Ritchie & Hoffman, 1996). The nature of these activities can differ a great deal, but one common theme that Web instructional designers and educational researchers advocate is the inclusion of learner centered activities (Siegel & Kirkley, 1997), which encourage the learner to actively create his or her own learning, and to relate the information to "real world" problems (National Research Council, 1996; Siegel & Kirkley, 1997).

External Resources

External sites. One genuinely unique strength of Web-based training is the potential to use the vast store of resources available on the Web (Butler, 1997). The use of external sites can serve as a powerful tool for providing a meaningful, "real world" context (Jonassen *et al.,* 1997), in that the foundational information included in the site can be linked to case examples from around the world (Jonassen *et al.,* 1997). These can be integrated into a fairly direct interactive task, in which the learner responds to specific questions or problems provided by the instructor about some external site (Hall, 1998). In contrast, the learner can also simply be directed to explore a site or group of sites, and to provide some sort of analysis, comparison, and/or synthesis (Dodge, 1995; Ritchie & Hoffman, 1996). Such exploratory activities, in which the learner is allowed to make the materials relevant to his or her own needs, can act to increase motivation (Cornell & Martin, 1997; Duchastel, 1997; Keller & Burkman, 1993). In any case, it is important to link the exploration of the site to some specific activity, to encourage the learner to actively process the information (Butler, 1997; Duchastel, 1997; Duchastel & Turcotte, 1996).

Communication. Communication activities carried out among learners on the Web also constitute one of the most powerful tools that Web-based trainers have at their disposal. First, decades of educational research point to the effectiveness of collaborative/cooperative learning (Johnson & Johnson, 1994; Slavin, 1995). In Web-based training, this is particularly important, since there is sometimes a tendency for the learner to feel isolated (Hill, 1997). The use of Web-based collaborative activities has proven to be one of the most rich and promising areas of Web-based instruction (Bonk & Reynolds, 1997; Eklund & Eklund, 1997; Harasim, 1990; Harasim, Calvert, & Groeneboer, 1997; Malikowski, 1997; Rheingold, 1995; Riel, 1990, 1993). There are some unique advantages of the Web with respect to collaborative interactions. First, these interactions can be structured and guided to a greater degree than they can in face-to-face interactions (Harasim, 1996), and providing structure in face-to-face cooperative learning is an important factor in determining its effectiveness (Hall *et al.* 1988; O'Donnell, 1996; Patterson, Dansereau, & Newborn, 1992). Second, the conversations among learners are available for the learners and instructors to view, increasing metacognitive awareness. Third, the anonymity of Web based collaboration can encourage learners who wouldn't otherwise participate to do so (McCollum, 1997).

Some important criteria have been identified that account for the effectiveness of cooperative learning via the Web. Consistent with a theme which runs through this review, the activity needs to be guided and structured (Jones & Farquhar, 1997; Jones & Okey, 1995). Just giving learners the opportunity to use e-mail will not guarantee productive interactive discussion (Sherry & Wilson, 1997). For this reason, instructors and designers have suggested that it is a good idea to require a minimum number of postings each week (Harasim, 1996; Malikowski, 1997; Paulsen, 1995). Also, learners can be assigned different roles for the completion of a group project (Bonk & Reynolds, 1997; Shotsberger, 1997). Another important factor is that the conferencing activity should be fully integrated with the class materials (Harasim, 1996).

Conclusion

A number of themes emerge from an examination of the existing literature which is relevant to Web-based training site design. One common theme is the importance of thoughtful site organization. The site designer must be careful to provide the learner with a modular environment consisting of short informational units, composed of text, directly supported by useful graphical representations, linked in a structured fashion. At the same time, the designer should take advantage of the hyperspace environment by allowing for flexibility and learner control, including interactive activities. Further, the designer should make use of the vast resources available on the Web to enrich the basic training materials with case examples. Finally, the designer should make use of the unique collaborative learning activities that are possible with the World Wide Web.

References

Berners-Lee, T. (1995). Style guide for online hypertext; w3.org/Provider/Style

Bonk, C. J., & Reynolds, T. H. (1997). Learner-centered Web instruction for higher-order thinking, teamwork, and apprenticeship. In B. H. Khan (Ed.), *Web-based instruction.* Englewood Cliffs: Educational Technology Publications.

Bostock, S. J. (1997). Designing Web-based instruction for active learning. In B. H. Khan (Ed.), *Web-based instruction*. Englewood Cliffs: Educational Technology Publications.

Burbules, N. C., & Callister, T. A. (1996). Knowledge at the crossroads: Some alternative futures of hypertext learning environments. *Educational Theory, 46,* 23–50.

Butler, B. S. (1997). Using the World Wide Web to support classroom-based education: Conclusions from a multiple-case study. In B. H. Khan (Ed.), *Web-based instruction*. Englewood Cliffs: Educational Technology Publications.

Cornell, R., & Martin, B. L. (1997). The role of motivation in Web-based instruction. In B. H. Khan (Ed.), *Web-based instruction*. Englewood Cliffs: Educational Technology Publications.

Cotrell, J., & Eisenberg, M. B. (1997). Web design for information problem-solving: Maximizing value for users. *Computers in Libraries, 17*(5), 52–57.

DeBra, P. M. (1996). *Hypermedia structures and systems.* Web Course, Eidenhoven University of Technology; wwwis.win.tue.nl/2L670/static

Dennison, R., Seyedmonir, M., & Meadows, G. (1998, April). Sequence and presentation effects of animation on learning from text. Paper presented at the annual meeting of the American Educational Research Association, San Diego, CA.

Dodge, B. (1995). Webquests: A technique for Internet-based learning. *Distance Educator, 1*(2), 10–13.

Duchastel, P. (1997). A motivational framework for Web-based instruction. In B. H. Khan (Ed.), *Web-based instruction*. Englewood Cliffs: Educational Technology Publications.

Duchastel, P., & Turcotte, S. (1996). On-line learning and teaching in an information-rich context. *Proceedings of the Ineti96 International Conference,* Montreal.

Eklund, J., & Eklund, P. (1997). Collaboration and networked technology: A case study in teaching educational computing. *Journal of Computing in Teacher Education, 13,* 14–19.

Everhart, N. (1997). Web page evaluation: Views from the field. *Technology Connection, 4*(3), 24–26.

Frick, T. W., Corry, M., & Bray, M. (1997). Preparing and managing a course Website: Understanding systematic change in education. In B. H. Khan (Ed.), *Web-based instruction*. Englewood Cliffs: Educational Technology Publications.

Gillani, B. B., & Relan, A. (1997). Incorporating interactivity and multimedia into Web-based instruction. In B. H. Khan (Ed.), *Web-based instruction,* Englewood Cliffs: Educational Technology Publications.

Goldberg, M. W. (1997). CALOS: First results from an experiment in computer-aided learning. *Proceedings of the ACM's 28th SIGCSE Technical Symposium on Computer Science Education.*

Hall, R. H. (1998, April). *A theory driven model for the Web-enhanced educational psychology class.* Paper presented at the annual meeting of the American Educational Research Association, San Diego, CA.

Hall, R. H., Rocklin, T. R., Dansereau, D. F., Skaggs, L. P., O'Donnell, A. M., Lambiotte, J. G., & Young, M. D. (1988). The role of individual differences in the cooperative learning of technical material. *Journal of Educational Psychology, 80,* 172–178.

Hansen, W. J., & Haas, C. (1988). Reading and writing with computers: A framework for explaining differences in performance. *CACM, 31,* 1080–1089.

Harasim, L. (1990). Online education: An environment for collaboration and intellectual amplification. In L. Harasim (Ed.), *Online education: Perspectives on a new environment* (pp. 39–64). New York: Praeger.

Harasim, L. (1996). Effectively using electronic conferencing; indiana.edu/ecopts/ectips.html

Harasim, L., Calvert, T., & Groeneboer, C. (1997). Virtual U: A Web-based system to support collaborative learning. In B. H. Khan (Ed.), *Web-based instruction*. Englewood Cliffs: Educational Technology Publications.

Hardman, L. (1989). Evaluating the usability of the Glasgow online hypertext. *Hypermedia, 1,* 34–63.

Hill, J. R. (1997). Distance learning environments via the World Wide Web. In B. H. Khan (Ed.), *Web-based instruction*. Englewood Cliffs: Educational Technology Publications.

Johnson, D. W., & Johnson, R. T. (1994). *Learning together and alone: Cooperative, competitive, and individualistic learning* (4th ed.). Boston: Allyn and Bacon.

Jonassen, D. H., Dyer, D., Peters, K., Robinson, T., Douglas, H., King, M., & Loughner, P. (1997). Cognitive flexibility hypertexts on the Web: Engaging learners in meaning making. In B. H. Khan (Ed.), *Web-based instruction*. Englewood Cliffs: Educational Technology Publications.

Jones, M. G., & Farquhar, J. D. (1997). User interface design for Web-based instruction. In B. H. Khan (Ed.), *Web-based instruction*. Englewood Cliffs: Educational Technology Publications.

Jones, M.G., & Okey, J.R. (1995). *Interface design for computer-based learning environments;* InTRO.html.

Keller, J., & Burkman, E. (1993). Motivation principles. In M. Fleming & W. H. Levie (Eds.), *Instructional message design: Principles from the behavioral and cognitive sciences* (pp. 3–53) (2nd ed.). Englewood Cliffs: Educational Technology Publications.

Large, A. (1996). Hypertext instructional programs and learner control: A research review. *Education for Information, 14*, 96–106.

Malikowski, S. (1997). Interacting in history's largest library: Web-based conferencing tools. In B. H. Khan (Ed.), *Web-based instruction*. Englewood Cliffs: Educational Technology Publications.

Mayer, R. E. (1997). Multimedia learning: Are we asking the right questions? *Educational Psychologist, 32*(1), 1–19.

Mayer, R. E., & Anderson, R. B. (1991). Animations need narrations: An experimental test of a dual-coding hypothesis. *Journal of Educational Psychology, 83*, 484–490.

McCollum, K. (1997). A professor divides his class in two to test value of online instruction. *The Chronicle of Higher Education, 43*(24), 23.

National Research Council. (1996). *National science education standards*. Washington, DC: National Academy Press.

Nichols, G. W. (1997). Formative evaluation of Web-based instruction. In B. H. Khan (Ed.), *Web-based instruction*. Englewood Cliffs: Educational Technology Publications.

Nielson, J. (1997). Be succinct! (writing for the Web). *Alertbox;* useit.com/alertbox/9703b.html

Nielson, J., & Lyngbaek, U. (1990). Two field studies of hypermedia usability. In C. Green & R. McAleese (Eds.), *Hypertext: Theory into practice II*. New York: Intellectual Press.

Niemiec, R. P., Sikorski, C., & Walberg, H. J. (1996). Learner-control effects: A review of reviews and a meta-analysis. *Journal of Educational Computing Research, 15*, 157–174.

O'Donnell, A. M. (1996). Effects of explicit incentives on scripted and unscripted cooperation. *Journal of Educational Psychology, 88*, 74–86.

Patterson, M. E., Dansereau, D. F., & Newborn, D. (1992). Effects of communication aids and strategies on cooperative teaching. *Journal of Educational Psychology, 84*, 453–461.

Paulsen, M. F. (1995). Moderating educational computer conferences. In Z. L. Berge & M. P. Collins (Eds.) *Computer mediated communication and the online classroom*. Cresskill, NJ: Hampton Press.

Reeves, T .C., & Reeves, P. M. (1997). Effective dimensions of interactive learning on the World Wide Web. In B. H. Khan (Ed.), *Web-based instruction*. Englewood Cliffs: Educational Technology Publications.

Rheingold, R. W. (1995). Moderating discussions in the electronic classroom. In Z. L. Berge & M. P. Collins (Eds.), *Computer mediated communication and the online classroom*. Cresskill, NJ: Hampton Press.

Riel, M. (1990). Cooperative learning across classrooms in electronic learning circles. *Instructional Science, 19*, 445–466.

Riel, M. (1993). *Global education through learning circles.* In L. Harasim, (Ed.), *Global networks.* Cambridge, MA: MIT Press.

Ritchie, D. C., & Hoffman, B. (1996, March) Using instructional design principles to amplify learning on the World Wide Web. *SITE 96 Conference;* edWeb.sdsu.edu/clrit/WWWInstrdesign/WWWInstrDesign.html

Shneiderman, B., & Kearsley, G. (1989). User interface design for the hyperties electronic encyclopedia. *Proceedings 1st ACM Conference on Hypertext,* 184–194.

Sherry, L., & Wilson, B. (1997). Transformative communication as a stimulus to Web innovations. In B. H. Khan (Ed.), *Web-based instruction.* Englewood Cliffs: Educational Technology Publications.

Shotsberger, P. G. (1996). Instructional uses of the World Wide Web: Exemplars and precautions. *Educational Technology, 36*(2), 47–50.

Shotsberger, P. G. (1997). Emerging roles for instructors and learners in the Web-based instruction classroom. In B. H. Khan (Ed.), *Web-based instruction.* Englewood Cliffs: Educational Technology Publications.

Siegel, M. A., & Kirkley, S. (1997). Moving toward the digital learning environment: The future of Web-based instruction. In B. H. Khan (Ed.), *Web-based instruction.* Englewood Cliffs: Educational Technology Publications.

Slavin, R. E. (1995). *Cooperative learning* (2nd ed.). Boston: Allyn and Bacon.

Smith, P. A., Newman, I. A., & Parks, L. M. (1997). Virtual hierarchies and virtual networks: Some lessons from hypermedia usability research applied to the World Wide Web. *Journal of Human-Computer Studies, 47,* 67–95.

User Interface Engineering. (1998). *Website usability: A designer's guide;* world.std.com/~vieweb

Wright, P., & Lickorish, A. (1983). Proof-reading texts on screen and paper. *Behavior and Information Technology, 2*(3), 227–235.

Young, F. L., & Watkins, S. E. (1997, April). *Electronic communication for educational and student organizations using the World Wide Web.* Paper presented at the annual Midwest Section Conference of the American Society for Engineering Education, Columbia, MO.

The Author

Richard H. Hall (e-mail: rhall@umr.edu; Web homepage: umr.edu/~rhall) is Associate Professor Research Associate at the Department of Psychology and the Instructional Software Development Center, University of Missouri–Rolla.

16

Developing Synchronous Web-Based Training for Adults in the Workplace

Margaret M. Driscoll

A great deal of confusion exists about Web-based training in the workplace. Managers, trainers, course developers, programmers, and subject-matter experts often talk about Web-based training as if it were a single, easy to recognize delivery medium. In reality, Web-based training can be described as four distinct delivery methods. Each type of Web-based training meets a specific educational goal and has unique educational strengths and limitations. Table 1 provides a matrix of the characteristics of the four kinds of Web-based training.

This chapter focuses primarily on the qualities of Web virtual synchronous classroom programs, because this delivery method offers benefits, tools, and strategies not available in the other Web environments. It is the most technically complex Web environment but the least understood, because potential developers have few opportunities to experience a Web virtual synchronous classroom program.

Before focusing on Web virtual synchronous classroom programs, let us examine the key distinctions among programs and the characteristics of each type.

Distinctions of Time and Learning Mode

There are two key distinctions among these programs. The first distinction is a time difference. Training on the Web takes place either synchronously (at the same time for all learners) or asynchronously (at each learner's convenience). For example, a synchronous class requires that learners and the instructor log in at an agreed upon time, such as 1:00 PM Pacific Standard Time. In contrast, an asynchronous class allows learners and the instructor to log on to examine class material and to communicate at different times of day and night.

The second distinction is the learning mode. Web-based training can be characterized as individual or group learning opportunities. Some topics are best learned by individuals working alone. For example, a bookkeeper learning to use a new spreadsheet program may engage in drill and practice, simulations, reading, and questioning and answering to learn how to create a spreadsheet template and to memorize keyboard shortcuts. Other topics, such as building supervisory skills and developing communication skills, generally are better suited to group

Table 1. Matrix of synchronous and asynchronous characteristics for four types of Web-based training.

	Types of Web-Based Training			
	Web/Computer-Based Training (W/CBT)	**Web/Electronic Performance Support Systems** (W/EPSS)	**Web/Virtual Asynchronous Classrooms** (W/VAC)	**Web/Virtual Synchronous Classrooms** (W/VSC)
PURPOSE	To provide learners with performance-based training with measurable goals and objectives.	To provide learners with practical knowledge and problem-solving skills when they are needed (just-in-time training).	To provide group learning at the learner's convenience, that is, without requiring the learner and instructor to be online together at a set time.	To provide group learning in which the learners and teacher are online together at an agreed upon time.
	Individual Learning		Group Learning	
Asynchronous	X	X	X	
Synchronous				X

Note: There are many variations of these approaches, and different approaches are often used in combination.

learning. For example, new managers may work in a group to learn how to deliver progressive discipline. Working collaboratively, managers can engage in role-plays and assess each other's delivery.

The major distinctions are synchronous vs. asynchronous meeting times and individual vs. group learning. Table 2 summarizes other differences among the four types of Web-based training.

Types of Web-Based Training

Web/Computer-Based Training (W/CBT). Web computer-based training is similar to traditional computer-based training programs; it provides individual learners with performance-based training keyed to measurable goals and objectives. This kind of learning employs drill and practice, simulations, reading, questioning, and answering as instructional strategies.

Many firms are revising existing multimedia CD-ROM programs and delivering them using the Internet. A serious drawback, however, is the limited ability of the network to relay large audio and video files.

Firms that do not have an existing inventory of courseware are creating new courses specifically designed for the Web. These programs use instructional strategies that work around bandwidth limitations and take advantage of communication tools such as e-mail. Web/computer-based training programs feature fast-loading graphics, small modules or lessons, and judicious use of multimedia features, such as sound and video. These programs do not offer complex interactions or rich multimedia elements but can be designed to be highly effective.

Table 2. Matrix of Web-based training types.

	Web-Based Training			
	Web/Computer-Based Training (W/CBT)	**Web/Electronic Performance Support System (W/EPSS)**	**Web/Virtual Asynchronous Classroom (W/VAC)**	**Web/Virtual Synchronous Classroom (W/VSC)**
Purpose	To provide learners performance-based training with measurable goals and objectives.	To provide learners practical knowledge and problem-solving skills in a just-in-time format.	To provide group learning in an asynchronous environment.	To provide collaborative learning in a real-time environment.
Types of learning	Problems that require transferring knowledge, building comprehension, and practicing application of skills.	Problems that require analysis and synthesis of elements, relationships, and organizational principles to produce solutions.	Problems that require application, analysis, synthesis, and evaluation to produce new ideas, plans, or products.	Problems that require the synthesis and evaluation of information and shared experience to produce new ideas, plans, or products.
Roles of facilitator or WBT designer	Manager of instruction: controls, predicts, directs, and assesses the learning outcomes; communicates with learner.	Organizer of content: locates, analyzes, abstracts, indexes, and classifies information into learning modules.	Facilitator of group learning: guides instruction, provides resources, evaluates outcomes, and communicates with learners.	Coordinator of learning experience: participates as a co-learner, recommends learning direction but does not determine direction or evaluate outcomes.
Relationship to learner	Contact with learner at instructor's convenience.	No direct contact with learner.	Contact with learner at instructor's convenience.	Live, real-time contact with learner.
Roles of learner	Learner takes active role in learning, practicing new behaviors; receiving feedback; and communicating with instructor.	Learner takes the initiative to direct own learning; determines the level of detail and assesses the success of instruction.	Learner is guided by facilitator as an individual or as a member of a group; participates in instructional activities, and receives feedback.	Learner is an active participant in a collaborative learning process with facilitator and peers; participates in dialog, and reflects on experience.
Methods/ Interactions	Drill and practice, simulations, reading, questioning, and answering.	Problem-solving, scientific method, experiential method, project method.	Experiential tasks, group discussions, team projects, self-directed learning, discovery method.	Dialog and discussions; problem-solving, and maximum interaction.
	Multimedia, hypertext, hypermedia, simulations, application exercises, e-mail, listserv, and bulletin-boards, communication with instructor.	Multimedia, hypertext, hypermedia, bulletin-boards, notes conferences, modules of Web-CBT, and e-mail access to facilitator and peers.	Multimedia, hypertext, hypermedia, bulletin-boards, notes conferences, modules of Web-CBT, and e-mail access to facilitator and peers.	Synchronous audio- and video-conferencing, shared whiteboards, shared applications.

Note: There are many variations of these approaches, and different approaches are often used in combination.

Web/Electronic Performance Support Systems (W/EPSS). Web/electronic performance support systems are high-tech job aids that provide individual learners with practical knowledge and problem-solving skills in a just-in-time format. This kind of learning employs problem solving, scientific method, experiential method, and project method and other instructional strategies to help learners solve immediate problems.

Using W/EPSS, a learner can find a Web page that provides step-by-step instructions for tasks as varied as completing a travel expense form or replacing a computer board. W/EPSS applications offer several advantages over paper-based job aids. The most obvious is that they are available worldwide. For example, an employee replacing a computer board at a customer site anywhere in the U.S. can log on to the Internet and call up the appropriate W/EPSS pages. Using hypertext and hypermedia, a W/EPSS page can be linked to more detailed information in repair manuals and engineering schematics or to short video clips demonstrating replacement procedures. Updates and revision control are also advantages of Web-based W/EPSS applications. Corporations can communicate changes to field personnel quickly by updating a single Web page or by replacing obsolete information uniformly, worldwide.

Web/Virtual Asynchronous Classrooms (W/VAC). Web/virtual asynchronous classroom programs mimic real classrooms. These are educational programs that bring students and teacher together at different times (asynchronously) to achieve a learning goal. Web virtual asynchronous classroom programs blends a variety of Web technologies, such as hypermedia, hypertext documents, online quizzes, modules of multimedia, notes conferences, and e-mail to create a learning experience. The program's design and the hardware limitations of the learners' systems largely determine the complexity and sophistication of the program.

Asynchronous virtual classroom programs are distinguished by their reliance on communication tools. Layering a variety of communication tools enables peer-to-peer learning, group learning, and student-facilitator coaching. As a result of so much communication and a shared goal, the geographically dispersed class forms a sense of community complete with norms for acceptable communications, interactions, and relationships outside of the virtual classroom.

Web/Virtual Synchronous Classrooms (W/VSC). Web/virtual synchronous classroom programs also mimic real classrooms. These are educational programs that bring students and teacher together at the same times (synchronously) to achieve a learning goal. This kind of learning employs live presentation of information, dialog, discussions, problem solving, brain storming, and other live interactive activities.

Synchronous classroom tools include whiteboards, application sharing, videoconferencing, audioconferencing, and/or chat rooms. Whiteboards are like chalkboards for the computer. The entire class can see the board and take turns writing on it. Application sharing is similar to whiteboards but more structured. Using a shared application such as a spreadsheet, learners work as a group to fill in cells, correct formulas, or modify column labels. Web-based videoconferencing and audioconferencing are conceptually similar to traditional room-based conferencing systems. Both allow students to interact in real time and to hear and/or see the instructor and class members. Chat rooms are a structured way for learners to carry on a dialog by typing comments in a running online discussion.

These tools allow learners from around the country or around the world to come together and learn in real-time. There are logistical and technical challenges to creating synchronous classrooms. Issues regarding setting a meeting time to accommodate the different time zones and addressing the limitations of network speeds for conferencing applications and other features raise special design considerations.

Each of type of Web-based training offers unique benefits and limitations related to educational objectives, technical infrastructure, and the roles of learners and facilitators. The remainder of this chapter examines the unique qualities of Web virtual synchronous classroom programs.

Benefits and Limitations of Web/Virtual Synchronous Classrooms

If you are considering a live, instructor-led program, it is important to weigh the benefits and limitations of Web/virtual synchronous classroom programs. In some cases, it may be appropriate to deliver an entire program using this medium, while in other cases, it may be more appropriate for a specific purpose, such as pre-class work, supplemental lessons, update training, or refresher training.

Benefits. The opportunities for live group learning and the immediacy of feedback are unique strengths of Web/virtual synchronous classroom programs. The ability to bring a group of learners together for discussions, brainstorming, case study analysis, debates, and project work in real time is only possible in this form of Web-based training. Unlike the other forms of Web-based training, W/VSC programs allow immediate feedback on ideas, extension of suggestions, and building of consensus. As a result of real-time interaction, students' responses reveal tone and personality, creating a greater sense of presence than other forms of Web-based training. Learners in W/VSC programs become part of a community complete with norms and netiquiette.

The just-in-time delivery capabilities of W/VSC are ideal for delivering skills and knowledge for which learners can not wait. Using tools such as Web-based audio conferencing, videoconferencing, and application sharing, corporations can deliver programs without long development cycles. For example, a software company can quickly provide sales representatives with the skills and knowledge needed to sell a new product. Using application sharing and live two-way audio, the company can demonstrate new software features and present subject-matter-experts to answer questions. Application sharing makes it possible to cost effectively demonstrate beta versions of software and to make scarce subject matter experts available worldwide. The asynchronous nature of other types of programs requires greater development efforts to anticipate learner needs, plan software demonstrations, and capture subject matter experts' knowledge.

The range of tools available in W/VSC programs makes complex topics manageable. Complex topics can be explained directly, using tools such as whiteboards, application sharing, text-chat, shared multipoint-audio, videoconferencing, video clips, text, images, animation, polling, and quizzing. These tools allow instructors and learners to illustrate their ideas and to take the class in unanticipated directions. For example, an instructor teaching a class of network engineers about routing may discover that many of the learners lack basic skills. The instructor can digress to review Internet protocol basics using a whiteboard and visit a Website that provides animated demonstrations of important concepts. Once all the learners have the prerequisite skills, the instructor can launch network configuration software and demonstrate routing options. While observing how the configuration software works, the instructor can ask learners to anticipate the effects of various routing decisions. Learners can respond to questions using polling tools such as yes/no buttons and real-time multi-point audio that allows the learner to talk to the instructor. In this environment, the tools are rich enough to allow the instructor to teach topics that are unexpected. The multimedia nature of W/VSC tools also makes it possible to examine complex topics using live audio, whiteboard drawings, application demonstrations, and videoconferencing.

The simplicity of the classroom metaphor is a benefit of Web virtual synchronous classroom programs. This form of Web-based training is most like a real classroom where learners and the instructor gather at the same time to share a learning experience. Unlike other types of Web-based training that rely on learners to be self-directed and motivated to log on and work alone, the virtual synchronous classroom provides a structured meeting time, and the support and encouragement of live peers. For example, busy store grocery managers who want to learn how to hire part-time help will take time out of their day to participate. The live, real-time class can not be put off indefinitely; learners are motivated to log on to be with peers.

Limitations. Limitations in Web/virtual synchronous classroom programs can be classified as educational, logistical, and technical. The educational limitations are the flip side of the virtual synchronous classroom's advantages. *Programs designed for individual learning and programs that employ passive instructional strategies do not work well in the virtual synchronous classroom.* There is little value in bringing learners together to work as individuals. Using passive strategies such as reading and drill and practice exercises are also of little value in this environment. The effectiveness of this technology is limited to instructional strategies that build on the synergy of group interaction.

Logistics can be a major limitation for organizations that want to offer programs to learners working in different time zones. For example, a class starting at 2:00 PM Pacific Standard Time in California would require those students in New York to log on at 5:00 PM Eastern Standard Time. Time zone difference can become an even greater issue when there are learners in Europe and Asia.

Web/virtual synchronous classroom programs require powerful networks and servers, multimedia computers, layers of software, and substantial technical support. Many of the software tools that enable W/VSC programs require powerful servers to host the programs and substantial bandwidth to accommodate video, audio, and application sharing. In addition, the computers used by learners may require sound cards, microphones, and color monitors. Because the software required to participate in a W/VSC is layered upon network software, browsers, and operating system software, substantial technical support may be required to install and troubleshoot programs.

Tools for the Synchronous Web Environment

Tools or software for the Web/virtual synchronous environment can be divided into eight basic functions (see Table 3) that are unique to the synchronous environment.* These tools can be used alone, in bundled software packages, and with other technologies such as the telephone or broadcast television.

The functions listed in Table 3 are general categories and the lines between them are sometimes hard to distinguish. For the purpose of this discussion, these tools have been presented in general terms, despite unique technical differences from vendor to vendor.

Before selecting a tool or tools to create a Web virtual synchronous classroom program, it is recommended that one participate in a training program using that tool. Try more than one vendor's version of a tool. For example, enroll in several classes that use Internet relay chat (IRC). Experience IRC software from commercial vendors and makers of shareware. Determine if the IRC technology will be easy or difficult for your learners.

---

*Many of the asynchronous tools (i.e., text, graphics, animation, video, images, hypertext, and hypermedia) also work in the synchronous environment but they are not the focus of this chapter.

Table 3. Eight basic functions unique to the synchronous environment.

Tool	Description
Application sharing	The ability to launch, view, and interact with a software program on the instructor's or student's desktop.
	For example, an instructor can launch a spreadsheet program from his or her desktop and ask learners at remote locations to take turns entering formulas in cells.
Whiteboards	The ability to bring up a blank screen, similar to a blank chalkboard, and invite a learner to draw on it while others watch.
	For example, an instructor could ask a learner to diagram the steps in the accounts payable process. A second student could then be asked to draw a line through the redundant steps and then circle the bottlenecks in the process.
Polling/Quizzing	The ability to ask yes/no questions and/or give multiple-choice quizzes during class that result in immediate feedback for the instructor and students.
	For example, an instructor can explain the difference between *synchronous* and *asynchronous, and* get immediate feedback on how well the concepts were understood by giving a short quiz. If the quiz results show that most students did not understand the difference, the instructor can spend more time reviewing the concept.
Guided Web Exploration	The ability to lead learners on a tour of Internet sites.
	For example, an instructor providing new hire training to sales representative may take the learners on a guided Web exploration. The exploration will familiarize them with the company's Web site and the resources available to sales representatives in the field.
Internet Relay Chat (IRC)	The ability to conduct a conversation among a group of learners by typing back and forth.
	For example, a group of human resource managers studying flexible benefit packages may be asked to discuss the advantages and disadvantages of cafeteria benefit plans.
Audioconferencing	The ability to conduct a live, multi-point, audio-based conversation with graphics.
	For example, a group of physicians learning about the benefits and side effects of a new drug would be able to discuss their results and ask questions of the researchers and developers from the pharmaceutical company.

(continued)

Table 3. Eight basic functions unique to the synchronous environment *(continued).*

Tool	Description
Videoconferencing	The ability to conduct a live one-way or multi-point conference in which the facilitator and learners can see and hear each other.
	For example, a large retailer is about to roll out new checkout stations with adjustable keyboards and scanners. Using videoconferencing, the company is able to show associates how to adjust the stations and take advantage of the ergonomics features designed to reduce back strain and carpal tunnel syndrome. Associates can ask questions of the facilitator and request more information on reducing workplace injuries.
Eventware	The ability to broadcast a program using graphics and live, one-way audio to learners, who are able to type questions and comments back to the instructor.
	For example, a program designed to introduce field service engineers to a new policy for improving response time to key customers could features images and live audio. The live audio may feature the V.P. of Services explaining the program and graphics that include maps of key metropolitan areas, text slides listing the exempt areas, and a photograph of the new service center. Service engineers would be invited to type in questions for the V.P. to answer live during the broadcast.

Separate Tools vs. Bundled Packages

The tools described above can be obtained as either separate software programs or as "bundled" software packages containing two or more of the tools. In addition to coming in a variety of combinations, the tools also span a continuum of functionality. Some tools offer bare-bones features and limited ability to customize the functions. Other tools offer deluxe features and the ability to customize the look and feel of the interface and the ability to determine instructors' and learners' level of control. Each tool and package has system specifications (e.g., hardware required, supported browser versions) that must be examined to determine if the tool or package is compatible with your systems.

Commercial vendors, university departments, shareware makers, freeware makers, and professional organizations produce tools. Because the list of tools is constantly changing and growing this chapter will not attempt to identify any tools. The most current list of tools can be found by searching combinations of the terms shown below using such Web portals as AltaVista, Yahoo, or Excite:

- forum

- Web-based training tools

- synchronous learning

- Web-based instruction

- Web videoconference

- real-time training

- live, instructor-led training

- eventware

- live audio

- Web videoconferencing

The tool(s) or package chosen for use on a Web virtual synchronous classroom program will determine what kind of strategies are possible. If one chooses a package with full videoconferencing and application sharing, he or she will have more options for instructional strategies than a separate tool for conducting class via Internet relay chat (IRC). Match the tool to the job to be done.

Strategies for the
Synchronous Web Environment

Many of the benefits of Web virtual synchronous classroom programs are related to high levels of interactivity. Interactivity is described by Moore and Kearsley (1996) as being distinguished by three types of interaction: learner-to-content interaction, learner-to-instructor interaction, and learner-to-learner interaction. Web virtual synchronous classroom programs offer new tools and instructional strategies. Table 4 provides an overview of the strategies and the types of interaction they employ.

Learner-to-content interactions are situations in which the student is involved with course materials. Listening to lectures, reading texts, solving problem, and viewing a video are examples of learner-content interactions. These kinds of interactions are most effectively done in an asynchronous environment where learners can access content at their convenience and complete it at their own pace.

Learner-to-instructor interactions are situation in which the student and teacher are engaged in communication. Feedback on assignments, questioning and answering, providing motivation, and gathering polling data are examples of learner-instructor interactions. These interactions are unique in the synchronous environment because they are done in real-time. The use of live-audio and live-video provides interactions that have immediacy. Training in the workplace is focused on problem-centered learning and helping learners quickly fill gaps in skills and knowledge. The W/VSC provides a means of quickly addressing learners' needs.

Learner-to-learner interactions are situations in which students work together to master new skills and knowledge. Synchronous classrooms are well suited for collaborative instructional strategies that foster peer-to-peer learning. Debates, case studies, problem solving, Delphi method exercises, brainstorming, and project work are excellent examples of learner-learner interactions.

How these instructional strategies are implemented depends on the tools or software packages used to deliver the training. For example, brainstorming can be done using an internet relay chat tool that allows learners to type back and forth, or it can be done using a software package that includes live multi-point audio and a shared whiteboard. Both solutions allow students to work in real-time to generate and capture ideas for analysis at a later point in the class.

Table 4. Strategies for the W/VSC environment.

STRATEGIES	Learner-to-Content	Learner-to-Instructor	Learner-to-Learner
		Interactions	
Debate			x
Case study analysis			x
Dialog/question & answer		x	x
Polling		x	x
Lecture	x		
Quizzing		x	
Problem solving	x		x
Application sharing		x	x
Brainstorming			x
Delphi method			x
Project work		x	x
Visual demonstration/presentation		x	x
Panel presentation		x	

Table 5. Summary of options.

	Asynchronous		Synchronous
	Individual	Group	Group
Web/Computer Based Training (W/CBT) *To provide learners performance-based training with measurable goals and objectives.*	X		
Web/Electronic Performance Support Systems (W/EPSS) *To provide learners practical knowledge and problem-solving skills when they are needed (just-in-time training).*	X		
Web/Virtual Asynchronous Classrooms (W/VAC) *To provide group learning at the learners' convenience, that is, without requiring the learners and instructor to be online together at a set time.*		X	
Web/Virtual Synchronous Classrooms (W/VSC) *To provide group learning in which the learners and teacher are online together at an agreed-upon time.*			X

Summary

Web-based training is flexible and robust delivery method for organizations seeking an online learning solution. Table 5 summarizes the options for asynchronous and synchronous learning. Consider the purpose of your program and the teaching strategies.

If your training program can benefit from just-in-time learning, immediate feedback, and robust tools to teach complex topics, then consider a Web virtual synchronous classroom program. Determine which W/VSC tools you need to accomplish your objective and assess the benefits and limitations of each. Be prepared to make trade-offs as you select tools and/or packages that work with your system specifications and within your price range.

References

Brookfield, S. D. (1991). *Understanding and facilitating adult learning: A comprehensive analysis of principles and effective practices.* San Francisco: Jossey-Bass.

Dede, C. (1996). Emerging technologies in distance education for business. *Journal of Education for Business, 71*(4), 197–204.

Driscoll, M. M. (1997). Defining Internet-based and Web-based training. *Performance and Instruction, 36*(4), 5–9.

Driscoll, M. M. (1997). Collaborative learning strategies for WBT. *Technical Training, 8*(8), 20–25.

Driscoll, M. M., & Alexander, L. (1998). *Web-based training: Using technology to design adult learning experiences.* San Francisco: Jossey-Bass.

Eastmond, D. V. (1995). *Alone but together: Adult distance study through computer conferencing.* Cresskill, NJ: Hampton Press.

Galbraith, M. W. (Ed.). (1991). *Adult learning methods: A guide for effective instruction.* Malabar, FL: Krieger Publishing Company.

Hall, B. (1997). *Web-based training cookbook.* New York: John Wiley & Sons.

Hannafin, M. J., & Peck, K. L. (1988). *The design, development, and evaluation of instructional software.* New York: Macmillan.

Harasim, L., Hiltz, S., Teles, L., & Turoff, M. (1995). *Learning networks.* Cambridge: MIT Press.

Harasim, L. (1993). Collaborating in cyberspace: Using computer-mediated conferences as a group learning environment. *Interactive Learning Environments, 3*(2), 119–130.

Henry, J. (1994). *Teaching through projects* (Open and Distance Learning Series). London: Kogan Page.

Hiltz, S. R. (1994). *The virtual classroom: Learning without limits via computer networks.* Norwood, NJ: Ablex Publications.

Moore, M. G., & Kearsley, G. (1996). *Distance education: A systems view.* Belmont, CA: Wadsworth.

Resnick, M., & Kafai, Y. (Eds.). (1996). *Constructionism in practice: Designing, thinking, and learning in a digital world.* Hillsdale, NJ: Lawrence Erlbaum Associates.

Rossman, M. H., & Rossman, M. E. (Eds.). (1995). *Facilitating distance education.* San Francisco: Jossey-Bass.

Wilkes, C. W., & Burnham, B. R. (1991). Adult learner motivations and electronic distance education. *The American Journal of Distance Education, 5*(1), 43–50.

The Author

Margaret M. Driscoll (e-mail: margaret.driscoll@umb.edu; Web homepage: 3phased.com) is Director of the Instructional Design Program, University of Massachusetts at Boston. She is the author, with Larry Alexander, of *Web-based training: Using technology to design adult learning experiences,* from Jossey-Bass.

17

Web-Based Instructional Methods for Corporate Training Curricula

Pamela D. Loughner, Douglas M. Harvey and William D. Milheim

Introduction

The instructional use of the Internet and intranets by corporations is expected to increase dramatically. In the next few years, a large number of training professionals will make decisions about whether a segment or an entire course is suited for delivery via an internal or external Web. Two important challenges in this area are: (1) knowing when and where to apply new learning technologies and (2) integrating new learning technologies with existing technologies. In this chapter, we provide a framework for identifying Web-based instructional methods suited for organizations' training curricula. This is accomplished by pairing Web-based technologies with instructional methods currently in use by corporate trainers.

Instructional Methods

Instructional methods can be defined as the procedures selected by trainers and instructional designers to help facilitate learning. To understand the various options for delivering a course or a segment of a course via Web-based training, it is important to first understand how learning is currently facilitated in a corporate setting. Described below are eight instructional methods often used in corporate training today.

Case Studies: A case study is a narrative description of a situation in which learners are asked to identify or solve a problem. While the case study may describe either a real or hypothetical situation, it must be pertinent to the learning experience (Rothwell & Kazanas, 1992).

Demonstrations: In a demonstration, the instructor shows the trainee how a task is performed through actual performance. Some examples of how demonstrations are used include teaching procedures, illustrating principles (why something works), teaching equipment operation (how something works), and setting standards for workmanship (Tracey, 1984).

Discussions/Debates: Discussion involves the exchange of ideas and feelings among learners and/or the instructor. Discussions can be used with small or large groups and at various stages of the instructional process (Heinich, Molenda, Russell, & Smaldino, 1996). Discussions are a popular method among corporate trainers, since adult learners particularly enjoy sharing personal experiences. Debates, a subset of discussions, force learners to select a position on an issue and develop an argument to defend that position.

Games: In a game, the learners follow a prescribed set of rules to try to attain a challenging goal. A game may involve one learner or a group of learners in the experience (Heinich *et al.,* 1996).

Presentations: In a presentation, the instructor presents facts, concepts, and principles; explores a problem; or explains relationships. This method is used primarily to transfer information from the trainer to the trainees, who participate in a presentation mainly as listeners (Tracey, 1984).

Role plays: A role play is a dramatic representation of a real situation that provides learners the opportunity to practice situations they face or will face on the job (Rothwell & Kazanas, 1992). This method is often used in instructor-led training to provide trainees with the opportunity to practice interacting with others.

Simulations: Simulations place the learner in a scaled down version of a real-life situation. They allow the learner to practice in a safe environment without the expense or risks that would be incurred in real life (Heinich *et al.,* 1996). Simulations can be computer-based or classroom-based.

Tutorials: A tutorial can be in the form of a computer-based lesson, printed instructional materials, or a personal tutor (Heinich *et al.,* 1996). Tutorials are designed to present the learner with new information and guide the learner through the use of the information. A typical flow in a tutorial lesson includes information presentation, question and response, judgment of response, feedback or remediation, and closing (Alessi & Trollip, 1991).

Web-Based Technologies

As training professionals decide how to transition to the Web, they have a host of technologies from which they can choose, beginning with the earliest use of the Internet, to the most technologically advanced capabilities. As with traditional training methods, Web-based technologies can be used in conjunction with other methods and media in the delivery of a training program. Each of these potential technologies is described below, in increasing order of technological sophistication.

Asynchronous Text Communication (e-mail, listservs, newsgroups): E-mail, listservs, and newsgroups are examples of asynchronous text communication. In this type of communication, trainers and trainees send and receive messages at different times. For example, a trainee may send a question to the trainer in the morning, and the trainer may respond to the question later in the day. While perhaps the least sophisticated of the Web-based technologies, there are advantages to communicating asynchronously. To begin with, trainers' and trainees' schedules need not be in synch; they can participate in the training program at different times. Asynchronous communication also allows trainees and trainers more time to formulate thoughtful questions, responses, and comments.

Synchronous Text Communication (chats): Synchronous text communication, also known as chatting, allows the sending of messages in real time. This technology allows for a discussion to take place at the same time among trainees and trainers connected via the World Wide Web. Since synchronous text communication more closely resembles a classroom discussion, exchanges among trainees are more spontaneous and less controlled.

Web Pages (HTML): Web pages are the cornerstone of the World Wide Web. A Web page typically consists of text and graphics (similar to what might appear on a written page), with a collection of Web pages being called a Website. Through the use of HTML, or HyperText

Markup Language, visitors to a Web page can click on specific text or images to gain access to other Web pages and files. As with other computer-based training programs, trainees can progress through the training at their own pace. Hypertext links may also be created to other Web sites external to the training program.

Web-Based Media Delivery (video/audio clips): Web pages can also be designed to deliver video and/or audio clips on a desktop or laptop computer, building upon the features of basic Web pages consisting of text and graphics.

Web-Based Interactive Multimedia: Web-based training can also be delivered as interactive computer-based training (CBT) modules (Fritz, 1997). They may be self-contained CBT programs which have been programmed to run directly through Web pages or as downloaded programs which execute on the trainee's desktop.

Web-Based Conferencing (groupware, synchronous video/audio): Taking the synchronous text communication technology to a higher level, Web-based conferencing allows text as well as other forms of communication to be exchanged among individuals. Groupware supports the sharing of documents and data (e.g., spreadsheets or software programs) so that several individuals in different locations can work with them at the same time. Synchronous audio and video enable individuals to see and hear one another, in a manner similar to audio and video conferencing systems. While this technology requires more computing power and technical support than other Web-based delivery methods, it most closely simulates trainers and trainees working together in the same classroom.

Table 1 identifies existing Web-based technologies that can be used to support the training methods described above. Types of training often delivered via each training method are also identified.

Examples

Provided below are several examples of different training methods delivered via the Web. Every attempt was made to provide examples of various types of training as well as different Web-based technologies. One example of Web-based training is provided for each of the eight training methods identified above.

Case Studies Using Web Pages: An example of a case study delivered through text and graphics Web pages is available on the Web (users.erols.com/robertwb/enzyme/ethics/ethics.htm). Such Websites provide a context for concepts and theories that might otherwise seem abstract. The case studies are presented in a text-based narrative format with review questions. Instructionally, case studies provide examples, generate discussion, and encourage higher-order thinking. Other examples where this method might be used include management development training, customer service training, and enabling skills training, among others.

Demonstrations Using Web-Based Interactive Multimedia: An example of a demonstration delivered through Web-based interactive multimedia is available on the Web (hhmi.org/grants/lectures/multimedia/). At this Website, The Howard Hughes Medical Institute's Virtual Lab, the trainee assumes the role of lab technician and is guided through a procedure to run tests for a chronic disease. Through the use of interactive animation, the trainee is prompted to click on various supplies (e.g., gloves and vials) that he or she will need to complete various steps of the procedure. Demonstrations can also be developed using less sophisticated Web-based technologies. For example, Web pages using text and graphics could be designed to prompt the trainee through a procedure, or audio and or video clips could be incorporated into a Web page to demonstrate a procedure. Demonstrations can be used in virtually every type of training (e.g., customer service, professional skills, sales and dealer), whenever the trainer shows the trainee how to do something or how something works.

Table 1. Training methods achieved with Web-based technologies.

This training method . . .	. . . can be achieved with these Web-based technologies . . .	. . . to deliver these types of training
Case Studies	Asynchronous Text Communication Web Pages Web-Based Media Delivery	Professional Skills Management/Supervisory Compliance/Regulatory Customer Service Sales and Dealer Enabling Skills
Demonstrations	Web Pages Web-Based Media Delivery Web-Based Interactive Multimedia Web-Based Conferencing	Technical Skills Professional Skills Computer Applications Management/Supervisory Compliance/Regulatory Customer Service Sales and Dealer Enabling Skills
Discussions/Debates	Asynchronous Text Communication Synchronous Text Communication Web-Based Conferencing	Professional Skills Management/Supervisory Customer Service Sales and Dealer Enabling Skills
Games	Web-Based Interactive Multimedia	Management/Supervisory Customer Service Sales and Dealer Enabling Skills
Presentations	Web Pages Web-Based Media Delivery Web-Based Conferencing	Technical Skills Professional Skills Computer Applications Management/Supervisory Compliance/Regulatory Customer Service Sales and Dealer Enabling Skills
Role Plays	Asynchronous Text Communication Synchronous Text Communication Web-Based Interactive Multimedia Web-Based Conferencing	Professional Skills Management/Supervisory Customer Service Sales and Dealer Enabling Skills
Simulations	Web-Based Interactive Multimedia	Technical Skills Professional Skills Management Supervisory Customer Service Sales and Dealer Enabling Skills
Tutorials	Web Pages Web-Based Media Delivery Web-Based Interactive Multimedia	Technical Skills Professional Skills Computer Applications Management/Supervisory Compliance/Regulatory Customer Service Sales and Dealer Enabling Skills

Discussions/Debates Using Asynchronous Text Communication: An example of training that uses Asynchronous Text Communication to generate discussions among trainers and trainees is available on the Web (apcoint1.org/institute/virtual/classes/demo/). This demonstration course was developed to provide training on public safety for personnel who take emergency phone calls, and uses a bulletin board approach for discussion. Trainers post assignments, trainees can ask questions, and the trainer and/or other trainees can post responses and comments via a moderated electronic discussion board. This simple, but effective, Web-based technology allows trainees to participate in the training session when their schedules permit. Discussions can also be held synchronously (at the same time) using other types of Web-based methods (e.g., synchronous text communication or Web-based conferencing). Discussions are an essential element of corporate training programs, not only because theyinvolve the learner, but also because they provide a forum through which trainees can learn from one another.

Games Using Web-Based Interactive Multimedia: An example of a training game delivered through Web-based interactive multimedia can be viewed on the Web (tej.com) (Hall, 1997). At this site, a game developed by Tobin, Erdmann, and Jacobsen for Motorola helps teach trainees Motorola manufacturing concepts and asks trainees to develop a water system for a simulated town. The object of the game is to design a system which provides water to all the town residents while showing a profit for the company. Games are an engaging way to allow trainees to learn important concepts and ideas and can be used for many different types of training.

Presentations Using Web-Based Media Delivery: An example of a presentation delivered through Web-based media delivery is available on the Web (training.dialog.com/). At this Website, audio is combined with a series of slides to deliver "quick tips" from experts. Presentations on the Web can take many forms, ranging from sharing text-based documents with trainees, to distributing audio and or video clips of the trainer, to actual videoconferencing over the Internet. Presentations are a popular instructional method, and generally allow for some interaction between trainer and trainee. It is suggested, therefore, that a communication link such as e-mail be established between the trainer and trainees.

Role-plays Using Web-Based Interactive Multimedia: An example of a role-play created through Web-based interactive multimedia can be viewed on the Web (macromedia.com/learning/examples/online_examples/training/). In this simulated air traffic control situation, a trainee is asked to assume the role of a radar operator. Given various scenarios, the trainee must provide the correct answers to avert problems and insure safe travel of various aircraft. Although no direct examples were found, role-plays can also be achieved through other Web-based technologies. Trainees can be asked to assume different roles and communicate with one another through synchronous, asynchronous, and conferencing technologies in the same way they would in a typical classroom.

Simulations Using Web-Based Interactive Multimedia: An example of a simulation delivered via Web-based interactive multimedia can be found on the Web (medicus.marshall.edu/medicus.htm). The Interactive Patient provides a simulated environment for those studying medicine to practice their diagnostic skills. At this site, a case is presented which allows students to request X-rays and run other tests so they can diagnosis the patient and prescribe a treatment. The learner e-mails the diagnosis and treatment to the instructor, who provides feedback. Simulated environments like The Interactive Patient immerses trainees in a realistic but scaled-down version of the actual workplace. These environments allow trainees to learn by doing and learn through their mistakes in a safe environment.

Tutorials Using Web Pages: An illustration of a tutorial delivered through Web pages is available on the Web (mce.be/wbt/demo/). At the Management Centre Europe Website, a sample module on financial ratios can be viewed. In this module, trainees read the information provided on the Web pages, and engage in calculation activities to apply what they have learned. Because tutorials are used to present and guide trainees on the use of new information (by asking questions and providing feedback) they can be adapted for nearly any training content. Also, while this example shows how tutorials can be delivered through Web-based pages using graphics and interactive forms, tutorials can also be *designed* using Web pages with graphics, sound and video, and interactive multimedia.

Conclusion

The goal of this chapter is to provide training professionals with a basic framework that they can reference as they begin investigating Web-based training methods. As Web-based training technologies continue to evolve, training professionals will likely develop new ways to combine instructional methods with these technologies.

References

Alessi, S., & Trollip, S. (1991). *Computer-based instruction: Methods and development.* Englewood Cliffs: Prentice-Hall.

Bassi, L., & Cheney, S. (1997). Benchmarking the best. *Training & Development, 51*(11), 60–64.

Bassi, L., Cheney, S., & Van Buren, M. (1997). Training industry trends 1997. *Training & Development, 51*(11), 46–59.

Fritz, M. (1997). Is Web-based training new hype in old wineskins? *Emedia Professional, 10*(6), 69–71.

Hall, B. (1997). *Web-based training cookbook.* New York: John Wiley & Sons.

Heinich, R., Molenda, M., Russell, J., & Smaldino, S. (1996). *Instructional media and technologies for learning.* Upper Saddle River, NJ: Prentice-Hall.

HRD executives forecast tremendous growth of learning technologies. (1997, November/December). *ASTD National Report on Human Resources, 3.*

Rothwell, W., & Kazanas, H. C. (1992). *Mastering the instructional design process.* San Francisco: Jossey-Bass.

Tracey, W. (1984). *Designing training and development systems.* New York: AMACOM.

The Authors

Pamela D. Loughner (e-mail: PDL110@psu.edu; Web homepage: personal.psu.edu/PDL110/) is a consultant in the design of training programs for business and industry and a doctoral candidate at Pennsylvania State University, University Park. **Douglas M. Harvey** (e-mail: harveyd@loki.stockton.edu; Web homepage: stockton.edu/~harveyd) is Assistant Professor of Instructional Technology at Richard Stockton College of New Jersey. **William D. Milheim** (e-mail: wdm2@psu.edu; Web homepage: personal.psu.edu/wdm2/) is Associate Professor of Education at Penn State Great Valley, Malvern, Pennsylvania.

18

Developing Web-Based Training for a Global Corporate Community

Judy Cossel Rice,

Miles Day Coleman,

Vincent E. Shrader,

Joanne P. Hall, Sharon A. Gibb,

and Reo H. McBride

Introduction

Instructional designers need to be aware that there are both cultural and individual differences which create obstacles to learning efficiency. A culture's general values, learning expectations, and verbal, nonverbal, and visual communication rules plus technology attitudes and access all influence the ways in which members of the culture interpret instruction (Reeves, 1997). Additionally, individual learning styles and modality preferences, physical needs, and personal values also affect the way learning occurs. This chapter discusses these differences, explains why they need to be addressed when designing Web-based training, and recommends strategies for creating universally accessible materials. Figure 1 illustrates how the perception of training materials is influenced by the interaction of cultural and individual factors.

The Assimilation Gap

The worth of a company is no longer determined simply by the monetary value of its inventory and holdings, but also by the knowledge-base of its employees (Sharp, 1998). The crucial job skills today are knowing how to learn and how to access information. We have gone from the industrial revolution, in which our principal resource was energy, to the knowledge revolution, in which our principal resource is information (Jones, 1998). With this information age comes an enormous need to maintain workers' skills so that they can use the plethora of ever more powerful information accessing and processing tools. Hodgins (1996) refers to the "assimilation gap" as the disparity between the rate at which new technology and tools are introduced and the rate at which users can assimilate them.

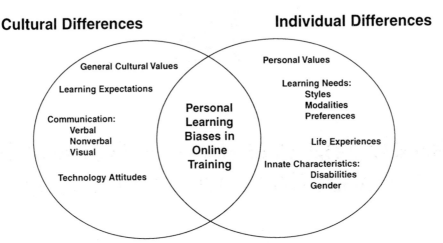

Figure 1. Personal learning biases in online training. All instruction must pass through this bias filter as it is processed by the brain. Instruction can create obstacles when it violates basic cultural and individual expectations.

Organizations dedicate an enormous amount of resources to overcome this gap. Corporations can no longer separate training from work; instead, it is an integral part of the work day. Companies, attempting to integrate the two activities, seek ways for employees to be trained in their own work space and at their own pace. Companies increasingly use their own intranets to provide this type of training (Hill Associates, 1998). The Web is a major medium for intranet-distributed training materials. The advantages of using the Web are fourfold: cost, time to market, time to distribute, and ease of revision. Organizations need to be aware, however, that while it is easy to create materials and place them on intranets or extranets for electronic distribution, it is not as easy to create *appropriate* training for all the employees those distribution networks will reach.

An obstacle to creating appropriate training is the fact that many corporations have a culturally and ethnically diverse workforce. Training developed in one country or for one group cannot simply be distributed to another. International trainers have long been aware of the need to avoid the "one shoe fits all" approach to instruction. They realize that to avoid cultural clashes and training failure, they need to customize their presentations (Harris & Moran, 1989). Addressing these issues will lead to better instruction and contribute to people becoming better, more efficient learners.

The Need to Develop a Culturally Pluralistic Approach to Training

Two forces drive the need for businesses to address diversity issues: (1) the globalization of corporations, and (2) the resulting diversity within the highly trained pool of workers. This global corporate community requires that workers form cooperative cross-cultural relationships. In addition, the U. S. work force has become more diverse as more skilled people immigrate and as assistive technology devices enable individuals with disabilities to be employed in mainstream jobs (Branch, 1997). Organizations face lost revenue when they fail to respond to problems of cross-cultural interactions (Slate, 1993). When Coca-Cola first introduced its beverage into China, the name was rendered in Chinese characters just as it sounds. Thousands of signs later, Coke discovered that the characters meant "bite the wax tadpole" or "female horse stuffed with wax," depending on the dialect (Ott, 1997). Occurrences such as this underscore the necessity for eliminating an ethnocentric mentality when participating in a global economy and for developing sensitivity to cultural differences.

Cultural sensitivity, however, is not merely awareness of cultural differences. It is a perspective, an attitude, that acknowledges and appreciates cultural diversity and accepts the fact that norms, roles, rules, values, attitudes, and expectations vary across cultures. This acceptance of the uniqueness of people and their culture is a key competency for cross-cultural trainers (Casse, 1981). Failure of such acceptance will result in poorly-trained employees and the loss of the firm's competitive edge. Training needs to respect the unique values inherent in different cultures (Reeves, 1997) and allow the trainees to learn in their own way without encountering offensive materials.

Problems Designing for Diverse Users

There are seven problems designers face when developing Web-based training for a global corporate community. These range from basic cultural and learning differences to individual and technology differences.

Basic Cultural Differences

The way individuals interact with training materials is partly influenced by their culture. Peoples' basic concepts of time, the amount of information they want to know about the world, their need for personal space, tolerance for ambiguity, attitude toward authority, perception of gender roles, and their ability to work collectively are all influenced by their culture. These culturally biased orientations can have a substantial impact on the outcome of any training program (Thiederman, 1988) and, if not addressed, can present insurmountable barriers to student learning. Table 1 presents general cultural differences affecting learning.

Learning Differences

Cultures vary in how they view learning atmosphere, interpersonal transactions, classroom structure, learner attitude, and learning activities (Powell, 1997). Students from different cultures react differently to both positive and negative feedback, competition, authority figures, and gender differences (Thiagarajan, 1988). Trainees bring these preconceived notions as to what constitutes learning and what is expected of them to the online instructional environment. It is easy to assume that since all cultures school their children, there would be no culturally-based educational differences. However, there are major differences, and failure to appreciate them leads to confused and frustrated learners. Table 2 presents some of the major educational differences affecting learning.

Verbal Communication Differences

Verbal communication refers to both spoken and written language, not only the words, but the nuances of words as well. Hall (1959) said, "I am convinced that much of our difficulty with people of other countries stems from the fact that so little is known about cross-cultural communication. Because of this lack, much of the good will and great effort of the nation has been wasted" (p. 7). There is an increasing amount of cross-cultural communication occurring today as the Internet provides an efficient means of connecting the world. As a result, people are more aware of communication difficulties as they are more personally involved in attempts to resolve miscommunications. Cross-cultural language issues are formidable challenges to information managers (Gollnick & Chin, 1986).

Table 1. General cultural differences affecting learning.

Time	*Monochronic time:* the view that time is linear, tangible, and divisible; preference for having things sequentially ordered with events occurring one at a time. Students prefer to finish one assignment before moving on to the next; task completion takes precedence over interpersonal relationships.
	Polychronic time: "the simultaneous occurrence of many things and by a great involvement with people" (Hall, 1990, p. 14); interpersonal relationships take precedence over task completion.
Context	How much information a person can comfortably manage. People in high context cultures are widely read and informed on many topics, whereas individuals in low context cultures tend not to be well informed on subjects outside of their own interests. Trainers may assume background information to be implicit in high context cultures but provide it explicitly in low ones. (Hall, 1990)
Space	How much personal space or territory an individual requires to be comfortable. Individuals from high space cultures tend to prefer assigned seats/desks, their own training materials, and less crowded meeting rooms. (Hall, 1990)
Uncertainty Avoidance	How comfortable people feel towards ambiguity. People with low tolerance will need explicit directions and clearly defined objectives. (Hofstede, 1980)
Power Distance	How well people accept hierarchical power structure. People with a low tolerance expect egalitarian structure and are uncomfortable with being addressed and treated as subordinates. (Hofstede & Bond, 1988)
Masculinity-Femininity	A culture's perceptions of gender roles. Masculine oriented cultures have rigid gender roles, while feminine cultures are more flexible in role expectations. Men in masculine cultures would be less tolerant of women leading training or women in positions of authority. (Hofstede, 1980)
Individualism-Collectivism	The willingness of individuals to work alone or in groups. A culture high in individualism would be uncomfortable with collaborative assignments. (Hofstede, 1980)

Rome (1980) concluded that language itself presents the most obvious obstacle for foreign technical training. Differences in writing conventions (style, format, content, and organization) between instructional designers and their audience can also often lead to miscommunication (Boiarsky, 1995). Developers will soon be able to incorporate more multimedia into their instruction as technology and bandwidth improves and as such they will need to consider verbal communication concepts as well as textual ones. To be truly effective, instructional designers must adapt their materials to both cultural and linguistic conventions (Hites, 1996).

Gudykunst (1994) presents five cultural and linguistic skills (mindfulness of others, tolerance of ambiguity, empathy, adaptability, and the ability to predict) that help reduce uncertainty and anxiety, both of which impede effective communication. Additionally, Table 3 provides Hites' (1996) recommendations for instructional designers to follow when designing and developing instruction across cultures.

Table 2. Some educational differences affecting learning.

Setting	• Classroom environment: decoration, furnishings • Location: classroom, home setting, outdoors • Personal space: closeness to other students and teacher • Defined and assigned areas: flexible or controlled spaces • Teacher characteristics: gender, age, marital status, involvement with students, accountability
Structure	• Noise level: amount of discussion and turn-taking rules • Spontaneity: flexibility versus strict lesson plans • Locus of control: teacher, student, or fate controls outcomes • Time concept: promptness, use of time, task, or time controlled class • Paradigm: constructivist, instructivist • Discipline: rational, natural consequences, capital • Rewards: verbal praise, intrinsic, grades, promotion
Learner attitudes	• Reverence for learning: sacred privilege, mandated by law or parents, priority assigned to education • Respect for teachers: permission to disagree, behaviors and rituals demonstrating respect
Learning activities	• Experience with collaborative activities • Preference for memorization: • Skill with problem solving activities • Amount of creativity encouraged or permitted
Learning style	• Concrete experiential • Reflective observational • Abstract conceptual • Active experimentation • Personal meaning: Why is it important? • Concepts and content: What are the facts? • Transferable application: How can it be used? • Integration of creation: What are the possibilities? • Field dependent • Field independent
Learning modality	• Auditory: learning by hearing • Visual: learning by seeing • Tactile: learning by feeling/touching • Kinetic: learning by doing

Nonverbal Communication Differences

Nonverbal communication refers to communication which transcends spoken or written language. Proxemics, physical appearance or characteristics, physical movements, paralanguage, touching behaviors, artifacts, and environment all communicate meaning (Knapp, 1978). Nonverbal communication emphasizes, complements, contradicts, regulates, or substitutes for verbal communication. People generally attribute intentionality and perception to nonverbal communications: They assume the message was meant to be sent, and that it is received and properly understood. Cross-communication or offense occurs when one person presumes intention or when a person assumes meaning is understood when, in fact, the other person is unaware of a message being sent or attributes a different meaning to it. Nonverbal

Table 3. Recommendations for cross-cultural verbal communication (from Hites, 1996).

1. Keep language simple and active. Abstract words can lead to difficulty in grasping ideas and in translating terminology.
2. Use consistent terminology rather than a variety of terms to refer to the same thing.
3. Reduce or totally avoid the use of jargon, idioms, and acronyms.
4. Define terms and provide glossaries.
5. Use relevant, specific examples familiar to the audience. A European would more easily understand the length of a meter than a yard.
6. Reiterate concepts in different ways. Using redundancy can overcome problems of weak translation.
7. Review and frequently summarize materials.
8. Provide translated summaries in student's native language.
9. Practice frequently in small chunks.
10. Check comprehension frequently by written exercises and student explanations of concepts and skills.
11. Use multimedia. Using multimedia to deliver the message through multiple senses can be an extremely effective way to reduce misunderstandings. Video is helpful to supplement the written material with animation, motion, and sound.
12. Allow students to work at their own pace (with asynchronous online help).
13. Allow more time than in non cross-cultural situations and provide frequent breaks in the instruction.
14. Develop and field test instruction and instruments with representatives of the cultures for which the material is written.
15. Encourage questions.
16. Use a variety of evaluation methods.

elements are incorporated into training materials as hand gestures and facial expressions on icons and graphics or in multimedia materials. Instructional designers need to be aware of potential misinterpretations these may present.

Visual Communication Differences

Language is not the only communication-related concern. We frequently use visual elements to convey meaning: directional placement, icons, graphics, color and white space. These visual elements generally do not transfer across cultures. For example, navigational images and text grouping intended to indicate the directional flow of information may confuse those whose native tongue is not English. Asian languages are traditionally written vertically, and their readers read from right to left. Thus, a directional arrow placed at the bottom right and pointing right for the next page may be counter intuitive to them (Slemp, 1998). Likewise, placing "important information" in the top right-hand section of a page may not be recognized by people in other cultures as a cognitive organizer.

Similar problems occur when using icons to convey meaning. Horton (1994) recommends thoroughly testing any icon before using it in training materials and avoiding icons represented by human anatomy altogether. Gorny (1997) identified many icons which cause problems internationally. A sample of problematic icons can be found in Table 4.

Table 4. Icons that don't transfer the meaning Americans might think.

Door handles	In many countries, round door knobs are very unusual. In continental Europe, door handles are long levers.
Folders	In many countries, folders do not look like the folders used as sub-directory icons. In Germany, the more common folder is designed like a ring book.
Rolodex	Practically unknown in Europe.
Animals	Owls are seen as wise birds in the U.S., but as brutal and stupid in Asia. Dogs symbolize loyalty or search and retrieve in the U.S., but are food in Asia. Pigs are used to represent a bank in the U.S., but are unclean and unholy to devout Muslims and Jews. Rabbits may be seen as symbols of ability to reproduce quickly in the U.S., but as food in Germany and vermin in Australia. (Horton, 1994)
Yearly Calendar Layout	One month is displayed as a matrix. In Germany the rows are the weekdays, the weeks are the columns. In the U.S.A. and Britain, it is the opposite.
Facial Expressions and Gestures	Expressions are heavily dependant on one's cultural background. "Some cultures forbid images of the human face or form . . ." An eye might be interpreted as "the evil eye." Foot prints may be offensive in the Orient as the underside of the foot is seen as crude and unprofessional, and hand gestures may be crude or obscene (Horton, 1994).

It is impossible to generalize the use of color across cultures. Color preferences, while heavily influenced by cultural norms, can still remain intensely personal. Table 5 is a small sampling of the potential difficulties in using colors to represent mood or meaning. Horton (1994) encourages designers to create icons first in black and white to ensure the intended meaning is not color dependent. Another strategy is to use a monochromatic color scheme when selecting pleasing color combinations. A sensitive designer is selective when using color to speed search, aid recognition, show organization, rate or qualify, or to create a pleasing design.

Individual Differences

Even within a given culture there is a range of individual variations created by preferences, religion, and innate differences such as gender and disabilities. It is not realistic for people to expect training materials to accommodate every preference. It is realistic, however, to expect materials to accommodate religion, gender and impairments. Religiously offensive and gender-biased materials can be identified by conducting user testing.

Similarly, individuals with impairments need to participate in the formative evaluation process. People with disabilities cannot access some Web pages because of the nature of their impairment. Sight, mobility, and auditory and cognitive limitations each present unique access barriers. Additionally, some assistive technology devices and specialized Web browsers are incapable of displaying common HTML features such as tables and frames. While assistive technology providers address these limitations, they still remain an issue when designing effective instruction. If designers are aware of these difficulties and take steps to address the design challenges presented by each, they can create universally accessible training materials. Table 6 presents design recommendations for creating materials for special populations.

Table 5. A representation of the complexity of color associations across cultures.

Red	• In Korea red is not used in the name of those who are alive. Red is only used in the names of those who have passed away. • Red and yellow are worn at weddings in most parts of India. • Chinese and Taiwanese use red for weddings and New Year. • Red generally represents danger in Western European cultures.
White	• White is the color of mourning in most parts of India. • The Chinese use white for funerals. • In Japan white is used for weddings and funerals. • Western cultures use white for purity and virtue.
Yellow	• In some parts of India, yellow, not black, is used for mourning. • Red and yellow are worn at weddings in most parts of India. • Yellow represents honor or royalty in China (Horton, 1994). • Yellow may symbolize either grace and nobility or childishness or gaiety in Japan (Horton, 1994). • Yellow is used to warn or caution and to symbolize cowardice in Western Europe.
Blue	• In the U.S.A., blue may mean tranquility, honor, masculinity, or authority (Horton, 1994). • Japan associates authority, virtue, truth, and villainy with blue.
Black	• In the U.S.A., black is associated with death, sin, gloom, dignity, and class.
Primary Colors	• Primary colors are preferred over earth tones in Saudi Arabia. • In the U.S.A., primary colors are often considered childlike or garish.

Technology Differences

Designers need to be aware of the technology difference among those who use their training materials. These differences include users' prior experience and the culture's and individual's attitudes about technology (O'Malley, 1995). Companies committed to Web-based training need to provide each potential trainee with a computer and network connection adequate to deliver the instruction without undue frustration. People's attitudes about technology can be positively changed as they see how the technology can be used as an effective and reliable tool for their job. Many user anxieties can be overcome with proper time to practice and gain confidence in accessing these media.

Recommendations

As a result of our study, four recommendations provide a framework for Web-based training in a global corporate community:

1. Use culturally diverse design teams. Drawing members from diverse groups not only enables the team to detect unacceptable elements in each person's own culture, but also allows all members of the team to become aware of their own prejudices, beliefs and preferences as they see where problems occur (Reeves, 1997). Understanding ethnocentricity begins with introspection. As team members recognizes their own biases, they will be better able to develop culturally sensitive materials. The design team's values determine the nature of the instructional materials as well as the learning activities (Powell, 1997). Branch (1997) states that the goal is

Table 6. Designing for special populations.

General Guidelines:	• use consistent/predictable layout • keep navigation minimally deep (number of clicks to access info) • provide site map and search feature • provide summaries at the top of the document with anchors to target subsections • use functional, descriptive, but concise anchors • avoid forms—if you must use them, provide an alternative for of submission, i.e., telephone number, e-mail • use full-text dating convention • avoid browser-specific tags
Mobility Impairments:	• provide large buttons • avoid using embedded links in text; alternately, use lists • use client-side image maps only and provide text alternative • avoid links requiring precise mouse control to select
Auditory Impairments:	• provide alternate anchor with descriptive text for videos • create captioned videos
Cognitive Impairments—Dyslexia:	• use controlled vocabulary • design graphics to illustrate concepts • utilize multimedia presentations
Cognition—Spatial organization:	• keep pages simple and consistent • use white space to clearly define units • provide uniform buttons to navigate
Cognition—Memory:	• use visual memory cues and metaphors to aid navigation • use consistent layout

not to develop culturally neutral instruction, but rather to create "learning environments that are enriched by the unique values that are inherent in different cultures" (p. 30).

2. Follow good design practices. Developers need to conduct frequent formative evaluations and a thorough assessment of the target audience (Kincaid & Horner, 1997). They can conduct virtual focus groups and virtual one-on-one online evaluations (Nichols, 1995). Users can fill out online questionnaires as another valuable way to test usability. Evaluators can track trainees' paths through the instruction by reviewing the server's user logs.

3. Create a three-tier intranet. A three-tier intranet consists of a client (the employee's computer), a Web server, and a database server. This structure allows for data to be inserted into HTML documents as needed rather than authoring each document individually.

4. Customize instructional components. Masie (1997) advocates designing for portability by breaking the instruction into small units. Designers can create the units and have a databank of culture-specific support components, such as color preferences, multimedia, exercises, examples, and metaphors, along with the culture profiles and impaired population guidelines. Users can be identified when they access the Web server and their identity and inquiry can be passed along to the database server. The database server can return information and user preferences back to the Web server. Style sheets can then layout HTML pages that conform to the user's requirements in much the same way as word processors are able to merge a form letter

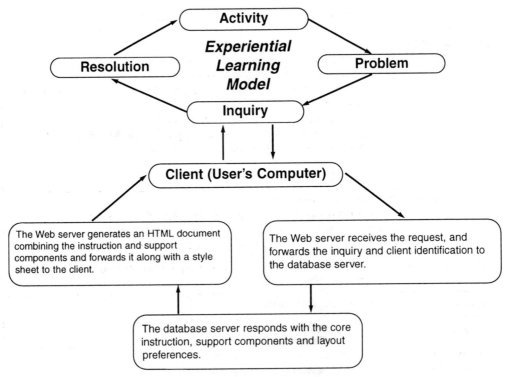

Figure 2. Customizing instruction.

with a database and produced individualized correspondence. Future Web technology may provide a means for an agent to communicate a complete individual learning profile to a server. Figure 2 illustrates how customized instruction can be delivered using a such a structure.

Conclusion

While we cannot presently deliver perfect instruction that will overcome every difference, we can deliver acceptable instruction. We can strive to become aware of the cultural and individual differences among people. Just as people tend to forgive the *faux pas* of trainers if they are perceived as not being arrogant, insensitive, and overbearingly ethnocentric (Copeland, 1985), we can suppose they will be equally tolerant of Web-based training if it is evident that the designers tried to avoid these same errors.

We invite the reader to visit our Web site (byu.edu/ipt/rice/papers/global.html) for additional charts, checklists, sample style sheets and Java code, and further discussion of the issues involved with ensuring universal access to Web sites.

References

Boiarsky, C. (1995). The relationship between cultural and rhetorical conventions: Engaging in international communication. *Technical Communication Quarterly, 4*(3).

Branch, R. M. (1997). Educational technology frameworks that facilitate culturally pluralistic instruction. *Educational Technology, 37*(2) 38–40.

Casse, P. (1981). *Training for the cross-cultural mind: A handbook for cross-cultural trainers and consultants.* Washington, DC: SETAR.

Copeland L. (1985). Training Americans to do business overseas. *Training, 22*(7), 22–23.

DO-IT: Disabilities, Opportunities, Internetworking & Technology. (1996). DO-IT HTML Guidelines; weber.u.washington.edu/~doit/Other/design.html

DO-IT: Disabilities, Opportunities, Internetworking & Technology. (1996). Universal design of World Wide Web Pages; weber.u.washington.edu/~doit/Brochers/universal.design.html

Fontaine, P. (1995). Writing accessible HTML documents; yuri.org/webable htmlcode.html

Gollnick, D. M., & Chin, P. C. (1986). *Multicultural education in a pluristic society* (2nd ed.). Columbus, OH: Charles Merrill Publishing Co.

Gorny, P. (1997, July 20). Discussion on culturally influenced user interfaces and color combinations in other cultures; e-mail: ist_students@indiana.edu

Gudykunst, W. B. (1994). *Bridging differences: Effective intergroup communication.* Thousand Oaks, CA: Sage Publications.

Hall, E.T. (1959). *The silent language.* Garden City, NY: Anchor Press/Doubleday.

Hall, E.T. (1990). *Understanding cultural differences.* Yarmouth, ME: Intercultural Press.

Harris, P., & Moran, R. (1989). *Managing cultural difference: High-performance strategies for today's global manager.* Houston: Gulf Publishing Company.

Hill Assoc. (1998). Fortune 500 survey; hill.com/press_releases/survey/

Hites, J. M. (1996). Design and delivery of training for international trainees: A case study. *Performance Improvement Quarterly, 9*(2), 57–74.

Hodgins, W. (1996). Quoted by Eric Skjel. Seeking a new kind of P&L. *Inside Track;* webgate.autodesk. com/solution/edu/ebd/fall96/ebdf9610.htm

Hodgins, W. (1998). Interview by Elliot Masie. *TechLearn 98 Live,* April 1, 1998, broadcast from Seattle, Washington.

Hofstede, G. (1980). Cultural differences in teaching and learning. *International Journal of Intercultural Relations,10,* 301–320.

Hofstede, G., & Bond, M. H. (1988). Confucius and economic growth: New trends in culture's consequences. *Organizational Dynamics, 16*(4), 4–21.

Horton, W. (1994). *The icon book: Visual symbols for computer systems and documentation.* New York: John Wiley & Sons.

Jones, G. R. (1998). *Cyberschools: An education renaissance* (4th ed.). Englewood, CO: Jones Digital Century.

Kincaid, T. M., & Horner, E. R. (1997). Designing, developing, and implementing diversity training: Guidelines for practitioners. *Educational Technology. 37*(2) 19–26.

Knapp, M. L. (1978). *Nonverbal communication in human interaction.* New York: Holt, Rinehart, and Winston.

Masie, E. (1997, May). Advice for designer of online learning—think small. *Technology for Learning.*

Masie, E. (1998). The bubble of concentration. *TechLearn Trends #32;* techlearn.com/trends/trends32. htm

National Center for Accessible Media (NCAM). (1999). Captioning and audio description on the Web; boston.com/wgbh/pages/ncam/captionedmovies.html

Nichols, G. (1995). Formative evaluation of Web-based training; acs.ucalgary.ca/~gwnichol/formeval/ formeval.html

Nielson, J. (1996). Accessible design for users with disabilities; eu.sun.com/columns/alertbox/9610.html

O'Malley, C. (1995). Designing computer support for collaborative learning. In C. O'Malley (Ed.), *Computer supported collaborative learning* (pp. 283–297). Berlin: Springer-Verlag.

Ott, L. (1997). "Bite the wax tadpole" and other translation boo-boos; stc.org/region2/pit/www/bpencil/vol34/01_sep/bitewax.htm

Powell, G. C. (1997). On being a culturally sensitive instructional designer and educator. *Educational Technology, 37*(2), 6–14.

Reeves, T. C. (1997). An evaluator looks at cultural diversity. *Educational Technology, 37*(2), 27–30.

Rome, D. (1980). International training: What is it? *The Bridge, 6*(1), 23–24.

Sharp J. (1998). Interview by Elliot Masie. *TechLearn 98 Live,* April 1, 1998, broadcast from Seattle, Washington.

Slate, E. (1993). Success depends on and understanding of cultural differences. *HR Focus, 70*(10), 16–17.

Slemp, C. (1998, February 18). Discussion on culturally influenced user interfaces and color combinations in other cultures; ist_students@indiana.edu

Starling Access. (1997). Accessible Web page design; igs.net/~starling/acc/

Thiagarajan, S. (1988). Performance technology in multicultural environments. *Performance & Instruction, 27*(7), 14–16.

Thiederman, S. (1988). Training foreigners. *Training & Development Journal, 42*(11), 81–84.

The Authors

Judy Cossel Rice (e-mail: Judy_Rice@byu.edu; Web homepage: byu.edu/ipt/rice/) is an Information Architect in the Instructional Psychology and Technology Department, Brigham Young University, Provo, Utah. **Miles Day Coleman** (e-mail: miles.coleman@ac.com; Web homepage: ac.com) is an Instructional Developer in Practice Innovation and Enablement with Andersen Consulting, St. Charles, Illinois. **Vincent E. Shrader** (e-mail: shraderv@ed.byu.edu; Web homepage: byu.edu/ipt/alumni/shraderv.html) is Instructional Designer at the Western Governors University, Provo, Utah. **Joanne P. Hall** (e-mail: ruttanj@ed.byu.edu; Web homepage: mse.byu.edu/ipt/students/ruttan/) is a Graduate Instructor in Instructional Psychology and Technology at Brigham Young University. **Sharon A. Gibb** (e-mail: Sharon_Gibb@byu.edu; Web homepage: byu.edu/edlf/people/faculty/gibb.html) is a Professor in Education Leadership and Foundations at Brigham Young University. **Reo H. McBride** (e-mail: reo.mcbride@hct.ac.ae; Web homepage: mse.byu.edu/ipt/students/mcbride/speedwagon/index.html) is an Instructor in Higher Colleges of Technology, Dubai, and a student at Brigham Young University.

19

Accommodating People with Disabilities in Web-Based Training Programs

Alan Cantor

Introduction

Access to the wealth of information on the World Wide Web for people with disabilities may be hindered—or entirely prevented—if their needs are not considered. To ensure that Web-based training programs are accessible to people with disabilities, curriculum planners and instructors need to be familiar with the range of technologies and techniques that enable people with disabilities to use Web resources. Similarly, people who create Web pages should have a basic understanding of the principles of universal Web page design—an approach to designing and coding sites that considers the needs of *all* users.

This chapter introduces educators and trainers to practical ways to accommodate people with disabilities in Web-based training programs. The chapter defines disability and outlines the various kinds of functional limitations and their effects on an individual's ability to use a computer; describes a variety of adaptive technologies and techniques that people with disabilities use to access computers and the Web; recommends common sense strategies for educators and trainers to make their Web-based programs more accessible to students with disabilities; and summarizes the principles of universal Web page design.

A Primer on Disability

What Is Disability?

Some individuals, due to accident, illness, or heredity, have difficulties performing—or cannot perform—certain tasks, such as moving their legs, seeing, hearing, talking, grasping, or lifting. When these functional limitations are severe enough to adversely affect a person's performance, and the natural and human environments fail to accommodate these functional limitations, the individual is said to have a *disability*.

Barriers

People with disabilities face *barriers* that prevent them from realizing their full potential. Barriers may be physical, architectural, cultural, political, informational, or attitudinal.

For people with disabilities in computer-based training programs, barriers frequently are due to poor planning or design. For example, most operating systems and software applications include poorly-designed features that compromise usability for people with certain disabilities; cyberspace is increasingly multimedia, and this characteristic works to the advantage of people with disabilities who might not otherwise be able to perceive everything on a site. However, if Web designers provide information in only one format, e.g., images without accompanying text, or optimize a site for one particular browser, some people may be unable to access all important information; access barriers result when Web designers do not consider all intended users. Making an accessible site is a matter of adhering to simple design principles.

Functional limitations

In addition to the barriers posed by poor design and planning, a person's functional limitations may make it physically hard to operate a keyboard or mouse, read a monitor or printout, or use other peripheral devices. Consider the functional limitations associated with seven different kinds of disability, and the effects of these limitations on an individual's ability to operate a computer:

Visual impairments. Visual impairments range from slightly reduced visual acuity to total blindness. A person with reduced visual acuity may have trouble reading the screen or distinguishing foreground text from background pattern on a Web page. People with more severe impairments rely on technologies that translate displayed text into synthesized speech, audible cues, or Braille.

Hearing impairments. Hearing impairments include problems distinguishing certain frequencies, sounds, or words, ringing in the ears, and total deafness. A computer user who is hard of hearing or deaf may miss audible prompts, or not hear music and speech that are conveyed through the PC loudspeakers.

Mobility impairments. Mobility impairments include minor difficulties moving or coordinating a part of the body, muscle weakness, tremors, and in extreme cases, paralysis in one or more parts of the body. Mobility impairments can be congenital, such as muscular dystrophy; or acquired, such as tendonitis. Computer users who have upper-body mobility impairments may be unable to manipulate a mouse, press two keys on the keyboard simultaneously, or reach certain areas of a keyboard. Others may tend to hit several keys at once, or press keys inadvertently.

Cognitive impairments. Cognitive disabilities affect an individual's ability to think and reason. They are caused by genetic factors (e.g., Down's syndrome), exposure to environmental toxins (as in fetal alcohol syndrome), brain trauma, and psychiatric conditions. Cognitive impairments include memory loss, perceptual difficulties, and inability to concentrate. A person whose memory has been adversely affected by, say, a head injury, may be unable to recall the function of an icon or the menu on which a frequently-used command appears.

Learning disabilities. People with learning disabilities may have average or above-average intelligence, but the ways they take in information, retain it, and express knowledge are affected. Learning disabilities affect reading comprehension, spelling, the mechanics of writing, manual dexterity, math computation, problem solving, processing speed, and the ability to organize space and manage time. Students in Web-based training programs who have learning disabilities may have trouble reading or understanding printed materials, picking out pertinent information on a busy computer screen, or using a keyboard or mouse.

Seizure disorders. People with certain kinds of epilepsy may have seizures when exposed to a monitor that refreshes or a cursor that flashes at particular frequencies, or to sounds that repeat at certain rates.

Speech impairments. Speech difficulties do not usually affect one's ability to use a computer. In the future, speech impairments might affect computer use if voice input technologies become more usable, or if telephone and PC applications become fully integrated.

Accommodations for People with Disabilities

Accommodations are bridges for overcoming design flaws in the environment and individual functional limitations. *Accommodation* is the process of modifying the environment to meet the needs of individuals who have difficulties performing tasks that many (perhaps most) other people can do. Accommodation involves removing or minimizing the adverse effects of barriers in the natural and human environments. These barriers prevent individuals with disabilities from achieving personal, educational, vocational, and recreational goals.

There are many ways to accommodate an individual in the home, workplace, library or classroom, including low-tech devices, spatial reorganization, work station modifications, and building modifications (see Cantor, 1996, 1998a). In computer-based training programs, most accommodations are likely to involve adaptive hardware and software.

Adaptive Technologies for Computer-Based Training Programs

Thousands of hardware and software products are available that allow people to overcome design flaws in the environment and their functional limitations. Adaptive technologies fall into two broad categories: input devices and techniques, and output hardware and software.

Input devices and techniques

- *Modified keyboards.* Miniature and enlarged keyboards; on-screen keyboards operated by switches, eye blinks, puff-and-sip devices, or a mouse; adjustable and split keyboards.

- *Mouse alternatives.* Touch pads, track balls, and graphic tablets.

- *Mouse emulators.* Software that modifies the keyboard so that the numeric keypad (or other keys) can be used to move and click the mouse.

- *Keyboard-only techniques.* Methods for operating a PC using keyboard shortcuts and equivalents instead of a mouse.

- *Speech recognition systems.* Software and hardware for entering text or issuing commands by voice.

- *Keyboard and mouse utilities.* Software for adjusting the sensitivity and behavior of the keyboard or mouse.

- *Word prediction and word completion software.* Keystroke-saving programs that generate a list of words (or expressions) in response to typing one or more letters. For example, typing "wo" displays a menu that includes "word," "word prediction," "work," and "would." The user selects the desired item from the menu by pressing a key or clicking the mouse.

- *Abbreviation expansion software.* Programs that instantly translate pre-defined codes into words or expressions. For example, typing "AES" yields "Abbreviation Expansion Software."

- *Macro software.* Programs that record a series of commands or keystrokes, and replay them by pressing a key or clicking the mouse.

Output hardware and software

- *Display properties utilities.* Software that alters the size, color, and contrast of information on the screen.

- *Text-to-speech systems.* Hardware and software that convert information displayed on the monitor into synthesized speech.

- *Text-to-Braille systems.* Hardware and software that convert information displayed on the monitor to Braille, either through a special printer or a refreshable display.

- *Visual warning utilities.* Software that converts auditory prompts into visual cues.

Each person's accommodation needs are unique, and the variations, even among people having similar functional limitations, are great. The most reliable way to determine an individual's accommodation needs is to ask. Assume that the person with a disability is the expert on his or her accommodation requirements.

Ideas for Curriculum Designers and Instructors

Common Sense Strategies

Although it is not possible to anticipate individual accommodation needs, there are many ways for curriculum designers and instructors to make their training programs generally more accessible:

Choose computers that can house adaptive technologies

- Get big tower cases for computers. A computer with room to add (or replace) a sound card, video card, or other peripheral can house a wider range of adaptive technologies.

Choose peripherals with an eye to enhancing accessibility

- Use 17-inch (or larger) monitors. For someone with low-vision, text enlargement and enhancement software works best with a large monitor. For a person who has trouble using a mouse, a large monitor displays more information than a small monitor, reducing the need to scroll through a document.

- Provide modified keyboards for those who have trouble using a regular keyboard. Alternatives include: keyboards with smaller and larger keys; with larger and smaller footprints; that are split in two or three sections; that have two or three independently-adjustable sections; that are designed for one-handed or left-handed typists.

- Offer track balls, touch pads, and other pointing devices to people who have trouble handling a mouse. For those who have difficulty holding down a mouse button, a pointing device with a "drag lock" feature is indispensable.

- Provide headphones for individuals who need to turn up the volume or filter out distracting noises. Headphones are also useful for those who use voice output systems in classroom and library settings.

Get to know the accessibility options built into the operating system of your PCs

- Basic accessibility features are incorporated into all modern PC operating systems. Standard accessibility options include adjustments to the sensitivity of the mouse and keyboard, and modifications to the size and color of menu bars, system fonts, and other visual elements. Also look for "Sticky keys," a feature that allows a modifier key (Shift, Ctrl, and Alt) to be pressed before, rather than at the same time, as an alphanumeric key; visual warnings (e.g., a menu bar flashes whenever the computer beeps); and audible key clicks.

Choose accessible Internet applications

- Choose Web browsers and e-mail programs that have built-in accessibility features. Some Internet applications are designed with accessibility in mind; others are extremely inaccessible. Look for applications that support:

  - mouse-free operation. In particular, ensure that all features can be activated without a mouse. In the most accessible browsers, the Tab-key advances the focus from one link to the next, and the Enter-key "clicks" it. Furthermore, the directional keys should scroll through a page;

  - user-configurable typefaces and font sizes; and

  - user-configurable screen layouts. For individuals with certain learning disabilities, it is helpful to eliminate visual clutter by hiding rarely-used toolbars and reducing the number of windows that are visible at one time.

Build a collection of accessibility utilities

- Oversize mouse pointers, simple magnification programs, basic on-screen keyboards, rudimentary text-to-speech applications, and keyboard-remapping/macro software are widely available—sometimes at no cost—from disability-related Websites. Refer to the Resources section at the end of this chapter.

Low- and No-Tech Accommodation Strategies

Not all accommodations involve high technology. Low-tech and no-tech accommodation strategies abound, all of which make the learning environment more conducive to people with disabilities:

Buy inexpensive low-tech devices

- Computer-based training programs for people with (and without) disabilities are greatly enhanced by ensuring that students have proper tools, such as book holders (available for a few dollars from office supply stores), cassette recorders (which serve as a notetaking machine), desk lamps (important for people with low-vision), and hand-held magnifiers.

Provide special training

- For students who cannot easily use a mouse, arrange for special training on keyboard-only techniques. See Cantor, 1998b; Snyder & Lowney, 1996.

Ensure that important Websites are accessible

- Ensure that Web pages that students must review as a course requirement are accessible. A fairly reliable accessibility test is to view Web pages with a text-only browser, such as Lynx. As a general rule, a page is accessible if (1) all links can be reached using keyboard commands, and (2) all important information on the site is visible. Note that not every site can be 100% accessible. However, sites that provide textual information are excellent candidates for being fully accessible. If a site is primarily textual but is not accessible, it is probably improperly designed.

Suggestions for Web Designers

Universal Design and the World Wide Web

To achieve a fully accessible Internet, all Web designers need to know principles of universal Website design.

Universal design is design for people of all ages and abilities. It is applicable to all design disciplines including architecture, landscape architecture, industrial design, graphic design, and Web page design. Universal design accommodates people with disabilities, older people, children, and others who are "non-average" in ways that are not stigmatizing and that benefit all users.

Universal Web page design means considering the needs of all intended users, and incorporating features that are useful to people with and without disabilities. A Website, page, or feature is considered accessible if it can be used by everyone—including people with sensory, mobility, and learning disabilities and people with injuries.

Thirteen Design Rules for Minimizing Web Barriers

Consider the following rules when creating Websites. For detailed information about universal Web page design, see the Resource section at the end of this Chapter.

Rule 1: Hypertext links. Use descriptive hypertext links. Links should make sense when read one at a time or out of context. Many people who are blind (and some people who have dyslexia) rely on screen reader technologies. A screen reader is a speech synthesizer that reads the contents of the screen. To get an overview of a Web page, the user presses a key (usually the Tab-key) to jump from link to link. Descriptive links make it easy for screen reader users to navigate a page, while vaguely-worded links complicate access. Examples of descriptive and non-descriptive hypertext links:

Good	*Bad*
"Click here for information about turtles."	*"Click here."*
"Contact the Vice-Principal."	*"VP"*
"Warning! Water quality alert!"	*"Warning!"*

Rule 2: Images and animations. Use the "Alt=text" element for all key images and image links. Alt-tags describe images that cannot otherwise be seen. They are indispensable for people who are blind, use text-only browsers, or prefer not to load images when viewing a page. (Note: It is not necessary to alt-tag purely decorative graphics.)

Rule 3: Backgrounds. Make Web pages more accessible by choosing simple, uncluttered background patterns, and selecting foreground text and images that contrast with background colors. People with certain learning disabilities have difficulties reading text against a heavily ornamented background. For this reason, choose simple backgrounds. Many people with low vision find that Web pages are easier to decipher when backgrounds are simple and background and foreground contrast sharply. A common form of color-blindness makes it hard to distinguish red from green, so avoid this color combination.

Rule 4: Image maps. Use client-side MAPs. Supplement image maps with a menu of text anchors that mirror the image map hot spots. Image maps are hard to access by users who cannot see the screen or have trouble manipulating a mouse. When including an image map on a Web page, ensure that the hotspots can be reached and activated without a mouse. Provide a corresponding "menu" of hypertext links as well.

Rule 5: Page organization. Use headers properly. Maintain a consistent page structure. Use Cascading Style Sheets (CSS) to lay out pages. Distinguish list items from sub-list items by, for example, labelling list items numerically and sub-list items alphabetically. Sighted users are able to understand the organization of a page at a glance. Contextual clues guide the eye to the most relevant parts of the screen without having to read a word. People who are blind cannot determine the organization of a page by seeing it as a whole. Screen reading software starts at the top of the page and reads downward. Screen readers cannot pick out contextual clues, such as lists. A list has a particular appearance, and this appearance signals its purpose. When each list item appears on a separate line, for example, screen reader users are better able to determine that they are reading a list. By labelling list items numerically and sub-list items alphabetically, a screen reader user receives additional clues about the organization of the page. A screen reader user can also get clues about page organization by studying its structure. Maintaining a consistent "look and feel" from page to page helps the user navigate a site. Using headers appropriately (e.g., H1 for a major heading, H2 for a subheading, and so on) guides the user to the most important information on a page.

Rule 6: Online forms. Make forms more accessible by (a) labelling fields clearly and consistently to indicate where they occur and what information is needed; (b) providing a form that can be downloaded, then mailed or e-mailed; and (c) offering telephone and TTY (Tele-type-writer) support. Screen reader users may have problems filling out online forms that are haphazardly formatted. Be consistent and clear when creating forms. Providing downloadable forms and offering telephone and TTY support make online forms more accessible.

Rule 7: Tables. Avoid using the Table element to format columns. Identify individual cells as containing data or header information. Provide abbreviations for header labels. Summarize table content. Ensure that a line-by-line reading of the Table makes sense. Screen readers, Braille displays, and some text-only browsers do not recognize boundaries between columns; they tend to read across columns, which renders the information unintelligible. Properly marked-up tables are fairly accessible. In a pinch, linearize simple two or three column tables by presenting each cell as a separate paragraph.

```
<NOFRAMES>
<BODY>

No Frames Version.
<P>
<H1>What do animals eat?</H1>

<A HREF="aardvarks.html">Find out more about aardvark's eating habits</A>
<P>
<A HREF="chimps.html">What does a chimpanzee eat for breakfast?</A>

 etc.

</BODY>
</NOFRAMES>
```

Figure 1. Using NOFRAMES to make frames more accessible.

Rule 8: Graphs and charts. Make graphs and charts more accessible by describing them. It is common practice in journals and textbooks to describe graphs and charts in the body of the text. For example, "In Figure 22, we see that the vehicle reached its maximum velocity after 3.25 seconds . . ." Web designers should follow the same convention.

Rule 9: Video. Make video more accessible by providing an audio description or by linking to a separate page that contains transcripts or descriptions of the video files. This strategy makes video more accessible to people with visual impairments.

Rule 10: Audio. Make audio more accessible by (a) linking to a separate page that contains transcripts, descriptions, or visual representations of the sound; and (b) stating the file format (.WAV, .AU, etc.), size (in kilobytes), and play length of audio files. Preparing textual or visual alternatives to audio enhances accessibility for people who are hard of hearing or deaf. Stating the size of audio files allows users with slow or intermittent internet access to decide whether or not to play an audio file.

Rule 11: Frames. Make frames more accessible by including an alternative set of HTML instructions that is displayed if the browser does not support frames. Assign meaningful titles to all frames. A page with frames is not necessarily inaccessible; however, frames complicate access for users of assistive technologies and alternative access techniques. For example, early versions of Lynx (a text-only browser still used by many people who are blind) are not frames-aware. Frames pose access problems similar to those caused by tables for users of screen readers, Braille displays, and some text-only browsers. If you include frames on your site, use NOFRAMES to advantage. See Figure 1.

Rule 12: Applets, scripts, and plug-ins. Provide alternative content if active features are inaccessible or unsupported. Some non-W3C Web technologies are not fully accessible to people with disabilities. Avoid them. If they must be used, provide accessible versions of the content.

Rule 13: Check accessibility. Test your site using different browsers—including text-based browsers—and without a mouse. Consult accessibility guidelines and checklists. Validate the

HTML. Accessibility guidelines and checklists are posted on the Web (w3.org/WAI). This site has links to other Web-based resources, including automated accessibility tools and page validators.

Conclusion

People with disabilities do well in Web-based training programs when their needs are accommodated. Throughout this chapter, I have suggested many strategies for enhancing the accessibility of Web-based training programs, such as providing adaptive technologies and low-tech devices; selecting monitors, keyboards, mice, and other peripherals that can serve to overcome individuals' functional limitations; using accessibility aids built into the operating system; choosing Internet programs that have built-in accessibility features; installing low-cost accessibility software on public computers; and adhering to the principles of universal Web page design when creating sites.

There is an unexpected dividend to considering accessibility when developing Web-based programs: Accommodation techniques also benefit people *without* disabilities. An accommodation consists of two things: better tools and smarter work practices. Many students find it easier to read slightly-enlarged screen fonts, manipulate a mouse when an oversized mouse pointer is installed, or use a trackball. For most tasks, keyboard-only techniques are significantly faster than point-and-click techniques. And everybody benefits from well-designed Web pages. In other words, by making simple hardware and software adjustments, by encouraging students to use alternative access techniques, and by providing accessible Web pages, the learning environment is enhanced for everyone.

References

Cantor, A. (1996). The ADAPTABLE approach: A practical guide to planning accessible libraries. *Library Hi Tech News, 14*(1), 41–45.

Cantor, A. (1998a). *Disability in the workplace: Effective and cost-effective accommodation planning.* Toronto: National Consultation on Career Development, University of Toronto.

Cantor, A. (1998b). *Avoiding the mousetrap: An evaluation of keyboard-only access to Windows.* 1998 CSUN International Technology and Persons with Disability Conference; interlog.com/~acantor/

Snyder, M. K., & Lowney, G. C. (1996, Oct. 17). *Microsoft Windows keyboard guide;* microsoft.com/

Resources

General Resources

The Internet: An inclusive magnet for teaching all students, by Betsy Bayha (1998) of the World Institute on Disability (WID), is an excellent resource. Free copies can be downloaded from the WID Website.

Internet Handbook
World Institute on Disability
510 Sixteenth St., Suite 100
Oakland, CA 94612
Tel: (510) 763-4100
TTY: (510) 208-9496
Fax: (510) 763-4109
e-mail: handbook@wid.org
Web: wid.org/tech/handbook

Adaptive Technologies

The Trace Center at the University of Wisconsin–Madison maintains a comprehensive Website about adaptive technologies. The Center publishes the *Trace Resource Book,* an encyclopedic guide to over 1,500 software, hardware and augmentative communication devices.

Trace Research and Development Center
University of Wisconsin–Madison
S-151 Waisman Center
1500 Highland Ave.
Madison, WI 53705-2280
Tel: (608) 263-6966
TTY: (608) 263-5408
Fax: (608) 262-8848
e-mail: info@trace.wisc.edu
Web: trace.wisc.edu

The Trace Center also maintains a library of adaptive freeware and shareware on the Web at: trace.wisc.edu/world/computer_access

Universal Web Page Design

The *Web Accessibility Initiative* was launched by the World Wide Web Consortium (W3C) to make the Web more accessible to people with disabilities. Their site lists guidelines for creating accessible Web pages: w3org/TR/WAI-WEBCONTENT

For more ideas about accessible Web page design, check the *National Center for Accessible Media* Website at WGBH in Boston: boston.com/wgbh/pages/ncam/currentprojects/wapindex.html

Acknowledgments

The author thanks Barbara L. Roberts, Disability Services Advisor, Queen's University in Kingston, for her superb editorial consultations; Dena Shumila of Burson-Marsteller, San Francisco, for sharing her expertise on text-to-speech/text-to-Braille technologies and universal Web page design; and colleagues in the Web Accessibility Initiative's Education and Outreach Working Group, for their passion for spinning stronger webs.

The Author

Alan Cantor (e-mail: acantor@interlog.com; Web homepage: interlog.com/~acantor) is President of Cantor Associates, Workplace Accommodation Consultants, Toronto, Canada.

20

An Instructional Design-Based Approach to Developing Online Learning Environments

Bob   Hoffman   and

Donn   C.   Ritchie

Introduction

Web-based training is burgeoning, but is Web-based *learning* keeping pace? With a grant from the California State University system, we set out to develop a systematic approach for applying traditional instructional design principles (Ritchie & Hoffman, 1997) to Web-based training across disciplines, organizations, and types of knowledge or skills being taught or learned.

We developed a system of templates, the so-called "I CARE" system (see below), that not only facilitates the technical development of Web-based courses and workshops, but, more importantly, also prompts trainers and/or workshop development teams to take advantage of what we know about how people learn. Moreover, it provides a system that helps trainees mentally organize their approach to course content and activities. The I CARE system is based on accepted learning theories that cut across disciplinary boundaries and adapt to different types of skills and knowledge.

Design Principles

A fundamental design principle underlying the I CARE approach is that both instructors and participants need a clear mental model or schema that helps them organize individual instructional activities, as well as whole courses, in their heads. In the case of a site-based, face-to-face course, trainees may construct their mental models around the materials used; the physical space associated with the workshop; other individuals involved in the course; or even the printed course schedule or outline.

Web-based training also benefits from a clear structure that facilitates both participants and trainers in constructing a clear mental model of the course. If the course structure also reflects the course pedagogy—the underlying instructional design—it further aids both instructors and trainees to think clearly and purposefully about the course.

The I CARE model is part of a system of course templates that are available free on the Web from: clipt.sdsu.edu/ (click on T3). The templates provide trainers with models and guidance for creating a clear, instructionally sound online course or workshop. In addition to instructional modules, the system includes a course "marketing" page, instructor home page, and other course documents, such as schedule, resource, and information pages. The templates may be used with any Web page editor.

The I CARE System

The central feature of the online course template is the instructional modules themselves. These instructional modules are based on a flexible five-step approach to lesson planning that we dubbed the I CARE system. I CARE stands for "Introduction, Connect, Apply, Reflect, and Extend" (see Figure 1). I CARE is distilled from basic instructional design practices that reflect what we know about how humans learn, adapted to serve Web-based training environments.

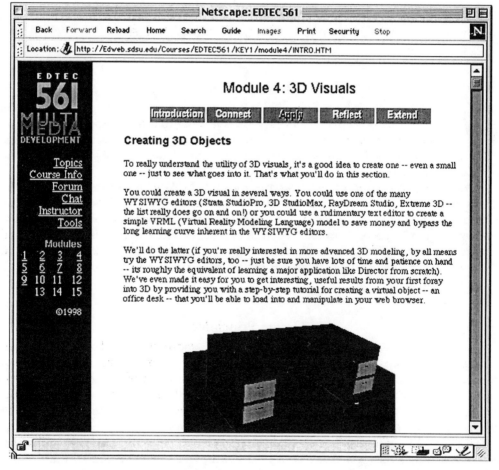

Figure 1. An example of the Apply section from an "I CARE" module on instructional 3D visualization from a Web-based course (San Diego State University's Educational Technology 561, Advanced Multimedia Development).

Some Web-based courses may be entirely asynchronous, or at least include asynchronous components. The system outlined here is organized around "modules" or "sessions" rather than "weeks" or "dates." This allows instructional designers to accommodate learners' needs to organize their course work around job schedules, family, and other commitments, while maintaining a modular, sequenced structure of "do-able chunks" or "objects."

Each module or object, in turn, represents a pedagogically complete "lesson" that learners can complete in roughly the equivalent time a trainee would devote to a face-to-face workshop session and associated on-the-job practice. The components of the I CARE system are described below, along with examples of how they help to increase learning during Web-based training.

Introduction

The Introductory section of the I CARE format serves to place the present learning in the context of the course or workshop as a whole, and enliven learners' prior knowledge with respect to the content. The introduction features clearly stated objectives for the module so learners know exactly what they are supposed to be learning. It may also provide motivational elements, such as a scenario that poses a familiar or relevant problem for learners.

Here is an Introduction section from a course on Business Statistics Basics, developed and taught by Professor Steven Pollard at Cal State Los Angeles:

> At the end of this module you will be able to explain how to collect, summarize, analyze, and report numerical findings relevant to a business decision or situation.
> We use statistics to help us make decisions:
>
> 1. Attainment of quality by a company.
>
> 2. Prediction of behavior of customers and competitors.
>
> 3. Making capital investments in face of uncertainty.
>
> 4. Determining if economic policy is having desired effects.
>
> Keep in mind that statistics is not a science! There are two distinct areas within statistics: Descriptive Statistics and Inferential Statistics. Descriptive statistics are summary measures that describe the characteristics of a set of data. Inferential statistics is a process that follows from data characteristics to making generalizations, estimates, forecasts, or other judgments about data.
> We will focus on descriptive statistics in this module. The modules on confidence interval estimation and hypothesis testing will cover inferential statistics.

Connect

In the I CARE's Connect section, learners encounter new information in a context that is relevant and meaningful to their professional or personal life. The Connect section may feature online text with appropriate charts, diagrams, illustrations, or visual analogies, as well as other media elements such as sound, video, multimedia representations, or virtual environments. Alternatively, it may consist primarily of instructions to read off-line text material, view a videocassette tape, or listen to a sound recording. The Connect section helps learners organize new material in the context of what they already know, preparing them to apply this information in the following section.

The Connect section should be rich with examples, and, if appropriate, non-examples. Both examples and non-examples should relate to learners' professional or personal need to know or do something.

Apply

In order to integrate new information into long-term memory, researchers have found un-equivocally that immediate, purposeful practice is essential. Practice may be rote rehearsal or may involve more complex levels of application, synthesis, and judgment. Regardless of the form it takes, it should be, like information in the Connect section, related to the real-life needs of the learners, be they professional or personal.

The Apply section of the online module is tailored to fit the requirements of the type of skill or knowledge offered in the module objectives. Learning a procedure, for instance, may require quite different types of practice than learning, say, to analyze the causes of industrial performance problems. While it is beyond the scope of this chapter to prescribe specific types of practice, the literature is replete with heuristics and examples to which online course de-signers may refer. The need for some type of practice, per se, however, is independent of the type of skill or knowledge being practiced.

In terms of modes of implementation, the Apply section may include a variety of meth-ods. It might involve writing a memo or preparing a presentation or report. It could involve a hands-on project such as classifying faulty product samples (virtual or actual), analyzing cus-tomer service patterns, or developing a Website. It might be an individual or small group pro-ject, or involve participants interviewing customers or subject experts. The Apply section might feature a *WebQuest* (Dodge, 1997), a prompted writing tool, an interactive online experiment, or simply provide instructions for an off-line activity you wish trainees to complete. Participants might create a concept map or draft a business plan. In short, any activity that gives learners a chance to exercise their new skills and knowledge in an appropriate context is fair game.

Figure 1 shows an Apply section from a module on instructional 3D visuals in an online course on Advanced Multimedia Development in the SDSU Department of Educational Tech-nology's masters degree program. In this case, the practice involves actually creating and ma-nipulating a 3D object to help participants understand the utility and affordances of such ob-jects for instructional purposes.

Reflect

Merely practicing a new skill is usually not enough to ensure retention in long-term memory. Learners often need to think about—and even talk about—the new knowledge with others to further process the new information and "wire it" securely into their existing cogni-tive framework. In a face-to-face workshop, this may indicate whole- or small-group discussion or the production of a "think piece" or other written report or memo.

In the context of Web-based training, the reflection might take the form of a thoughtful response to a carefully crafted question from the instructor, or a peer exchange about lessons learned, insights gained, applications in the learners' own job activities, and so forth. It might be implemented through an online chat or a more deliberative threaded discussion. Asking par-ticipants to keep an electronic journal to submit or use in a later assignment could also be con-sidered a form of reflection. The important idea here is to provide the trainees a chance to ar-ticulate their newly developed knowledge to help stabilize and strengthen the links between their existing mental models and the new information

Extend

Several other important elements of instruction are included in the Extend section of the I CARE model. The Extend section might offer remediation, encourage enrichment activities, assess participants' learning, prompt trainees to evaluate their own learning and the course module itself, or all of the above. This is a good place to provide references or resources "for further information" or for advanced work on the topic.

Extend activities may be implemented using Web-based forms (for self- or instructor-administered tests, quizzes, and surveys), e-mail, threaded discussions, or off-line activities, depending on the circumstances.

Online Course Development

The original workshop for which the I CARE model was developed and first disseminated taught us that a team approach to Web-based course development is not only convenient and helpful, but perhaps necessary to ensure quality instruction in this emerging medium.

Many instructors and instructional designers not only lack the requisite skills to single-handedly author Web-based workshops and courses, but they are unlikely to develop those skills to any significant degree through a short workshop, online or otherwise, or, indeed, through any other instructional method.

Successful Web-based training development teams with which we have worked or which we have observed evidence four skill sets. The first characteristic is common to every team—expert content knowledge. In a corporate training environment, this may involve internal or external experts, who may or may not be regular members of the course development team.

A second skill that is important to include in Web-based training development team is the ability to structure pedagogically effective instructional modules. Including an instructional designer on the development team is the most obvious solution. Instructional designers bring a broad, discipline-independent perspective and a multi-purpose instructional tool kit to the online course development process. If that is not possible, the I CARE system templates can prompt content experts with little experience or interest in pedagogy or instructional design to incorporate appropriate methods and strategies to facilitate novices' learning.

Online courses rely almost exclusively on media products, be they print material, Web pages, videotapes, or CD-ROMs. Consequently, the third skill set to include in a Web-based training development team is media production. Creating attractive, useable, media elements or objects requires competent artists, video production personnel, and/or multimedia developers.

The fourth skill set to include in a Web-based training development team is that of a computer programmer and/or Webmaster. These professionals bring the ability to incorporate the ever-expanding kit of Web-based technologies. What was once confined to a few strategic HTML tags has become a staggering array of complex technologies, such as Java applets and JavaScript, "plug-ins," CGIs, forms, database interactions, frames, layers, image maps, streaming audio and video, and much more. Successful online course development teams will include a dedicated technical support person who can program advanced computer interactions, help set up and maintain servers, load and maintain software, and consult on bandwidth and compatibility issues. We distinguish such an individual from a media producer, who may have multimedia authoring, or video or graphic production skills, but whose computer programming skills may fall short when attempting to implement, for example, a complex database system to serve learners' and/or instructors' needs.

Conclusion

The I CARE model represents a pedagogically sound approach to creating Web-based training modules. The model is free for use by anyone with an interest in developing online instruction. Moreover, the original T3 (tools, templates, and training) CSU Faculty Development Institute, for which I CARE was first developed, is available free, online, and includes course and module templates that may be adopted, adapted, or significantly transformed.

References

Dodge, B. (1997). The *WebQuest* Page; edweb.sdsu.edu/webquest/webquest.html

Ritchie, D., & Hoffman, B. (1997). Incorporating instructional design principles with the World Wide Web. In B. Kahn (Ed.), *Web-based instruction* (pp. 135–138). Englewood Cliffs: Educational Technology Publications.

The Authors

Bob Hoffman (e-mail: Bob.Hoffman@sdsu.edu; Web homepage: edweb.sdsu.edu/people/bhoffman/) is Associate Professor, Department of Educational Technology, San Diego State University, San Diego, California. **Donn Ritchie (e-mail: DonnRitchie@sdsu.edu; Web homepage: edweb.sdsu.edu/people/dritchie/)** is Chair, Department of Educational Technology at San Diego State University.

21

Playing Interactive Training Games on the Web

Sivasailam Thiagarajan and Raja Thiagarajan

nteractivity is touted as one of the most valuable features of Web-based instruction. However, even a cursory examination of most instructional offerings on the Web reveals that the provided interactivity is of the mindless variety that connects the learner with the content. Instructional designers on the Web appear to be intent on repeating the mistakes of their teaching-machines and programmed-learning predecessors from four decades ago. These designers seem to have forgotten that the only guaranteed improvement in performance that arises from interacting with multiple-choice questions is increased fluency in clicking the left mouse button.

True instructional interactivity should involve examples of learner-to-learner and learner-to-facilitator interaction. We should move away from such irrelevant questions as *What are the four stages of team development?* and *By what percent did the Asian population in the U. S. grow in the 1980s?* toward such job-relevant questions as *How would you facilitate your team during its brainstorming stage?* and *How might we sell more products to people of Asian origin?* Current Web-based instruction is replete with closed, convergent questions that fall in the one-correct-answer category. This state of affairs is due to the fact the computer can be easily programmed to check a single answer. It is much more challenging to evaluate answers to open-ended, divergent questions that require application, analysis, synthesis, and problem solving.

During the past 30 years, we have been designing training games for corporate employees that encourage meaningful people-to-people interaction through the use of open-ended questions. We have used these types of questions and interactions not only to check participants' understanding, but also help them create content. For the past few years, we have been applying the same principles to the design of Web-based training games.

P3: Pool, Poll, Predict

One of our early Internet games, called *P3*, is designed to elicit and process open-ended responses from players. The game uses e-mail notes to require participant-to-facilitator interaction. Although there is no direct interaction among participants, they generate and process the content. The basic flow of the game consists of three rounds during which participants generate content items, select the top three items, and predict the top five, as follows:

Round 1: Pool

The facilitator sends an e-mail note to all participants. This note contains an open-ended question (example: *How do we improve the performance of a team?*), invites each participant to send three suggestions or responses, and announces a deadline. Each participant sends an e-mail with his or her responses to the facilitator, who records the responses, removes redundant ones, and prepares a pool of 10–20 items.

Round 2: Poll

At the beginning of this round, the facilitator sends an e-mail to each participant containing the pool of items and instructions to reply with a list of three items that the participant finds most personally appealing. The facilitator tabulates the replies and arranges the items in a "popularity list" in order of the number of choices. (This popularity list is not shared with the participants until the end of the game.)

Round 3: Predict

At the beginning of this round, the facilitator sends another e-mail to each participant repeating the original pool of items and instructions to reply with a list of the five items the participant predicts were the most popular. For each reply, the facilitator computes the correlation coefficient between the predicted order and the actual order in the popularity list. The player with the highest correlation coefficient is identified as winner.

The facilitator sends a final e-mail note identifying and congratulating the player with the most accurate prediction (the highest correlation coefficient) as the winner. This e-mail note also includes the popularity list along with the names of the players who originally contributed the top five items.

Making the Most of Available Resources

Most designers of Web-based instruction avoid developing interactive games because they feel that they don't have sophisticated technology and appropriate resources. We believe that we can design Web-based games that work around local limitations and make the optimum use of available resources. The version of *P3* described above uses the most basic e-mail technology. As more sophisticated resources became available to us, we adapted the *P3* game to exploit these resources. Here are different variations of the same game:

Listserv version. The game is played as in the original version, but with the listserv making the e-mail distribution task easier. In addition, this approach permits introverted listserv members to vicariously participate in the game by reading the notes and tracking the progress. It also permits selective participation in any of the rounds. For example, a listserv member may not respond during the first round but may participate in the two subsequent rounds. Another member may respond during the first round and drop out of the later rounds.

Web-based version. This version uses a Website to deliver the game. A page on the Web introduces the activity, asks an open-ended question, and provides a form for the participants to submit their three responses. The Webmaster collects, edits, and pools these responses. A new Web-page displays the pool of 10–20 items. Participants choose their three items by clicking buttons on the Web-page. A computer program tabulates the data and creates the "popularity list." The next Web-page reproduces the original pool and asks participants to predict the five most popular items in the correct order. Another computer program calculates the correlation coefficient between each participant's predictions with the order of items in the popularity list.

A new Web-page displays the names of the participants along with their correlation coefficients—from the most accurate prediction to the least accurate.

Chat room. This is a synchronous version of *P3* using a chat room facility. The facilitator types in an open-ended question and sets up a five-minute time limit. Participant responses are not displayed on screen. The facilitator randomly displays 10 items and invites participants to select their three personal favorites within a two-minute time limit. These selections are not displayed on the screen. The facilitator now asks participants to identify the five most popular items in the correct order within a three-minute time limit. At the end of this time period, the facilitator displays the "popularity list" and identifies the winner.

Chat room with enhanced interaction. This version begins as the previous one, but asks participants to collaboratively brainstorm 10 different responses to the open-ended question. Participants' responses are displayed on the screen as they are typed in. When this list contains 10 items, the facilitator asks participants to individually predict the top five items. These predictions are stored but not displayed. The facilitator now encourages participants to chat with each other and identify the top five items. Once this task is completed, the facilitator displays each participant's prediction and asks the group to identify the player who made the most accurate prediction.

Electronic auditorium. The facilitator introduces *P3* using audio through a telephone line and displays the open-ended question on the screen. Participants type in their responses using the feedback window, which keeps the items hidden from the other participants but makes them available to the facilitator. The facilitator quickly reviews the responses and displays 10 different items on a polling slide. This slide permits participants to select their three personal choices and automatically creates a bar graph for each choice. The results are kept hidden while the facilitator asks each participant to predict the top five items. After a suitable pause, the facilitator displays a bar graph showing the actual popularity of each item and invites participants to judge how accurate their predictions were.

Ten years in the future. The open-ended question is flashed on the video wall. Participants speak their responses into the built-in microphone. The computer converts the items into text and displays 10 of the items in a random order. Participants announce their secret predictions into the microphone and then talk to each other to arrive at a consensus about the top five items. The computer instantaneously calculates the correlation coefficients and displays each participant's score on his or her individual video wall. It also flashes the names of the winners (who made the most accurate prediction) and the names of the participants who originally contributed each of the top five items.

Flexible Use of *P3*

The heart of *P3* is an open-ended question that elicits alternative answers. Players respond to the question and process the pool of their responses. Obviously, by changing the initial question, you can use this game to explore different instructional topics. Also, as an instructional game, *P3* can be used in a variety of situations to serve a variety of purposes. You can use this game at the beginning of a Web-based instructional module as an advance organizer or as a pretest. You can also use this game as an indirect needs analysis tool and rearrange the instructional sequence to remove misconceptions revealed in the players' responses and to reinforce accurate perceptions and principles. At the end of a Web-based instructional module, you can use *P3* as a review, summary, posttest, or tool for collecting formative-evaluation data. Outside the instructional context, you can use *P3* as a collaborative strategy for goal setting, problem solving, and decision-making. Recently, for example, we invited members of the North American Simulation and Gaming Association (NASAGA) through their listserv to participate in a *P3* game to identify elements of NASAGA's mission and to arrange them in order of priority.

Perhaps the most desirable competency for Web-game designers is the flexibility to re-purpose the same game for delivery through different technologies to achieve different goals. This principle applies to our most recent Web game, described below.

The Change Game

Internet stories (also known as *interactive novels* or *Internet novels*) are a way of presenting nonlinear fiction on the Web. This type of fiction is usually written by a group of authors and read by individuals in an interactive, nonlinear fashion.

Recently, we designed a Web-based learning game that involves the collaborative development of an interactive story. The object of the game is to explore the stages in organizational change management. Unlike the typical piece of Internet fiction, our game involved a specific number of players with specific assignments and deadlines.

Players begin *The Change Game* by reading a short description of different types of people involved in organizational changes and different steps in the change process. The actual play of the game involves 10 rounds, each round presented once a day or week, depending on the schedule. Each round requires the application of specific concepts and principles related to organizational change to the continuous development of an interactive story.

Initial Version of the Story

The play site on the Web presents a skeletal story with an advance organizer for systematic change. This piece of fiction sets up the organizational context of a large multinational publishing company. It also provides brief background information about an innovative e-commerce system that will be implemented in the corporation. The story line identifies sponsors and change agents working on the project.

The skeletal story outlines six chapters, corresponding to six stages in the organizational change process:

- **Chapter 1.** Employees are ignorant of the e-commerce initiative; change agents provide short pieces of information to increase their level of awareness.

- **Chapter 2.** Employees are anxious about how the large-scale implementation of e-commerce strategies will affect them personally; change agents use different techniques to reassure them.

- **Chapter 3.** Employees are curious about e-commerce; change agents demonstrate how the new system works and what types of results it produces.

- **Chapter 4.** Employees are ready to learn about e-commerce; change agents coordinate the training program.

- **Chapter 5.** Employees are capable of using e-commerce; change agents coordinate the installation of the system.

- **Chapter 6.** Several months after the system is installed, employees are jaded; change agents work with technical experts to upgrade the system based on employee feedback.

Final Version of the Story

The final version of the story is a complex piece of hypertext fiction that can be entered from different locations and sequenced in different orders. This version contains several characters and you can track the story from the point of view of any one of these characters. The changes of fortune of one character will be different from those of any other character, reflecting the realities of organizational transformation. You can also navigate through the chronological events in the story, following each stage in the change process and investigating how it affects different characters.

Flow of the Game

The critical feature of *The Change Game* is that the initial version of the story is transformed into the final version by participants themselves, in response to their periodic assignments.

The first round requires participants to populate the story with a cast of characters. Depending on the number of participants and available time, each player is to create one to five characters associated with the publishing company and representing a variety of types, including sponsors, champions, change agents, skeptical managers, enthusiastic managers, technical experts, customer advocates, change-management consultants, employees who are not affected by the change, employees who are directly affected by the change, employees who are negatively affected by the change, employees who are positively affected by the change, innovative employees who are eager to embrace the change, laggards who are afraid of the change, gatekeepers who control the flow of information, stockholders, and customers. Each player creates appropriate characters by giving them names, job titles, personality types, psychological characteristics, status in the organization, and current relationships toward the new system.

The second round randomly distributes a set of characters to each player and asks them to describe how each character initially perceives the proposed e-commerce system in terms of its costs and benefits; complexity; compatibility with corporate policies, procedures, traditions, and values; adaptability; and potential impact on social relationships and interaction patterns. The assignment gives sparse information about the new system and encourages players to create multiple realities.

Later rounds follow the plot line through the six stages of the change process. During each round, players are assigned different characters to increase their ability to analyze the context and to apply change principles. Players are encouraged to create a realistic story rather than follow a predictable turn of events in which the change agents are heroes and all employees live happily ever after.

Once the story is developed through all stages of the change process, following rounds require players to create alternate versions by imposing unexpected external events such as changes in copyright laws, availability of free books on the Internet, and the sale of the publishing company to an entertainment conglomerate.

Eventually, the game comes to an end when the group of players "completes" the story. The next group begins with the original skeletal version and creates its own final version. Our eventual goal is develop a giant repository that includes all alternate versions of the story from all groups of players, clearly demonstrating that change is a complex, never-ending process.

Flexible Use of Internet Stories

You can easily create effective interactive exercises by replacing the content of the preceding exercise *(change process)* by other processes to be explored. For example, we are currently working on Internet fiction games on creativity, team development, human performance technology, and intercultural sensitivity. Participant feedback indicates that the games have the unique (and discomfitting) benefit of reminding everyone that real-world processes are far more complex, chaotic, unreliable, and multidimensional than narrative models and graphical flow-charts in textbooks suggest.

Conclusion

P3 and the *The Change Game* are just two examples of truly interactive training games that can be played on the Web. The secret to effective play on the Web is to work around local limitations and to fully exploit available opportunities.

The Authors

Sivasailam "Thiagi" Thiagarajan (e-mail: thiagi@thiagi.com; Web homepage: thiagi.com) is President, Workshops by Thiagi, Inc. He also writes a monthly newsletter, *Thiagi GameLetter*, published by Jossey-Bass/Pfeiffer. **Raja Thiagarajan (e-mail: raja@thiagi.com; Web homepage: thiagi.com)** is vice-president for research and development, Workshops by Thiagi, Inc.

22

Simulations for Web-Based Training

Harry A. Pappo

nteractive, reality-driven, computer-based simulations have proved successful and have served us well as vehicles for the training of skills. Aimed at improving our decision-making and problem-solving capability under diverse environmental circumstances, they have already been used to train airline pilots, military personnel, and spacecraft crews, among others. To date, however, the techniques have been applied mainly to stand-alone computers, though there have been some network applications in the training of organizations.

In a recently published book, *Simulations for Skills Training*, published by Educational Technology Publications, I dealt with the problem of building simulations for the study and training of skills, generally, either for stand-alone or network training. I developed techniques for analyzing and modeling the environments of the skills for the simulations. I have since continued that work, using my Website, *Simulations Research*, as a research station, but have now directed my attention more pointedly to the use of the Web as the training mode. At that site, I examine a number of special aspects and problems relating to the construction of simulations for Web-based training. My aim, here, is to review some of those topics. A more extensive treatment of the subject is available at the Website (home1.gte.net/simres).

Simulation Design Considerations

Building a training simulation requires dedication, not to mention a lot of work. This is to say, you must have, or develop, an abiding interest, if not a professional specialty, in the skill (or skill group) toward which the training is geared. The reason is that the training vehicle, like the skill itself, is extremely complex, centered as it is on a simulation of the environment in which the skill is normally performed. Indeed, the complexity is sufficient to warrant use of complexity theory as a tool of analysis.

Complexity of the Skill Environments

In themselves, skill environments more than satisfy the meaning of a complex object, both in structure and dynamics. At a minimum they are highly interactive, having diverse effects, both short and long term, and at times even well into the future. They usually exhibit many feedback loops, as well. And they demonstrate chaotic behavior plus a significant degree of adaptability.

With behavioral environments, too, the closer they are examined, the more detail that remains to be found. In fact, there are literally orders of magnitude differences in levels of complexity. You need only look at the structure of the human organism, with its many bones, muscles, and nerves—not to mention the billions of neuronal cells in the brain—to appreciate the range of complexity it displays. This is characteristic of fractals, the theory of which has become an integral part of complexity theory.

Given the interactive nature of the many components, you can see that the dynamics are unquestionably nonlinear and display common characteristics of nonlinearity. And when it is recognized that the individual is only part of the larger, behavioral environment, the complexity of the latter can be seen in its true proportions. It can also be understood that a science of complexity is not simply valuable for the study of behavioral environments, but absolutely essential, if progress is to be made in understanding them.

Complexity of the Simulation

To provide adequate training, the simulated environment has to be detailed enough to be a reasonable equivalent to the natural setting of the skill and provide a meaningful challenge to the trainee. That is, the quality of representation has to be commensurate with the subtlety of the skill being trained and the competence level of the trainee. The more subtle or more difficult the problem to be dealt with, the more detailed the program has to be to handle it. The simulation has to allow choices to be made among relevant behavior alternatives. Anything short of that quality will produce inadequate results and be unacceptable as a training vehicle. Continued analysis, formulation, and programming are required to put together such a system. It follows that a thorough understanding of the skill, intimate knowledge of related formal models, working familiarity with one or more program development tools, and considerable time and effort are needed to generate the necessary detail. The project should not be taken lightly.

Any project engaged in building simulations for training, whether for the Web or for stand-alone computers, thus has to take into account:

- The nature of the environment of the skills.

- The problem situations, or how, where, and when the skills are to be applied.

- The training or competence-level requirements for the skills.

- The processing capability of the computer to be used for the training.

Should the processing capability change, the operating limits would likely change, too, and this change could directly affect the nature and quality of the simulation. Changes here, in turn, could alter the training techniques and perhaps affect the training quality. For this reason, it would seem that a reduction of the computer capability would degrade the training, while an enhanced computer capability would significantly heighten the training opportunities.

Nevertheless, the central controlling factor—the standard of measurement of difficulty for the construction project—is still the complexity of the real environment of the skills. Whatever computer system you use, you still have to ferret out the essential aspects of the environment—the properties that affect performance in some way, either positively or negatively. These are the elements that have to be simulated. To uncover them—to become aware of them—you need to acquire considerable knowledge of the real operations of the system.

Simulating the processes also calls for extensive use of the principles of traditional science, because the make-believe environments have to be expressed in terms of formal models. That is, you have to formulate the equations that define the dynamics of the real-world situations—

arenas like a workstation, tennis court, surgery, etc., in which the skills in question are performed. And you have to convert the equations into a form suitable for processing. The models are, of course, stand-ins for the real operational environment and therefore must be rich enough—detailed enough and accurate enough—to accommodate the required level of decision-making in the skills being trained. Otherwise, the patterns of behavior that unfold in the learning process will be inappropriate for the real contexts.

But the simulations still must fit within the environment of the computer used to do the training. A great deal of programming is normally required, so the more powerful and capable the computer, the more complete and better the simulations can be, all other things being equal. This applies as much to the Web as to any network or stand-alone system. As the Internet improves, it will become more and more productive and more useful in training. Because of the inherent limitations of the equipment, you may have to limit the scope of the study or training program. So it's still important to ask how the characteristics of the Internet affect the design conditions.

The Web as a Training Platform

The World Wide Web is already sophisticated enough to permit the use of motion picture clips along with text and graphics as vehicles of communication. Although it is still quite limited in the kind and speed of user interaction, it is encouragingly more tolerant in this regard. Anticipated improvement in the capabilities makes the system an ideal vehicle for training.

The Web as an Extension of Your Computer

You can think of the Web—or any network, for that matter—as an *extension or enhancement of the processing capacity of your own computer.* Using hyperlinks, for instance, you now access data from other computers in the network and in that way multiply your effective storage capacity many-fold. Yet, the procedure still feels much like calling for a file located on your CD-ROM, hard drive, or floppy drive.

Limitations. Unfortunately, information access through the links is still limited by the bandwidth of one's modem, the power and speed of the central processing unit, the quality of the display system, and the capabilities of the browser. Within these limits, though, the easier it is to acquire or transmit the data, the more like working on a stand-alone system the process becomes and, in effect, the more powerful a computer becomes.

Effort Sharing. In a similar way, a stand-alone computer can be made more powerful by sharing processing tasks with other systems. Distributing the processing load among several machines running in parallel can decrease the program running time and possibly solve problems that otherwise wouldn't yield timely results.

This capability could be particularly helpful when training skills, particularly subtle skills, simply because the processing that is required places heavy demands on the computer. Due to the complexity of the environments of such skills, generally, a stand-alone computer could easily be overwhelmed by the amount of computing required to simulate the dynamics. But if the work is shared with other computers, the results could be much improved.

It is this enhanced capability that provides the hope for extended classroom, living room, or workplace training of skills via the Net, despite the possible tunnel effect produced by the hardware. But the added capability requires new standards of cooperation and/or remuneration among the participants, as well as technical considerations in parallel or distributed program design.

Internet Issues

Since the Internet generally enhances the utility of a stand-alone computer, the design considerations should change for the better with a network. But the Internet itself, being a network of computers and browsers with varying levels of power and capability, introduces its own set of problems. These factors call for program simplifications and special compensating mechanisms if the training is to be universal. This raises a number of questions that have to be addressed eventually: What adjustments and/or agreements need to be made? How is the workload to be distributed? More basically, what program development system should be used? Java? Visual Basic? HTML?

Java. An important characteristic of Java, for example, is that it is compiled into a *byte* code (rather than basic machine code). Byte code is an intermediate representation that's interpreted by a so-called virtual machine—a program executing on a real machine. Given an *interpreter* for the particular platform, any Java code distributed over the Internet will run on the machine. An interpreter is a program that literally interprets the succession of lines of code of a program as the program is being run. It reads the code and converts it on the spot into the language of the computer on which the program is being run, so it has to "know" both languages. It is the interpreted version of the code that operates the computer.

Visual Basic. While very similar to Java in many respects (as in its object-oriented approach to programming or in its encapsulated units of code), Visual Basic is different in that it doesn't work through a virtual machine. So it lacks that Internet advantage. On the other hand, it provides the means to let one develop a graphics user interface with relative ease and with relatively little code, whereas Java can be cumbersome in this regard, if not difficult.

HTML. Despite these advantages, it is quite likely that HTML will remain the Internet language of choice. This is the opinion expressed by Jon DeVaan, head of Microsoft's Desktop Applications Division, in response to a question asked in an interview (Summer 1998 edition of *Microsoft Magazine*):

> We've decided that since HTML is the agreed-upon language of the Internet—the agreed way of writing things down—we're going to use HTML as a companion file format. Today, when a document is on the Web or a company intranet in HTML, your software has to convert the HTML to a file format so you can read it. When we use HTML as our standard, that won't be necessary. You'll be able to download documents from the Web or an intranet without converting them from HTML to Word or Excel documents. This will make it faster and easier to share information.

Future of the Web

It is predicted that the Internet of the future will be a more intelligent network, and that communication will take place between *people*—by voice, say—rather than between devices, as it is today. The number of subscribers to the Net will no doubt continue to increase, and the bandwidth will surely increase to accommodate them. What, exactly, the system will ultimately look like is anybody's guess, but its structure will no doubt be driven both by advances in technology and by demands of its subscribers on how it is to be used.

The Author

Harry A. Pappo (e-mail: simres@gte.net; **Web homepage: home1.gte.net/simres**), an independent researcher, is based in Torrance, California.

23

HyperInquiry:
Surfing Below the Surface
of the Web

John V. Dempsey and
Brenda C. Litchfield

Most training activities using the Internet or intranets are composed of verbal information or other relatively lower-level learning outcomes. One explanation is that even Web-savvy training organizations do not follow appropriate design models or incorporate instructional theory. In essence, we are enamored with the Web, but we are just skimming the surface of the possible ways it can be used in training.

We often look at the Web as a way to get to hyperlinked information. That is the Web's most obvious use and it is very effective in that function. From this view we make two assertions. First, learning that takes place on the Web is often confined to what Gagné (1985) refers to as verbal information. This is not only the chief learning outcome of informal Web surfing, it is the way trainers typically teach others in the workforce to use the Web. Secondly, few deliberate instructional or learning strategies (excluding search engines) are used to organize or deliver training experiences.

Why is this? Perhaps more than any other medium, the Web gives the control of a learning experience to the learner. Our most common models of training use media such as platform instruction, video, printed courseware materials, or fairly linear computer-based tutorials. In these media, where control of the learning situation is retained by the trainer, behaviorally-oriented approaches, particularly with technical training, are the norm. Because navigation within the Web is primarily controlled by users and guided by their motives, intuition, and experiences, behavioral training models are not likely to be as effective.

Adult learning theory, or andragogy, has for some years been used in "soft skill" domains such as management training. Many of its precepts are consistent with training using the Web. For example, Knowles (1984) has proposed four basic principles of adult learning. First, adults need to be involved in the planning and evaluation of their instruction. Second, experience (including mistakes) provides the basis for learning activities. Third, adults are most interested in learning subjects that have immediate relevance to their jobs or personal lives. Fourth, adult learning is problem-centered rather than content-oriented.

All of Knowles' four principles are relevant to training programs delivered via the Web or a combination of the Web and other media. In our increasingly complex work environments, new knowledge, skills, or attitudes (KSAs) are ill-defined and require that trainees customize learning goals based on their experiences. Most training programs are relevant to the job in that they provide KSAs that can be transferred to job-related activities. The problem centered approach, Knowles' fourth principle, can be integrated into programs using the inductive inquiry method that we discuss later in this chapter.

In using Web-based training, therefore, the trainer becomes a facilitator and a partner in structuring the learning experience, not the purveyor of that experience. Increasingly, trainers will not be able to lay out the content of training in all its detail, but will instead provide the framework by which training goals can be met. Among the most conspicuous challenges facing effective Web trainers are:

- to match effective training models and strategies with specific learning outcomes;

- to assure that using the Web is an integrated, meaningful learning experience and not just isolated pieces of information;

- to integrate print-based and other adjunct learning materials to support Web-based training; and

- to help trainees overcome the "lost in hyperspace" state that accompanies many Web-based activities.

One instructional model that addresses these and related challenges is the inquiry learning model, or in the context of the Web, a HyperInquiry model. We have used this model most recently in an educational Website (oar.noaa.gov/k12) for the Office of Oceanic and Atmospheric Research, part of the National Oceanic and Atmospheric Administration (NOAA). The goal of this site was to use the enormous amount of data and information available in NOAA and other government sites to investigate a dozen or so domains such as El Nino, tornadoes, and the oceans.

An Inductive Inquiry Model

Inquiry is often patterned on either inductive or deductive thinking. A deductive approach begins with a principle or concept. Activities or investigations are designed to prove or discover that main idea. Inductive inquiry is the converse. It begins with discrete and often disparate ideas. Through activities and investigation, a person or group shapes a main idea or principle. Both methods of inquiry are extremely useful for facilitating thinking in learners because the methods require thought, decision, and synthesis on their part.

Taba (1967) is often credited with developing the inductive inquiry teaching model. It was designed to improve learners' abilities to think, handle information, and synthesize ideas. By employing inductive inquiry to training situations, learners are guided through concept formation, data interpretation, and application of principles. Although the phases appear to be steps followed in a scientific investigation, essentially any training or instructional topic can be designed and delivered using this method. What the inductive inquiry approach does is answer the question, "How do I create a Web-based training experience that goes beyond verbal information and simple concepts?"

There are many variations of the inductive inquiry model. Even so, a trainer generally could conceive this approach in three phases with several components in each phase (see Table 1). *Observed processes* constitute the learning environment. Questions, probing, and guid-

Table 1. Phases of the HyperInquiry Model (adapted from Taba, 1967).

	Observed Processes	Mental Processes	Probing Questions
Forming Concepts	A. Initial identification	Identifying discrete examples	What is going on here? What is happening?
	B. Identifying commonalities	Identifying common characteristics	What examples are the same?
	C. Naming, categorizing	Deciding what happens first, second, etc. . . .	What would you name these groups? What tasks are related to each other?
Interpreting Data/Info	A. Indicating important relationships	Comparing and contrasting	What do you think is important here? What is not important?
	B. Investigating relationships	Combining categories, as certain cause-and-effect relationships	Why did this occur? What caused this to happen?
	C. Formulating inferences and assumptions	Synthesizing beyond given information, determining reasons, deducing	What do you think about this? What is your conclusion?
Applying Principles	A. Hypothesizing, conjecturing, predicting	Dissect the problem or example, retrieving pertinent information	What would happen when, if . . . ? What would be the effect of . . . ?
	B. Explaining, supporting hypotheses, predicting	Establish what relates to what to achieve hypothesis	Why would these events happen?
	C. Justify hypothesis, prediction	Using relevant KSAs to evaluate prediction	What would need to happen for this situation to continue?

ing by the Web program or adjunct materials (e.g., a printed activity book) take place by using the *probing questions.* While learners are engaged in overt activities, cognitive processes or covert mental operations are taking place within the learners. These *mental processes* encourage what Schön (1983) refers to as reflective activities.

The first phase in inductive inquiry model, *Forming Concepts,* develops the general ideas and knowledge base of the topic. Learners are directed to locate information about the topic and build a foundation of concepts. They identify common properties or characteristics of examples and determine their hierarchial relationships.

Phase two is *Interpreting Data or Information.* In this phase, trainees identify the critical relationship among examples or information. After doing this, they look for cause-and-effect relationships and explore how and why they work or do not work. Essential in this phase is making inferences about the topic and going beyond what is given to develop conclusions.

The final phase of the model is *Applying Principles.* In this phase, learners use what they have explored in the previous phases. With this information they make predictions or hypotheses and support or explain these predictions. In addition, they are guided to verify their predictions by using logical principles or factual knowledge to determine necessary and sufficient conditions for their predictions to be true.

An Example: Time Management

Although the model seems complex, delivery can be fairly simple. For example, trainers or instructional designers could design cases that use audio or written format delivered via the Web or a combination of Web and printed activity book. Research contracts or agreements could be negotiated with trainees that structure the inquiry process and yet provide a maximum amount of exploration. Web-based simulations could provide the method of collecting data and trying out predictions. Structured role-playing using Web-based chat lines with trainers and trainees at remote locations could generate scenarios that act as a vehicle for inquiry training.

As an example, let's consider a situation in which you, the trainer, are tasked with designing a seminar on time management. After careful consideration, you have decided to use a case study approach to facilitate inductive inquiry. For our purposes, we'll consider Web-based case study to be comprehensive written, audio, illustrated, and/or video accounts of events which pose the problem to be solved. The case could be trainee-centered, where the individual or a group analyzes and solves the problem with little guidance but using the general parameters of inductive inquiry. Alternately, the case could be trainer-centered, where the problem is solved by following a series of carefully constructed questions. In our time management example, we'll use a simple trainer-centered approach.

Start out by clearly stating the purposes of the case study. If you are not clear about the purposes, involve your learners and content experts in the process until you are. Generate simple, plain English objectives for each phase of the inquiry process. Next, generate a list of questions for each phase of the HyperInquiry process. Examples of the types of questions that you might develop are included in Table 2.

If there are supplementary printed materials, make sure all trainees have access to them and know how to use the different media together. You could also place the printed supplementary materials on the Web for downloading. It is essential to make sure that users have all the information and software they need to successfully use your site.

During Phase 1 (concept formation) encourage the learners to establish a well-researched definition of what time management is. For this, you could set up links to sources on the Web or you could use a conference board and post some definitions. Present examples and nonexamples of time management. In effect, these are short cases. These could be in text form on a Website you develop for that purpose. If your resources are more liberal, enable your learners to use other modalities such as photos or digitized video to make your examples more concrete and encourage dual coding (Clark & Pavio, 1991). Make sure the examples are either from the workplace or the trainees' everyday life. For instance, on one medical training project in which we participated, we used specific example scenarios from medical cases and other examples. We did this because our prototype tests suggested that some physicians tended to get caught up in the minutiae of medical technique and were sometime missing the point of the examples and nonexamples. Finish the phase by connecting trainees with resources related to the other Phase 1 questions in Table 2. You could use a chat or conference board to address these activity questions, as well as a printed activity book.

To begin Phase 2 (interpreting data/information), present a more complex "real-life" case. Make sure your case is a detailed incident with a well-sequenced set of events. Also, make sure that potential solutions to the problem are contained within the presentation of the case. Again, text is fine to present the case if costs are an issue, but there is some research to support the use of multiple modalities (Austin, 1994; Chadwick, 1992; Hannafin & Phillips, 1987) such as text,

Table 2. Examples of eliciting questions for a time management topic.

Phase 1—Forming Concepts

What is time management?
What are examples of **poor** time management?
What are examples of **good** time management?
What are some of the first things you should do to manage your time?
What would you concentrate on next?
What would be some final things you could do?

Phase 2—Interpreting Data/Information

What did the person do that would be considered **poor** time management?
Why do you think this was a poor example?
What would be the long-term effect(s) of this action?
What did the person do that would be considered **good** time management?
Why do you think this was a good example?
What would be the long-term effect(s) of this action?

Phase 3—Applying Principles

What would happen if the person applied time management skill "A"?
What would happen if the person applied time management skill "B"?
Which aspects of daily routines would be improved?
What would be long-term benefits of this?
What would it take for this person's life to become more efficient?

---

illustrations, and audio. After presenting the case, point trainees to sources of data that correspond to the Phase 2 questions (see Table 2). The resources should be available to help trainees answer the question, "How can we set up time management systems appropriate for our jobs?"

During Phase 3 (applying principles), your job will be to help trainees make predictions (What would happen if . . . ?) and improvement plans (How could specific time management schemes have benefited the characters in the case study?) that solve the problems presented in the case. In this part of the process you will need to provide feedback, clarify issues, and arbitrate in technical disputes. You could do this through a conference board. It could also be achieved by providing the trainee with a detailed self-check job aid. Focus on process and outcome, particularly the KSAs that the characters presented in the case study would need to solve the time management problem.

Summary

In this chapter, we have proposed a model of inductive inquiry that uses the associative hyperlinks of the Web and related media. A primary benefit of this three-phase model is to present a structured problem-centered approach to Web-based training which offers learners maximum flexibility to attain complex learning outcomes.

References

Austin, M. B. (1994). A comparison of three interactive media formats in an RTV/DVI computer-mediated lesson. *Computers in Education, 22*(4), 319–333.

Chadwick, J. (1992). The development of a museum multimedia program and the effect of audio on user completion rate. *Journal of Educational Multimedia and Hypermedia, 1,* 331–340.

Clark, J. M., & Pavio, A. (1991). Dual coding theory and education. *Educational Psychology Review, 37,* 250–263.

Gagné, R. M. (1985). *The conditions of learning and theory of instruction.* New York: Holt, Rinehart, and Winston.

Hannafin, M. J. , & Phillips, T. L. (1987). Perspectives in the design of interactive video: Beyond tape versus disc. *Journal of Research and Development in Education, 21,* 44–60.

Knowles, M. (1984). *The adult learner: A neglected species* (3rd. ed.). Houston, TX: Gulf Publishing.

Schön, D. A. (1983). *The reflective practitioner: How professionals think in action.* New York: Basic Books.

Taba, H. (1967). *Teacher's handbook for elementary social studies.* Reading, MA: Addison-Wesley Publishing Co.

The Authors

John V. Dempsey (e-mail: jdempsey@jaguar1.usouthal.edu; Web homepage: coe.usouthal.edu/faculty/ jack_dempsey/jack.html) is Associate Professor, Instructional Design and Development Program, University of South Alabama, Mobile, Alabama. **Brenda C. Litchfield (e-mail: bcl@jaguar1.usouthal.edu)** is Assistant Professor in the Instructional Design and Development Program at the University of South Alabama.

24

Practical Guidelines for Facilitating Team Activities in Web-Based Training

M a r g a r e t   B a i l e y   a n d

L a r a   L u e t k e h a n s

Introduction

Today's trainers are expected to adapt and develop effective training techniques for a variety of new delivery systems, particularly Web-based training (WBT). An article in *Training and Development* has reported "advances in technology that will revolutionize the way training is delivered" to be one of the top ten trends affecting the future of training and development in the U.S. (Bassi, Benson, & Cheney, 1996). "But in order to use technology effectively, training professionals must know the appropriate situations and content for each learning platform" (p. 28).

This chapter provides a set of practical techniques for the Web-based trainer/facilitator faced with such a challenge. The techniques are grounded in the theories of constructivism, systems theory, and group dynamics, and have been tested by field trainers and educators. Included are specific techniques for facilitating (a) virtual learning teams (VLTs), (b) assembled for the purpose of formal training (knowledge/skills/attitudes), and (c) supported by access to text-based communication tools on the World Wide Web.

Facilitation. To facilitate is "to free from difficulties or obstacles; to make easier; to aid; to assist" (Bailey & Hannah, 1996). The role of the facilitator in WBT environments is different from that of face-to-face training. WBT provides two unique elements for the facilitator to consider: distant learners who are independent and self-directed, and communications mediated through technology.

WBT team members are distant from the facilitator and other learners, and thus must rely more heavily on internal motivation for participation and success in WBT courses. Also due to distance, the trainer is likely to feel less in control of teams and activities, as well as experiencing a loss in status as the trainer (Hatcher, 1997). Because communication in Web-based training environment is mediated, team members may not find it as easy to seek help from the facilitator. These challenges require the facilitator to be skilled in identifying struggling teams and assisting them in getting on track.

For purposes of this chapter, the facilitator's primary functions are defined as: (1) ensuring that no barriers exist to individual and team learning; (2) making essentials to learning accessible (such as interaction, information, feedback); (3) aiding learners and teams in times of conflict; and (4) assisting individuals and teams in all types of instructional activities.

Virtual Learning Teams (VLTs). Virtual learning teams are groups of workers assembled for the purpose of learning and problem solving who "meet" virtually through the support of electronic communications rather than face-to-face. VLTs can be assembled for formal learning (as represented by a defined set of training goals and scheduled as a training event) or informal learning. VLTs can be externally facilitated (e.g., by a non-participating team member such as a trainer) or internally facilitated (e.g., self-directed virtual learning teams or SVLTs). This chapter will address VLTs assembled for formal learning, and discuss methods for both external and internal facilitation.

Group Dynamics. As with any face-to-face team, VLTs are governed, in part, by the dynamics of group communication. The skilled facilitator is able to recognize elements of group dynamics such as: (a) the roles and relationships among members (e.g., affirming, leading, dominating, withdrawing), (b) the development and enforcement of group norms (e.g., acceptable and unacceptable communicative behaviors), and (c) patterns of interaction (Bailey & Hannah, 1996; Blanchard, Carew, & Parisi-Carew, 1996). While this chapter will not provide a complete primer on group dynamics, it will refer to these foundations in the techniques presented.

Planning and Selecting Tools and Activities

When planning team-based instructional activities to create interactive WBT environments, consideration should be made for tools available to teams matched with the primary purpose and learning goals of each team. The skilled facilitator must be familiar with the opportunities that a variety of Web-based communication tools can provide, yet keep in mind that the learning goals, not the tools, drive the appropriate selection of activities. See Table 1 for a listing of WBT activities supported by appropriate Web-based communication tools.

Web-Based Communication Tools. World Wide Web technology offers at least three categories of communication tools: synchronous, asynchronous, and hypertext resources. Such tools make one-to-one, one-to-many, and many-to-many models of communication possible. The capabilities of each tool can have a great deal of impact on the communication patterns of participants (Danielsen, 1994; Romiszowski & Mason, 1996).

Synchronous Tools. Synchronous communication tools allow groups to interact independent of each learner's location, but at the same time. This allows real-time communication to take place. Such tools might include multi-user domains, chat forums, or shared editors and whiteboards. Some also include desktop audio or video transmission.

Asynchronous Tools. Asynchronous communication tools provide a means for teams to interact independently of location and time. They are generally text-based, such as electronic mail and bulletin boards. Among the various asynchronous tools, each can vary in the amount of structure it provides to a team. For example, e-mail and listservs provide no threading of the discussion or archival record. Other asynchronous tools, such as *NetForum* (see Figure 1), a tool designed specifically for Web-based asynchronous discussions, include functions for keeping a group record, identifying new messages, threading a particular discussion, and allowing subsets of groups to have private discussion areas.

Table 1. WBT activities and supporting communication tools.

Training Activities	Supporting Communication Tools
Knowledge Construction	
Accessing Readings	Threaded Discussions
Adding Links to Web Resources	E-mail
Concept Exploration	Listservs
Questioning/Inquiry	Newsgroups
Gathering Data Through Surveys	Chat Forums
Sharing Information	Hypertext Resources
Posting Course Content and Examples	
Reflection	
Whole Class Discussions	
Team Based Discussions	
Searching for Information	
Mindmaps	
Skill Development	
Constructing or Producing Artifacts	Hypertext Resources
Creating Web Resources	Shared Editors
Gathering Data Through Surveys	White Boards
Reflection and Debriefing	Chat Forums
Role Playing	Threaded Discussions
Expert Modeling	
Posted Examples	
Tutorials/Worksheets	
Status Reporting	
Submitting Course Work	
Problem Solving	
Brainstorming	Chat Forums
Constructing or Producing Artifacts	Shared Editors
Creating Web Resources	White Boards
Gathering Data Through Surveys	Hypertext Resources
Sharing Information	Threaded Discussions
Consensus Building	E-mail
Negotiation and Decision Making	Listservs
Reflection and Debriefing	Newsgroups
Research	
Simulation/Scenario-based Exercises	
Status Reporting	
Submitting Course Work	
Motivation and Attitude Development	
Sharing Information	Threaded Discussions
Instructor and Peer Support	E-mail
Reflection and Debriefing	Listservs
Role Playing	Newsgroups
Ice Breakers	Hypertext Resources
Ground Rules	
Team Building	
Whole Class Discussions	

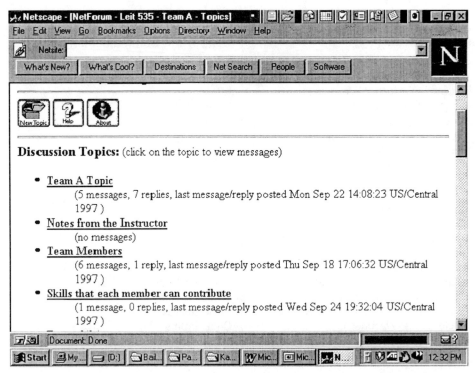

Figure 1. Example of threaded discussion in NetForum.

Hypertext Resources. The hypertext nature of the World Wide Web is one of its greatest strengths for educational use. Hypertext links make it possible for participants to access course and related resources, search for new information, contribute resources, post their own projects, interact through electronic forms, or gather data and participate in experimentation (Bannan & Milheim, 1997; Spiro, Feltovich, Jacobson, & Coulson, 1991).

Techniques for Facilitating Virtual Learning Team (VLTs) Activities

Instructional activities in WBT can be classified by the type of learning (Bannan & Milheim, 1997). For our purposes, WBT activities can be classified as those designed for (a) knowledge construction, (b) skill development, (c) problem-solving, and (d) motivation or attitude development.

Techniques for facilitating knowledge construction. Activities which develop new concepts, contexts, and meaning may include reading, information searching and sharing, Web-based discussion, inquiry, and reflection. The facilitator of knowledge construction must be skilled at scaffolding discussion, and encouraging exploration and elaboration.

• Use an asynchronous communication tool (such as a threaded discussion) to scaffold topical discussions.

—*Provide a minimal scaffold or structure for the discussion.* If the discussion topic is new to learners, post a topic name along with one or two open-ended questions to stimulate thinking. Use questions that elicit opinions and diverse viewpoints early, such as

"What makes a good sale?" Don't overdo the structure. Allow students to construct the concepts and detail.

—*Encourage learners to build off each response.* Use questioning to encourage elaboration, such as, "Jack, you indicated 'that a smile and a handshake are important.' What other techniques for building rapport with the client are essential?"

—*Encourage learner-to-learner interaction.* Use relay questioning techniques to avoid a discussion that is dominated by direct responses to the trainer. For example, "Lois asks if some clients are more approachable than others. Who can describe an 'approachable client'?"

—*Reward thoughtful contributions to the discussion.* One of the powers of asynchronous tools is that learners can take the time to frame a thoughtful response. Encourage this by short affirmations such as, "Karen, thank you for supporting your last point with a reference to our assigned reading. An effective reminder!"

—*Summarize key concepts for reinforcement.* When discussion objectives have been met, quickly "point to" the learning with a quick summary such as, "Each of you has described a variety of elements of the sale. To summarize, these can be classified as: establishing rapport, analyzing client needs, matching product to needs, handling objections, and closing the sale."

• **Use hypertext linking to encourage exploration and elaboration.**

—*Encourage students to provide hyperlinks in responses.* Many Web communication tools accept HTML links within the message body. Model the use of hypertext in your own responses. For example: "A good example of what Frank is talking about can be found on the Web at: coe.cedu.niu.edu/~luetke."

—*Invite students to solicit expert opinions through e-mail links.* Establish an area on your course Website that provides e-mail links to topical experts within and outside your organization. Encourage e-mail interaction with experts as part of discussion.

Techniques for facilitating skill development. WBT activities for skill development typically require levels of interactivity to support modeling, practice, and feedback. Activities that allow for the development of workplace competencies and skills may include expert modeling, interactive worksheets and forms, tutorials, role-plays, and small team projects. The facilitator of skill development must be expert at designing authentic projects, modeling, offering timely and meaningful feedback, and leading effective reflection and debriefs of skill activities.

• **Assemble Self-directed Virtual Learning Teams (SVLT) to produce or create an artifact using new skills.**

—*Assemble SVLTs strategically.* Break learners into SVLTs of 3–4 members. Larger teams are less productive and have more difficulty arriving at consensus (Dennis & Gallupe, 1993). Assemble teams according to experience (e.g., with HTML) so that an "expert" in the team is able to provide modeling of the skills and scaffolding for other team members.

—*Provide each team with a clear goal.* Give each SVLT the goal of producing a product or artifact. For example, for a competency in Web page development, have the SVLTs develop a Website, requiring each team member to take part in the Web page development. This activity also promotes skills in teamwork.

- **Model difficult tasks and behaviors.**

  —*Provide hyperlinks to models and examples.* Provide links to completed projects, forms, or reports on the training Website or in threaded discussion.

  —*Continuously model effective text-based communication.* In your own postings, use clear, concise language; avoid criticism and judgment in your responses; use complete sentences; restate key points from prior postings to provide connections to the reader; and affirm contributions that are thoughtful, diverse, and unique.

  —*Model unfamiliar tools and functions.* Be aware of tools and functions in the Web-based environment that may be unfamiliar to the new Web-based learner. Provide introductory assignments that allow safe exploration and modeling of tools, such as a threaded discussion, prior to relying on the tool for an instructional purpose.

- **Provide timely and meaningful feedback to teams and team members.**

  —*Use semi-private and private communications for feedback.* Semi-private communications can be established by providing "exclusive" threaded discussions, chat rooms, or listservs that can be accessed only by team members. Individual feedback, particularly training performance evaluations, should be conducted via private e-mail.

  —*Plan and use process checks as part of project activities.* A process check is a planned "check point" for communication, reporting, and questioning on a project's progress. Synchronous tools are effective for conducting process checks.

  —*Conduct an activity debrief.* When the activity is complete, conduct an asynchronous debrief discussion. Post questions that stimulate reflection and processing. Use hyperlinks to areas on the course Website to reinforce critical points. Refer to prior discussion points to personalize the discussion. For example, "Doris stated that her team experienced frustration as the client in this role-play. How does this relate to last week's discussion about what makes a disgruntled client?"

Techniques for facilitating problem solving. WBT activities for problem solving typically require methods that encourage both creativity and decision making. Activities which integrate knowledge and skill sets with real problems and contexts may include case scenarios, simulations, team research and reporting, negotiation, and decision making. The facilitator of problem solving must be skilled at encouraging creativity, diversity and participation, and managing conflict.

- **Plan authentic problem-based activities that culminate in a team decision or solution.**

  —*Provide teams an area on the course Website for posting resources and developing solutions.* Because problem solving requires both exploration and consensus, SVLTs should have the ability to access and post hypertext resources for information searching and sharing, as well as tools to develop and debate solutions.

  —*Provide a combination of tools for different stages of problem solving.* If the problem or case study will take several sessions to solve, teams will benefit from access to an asynchronous tool that can be used to keep records of the team's discussions and negotiations. If the case study can be resolved in a single sitting, a synchronous tool for discussing and defending individual perspectives or even voting can be useful. Asynchronous problem solving is best supplemented with a synchronous tool during stages of negotiation and decision making.

```
┌─────────────────────────────────────┐
│  ┌───────────────────────────────┐  │
│  │        Ground Rules           │  │
│  └───────────────────────────────┘  │
│                                      │
│  ☑ All ideas are welcome. Honesty    │
│    and critical reflection are       │
│    valued.                           │
│  ☑ Participate frequently. Both      │
│    reading and responding            │
│    activities are vital to this      │
│    discussion.                       │
│  ☑ Build on each others' ideas. This │
│    is the central strength of a      │
│    forum. Feel free to question,     │
│    react to, and build on each       │
│    others' thoughts.                 │
│  ☑ Let yourself discover a personal  │
│    style for reading and responding. │
│    I encourage you to start by       │
│    looking for a thread that         │
│    interests you. Start a new thread │
│    if your idea is different from     │
│    those already posted.             │
│  ☑ Please use e-mail for private     │
│    communication.                    │
│  ☑ Please no personal attacks or     │
│    flaming.                          │
│  ☑ Facilitators will monitor the     │
│    forum throughout the discussion.  │
└─────────────────────────────────────┘
```

Figure 2. Example ground rules for a threaded discussion.

- **Establish ground rules for communications to encourage creativity.**

  —*Post ground rules in an area where all team members will read it.* Creative problem solving requires a certain level of trust among members that all ideas, no matter how diverse or unique, will be accepted. Establishing ground rules that encourage members to suspend judgment and accept diverse views are important. Post the rules at the beginning of a topic or on the course Website. Monitor the interaction and remind members when a contribution is outside of the accepted rules. See Figure 2 for an example of WBT ground rules.

- **Intervene when conflicts arise.** (It is the facilitator's primary function to remove obstacles to learning. Conflict can be the greatest obstacle to problem solving and problem-based learning.)

  —*Discourage personal criticism and attacks.* Carefully phrase responses to comments that are clearly not constructive. For example, "While I realize we will not always agree with all points of view expressed on this forum, this is a reminder to reflect and build on the IDEAS, not judge the PERSON."

  —*Intervene to highlight areas of common ground among conflicting team members.* Team members will expect the facilitator to intervene when conflicts get personal or unproductive. Start by helping team members see areas within their conflict that they agree upon. For example, "Sara and Tom, you seem to be at a standstill. In reviewing your discussion, it appears that you are both concerned that the client is satisfied. Is that correct?" Encourage the use of synchronous tools to resolve heated conflict in a timely fashion.

Techniques for facilitating motivation and attitude development. WBT activities for motivation and attitude development typically require methods which eliminate barriers to learning. These barriers may come from fear, apathy, or from being on unfamiliar ground (such as the first time with a team or the first time as a learner in WBT.) The skilled facilitator has a variety of techniques to support learners in establishing relationships, team building, interacting with the Web environment, and overcoming issues of procrastination.

- **Help learners overcome initial fears through an advance e-mail.** (Include the following: welcome; introduction and some personal data; a brief description of course expectations; and tips on being a successful learner in WBT. Provide your e-mail address and the URL to the course Web site so learners can greet you and explore the site before the course begins.)

- **Personalize team members through posted biographies and photos.** (As one of the first course or team activities, have each learner use the selected communication tools to post a brief introduction or biographical sketch of themselves or another learner.)

  —*Ask learners to post a biographical sketch.* The biography might include a photo and information regarding background, interests and personal learning goals. By doing this, the learners become acquainted with the tools and the facilitator now has a bank of information for assembling SVLTs based on interest and expertise.

  —*Ask learners to interview a fellow learner and introduce the individual to the rest of the team.* This, too, orients the learner to the communication tools, but in addition, expedites relationship building among learners.

- **Plan frequent e-mail prompts to help team members overcome procrastination.** (A challenge in WBT is encouraging team members to sustain participation throughout the length of a course. E-mail reminders are useful in helping to keep the course in the forefront of learner's thoughts. E-mails should not be nagging, but serve as friendly reminders to log-on to the site. For example, "There has been some excellent discussion taking place this week in the Week Five Forum! Check out the new topics under 'Handling Objections.' I will be online from 2–5 PM CDT today to answer project questions in Course Chat.")

Conclusion

Drawing on a theoretical framework emergent from constructivism, systems theory, and group dynamics as well as the authors' own experiences, this chapter presented some practical guidelines for facilitating team activities in Web-based training. A facilitator's required skills range from planning and selecting appropriate learning activities and communication tools to developing electronic materials and managing online discussions. In planning WBT, the facilitator's focus should be on selecting activities that address the learning goals, supported by the unique capabilities of an appropriate communication tool. As the training moves into implementation, the facilitator's focus should be on removing obstacles to team learning.

The specific skills and techniques outlined in this chapter are presented for use during formal WBT. However, a great deal of organizational learning occurs informally. WBT can be used to support both formal and informal learning opportunities. Continued investigation and thought should be given to specific skills and techniques to be used in facilitating continuous learning.

References

Bailey, M., & Hannah, M. H. (1996). Instructional technology workshop: Group facilitation. Unpublished manuscript.

Bannan, B., & Milheim, W. D. (1997). Existing Web-based instruction courses and their design. In B. H. Khan (Ed.), *Web-based instruction* (pp. 381–387). Englewood Cliffs: Educational Technology Publications.

Bassi, L. J., Benson, G., & Cheney, S. (1996). The top ten trends. *Training & Development, 50*(11), 28–42.

Blanchard, K., Carew, D., & Parisi–Carew, E. (1996). How to get your group to perform like a team. *Training & Development, 50*(9), 34–37.

Danielsen, T. (1994). Computer support for collaboration. In M. F. Verdejo, & S. A. Cerri (Eds.), *Collaborative dialogue technologies in distance learning.* New York: Springer–Verlag.

Dennis, A., & Gallupe, R. B. (1993). A history of group support systems empirical research: Lessons learned and future directions. In L. M. Jessup & J. S. Valacich (Eds.), *Group support systems: New perspectives* (pp. 59–77). New York: Macmillan.

Hatcher, T. G. (1997). The ins and outs of self-directed learning. *Training & Development, 51*(2), 35–39.

Romiszowski, A. J., & Mason, R. (1996). Computer-mediated communication. In D. Jonassen (Ed.), *Handbook of research in educational communication and technology* (pp. 438–456). New York: Macmillan.

Spiro, R. J., Feltovich, P. J., Jacobson, M. L., & Coulson, R. L. (1991). Cognitive flexibility, constructivism, and hypertext: Random access instruction for advanced knowledge acquisition in ill-structured domains. *Educational Technology, 31*(5), 24–33.

The Authors

Margaret Bailey (e-mail: pbailey@niu.edu; Web homepage: coe.niu.edu/~bailey) is Assistant Chair for Special Projects at Northern Illinois University, DeKalb. **Lara Luetkehans** (e-mail: luetke@niu.edu; Web homepage: coe.niu.edu/~luetke) is Assistant Professor at NIU.

25

Industry-University Partnerships in Web-Based Learning: A Working Model

Colla J. MacDonald and

Martha Gabriel

I n the midst of rapid technological change, new approaches to education and training are being demanded (Eastmond & Ziegahn, 1995). Lifelong learning and constant upgrading and training have become the norm in the Information Society. These demands are being advanced both by employees struggling to maintain their present jobs or seeking career advancement, and by employers searching for appropriate, technically skilled workers to ensure economic survival. The World Wide Web is a major force that focuses attention on how global networks will transform educational and training experiences (Haughey & Anderson, 1998; Kearsley, 1996; Khan, 1997; Romiszowski, 1997). Web-based learning, when driven by sound concepts of pedagogy, is a form of distance education offering an extensive range of educational possibilities. This approach is strongly supported by current growth trends in distance education, as well as the rapid development and success of specific educational programs utilizing high-end information technologies.

The advanced technology sector is an example of one group of knowledge-based employees with specific training needs. A major problem facing today's advanced technology companies is the management gap (MacDonald, Cousins, Bailetti, & Rahman, 1995). Firms are frequently very capable in the technical areas of advanced technology, but weak in management areas, especially at the product or project level. Rapid changes in the advanced technology industry make it imperative that companies have cross functionally-trained managers who can successfully create and market new products (MacDonald & Cousins, 1998/1999).

The allocation of time for training becomes problematic, given the heavy workloads of employees in advanced technology companies. A need exists for flexible industry-specific education and training programs in these companies. A critical consideration will be programs enabled through alternate distributive methods that allow training to be accomplished any time and any place (MacDonald, Cousins, Bucknell, & Nariman, 1998). If the training is flexible, relevant, and also holds the prestige of an accredited university degree, all stakeholders will benefit. A substantial opportunity exists to design a graduate level program in advanced technology management delivered by distance education to fulfill the education and training needs of the advanced technology sector.

245

The time is right to develop alternative models of delivering university education to accommodate the demands of both employees and corporations. In this chapter, we propose partnerships between private industry and accredited universities as an effective model to deliver such programs. The model will accommodate professionals wanting to attain a university degree while maintaining their place in the workforce. The model can be generalized to many diverse fields, such as nursing, education, law, and medicine. Combining the strengths of content experts from academia and private industry will ensure that all students, regardless of location, will have the best possible learning experience. The main objective of the model is to incorporate pedagogical and technological considerations to maintain the benefits of the synchronous classroom experience while gaining the benefits of asynchronous learning and interactivity (Burge & Roberts, 1998; Eastmond & Ziegahn, 1995).

The model is discussed in relation to a program based on a partnership between collaborating east coast Canadian universities and a private advanced technology training company. This model was initially conceived for and will first be piloted on a specific program with great market demand—management education and training in the advanced technology sector. The model was developed because there was no one existing model that successfully addressed the diversified needs of adult learners in the Web-based learning experience envisioned in the program. The model could be adopted by or adapted to many Web-based learning courses or programs. For the purpose of this chapter, however, the learning model is used as a framework to design and effectively operationalize a Web-based MBA for advanced technology professionals. By piloting this model, we hope to contribute to an understanding of the salient features of learning in a Web-based environment, in an effort to improve distance educators' practice.

The Partnership Learning Model: Web-Based

The aim of applying the Partnership Learning Model (PLM) to a Web-based format is to establish a platform to improve the quality of Web-based learning from the standpoint of both technology and pedagogy. To meet this objective, the model incorporates several aspects of existing learning models and approaches. However, the PLM focuses on three distinct variables: superior content—industry driven, relevant, applicable, researched content; superior delivery—fourth generation technology which is engaging and interactive; and superior service—consistent quality, immediate response, constant support, and convenience for the customer. These three variables are enabled through a fourth variable—a partnership between private industry and an accredited learning institution (Figure 1).

The PLM utilizes "fourth generation" distance education. Fourth generation distance education incorporates the possibilities of global networking in an interactive distance classroom (Shimabukuro, 1995). This technology allows a qualitative shift from technologies employed in third generation computer mediated distance education (Bates, 1991; Kaufman, 1989; Kaye, 1989; Nipper, 1989). Within the concept of the virtual classroom, distance education can be superior to the best available on-site courses.

Superior Content

The PLM responds to the demands of both employees striving to acquire a degree while working and meeting family responsibilities, and corporations seeking the appropriate technically skilled workers to assure economic survival. The PLM, like just-in-time learning approaches, adheres to adult learning principles of relevant and applicable content (Knowles, 1984).

A distinctive feature of the PLM is that it creates competitive advantage because it is demand driven. Members of a curriculum advisory board of both industry and academic leaders

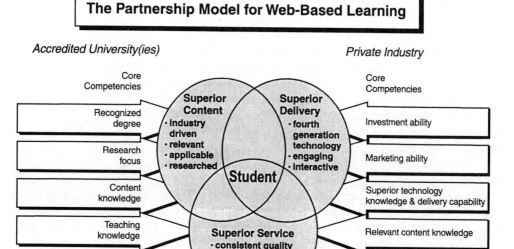

Figure 1. The Partnership Model for Web-Based Learning focuses on three distinct variables: superior content (industry driven, relevant, applicable, researched); superior delivery (fourth generation technology, engaging, interactive); and superior service (consistent quality, immediate response, constant support, and convenience for the student). These three variables are enabled through a fourth variable, a partnership between private industry and accredited learning institution(s).

collaborate on an ongoing basis to ensure that key topic coverage in the degree program meets the core needs of the specific industry. Having identified the requisite topic areas and specific content needs, subject matter experts are invited to design specific course modules. Content creators are recognized content experts and are drawn from both academia and industry. PLM solicits the direct input of industry professionals to address the education needs of the companies within specific industries, under the auspices and guidance of university academics. This will insure that the program will incorporate an appropriate balance of relevant, practical, up-to-date skills and theory, making it credible and attractive to professionals. Suggested or necessary changes to content are identified and modifications are made on a continual basis through ongoing review.

Action research is an essential element of the superior content component of the PLM. Continual research into learning processes and strategies of Web-based learning are an integral component of the model. Summative and formative evaluations of knowledge learned, retained, and transferred to the workplace are incorporated into the learning process (Cousins & MacDonald, 1998). The research findings associated with this particular program will be disseminated to both academic and professional audiences.

The focus of the content is on the specific requirements of the client, in an effort to develop the most effective global education program possible. Developing a learning model that is industry-driven produces a program providing university graduates, for example, in engineering and computer science, with technical knowledge of and experience in business administration. Due to the scarcity of graduates in computer science and engineering at universities in recent years, employees are often promoted to managers at a relatively young age. However, these individuals sometimes lack necessary skills in marketing, finance, economics, and management. The PLM is designed to support the development of a program that will bridge this gap.

A learning model with an industry-driven focus permits the integration of content, theory, and practice. This integration brings the learning closer to the workplace, and fosters the development and application of job-related skills. A group with similar work experience, such as computer scientists and engineers, allows appropriate content to be tailored to the needs of those working in the high technology industry. The superior content will satisfy employers' needs in the industry, as well as motivating the learner, increasing retention, and justifying costs on a third level evaluation.

Superior Delivery

The application of fourth generation technology is another distinguishing characteristic of the PLM. When fourth generation technology is utilized, traditional college campuses are no longer the focal point of instructional delivery (Shimabukuro, 1995). Instructors and students are electronically linked around the world and seldom, if ever, meet face to face. In this model, the application of fourth generation technology is enabled by a partnership association with industry.

The PLM delivers learning experiences which allow students to critically assess the quality and utility of information and then synthesize it with prior experiential knowledge, similar to both constructivist and just-in-time approaches to learning (Duffy & Jonassen, 1992). This interactive learning process utilizes the most current tools available for distance education (Berge & Collins, 1995). Learning activities in this model include: instructor-led group discussions; brainstorming; guest lectures; project-based instruction; small group discussions; individual presentations; peer review of writing; public conferencing; interactive chat; question and answer sessions; simulations; retrieving information from online databases; electronic journals, and high-end interactive video and graphics. Thousands of hours of labor and millions of dollars are required to support the effective development and delivery of such a program.

In this economic climate, most universities do not have the resources required to develop or deliver the kind of high-end technology program described here. Therefore, many of the university courses or programs which currently exist online do not effectively utilize available technology. For the most part, the delivery of these distance education programs is limited to e-mail communication with professors and teaching assistants. Many students are left reading content on the Internet with little or no interactivity. In the PLM, a common vision to deliver superior industry-driven content, by way of cutting edge technology delivery mechanisms, is realized through a collaborative partnership between universities and private industry.

Superior Service

The PLM offers a high quality service to the adult learner in a number of ways. Courses are designed in modular format; students have the option to take a particular module, a course, or an entire degree. Turn-around on assignments is short. Students feel a responsiveness equal to, or superior to, on-site instruction. Course delivery utilizes the full power of the World Wide Web as a delivery tool, providing printable course notes, and augmenting course content through links to online resources.

The PLM supports the adult learner by providing a flexible industry-specific program with delivery accomplished through alternate distributive methods that permit student participation at any time or place. The learning model improves access to lifelong education opportunities for many adult learners (part-time, full-time, retraining, individuals desiring career change, senior level staff affected by downsizing). This learning model is cost effective for firms, since it requires limited time away from work. This flexible delivery structure also encourages the learner to apply skills back in the workplace between units, as learners discuss experiences with instructors and peers online. By linking theory and practice in this way, this approach further increases the probability that genuine, long-lasting impact will occur in the workplace (MacDonald & Cousins, 1998/1999).

In the PLM, the learner is provided with effective, online quality services, such as: electronic registration, question and answer sessions, extensive and fast feedback on assignments, direct access to professors via e-mail and telephone, bulletin board announcements, and a bookstore. The latter provides the convenience of browsing an online bookstore cross-referenced to course codes, allowing students to order their texts online. Additional relevant resources are supplied in the virtual library for students' interest, or to assist with research papers and assignments. An extensive bibliography of industry-specific related resources is also provided. The literature suggests that these forms of support help increase the effectiveness of the learning process (Eastmond & Ziegahn, 1995; Haughey & Anderson, 1998).

Partnership Between Industry and University

The PLM is distinctive through the combination of quality content, reliance on the most effective technology to support learning, and the development of cooperative partnerships. Superior content, delivery, and service are enabled through a partnership between the university and private industry. Both parties have diverse and valuable core competencies. This learning model addresses clients' perceived need for university accreditation—brand identity enhanced by university infrastructures provide a research focus, course delivery, and support. At the same time, the learning model maximizes the value of core competencies and credibility in the advanced technology sector—relevant applicable content and the ability to raise funds to develop and deliver superior interactive content. Thus, the PLM merges the strengths of content experts from academia and private industry to ensure all students have access to the best possible learning experiences, regardless of geographic location.

References

Bates, A. W. (1991). Third generation distance education: The challenge of new technology. *Research in Distance Education, 3*(2), 10–15.

Berge, Z. L., & Collins, M. P. (Eds.). (1995). *Computer mediated communication and the online classroom: Vol. III. Distance learning.* Cresskill, NJ: Hampton Press.

Burge, E. J., & Roberts, J. M. (1998). *Classrooms with a difference: Facilitating learning on the information highway* (2nd ed.). Toronto: McGraw-Hill.

Cousins, J. B., & MacDonald, C. J. (1998). Conceptualizing outcomes for the evaluation of management training in technology-based companies: A participatory concept mapping application. *Evaluation and Program Planning Journal, 21*(3).

Duffy, T. M., & Jonassen, D. H. (Eds.). (1992). *Constructivism and the technology of instruction: A conversation.* Hillsdale, NJ: Lawrence Erlbaum Associates.

Eastmond, D., & Ziegahn, L. (1995). Instructional design for the online classroom. In Z. L. Berge & M. P. Collins (Eds.), *Computer mediated communication and the online classroom: Vol. III. Distance learning* (pp. 59–80). Cresskill, NJ: Hampton Press.

Haughey, M., & Anderson, T. (1998). *Networked learning: The pedagogy of the Internet.* Toronto: McGraw-Hill.

Kaufman, D. M. (1989). Third generation course design in distance education. In R. Sweet (Ed.), *Post-secondary distance education in Canada: Policies, practices, and priorities* (pp. 61–78). Alberta: Athabasca University and Canadian Society for Studies in Education.

Kaye, A. (1989). Computer-mediated communication and distance education. In R. Mason & A. Kaye (Eds.), *Mindweave: Communication, computers, and distance education* (pp. 3–21). Oxford: Pergamon Press.

Kearsley, G. (1996). The World Wide Web: Global access to education. *Educational Technology Review, 5*(5), 26–30.

Khan, B. H. (1997). Web-based instruction (WBI): What is it and why is it? In B. H. Khan (Ed.), *Web-based instruction* (pp. 5–18). Englewood Cliffs: Educational Technology Publications.

Knowles, M. S. (1984) *Andragogy in action.* San Francisco: Jossey-Bass.

MacDonald, C. J., & Cousins, J. B. (1998/1999). Predictors and outcomes of successful product development projects. *Training Research Journal, 4,* 117–134.

MacDonald, C. J., Cousins, J. B., Bailetti, A. J., & Rahman, A. H. (1995). *Toward meaningful evaluation of manager training in technology-based companies.* Training in Business and Industry: Selected Research Papers, AERA Special Interest Groups Conference proceedings (pp. 69–98).

MacDonald, C. J., Cousins, J. B., Bucknell, T., & Nariman, N. (1998). Technicians learn to lead. *Technical Training, 9*(5), 48–51.

Nipper, S. (1989). Third generation distance learning and computer conferencing. In R. Mason & A. Kaye (Eds.), *Mindweave: Communication, computers, and distance education* (pp. 63–73). Oxford: Pergamon Press.

Romiszowski, A. J. (1997). Web-based distance learning and teaching: Revolutionary invention or reaction to necessity? In B. H. Khan (Ed.), *Web-based instruction* (pp. 25–37). Englewood Cliffs: Educational Technology Publications.

Shimabukuro, J. (1995). CMC and writing instruction: A future scenario. In Z. L. Berge & M. P. Collins (Eds.), *Computer mediated communication and the online classroom: Vol. I. Overview and Perspectives* (pp. 37–52). Cresskill, NJ: Hampton Press.

Authors' Note

Contributions made to the design and interpretation phases of this model by Michael Gaffney of Learnsoft Corporation and François Desjardins of the Faculty of Education at the University of Ottawa are appreciated.

The Authors

Colla J. MacDonald (e-mail: cjmacdon@uottawa.ca) is Associate Professor, Faculty of Education, at the University of Ottawa, Canada. **Martha Gabriel** (e-mail: mgabriel@upei.ca) is with the Faculty of Education at the University of Prince Edward Island, Canada.

26

Managing the Development and Evolution of Web-Based Training: A Service Bureau Concept

Thomas M. Welsh and

Ben L. Anderson

Introduction

With the advent of the World Wide Web as a vehicle for the delivery of training, important issues are being raised which were unforeseen prior to this first widely used and completely networked medium. Training professionals are finding that the systematic development of Web-based training requires a great deal of cooperation between instructional designers, MIS personnel, and instructors. More than ever before, instructional designers are required to acknowledge the systemic nature of the training process due to the high degree of interaction between the technology infrastructure available for training and the needs of trainees, managers, and the training organization. In order to be successful, Web-based training must be convenient for students and their managers. It must be compatible with local or wide area networks, depending on the degree of freedom you wish to give students as to when and where they attend Web-based courses. Also, it must be revisable, allowing easy integration of new technologies that better facilitate learning, convenience, management, and student tracking.

These goals can be facilitated through the creation of a service bureau for Web-based training. The service bureau coordinates its activities with the training department and ensures the quality of Web-based training for all stakeholders, while keeping a keen eye on future developments that can enhance learning and training management. Integration of the service bureau concept, however, demands a rethinking of the traditional instructional design process to accommodate the capabilities of the Web as a dynamic, updatable, single source training delivery system. The authors have been pilot testing the service bureau concept by using the Event Oriented Design (EOD) model for Web-based training development (Welsh, 1997). The EOD model has evolved based on our experience and now includes the elements depicted in Table 1. This chapter explores the service bureau concept in relation to the EOD model and its potential benefits for the development, delivery, and revision of Web-based training.

Table 1. A service bureau concept based on the EOD model.*

Course Specific Development Steps	Ongoing Activities
1. Specify instructional goal and performance objectives of the course using traditional instructional design methods.	
2. Sequence and chunk performance objectives into a series of instructional units, each of which results in assessment of student ability to meet specific performance objectives.	• Determine organizational standards for supported WBT technologies.
3. Divide each instructional unit into a series of chronological instructional events.	• Maintain and revise existing online courses.
4. For each event, specify appropriate Web-based training technologies to enable event. Care should be taken to choose only from technologies available to instructor and all students and supportable by available bandwidth.	• Explore and recommend emerging technologies to better enable instructional events, assessment, and tracking.
5. For each event, develop content where needed and define procedures that ensure smooth completion of event.	
6. Pilot test as necessary to verify that each event is robust pedagogically and procedurally.	

*See Welsh (1997) for a detailed application of the EOD model to an instructional development scenario.

The Service Bureau Concept

With the advent of Web-based delivery formats, the traditional training organization must concern itself with course maintenance issues that were nonexistent in past course delivery formats. In the past, training organization tasks revolved around traditional concerns related to training needs assessment, development, and distribution. Usually, once a course was developed, it required relatively little ongoing maintenance. The service bureau concept reflects the need for the training organization to maintain and revise active Web-based courses in addition to developing them. In the development capacity, the service bureau assists the course development team in defining Web-based training technology standards for the organization and in assisting the instructional design team in defining delivery formats for training. In the maintenance and revision capacity, the service bureau takes on tasks related to maintaining and updating the content and operational characteristics of course Websites (Kilby, 1997). It also explores and recommends new Web-based technologies that better facilitate learning.

Course Design and Development

A fundamental role played by the service bureau in terms of course design and development is in establishing standards for supported technologies and a plan for accommodating newly emerging technologies into existing courses. Hall (1997) describes a plethora of potential hardware and software configurations on both the server and client sides of the Web-based training scenario. Decisions on which Web-based technologies to use depend on the capabilities and limitations of the server, network, and user (or client) platforms. Once these capabilities and limitations are defined, the service bureau can recommend a feasible technology mix that enables desired learning activities.

Once the technology mix is defined, organizing the content of online courses into units and instructional events using the EOD model permits quick and easy maintenance and revision of course content and allows for the integration of new technologies. However, a strategy that enables easy revision and modification of course content must be considered and planned for early in the development process. Templates should be created that include standard navigational controls and enable rapid development of new instruction. In addition, the service bureau must define naming conventions and standards for content organization.

The key to designing training content for network delivery revolves around the idea of "chunking" content into small, manageable units (Filipczak, 1996; Kilby, 1997). Units should be designed as relatively freestanding. This allows changes to be made in one unit while not affecting other units or the course as a whole. Instructional events should consist of learning activities that stand alone and are not overly dependent on the other activities within the module. This way, individual events can be deleted or modified, or new events can be inserted into modules without necessitating changes throughout the course. Structuring content in this manner allows it to be easily revised and ensures that users have access to the most up-to-date training. In fact, training on one unit can be updated while users are completing other modules in the training program!

Course Maintenance

After the Web-based training program has been implemented, the role of the service bureau changes to one of maintaining the online course, revising course content, and integrating new technologies that may enhance instruction. When the organization decides that content has become obsolete or needs modification, or that new content needs to be added, the revision process becomes one of deleting old instructional events, modifying others, and inserting new events. And when new technologies emerge that allow more effective instruction or rapid transmission of multimedia, revising the content is simply a matter of replacing existing events with new ones that utilize the new technologies. It is not necessary to rewrite an entire course, only those instructional events that require revision.

Sales Training: A Content Revision Scenario

Consider the case of a traveling pharmaceutical sales representative. In the evening, Sandy Johnson sits in her motel room with her laptop computer, planning for the next day's calls. Using her contact database, she identifies each physician's prescribing habits and reviews her previous call notes. Among other things, she notes that many of her clients have been raising objections to the described benefits of Acetaminophen. As part of her ongoing training plan, Sandy logs onto the company Web site. Her laptop modem comes to life and dials into the sales training department's computer. She clicks on the link labeled "Sales Training Online."

Meanwhile, back at company headquarters, the sales department in recent months had received similar objections to the company's line on the benefits of Acetaminophen. Earlier, headquarters had asked the training department to address those objections in the training. In response, the training department designed an instructional module about handling objections to Acetaminophen. The service bureau, using pre-existing templates and current Web-based technologies, produced the Web pages and inserted the necessary instructional events into the existing sales training course.

When Sandy accesses the online training from her motel room, she sees a screen filled with icons and links to a variety of training modules. Upon selecting the module "Handling Objections," she sees the issue that many of her clients had been raising. After completing the

30-minute online tutorial about handling objections, Sandy turns off her computer and begins to unwind for the evening, confident that she is prepared to respond to her clients' objections.

What happened in this scenario? From Sandy's perspective, she was able to access the most up-to-date training available from her company. Because the training was organized in modular form with discrete instructional units and events, maintenance and revision of the content was easy. By following the conventions and standards for chunking content and instructional events that were established in the development of the training, the service bureau was able to produce new instructional events and easily insert them into the existing Web-based training site.

Integration of New Technologies

As new technologies emerge that enable more effective online instruction, assessment, and tracking, the service bureau is responsible for facilitating the integration of those technologies into the training department's current repertoire. Therefore, the service bureau must develop a strategy for integrating new technologies and for addressing the likely issues involved with their adoption. It must look ahead to see how changes in technology will affect the future of the Web-based training program. This involves developing a technology plan and includes considering all pieces of technology needed to plan, design, author, deliver, and maintain Web-based training. Hall (1997) recommends looking ahead three years to assess the likely impact of technology on training. The technology plan must address how emerging technologies will be integrated into the training program and it should revolve around how the training will be delivered and accessed by the end user. The goal of the service bureau should be to choose the most appropriate and effective technologies for a given instructional task (Ahern, 1996). And the key determinant for choosing any new technology should be the effectiveness with which it can communicate/deliver the experiences that enable students to achieve a course's goals and objectives (Boettcher & Cartwright, 1997).

There are many issues that must be considered by the service bureau before integrating new technologies. What impact will it have on server and client machines? What software is necessary on both sides? Will new software need to be installed and maintained on the company server? Are external applications and plug-ins beyond the currently installed Web browser necessary for client machines? Does the new technology fit within the technical expertise of the end users? Employees may not have the computer skills or Internet knowledge to use sophisticated technologies (Wulf, 1996). Installing and configuring plug-ins may be beyond the employees' ability. Is the bandwidth sufficient to enable the technology to be effective? Limited bandwidth means slower performance than is possible with stand-alone computer-based training, especially when incorporating sound, video, and elaborate graphics into the training (Wulf, 1996). These are just some of the concerns that must be addressed by the service bureau.

Sale Training: A Technology Revision Scenario

In the previously introduced scenario, Sandy Johnson, the pharmaceutical sales representative, accessed her company's online training site over a modem on her laptop computer. Suppose that part of the tutorial included real-time (or streaming*) audio delivered using Macromedia's Shockwave multimedia technology. The company has been considering converting from Shockwave to a different technology, Real Audio, for its streaming audio needs. What issues must the service bureau consider before it integrates the new technology?

---

*Streaming audio refers to a process by which a server "feeds" audio to the client machine in real time. The end user can almost immediately listen to the beginning of the audio file while the server continues to download the remaining data.

On the server side, the service bureau must first consider the benefits of Real Audio over Shockwave. It must consider the added expense and maintenance of a Real Audio server. On the client side, Sandy Johnson would need to possess enough technical knowledge to download and install the Real Audio player on her computer and configure her browser to play Real Audio files. Or at least she must have access to a technical support person who can reconfigure her computer. Her computer would need sufficient memory and the necessary system requirements to play Real Audio. Bandwidth issues would also need to be considered. Does Real Audio require increased bandwidth? Is Sandy's modem sufficient to play Real Audio without it breaking up? These are some of the issues that must be addressed by the service bureau personnel as they consider integrating a new technology into the Web-based training program.

Pilot testing the new training materials on a small group of sales representatives can resolve these issues. Through pilot testing, the service bureau may find that Real Audio is a better technology to use than Shockwave. Or they may discover that Shockwave works well and there is no advantage in converting to Real Audio. Pilot testing may reveal other issues that were not even considered previously. After pilot testing shows that the issues surrounding the new technology have been resolved, then the new technology can be integrated into the training program. Future instructional events and modules can be developed that incorporate the new technology, and it would be a relatively simple task to modify existing instructional events to take advantage of this technology.

Conclusion

The speed at which Web-based technologies are changing requires constant attention to prevent online training from becoming stale and out of date. The service bureau concept provides a means by which training departments can address the issues involved in developing, maintaining, and revising content and integrating new technologies. By conducting ongoing evaluation and analysis of new technologies, and by having a technology plan and a strategy for implementing new technologies, the service bureau can assist the training department in keeping its online training on the cutting edge.

References

Ahern, T. C. (1996). A framework for improving the task-to-technology fit in distance education. *TechTrends, 41*, 23–26.

Boettcher, J., & Cartwright, G. (1997). Designing and supporting courses on the Web. *Change, 29(9)*, 10–14.

Filipczak, B. (1996). Training on intranets: The hope and the hype. *Training, 33(9)*, 24–32.

Hall, B. (1997). *Web-based training cookbook.* New York: John Wiley & Sons.

Kilby, T. (1997). The development process, *WBT Information Center;* filename.com/wbt/_private/process.htm

Welsh, T. (1997). An event-oriented design model for Web-based instruction. In B. H. Khan (Ed.), *Web-based instruction.* Englewood Cliffs: Educational Technology Publications.

Wulf, K. (1996). Training via the Internet: Where are we? *Training & Development, 50(5)*, 50–60.

The Authors

Thomas M. Welsh (e-mail: twelsh@csuchico.edu; Web homepage: csuchico.edu/~twelsh/vital.htm) is an Assistant Professor of Instructional Technology at California State University, Chico. **Ben L. Anderson** (e-mail: banders@lcoe.butte.k12.ca.us; Web homepage: ctap2.bcol.butte.k12.ea.us) is Coordinator of the California Technology Assistance Project, Center for Distributed Learning, Butte County Office of Education, Oraville, California.

27

Designing Practical Websites for Interactive Training

John G. Hedberg,

Christine Brown,

John L. Larkin, and

Shirley Agostinho

Any manager who does not forward the information to the interested parties, and any manager that does not have a system to use information, is doing a great disservice to the company and creating massive waste in the form of lost opportunities and wasted executive time. (Imai, 1986, p. 93)

One man gives freely yet gains even more. Another withholds unduly, but comes to poverty. (Proverbs 11:24)

Introduction

When you think about introducing Web-based training into an organization, there are many options that flow from what might seem a simple decision requiring only incremental change. In our work on a series of projects, we have been amazed at how the decision to introduce Web-based training might generate a powerful strategic plan for the training function of an organization. Further, strategy changes can even instigate a shift in the culture of the organization from one which merely adopts a technological framework for content delivery (Scenario A) to one in which technology facilitates the emergence and evolution of a progressive learning-centered organization (Scenario B). *A typical scenario might flow along the lines in Scenario A on the following page.* The training manager for **Quality Quiche Company** views the Web as an information source or a means of updating training information. It is considered an appropriate electronic storage mechanism, with the advantage that trainees do not have to attend classes.

The extent of the use of the Web in training in an organization can start with the simple conversion of training materials into pages that might be provided to all members of the organization through an intranet Web server. But much more is possible than a simple conversion with the use of computer delivery technologies like the Web. Not only are training materials instantly available anywhere throughout the network, but also they can be updated rapidly and

257

Scenario A: The Quality Quiche Company

At the Quality Quiche Company, George, the training manager, has decided that the Web is a good storage mechanism for his training materials. He can continue to use his existing paper-based training materials, but with the Web as his storage mechanism, he can institute a technological approach. The trainees can access the materials at their own convenience, from their own work-stations, or even from home. This will enable the training department to save money on adminis-tration costs, as the cumbersome and wordy manuals no longer need to be printed and distributed to trainees. Employees can continue to attend the face-to-face training workshops if their work schedule allows them, or they can undertake the training on their own by accessing the materials on the Web. When they have completed their assessment tasks, they can e-mail their work to George via the company's e-mail infrastructure, which resides on the company management system.

By structuring training in this way, a more flexible training program can be offered to employees and George can maintain control of the information that is put on the Web. His trainees' knowledge base will remain consistent over time, and he can make the required changes as new training re-quirements are identified. The Web will allow him to update information at his convenience. As train-ing is his domain, it is only fitting that he should control the Web on his own server, independent of the company's management system.

Employees will have their skills updated as the company or, more importantly, the training man-ager, sees fit. Thus, when there is a need, George will devise the new training programs and store the materials on the Web. Self-motivation from the trainees will naturally be expected with their use of the Web. The trainees will be thus seen as computer literate and suitable candidates for promo-tion. Therefore, the use of the Web for training is integral to his work practices, as George's phi-losophy maintains that the company's training will deal with only those skills that relate directly to the specifications of the job.

Trainees are not expected to interact with the technology of the Web, just simply to receive infor-mation from it. If the trainees need further assistance, they can always send George an e-mail.

---

augmented easily to adjust to the changing economic and strategic goals of the company. Even in manufacturing industries, it is possible to modify parameters for a production process dur-ing one shift and pass the changes on to the next shift without the requirement of major train-ing or down time. Simple advantages grow rapidly as more aspects of Web-based training are incorporated into the organization. The following discussion explores some of the possibilities.

While not diminishing the importance of the simple training focus in Web-based imple-mentations, some alternative contemporary thinking is driving innovative organizations (both large and small) to re-conceptualize the use of their training resources. This thinking is creating a learning organization that utilizes the combined knowledge of all members of the organization through Web-based training. The essence of Web-based training is about how *both* information and learning that occur during the working day can be shared across an organization.

We use the example of the OzFuture Technologies company to illustrate these pos-sibilities.

See Scenario B, on the following two pages, for ideas on creating a learning organization through Web-based training (OzFuture Technologies).

Scenario B (Part 1): OzFuture Technologies

OzFuture Technologies has widely disseminated offices and manufacturing plants across the state and nation. They are currently developing a revolutionary manufacturing process for their computer hardware (code named Project "M"). They also propose to license this manufacturing process offshore.

This revolutionary manufacturing process is constantly evolving, and the core engineering staff working on Project "M" sees the need for the development of a training package for the operators who will be working in relatively new environments with the development and ongoing implementation of the new process. Operators recruited for these new work environments may have few skills or experience in this type of work environment.

Company management realizes that it will have to prepare training materials to accompany the machinery and manufacturing components when they are licensed for manufacture elsewhere. The training package is to be shipped with machinery and manufacturing components so that newly licensed manufacturers can be brought up to speed in the mechanics of the new manufacturing process rapidly and efficiently.

Company management also realizes its own staff also requires the training across the various manufacturing plants located around the country.

So, the OzFuture Technologies company's training system will be used to train:

- Existing staff in the current work environment (enhancing their skills, getting them to learn about other areas of operation, how to solve current problems, etc.).

- New staff in the current work environment of the company.

- New staff in a new work environment licensed to manufacture the new hardware.

The training system and materials have to be malleable. The company wants a training package that could evolve to incorporate:

- Changes in the manufacturing process.

- Technological development. (It cannot be too dependent on the current processes or systems.)

- Documentation of new staff knowledge and new staff experiences.

- Ready access to the Document Management System that is a repository for Standard Operating Procedures or Functional Descriptors. (Most of the company's information about the project is stored in their document management system that acts like an "organizational memory"; however, there is also a wealth of staff expertise and knowledge that is not formally documented.)

Therefore, the task is to take the existing body of knowledge, transplant it to each new context, and then develop something that will enable this new training context to operate.

The training materials will be developed concurrently with the products, so once they are perfected, the training system is complete ("concurrent design").

Scenario B (Part 2): Implementing Web-Based Training at OzFuture Technologies

Wendy is an engineer within Project "M" who is heavily involved in trying to perfect one aspect of the manufacturing process. She has been given the training charter. Wendy is not sure where to start. She knows a little about the Web.

She knows all company staff have access to the company's computer network and workstations. She has had exposure to multimedia CD-ROM training packages produced internally within the organization. After being given the charter, she attends a Computer Based Learning conference, gets some ideas and makes a few contacts. Wendy is convinced that CD-ROM delivery would not be suitable, as the manufacturing process is constantly evolving and improving over time. She also does not want to develop this training system using a proprietary authoring tool. In the past, authoring tools had been employed to produce and deliver training materials, but when the development team left, the training materials were forever cast and no changes were ever made, as there was no provision for maintenance. She also wants to use tools that are machine independent (cross platform), so the final resources will not be bound to a particular manufacturer.

Wendy is attracted to the Web because of the growing interest in HTML, its universality, its perceived longevity, and its multi-platform capability. But she is not sure how to use it or integrate it into the organization. As OzFuture Technologies has an existing intranet system which is relatively new, and also has a comprehensive document management system, the idea of integrating the training materials with the document management system has distinct appeal. Although she feels she is treading in unknown waters, Wendy asks the "techies" to see if they can store and retrieve HTML documents from the document management system.

Being a proactive employee, she also produces a document stating some estimates of the number of Web pages that would be required for the training system. She attempts an "environmental or infrastructure analysis" to determine what bandwidth the intranet can handle, how much of the server(s) space can be allocated to "training" functions, and what recommendations for hardware purchases (if any) to make.

As a non-professional training designer, Wendy realizes her own limitations in developing resources, although she has developed print-based training materials for another project. For this current product, her target audience is new recruits to the manufacturing process with potentially little or no experience with the manufacture and development of the revolutionary computer hardware device and who may have limited knowledge of English (as the intention is to license the manufacturing process internationally). It is also probable that many new recruits would be entering a brand new work environment, so there will be an opportunity to provide not only technical training but to instill some organizational cultural aspects about working with the product, such as:

- Encouraging everyone to work as a part of team (stifling the "this is my job, that is your job" attitude).

- Facilitating ownership over one's own work and exhibiting what one knows to others.

Wendy expects a minimum level of skill in using the training materials via the intranet and the Web (basic operation of a computer and Web browser) by the newly recruited operators. This means that by employing a Web browser to gain access to the training resources, the learning requirements would be reduced.

So the process begins . . .

Figure 1. Phases in Website development.

The scenario on the preceding two pages has the potential to move the role of Web-based training into new areas and to be of strategic importance within OzFuture Technologies. The first step is to identify the key personnel who are to take the project along the development path.

In exploring the potential design of practical Websites for interactive training, we'll "unpack" the OzFuture Technologies case study. The framework we have generated to discuss this case study consists of two phases depicted in Figure 1.

From the framework, it is obvious that many decisions are made as a project develops. In practical outcomes, it is useful to consider the decisions as they may apply to the initial set-up and design of a Web-based training system, compared with its implementation and ongoing maintenance. The following heuristics are developed in response to the needs and context as Project "M" unfolds.

Within the following discussion, it should be noted that while the phases are used as headings for ease of discussion, in practice these phases are interwoven and are cyclical. Further, before we venture into the phases there are some early considerations, which need to be determined.

Wendy's thoughts are indicative of some of the concerns those tasked with training have expressed in considering computer-based training. Such products have been traditionally very expensive to produce and very difficult, if not impossible, to modify by simple means. Often a specialist designer/programmer would need to be called in to create and modify the software. Most of the time, the parameters upon which the training was generated employed old and rather rudimentary instructional strategies and often ignored higher order skills such as problem solving. This latter aspect is largely related to the time (and consequent costs) needed to generate such complex learning systems. But as Wendy illustrates, many have heard lots about the World Wide Web and organizations devising their own intranet systems, and while cautious about costs, she believes that these technologies could potentially be suitable delivery mechanisms.

But Wendy is not too sure where to start and not too sure how the Web options can best be used to meet her company's needs. We would propose some basic thoughts:

Early Considerations

H1: Web-based training supports a view of training that it is more than just passing on information to a recipient trainee. It is sharing the understandings of different people at all levels in the organization and providing the information aggregated at the level required to help each person contribute to the organizational mission.

OzFuture Technologies has, in establishing the preface for the development of its Web-based training system, recognized that the expertise of the company is not simply in the product it is producing (as stored in the Document Management System). Rather, the expertise resides intuitively in the minds of all the staff working on the project. Wendy's brief therefore encompasses acknowledgment that the training system should support the sharing of resources and ideas not simply from the trainer as designer of resources, but also should incorporate employee contributions.

This first heuristic sets the framework for the development of the Web-based training and underpins the set-up and design phase.

Set-up

Recognition of the involvement and contribution of all staff in training suggests a fundamental consideration that an organization must ensure in developing practical Websites for interactive training. The fundamental consideration is that all members of the organization need to have ready and easy access to a workstation through which they can access an intranet or the Web. Given this practicality, they can then begin to shape the training.

> H2: *Seek to develop a training system that acts both as a learning tool and as a reference tool (like an encyclopedia).*

Wendy and OzFuture Technologies have recognized that their intranet Website can be used both as storage for the ongoing work on the project and at the same time as a valuable learning resource and electronic performance support system (EPSS). Thus, while it can function for initial training, it also acts as a speedy reference resource, so that if a user wanted to review a piece of information at a later date, he or she would not have to sit through an entire lesson again. Users should be able to go directly to the information they are seeking.

> H3: *The more useful the Web-based training site, the more it will formalize organizational memory.*

The OzFuture Technologies company has several levels of need in its training specifications. It will be dealing with users with different levels of skill and expertise and with a variety of task requirements.

From the outset, any Web-based training environment needs to:

- Be easy to navigate yet afford the opportunity to augment and add new components without destroying the fundamental information structure.

- Enable users to have flexible paths through the training and to access further information when necessary (just-in-time training).

- Use an interface that allows users to follow a path (like a "yellow brick road") but does not force them to follow that path—allow users the freedom to explore other information, as it might be relevant to the questions they are seeking to answer.

- Be maintained by training staff with little specialized training. (Wendy did not see herself as a training expert.)

- Be accessible by trainees/users so that they can contribute to modifications and updates.

All these elements can be woven into a Website. No longer do operational procedures have to be separate from training documents. Often, multiple users can access the same set of resources through different "front ends."

Design

The OzFuture Technologies Case Study suggests a number of design heuristics. Underpinning these heuristics is the idea that the Web is not a book, so don't write one unless you need to be very complex in your explanation.

> H4: *Starting with a simple set of Web pages, it is possible for the Website to grow into a complete and useful venue.*

Wendy's dilemma of where to begin and how to go about her task suggests the need to begin simply. The company already has a substantial bank of resources in its document repository, and more in the "minds" of its staff. Simply begin by organizing resources as you go. The resources and learning activities can be generated over time, and may include guides to Websites that are useful, exercises specific to the organization, and collaboration tools to support social learning outcomes.

These can often be later aggregated into relevant and professional course materials that are derived from the specific learning experiences of trainees by accumulating the materials that will help as part of the training, collecting them into resource bank and making them accessible on demand.

> H5: *Consider that the dynamic Website is essentially standing upon the shoulders of the previous trainees.*

OzFuture Technologies has already undertaken substantial development of its software and the accompanying materials. All of these experiences formed valuable training information. Problems the development team experienced and insights it generated can all be captured and stored for later groups or individuals. The development of the Web-based training site might also require the expert input of those who designed the products or, in this case, the manufacturing process the organization is evolving and also licensing for use. Each person can immediately "see" from his or her own and other's perspectives how the product, process, or service is described; how it can be presented to customers and clients; and how changes to the product, process or service may influence the outcomes for the organization.

Consider also creating supportive Web structures such as a Frequently Asked Questions (FAQs) section. FAQs enable trainees to review all the other questions previously asked and to learn from the problems experienced by others. If a company generates a new product, for example, questions asked of the sales people can be submitted to a FAQs section and answered by the "expert." This teamwork will also test out the product and its likely acceptance by potential customers. Often, new service products many be released to compete with other firms. The use of a quick summary and likely customers, specific conditions, etc., can be communicated to all branches without massive investment in face-to-face training.

So we are talking about supporting, in a very concrete way, through the training and development function, a learning organization, possibly not even envisaged by Senge (1992) when he introduced the concept. The notion of "teamwork" is central to the ideas of Web-based training. It is important to note the bias that might apply to the design of a Website. Based on the organizational solutions we have seen, Website development requires a partnership among training designers, workers, and managers.

> H6: *Encourage activity; allow trainees to actively process information.*

One of Wendy's and OzFuture Technologies' considerations was "how can everyone work as a part of the team and take ownership over their work and share it with others?" As a mechanism for generating teamwork, trainees should be asked to compare, classify, induce, deduce, analyze, construct, or make abstractions. Create a site with the ability to allow comment and high levels of interaction.

> H7: *Ensure that computer-based collaboration is encouraged and supported through simple communications software.*

The OzFuture Technologies company has an already existing communications system, with which experienced staff is familiar. But Wendy recognizes the need for new trainees to have support in interacting with the training materials. One of the often overlooked aspects of online training is the use of online feedback. Establishing chat spaces, online discussion forums, and sharing sessions can usefully focus on organizational learning issues. Improvements in communication between the trainers and the trainees or the impact of such communication can be quickly documented. In fact, via the use of listservers, chat spaces, and e-mail, tacit knowledge can be made more explicit as users exchange views and experiences with one another (Oliver, Herrington, & Omari, 1996).

> H8: *Design a navigation structure so that after three clicks, you are not lost in hyperspace.*

> H9: *Create a simple structure that allows changes to be made at the top level (home page menu).*

In acknowledging the possible language limitations and inexperience of new recruits, Wendy establishes a picture of the type of structures and functionality the training site requires. By ensuring that the trainees/users are oriented at all times, learning is made more important than simply finding your way around. The relationship between the page users are on and other related supportive information should be demonstrated visually, using placement cues representing positions through hierarchies and indexes, or locating them within a picture such as an image map. For more sophisticated users, you might seek to get them to draw up a concept map or semantic net.

> H10: *Consider providing a holistic picture of the training task, in which the learner is guided through a series of iterations of increasing complexity.*

As a training non-specialist, Wendy realizes her own limitations and requires a comprehensive model. The Web interface should match this model. Using frames whereby the left hand frame provides the synopsis and the right hand frame provides the details enables the trainee to "see" at a number of levels. Within the information in the right hand window, there can also be hyperlinks to further detailed information. But don't enthusiastically run away with the HTML coding without a strong underlying knowledge of how the information is structured and accessed. Figure 2 provides an example of this idea.

The frame concept also simplifies maintenance; each index item on the left can point to a separate file/document. This system allows the users to track backwards and forwards through the material, providing them with opportunities to get back on track.

The frame-based menu on the left-hand side of the page allows the user to remain oriented to the underlying conceptual model of the training, whereas the reference/training material in the main window on the right provides the materials to be learned, examples, and activities. The left-hand frame allows hierarchies to be always in view so that the user has constant access to the overall information structure, and knowledge of position and history of use within the information structure, as selected links (topics) are highlighted in a different color (Oliver,

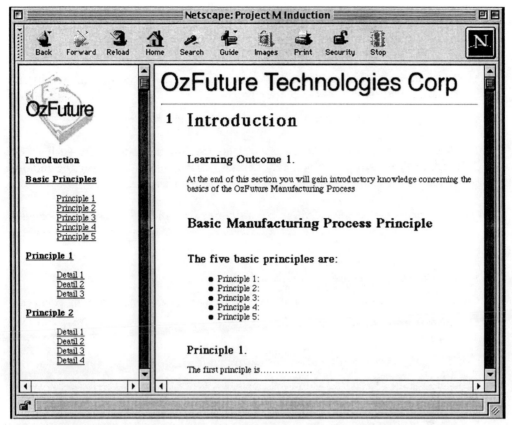

Figure 2. Using frames to place the trainee within a knowledge structure.

Herrington, & Omari, 1996). This two-frame organization also reduces maintenance, as changes can occur in the detail without major shifts in the conceptual structure in the left frame.

> *H11: Aim for self-regulated learning as part of the concept of the learning organization, thus ensuring ownership and total quality management.*

Wendy notes the need for the OzFuture Technologies Company's training package to encourage teamwork as opposed to individual "jobs," and for the trainees to have an understanding of all parts of the company operations. However, in completely allowing learners to set their own learning objectives, the designer is unable to assess whether those objectives have been met. Therefore, the training needs to encourage learner self-reflection by providing questions and guidance to help foster this sort of self-evaluation. And the design should include tools that help the learner decide what to do next, based on this reflection (McManus, 1997).

> *H12: Design for self-assessment, so that users can communicate with other learners via discussion spaces, etc. Seek to incorporate a management system to monitor progress.*

Wendy acknowledges her lack of trainer experience. Given preferences, any trainer would like a Training Management System that would:

- Manage who has done what.

- Identify when trainees have completed required sections of the training, and what level of competency was achieved on those sections.

- Record all assessment results and allow trainers to enter in assessment results from practical activities or face-to-face training.

- Alert users to modified parts of the training that need revisiting.

The Website is a tool, and its success as a training medium depends on how such a tool is used. Although the Web purports to be a very flexible design environment, planning and organization are still critical elements in the set-up of a Website for training.

> H13: *Web pages employing HTML as the authoring code provide a useful and extensible set of resources which can be easily edited and revised by both trainer and trainee.*

Since . . .

- They can be easily coded via a Web authoring package.

- Staff can be trained quickly in authoring using a visually driven authoring package.

- Staff members can work at home on the their own personal computer, regardless of platform.

- Individual files are small and easily transportable via floppy disk, e-mail, or across a network.

- Pages can incorporate text, images, audio, and video.

- Computer programmers can integrate more complex code after initial authoring or as the need arises.

- Pages can be included in a document management system (thus automatically handling version control and ensuring accountability).

A typical page describing a particular process can have embedded links to materials conveying additional detail describing the process in a variety of formats, such as text documents, images, audio, video, listservers, chat spaces, and e-mail.

Having established the set-up and design of the Web-based training site, there is a need for consideration of the ongoing, dynamic, and evolving nature of the environment.

Maintain and Evolve

> H14: *Maintenance is a responsibility shared by learner and trainer.*

The OzFuture Technologies Corp. saw its manufacturing process as one which, although the products would be shipped as a finished package, would continue to advance as changes in the manufacturing process and associated technologies developed. Its Web training site would need to reflect the ongoing nature of this undertaking.

With Web-based training, users can be given a template and a copy of a Web page editor. If they are familiar with word processing, then they can add information relatively easily at their convenience. They don't need a copy of an authoring tool on their machine. Each contributor can work on separate parts of the training system at the same time, and need not worry how it is incorporated into the whole training system. The Web allows concurrent design due to its relative ease of use. Trainers and trainees/users can both become producers. Once the Website gains momentum, it will be self-sustainable, if everyone in the organization finds the training system of value.

> *H15: Involve the learner in the design of the training, and, in return, the learner will be more involved/engaged in the training.*

Consider that learners may want to make their own learning objectives; therefore, provide opportunities in the training system so that learners can access/explore information that is relevant to them. Tools, through which learners can explore on their own, may include keyword search engines, concept maps which the learner can restructure, and possibly random link editors (McManus, 1997).

> *H16: The training system can be an organic entity, and the system will be able to grow as your training needs grow.*

Web-based training is more than putting resources online. The training system can be an organic entity and the system will be able to grow as your training needs grow.

The training materials need to be maintainable, possibly transportable across the globe, and accurate, and must include a training management system to track learners' progress and ensure that all learners are exposed to the updates of the system. A critical aspect of the training materials is that if a change has to be made to the training materials, that change should only be made in one central place, therefore avoiding duplication of the same documents/information in the training system.

There should be a master file. Any updates should require authorization from a single source. This will assist with any audits. Many document management systems can be set up to ensure that versioning history is easy to follow and also to ensure changes to the server software have a limited or nil impact upon the Web-based training documents.

Use the last training course's Web-based training resources, including work from trainees, as the basis for the next course. Due to the nature of the medium (electronic), this allows easy collection, thus creating a body of class products which instructors can use to evaluate, refine, and evolve the teaching/learning mechanism/strategies.

Unlike traditional computer-based training development, which can be expensive, difficult to modify, etc., Web-based training development is being put into the hands of the user with the training need. Traditionally, an outside consultant would be commissioned, the subject matter expert would explain the content to the consultant, and the consultant would then go away and return with a training module. With Web-based training, the consultant can now advise the user how to best set up the information, and the user/subject matter expert can enter the content directly. As the tools become easier to use, it is more time-efficient for the user to learn how to use the tool than to employ a separate consultant/developer to learn the specific content.

Conclusion

The previous discussion has served to illustrate what might be seen as two somewhat different training environments, that of the Quality Quiche Company and the OzFuture Technologies Corp. Figure 3 summarizes the different perspective of Web-based training that has been encountered in each case. The determination of the extent and success of Web-based training will depend on the perspective of the company.

Learning with a Training Course Focus	Learning with a "Learning Organization" Focus
Episodic training sessions	Evolving online training and continuous learning
Fixed period of time on specific task	Daily/weekly access with frequent self-checking on current knowledge
Trainee is recipient of knowledge base	Trainee uses and contributes to knowledge
Static knowledge base (but as new materials are generated, they can be accessed)	Dynamic knowledge base and links to simplified ways of data capture which are easy for non-specialist trainees
Separate system from the Management Information Systems (MIS)	Links to MIS functions
Development of specific skills	Development of an organizational resource for current and future learning
Motivation to receive someone else's knowledge base	Motivation to give and share ownership; as trainees learn from their forerunners, they realize the importance of each contribution
Productivity limited to skills remembered	Productivity limited only by relevance to the user and the effort each member of the team makes towards ideas and information collection
Learning determined by trainer	Learning determined by trainee/user/contributor and enhanced by a variety of different experiences

Figure 3. Changing learning environments with Web-based training.

As seen in Figure 3, the training course focus might be characterized as a somewhat narrow, fixed, and individual perspective, whereas the learning organization perspective presents a more holistic and dynamic undertaking, in which the entire organization is actively involved in the ongoing learning experience. It is from this latter perspective that perhaps the design of the most productive and practical Websites for interactive training should be generated.

When considering Web-based training, you should first examine:

- the scale of operation (large scale project or smaller short term projects);

- the level of knowledge of the trainees/learners;

- the level of competency (survival, operation or higher order); and

- whether the purpose is creating new understanding or capturing existing knowledge base (or both).

The heuristics we have developed can be devised for your own training challenge. Consider the issues of *Set-up and Design* separately from *Maintenance and Evolution,* although the design will inform and set the scene for what can be easily maintained and contained.

On the horizon, there are some interesting possible extensions of Web-based technologies that might prove useful for the next generation of training systems. Consider the "push" technologies, which could inform employees of changes made to the training materials and what new developments are planned. The use of push technologies act as a sort of daily news and current affairs bulletin without the need to formally request or try to find out what differences have occurred. This would avoid the need for other forms of probably more annoying, awareness generating methods.

Another possibility is the use of "pull" technologies. Instead of using the more general broadcast of the push technologies, it is possible to provide each user with a unique view of the Website, customized (through the use of integrated database and server technology) to meet their own needs and what aspects of the training resources they wish to monitor. Using these emerging techniques as an extension to Web-based training might provide for other aspects, such as urgent and critical requirements in addition to standard information and learning requirements.

Acknowledgment

We wish to thank those who employed us on different projects and in so doing enabled us to learn, and Dr. Suzanne McNamara, who read and commented extensively on an earlier draft.

References

Imai, M. (1986). *Kaizen. The key to Japan's competitive success.* New York: McGraw-Hill Publishing Company.

McManus, T. F. (1997). Delivering instruction on the World Wide Web; ccwf.cc.utexas.edu/~mcmanus/wbi.html

Oliver, R., Herrington, J., & Omari, A. (1996). Creating effective instructional materials for the World Wide Web; scu.edu.au/sponsored/ausweb/ausweb96/educn/oliver

Parson, R., (1997). An investigation into instruction available on the World Wide Web; oise.on.ca/~rparson/designin.html

Senge, P. M. (1992). *The fifth discipline: The art and practice of the learning organization.* Sydney: Random House.

The Authors

John G. Hedberg and Christine Brown are members of the Graduate School of Education, and John L. Larkin and Shirley Agostinho are doctoral students with the Faculty of Education, University of Wollongong, New South Wales, Australia (e-mail: john_hedberg@uow.edu.au; christine_brown@uow.edu.au; john_larkin@uow.edu.au; shirley.agostinho@uow.edu.au; Web homepage: immll.uow.edu.au/).

28

Design Strategies for Web-Based Training: Using Bandwidth Effectively

David R. Moore and

Barbara B. Lockee

The movement of training to the desktop computer reflects the growing demand for instruction that is time and place independent. The convergence of audio, video, text, and graphics in a networked, readily accessible virtual space has prompted a variety of instructional packaging solutions, from asynchronous (*time independent*) text-based interactions to real-time desktop videoconferencing, enhanced by a never-ending array of peripherals such as electronic whiteboards and application sharing capabilities. Web-based training has the capability to deliver all of these media to the desktop at virtually any location.

While networked instruction to the desktop offers a variety of possibilities for training delivery, it is not without flaws. Slow download time, delayed audio, and jerky video images are the result of such a system's primary limitation—bandwidth. To put it simply, bandwidth places a limit on what can occur at any particular time throughout the instructional event. In an interview about the development of Web-based training, Steve Bradley, president of Gartner Group Learning, stated: "The real breakthroughs will be about managing the bandwidth challenge. That's really nothing new, and it won't be old for a long time" (Cohen, 1997, p. 43). As the demands on local and global networks soar, so will the quest for solutions to bandwidth constraints. Our task as trainers is to identify this limitation and to use appropriate strategies to compensate for it.

The Interaction of Bandwidth and Instruction

Bandwidth is a volume measure of information flow. On a digital network, it is the number of bits that can be transported in a given period of time. Digital networks are composed of a number of components that may include a sender's computer, a connection from the sender's computer to a router(s), a connection from the router(s) to the receiver's computer, and finally, the receiver's computer. The slowest link in that path will define the system's available bandwidth. When planning network use, one should keep in mind that effective bandwidth is determined by the weakest link in a system.

Instructional design theories recommend that instruction be designed before media are chosen (Smith & Ragan, 1999). Unfortunately, in the practice of computer-based training programs, such procedures are rarely possible. In many organizations, the pervasiveness of the Internet has made the Web a default delivery medium. Currently, distributed training developers must have knowledge of the network over which instruction will be delivered and its capabilities and limitations in order to make important instructional development decisions. Whether creating instruction for delivery over a company intranet or via the globally accessible Internet, knowledge of strategies, trends, and trade-offs in bandwidth consumption is essential to produce courseware that is both technically and instructionally effective.

Trends in Training

Recent trends in the design and delivery of training may have a positive impact in reducing the amount of bandwidth necessary to deliver Web-based offerings. These trends involve the time at which the training is encountered, as well as the size of the instructional unit. Both provide increased flexibility for a trainer attempting to maximize limited bandwidth by minimizing the amount of user demand on a server at any given time.

Temporal Distribution

The power of Web-based training is its ability to provide effective learning experiences in a more convenient and cost-saving manner than classroom training. Until recently, distributed teaching technologies have focused on replicating traditional instructor-led models through the use of synchronous *(at the same time)* tools such as satellite delivery or interactive videoconferencing. New models of distance education emphasize the ability to engage in training that is not time-dependent. Because participants in asynchronous instruction will utilize Web-based courseware at a time that is personally convenient for them, demands on the providing network will be more distributed, thus reducing demands on bandwidth.

Modular Instruction

Another trend that reflects the need for efficiency in training is the creation of modular instruction, offerings that are customized to obtain a limited set of very specific learning outcomes. This method is also called "chunking" (Cohen, 1997) or the "granularization" of content (Gordon, 1997). The benefits of a modular approach related to bandwidth are gained when learners are accessing only necessary information at the time it is needed instead of attempting to utilize a larger, more comprehensive program of instruction.

Bandwidth Management Strategies

Bandwidth brings logistics into instructional design simply because successful instruction may be compromised if instructional materials are delivered at a rate at which learners are incapable of consuming them. Learner attention, motivation, and comprehension may suffer when participants are forced to continually wait for an instructional event to occur. Fortunately, trainers have a number of strategies for eliminating or reducing these delays. These strategies can be organized into the following categories. *Pre-distribution* strategies attempt to overcome delays by delivering instructional materials and images in advance of the instructional event. *Parsing* strategies emphasize designing materials according to their instructional essence in order to remove extraneous information and data. *Choreographic* strategies attempt to present instructional materials at a rate equal to the rate at which they are consumed (Lockee, Moore, & Moore, in press).

Pre-distribution Strategies

Pre-distribution strategies are techniques that assist in the avoidance of bandwidth bottlenecks by distributing data through other means. Strategic use of alternative media such as print materials, CD-ROMs, and videotapes can dramatically increase the volume of instructional materials to which learners have access while reducing demands on the delivery network. This technique has been called a "hybrid approach" (Douglas, 1993) to distance education because it incorporates the instructional strengths of a variety of teaching technologies. However, traditional distribution routes are required for this strategy to have a successful impact. Also, these tools have the disadvantage of having to be developed or purchased well in advance of the instructional event. To produce these materials, a number of skills and tools may be required. Perhaps most important in using these tools is the ability to evaluate commercial or previously created instructional materials.

Pre-distribution strategies have the disadvantage of increasing the planning time of an online course in order to carry out the logistics of traditional materials delivery (library checkout, postal service, etc.). However, pre-distribution has the advantage of encouraging pre-planning and creating contingency plans.

Parsing Strategies

A brief look at many Web-based training sites reveals that a large percentage of the Web-site components are extraneous to instructional goals, such as the inclusion of images for aesthetic purposes. By eliminating Web-site content that is aesthetic but not instructional, relevant data throughput can be maximized.

The next step is to reduce unnecessary data within instructional content. Training developers must ask themselves what media attributes are essential to the facilitation of learning. For example, is animation needed to convey a process or will a series of still photographs serve the same purpose? In her article "Web-based Training on a Shoestring," Sarah Fister (1998) directs training developers to include only the media elements that are necessary to convey the intended instructional message. The advantages of doing so are functional as well as monetary. Providing information through text instead of a video clip of a talking head is equally effective and consumes only a small portion of bandwidth compared to digital video.

Choreographic Strategies

The final Web-based delivery strategy is called choreographic because it deals with the order in which training is delivered. Images and other media that are data intensive can be strategically interspersed with text. A large volume of text can be transmitted relative to images. In terms of data, text delivers more content than an equivalent amount of data in an image. While students are reading textual material, images can be downloaded and be ready to be examined once the text has been consumed. This strategy may make the educational experience seamless, and the delays imposed by bandwidth may not be noticed. A similar strategy is often used at amusement parks. Many rides require a long wait. Parks are now using this wait time to prepare the audience for the experience by showing background videos and other contextual information. The result is an entertainment experience that is holistically enhanced while reducing the frustration of waiting. The same can be done in an online environment. Secondary presentation forms that augment the instructional message can be included when a data-heavy image is required.

Conclusion

In a Web-training environment, the delivery network infrastructure must be considered so that training developers can avoid creating instruction that diverts a learner's attention due to unnecessary delays. Taking advantage of training trends that compensate for bandwidth constraints, instead of replicating traditional teaching models, is effective in creating immediately useful training experiences. While the strategies we have mentioned can be implemented to utilize bandwidth more efficiently, it is important to remember a point well-made by Cohen and Rustad, that "technology should function as a tool for learning, not as the blueprint that drives the learning agenda" (1998, p. 32). The wise use of these bandwidth strategies increases control over the learning event while reducing the influence that media have on instructional goals and objectives.

References

Cohen, S. (1997). A guide to multimedia in the next millenium. *Training and Development, 51*(8), 33–44.

Cohen, S. L., & Rustad, J. M. (1998). High-tech, high-touch, high-time? *Training and Development, 52*(12), 30–37.

Douglas, S. (1993). Digital soup: The new ABCs of distance learning. *EDUCOM Review, 28*(4), 22–25.

Fister, S. (1998). Web-based training on a shoestring. *Training, 35*(12), 42–47.

Gordon, J. (1997). Infonuggets: The bite-sized future of corporate training? *Training, 34*(7), 26–33.

Lockee, B., Moore, D., & Moore, D. M. (in press). Instructional image development for network-based distance education. *International Journal of Instructional Media.*

Smith, P. L., & Ragan, T. J. (1999). *Instructional design* (2nd ed.). Upper Saddle River, NJ: Merrill/Prentice-Hall.

The Authors

David R. Moore (e-mail: moored@pdx.edu; Web homepage: web.pdx.edu/~mooredr/) is an instructional designer with the Office of Information Technologies at Portland State University, Portland, Oregon. **Barbara B. Lockee (e-mail: Barbara.Lockee@vt.edu)** is Assistant Professor, Instructional Systems Development, College of Human Resources and Education, Virginia Tech, Blacksburg, Virginia.

29

Ideas on Designing Web Pages for Online Training

Don E. Descy

Web-based training is now a reality. Many companies, large and small, are training their employees online. National Car Rental uses the Internet to train its employees in customer service skills. Employees at Motorola learn manufacturing and design skills, and General Motors and DaimlerChrysler train their workers in quality-standards compliance over the Web. Dunkin' Donuts, Travelers, IBM, Ford, Andersen Consulting, United Technologies, and many others have all climbed on board.

It is not always easy to introduce online training to a corporation. There are at least two variables that must be present: forward-thinking management and risk-taking trainers. There are now plenty of pioneers online, but the path is not clear of hazards.

A major problem in online training is money. There are several good arguments that can be used to make high start-up costs more palatable to top-level management. First, online training will save money in the long run by reducing expenses usually associated with travel to the training facility. This savings is not only in the tangible costs such as airline tickets, car rental, and hotel rooms, but also the intangible costs associated with the absence of that employee from his or her regular workstation. One corporate trainer projected that by converting 120 hours of classroom to multimedia simulations, she could recover all start-up costs by the 350th enrollee and save her company $55 million over five years (Hall, 1998).

The most efficient means for online training is using browser-based (Web) technology. Many more desktop computers are connected to the company intranet than have a CD-ROM drive, and that is all that is needed, other than the browser software. Placing your training programs on your company's intranet is not difficult. As a matter of fact, it is very easy to create Web pages. It is no wonder that there are so many terrible Web pages out there! Though it may not be as important to have an esthetically pleasing page for training as it would be for sales, we do not want our pages to be confusing or overloaded. Let us take a look at some simple rules to follow as you design your Web pages and Website. These are not rigid rules, but rather suggestions that will make pages more pleasing to users.

General Design Decisions

There are several things that you should take into consideration as you are preplanning your Website. These fall into two large categories: the audience and the content.

First, think about your intended audience. How sophisticated are their Internet skills and equipment? Can they access and view pages that contain Java, Shockwave, imagemaps, and frames? Will your intended audience access the pages the same way, perhaps over the company intranet, or will they use a wide variety of means from T1 at work to third-party dial-up at home? Dial-up connections can be slow, so limit the size and number of images (i.e., smaller pictures and fewer variations in lines or buttons) for faster access. You should also think about making your site disability friendly. This is not only the correct thing to do, but disability friendly sites are also easier for the general trainee to navigate (Auerbach, 1999). A good place to find information to make your site more disability friendly is the Equal Access to Software and Information (EASI) site on the Web (rit.edu/~easi).

The second category is content. You are developing these pages for a particular purpose. Design them in the most meaningful and efficient way possible. Preplan your site as carefully as you preplan all of your pages.

After you have outlined the skills, knowledge, and other information about your target audience and have a good idea about the content, there are two more steps to follow:

Outline the Material: On a pad of paper, outline the material that you want to place on the site. Try to divide the information into three to five sections or pages. Try not to have more than six or seven sections. Content-heavy sites will, of course, contain more sections. Organize the material in a logical order so that others can easily understand the order and flow.

Map Out the Site: Now draw a map or sketch of your site, showing the relationship of different pages to each other. Don't forget links back to the index page. There should be no dead-ends. A toolbar or small clickable index on the top or bottom of each page is very useful. Outline the material that you will cover on each page on a separate (large) index card.

Once you have gotten this far, you are now ready to start developing your pages.

Developing Your Web Pages

Objectives: Remember that you have a relatively captive audience. You do not have to add interest to your pages as an advertiser might. You are not selling a product to a customer but rather you are using the Web to transmit information. Use the most efficient means to get your information across. Most times, simple equals better. Every added picture or line adds to the download time and distraction potential. That is not to say that you don't want your material to be pleasing. Pleasing—yes: distracting—no. First, start with your objectives. Second, outline what you want to say. Only after you have done these two steps will you be set to develop your pages.

Consistency: A well-designed site has consistency. You don't want your site to look like a group of unrelated pages. Decide on the general layout. Sketch out a "template" page. Will you have a logo at the top (bottom, side) of each page? Backgrounds should be consistent. Many sites now use a vertical strip, stripe, or graphic down the left side of the page. Placing a menu bar on the left (top or bottom) of each page makes for easier navigation and is appreciated by all. Many sites place the menu in a frame at the left of the page. Don't forget to place the URL, copyright notice, and the name of the contact person/agency at the bottom of each page.

Size: Size of computer files can be a serious problem. The slower the connection and/or the larger your pages, the slower your pages will load. After you have put your pages together, add together the size of your text and graphics. Try to keep the total size down.

Information Placement: The most important part of your page is the top. This is the part that people see first, so this must be the part of the page that will grab and hold their attention. Why do you think that advertising graphics are placed at the top of the page? This is especially important if you have a page that people may come across as they surf the net for information; i.e., your company home page. Many people glance at this part of the page on their browser and won't bother (or wish) to scroll any further down *unless* something catches their eye. It is not as important in Web-based training. Your viewers have little choice but to view the pages. But remember, the top part of the page will be their first impression of the training site and training materials.

Backgrounds: A well-tailored page has a background. These are very easy to put on a page. The simplest background is just a solid color. It is also possible to have an image as your background. This is sometimes called "wallpaper." One way to do this is to have a huge image that covers the whole background. It is far easier to send one small graphic and have it run across the background of the page to create a seamless effect. Many of these background graphics are very small and take just a few seconds to load.

Interactivity: One of the most important features of any Web-based training module is interactivity. Design this in from the start. Your trainees will be interacting with the material. They will be reading, watching a simulation or QuickTime movie, manipulating physical entities or information when prompted by the screen, or doing any number of things. Your trainees may be interacting with you and perhaps other trainees. This may be through e-mail, chat, or discussion groups. Your trainees may even be interacting with the software. Choose the instructional software with care. Developments in instructional and training software over the past few years have taken much of the drudgery out of training. Modern software can keep track of the trainees' progress, notifying them and you of how they are doing. It can test the trainees and add material to remediate, reinforce, or enrich the training sequence.

Tips to Make Web Pages
Easier to View and Maintain

First, keep the names of your pages, images, icons, and directories (folders) simple. For example, the YNT (YourName Training) directory (folder) at your Website may contain several directories (folders). One directory may contain general introductory pages for your site. Each class or training program should have a separate directory.

Second, do not name your files, folders, or pages using capital letters. Most people type in lower case and most servers are not case specific.

Third, organize Web pages, directories, and files. Don't just place everything in one long directory. One training group that I know of did this. A person viewing the directory on the server would be confronted with one huge list of 95 (at last count) pages, bars, buttons, logos, etc. It is a nightmare. It is a better idea to place *closely related* pages in one directory and place the images, icons, sounds, etc., used on these pages in separate sub-directories within this overall directory.

Remember, Web pages are not going to be static. They will need some revision at regular intervals. Your copy will be revised and links to other Web resources are always changing. Is your corporate training site ready for this? Will someone check and update the site on a regular basis? Have you designed it so that it is easy to do?

References

Auerbach, S. (1999, January). Learning online: Site unseen. *Inside Technology Training, 3*(1), p. 36.

Hall, B. (1998, April). Enterprise: Win friends, gain funds. *Inside Technology Training, 2*(4), p. 30.

The Author

Don E. Descy (e-mail: descy@mankato.msus.edu; Web homepage: ime.mankato.msus.edu/ded/don.html) is Professor, Minnesota State University, Mankato.

30

Web-Based Training: Current Status of This Instructional Tool

William D. Milheim and
Brenda Bannan-Ritland

Introduction

As described in other chapters in this book, one of the most useful functions of the multi-purpose resource known as the World Wide Web is Web-based training, in which instructional materials are delivered via the Web, generally to geographically dispersed learners. While many of the previous offerings in this area have focused on higher education or various independent Web sites (see Khan, 1997), there is a rapidly growing interest in corporate organizations concerning the potential of the Web to provide training for employees at multiple locations. The current status of this corporate or other large organizational focus on Web-based training is the topic of discussion in this chapter.

Description of Web-Based Training

By definition, Web-based training is the design, development, and delivery of corporate-based instruction through various World Wide Web-based technologies to employees at various locations within a given organization. While new strategies and technologies are constantly becoming available, this type of instruction generally includes the ability for employees to learn on their own via online instructional materials, multimedia presentations, hypermedia links, electronic mail (e-mail), and real-time conferencing (Munger, 1997). Many content areas have already been addressed with this new delivery format, including computer and technical training as well as soft skills instruction (Hall, 1997). In addition, a number of organizations and tools also exist to support Web-based training design and development (see Table 1 for a list of Internet resource sites related to Web-based training, and Table 2 for a list of Web-based training authoring products.)

In many ways, this instructional methodology is in direct contrast with traditional corporate practices in which training is delivered through classroom-based instruction conducted by a human facilitator at the organization's home location, the vendor's company, a central metropolitan site, or in conjunction with a conference (Hawkins, 1997). The American Society for

Table 1. Resource sites for Web-based training.

Site Name	Web Site URL
American Society for Training and Development	astd.org
Association for Educational Communications and Technology	aect.org
Discussion Group for Training and Development	train.ed.psu.edu/trdev-l
Distance Education Clearinghouse	uwex.edu/disted/home.html
Distance Learning on the Net	homepage.interaccess.com/~ghoyle
EdWeb Home Room	edweb.cnidr.org/resource.cntnts.html
Instructional Software Development Group	uiowa.edu:80/~itsisdg/index.html
International Interactive Communications Society	iics.org
International Society for Performance Improvement	ispi.org
Links to Training-Related Organizations	infoweb.magi.com/~mmilette/other.htm
New Tools for Teaching	ccat.sas.upenn.edu/teachdemo
Training & Development Resource Center	tcm.com/trdev
U. S. Distance Learning Association	usdla.org
Web-Based Instruction Resource Site	personal.psu.edu/wdm2/main.htm
Web-Based Training Information Center	webbasedtraining.com
Web-Based Training Information Site	brandon-hall.com/training.html
Webmaster's Resources	cio.com/resources

Training and Development estimated in 1996 that when considering training time by delivery system, classroom instruction remained the primary delivery mode for 70 percent of training, while interactive multimedia CBT accounted for only four percent, and Internet/network electronic distance learning accounted for a mere two percent of training time (Bassi, Benson, & Cheney, 1996). However, many organizations seemed poised to investigate and utilize Web-based training in the near future, since it was projected that the overall use of Internet/Web training would increase to 47.9 percent by the year 2000 (Bassi, Cheney, & Van Buren, 1997).

One reason for this projected increase in Web-based training may be the higher costs associated with traditional instruction, which can include significant expenses for the trainer, required travel, necessary equipment, training facilities, and time away from the job (Hawkins, 1997). Although development costs of multimedia or Web-based training may be higher initially, final delivery costs are often lower when compared to instructor-led training.

While Web-based training does allow for the widespread utilization of materials by widely dispersed students, it may also be available through private, in-house systems known as intranets which use Internet technology to provide information to specified users and/or locations. According to Wulf (1996), intranets are an effective way to communicate within a given organization since they allow employees to use standard Web browsers for navigating through protected company information as if it were on the Internet. In fact, intranets are able to mimic

Table 2. Web-based training authoring products.

Company	Product(s)	Web Site URL
Asymetrix	ToolBook	asymetrix.com
Center for Complex Systems Research	CyberProf	cyber.ccsr.uiuc.edu/cyberprof
CourseInfo	Teachers ToolBox	courseinfo.com
ForeFront Group	WebSeeker WebWhacker	ffg.com
Lotus	LearningSpace Lotus Notes	lotus.com
Macromedia	Authorware Director	macromedia.com
Roger Wagner Publishing	HyperStudio	hyperstudio.com
University of British Columbia	WebCT	homebrew1.cs.ubc.ca/webct
Virginia Commonwealth University	Web Course in a Box	views.vcu.edu/wcb/intro/wcbintro.html
WBT Systems	TopClass	wbtsystems.com

the overall Internet in terms of accessibility and platform independence while safely protecting this information behind security software (firewalls) that allow only authorized employees into a specific system (Filipczak, 1996).

Advantages of Web-Based Training

With the incredibly rapid growth of the Internet and the World Wide Web during the past several years, training delivered via the Internet and intranet technology is still very much in its infancy in terms of the delivery of actual modules and courses. However, even during this relatively short period of time, this technology has begun to offer a number of advantages compared to other more traditional training methodologies currently utilized by corporate organizations.

Kruse (1997), for example, offers three broad characteristics of this technology that make it very appropriate for the design and development of corporate-based training. These advantages include: (1) the use of HyperText Markup Language (HTML), which allows for the delivery of Web-based training on most computers and operating systems (Macintosh, Windows, and UNIX) with only one version of the actual program being built and maintained on a centralized server; (2) instant distribution of the instructional content to an unlimited number of worldwide trainees, with no required time or expense for duplicating, packaging, or mailing of the material; and (3) affordable technology which does not require costly new hardware or software, but, instead, simply the utilization of free or inexpensive browser software such as Microsoft Internet Explorer or Netscape Navigator. Hawkins (1997) adds that Web-based training has fewer limitations based on class size, since there are no problems with room capacity, scheduling, or the number of available instructors.

In addition to the above characteristics, Wulf (1996) describes the following advantages for Web-based training:

(1) immediate access by corporate trainees to a wealth of information in a given content area;

(2) the ability to create links to external Web resources from a given Web page;

(3) time and place independence, allowing users to log on whenever and wherever they want;

(4) savings on costs and productivity losses that occur when employees need to travel for training;

(5) opportunities for collaborative learning and instruction where groups of learners can be brought together from around the globe;

(6) utilization of various Internet and Web-based tools, including e-mail, bulletin boards, real-time conferencing, and interactive tutorials;

(7) a high degree of learner control, which provides participants with more control of the pace of a course and the ability to come back online at any time for more help and clarification; and

(8) asynchronous conferencing where students can read materials, then reflect on them for a period of time before posting comments and/or replies.

Disadvantages of Web-Based Training

While the characteristics described above strongly indicate the positive points of Web-based training, there are also a number of authors who describe the potential negative aspects of this training format. Wulf (1996), for example, describes a number of disadvantages for Internet-based training, including:

(1) relatively high development costs for those Web pages with complex graphics, multi-media, or other features (e.g., elaborate tutorials);

(2) limited available bandwidth, which may mean relatively slow performance, particularly when incorporating sound, video, and elaborate graphics;

(3) new and generally unsophisticated authoring systems for Web-based training as compared to similar software for computer-based training materials;

(4) potentially unreliable Internet links due to changing addresses or sites which have completely disappeared;

(5) lack of Internet knowledge or other computer skills in those corporate employees who would be using this training; and

(6) increased reliance on student initiative, since Web-based students have more responsibility for choosing when and how to participate in training.

Appleton (1997) adds several technological concerns for Web-based training, including the potential use of out-of-date equipment by trainees, the slow speed of users' modems, and various compatibility issues relating to the use of specific software browsers and computer operating systems. In addition, Munger (1997) suggests that many companies may need to add firewall protection to their networks to keep unwanted outsiders and/or software viruses away from their organization. Finally, several authors (Horowitz, 1997; McKegney, 1997) describe the disadvantages resulting from the lack of face-to-face interaction among instructors and trainees in Web-based training, potentially affecting learners who may not have the motivation to learn without a trainer being physically present in the classroom.

Implementation of Web-Based Training

While there are a number of advantages and disadvantages concerning the use of the World Wide Web for corporate training, its actual application should be based on specific criteria that match this delivery system with particular instructional or organizational needs. These criteria become particularly important in the early design phases of a new project, since they can assist the instructional designer in the choice of an educational medium (e.g., the World Wide Web) as well as specific instructional strategies to be used in the final training program.

Adams (1997), for example, provides a number of specific criteria related to intended learners for use when considering the World Wide Web for the delivery of corporate training. This author suggests using Web-based training for trainees who:

(1) are housed at individual locations, rather than a single corporate site;

(2) prefer independent learning;

(3) are able to set their own schedules;

(4) have widely varying skill levels;

(5) have favorable past experiences with technology-based training; and

(6) use the Web on a regular basis.

In terms of program development criteria, Adams (1997) suggests using Web-based training in those situations where:

(1) the instructional program will change frequently;

(2) the instruction requires text, graphics, and animation, but not sound or motion video;

(3) the content would benefit from links to other World Wide Web sites;

(4) hardware is readily available at the learner site;

(5) performance needs to be tracked across multiple courses or modules;

(6) consistency across individual training segments is very important; and

(7) the company has implemented previous network-based, multimedia training programs.

Finally, Adams (1997) adds a number of important organizational or management issues related to Web-based training, suggesting that Web-based training will be successful when:

(1) strong support for technology is provided by corporate management;

(2) development costs are included with delivery costs;

(3) sponsors have a successful track record;

(4) existing trainers are used;

(5) troubleshooters are made readily available; and

(6) managers and administrators have Internet experience, and their staff can design and author Web-based instructional applications.

Instructional Design Considerations

Once the decision to utilize Web-based training has been made, there are a number of design issues that need to be addressed before any instructional development is undertaken. Each of these issues should be carefully considered in order to insure the integrity of the development process and the effective delivery of the instructional materials to the targeted learners.

Cohen (1997), for example, discusses the importance of overall interactivity, particularly in terms of intranet technology, even though many corporate sites still include primarily static information rather than truly interactive instruction. Fryer (1997) also describes interactivity as a critical design component, further describing the importance of a good match between a given content area and Web-based training in general, a strong focus on learners' needs, a reduction in the use of simple "page-turning" and unfocused animation, and, in general, the utilization of well-planned and exhaustively-tested training materials.

In addition, Hall and Sprenger (1997) suggest a number of other issues related to successful learning, including:

(1) high quality content presented at the correct depth;

(2) appropriate navigation in terms of icons, labels, and hyperlinks;

(3) program aesthetics to entice students and hold their attention;

(4) an appropriate tone for the training program which does not "talk down" to trainees;

(5) effective motivational components that use novelty, humor, and/or adventure to "hook" users in some way;

(6) the appropriate use of graphics, animation, audio, and video;

(7) record-keeping procedures that are readily available to course managers; and

(8) an evaluation process that indicates whether trainees have actually learned the targeted skills.

Hawkins (1997) also describes a number of specific guidelines for the development of Web-based training, including the need to check for blind paths or erroneous hyperlinks, the ability of students to suspend training in part of the course when desired, the need to provide students with links to the main instructional page and various portions of the course, and the ability to demonstrate actual computer screens and mouse clicks within Web-based training courses.

Communication Technology Options

In addition to various design concerns, there are a number of technological features and components as described by Khan (1997) that should be considered during the overall Web-based training development process. One of the most important of these Web-based features is the general type of interaction within a given training course, which can be described as either synchronous or asynchronous, depending on the overall form of communication within a specific Web application.

Synchronous communication in this context refers to the utilization of various media components that permit "live" connections between various Web-based users involved in a specific instructional session. According to Fritz (1997), this type of Web-based training extends the reach of traditional classroom instruction in an attempt to create "virtual classroom" learning environments. Media components in this category would include audio and videoconferencing, for example, since they permit instructors and trainees to interact in real time during an instructional sequence.

Asynchronous learning, on the other hand, refers to instruction where trainers have no simultaneous communication with their learners, with the educational materials being received at times chosen by each trainee.

Kruse (1997) provides a slightly different instructional framework related to various technology-related options for Web-based training. The levels in this hierarchical framework include:

(1) basic communication at either a simple level (using electronic mail to provide messages between instructional participants as well as the distribution of course materials) or a more advanced level (including real-time, synchronous electronic conferencing or "chat" sessions);

(2) online reference sites with libraries of hyperlinked resources for product manuals, technical documentation, and other similar information;

(3) testing and assessment locations where tests or surveys reside;

(4) computer-based training sites for the distribution and downloading of instructional modules; and

(5) multimedia materials, including the delivery of interactive audio and video programs.

Wulf (1996) also describes a number of technology components that should be considered for Web-based training applications. These include:

(1) *e-mail*—for the distribution of class-related messages and course content, including mass distribution lists (listservs);

(2) *bulletin boards or newsgroups*—where messages are sent (posted) to a central server for later retrieval by users (instructors and students);

(3) *software distribution*—which permits documents, tutorials, or software to be transferred to individual users via File Transfer Protocol (FTP) for later printing or reading;

(4) *interactive tutorials*—where students log on to an Internet site and work through lessons online, involving tasks such as reading new material, taking tests, and linking to other World Wide Web sites; and, finally,

(5) *real-time conferencing*—which provides live communication among participants in an audio and/or video format, potentially facilitated through Multi-user Object Oriented (MOO) environments or Internet Relay Chat (IRC) options.

Hybrid instructional delivery models that incorporate a number of the above technological features and components using the most effective characteristics of each are also being discussed.

Conclusion

Corporate organizations are beginning to realize the potential of the Internet and the World Wide Web for the delivery of training to their employees. While a growing number of instructional providers and universities are hoping to produce materials for this potentially large market, it may be some time before widespread utilization has been attained. Web-based training may also not be the most effective option when compared to live instruction in many situations, since real-time training over the World Wide Web is currently restricted by bandwidth considerations. In fact, the most effective utilization of this technology may be its use in conjunction with other training strategies, such as CD-ROMs (Fritz, 1997), which would allow relatively permanent information and large computer files (including audio and video) to reside on a local CD-ROM, while current topics and smaller files (such as text and small graphics) would reside on a central server.

Overall, Web-based instruction is becoming one of the major delivery mechanisms for corporate organizations seeking to train their employees as efficiently and effectively as possible in a variety of required content areas. While there are several technological concerns that must be addressed, this form of instruction has significant potential for providing widespread, high-quality instruction to learners dispersed by space or time.

References

Adams, N. (1997). Take the Web test. *Inside Technology Training, 1*(2), 32–33.

Appleton, E. L. (1997). New recipes for learning. *Inside Technology Training, 1*(1), 12–18.

Bassi, L. J., Benson, G., & Cheney, S. (1996). Position yourself for the future. *Training and Development, 50*(11), 28–43.

Bassi, L. J., Cheney, S., & Van Buren, M. (1997). Training industry trends 1997. *Training and Development, 51*(11), 46–59.

Cohen, S. (1997). Intranets uncovered. *Training and Development, 51*(2), 48–50.

Filipczak, B. (1996). Training on intranets: The hope and the hype. *Training, 33*(9), 24–32.

Fritz, M. (1997). Is Web-based training new hype in old wineskins? *EMedia Professional, 10*(6), 69–71.

Fryer, B. (1997). Caught in the Web? *Inside Technology Training, 1*(6), 10–14.

Hall, B. (1997). *Web-based training cookbook.* New York: Wiley Computer Publishing

Hall, B., & Sprenger, P. (1997). Team training. *Internet World, 8*(7), 58–60.

Hawkins, D. T. (1997). Web-based training for online retrieval: An idea whose time is coming. *Online, 21*(3), 68–69.

Horowitz, A. S. (1997). Net train, net gain? *Computerworld, 31*(5), 63–66.

Khan, B. H. (Ed.). (1997). *Web-based instruction.* Englewood Cliffs: Educational Technology Publications.

Kruse, K. (1997). Five levels of Internet-based training. *Training and Development, 51*(2), 60–61.

McKegney, M. (1997). Training via nets starts to heat up. *Web Week, 3*(28), 17–18.

Munger, P. D. (1997). High-tech training delivery methods: When to use them. *Training and Development, 51*(1), 46–47.

Wulf, K. (1996). Training via the Internet: Where are we? *Training and Development, 50*(5), 50–55.

The Authors

William D. Milheim (e-mail: wdm2@psu.edu; Web homepage: personal.psu.edu/wdm2/) is Associate Professor/Division Head, Education (Instructional Systems), Penn State Great Valley, Malvern, Pennsylvania. **Brenda Bannan-Ritland** (e-mail: bannan@gmu.edu; Web homepage: gse.gmu.edu/programs/it/faculty/bannan.htm) is Assistant Professor, Instructional Technology, George Mason University, Fairfax, Virginia.

31

Review of Web-Based Assessment Tools

Jianping Zhang, Badrul H. Khan,
Andrew S. Gibbons, and
Yun Ni

Introduction

As instruction migrates rapidly to the Web, so also do most assessments of instructional effectiveness. There is a long history of construction of automated systems to administer student assessments, store them, provide reports to a variety of information users, and store the results for later use (Bunderson *et al.*, 1989). This function was seen as integral and inseparable from the instructional functions by early pioneers of computer-based instructional technology (Atkinson & Wilson, 1969). They describe a form of adaptive instruction whose defining characteristic was a moment-to-moment adjustment of the instructional prescription based on built-in assessment, judging, and recordkeeping. Even today's stand-alone educational products are supplied with automated systems that assess progress, prescribe the path of instruction, and maintain records on achievement for individuals. Educational suites, called integrated learning systems, have long employed such mechanisms at the heart of their operations. Industrial CBI users have long been aware that instruction is difficult to manage in cases where there are more than two or three instructional segments to administer, unless testing and management software is used. This connection is in direct proportion to the number of students to be instructed.

Despite the importance of assessment and recordkeeping software, it has received relatively little attention in the academic literature, perhaps because it seems to lack the glamour of theory. Nonetheless, its practical value has led to the development of numerous test-administration packages. Now the movement toward Web-based packages is clearly apparent.

As networking/Web and multimedia technologies converge, the use of Web-based training and education has been experiencing a corresponding and dramatic increase. There is no doubt that Internet and Web technology can provide new incentives and unprecedented opportunities for innovation in the field of education (Trentin, 1996). As a part of Web-based instruction (Khan, 1997), Web-based assessment is also becoming more popular. The need for Web-based assessment can be demonstrated by the following example: Cooley and Zhang (1996) have implemented a computer-based test tool, called *ConTest*, that delivers tests over a local area network. *ConTest* is in use for Civil Engineering Air Force personnel. These tests are being given at many different Air Force bases throughout the world. In this case, each site must have its own test and student databases. Problems arise in maintaining the consistency of the test databases and creating difficulties for collecting statistical data. A study conducted on a pilot project statewide in Pennsylvania (Bicanich *et al.*, 1997) shows that students preferred Web-based tests to paper-and-pencil tests by a 3-to-1 margin and that Web-based testing required somewhat less preparation time, effort, and class time, as well as substantially less effort for data analysis.

Development and maintenance of Web-based tests are time consuming and labor intensive and require technical skills. This fact has led to many efforts expended to develop Web-based assessment tools that reduce the time and cost in developing and maintaining Web-based tests. This chapter aims to provide readers with a comparison of the features and capabilities of a sample of Web-based assessment tools. The tools reviewed in this chapter include: *Internet Test System, MicroTest, NetTest, QuestionMark, QuizMaker, RAGs, Tutorial Gateway, WWWAssign, Web@ssessor,* and *WebTester.*

Web-Based Assessment

Web-based assessment uses the World Wide Web to deliver instructional assessment questions to students and collect student answers. Because assessments must be interactive, Web-based assessments cannot be implemented using only HTML. CGI scripts, Javascript, VBscript, or Java must be used along with HTML in developing a Web-based assessment.

Web-based assessment has a number of advantages over paper-based and computer-based assessment. Web-based assessment can reach a large student population, especially students in rural areas and underrepresented students. A student can access a Web-based assessment from anywhere in the world as long as he or she has a computer with Internet connection and a Web browser.

Web-based assessment is time and place independent. A student does not need to attend an assessment at a given time and a specific location. Instead, the student may access a Web-based assessment at home or office during working hours or at night. This advantage is especially important for adult education and life long learning.

Web-based assessment is platform independent and no special software is needed. A student can access a Web-based assessment from his or her PC, Mac, or Unix-based system, using a graphical Web browser such as Netscape or Internet Explorer.

Management, maintenance, and update of a Web-based assessment are relatively easy. All test items, answers, and assessment related information are stored on one site (the Web server); therefore, modification and update of a Web-based assessment only need to be performed at this site. Similarly, management, maintenance, and update of student records are also easy.

Feedback from students and assessment statistical data can be easily collected and analyzed. This is because all feedback and results are sent back to the Web server. The feedback and assessment statistical data can be used for the instructor to evaluate the instruction and the assessment so as to improve them.

We now propose a simple framework of Web-based assessment tools. A Web-based assessment tool may consist of three modules and two databases. The three modules are the student module, the instructor module, and the manager module. The two databases are the test database and the student information database. The test database stores all test items and statistical information about individual tests and items. The student information database contains student information for log-on security, class status, test results, etc.

The student module provides an environment for the student to take a test and view his or her record stored in the student information database. The student module is also responsible for selecting test items from the test database and grading the test automatically. With the instructor module, the instructor can create and delete tests and test items, configure a test by setting up test parameters, grade tests manually, and access student information and test item statistics. The manager module provides various functions for the manager to manage the test and student information databases. All these three modules may be implemented using Java, Javascript, VB script, or CGI script, and accessed using a Web browser.

Review Criteria

Assessment tools may be compared on many points, the most important being test type. Assessments are of two major types: performance and nonperformance assessments of knowledge. Performance tests provide realistic action demands on realistic problems staged in settings with some degree of realism. Nonperformance knowledge tests are normally made up of traditional objective test item types that are described later. Some tests mix both performance and nonperformance varieties to ensure more complete testing coverage. The focus of this chapter is nonperformance tests.

In this section, we discuss the criteria, which we use to review Web-based assessment tools. There are many criteria that can be used to review Web-based assessment tools. The most basic dimensional for the comparison of assessment tools include the following:

Test Item Type. Test item types refer to the types of test items supported by a Web-based assessment tool. The most common test item types supported by Web-based assessment tools are True/False, Multiple Choice (one or multiple answers), Fill-in-the-Blank (Short Answer), and Essay. Other types of questions supported include Matching and Sequencing. For a matching test item, the student matches items in column "A" with those shown in column "B." For a sequencing test item, the student places the shown steps in proper order.

Scoring/Grading Capability. One of the advantages of computer/Web-based assessment is that test items can be scored automatically. This automation saves instructor time and makes it possible to return test results and feedback instantly to the student if desired. Some types of items, such as essays, are difficult to mark automatically, and often the only practical solution is to store responses for later checking or to e-mail responses to an instructor. Saving responses for all test items allows the instructor to track student performance over time, review test item performance, and calibrate tests.

Feedback. Different levels of feedback may be provided after a test is finished. A Web-based assessment tool can: (1) indicate the acceptability of a response, (2) indicate whether the answer supplied by the student is correct or incorrect, and (3) provide the correct answer for incorrectly answered items. Remedial messages may be given for incorrectly answered items. References for supplementary study materials can be supplied. Feedback may be provided for individual items, and a summary may be given for sections or the entire test.

Multimedia. A Web-based assessment tool may support different media, such as plain text, rich text format, still image, video, and audio, in representing the items.

Statistical Analysis. Statistical data about tests and test items are easy to collect in Web-based tests. These statistical data may include the numbers of students taking, passing, and failing a test, and the number of times an item is correctly and incorrectly answered. These data can be used by the instructor to improve instruction and assessment items themselves.

Security. Security is an important issue for a Web-based assessment tool. The security policy of a Web-based assessment tool specifies who may take a test, when, and where. Security also controls access to test authoring and scoring systems and test records. There could be several levels of security provided by a Web-based assessment tool. The lowest level security is the student account. To take a test, a student must have an account and the student must log on with a username and a password when taking a test.

Performance Tracking and Reporting. A student's record can be maintained in raw or summarized form for the instructor and student review. Records can store pass/fail status of the test, scores, or answers to specific items. Automated assessment packages differ in their ability to create reports and in the types and amounts of data reported. Performance tracking data can be summarized and reported as well for tests and test items themselves.

Authoring Environment. An authoring environment is the environment in which an instructor creates a new test or a test specification. Authoring includes creating and editing items and specifying test recipes and parameters. Some Web-based assessment tools accept text files of test items with predefined format; some accept HTML files with expanded tags; others provide a GUI interface with templates of different types of items.

In addition to these basic dimensions of assessment tools, Web-based assessment tools must measure up in the following additional areas:

Implementation. A Web-based assessment tool may be implemented using Java, Javascript/Vbscript, or CGI script.

Server Requirement. Server requirements include platform and database requirements.

Client Requirement. Client requirements include platform and software requirements.

Web-Based Assessment Tools

A survey of available automated assessment and recordkeeping tools for use with the Web has identified over 30 products developed by commercial, university-based, or government contractor teams (see Table 2 for a complete listing). These tools represent a wide variety of configurations combining the features listed earlier. Of these systems, we have selected ten systems for more detailed review. These ten systems best exemplify one or more of these features in a particularly interesting or instructive way and are listed in Table 1.

Internet Test System (ITS) supports two types of questions: true/false and multiple choice with single or multiple answers. ITS automatically scores the test and can e-mail the test results to three different e-mail addresses (e.g., the student, the teacher, and the parents). E-mailed results include the student name, scores, missed questions, time required to complete the test and IP address of the machine where the test was taken. ITS informs the student of the incorrectly answered questions with the reference to the chapter source in which the correct answer can be found. ITS was implemented in Java and can be accessed using a Java-capable Web browser.

MicroTest Pro is expanded from the computer-based test tool MicroTest III to deliver Internet-based tests and is currently under development. MicroTest III supports true/false, multiple choice, fill-in-the-blank, short answer, matching, and essay questions. MicroTest Pro grades a test automatically and saves the score in the database. Correct answers or feedback can be provided, depending on the setting of the tests. Graphics and mathematical formulas can be used in representing questions. Statistics for individual questions and tests can be generated. For security, a student must have an access ID and password to take a test. MicroTest Pro collects test

Table 1. List of Web-based assessment tools reviewed.

Product Name	Company	Website
Internet Test System	Knowlton & Associates, Inc.	studio-ide.com/
MicroTest Pro	Chariot Software Group	chariot.com/sindex.html
NetTest	Utah State University	ntserver.cs.usu.edu/netest
QuestionMark	AssessNet	assessnet.com/
QuizMaker	University of Hawaii	motted.hawaii.edu
RAGS	Clark Atlanta University	stargate.jpl.nasa.gov:1084/RAGS/
Tutorial Gateway	Carleton University	civeng.carleton.ca/~nholtz/tut/doc/doc.html
WWWAssign	North Park University	northpark.edu/~martin/WWWAssign/
Web@ssessor	ComputerPREP, Inc.	webassessor.com
WebTester	Weber State University	webtesterdev.weber.edu/

results and other information for each test to create a series of student performance and results reports. MicroTest Pro uses MicroTest III for test creation. MicroTest III is not Web-based, meaning it cannot be accessed using a Web browser. MicroTest Pro uses an NT server.

NetTest (Zhang *et al.*, in press) supports six different types of questions: true/false, multiple choice (with single and multiple answers), fill-in-the-blank, matching, sequencing, and essay. NetTest marks all questions except essay questions automatically and partial scores for matching questions are allowed. It also saves all answers with questions in the Web server for the instructor to review and regrade the student's test. A Web-based environment is provided for the instructor to review and regrade a student test. Essay questions are marked manually by the instructor. NetTest can inform the student of all incorrectly answered questions and their correct answers. Images and graphics may be used to represent questions. Statistics about individual questions and tests are collected and stored. NetTest supports several levels of test security. Every user (including students, instructors, and managers) of NetTest must have an account in order to access it. The student can only take a test which is assigned to him or her by the instructor. A secured test is usually proctored and can be only taken in some specified test sites managed by proctors. To take a secured test, the student has to go to one of these test sites and show his/her picture ID to the proctor. Then, the proctor unlocks the test for the student. After the student finishes the test, the test becomes locked again for the student. When unlocking a test, the proctor may specify the IP address of the machine on which the student can take the test and the time period when the student can take the test. For each student, NetTest maintains a record which stores the test status (taken/pass/fail/incomplete), test scores, and test answers. A Web-based graphic user interface is available for the test author to create and edit tests. Templates of different types of questions are provided to add different types of new questions. NetTest is fully implemented in Java and runs on Windows NT server. It can be accessed using Netscape Navigator.

QuestionMark supports many different types of questions, and templates are available for multiple choice (with single and multiple answers) and fill-in-the-blank questions. It also provides the Question Markup Language for the author to create other types of questions.

Questions are automatically marked and a different score may be attached with a different answer to a multiple choice question. Detailed feedback such as why the answer is correct or incorrect could be associated with each answer of a multiple choice question. Graphics may be used in representing questions. QuestionMark has the capability to produce statistics for individual questions and tests. For a secured test, a student account with username and password is required and a test may be scheduled in a given period of time for a student. QuestionMark can generate student reports, which include the answers and scores for every question. Its test authoring environment is not Web-based and runs under the windows PC environment. An HTML forms-compliant and cookie-capable browser is required for students to take tests. Several Web browsers provide a mechanism that allows server-side programs to store simple information on the client machine. This mechanism is called a cookie. An NT server with an ISAPI compliant Web server and an active server pages server is required. ISAPI (Information Server Application Program Interface) allows Dynamic Linked Libraries (DLLs) to be associated with the server and accessed at predefined entry points when certain requests are made.

QuizMaker supports true/false, multiple choice, fill-in-the-blank, and essay questions. QuizMaker can grade a test automatically and/or e-mail the answers to the instructor depending on the setting of the test. Correct answers for incorrectly answered questions can be displayed for the student. References to related instructional materials can be provided. Graphics and images can be included in questions. Passwords may be required to take a test. A simple interactive test authoring is available for the instructor to create tests. QuizMaker is available for UNIX-based Web servers only.

RAGS (Kerven *et al.,* 1998) supports three types of questions: true/false, multiple choice (with single and multiple answers), and essay. It provides automatic grading of multiple-choice and true/false questions and e-mails student true/false question "Why?" responses and essay question responses to the grader. For each incorrectly answered question, the prescribed review material may be provided. Images and graphics can be used in representing questions. Currently, a text editor is used to create tests and the author must have knowledge about HTML and the language used for representing a test.

Tutorial Gateway supports true/false and multiple choice questions. In addition, it also supports questions with numeric algebraic expression answers. Numeric answers can be exact or approximate. Feedback can be provided for correct or incorrect answers or it can depend on the actual answers of a question. A question may have several hints that are revealed one at a time on request from the student. Test questions are created using an extended version of HTML. Additional tags have been invented to markup the various parts of questions in various ways. Therefore, graphics and other medium representation may be used to represent questions. To create a test, the instructor uses a text editor to create an HTML file. Tutorial Gateway is implemented as CGI scripts using Perl.

WWWAssign supports true/false, multiple choice, fill-in-blank, numeric, and essay questions. Numeric questions allow exact or approximate answers. In addition, proofreading questions are also supported. All but essay questions are marked automatically. An interface is provided for the instructor to grade essay questions. A report of each student's score on each assignment may be available for the teacher. Several statistics are also given on each question for item analysis. To take a test, a student needs to have a username and password. Test questions are stored in an HTML file. To create a test, the instructor uses a text editor to create an HTML file. WWWAssign is implemented as CGI scripts using Perl.

Web@ssessor supports true/false, multiple choice, and fill-in-blank questions. All questions are marked automatically. Feedback of a test includes whether a question is answered correctly or incorrectly or is skipped. It supports video, audio, and images. An authoring environment with question template is provided for the instructor to create a test. For a private test, username and password are required. Web@ssessor is implemented in Java on Windows NT 4.0, Internet Information Web Server, and MS SQL Database Sever are required. Netscape Navigator 3.0 or 3.01 on Windows 95 (or later) is required to access Web@ssessor.

WebTester supports multiple choice (with single and multiple answers), fill-in-blank, and essay questions. All but essay questions are graded automatically. Feedback includes explanations for incorrect answers and hints may also be provided. Reports of student test results may be e-mailed to the instructor. Test statistics may be generated. For a secured test, username and password are required and sites and time periods in which a test may be taken can be specified. Images, video, animation, and audio may be used to represent questions. Tests are authored using a word processor and then e-mailed to the server. WebTester server must be a Macintosh capable of running Userland Frontier database system and WebSTAR Web server software.

Summary and Conclusions

This chapter reviewed ten different Web-based assessment tools. Still, many other Web-based assessment tools are available, and Table 2 is a more complete list of Web-based assessment tools and their Web sites. With these tools, instructors are able to develop Web-based assessments in a timely and cost-effective way.

Our review of Web-based assessment and record-keeping tools showed that in a very short time, numerous products have emerged, many of them possessing interesting and sophisticated capabilities for creating and administering nonperformance knowledge tests. This review could not consider systems for the creation of performance tests, which is the appropriate subject matter for a different article. In summary, we would say that tools for the development of performance assessments lag far behind tools for the development of objective item type assessments.

Web-based assessments/tests are the obvious trend in the future. However, there are still some issues that need to be addressed. Some examples of these issues are

- What are the differences, if any, in student performance and attitudes toward Web-based tests compared to paper-and-pencil tests?

- How can student privacy and security be assured?

- Are Web-based tests really cost-effective? What are the cost differences between Web-based tests and traditional paper-and-pencil tests?

We believe that as tool improvements are made and tools continue to mature, the importance of Web-based testing in general of both performance and nonperformance varieties will increase dramatically. We especially believe this will be important in support of certification testing in many areas, which was one of the reasons we were anxious to include in our review specific systems designed for high accuracy and high security uses.

The development of Web-based assessment building tools is driven by necessity and not by economics at present. However, over time, we believe that organizations will find that their assessments can be improved, standardized, and speeded up in addition to reducing the cost of delivering those assessments, while at the same time improving the security conditions of giving assessments. This result remains to be measured. One issue which stands as a difficult limitation

Table 2. List of existing Web-based assessment tools.

Product Name	Company	Website
CASTLE	Leicester University	le.ac.uk/cc/ltg/castle/
CyberExam	Virtual Learning Technologies	ecmtest.com/cyberexam.html
CVU Assessment Engine	The Clyde Virtual University	cvu.strath.ac.uk/ae/
ExamMail	Oyston	oyston.com/ExamMail/home.html
Exam Writer	University of Montreal	igb.umontreal.ca/~leon/exam.html
Internet Test System	Knowlton & Associates, Inc.	studio-ide.com/
JBC	Half-Baked Software	net-shopper.co.uk/creative/education/ languages/martin/jbc.htm
HTML to Quiz	University of Virginia	landau1.phys.virginia.edu/teaching/quiz/ home.html
MicroTest Pro	Chariot Software Group	chariot.com/sindex.html
NetTest	Utah State University	ntserver.cs.usu.edu/netest
Online Exercises	University of Cincinnati	math.uc.edu/onex/demo.html
QuestionMark	AssessNet	assessnet.com/
Question Mark	Question Mark Computing	questionmark.com/
QuestWriter	Oregon State University	iq.orst.edu/meta/
QuickQuiz/Quiz Engine	Bytes Interactive	bytesinteractive.com/
Quick Quiz Maker	Internet Protocol	interpro.net.au/zquiz/
Quiz Form Maker	University of North Carolina	cs.unc.edu/~tobacco
QuizMaker	University of Hawaii	motted.hawaii.edu
QuizMaker	North Dakota State University	ndsu.nodak.edu/instruct/wwwinstr/tools/ qmmail2/
QuizMaker	Attotron Biosensor Corporation	attotron.com/pub/Quizmaker.html
QuizPlease	MoneyTree Software	quizplease.com/
RAGS	Clark Atlanta University	stargate.jpl.nasa.gov:1084/RAGS/
Test Pilot	Purdue University	clearcutsoft.com/TestPilot/
Tutorial Gateway	Carleton University	civeng.carleton.ca/~nholtz/tut/doc/ doc.html
WebQuiz Writer	Eon Communications	server.getbiz.com/~chester/
Web Worksheet	University of Washington	weber.u.washington.edu/~lspace/
WhizQuiz	Virginia Tech	cals.agnis.vt.edu/whizquiz/
WWWAssign	North Park University	northpark.edu/~martin/WWWAssign/
Web@ssessor	ComputerPREP, Inc.	webassessor.com
WebTest	University of Waterloo	fpg.uwaterloo.ca/WEBTEST
WebTester	Weber State University	webtesterdev.weber.edu/

of Web-based assessment systems is the authenticating of student identity at the time of testing. Instructors in classrooms can make identifications personally; Web-based testing systems always have the difficulty of personal identification. We expect that recent developments in identity-matching tool will be a factor in the improvement of authentication.

Several special challenges face the industry in the development of improved Web-based assessment tools in the future:

- Performance testing

- Security and student identification

- Advanced graphics user interface for both students and instructors

- Intelligent testing techniques

- Automated test item generation

In general, then, the future points to a good market for Web-based testing tools.

References

Atkinson, R. C., & Wilson, H. (1969). *Computer-assisted instruction.* New York: Academic Press.

Bicanich, E., Hardwicke, S. B., Slivinski, T., & Kapes, J. T. (1997, Sept.). Internet-based testing: A vision or reality? *Journal of Technological Horizons in Education.*

Bunderson, C. V., Inouye, D. K., & Olsen, J. B. (1989). The four generations of computerized educational measurement. In R. E. Linn (Ed.), *Educational measurement* (3rd ed.). New York: American Council on Education and Macmillan Publishing Company.

Cooley, D. H., & Zhang, J. (1996, June). ConTest: A multimedia computer-based test generation system. *Proceedings of World Conference on Educational Multimedia and Hypermedia.*

Kerven, D., Ambos, E., & Frost E. (1998). Interactive Web-based quizzes using the review automated generation system (RAGS). *International Journal of Educational Telecommunications, 4*(1), 31–44.

Khan, B. H. (Ed.). (1997). *Web-based instruction.* Englewood Cliffs: Educational Technology Publications.

Trentin, G. (1996). The Internet: Does it really bring added value to education? *Educational Technology Review,* No. 6.

Zhang J., Cooley, D. H., & Ni, Y. (in press). NetTest: An integrated Web-based assessment tool. *International Journal of Educational Telecommunications.*

Acknowledgment

The authors wish to thank David Twitchell for many useful comments and suggestions.

The Authors

Jianping Zhang (e-mail: jianping@zhang.cs.usu.edu; Web homepage: leimeng.cs.usu.edu/zhang/) is Associate Professor, Department of Computer Science, Utah State University, Logan, Utah. Badrul H. Khan (e-mail: khanb@gwu.edu, or khanb@BooksToRead.com/khan; Web homepage: BooksToRead.com/khan) is Associate Professor and Director, Educational Technology Leadership cohort graduate program, George Washington University, Washington, D.C. He is the founder of BooksToRead.com, a recommended readings site on the Internet. Andrew S. Gibbons (e-mail: gibbons@cc.usu.edu) is Professor, Instructional Technology Department, Utah State University, Logan, Utah. Yun Ni is Senior Software Engineer, Salt Lake City Branch, Federal Reserve Bank of San Francisco.

32

Online Testing Methods in Web-Based Training Courses

Sunil Hazari

Introduction

Testing and assessment remain an integral part of instructional systems design for traditional classroom courses as well as Web-based training courses. The goal of testing is to determine if learning objectives have been accomplished. Formative evaluation using online testing can be used to help students assess their level of knowledge of course material. In addition, it gives the instructor a better idea of what students are understanding, as well as the concepts that still need clarification.

Although there are commercial Web authoring tools available that include testing, many are proprietary in nature and not available to instructors and trainers who would like to integrate only the testing component without using the entire suite of embedded tools of commercial programs. Two methods that can be used for online testing will be the focus of this chapter, along with a discussion of the benefits of using online testing for Web-based training.

Online testing can be broadly categorized according to the use of either client-side or server-side processing. For the client-side method, JavaScript is a standard scripting language commonly used today that continues to be very popular, since it works with all browsers with a graphical user interface. As a result, it is attractive to most trainers and instructors who are interested in integrating testing in training courses delivered on the Web. Server-side method, on the other hand, relies on a back-end machine to process test results and return the output in HTML format to the user. A non-proprietary technology called Common Gateway Interface (CGI) is used to implement server based assessment.

A comparison of these two methods will be given citing advantages, disadvantages, and examples of each. While this chapter will not teach a programming language, it will give readers an insight into the work that needs to be done to incorporate interactivity and online testing into Web-based training materials. Supplementary materials, including an extensive annotated resource list with demos and working models, is available to readers on the author's Web site (sunil.umd.edu).

Assessment and Evaluation

With exponential growth of the Internet, intranets, and extranets, Web-based training offers tremendous opportunities for training of employees by using the Web as a training medium. Advantages such as flexibility, convenience, updated material delivery, cross-platform compatibility, and world-wide distribution have led to many new courses being designed for the Web, and existing courses being modified for Web-based delivery.

The first generation of Web-based courses were "static" in nature. Most were a result of paper-based material scanned into electronic format and uploaded to the Web server. Information in these courses was only presented to be browsed, without the user being actively involved with changing and manipulating information online. Although effective Web-based educational systems must provide basic instructional functionalities (Overbaugh, 1994), one of the challenges for Web-based training courses remains the use of *interactivity* within courses. Interactivity, defined here within the context of Web-based training, can be said to be a process in which the learner is part of an active system that supports learning by encouraging user participation. Interactivity can be built into Web-based training by the use of discussion groups, bulletin boards, synchronous communication tools such as chat forums, quizzes, and evaluation/feedback instruments.

In traditional courses, once learning objectives to be accomplished have been identified, there usually is an assessment process to measure the degree to which learners have acquired knowledge and can perform skills as required by the objectives (Kemp, 1985). Gagné and Briggs (1979) stress the need for evaluating a student's understanding, providing feedback during evaluation, and assessing complete understanding of each concept as part of an effective learning process. Web-based training courses that follow models of traditional course instructional design should also have a component for evaluation, assessment, or testing. The purpose of this component is to determine if learning objectives have been met from Web-based learning.

Most cognitive-domain objectives in Web-based training can be evaluated by tests that can be delivered online. Objective tests, such as multiple choice, true or false, or fill-in-the-blanks, can be implemented on the Web. Feedback can also be built in so that users can check answers. The role of these tests cannot only be for formal assessment, but also can serve an important role if used for student self-evaluation. Depending on the role, this self-evaluation can help the student (or instructor) monitor progress, recognize difficulties, or serve as review material to better ensure learner preparation for alternative formal assessment instruments. In addition, online tests also offer an option of delivering multimedia content, such as audio and video clips, that can be directly tied to learning outcomes. This may not be possible when paper-based traditional testing methods are used. Examples of some subject areas that can benefit from multimedia-enabled online tests are language learning and music education, in which audio clips can be used to test pronunciation of foreign languages or musical notes and pitch. Similarly, video clips can be used to provide instruction as well as assessment of topics such as non-verbal communication, posture, hand position, slide position, and proper breathing.

Ideally, commercial full-fledged Web course development programs include course administration and assessment tools that integrate student registration with password authentication, question delivery in various formats, randomization of question items, real-time grading, statistical analysis of responses, and storage of results in a standard database format that can be accessed by the instructor at a later date. User-centered learning systems use some or all of these components within Web-based courses to address one of the needs (i.e., testing) for learner engagement. But issues such as the viability of applying these tools also have to be considered (Norman & Spohrer, 1996). To trainers and instructors not using proprietary commercial tools, assessment can be built in to Web-based training courses by using one of two methods: either a scripting language such as JavaScript, in which processing is done on the client side, or another technique that uses Common Gateway Interface (CGI) technology on the server side.

JavaScript

JavaScript is an interpreted scripting language (similar to dBase or HyperCard program languages) that is embedded with HTML code to develop interactive pages. It is supported by popular browsers such as Netscape 2.0 and higher or Microsoft Internet Explorer 3.0 and higher. JavaScript is completely different from "Java," which is an object oriented programming language that is used to create applets. JavaScript is also different in that it works with HTML without having to open other helper applications. Similar to other programming languages, JavaScript uses identifiers, literals, variables, functions, objects, properties, and arrays. Although detailed explanation of each feature is beyond the scope of this chapter, the reader is referred to online documentation and frequently asked questions on JavaScript available on various sites on the Internet. Once the HTML/JavaScript code is downloaded from the server, all processing is done on the client side. This saves bandwidth since all work is done locally. A typical example in which this could be useful is when many students are required to access the page and be assessed individually at the same time.

Multiple choice, fill-in-the-blank, and true/false type questions can be developed using JavaScript functions. Another advantage of JavaScript is that form validation can be built in, which allows immediate feedback to be given to the students based on their responses. Aronson and Briggs (1983) identify feedback as a vital and indispensable instructional activity in the learning process. Using appropriate code, incorrect answers can be made to pop up in another small browser window, informing the student that the response was incorrect and providing hints to guide student to the correct response. It is also possible to integrate features that limit the number of attempts on each question, keep track of elapsed time, and calculate total score for the entire test. One main disadvantage of using JavaScript is that the code cannot be hidden completely. A user could view source from one of the browser menus and find answers in the source code. However, this can be overcome by using advanced coding techniques such as "cookies" that hide answers from users.

Although JavaScript processes information on the client side, most of the processing (such as checking correct answers) takes place on the user's browser. For self-assessment, the student gets to see what questions were marked correct or incorrect. Depending on the purpose of assessment, there may have to be grades that are recorded by the instructor or administrator software. This can be achieved by using the "Forms" feature of HTML. After the test has been completed, the user clicks a "Submit" button that sends results of the quiz to an e-mail address.

Picking up a new programming language is difficult, even for experienced programmers. Fortunately, there are many pre-designed JavaScript templates that are made freely available for instructors/trainers to use and customize. A list of these programs is available from the author's Website (sunil.umd.edu). For more sophisticated use of assessment techniques that rival those built into high-end Web authoring programs, a technique called CGI is used.

Common Gateway Interface (CGI)

CGI is a server-based method that can be used to implement online testing. A student would connect to the Quiz page and fill out a HTML form that might ask for student name and identification number. A series of questions (multiple choice, true or false, fill in the blanks) are presented to the student by the browser and, using mouse clicks or keystrokes, the student enters answers to questions displayed on the screen. When all questions have been answered, the test is submitted for "grading." Results of the quiz are then displayed on student screen, mailed to the instructor, and/or stored in a file on the server for instructor records. These apparently simple procedures on the user's side hide the complex sequence of database queries on the server side to generate a complete graded test. The sequence is shown in Figure 1.

(1) Student connects to the Web server using a browser such as Netscape Navigator or Microsoft Internet Explorer.

(2) Server presents form data to student's browser.

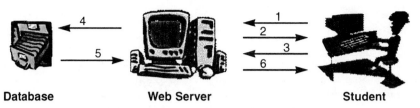

Figure 1. CGI script execution sequence.

(3) Student selects answers from form items and submits data to server.

(4) Server performs the following actions:

   (a) Data is parsed into variables

   (b) Query is generated by gateway script

   (c) Query is submitted to database.

(5) Database returns dataset items that match query.

(6) Dataset is formatted to HyperText Markup Language (HTML):

   (a) Server sends formatted output to client

   (b) Client displays result page on buyer's browser.

In most cases, CGI scripts are written using the Perl scripting language because Perl is a common programming language, fairly easy to learn and modify, and is portable across operating systems. If set up correctly, almost all Web servers on the market today understand CGI interface.

Case Study

Use of both these testing methods can be seen in a sample course, *EDIT 530: Scripting Languages in Authoring Educational Material* (available from sunil.umd.edu). In this course, students are required to develop computer-based educational materials using widely known educational scripting languages. Course requirements also call for students to explore basic authoring capabilities, and to learn and apply those capabilities by designing and producing material using commands, procedures, and functions of scripting language.

Since EDIT 530 is primarily a skills based course, a majority of the course grade is based on projects and products created by students, individually or in groups. However, surveys of authoring tools, programs, scripts, systems, and topics such as multimedia video, sound formats, graphical user interface design, flowcharting, storyboards, and instructional design process are also studied. Students are tested on these topics by using online assessment instead of traditional paper-based assessment. There are two types of testing used: one for student progress intended solely for reinforcing student concepts (no grade assigned), and the other as part of the course grade. In this case, because of better reporting capabilities, the CGI script is used for recording grades, and the JavaScript program for self-monitoring by students.

As previously explained, tests can be presented to the students, who select answers and submit the form to the server for processing. For the instructor, there are various options available to collect data of for scored tests. These include displaying the test, listing all results, clearing all results for use of the test in a new course, or downloading results into a spreadsheet software. With data collected and stored on the server, further analysis can be done on the tests by downloading it to a spreadsheet, using tab-delimited or comma-separated values that can be imported into any desktop spreadsheet or database application for viewing individual data online.

When analyzing student data, other demographic information is utilized, such as date and time the test is taken and time required by the students to complete the test (in seconds). In addition, the program also calculates the score and percentage of correct answers. This type of reported data provides the instructor additional options, such as calculating mean scores, standard deviation, determining internal consistency, distribution, and item analysis for each question, if required.

Chickering and Ehrmann (1998) suggest that while using technology to teach, faculty members should eschew materials that are didactic and instead search for technology-assisted interactions that are interactive, problem oriented, and that evoke student motivation. Online self-assessment techniques help engage students in active application of knowledge, principles, and values, and provide them with feedback that may enable their understanding to grow and evolve.

Interactive Web environments parallel ideas of the constructivist theory. In designing learning environments, researchers (Honebein, 1996; Knuth & Cunningham, 1993; Lebow, 1993) have recommended using constructivist theory for effective learning. The constructivist approach incorporates pedagogical goals in the knowledge construction process by providing appreciation for multiple perspectives, embedding learning in relevant contexts, encouraging ownership in the learning process, embedding learning in social experience, encouraging use of multiple modes of representation, and encouraging self-awareness of the knowledge construction process (Bruner, 1990; Vygotsky, 1986). Interaction and feedback have significant impact on the learning process since they add value that results in improving quality and success in Web courses. Moore and Kearsley (1996) and Cornell and Martin (1997) have specifically identified interaction and feedback components as factors that influence student motivation in completing a course. In a research study, Comeaux (1995) also found that interaction and involvement lessened the psychological distance for students at remote learning sites.

Conclusion

Web-based training, when used as an instructional tool, must have some means of assessing how much learning is taking place. For interactive sites, there are many different methods of integrating Web-based testing and evaluation as part of the online learning process. JavaScript and CGI are two of the most effective and easily implemented options available. For the instructional designer or trainer, final decisions on which tool to use will depend on variables such as learning outcomes to be measured, type of server available and its capabilities, degree of complexity required, and instructor or design team programming expertise.

At the beginning of a course, interactive assessment techniques can be used to collect data on initial student competencies. This may identify potential issues with students or technology application. One of the goals in using online assessment is to provide opportunities for students to test mastery of concepts being studied in the Web learning environment. Online self-assessment technique provides a non-threatening means of helping students gauge their understanding of the subject matter. By providing assessment mechanisms to students, their motivation is increased, since measurement of success is clear. Graded assessment results analyzed during the term can give the instructor a better idea of what students are understanding, as well as concepts that still need clarification to help plan follow-up modules.

Web-based online testing is gaining momentum as paper-based tests become an obsolete form of testing. IT training and certification is increasingly relying on computer-based tests that are more efficient to deliver and provide fast results while maintaining a record of not only scores, but also other student information that can be analyzed further, with results used to improve training. Students also benefit because of instantaneous feedback. Because of the advantages offered, trainers should realize the potential of using Web-based online testing and implement it as an integral part of training that not only provides evidence of learning outcomes, but also enhances student learning.

References

Aronson, D. T., & Briggs, L. J. (1983). Contributions of Gagné and Briggs to a prescriptive model of instruction. In C. Reigeluth (Ed.), *Instructional-design theories and models: An overview of their current status.* Hillsdale, NJ: Lawrence Erlbaum Associates.

Bruner, J. (1990). *Acts of meaning.* Cambridge, MA: Harvard University Press.

Chickering, A., & Ehrmann, S. (1998). Implementing the seven principles: Technology as a lever; tltgroup.org/ehrmann.htm

Comeaux, P. (1995). The impact of an interactive distance learning network on classroom communication. *Communication Education, 44,* 355–361.

Cornell, R., & Martin, B. (1997). The role of motivation in Web-based instruction. In B. H. Khan (Ed.), *Web-based instruction* (pp. 93–100). Englewood Cliffs: Educational Technology Publications.

Gagné, R. M., & Briggs, L. J. (1979). *Principles of instructional design* (2nd ed.). New York: Holt, Rinehart, & Winston.

Honebein, P. C. (1996). Seven goals for the design of constructivist learning environments. In B. G. Wilson (Ed.), *Constructivist learning environments: Case studies in instructional design* (pp. 11–24). Englewood Cliffs: Educational Technology Publications.

Kemp, J. E. (1985). *The instructional design process.* New York: Harper & Row.

Knuth, R. A., & Cunningham, D. J. (1993). Tools for constructivism. In T. Duffy, J. Lowyck, & D. Jonassen (Eds.), *Designing environments for constructivist learning* (pp. 163–187). Berlin: Springer-Verlag.

Lebow, D. (1993). Constructivist values for instructional systems design: Five principles for a new mindset. *Educational Technology Research and Development, 41*(3), 4–16.

Moore, M., & Kearsley, G. (1996). *Distance education: A systems view.* Belmont, CA: Wadsworth Publishing.

Norman, D. A., & Spohrer, J. C. (1996). Learner centered education. *Communications of ACM, 39*(4), 24–27.

Overbaugh, R. C. (1994). Research-based guidelines for computer-based instruction development. *Journal of Research on Computing in Education, 27*(1), 29–47.

Vygotsky, L. (1986). *Thought and language.* Cambridge, MA: MIT Press.

The Author

Sunil Hazari (e-mail: shazari@glue.umd.edu; Web homepage: sunil.umd.edu) is Campus Computing Faculty Research Associate, School of Business and Management, at the University of Maryland, College Park.

33

Software Tools for Online Course Management and Delivery

Ann E. Barron

and Chet Lyskawa

The number of distance learning options offered in industrial and academic environments is increasing at a rapid pace. In the past, the primary technologies used to deliver distance learning courses, in addition to various forms of printed materials, were two-way interactive video and one-way prerecorded video. Although effective, these technologies have their limitations. For example, two-way interactive video requires expensive equipment, and prerecorded video does not offer interactions with the instructor. Today, the Internet and its World Wide Web offer a new, accessible mechanism for delivering instruction. This chapter will explore current options for educators interested in Web course development, focusing specifically on four popular integrated Web course management systems: LearningSpace, TopClass, Web Course in a Box, and WebCT.

The Need for New Software Tools for Online Course Management and Delivery

Despite the increased pressure on trainers and educators to produce Web-based courses, the options for developing the courses have been limited in the past. Very few industrial trainers or faculty members have the time (or experience) to develop entire courses in HTML or other Internet-based development tools, such as JavaScript, Java, or Shockwave. In addition, the management and recordkeeping aspects of online courses often require sophisticated programming.

To meet the need for the development and management of online courses, several software programs have been released. These tools provide a relatively easy, effective means of creating, managing, and updating courses. Many of them also offer features related to student and faculty collaboration, such as chat rooms, discussion groups, and videoconferencing.

Overview of Current Software Options

The software for online education is still evolving. The products reviewed in this section (LearningSpace, TopClass, Web Course in a Box, and WebCT) all provide similar functions for managing Web-based courses. They were all designed specifically for this purpose, and they can be accessed through Web browsers without any additional client-side software. Another similarity is that they all require an HTTP (Web) server. In most cases, the company or university would download the server software and install it on a local server. Some of the products also provide the option of hosting the courses on a server at the manufacturer's site.

The Web course management products and tools featured in this chapter are described as they existed at the time of this writing. Web course software is an evolving industry and is changing daily. The chapter is written as an overview of the possibilities, not as user documentation.

LearningSpace. LearningSpace is IBM's contribution to development tools for Internet-based courses. The software is based on Lotus Notes, using the Lotus Domino server to provide a secure environment for Web-based applications. The application includes five specialized Domino databases that provide for the management and evaluation of online courses. For more information, visit on the Web: lotus.com/home.nsf/tabs/learnspace

TopClass. TopClass is distributed by WBTSystems. The software is database-driven and allows for remote access, management, and tracking. TopClass runs on multiple operating systems (UNIX, Windows NT, Windows 95, and Macintosh), while supporting numerous browsers. For more information, visit on the Web: wbtsystems.com/

Web Course in a Box. Web Course in a Box (WCB) was created by the Instructional Development Center at Virginia Commonwealth University. The software is a template-based authoring tool and is available for download and use at no charge to educational institutions. For more information, visit on the Web: madduck.com/wcbinfo/wcb.html

WebCT. Web Course Tools (WebCT) was developed in the Department of Computer Science at the University of British Columbia. WebCT had been used in the beta test stage by several universities and is now a commercial product. For more information, visit on the Web: homebrew1.cs.ubc.ca/webct/

Implementation

It is important to note that these software tools were developed using a variety of other Web languages. For example, WebCT uses Java for the chat feature and JavaScript for other functions. The products reviewed in this chapter are not competitors of HTML, Java, etc. Instead, they use the features of Web authoring tools to create an environment for tracking, delivering, and managing online instruction.

These products can be implemented with various levels of complexity, ranging from a supplementary collaboration tool to complete course delivery. For example, one instructor may wish to use TopClass as a collaboration tool for a traditional class that meets on a regular basis. Another instructor may use TopClass as a collaboration and management tool for an online class that uses textbooks or video for the content delivery, and a third instructor may use TopClass to deliver all of the instructional content.

The procedure for adding content to the products generally involves writing the content in a word processor, saving the file as HTML, uploading the file to the server, and adding it to a pre-established course structure. After the file has been added to the course structure, it is accessible by all of the students who are registered for the course.

Overview of Course Management Software Features

Course management software applications provide both the framework and the back-end programming that make the task of delivering instruction via the Web easier. The software applications integrate the design and management tasks into one convenient interface. In most cases, the Web browser is the only tool an instructor needs to create, deliver, and manage an entire Web-based course. The applications are evolving, and new products have appeared and will continue to appear on the market, making the chore of choosing the right product for an institution a formidable task. The following features are integral to all course management software applications:

- Asynchronous Communication
- Synchronous Communication
- Online Testing
- Home Pages
- Security
- Course Design and Management
- Student Management
- Student and Site Tracking

Asynchronous Communication

Asynchronous communication facilities, such as e-mail and bulletin boards, are the backbone of any Web-based course delivery system. Instructors can create a self-contained, collaborative environment for students. E-mail systems are built into the software applications. Students are not required to have an external e-mail account to participate in the course, although external accounts can be used in conjunction with the internal e-mail. Bulletin boards that provide for threaded discussions are also a built-in feature. Students and instructors can easily post messages to one another without the aid of newsgroups or listservs. LearningSpace, TopClass, Web Course in a Box, and WebCT all have built-in e-mail and bulletin board capabilities.

Synchronous Communication

Synchronous communication provides for "real time" collaboration between students and instructors. Synchronous communication can take the form of video conferencing, audio conferencing, white boards, chat rooms, and application sharing. While most of the software applications plan for the future integration of more utilities, synchronous communication at the time of this writing is limited to the use of chat facilities. Text is entered by each participant and displayed on the screen instantly. In this manner, students and instructors can log in to chat rooms and discuss topics in real time. Instructors can also hold virtual office hours by informing students of a meeting time in the chat facility.

WebCT affords the most extensive use of chat. The WebCT chat facility is organized into six separate rooms (see Figure 1). Four private meeting rooms are provided for students. The private rooms are logged, allowing the instructor to read and/or print the discussion that took place among participants. The fifth and sixth are public rooms—for the class and the entire WebCT course site, respectively. Web Course in a Box also employs a limited chat facility.

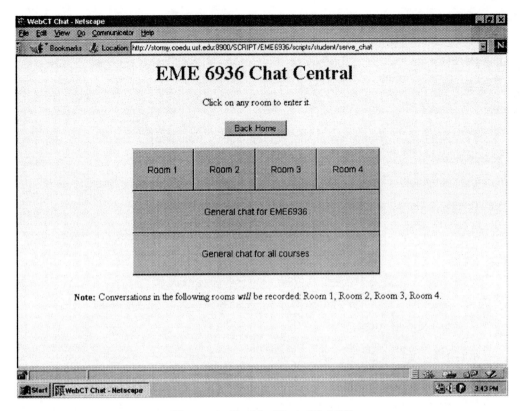

Figure 1. Chat facility in WebCT.

Online Testing

One of the nicest features of the course management software lies in integrated online testing capabilities. Student progress can be tracked and evaluated through a variety of quizzes and surveys. True and false, multiple choice, short-answer, and essay tests can all be offered on-line. Tests can be presented at the discretion of the instructor/designer. If the tests are true and false, multiple choice, or short answer, the tests will be scored immediately. Depending on the software package, scores can be revealed to students as immediate feedback or reported at a later date.

LearningSpace, TopClass, Web Course in a Box, and WebCT all have built-in online testing capabilities. The software applications differ in the degree of flexibility afforded to instructors. TopClass allows instructors to add a quiz page anywhere within the content folders. WebCT provides a very tailored presentation configuration, allowing instructors to limit the time allowed for students to complete the quiz, set a date range for test availability, set the number of times students are allowed to take the quiz, determine when test results will be reported, etc.

Home Pages

Most applications provide templates for student and instructor home pages. Class members can supply personal information about hobbies, interests, studies, etc. Photographs can be added to make participation in the class less impersonal. In most cases, the student or instruc-

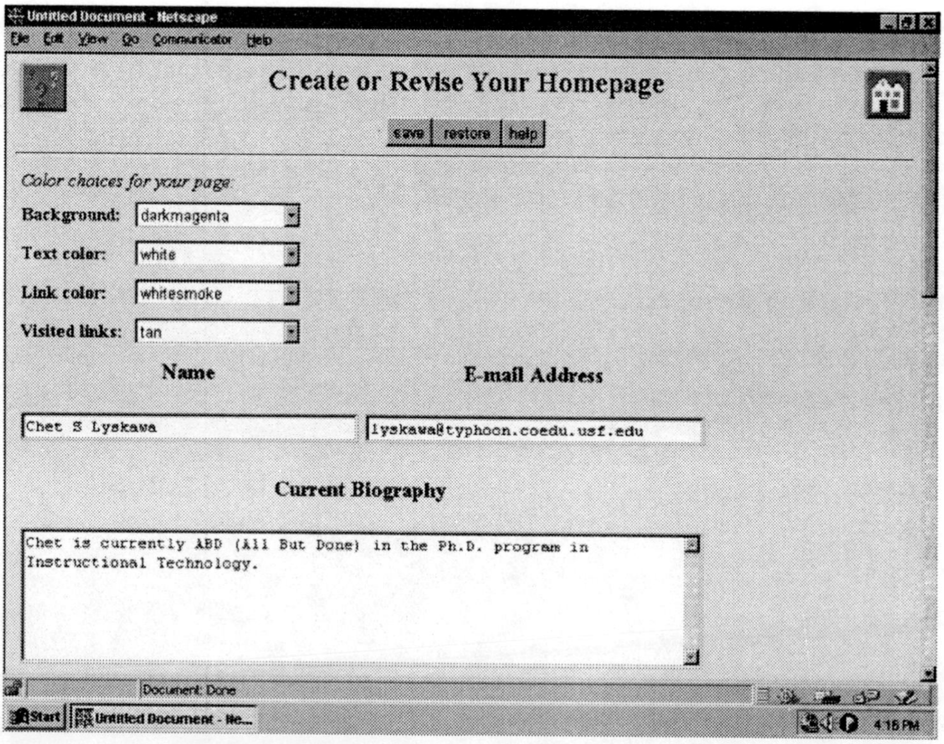

Figure 2. Home page option in Web Course in a Box.

tor simply clicks on a button or link and is presented with a Web template that can be customized to suit the needs of the class member.

Web Course in a Box has an intuitive, easy to learn interface for students to create home pages (see Figure 2). The path to student pages is provided by a graphical link directly from the course home page. WebCT also provides a template that can be accessed from the home page. TopClass provides an easy method for uploading a student photograph that can be viewed by all. LearningSpace provides a customizable individual component for student and instructor information.

Security

The protection of intellectual property rights and copyrights are major issues in the delivery of Web-based training or instruction. Password secured sites offer some protection for the instructor. Course sites can be configured to allow access to only those who are members of the course. Password protection also provides a more secure method for tracking who is receiving the materials or taking the quizzes than an ordinary, unprotected Website.

LearningSpace, TopClass, Web Course in a Box, and WebCT all provide password protection (see Figure 3). TopClass provides a log-out feature, allowing students and instructors to log out manually. TopClass also provides a time-out feature, automatically logging out inactive users after a stipulated length of time. The time-out feature may be important in a lab situation where many students use the same machines. For example, a student must actually close the Web browser to log out of WebCT. If the browser is not closed properly, the student's account remains active.

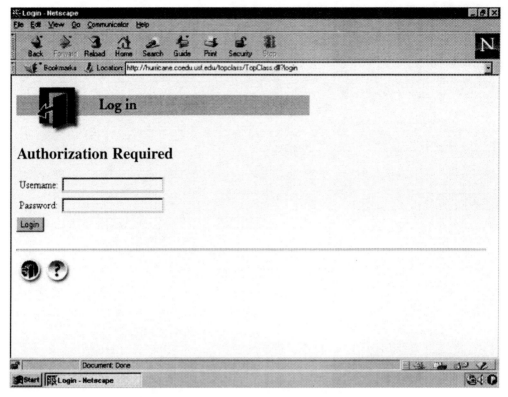

Figure 3. Password protection in TopClass.

Course Design and Management

Course management features of the software provide an administrator account to administer courses, set application properties, create instructor/designer accounts, change passwords, etc. After the course is created, the instructor maintains complete control over its design and administration. Each software application provides a separate interface for instructors and students. On log in, the application checks for instructor privileges and displays the appropriate interface, presenting the designer/instructor with numerous tools to create and customize the course.

In TopClass, multiple instructors can be assigned to an individual class, and multiple classes can be assigned to an individual instructor. Instructors can also be granted privileges to create new courses. LearningSpace and Web Course in a Box also allow instructors to create courses. The administrator must create the course account in WebCT.

Student Management

Once the course is created, instructors have complete control over the student database. Student accounts are created and administered by the instructor. Student accounts can be created individually or in a batch upload, entering the names into the database through a delimited digital text file. In most software packages, students can then be assigned into groups if desired. Permissions on pages, folders, tools, quizzes, etc., can be individually configured for group use or open use.

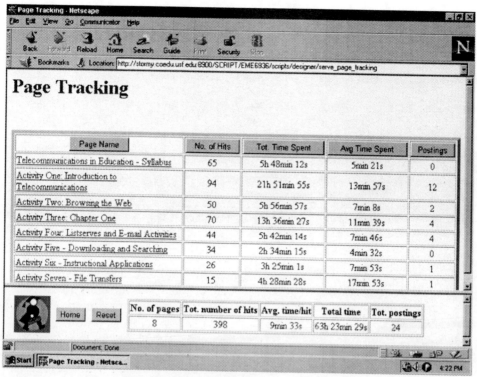

Figure 4. Tracking information in WebCT.

LearningSpace, TopClass, Web Course in a Box, and WebCT provide features for student account management. All four software packages allow for batch account creation as well as for individual account creation.

Student and Site Tracking

Student progress and site use is tracked to some degree by all of the course management software reviewed. However, the packages differ in the degree to which they track individual items. Statistics can be collected that track how many times students have logged on, how long they spent online, how many times they visited a certain page, how many assignments they have completed, etc. Statistics can also track the use of the course site. Records can track the total number of times the site was accessed by students, the total number of hits to each individual page, the total time spent on certain page, and the total number of time spent on site. LearningSpace, TopClass, Web Course in a Box, and WebCT all provide some form of student and site tracking. See Figure 4 for a summary of major system features, which are subject to change in later versions, produced after this chapter was written.

Summary

Each of the software applications reviewed in this chapter differs mainly in the degree to which it offers services. One may afford more capabilities for online quizzing, while another may provide better interaction with synchronous communication capabilities. Rather than choosing one as a clear-cut winner, perhaps a better approach may include determining the best software

Table 1. Major system features.*

	WebCT	TopClass	LearningSpace	Web Course in a Box
E-mail	Yes	Yes	Yes	Yes
Bulletin board	Yes	Yes	Yes	Yes
Chat	Yes	No	No	Yes
Online testing	Yes	Yes	Yes	Yes
Home pages	Yes	No	Yes	Yes
Security	Yes	Yes	Yes	Yes
Student management	Yes	Yes	Yes	Yes
Course management	Yes	Yes	Yes	Yes
Site tracking	Yes	Yes	Yes	Yes
Student tracking	Yes	Yes	Yes	Yes

*Due to the dynamic nature of this evolving field, these features may have been revised in versions offered after this chapter was prepared.

application for each individual instructional approach. Multiple course management applications can coexist on a single server, providing administrators with the tools necessary to provide a wide range of choice for designers and instructors. Table 1 summarizes major features of the four applications.

Obviously, the software packages reviewed are in a constant state of flux. Improvements are being made daily. New systems are being developed. Fortunately, many online resources are available for the Web course developer. Online resources can provide a much more current assessment of available Web course management packages. The following Websites are offered as a starting point for making more detailed comparisons:

- The Virtual Companion (ntlf.com/html/sf/vcslinks.htm)

- Online Educational Delivery Applications: A Web Tool for Comparative Analysis (ctt.bc.ca/landonline/index.html)

- Tools for Developing Interactive Academic Web Courses (umanitoba.ca/ip/tools/courseware/)

The Authors

Ann E. Barron (e-mail: barron@tempest.coedu.usf.edu; Web homepage: coedu.usf.edu/inst_tech/faculty/barron) is Associate Professor of Instructional Technology at the University of South Florida, Tampa, Florida. Chet Lyskawa (e-mail: lyskawa@typhoon.coedu.usf.edu) is Director of VITAL Services for the Florida Center for Instructional Technology in Tampa.

34

Planning for Web-Based Course Management

Henryk R. Marcinkiewicz and

Eva M. Ross

The purpose of this chapter is to provide a set of strategies for initiating and implementing Web-based course management software. The planning process that follows was drawn from established ideas and conventions and, while they were further developed and applied in a university setting, we expect there will be generalizability to training settings.

The challenge that you may be facing, and for which these steps were specifically developed, is the implementation of Web-based course management software. These are the steps:

1. Determine the needs.
2. Determine the resources and evaluate the products.
3. Train the trainers.
4. Evaluate the needs being met.

Determine the Needs

Do we need online instruction? Establish the need. Whether or not you need to be involved with online instruction is the question that ought to initiate your planning. It is recommended that you formulate an answer to this question because it will help you structure your plan and identify procedures, personnel, and resources. Someone in your company may claim a need and is seeking satisfaction of the need without verifying or justifying it. You may even be pressured into action without establishing the justification. The advice—resist the urge!

There is an entire field of study concerned with needs assessment. The consequences of not assessing the need include inaction and missed opportunity where there truly was a need or unnecessary expense, time, and effort where there was not a need. In short, it is irresponsible to act without establishing a need. Awareness of the five need categories below will help you to organize your thinking about what you consider a legitimate basis for a need (Briggs & Wager, 1981). Then, prioritize these need categories according to the demands of your company.

Categories of needs:

- Normative: relative to established standards.

- Felt: based on perceptions.

- Expressed or demanded: demonstrated by specific request.

- Anticipated: projection based on past or current information.

- Comparative: relative to similar institutions.

Who knows whether you need online instruction? Ask the key influencers. You have likely already been persuaded of the need for online instruction; the external factors are compelling. In order to be competitive, you need to meet the demands of a changing population. Often employees are hired on the basis of the unique and diverse characteristics that they bring to a company rather than for their ability to conform (Scheinholtz, 1998). There are more location-independent employees. Many employees expect educational technology, or technology capable of presenting information in a variety of ways. You must be aware of these factors, but in order to make a thorough assessment of whether your company needs to be involved with online instruction, you must research your company internally.

The least practical and least informative approach would be to ask everyone at your company. In fact, it may not be possible to identify all individuals who are related to the company. A useful model to structure the set of individuals to include in your assessment process is the "significant others" (key influencers) suggested by the "Theory of Reasoned Action" (Ajzen & Fishbein, 1980). These are the individuals or groups who create the expectations at an institution, and, by doing so, create the culture. Drawing from research on adoption of educational technology (Marcinkiewicz, 1996), the significant others whose views can be sought concerning online instruction are the administration, trainers, professional societies, and students.

Your needs assessment may reveal that not all key influencers are supportive. In the midst of the avalanche of enthusiasm for online instruction in general from external sources (such as members of professional organizations or scholars), support is not unanimous (see Cuban, 1998; Noble, 1997). You must decide whether, from the standpoint of cost and benefits, the concerns do not outweigh the previously-determined advantages.

To what degree can instruction be online? A variation of this question is, "How much needs to be online?" There are three degrees of Web-based instruction: (1) Web-Presence, (2) Web-Enabled, and (3) Web-Integrated (Schumann, 1998). The distinguishing characteristics of these categories are interaction, stability of content, and classroom independence.

- Web-Presence has no interaction, and the content is stable. Some examples are course syllabi or the periodic table of elements.

- Web-Enabled has interaction, dynamic content, and is a component of instruction. An example is a classroom exercise requiring the identification of the parts of the human anatomy.

- Web-Integrated has interaction, dynamic content, and is independent. An example is an electronic discussion group's members solving a problem from their homes.

Identifying the degree of online instruction is critical because it guides planning for expenses of money and time. It also helps determine whether the instructional components will be developed by the training staff, instructional developers, or both.

Determine the Resources and Evaluate the Products

We recommend the steps provided below for resource determination. You can expect that there will be a large amount of information available and competing products for enabling online instruction; therefore, a purposeful effort must be made to sort through the information. Accordingly, these steps will organize the searching and sorting process.

    (a) Solicit opinions among colleagues via the Internet—Listservs and Web sites.

    (b) Identify companies and vendors.

    (c) Identify, form, or empower a decision-making body at the company.

    (d) Arrange for presentations about the products.

    (e) Prepare evaluation forms with most pertinent criteria.

    (f) Evaluate the software.

    (g) Select the product.

With regard to step "(d)," arranging for presentations, you will find that some products do not have a sales unit that will conduct a product demonstration either live or via teleconference. Under these circumstances, you will need to seek private consultants or third party enterprises. Private consultants for Web-based course management software can often be identified at universities or community colleges. Many universities now post referral lists of experts. There are also small businesses that provide product demonstration as well as training.

With regard to the preparation of evaluation forms and software evaluation, we recommend you use the provided form in Table 1. It was developed based on the goal of instructional needs guiding technology selection. The evaluation should proceed in two stages. In the first stage, the evaluation form sorts software according to its functionality. What will likely emerge is a handful of programs that are very similar in terms of capabilities and ease of use. The programs identified at the end of the first evaluation will meet your needs in general.

In the second stage, evaluate the software selected considering broader company concerns, such as cost, time, effort, ease of installation, and technical support. Due to the lack of variation among software in terms of capabilities and functions, this step is necessary to help differentiate among the software.

Train the Trainers

Schedule training and follow-up. In scheduling training and follow-up, these are key points to consider:

Organize by skill level. The importance of organizing participants by skill level is critical. It may be necessary to organize according to general computer ability in addition to the participants' familiarity with the software.

Consider the needs of individual learners. Training in the use of computer software is most successful under the conditions where each learner is working with an individual machine, clear learning goals are set, and the instructor-to-learner ratio is low. Assume that learning to use the software will be an continuous process and provide opportunities to support ongoing learning. Plan to have follow up training sessions and form "interest groups" of trainers.

Consider the match of software to learner needs. You may be inclined to organize your training by focusing on the features of the Web management software. Because Web management software is so feature laden, the learners will find it overwhelming. Instead, focus on creating documents first, then on, uploading documents and later on providing an overview of Web management features.

Table 1. Rating scale for Web courseware.
(*RATING: 0 = low; 1 = adequate; 2 = exceptional)

PEDAGOGICAL FEATURES	RATING*	COMMENT	N/A
I. TESTING			
a. item banking			
b. random generation of questions from pool			
c. score reporting online			
d. customized feedback for test items			
e. score analysis			
f. variety of formats: fill blanks, multiple choice			
g. scoring online			
h. timed quizzes			
II. INSTRUCTION			
A. Presentation			
a. ease of composition			
b. HTML necessary			
c. ease of editing			
d. all data: graphics, etc.			
e. automated glossary			
f. automated index			
g. search tool			
h. students can annotate material			
i. students can upload presentations			
B. PRACTICE & PRODUCTION			
a. instructor to student feedback			
b. student to student feedback (group work)			
c. retries possible			
d. path of tutorial follows responses			
e. ease of use for students			
f. ease of use for teachers			
g. student access and progress data monitored			
h. students can self-assess			
i. ease of course revision			

(continued)

Table 1. *(Continued).*

PEDAGOGICAL FEATURES *(continued)*	RATING*	COMMENT	N/A
C. DISCUSSION			
a. synchronous: chat room			
b. simultaneous groups possible			
c. asynchronous: e-mail			
d. thread tracking possible			
e. posting categories of responses possible			
f. bulletin board			
TECHNICAL FEATURES			
III. SERVER			
a. installation			
b. maintenance			
c. upgrading software			
d. crash recovery			
IV. SECURITY			
a. individual and group enabled			
b. ease of access, not a bottleneck			
V. SERVER SUPPORT			
a. cost			
b. terms (duration)			
c. 24-hour availability			
d. transferability to Help Desk			
VI. HOW-TO SUPPORT			
a. cost			
b. terms (duration)			
c. 24-hour availability			
d. transferability to Help Desk			
VII. CLIENT EQUIPMENT			
a. faculty needs			
b. student needs			
VIII. COST			

Have necessary equipment available. Consider a dedicated server that would operate independently from administrative, business, and e-mail components of the complete server system. Also have available support resources available, such as a Webmaster or early adopting staff. Technical support personnel are always necessary, but especially with Web-based course management software because few of the software companies provide live support. You can expect some personnel to emerge as leaders; encourage them in that role by perhaps allowing them to conduct continued training. Hold "user group" meetings.

Evaluate the Needs Being Met

The assessment of your plan should reveal whether you have a workable plan, that you are following it, that you are achieving the desired results, and that any of your concerns are being mitigated.

Summary

It is our hope that these strategies will enable all trainers to successfully implement Web-based instruction courses. Two final points: (1) market the plan to sustain interest, and (2) continue to communicate with and gain feedback from all the key influencers.

References

Ajzen, I., & Fishbein, M. (1980). *Understanding attitudes and predicting social behavior.* Englewood Cliffs: Prentice-Hall.

Briggs, L. J., & Wager, W. W. (1981). *Handbook of procedures for the design of instruction* (2nd ed.). Englewood Cliffs: Educational Technology Publications.

Cuban, L. (1998). High-tech schools and low-tech teaching. *Journal of Computing in Teacher Education, 14*(2), 6–7.

Marcinkiewicz, H. R. (1996). Using subjective norms to predict teachers' computer use. *Journal of Computing in Teacher Education, 13*(1), 27–33.

Noble, D. (1997). Education as a commodity. *Adult Assessment Forum, 7*(4), 12–17.

Scheinholtz, D. (1998, November 16). Diversity: The bottom line. Part III. Leveraging diversity: Opportunities in the new market [Special advertising section]. *Forbes, 162,* 1–30.

Schumann, T. K. (1998). Resources for building Web-based environments; ttc.ferris.edu/WB2/resources/index.htm

The Authors

Henryk R. Marcinkiewicz (e-mail: marcinkh@ferris.edu; Web homepage: ferris.edu/html/academics/center/center.htm) is Director, Center for Teaching, Learning, and Faculty Development, Ferris State University, Big Rapids, Michigan. **Eva M. Ross** (e-mail: emross@purdue.edu) is an Instructional Developer, Center for Instructional Excellence, Purdue University, West Lafayette, Indiana.

35

Web-Based Training Administration

Jason D. Baker

Many organizations have neglected to notice the administrative advantages of WBT. In addition to using the Web to deliver instruction, the Web can also be harnessed to manage the overall scheduling of a corporate training program. In an effort to reduce administrative costs, the Information Services (IS) department of Loyola College in Maryland converted its entire technology training administrative database to a Web-based system in 1996. The result was not only a reduction in administrative costs but also improved service to the user community of College employees.

Preliminary Design

Prior to Loyola's Web-based administrative system, a user was required to telephone the Technology Helpdesk in order to determine the availability of a particular training class. The Helpdesk employee then registered the user for the class by hand-writing the user's name into the registration logbook. Subsequently, the training coordinator was responsible for comparing the registration list to the actual attendance sign-in sheet and entering the names into the training database. Clearly, this was a labor-intensive procedure, and it contained numerous stumbling blocks, such as the time when one Helpdesk worker misplaced the registration book and we lost dozens of rosters for upcoming classes.

The original plan was simply to make the training database a shared Helpdesk resource, thereby eliminating the paper registration book. However, after examining the possibilities of using this as Loyola's first intranet application, it was determined that a Web-based approach would be superior. The concept was simple—a self-service training registration system. Employees would visit the Information Services Technology Training Web site and find descriptions of current seminars, an up-to-date schedule of course offerings, a registration section where they could view the attendance roster and enroll in (or remove themselves from) a particular class, and a transcript area where they could view or print a list of all training seminars that they have attended.

The first step was to modify the existing training registration database in preparation for connecting it to the Web. Because the database was increased from a basic attendance list to an integrated registration system, it was easier to simply build a new relational database with tables for course descriptions, schedules, course registration, and an employee directory. Building the database enabled us to prototype the various aspects of the online registration system prior to connecting the database to the Web. Over a period of weeks, the database underwent extensive testing and modification to meet the system requirements and needs of the users. Once the database was designed and the user services (e.g., view course schedule, view personal transcript, etc.) had been tested, it was time to place the database online.

Web Database Connectivity

Connecting a database to the Web generally involves a "middleware" component. There needs to be a piece of software in between the Web server and the database to pass information back and forth. Since the standard HTML language is primarily for text markup and doesn't support database queries, most database connectivity software programs include special HTML tags which enable Structured Query Language (SQL) commands to be sent to the database. SQL commands, supported by most databases, permit a user to search fields and records within a database, add or delete records, or modify existing entries. For instance, there might be a special HTML tag called <DBQUERY> which can pass an SQL Select command to the database or <DBUPDATE> to edit the fields within a particular record. The Web developer would then create HTML forms using these special SQL tags in order to permit real-time interaction with the database.

A typical example of the database interaction occurs when a user would like to find out when the next Introduction to Microsoft Word class is being held. The user first examines the Technology Training Schedule Web page (see Figure 1) and selects the Introduction to Word class. When the user presses the View button, a special SQL query HTML command is passed from the Web page, to the Web server, and on to the database connectivity software. The data-

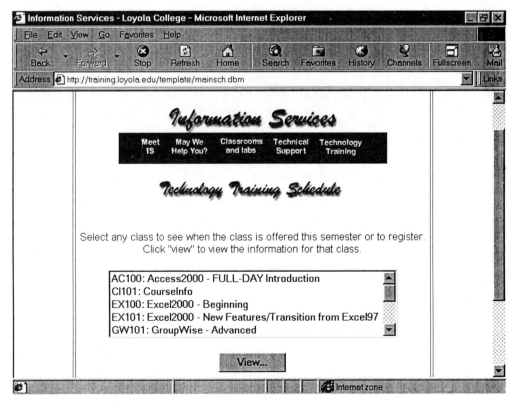

Figure 1. The technology training schedule Web page.

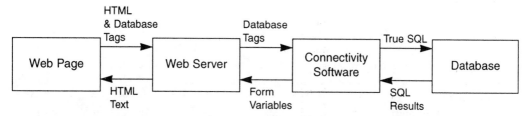

Figure 2. A model of a database query being conducted through the Web.

base connectivity software translates this request into a true SQL command and thereby queries the database to determine when the upcoming Word classes are scheduled. The results are returned by the database, assigned to HTML form variables by the connectivity software, and passed back to the browser. (This sequence is shown in Figure 2.) Finally, the user sees a resulting Web page that lists the class offerings for that course (see Figure 3).

System Implementation

Once the training database was connected to the Web, the Web pages and online forms were designed and published. Basic security was added to the system to prevent those outside of the Loyola employees community from registering for classes. The system was tested and then released to the campus community with instructions about the new registration system.

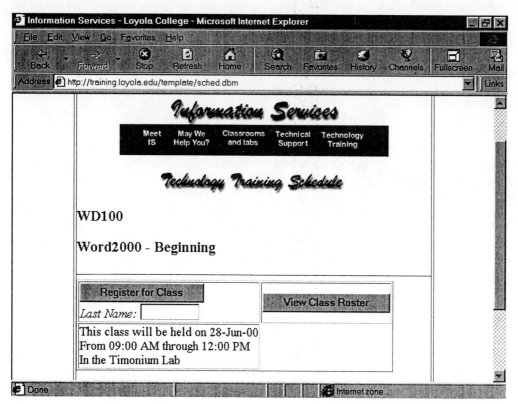

Figure 3. The resulting course schedule generated from the query conducted in Figure 1.

The result is that at the beginning of each semester, a technology training bulletin, featuring course titles and times, is published in both print and electronic form. Employees can then visit the training Web site, get more details about the seminars, and register for a course. The registration process is fairly straightforward. After an employee selects the title of the desired seminar and presses the View button, a list of course dates appear. He or she then has the option of viewing the existing registration list, to see who else is planning to attend on a particular date, or sign up by entering his or her last name and pressing Register. A verification list of names appears, the user selects his or her name, and then completes the registration. If the course is full, then the user is informed of such and encouraged to sign-up for another offering. Furthermore, at any time prior to the seminar, the user can return to the registration site and remove his or her name from the roster. However, a password system prevents users from deleting any names but their own. Users can also view a transcript of all seminars that they've attended.

In parallel with the user interface, a Web-based configuration page was designed. This permitted the training coordinator to add, edit, or delete classes to the schedule. Furthermore, the coordinator or Helpdesk could override a full class and register a user. In addition, the instructor can use the configuration page to mark those who actually attended the class and remove the absentee names.

Results

The reaction to the Web-based registration system has been positive. The new system has reduced the administrative efforts of the Helpdesk and training coordinator by empowering the employees to manage their own course registration. Furthermore, employees always have a way of checking the latest updates to the training schedule, even if they are away from campus. The transcript request form has proved to be most beneficial in conjunction with the performance appraisal process to demonstrate employees' professional development efforts during the previous year. In addition to sparking numerous other intranet Web database projects, the registration system became the foundation of a WBT program which supplements traditional classroom instruction.

Conclusion

Using Web-based course administration offers many benefits to an organization. It gives employees complete control over their professional development training plans from their desktops. By combining a Web front-end with a back-end database, the training group can serve the needs of the users as well as manage the training course registration with a single system. By eliminating redundant efforts and reducing paperwork, online course administration can reduce costs and improve the overall return on investment. Finally, online course administration can be combined with other intranet applications to offer employees a complete suite of services on the Web.

The Author

Jason D. Baker (e-mail: jasobak@regent.edu; Web homepage: bakersguide.com), formerly at Loyola College in Maryland, is an Assistant Professor in the College of Communication and the Arts at Regent University, Virginia Beach, Virginia.

36

Project Support Sites: A Project Management Tool for Constructing Web-Based Training

Lee T. Gotcher

O nce the process of designing and developing online instruction begins, coordinating people, resources, and document revisions can become overwhelming. A manager developing online instruction must not only manage logistics, but also be able to offer technical and managerial insight to the project team members as their problems emerge during development. With the amount of information being exchanged about creating and using Websites in a training or instructional context, little information exists about co-developing a project support site (PSS) in conjunction with building the actual instructional Website itself.

A Project Support Site Defined

A PSS is a specially constructed Website used to assist all project team members to access and share organized information and communicate with other team members for the duration of a project. A PSS is developed at the same time that the instructional Website is created. The PSS will assist in the instructional Website construction process and is used in addition to regular face-to-face meetings.

Functions of a PSS

The primary reason to create a project support site is to provide a one-stop-shopping node for project notes, proposals, design standards, graphics, media files, documents, or any other materials that assist the development team in making the instructional site a reality. Some projects may have team members who cannot attend meetings on a regular basis. By having the PSS available, those members can still have access to resources available to everyone else during face-to-face meetings.

A PSS will keep all interested parties informed of project progress, such as the latest news regarding the project and special updates of documents or standards. With all relevant course development materials available on the site, everyone "knows everything" about the project and every team member can see where his or her tasks fit in. The PSS that is co-developed with the instructional site MUST be considered an "open site." That is, no information on the site is "exclusive" to any one person or group in the team. All information must be shared with everyone on the team. By holding back information, the project manager in effect excludes everyone on the team, which means that the project manager is the only one who knows what is really going on.

Maintaining a PSS during a project results in an archive of information sources on how processes were completed, best practices, how NOT to do things, or what went wrong. This captured information serves as a reference system for designing and building future Internet projects. No need re-inventing the wheel every time a project begins when a dynamic reference exists that includes information and tricks and tips learned from previous successes and failures.

PSS Management

Project support sites are maintained by the Web architect, project manager, or in many cases these days, the dual role of project manager/Webmaster. Maintaining a PSS results in a site that provides a status picture of the project at any given moment. The site must be updated within 24 hours of the previous face-to-face meeting to keep all members abreast of the updates of new resources and documents delivered or presented during these meetings. The PSS is only as good as its accuracy, currency, and usefulness to the team.

The PSS site grows only as large and complex as the team dynamics dictate. A wise manager will not put a lot of energy into developing the project support site, but will save the creative energy for the actual instructional Website itself. Remember, this type of site is most successful as an addition to regular face-to-face meetings, not as a solo communication solution or to replace regular meetings.

After the completion of the instructional Website, the supporting PSS site will be "closed." That is, no new entries or additions to the PSS will be made, and the site is ready to serve as an information archive for additional projects.

PSS Construction

The best way to construct a PSS is to use HTML code to construct a primitive Website. Add to these Web pages hyperlinks to documents, information, or graphics that need to be made available to the team, but not for the general public. Create hypertext links to form a simple Website—and that's all. Of course, if manpower and time permit efforts for a more attractive site, by all means do so. The best advice is to keep it simple.

Special Features in PSSs

There are several features to consider adding to a PSS. Development and maintenance time may be the barrier from using all of the following features. Use only the items necessary at the time needed:

1. Team-member access, which includes e-mail addresses, phone, fax, and pager numbers, or any relevant information needed to contact anyone involved with the project.
2. Work delegation and responsibilities: who does what and where it fits into the project.
3. Project milestones and task due dates.
4. Delivery dates—when the actual course is scheduled to be delivered. To see the impending delivery date getting closer every time the user accesses the site will be motivating.
5. If meeting rooms change location, include the time, date, and location of the next meeting.

6. Archive of previous meetings minutes—a great feature for members who were not able to attend a certain meeting, or for reviewing the historical process of developing an instructional Website.

7. Text and memos related to the course, such as archived e-mail, handouts, and notes of reminder.

8. Links to relevant Websites.

9. Pictures and graphics relevant to the course.

10. A file upload feature to exchange documents, graphics for review or post

11. Copies of templates, tools, software, and job aids.

12. A General Announcements Web page could reiterate what was sent via e-mail or list-serv so no one has an excuse for not knowing about something. A bulletin board may also serve a similar function. When team members access the PSS, make reading the Announcement page or bulletin board mandatory.

13. Another beneficial item is a chat feature. This is an excellent addition to accommodate remote members not able to attend the regular face-to-face meetings. Team members could meet at an alternate date and time for a second online meeting, or conduct quickie follow-up meetings. Announce the date and time for the alternate chat meetings on the Announcements page or bulletin board.

Advance Organizers

On the splash page, use a navigation aid to take users to specific areas within the site. Consider including these advance organizer links on the splash page:

- information or announcements;
- tools;
- schedule and due dates;
- announcements;
- a section for graphic artists, instructional designers, and programmers; and
- data or instructional content files.

Providing this feature on the site will speed up navigation and browsing of the site. When the users first log on, these advanced organizers will quickly guide users to the information they need.

Site Design Hierarchy

To design a PSS, consider using a directory/folder hierarchy (Figure 1) to construct a simple site. Feel free to add directories or subdirectories as the needs of the project or PSS dictate:

- *Home.* This is the splash or opening page for the site. At this level are the advance organizers for the team.
- *Pix.* Pictures for the graphic artists or site designers.
- *HTML.* The HTML pages that make up the PSS here. This directory would include the Information.htm and Announcements.htm files.
- *Team.* Web page that includes phone numbers, pagers, faxes, and e-mail addresses of all team members.
- *Misc.* Everything else, which may include standards documents, content files, etc.

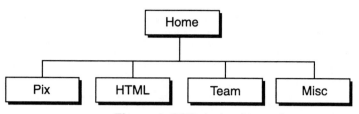

Figure 1. PSS design hierarchy.

Exchanging Files Between Team Members

If development times permit, another benefit to the PSS is a feature to exchange files. Either an FTP server or a script that allows file transfers through the Web will serve well. FTP server software is available from shareware.com, and there are several scripts from cgi-resources.com/ that provide Web file transfer. The Web file transfer scripts allow file exchange through the Web. These scripts take advantage of a feature called "http upload." These scripts will allow users to upload files from their computer to the server from an HTML Web page. Users can browse for a file on their computer and click the Submit button, and the selected file is uploaded to the server.

Joint Contributions

One problem with exchanging files between many users is the misfortune of overwriting someone else's files on the PSS Website. The best way to work with multiple submissions is to have each worker be responsible only for specific files and by using specific file naming conventions. If any issues arise regarding the file or its content, accountability is easily accomplished. To further remove the possibility of file overwrite, each team or team member could have a separate proprietary directory to store files related to the project. A sub-directory nested inside each of the user directories called "In" and "Out" may also be useful to control file and work flow. A separate but similar directory structure could be created that is accessible by all users.

Observations on Using PSSs

Personal dynamics of the team and regular meetings will dictate whether a PSS is needed or not. Usually within the first couple of meetings, team members will ask "How do I get this item to you?" or "How can I get with you about . . . ." This is the sign that a PSS needs to be constructed. The simplest PSS should at least include e-mail and phone information for members, and links to a few important project documents, and if time permits, include a method for exchanging files. An important point to remember is that a PSS doesn't necessarily have to be a fancy site. This site is not used by the general public for browsing but as an internal quick-and-dirty communication medium for all members on a Web development project. Use PSSs for prompting and answering questions between meetings and announcing items relevant to project development. This tool should be used to guide the team through the "rough spots," which usually occur at the beginning of the project.

The Author

Lee T. Gotcher (e-mail: gotcher@net1.net; Web homepage: cl.uh.edu) is an instructional programmer with the University of Houston Clear Lake, Houston, Texas.

37

Current and Ideal Practices in Designing, Developing, and Delivering Web-Based Training

Carlos Villalba and Alexander J. Romiszowski

Introduction

The recent explosion in the use of the Internet is being accompanied by a parallel increase in the use of distance education, especially in higher education, adult continuing education, and corporate training. Recent studies estimate that over four million North American university students now use the Internet as an integral and regular course component, to access the vast resources of information now available on the Web, and also to interact with their professors and colleagues outside of normally scheduled classes. The number of students who study entirely at a distance is, of course, smaller, but is rapidly increasing. One indicator of this growth is the number of U.S. higher education institutions that offer distance learning courses and programs. In 1993 this was below 100; by 1996 it had grown to over 700, and the estimate for 1999 is in the region of 1500 (*Peterson's Distance Learning Catalog,* 1996, 1998).

In the corporate training and business education world, the growth is even more rapid, and the predictions of further growth are quite staggering. A recent report (Julian & Capozzi, 1998) estimated a fourfold growth in the Web-based training market from 1997 to 1999, from some $197 million to just short of $1 billion, and predicts a similar continuing growth that will take the market to somewhere in the region of $6 billion by the year 2002. This scenario is fascinating, and even to some extent confusing, when one perceives that this report seems to view Web-based training (WBT) as being principally the individualized self-study of computer-based training (CBT) packages, accessed by the trainee via the Web. The report does not thus define WBT, but all the content providers reviewed and analyzed are the current CBT market leaders (e.g., CBT Systems, Gartner Group, NETg), and most of the technological support organizations reviewed are the leading providers of CBT authoring software (e.g., Asymetrix, Macromedia). It is true that some client-server environments that support instructor-led "virtual" group instruction (e.g., Lotus LearningSpace, WBT Systems) are also reviewed in the appendices, but this form of WBT is not mentioned anywhere else in the report. It is not clear, therefore, whether the growth figures in this report refer to just the Web-delivered CBT variety of WBT, or to all possible forms of WBT. We start therefore by attempting to define WBT more comprehensively and to delineate the specific focus we should adopt in this chapter.

Web-based training (WBT) is defined in many different ways in the literature, the only common denominator being the use of the Web as a means of storing and distributing information and also as an environment to support interpersonal message exchanges. It may be useful to define three categories of WBT that are identifiable through both existing practical examples and the more theoretical literature of the field. These three categories reflect three forms of training systems, whether they are Web-based or not.

CATEGORY 1: Individualized, self-instructional, or job-performance aid systems. This category includes the full range of self-study CBT forms (drill-and-practice, tutorials, simulation exercises, projects, etc.) that are well-known to the technology-based training specialist and that, for many trainers, have represented the total universe of computer-based training alternatives. The category also includes the plethora of computer-based electronic performance support systems (EPSS), although in many cases, these are not so much "training systems" as "training substitutes." However, in the real world, they do get used as components in learner-directed training, in that the user, by making use of the online support, in effect organizes his or her own just-in-time training program. The only novelty in this category is that the trainees or users access the materials via the Web instead of other alternatives, such as LANs or CD-ROMs.

CATEGORY 2: Individual and group study in a "virtual classroom" environment. This category includes the emerging online learning environments that combine the Web's rich (Hypertext/Hypermedia) information resources and its potential to support a variety of modes of Computer-Mediated Communication (CMC) to create something akin to the conventional "classroom-plus homework-plus group exercises" experience. We all used such learning environments in our formal education, and they still form the bulk of corporate training activity (the current size of the individualized WBT/CBT market, estimated in the aforementioned IDC report as about $1 billion, hardly represents 2% of the total USA expenditure on corporate training). This category has earned the not-too-accurate title of "virtual classroom," and now we hear of an ever increasing number of "virtual" schools, universities, and corporate training centers being established.

CATEGORY 3: Collaborative small-group learning environments. This category is the one that is perhaps least practiced but most written about in the current literature of Web-based learning. We use the word "learning" intentionally to emphasize the theoretical and the practical focus of this category. Much of the literature and research is occurring not in corporate training contexts but in formal education. However, as the corporate world moves inexorably toward the globalized "networked society," and "knowledge work" becomes the rule, training needs will ever more require the use of such collaborative group-learning methodologies (Romiszowski, 1997). One well-known growth area here is the use of case-study methodology, not only in top management training, but right across the board.

In this chapter, we shall concentrate our attention on CATEGORY 2. As mentioned above, there is little new to analyze and report in relation to the first category, except for the novel technical aspects of delivery, tracking, control and evaluation of the use of CBT over the Web. We leave this to other authors. The third category is, as mentioned above, of great and increasing importance. However, it is addressed by one of the present authors in another chapter in this book. We choose to concentrate our attention here on the second category, not only because it is analogous to the greater part of conventional training activities, but also because we have recently had the opportunity to perform some comparative studies of several of the currently available "virtual classroom" environments.

Learning Theories and the Design of WBT

There are many different learning theories that can serve as a basis for designing instruction. Three schools of thought have been widely used and explored to provide guidance for instructional practice: behaviorism, cognitive psychology, and constructivism. From these three viewpoints, learning can be seen as shown in Figure 1.

In a very loose sense, these three categories of learning theory and their associated assumptions and practical implementation approaches (see Table 1) may be mapped onto the three categories of WBT as we defined them above. This mapping is loose in that there is every reason, both theoretical and practical, to draw on many theoretical sources for the planning of instruction in any one of the three WBT categories. However, it is nevertheless observable that the professionals who work in the emerging field of WBT are aligning themselves fairly rigidly by theoretical views on learning theory and therefore are interested in promoting only one or other of the three categories of WBT environments. Whereas this may be a very appropriate position to adopt for a researcher or theoretician, we argue that the range of real-life training needs in the corporate world leads to all three categories of WBT being of equal importance. We do not intend to adopt any partisan positions regarding the theory/practice issues we have raised, but just leave what we have said as an issue for the reader's reflection.

Teaching Models and the Development of WBT

Instructional Development is a systemic process for developing successful training. The process has two main characteristics that focus on performance and cost effectiveness. First, it is designed to emphasize performance-based training. That is, when properly implemented, the process will result in a training program that maximizes the quality and efficiency of on-the-job performance achieved by trainees. Second, the various steps, activities, and decisions that make up this process have been designed to produce the most cost-effective training program possible. Specifically, it seeks to minimize the resources (including trainer and trainee time) required to produce the desired level of job performance. The typical instructional development process consists of six phases that are important for successfully developing effective and efficient instruction. The six phases are: (1) analysis, (2) design, (3) development, (4) implementation, (5) evaluation, and (6) management. Figure 2 shows the manner in which these phases are integrated into a systemic instructional development process. Table 2 presents, in summary, a functional definition of each of the phases and its expected outcome.

It is interesting to conjecture whether this basic development model is as applicable to the category 2 and 3 definition of WBT (the virtual classroom and collaborative small group) as it is to category 1 (CBT). In the authors' opinion, the six phases and the overall systemic nature of the way they should be implemented do indeed serve as a generic model for all forms of training design. As instructional designers, we believe that the world is changing at an ever accelerating rate; therefore, it is very difficult to update educational goals and select teaching/learning methods to attend to emerging needs for new information processing skills. We believe that education and training should emphasize more general capabilities for "learning to learn" that will help the future citizens adapt themselves to this never-ending change process. However, that does not mean that future training (or indeed education) is excused from setting goals, planning the teaching/learning process, and evaluating the outcomes.

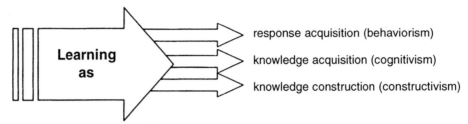

Figure 1. Assumptions about learning.

Table 1. Approaches to instruction.

Learning theory	Overall assumption/paradigm	Basic instructional approach
Behaviorism	• Basically, behavior is a function of its consequences. Learning is achieved through frequent response and immediate reinforcement of appropriate behavior. • Essentially, behavior and performance are either seen as synonymous or performance is seen as the useful outcome of learning behavior.	• Instruction is designed to promote individual pacing and progress. • Instruction is designed using a task analysis, which breaks down the behavior into a sequence of observable actions. • Assessment practices measure objectives in which behavior is operationally defined and measured according to some performance indicators.
Cognitivism	• New information is built on existing knowledge structures. Relevant processing activities are stimulated and specific strategies are taught to ensure that the learner efficiently acquires the information or solves the problem.	• Instruction is designed to promote processing activity akin to that of an expert. • Assessment practices rely on observable behavior but infer specific mental operations based on the design of the test.
Constructivism	• Learning is understood as interpretative and emergent, and under the control of the learner. Cognition is situated and must be understood in terms of the setting, purposes, tools, and tasks in which the knowledge is to be learned. • Knowledge is to a large extent a negotiated meaning ascribed to reality and should be achieved via collaborative group work.	• The goal structures need to be negotiated through teacher-learner interaction. • Learners are at the center of the design activity. Some forms of constructivism stress cooperative learning. • Assessment practices are designed around real-life problems and promote self-evaluation and reflection to maximize learner responsibility.

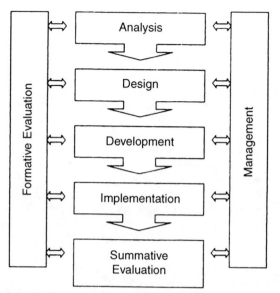

Figure 2. A generic instructional development model.

The Virtual Classroom and the Delivery of WBT

The explosion in Web-based distance education is accompanied by a parallel explosion in the number and variety of software, systems, and environments for online study. This is in part a natural response to market demand, but is also fueled by the rapid technological developments occurring in the fields of computing and communications. In addition to the already well known forms of asynchronous Computer-Mediated-Communication (CMC) systems, such as e-mail, discussion lists, and BBS, we now use a variety of new synchronous communication alternatives, such as electronic whiteboards, Internet Relay Chat, Web-based audio and video conferencing, and a growing variety of "groupware" packages. In addition to the previously predominant medium of text, we now communicate and intercommunicate by means of multimedia, thus diminishing the differences between distance and conventional education environments.

However, in this apparent revolution in delivery systems, there is another aspect to consider. Are technological innovations and economic realities driving the changes without due consideration for the social, pedagogical, and psychological factors that govern the viability and effectiveness of the learning process? Technology may be revolutionizing the possible ways of communication and teaching, but one element in the process—the learner—remains much the same as ever, evolving almost imperceptibly from one generation to the next in terms of thought processes, learning styles, motivation for study, and so on. Are the designers of the new online learning environments taking into due consideration the relevant characteristics, needs, and preferences of the trainee?

The authors of this study have had the opportunity to use and compare several online learning environments, from early mainframe-based systems, such as CoSy and PARTI, to currently available client-server and Web-based systems, such as LotusNotes, WebCT, TopClass, FirstClass, Embanet, and TangoInteractive. Most recently, they have implemented some of the first English-language applications of the AulaNet environment, developed in Brazil at the Catholic University of Rio de Janeiro (Lucena *et al.*, 1999). The following sections present some of the findings of these studies, concentrating on the most recent generation of online learning environments that seek to promote "the best of classroom instruction within WBT."

Table 2. Summary of steps in instructional development.

PHASE I: ANALYSIS	The process of finding out what tasks or functions are performed, which of these tasks require training or other actions, measuring the results of job performance, and deciding the setting in which the training or other actions should take place. This process is often referred to as "front-end analysis." Front-end analysis is concerned with data gathering and analysis, priority setting, and establishing measurement procedures to use for evaluation. The outcome of a front-end-analysis is a clear description of a problem, evidence of the validity of the problem, and alternative solutions.
PHASE II: DESIGN	The process of integrating principles, processes, and products as a means to create solution alternatives. Taking the "output" of analysis—the verified performance requirements or discrepancies—it is the designer's job to write the specifications for how the problem is to be solved. Design is concerned with specifying performance objectives, assessment instruments, instructional strategies, materials, and delivery (media) systems.
PHASE III: DEVELOPMENT	The process of creating training systems that conform to design specifications. Development is an interactive process between subject matter experts and designers to ensure specifications are understood and attained within the time and resource constraints. Development may involve original construction of instructional elements, or adaptive revision of existing instructional elements. It is also concerned with authoring and producing instructional materials, adapting or modifying selected media to fit with objectives and strategies, and specifying the roles, strategies, and procedures to be executed by instructors, facilitators, and mentors.
PHASE IV: IMPLEMENTATION	The process of developing plans for delivering the project in the real-world context and maintaining the quality of instruction. Plans are developed for monitoring, directing, and controlling instructional activities until the completion of the project. Emphasis in the implementation phase is on training the instructor or teacher, student tryout, and maintaining the quality of instruction once it has been implemented.
PHASE V: EVALUATION	The process of gathering and analyzing information that can be used for making decisions or judgments about people, products, procedures, or processes. Evaluation is an ongoing process throughout instructional development that has two unique methods for conducting a study: *formative* and *summative*. *Formative* evaluation is used to obtain data that can be used to revise the instruction to make it more efficient and effective. *Summative* evaluation is collecting data and information in order to make decisions about the acquisition or continued use of some instruction.

The Initial Study: Structure of
Three Representative Online Environments

Three computer software packages commonly used to facilitate the delivery of instruction over the World Wide Web were selected for study: LotusNotes Domino, WebCT, and TopClass. These were selected because of the availability of a significant number of online courses that could be accessed for the purpose of analysis. First, a comparative analysis was conducted of the functionality of the systems, by reviewing which course characteristics were exemplified by each of the three packages. The characteristics are related to instructional content, appropriateness, formats and the integration of multimedia attributes to this content to support teaching pedagogy. Each course delivery package utilized the Web in a different fashion, ranging from the support of particular activities to the online provision of all course materials. From these cases, we have identified several common online course components (Table 3).

The list of common features and suggestions on how to implement them, presented in Table 3, was derived from a review of existing literature on the design of online learning environments (Averman, 1996; Hales, 1997; Hites & Ewing, 1995; McManus 1995; Parson, 1997) as well as from the authors' personal experience as users of a wide variety of systems. The three packages selected for comparison were analyzed to see how closely they matched this "mainstream" model and also to identify any key differences between the three exemplars. A summary of this analysis is presented in Table 4. (It should be noted that as software packages in general and online learning environments in particular are in constant evaluation, development, and upgrading, the data and observations presented in this table may no longer be accurate subsequent to publication of this volume. However, the data are not presented as technical specifications for the products reviewed, but merely to illustrate the similarities or differences that may be found among the products available at one university at one time.) This shows a surprising amount of divergence between the packages in terms of the capabilities implemented, especially in regard to the practical application of knowledge to tasks and exercises and the provisions for online interaction between the participants. The packages are much more similar in relation to the facilities they offer for the presentation of content. It would seem, on face value, that the designers of two of the packages were more concerned with the provision of a vehicle for the communication of content in a format that made use of the hypertext/hypermedia characteristics of the Web than with the provision of appropriate exercise and discussion environments that would allow instructors to easily implement, track, and evaluate relevant learning activities for their students. The third package, TopClass, seems to have given equal consideration to both the communication and the application of knowledge, as well as providing superior tracking and evaluation tools for both instructors and participants.

Second Study: Design Characteristics of
Representative Online Courses

Today, almost any instructor may easily publish course information on the Web. However, if this information does not guide the learner toward efficient learning and attainment of worthwhile goals, this publishing effort may be largely ineffective. When designing WBT, or indeed any course, it is critical to consider learning theories and instructional principles and use them to effectively organize and present relevant information and also design relevant learning activities for the students. The choice of instructional strategies varies according to different types of learning domain. However, Smith and Ragan (1993) claim that there is at least one thing all instruction has in common. No matter what the learning domain is, all instruction has a "pattern of instruction" (Smith & Ragan, 1993, p. 161) which consists of a set of instructional events.

Table 3. Characteristics and standards for WBT delivery systems.

The Online Syllabus	An online course syllabus provides the instructor with a way to change course material easily, and the student with a complete and up-to-date picture of the course requirements. The format need not (and probably should not) duplicate the print version. Hypertext links to sample relevant disciplinary Websites may be helpful in giving students (and prospective students) a sense of the disciplinary context for the course.
Assignments	A Web page listing homework assignments, upcoming events, and exams can be more interactive than the familiar print version. If some homework assignments, for example, are based on online materials, they can be directly linked to the class schedule.
Announcements	To be effective, announcements need to be read; for that to happen, the students need to know when a new announcement has been posted. Alert boxes or running footers (using JavaScript) or a blinking link added to a page can let students know when there are new announcements.
Personal Home Pages	Personal home pages can be used to foster the sense that the class is not just a collection of isolated individuals, but a community of learners who can profit from interacting with one another. Home pages encourage students to learn about each other so as to encourage contact and mutual curiosity.
Interactivity	Adding discussion forums and chat sessions is a common way to add an interactive component to a Web-based course. There are many implementations of bulletin board and chat session software to choose from, but we recommend those that allow the sharing files and also the "threading" of discussions. A second method of interactivity is, of course, e-mail. It is common practice to have an online list of all registered students (and the instructor) with their e-mail addresses.
Testing	Online drill and practice or testing can be used to reinforce material, even if not used as part of a grade. Comprehension questions, for example, in short answer or multiple-choice formats can provide students with self-assessment of their understanding of the text.
Course Management	Software should be available to add/delete students from a course, assign user IDs and passwords, create/edit homepages, manage the interactive discussion groups, and generate progress reports.
Content	Perhaps the most difficult part of developing a Web-based course is creating the online content. One often begins by translating the basic lecture materials to the Web and integrating media, such as sound, images, and even video. One should also experiment with incorporating some of the new Web-based learning paradigms.

Table 4. Characteristics and capabilities of three WBI delivery systems.

Features	LotusNotes Domino	WebCT	TopClass
The Online Syllabus	Present and well-defined; however, not very attractive in layout. Without links to class assignments or lectures.	Present and well-planned. The calendar may contain direct links to relevant course content.	Not automatically present. Generally implemented as a separate Web page or as part of the instructor's homepage.
Assignments	Present, with powerful file transfer capabilities. Assignments are embedded within class discussions, achieving a very good sequence in the content.	Present, embedded with course content. Not always easy to locate an assignment out of context of the course material.	Present, embedded with course contents.
Announcements	Present, and easy to use.	Not present as a separate capability. Use of the bulletin board facility for posting announcements.	Present, easy to use, attractive interface.
Personal Home Pages	Not integrated. Class rosters are used so students know their classmates.	Not present.	As a rule, only the instructor has one.
Interactivity	No chatroom capabilities. Bulletin board and discussion lists are present.	Chatroom, e-mail, and bulletin boards are all implemented.	Chatroom capabilities are not available. Internal e-mail and discussion lists are present.
Testing	Moderate self-assessment facilities, but not very attractive, and progress tracking facilities are limited.	Student assessment facilities are present and keeping track of that self-assessment is relatively easy.	Self-assessment capability is attractive and powerful. Tools to keep track of students' progress are very powerful and versatile.
Course Management	Information not available to instructors. Additional programming is required.	Administrative tools, students' records, and student profile are present and functional.	Capabilities are outstanding, allowing modifications in almost anything.
Content	Well-presented, structured, and sequenced. Navigation is very good and simple.	Attractive. Navigation system excellent. Search capabilities and glossary facilitate browsing. Content structured.	Very attractive. Content is structured and sequenced. Navigation is complicated with many graphic links.

Note: As software packages in general and online learning environments in particular are in constant evaluation, development, and upgrading, the data and observations presented in this table may no longer be accurate subsequent to publication of this volume. However, the data are not presented as technical specifications for the products reviewed, but merely to illustrate the similarities or differences that may be found among the products available at one university at one time.

Table 5. Implementation methods for the instructional events in courses reviewed.

Instructional Events	Implementation Methods
1. Gaining attention	Attention was gained by presenting various opening stimuli (e.g., multimedia effects).
2. Informing learner of instructional purpose	The only strategy used to implement this event was informing the learner of the learning objectives directly.
3. Stimulating learner's attention	This event was implemented primarily by change of stimulus (e.g., from text to audio).
4. Providing overview	Strategies in this event included providing outlines, syllabi, and descriptions of the proposed course of instruction.
5. Stimulating recall of prior knowledge	No observable evidence of employing this event was found in any of the WBT sites evaluated.
6. Presenting new information relevant to the learning goals	Strategies in this stage included presentation, discussion, definition, giving examples and non-examples, and contributions from learners.
7. Guiding learning strategies	Strategies used to implement this event included directing the learner by refocusing attention, embedding structural aids, and employing multiple layers in presentation.
8. Eliciting responses that may be used to monitor the progress of learning	Accomplished by way of assigning projects, simulations, quizzes, and opportunities for engaging in online discussion.
9. Providing feedback and guidance to aid the learning process	Feedback of results was often provided in the case of quizzes or self-evaluation tests, but it was often missing in online discussions.
10. Providing a summary	Very occasionally provided by summarizing key points of the instruction in tables, etc.
11. Enhancing transfer of learning	Implemented by providing a forum for learners and the instructor to discuss further on a specific topic.
12. Conducting assessment and course evaluation	Assessments usually conducted by means of assignments or tests of a relatively conventional form.
13. Providing feedback and remediation at the end of a lesson, module, or study unit	WBT with specific registered audiences and live instructors tended to provide feedback, whereas WBT of a more open, self-study format provided little or no feedback. This was particularly true in the absence of automatic performance tracking capabilities.

Gagné developed a well-known lesson-planning model consisting of nine types of instructional events, based on his study of the conditions for effective and efficient learning (Gagné, 1985). Traditional instruction in military training environments has for some time used a similar list of instructional events as a basis for the planning of lessons and other learning activities. Smith and Ragan (1993) combine these two lists to form an "expanded instructional events" model that defines what a lesson should include. Smith and Ragan's expanded instructional events are often integrated with each other in practice, although they are conceptually discrete. An analysis of several online courses was conducted in order to identify the instructional events implemented in current WBT practice and the methods most frequently used to implement these events.

The courses included content areas such as Computing, Networking, Remote Administration, Aging and Disability, Instructional Product Development, Time Management, Distance Education, Project Management, and Relational Databases Design.

The data in Table 5 provide a list of the implementation methods utilized for the instructional events incorporated in the WBT courses analyzed in the study. Without the presence of a live instructor, the responsibility for the stimulus presentation was dependent on the computer screen to gain the learner's attention. The instructional designers manipulated a variety of both visual and auditory stimuli, including text fonts and colors, to direct the learner's attention. Learners almost always were clearly informed of the learning objectives upfront. All of the WBT sites offered course descriptions, course outlines, or syllabi. However, there was no apparent effort in any of the courses analyzed to stimulate the recall of prior knowledge. Methods used to present new information included presentation, asynchronous online discussion, giving examples and non-examples, and the learner's participative contributions. The WBT sites either presented limited amounts of information at a time by using short pages, or provided embedded structural aids or site maps to guide the learner's navigation. There were assignments to be turned in electronically, quizzes, and online discussions to elicit responses from the learner. The quizzes were usually followed by immediate feedback upon the learner's submission of his/her answers. The grading of the assignments was either sent to the learner individually or posted to the site, which could be accessed with a valid user ID and password. Some WBT sites reviewed summarized key points of the instruction. Enhancing transfer was accomplished only by further discussions, if at all. Assignments were the major tool of assessment. Depending on the instructional goals and course management styles, courses with a specific registered audience and live participation of instructors tended to provide a modicum of evaluative feedback, whereas courses open to an unspecified and unselected audience provided very limited feedback.

In addition to lesson planning models based on "instructional events," it is possible to describe instruction in terms of the specific strategies employed to achieve certain teaching-learning goals (McKeague & Di Vesta, 1996). Table 6 identifies some important instructional strategies and the extent to which they were used in the WBT sites evaluated. The left-hand column lists the strategies, and the right-hand column comments on whether and how they were implemented in the reviewed courses.

Summarizing the data from the previous two tables:

1. Except for one event, all of Smith and Ragan's expanded list of instructional events were utilized in at least some of the Web-based instruction examined. The one event that could not be identified was "stimulating recall of prior knowledge."

2. Because of the absence of the event of "stimulating recall of prior knowledge," none of the instructional strategies typically used to implement this event could be identi-

Table 6. Implementation methods for selected instructional strategies in courses.

Instructional Strategies	Implementation Methods
1. Alert learners, gain their attention and interest (the A of the ARCS model for motivational instruction).	Accomplished by using large graphics or strong contrast in color or text size. Some WBT sites employed video or audio clips.
2. Change of stimulus in order to maintain attention, interest, and motivation.	Accomplished by using different textual fonts, sizes, colors, and styles and by employing graphics and animation.
3. Appealing to learners' interests and needs (the R of the ARCS model).	Used textual explanation of target skills or included graphic and relevant illustrations.
4. Game-playing, or use of interactive simulations.	Game-playing and simulation were not found in the WBT sites evaluated.
5. Informing learners of the objectives (part of the R of the ARCS model).	Done by either stating the learning objective up front or by setting an expectancy of what will be learned.
6. Providing a lesson overview	Overviews were provided in several ways: course outlines and syllabi; hyperlinks to respective instruction sections; site maps; suggested learning routes.
7. Showing novelty, using humor and anecdotes.	Such strategies were not found in the reviewed sites.
8. Summarizing previous knowledge.	This strategy was not formally and systematically implemented in the courses analyzed. Some courses occasionally (not systematically) presented summary tables.
9. Use of examples or non-examples of new concepts and principles	Some sites provided hyperlinks between examples and non-examples or examples in other parts of the material for the learner to make comparison.
10. Feature emphasizing	Key features were emphasized with cues, graphical illustrations, changes in font and size, and hyperlinks to further explanations.
11. Human modeling	Such strategies were not found in the reviewed WBI sites.
12. Learner participation and discussion	Accomplished by online discussion and practice exercises, synchronous and asynchronous forums where a learner could "talk" to other learners and the instructor either publicly or privately, and by electronic newsletters.

Table 6. Implementation methods for selected instructional strategies *(continued)*.

Instructional Strategies	Implementation Methods
13. Refocus of attention	Attention was focused mainly by change of textual font or size and graphics.
14. Embedded structural aids	Accomplished by suggesting learning paths, implementing templates, and using headings.
15. Multiple layers in presentation instruction or by short page design.	Accomplished by optional links to more advanced content.
16. Integrating new information with previous knowledge	Accomplished in a few cases by combining previously learned skills with the new ones, but by and large not implemented.
17. Quizzes and tests	Generally implemented by true/false or multiple-choice questions, thus being restricted to recall and comprehension of knowledge and neglecting its application.
18. Case studies, interactive simulations, and role-play exercises	Simulations found in this study were all process simulations that the students could observe and control by manipulating inputs to the computer generated model. No complex interactive case-based simulations were encountered in the courses analyzed.
19. Engaging the learner in relevant learning activities	E-mail was the most popular discussion form employed. Listservs, chat rooms, and asynchronous forums were other common means of discussion. These activities are often student-driven rather than closely controlled by the instructors, and process-oriented rather than outcomes-oriented. Often they are only very loosely related to the supposed objectives of the lesson.
20. Corrective and constructive feedback strategies	Usually, only test-question-related feedback was provided. Sometimes there was a qualitative judgment on the learner's performance, but few opportunities for a true "Socratic Dialogue" were seized.

fied within the WBI sites reviewed. These missing strategies include, for example, summarizing previous knowledge, pretests, and warm-up exercises.

3. Other instructional strategies that were not identified in this review were: simulations and game-playing; showing novelty; using analogies; human modeling; and real life practical application of the knowledge and skill being learned.

The Current State of the Art

It is interesting to consider the events and strategies that were not used, or used very little, by the designers of these courses. Some of the strategies that were not implemented are those that typically require close personal contact and profound interaction at the level of observation of other participants' actions and reactions. These strategies may have been avoided by the course designers because they are difficult if not impossible to implement within the communication infrastructure of the available online learning environments. Role modeling and learning by example is difficult without intensive personal contact between the teacher/model and the student/observer. Group role-play exercises that focus on the development of interpersonal skills, such as interviewing or leadership, may be rarely implemented for the same reasons.

However, the rarity of examples of interactive case study exercises and simulations in content areas such as management decision-making is less easy to understand. Research has shown that decision-making exercises and case study discussions can be conducted effectively in online learning environments, including asynchronous computer-mediated-communication (CMC) environments such as listserv and BBS (Romiszowski & Jost, 1989; Romiszowski & Mason, 1996). Given that such small group "conversational" learning methodologies are of increasing importance for the adult continuing education and professional training systems of today, it is surprising that the opportunity to implement such learning strategies on the Web has not been seized. However, research has also demonstrated that the CMC environments that best support deep, conversational interactions, such as those involved in an in-depth case study discussion, should be specially planned. In order to promote, support, and automatically moderate the in-depth interactions between small groups of participants, such environments and the study exercises they support should be pre-programmed to some extent (Romiszowski & Chang, 1992, 1995). Thus, the relative rarity of organized small group conversations in the online courses analyzed may be due in part to the inadequacy of the online course delivery systems used, and partly to the lack of experience or expertise of the course designers, inhibiting them from attempting to develop such exercises.

Thirdly, the total absence, in the sample of courses analyzed, of recall and review strategies to bring to mind relevant pre-requisite knowledge that may have been forgotten by students is particularly strange. Such strategies are well known, well established (and often necessary) components of conventional classroom instruction, and the hypertext-like environment of the Web is most suitable for their implementation in distance education. It would seem to us that the absence of these strategies is more a sign of incomplete, or inexpert, course design, than of any inadequacy of the online learning environments we analyzed.

AulaNet: Towards a Richer Online Environment

AulaNet is an environment for the creation and maintenance of Web-based courses that is "designed for the layman" (Lucena *et al.*, 1999). The objectives of AulaNet are to adopt the Web as an environment in which to foster a workable transition from conventional classrooms to virtual classrooms, giving the opportunity to reuse existing material and to create knowledge communities. While most systems emphasize courseware aspects, AulaNet, according to its creators, emphasizes "learningware," which combines courseware with peer and teacher/student interaction. An AulaNet course provides instructors and students with a variety of communication mechanisms:

- Course discussion lists present sets of messages posted by any member of that community, in exactly the same way as the lists that have been available for many years on every computer network.

- Special interest discussion areas that may be defined by the instructor, each containing messages on a specific subject of interest to the community. Unlike the discussion lists, these special interest areas support threaded discussions, which helps to keep order among messages and facilitates the online discussion process.

- A news feature, to which any participant may post short announcements of general interest.

- An agenda or diary, which carries information about commitments established for the community. Announcements are posted by the instructor to inform the community about course activities.

- Webchat and CU-SeeMe videoconferencing technologies are bundled with AulaNet to offer synchronous forms of distance communication.

- Virtual lecture rooms, where the teacher may place any combination of text and graphic communication, PowerPoint slides, and the Real Media technology that allows the streaming of audio or video materials across the Internet to all the course participants.

Compared to the three online learning systems analyzed earlier, AulaNet offers all the communication options included in any of the other three (see Table 2), plus a few more. The most interesting extra capabilities are the seamless integration of desktop audio and video and the ability to stream video and audiovisual information over the Internet. All the separate Internet-based communication technologies that are currently available are bundled as an integrated package, giving the course designer a wide variety of options to choose from as regards message delivery and intercommunication.

In addition to the communication options, AulaNet also offers a range of course coordination and evaluation options. When designing a course, the professor/designer can choose the options that are required from an extensive menu, including special areas for posting tests, exercises and assignments, the marks or grades for these tests and assignments, and so on. As a result, the AulaNet environment may, according to its creators, be more closely compared to a conventional course environment than most of the other online learning environments currently available.

The present authors have observed and analyzed the use of AulaNet as the delivery system for two courses running through the spring semester of 1999. Both these courses form part of a graduate (Masters and Doctorate) program in Educational Technology in a leading North American research university. Whereas the courses are offered in the higher education context, the content and objectives qualify then to be considered examples of WBT systems. In one of the courses (Instructional Product Development), the students learn to design, develop, and implement a set of learning materials for a course and context of their choosing. In the other course (Distance Education), the students learn to select and evaluate systems and methodologies for the distance delivery of education. In addition, both these courses are currently taught partially by distance learning. AulaNet was used as the delivery platform. Therefore, the students in these courses obtained experience of AulaNet both as system of course delivery and as subject of study.

In regard to the first claim mentioned in this section (online course design and development system "for the layman"), Aulanet already comes close. It is totally menu-driven and very easy to master. It does, of course, rely on the existence of previously prepared materials that are then imported into the Aulanet shell. So, in addition to mastering Aulanet, which may take only an hour or two, the course developer, or team, must master:

- the efficient use of PowerPoint (including its special and multimedia effects if full benefits are to be derived);

- the storyboarding, shooting, editing, and digitizing of video (and audio) tapes of acceptable quality;

- the use of supplementary software packages such as Cu-See-Me, Real Media, and several others (as well as the skills of desktop video presentation); and

- some HTML document production skills if any text or graphic material more complex than a simple Word document is to be uploaded.

All in all, therefore, despite AulaNet's basic simplicity, the construction of a full course can be a complex and time-consuming process that requires a multiplicity of special skills.

There is also the danger of over-using the many extra capabilities to the detriment of the course as a whole. For example, our initial experience with the use of Real Video as a lesson component was that the instructor's videos were little used by the students. There was little important visual content in the lectures—that was in the accompanying PowerPoint slides. The visual of the "talking head" distracted attention from the slides. The audio message was the important part, but that was deemed to be too long to listen to in one go and was generally required to be repeated for students to capture all the important information. Also, the audio track was not always sufficiently clearly recorded and/or reproduced to allow for once-only listening. All in all, the students voted to discontinue the use of video commentaries supporting the PowerPoint presentations, in favor of short textual messages to accompany each slide. Video, they felt, should be reserved for when there is a message to be communicated that will be clearer if illustrated with motion pictures, or if there is a multi-person discussion or debate that cannot be attended "live."

The students also made some quite significant suggestions for enhancement of the learning environment. The fact that AulaNet is still in the development stages may be seen as a positive aspect, in that modifications and enhancements may still be added before widespread dissemination takes place.

The first major observation concerned control and evaluation. These two terms are sometimes viewed in a bad light, as they conjure up pictures of some autocratic, system-imposed rigidity. But they need not do so. It is significant that the observations of the need for greater functionality of AulaNet in relation to its control and evaluation aspects came from the students more than from the faculty. They asked questions such as "How do I control my progress?" and "How can I bookmark or otherwise identify those parts of the course that I have studied and those I have not?" or "How can I link directly from specific topics listed on the syllabus to the relevant study materials?" The professors/administrators asked "I can see how many times a given student has accessed the course, but how do I know what that student did there?" "Did the students study all or only parts of the material?" "How much time did they devote to their studies?" "What are the major problems they are encountering with the material?" "Can I keep a cumulative record of the progress through the course, and the success rate, of a given student or of the whole group?" In this respect, there are many possible enhancements that may yet be added to ensure that in terms of tracking student progress and course quality, AulaNet stands out "above the competition," just as it already stands out in terms of many other factors.

The second major observation concerned the structure of facilities for constructive educational "conversations." The many and various components of AulaNet that permit both synchronous and asynchronous student/teacher and student/student interaction are no different from the facilities that exist in many other online learning packages currently on the market. AulaNet has a greater variety of options in one integrated package than most of the others, but it does not offer any innovations beyond what already has existed. There is considerable evidence from recent research, however, that it is possible to design online learning environments that do offer significant and useful innovations and that may even lead to online learning becoming not only equal but in some aspects superior to the best of conventional face-to-face learning. One area of research and development which has already shown such possibilities is that of advanced computer-based simulations, including, for example, some applications of virtual reality technologies. Another area is the application of the science of artificial intelligence to the creation of virtual learning assistants, or avatars, as well as various forms of performance support systems that may reduce the difficulty and the quantity of job-related learning. In this respect, the structure of AulaNet will enable the easy presentation of such an interactive package, provided the necessary plug-ins are also loaded.

Another important area for improvement of existing online learning environments is the area of effective "conversational" interaction between groups of students (and instructors) engaged in a joint project, such as analyzing a Harvard business case or engaging in the new profession of "Knowledge Work," but doing it at a distance (and usually in the asynchronous mode). In this first experience using Aulanet as a delivery platform, both faculty and students have come across limitations in the available group communication facilities that limit what they can implement in the way of "creative group work at a distance." We are seeking, and are finding, ways around these limitations. Some of these suggestions are included in the chapter in this book by Romiszowski and Chang, which, in a sense, takes off where this chapter closes.

References

Averman, D. (1996). Reviewing the research on hypermedia-based learning. *Journal of Research on Computers in Education, 28*(4), 500–525.

Gagné, R. M. (1985). *The conditions of learning* (3rd ed.). New York: Holt, Rinehart, and Winston.

Hales, R. (1997). Delivering coursework via the Web; serc.gws.uky.edu/www/ukat/topclass

Hites, A., & Ewing, M. (1995). Designing and implementing instruction on the World Wide Web: A case study; lrs.stcloudstate.edu/ispi/proceeding.html

Julian, E. H., & Capozzi, M. (1998, March). The emerging market for Web-based learning, 1996–2002. International Data Corporation, report No. 15602; idc.com

Lucena, C., Fuks, H., Milidiú, R., Laufer, C., Blois, M., Choren, R., Torres, V., & Daflon, L. (1999). *Multimedia computer techniques in engineering education*. Proceedings of a workshop held in Graz, Austria.

McKeague, C., & Di Vesta, F. J. (1996). Strategy orientations, learning activity, and learning outcomes: Implications for instructional support of learning. *Educational Technology Research and Development, 44*(2), 29–42.

McManus, T. (1995). Special considerations for designing Internet-based instruction; ualberta.ca/coe/depts/ci/itlprojects/papers/special.html

Parson, R. (1997). An investigation into instruction available on the World Wide Web; oise.utoronto.cai.edu

Peterson's (1996, 1998). *Distance learning in higher education catalog.* Princeton, NJ: Peterson's.

Romiszowski, A. J. (1981). *Designing instructional systems: Decision making in course planning and curriculum design.* New York: Nichols Publishing Company.

Romiszowski, A. J. (1997). Instructional development for a networked society. In C. Dills & A. J. Romiszowski (Eds.), *Instructional development paradigms.* Englewood Cliffs: Educational Technology Publications.

Romiszowski, A. J., & Chang, E. (1992). Hypertext's contribution to computer mediated communication: In search of an instructional model. Proceedings of the NATO Advanced Research Workshop on Interactive Multimedia Learning Environments, Laval University, Quebec, June 1991. In M. Giardina (Ed.), *Interactive multimedia learning environments: Human factors and technical considerations on design issues.* Berlin: Springer-Verlag.

Romiszowski, A. J., & Chang, E. (1995). Use of Hypermedia and telecommunications for case-study discussions in distance education. *Proceedings of the 17th World Distance Education Conference,* Birmingham, UK. International Council for Distance Education (ICDE), Norway, 1995.

Romiszowski, A. J., & Jost K. L. (1989). Computer conferencing and the distance learner: Problems of structure and control. *Proceedings of the Conference on Distance Education, University of Wisconsin.*

Romiszowski, A. J., & Mason R. (1996). Research on computer mediated communication. In D. H. Jonassen (Ed.), *Handbook of research for educational communication and technology.* New York: Macmillan.

Seels, B., & Glasgow, Z., (1990). *Exercises in instructional design.* Columbus, OH: Merrill Publishing Company.

Smith, P., & Ragan, T. (1993). *Instructional design.* Columbus, OH: Merrill Publishing Company.

The Authors

Carlos Villalba (e-mail: cavallal@mailbox.syr.edu) is a doctoral student in the Instructional Design, Development, and Evaluation program at Syracuse University, Syracuse, New York. **Alexander J. Romiszowski (e-mail: alexromi@sued.syr.edu; Web homepage: tts-global.com)** is Director, Technology-Based Training Systems, Rio de Janeiro, Brazil, and Adjunct Professor, Instructional Design, Development, and Evaluation at Syracuse University. He serves as Coordinator of the Syracuse University IDD&E distance-education program for students in Latin America.

38

Pedagogy and Web-Based Course Authoring Tools: Issues and Implications

Nada H. Dabbagh,

Brenda Bannan-Ritland, and

Kate Flannery Silc

Introduction

The move to online technologies is an evolving and dynamic process of investigation, particularly in the area of examining the ability of such technologies to improve the teaching and learning process. In the case of Web-based course authoring tools (also known as Internet-based training tools), several evaluation frameworks or guidelines have been used to determine the degree of success of those tools in designing, delivering, and managing instruction. For example, Hansen and Frick (1997) suggest four areas that should be addressed by a Web-based course authoring tool for it to become a standard for the development of Web-based instruction (WBI): presenting information, providing human interaction, assessment of learning, and course management. Another example is the framework used by PC Week Labs (1997) in conjunction with its corporate partner, Wisconsin Technical College System, to evaluate courseware authoring systems for Web-based training. The products used to create the training programs and the resulting programs themselves were judged on conformity to the corporate and education landscape, exploitation of the Internet/intranet, manageability, flexibility, and ease of use. In another effort aimed at helping educators and administrators select new online delivery methods, Landon (1998) conducted an analysis of online delivery software in which he described and compared these applications by focusing on their technical specifications, instructional design values, media capabilities, features/tools, ease of use, accessibility to persons with disabilities, and potential for collaboration and connectivity.

Although useful, these frameworks (and others) have focused on the technological aspects of the features that enable the development of online instruction (Dabbagh & Schmitt, 1998), and have adopted a piecemeal approach to the evaluation process, which makes it difficult to form an authentic representation of the learning environment generated. As asserted by the Australian National Training Authority (ANTA, 1998), Web-based authoring tools seem to be adhering to a common pattern of development and analysis:

An emerging pattern for the development of online courses is that of a staged and incremental process. In the first round of investigations, the focus for developers is more on understanding the potential of the technology and exploring its features.

The purpose of this chapter is to use a more comprehensive framework to evaluate Web-based course authoring tools, encompassing pedagogical, institutional, and ethical aspects, among others, and to examine the instructional effectiveness of the online learning environment by applying the framework to *completed courses* rather than assessing the specific features of the tool under investigation. The term used to describe such courses in this discussion will be Web-based training (WBT).

The Framework

According to Hall (1998), WBT is "instruction that is delivered via a Web browser, such as Netscape Navigator, through the Internet or an intranet." Other terms that have been used to define this type of instruction include Internet-based training (IBT), Web-based learning (WBL), and Web-based instruction (WBI) (Barron, 1998). The proposed framework can be used to guide the design, development, and evaluation of any instructional program that utilizes the attributes and resources of the Internet and the World Wide Web to create a meaningful learning environment.

The proposed framework known as the Framework for WBL (hereafter referred to as WBL Framework) was developed by Khan and consists of eight dimensions: pedagogical, technological, interface design, evaluation, management, resource support, ethical, and institutional (see Khan's chapter, A Framework for Web-Based Learning, Chapter 8). Each dimension has various items addressing its constituents in relation to Web-based learning environments. For example, the pedagogical dimension addresses issues such as instructional goals and objectives, the overall design approach of the course, content sequencing and organization, instructional methods and strategies, the instructional medium (the Web in this case), and the extent to which the course uses its attributes, accuracy of subject matter, and learner assessment. The interface design dimension addresses issues pertaining to the "creation of a seamless integration of content and control" through the physical layout of the information and the conceptualization and implementation of the navigation of the instructional program (Jones & Farquhar, 1997). The management dimension refers to the administration, maintenance, and operation of Web-based courses, which includes security issues, updating of course information, provision of course evaluation, tracking of student progress, and feedback on student progress. The ethical dimension addresses issues such as course sensitivity to diverse populations, copyright issues, netiquette, and provision for representation of concepts for a worldwide audience. The resource support dimension addresses issues related to various online and offline learning resources which include archives, bibliographies of related books/journals, searchable glossaries, class distribution lists, and other resources related to WBI. The technological dimension addresses issues related to infrastructure planning, hardware, and software. The institutional dimension addresses issues related to institutional policy in delivering WBI. And the evaluation dimension addresses issues related to assessment of learners and evaluation of the instruction and learning environment.

The framework began as a survey, the intent of which was to create a list of concerns that students, developers, and instructors have regarding Web-based instruction (Khan & Vega, 1997). The framework continued to evolve and expand as a result of further queries and commentaries on WBI directed to Khan from readers of his first book, *Web-Based Instruction* (1997). Khan compiled those queries and refined them, based on the underlying theories and concepts of the book, to form the eight dimensions and their constituents. The initial survey resulted in 36 criteria prioritized in order of frequency of occurrences of responses, with the first five criteria being clarity of course objectives, degree of interactivity, quality of content, quality of structure, and ease of accessibility. With the exception of the last criteria, it appears that evaluating a Web-based course is very similar to evaluating a traditional classroom course. This may well be the case, considering that most Web-based courses are a result of redesigning traditional classroom courses, with the developers focusing on adapting the course content to the medium rather than preserving or defining the underlying pedagogy of instruction. According to ANTA (1998), "there is a natural tendency to adapt an existing and familiar methodology to the technology—often the focus is on the content to be learned rather than the process of learning." This suggests two cautionary situations: that the methodology applied may not capitalize on the attributes of the medium, or the opposite case, where the medium may drive the methodology (Winn, 1990). Care in designing and evaluating these courses needs to be taken regardless of approach. Should frameworks for guiding the design and evaluation of WBI then be less rigorous than those used to design and evaluate traditional classroom courses?

There are three issues to consider when attempting to answer this question. First is the issue of the transformation that traditional courses experience when redesigned for Web delivery. Typically, such courses undergo a "pedagogical reengineering" (Collis, 1997) because of some of the inherent features of the Web that are integral to the design of WBI (Dabbagh & Schmitt, 1998). Second is the purpose of the Web-based course in the learning environment. Is the course a supplement to on-campus/on-site instruction or is it intended as a distance learning alternative in which the instruction, interactions, and feedback are delivered via the Web? Third is the type of authoring tool used to develop the course for Web-delivery and the features it affords the developer. For example, integrated application suites (authoring tools) refer to applications that provide specific tools designed for each of three user groups: learners, instructors, and technical administrators, whereas component applications refer to more specialized applications that generally provide few instructor tools (Center for Curriculum Transfer & Technology, ctt.bc.ca/landonline). We will address these issues by applying the WBL Framework to six WBT sites that have been developed using six different Web-based course authoring tools (see Table 1). We will then use the results of this evaluation to determine the

Table 1. Courses and authoring tools.

Course Name	Authoring Tool
Marketing Certificate in Small Business Management tafe.sa.edu.au:8900/public/demo/	WebCT
SUNY TopClass Virtual Lounge & HelpDesk topclass.itec.suny.edu:800/topclass/	TopClass
Effective Business Writing English 1007 virtual-u.cs.sfu.ca/vuexchange/	Virtual-U
Health Care Management madduck.com/wcb/schools/TST/tst/spolyson/1/index.html	Web Course in a Box (WCB)
Hospitality Industry Law and Liability lotus.com/demos/law/schedule.nsf	LearningSpace
Programming Your Avilar VCR avilar.com/avilar/msubfrm.html	Web Mentor

extent to which the technology of delivery, in this case the Web-based authoring tools, can shape the pedagogy of courses and assist course developers in focusing on instructional considerations when capitalizing on the attributes of the medium.

The Authoring Tools

Hedberg and Harper (1998) argue that the visual metaphors employed by Web-authoring tools restrict the learning environment by placing constraints on the organization of content and the learning strategies. For the sake of consistency, we have selected course authoring tools whose visual metaphors are somewhat comparable and whose functions are similar, in that they offer features related to student and faculty collaboration and allow tracking of student records and management of course information and materials. We have also elected not to include multimedia-authoring tools that require plug-ins for viewing, such as Director, Authorware, or Tool-Book. We feel that courseware developed using such tools was *not* designed to take advantage of the inherent and unique features of the Web and therefore does not fall under the category of WBT. The tools under investigation are WebCT, TopClass, Virtual-U, WCB (Web Course in a Box), LearningSpace, and Web Mentor. These tools are similar in that they provide instructor tools, learner tools, and technical administration tools, and they also use features that are intrinsic to the Web medium and can be conducive to learning environments. Such features include interactivity, multimodal representation of information, online searching, electronic publishing, global accessibility, learner control, worldwide uniformity, and multiple expertise or resources (Khan, 1997). Use of these features can promote collaborative learning, enhance critical thinking skills, and give every student an equal opportunity to participate in classroom discussions. Following is a brief description of each of these tools and its features:

Web-CT (homebrew.cs.ubc.ca/webct/webct.html). In addition to facilitating the organization of course material on the Web, WebCT also provides a variety of tools and features that can be added to a course. Examples include a conferencing system, online chat, student progress tracking, group project organization, student self-evaluation, grade maintenance and distribution, access control, navigation tools, auto-marked quizzes, electronic mail, automatic index generation, course calendar, student homepages, course content searches, and more.

TopClass (wbtsystems.com/products/overvie1.htm). TopClass provides a virtual environment to manage all aspects of content and class management and to deliver a flexible learning environment built upon Web standards. It includes features such as security (unique user ID), online registration and enrollment, collaborative tools (e-mail, threaded discussion groups, bulletin board), a testing engine, student progress tracking, content and user searching, summary reporting, and course assembly tools that are platform independent.

Virtual-U (virtual-u.cs.sfu.ca/vuweb/). Virtual-U is an online learning application made up of various integrated components. These include the VGroups conferencing system, which gives instructors the ability to easily set up collaborative groups and define structures, tasks and objectives; course structuring tools (the Workspace and the Course Syllabus), which enable instructors to create complete courses online without programming knowledge; student performance tracking (the Gradebook); and system administration tools.

Web Course in a Box (madduck.com/). Web Course in a Box, created by faculty members at Virginia Commonwealth University in 1996, was one of the first template-based Web-authoring tools. It is an integrated system that includes a sophisticated lesson builder for con-

The course overview encourages contributions through e-mail (which is always available on the tool bar at the bottom of each screen), and discussions can be accessed through the course homepage; however, group interaction and collaboration (WBL Framework) are not an integral part of the course design. Only one folder, the "live interactive tutorial," appears to provide interaction between student and instructor. Unfortunately, access to this tutorial is restricted to the SUNY community. Another weakness of the course is the absence of a search engine, index, or glossary to help students with specific questions sift through the profusion of information presented under each topic/unit. Also, considering the amount of information in some folders, the topic of Online Education could have provided many more *outside links* to resources on distance learning and instructional design strategies relevant to this delivery medium.

Effective Business Writing English. The purpose of this course is to be delivered half the time in a face-to-face format and the other half fully online. This is known as the *mixed mode,* compared to an adjunct or an online mode. In an *adjunct mode,* the online portion of the course is intended as a supplement to enhance traditional classroom instruction. The *online mode,* is when the network serves as the primary environment for course discussions, assignments and interactions. These modes are referred to as 'modes of teaching' by Virtual-U, the tool used to develop this course, and are offered as guidelines for instructors in the *Instructor Tools and Support* component of the tool.

The course begins with four options to choose from: course syllabus, course overview, course calendar, and glossary. These options are not standard. They can be customized to reflect different choices based on the content of the course, thus providing structural flexibility (WBL Framework). The *course syllabus* is an advance organizer and contains hypertext links to the course topics, units, assignments, tests, activities, resources, and online conferences and discussions. The links encompass a wide variety of electronic media, utilizing virtually every attribute of the Internet and the World Wide Web. They include text files, tutorials, audio files, video clips, animations, graphics, online resources (with built-in search engines), and Power-Point files to present course content and learning activities, as well as synchronous and asynchronous communication forums, ranging from e-mail to a virtual café for socializing. Although intricately rich in multimodal representations and interaction levels, the variety is overwhelming and could present too much complexity for first time users. However, it is evident that online support, resource support, and inside and outside collaboration are demonstrated through the use of these features (WBL Framework). The *course overview* reorganizes the information presented in the *course syllabus* into a condensed and perhaps more comprehensible format. It presents a list of course topics, course resources and conferences, and course assignments, tests, and activities. The same links are accessible through both views. The *course calendar* is an active timeline of when the topics are discussed and the assignments and activities are due. And finally, the *glossary* is a searchable index of course related terms.

With each of these views, there are *Use* features that can be accessed by the student and the instructor to perform certain activities. Some are intended for instructors only (e.g., the gradebook and the course editing features), others for students only (e.g., assignment submissions), and some are for both groups of users. One of the areas accessible to both the instructor and the student is called the *workspace.* In the workspace, students can bookmark their favorite Websites, upload assignment files, organize and edit files, and access the course syllabus, calendar, and glossary. This *Use* feature promotes a student-centered approach to learning, which is one of the underlying instructional principles that Virtual-U supports. The workspace interface is a good anchor point for the user and perhaps should serve as the primary navigational structure for the course. It will improve the user friendliness of the interface.

Other features that could be improved in this course are: providing a student orientation module on how to use the course interface; stating up front the hardware/software requirements needed to use the various modalities of information representation and levels of interactions and communication; and sequencing the order of activities or at least suggesting a learner path for students who are not self-directed learners.

Health Care Management. Health Care Management, first conducted in the fall of 1997, provides an example of a course delivered via Web Course in a Box (WCB) authoring software. The course is structured using face-to-face class sessions interspersed with at least five electronic seminar discussions. This demonstration course highlights the main features and aspects of the WCB software but is currently deliberately restricted in content and resources as well as corrupted by multiple users experimenting with the authoring tool. However, in reviewing the structure and content that is available, many attributes of the course and the software are revealed.

The primary strengths of this course are the instructor's apparent attempts at management and organization of the content within the software constraints in addition to adequately addressing the online support issues necessary for student participation. These factors have pedagogical as well as interface usability implications. The electronic seminars focus on discussions about the off-line readings. These discussions are well directed with specific objectives and clearly outlined expectations established prior to providing a link directly to the conference on that topic. This organization facilitates the discussion of a specific topic focusing student contributions and easily directs students to the related conference session. Additional management issues are addressed in the course, such as providing a help section and learning links dealing with Web development skills; however, the relationship of these skills to the required assignments could not be clearly determined. Inside collaboration (WBL Framework) between students in the course is fostered by WCB's providing space for personal biographies as well as individual and public class e-mail capabilities.

The main menu layout of the course illustrates the six basic areas of the course represented by the software's simplistic but relevant icons. This screen design is easily navigable but may not compete well in a marketing comparison with other Web authoring tools projecting a more sophisticated or customizable interface. Although simplistic in representation, the functional segments of this course may still permit confusion on the part of the user. For example, the assignment section contains a description of some of the assignments as well as links to various resources that are not annotated. These links seem unrelated to the assignments, making it difficult to discern their importance. The learning links section contains course resources as well as course activities, instead of placing these elements in separate areas. This potential for misinterpretation of a section's elements may result from forcing content into pre-established structure set by the software and not providing structural flexibility.

Hospitality Industry Law and Liability. LearningSpace featured Hospitality Industry Law and Liability, a course from the University of Wisconsin-Stout, Department of Hospitality and Tourism. The course was entirely Web-based, having no classroom component. The class databases were modified to remove copyright material, student discussions, and student profiles. Only a few units of the course are shown in their complete form; however, those sections demonstrate both the efficient ordering of content to help the learner achieve the objectives (Kemp, Morrison, & Ross, 1994) and clear expectations of what the student is required to do. The units featured in the "Schedule" section provide reading assignments, content and process objectives, the purpose of the unit, as well as student and instructor evaluation criteria. The WBL Framework suggests that online courses promote inside collaboration for working on joint projects. The instructor of this course requires collaboration with team members on many assignments, such as critiquing case studies. Collaboration is facilitated by the LearningSpace structure. It provides a shared workspace for team assignments. Teams may choose to restrict access to this space to members only. A message appears on the assignment link to indicate whether the work is "In Progress," "Ready for Grading," or ready for "Instructor Review." Collaboration is further promoted through discussion, which may be directed to the entire class or to team members. The course also provides metacognitive support by allowing annotations on the documents in the "Media Center." The student may type notes directly into a document, but leave the original unchanged. The student may then specify which course participants have access to the annotations.

The interface design does not always provide cues for navigation. Although frames guide the student back to the course after visiting external links, internal navigation is sometimes confusing. Various icons are used to represent different course sections, status of documents, internal navigation, and many other functions. The purpose of each of the icons is difficult to remember. In addition, should the course be offered to a diverse worldwide audience, the use of Caucasians for all of the people icons may be seen as discriminatory. The course uses a mixture of media to create a rich environment for active learning (WBL Framework), including PowerPoint slides, MS Word documents, and Web sites, yet this variety cannot be accessed without the correct applications and plug-ins.

Programming Your Avilar VCR. This course, which was developed by Web Mentor, is intended as stand-alone instruction. It is self-contained and designed using tried-and-true instructional design principles. The pedagogical philosophy used in the overall design of the course actually shapes the learning environment (WBL Framework). The course starts out with clear instructional objectives and user directions on "how to take the course." Using a frame-based interface, the course is conveniently divided into six modules: lesson, exercises, questions, review, resources, and assessment. Buttons for each of these modules remain accessible throughout the entire lesson; however, they are disabled and enabled based on *where the learner* is in the lesson. One must complete a lesson module first; then complete related exercises, answer questions, get feedback, review the lesson, and take the assessment. The progress through the lesson is therefore dictated by the organization of the content (to a large extent) and proceeds from basic to more complex learning outcomes. Although there is not much structural flexibility, it is possible to jump between course modules using embedded hypertext or the Course Contents menu. It is recommended, however, that first-time learners complete the course in the intended sequence. The modules can later be used as a reference or a job aid if one forgets how to perform a certain function.

The course makes excellent use of text, graphics, tables, and technical diagrams to explicate the content, which is technical and procedural in nature. The amount and layout of information is just right for a computer screen. The interface is very user-friendly and has been customized to reflect the instructional sequence of the course. This is a good feature of Web Mentor. Although animations and simulations are not used in this course, there is a demo of how RealAudio and RealVideo can be incorporated into instruction. The course also has an online help feature for students, a glossary, a user's guide, and a troubleshooting guide related to the instructional objectives of the lesson. Online support is evident.

The *assessment* and *questions* modules demonstrate a variety of multiple-choice question formats that can be used to evaluate learners' mastery of learning outcomes. Equally evident is the feedback feature after each response and the instant grade reporting that follows an assessment. Throughout the lesson there are trivia questions and other embedded questions and pop-up windows that elaborate on the content. Although these questions attempt to engage the learner by provoking meaningful thought, they do not seem to enhance the overall objectivist pedagogy of the course. Other negative attributes of the course are the absence of outside links to relevant Web sites, interactivity, and collaboration. The course designer may not have perceived a need for these elements to help learners achieve the lesson objectives; however, being a Web-based course, it is anticipated that such inherent features of the medium would be incorporated. Web Mentor supports the use of e-mail, conferencing, chat rooms, application sharing, and other synchronous and asynchronous interactions that foster collaboration and interactivity. The course content, however, was not appropriately matched to the capabilities of the delivery medium (WBL Framework), and the use of a familiar methodology in designing instruction for a new technology may have once again contributed to the under-utilization of the tool.

Discussion and Implications

As is often evident in face-to-face courses, the Web-based courses demonstrated a mix of methods, strategies, and pedagogical approaches. Various strengths and weaknesses were noted in each case when mapped against the WBL Framework. Some courses adopted an objectivist, straightforward approach of content segmentation and delivery for mastery (see Programming VCR—Web Mentor), while others capitalized more fully on the inherent collaborative attributes of the Web in providing students with shared workspace (Hospitality Industry Law and Liability—LearningSpace) and a constructivist student-centered approach (Effective Business Writing—Virtual U). Most presented a clear, logical and organized format (SUNY Top Class Virtual Lounge and Help—TopClass) and well-directed objectives and expectations (Health Care Management—WCB) while some provided exceptional guidance for learners with recommended approaches to the material (Marketing Certificate in Small Business Management—WebCT).

Primary weaknesses that emerged in the courses included confusing interface features such as indistinguishable icons and repetition of content in several simultaneous frames, as well as a lack of structural flexibility in regard to multiple ways to access information. Those courses that did provide structural flexibility in content organization and representation, such as SUNY Top Class Virtual Lounge and Help and Effective Business Writing, lacked advice for novice online learners on how to initially proceed with the course in order to take advantage of its instructional strengths. The principal caution for designers, which emerged from our investigation, is that students may need additional orientation and guidance, particularly when interacting with a complex course and tools that provide a variety of Web-based delivery media. In addition, it is recommended that designers capitalize on the unique attributes of Web-delivery (such as opportunities for collaboration) when developing with this medium. Without this focus in mind, many courses may be more appropriately delivered with stand-alone multimedia software and technology.

In examining the courses and hence the Web-based authoring tools, we found that the WBL Framework is an effective review tool and a good guiding mechanism for the development of Web-based courses. Our position is clear in attempting to promote a more comprehensive evaluation of courses developed with these authoring tools rather than examining the tool itself. Educators do not evaluate a classroom course merely by the technology of delivery (e.g., attributes of overheads, LCD display, teacher-directed discussion), therefore we should not discern the effectiveness of online learning environments merely by dissecting the delivery tool.

Our review of these courses and the attributes of the tools used to deliver them revealed several conclusions. In order for WBI to be effective, it must be pedagogically driven, dynamically designed, interaction oriented, and content specific. Focus should be placed on designing a pedagogical approach appropriate for the content, inclusion of organization and interaction strategies that enhance the student's processing of the information, and integration of the medium's attributes to support the designated goals and objectives of the course. Developers of Web-based training and educational materials need to place emphasis on these tasks and view the technology in relation to its capacity to deliver the planned design. This focus is perhaps best promoted by ANTA (1998):

> While we are constantly reminded that learning must be developed around learning needs, meeting educational objectives and producing viable graduates, the lure of "exploring the technology" is often at the expense of equal investment in the underpinning educational design.

The intersection between pedagogical considerations and the attributes of the Web-based authoring tools may, in fact, yield the most educational impact. Our reviews of these courses showed that attributes of the technological tools may also influence the pedagogical aspects of the course. This has been previously demonstrated in a case study by Dabbagh and Schmitt (1998), whereby a course that was redesigned for Web delivery underwent a *pedagogical reengineering* from a primarily instructivist pedagogy to a more constructivist one due to the focusing of the developer on the inherent attributes of the Web through the use of the authoring tool. Web authoring tools which include components that facilitate the team process, such as LearningSpace, promote the inclusion of collaboration as an instructional strategy. Therefore, if the content and planned strategy dictate a strong focus on students working together, then taking advantage of the attributes of this particular authoring tool may, in fact, enhance the educational effectiveness of the course.

Unfortunately, no one tool can deliver every possible instructional approach. The software tools seem to have some common attributes as well as individual strengths and weaknesses. Most current Web-based course authoring tools can also be viewed as restrictive in nature due to their visual metaphors, which place constraints on the organization of content and the potential learning strategies employed. This factor certainly can restrict the learning environment produced and may prompt the need for Web-based tools that are more open-ended, comprehensive, and customizable. Hedberg and Harper (1998) make the valuable suggestion that new metaphors for authoring should be developed to match current theory. This notion seems to be a good start; however, a comprehensive advisement mechanism included within Web-based authoring tools, providing guidance in the areas of pedagogical approach, instructional strategy, and online support and resources, may go further to support the developer who is lacking instructional design skills.

At least one Web-based authoring tool (Virtual U) indicates evidence of some pedagogical advisement capability for developers to help them shape the online learning environment into a student-centered approach. In the rest of the courses, the knowledge of the instructor or developer seemed to be the determining factor in utilizing the medium to its instructional capacity. Many revealed the common, less effective objectivist approach of directly transposing content delivered in a face-to-face situation to online Web delivery. A more comprehensive advising system, possibly aligning with Khan's Web-Based Learning Framework, may avoid this type of approach and permit the inclusion of more effective and engaging instructional methods in Web-based courses.

References

Australian National Training Authority (ANTA). (1998, March). *Teaching and learning styles that facilitate online learning;* tafe.sa.edu.au/lsrsc/one/natproj/tal/

Avilar Technologies, Inc. (1997). *Web Mentor;* avilar.com

Barron, A. (1998). *Designing Web-based training.* ITFORUM [electronic listserv]. Athens, GA: The University of Georgia; itech1.coe.uga.edu/ITFORUM/home.html

Dabbagh, N. H., & Schmitt, J. (1998). Redesigning instruction through Web-based course authoring tools. *Educational Media International, 35*(2), 106–110.

Center for Curriculum Transfer & Technology (May, 1998). *Online educational delivery applications: A Web tool for comparative analysis;* ctt.bc.ca/landonline

Collis, B. (1997, Autumn–Winter). Pedagogical reengineering: A pedagogical approach to course enrichment and redesign with the WWW. *Educational Technology Review.*

Hall, B. (1998). *FAQ about Web-Based Training. Brandon Hall Resources;* multimediatraining.com/

Hansen, L., & Frick, T. W. (1997). Evaluation guidelines for Web-based course authoring systems. In B. H. Khan (Ed.), *Web-based instruction* (pp. 299–306). Englewood Cliffs: Educational Technology Publications.

Hedberg, J., & Harper, B. (1998, March). *Visual metaphors and authoring;* itech1.coe.uga.edu/itforum/paper25/paper25.html

Jones, M. G., & Farquhar, J. D. (1997). User interface design for Web-based instruction. In B. H. Khan (Ed.), *Web-based instruction* (pp. 239–244). Englewood Cliffs: Educational Technology Publications.

Kemp, J. E., Morrison, G.R., & Ross, S.M. (1994). *Designing effective instruction.* New York: Macmillan College Publishing Company.

Khan, B. H. (1997). Web-based instruction (WBI): What is it and why is it? In B. H. Khan (Ed.), *Web-based instruction* (pp. 5–18). Englewood Cliffs: Educational Technology Publications.

Khan, B. H. (2000). A framework for Web-based learning. In B. H. Khan (Ed.), *Web-based training.* Englewood Cliffs: Educational Technology Publications.

Khan, B. H., & Vega, R. (1997). *Factors to consider when evaluating Web-based instruction courses: A survey.* In B. H. Khan (Ed.), *Web-based instruction* (pp. 375–378). Englewood Cliffs: Educational Technology Publications.

Landon B. (1998). Online educational delivery applications: A Web tool for comparative analysis; ctt.bc.ca/landonline/

Lotus Corporation (n.d.) *LearningSpace;* lotus.com/home.nsf/welcome/learnspace/

MadDuck Technologies (December, 1997). *Web Course in a Box;* madduck.com/

PC Week Labs (1997, August). *Evaluation of Internet based training systems;* 8.zdnet.com/pcweek/reviews/ibt.html

Simon Fraser University (n.d.) Virtual-U; virtual-u.cs.sfu.ca/vuweb/

WBT Systems (n.d.) *TopClass;* wbtsystems.com/products/overvie1.htm

Winn, W. (1990). Media and instructional methods. In D. R. Garrison & D. Shale (Eds.), *Education at a distance: From issues to practice* (pp. 53–66). Malabar, FL: Robert E. Krieger Publishing Company.

World Wide Web Course Tools (n.d.) *Web-CT;* homebrew.cs.ubc.ca/webct/webct.html

The Authors

Nada H. Dabbagh (e-mail: ndabbagh@gmu.edu; Web homepage: mason.gmu/~ndabbagh) is Assistant Professor, Instructional Technology, George Mason University, Fairfax, Virginia. **Brenda Bannan-Ritland (e-mail: bbannan@gmu.edu; Web homepage: gse.gmu.edu/profiles/bannan.htm)** is Assistant Professor, Instructional Design and Development at George Mason University. **Kate Flannery Silc (e-mail: ksilc@concentric.net; Web homepage: concentric.net/~ksilc)** is an independent instructional designer and distance learning consultant based in Falls Church, Virginia.

39

A Framework for a Comprehensive Web-Based Authoring System

B a d r u l   H .   K h a n   a n d

D a v i d   A .   E a l y

Introduction

As the Internet is rapidly emerging, the World Wide Web, commonly known as the Web, has become an increasingly prolific and dynamic medium for sharing information (Khan, 1997a). The recent emergence of the Web as a new learning medium (delivery system) is definitely a blessing for education and training. The Web provides an open, dynamic, and flexible learning environment with implications for countless applications with respect to education and training. Numerous names are used to describe Web-based learning (WBL) activities, including Web-based training (WBT), Web-based instruction (WBI), Internet-based training (IBT), online training (OT), advanced distributed learning (ADL), online learning (OL), e-learning, and distributed learning (DL), to name a few; for our purposes, however, we will use WBT.

The design, development, and implementation of WBT for a distributed, open, and flexible environment would greatly benefit from an authoring system which allows designers to create meaningful educational/training materials (Khan, 2000; in press). This chapter discusses important aspects of authoring environments for open and distributed systems. In creating WBT, we must explore the similarities and differences between open and closed systems. An understanding of open systems and their systemic relationship with various components of the learning environment would play a very critical role in WBT design and development.

Open Vs. Closed Authoring Tools

Most of the larger and more established authoring tools that currently exist, such as *ToolBook* and *Authorware,* were developed with a closed system in mind. In addition, this older generation of authoring tools was designed to accommodate the assumption that the learning resulting from computer-based training (CBT) would take place in a state of solitary confinement. These tools were instrumental in helping a designer to create computer-based instruction (CBI), computer-assisted instruction (CAI), or computer-based training (CBT), which almost always called for some degree of interaction between the learner and content to meet the instructional goals (Phillips, 1998). WBT challenges us to break the solitary confinement of closed systems (CBT) by designing for an open, flexible, and distributed learning environment. Phillips (1998) contends that the Web provides opportunities for learners to experience instruction on three levels:

- Between the learner and content.
- Between the learner and instructor.
- Among other learners.

"One of the challenges for instructional designers charged with the task of suggesting the best use of an instructional medium such as the World Wide Web is the inevitable and incessant rate of change of information technologies" (Welsh, 1997, p. 159). The Web as a learning medium has tremendous potential for delivering instructional materials, but it becomes problematic for designers and developers when using authoring software that may not be able to accommodate the new functionality of emerging information technologies.

Web-Based Authoring for Open Systems

The demand within the past five years has sharply increased for WBT (virtual universities, corporate intranets and extranets). According to McGee (1999), "Technology-based training, including Web-based solutions, will represent half of all training by the year 2002, up from 25% [in 1998]." For example, The White House Office of Science and Technology Policy (OSTP) and the Department of Defense (DOD) launched the Advanced Distributed Learning (ADL) initiative to ensure ready public access to high-quality education and training materials on the Web that can be tailored to individual learner needs. This ADL initiative and most of the literature surrounding WBT address several common goals. At present, there is not a single authoring tool that adequately addresses all issues concerning Web-based learning environments.

Because the Web is a new medium and many of us in the field of education and training are used to developing learning materials for closed systems (e.g., CAI, CBT, etc.), developing learning materials for open systems (e.g., WBI, WBT, etc.) can pose a new set of challenges, for which solutions are still in the formative stage. "While having an open system has its appeal, it can make designing for it extremely difficult, because in an open system, the designer agrees to give up a certain amount of control to the user" (Jones & Farquhar, 1997). Instructional designers now face difficult choices regarding tool selection, with particular concern as to whether a given tool will be stable enough in the future not to require adjustments and re-programming to their products. Even more importantly, many designers are wondering how they will be able to implement with success a newer instructional paradigm (indirect instruction) in a medium that is not yet fully comparable (in terms of productivity) with the high interactive functionality of the old paradigm (direct instruction) (Gibbons, Lawless, Anderson, & Duffin, 2001).

In designing WBT, we must focus on issues important to learners and how to use the Web's potential in concert with instructional design principles (Ritchie & Hoffman, cited in Khan, 1997a). Khan has been researching the question, "What does it take to provide the best and most meaningful flexible learning environments for learners worldwide?" He learned that there are numerous factors that help to create a meaningful learning environment (see Chapter 8), many of which are systemically interrelated and interdependent. A systemic understanding of these factors can help designers create meaningful distributed learning environments. In addressing these systemically interrelated issues for WBT, we should seek support from the following knowledge bases (but not limited to these): Instructional design, cognitive and educational psychology, curriculum development, distance education, innovation and change, telecommunication, information databases, artificial intelligence, software engineering, and media production.

Status of Web-Based Authoring Tools

To date, many of the existing Web-based authoring tools do not seem to address many of the aforementioned critical factors surrounding WBT. Some authoring packages for closed systems are trying to expand their capabilities for the Web by allowing designers to simply "upload" current CBT to the Web, for example. However, as we already learned years ago in translating print-based materials to CBT, it is again important to note that authoring tools not initially developed to accommodate an open and flexible system may not be able to address the scope and needs involved in designing purely Web-based instructional and training materials.

Currently, existing Web-based authoring tools do not support the pedagogical and other critical issues that arise when instructional materials are transported to the Web. At a recent *PC Week Magazine PC Week Shoot-Out* held at the Institute for Defense Analysis in conjunction with the U.S. Department of Defense, PC Week Labs and Shoot-Out judges from the corporate, higher education, and government sectors evaluated systems designed to manage the distributed learning process. Several judges emphasized concerns surrounding pedagogical implications and other issues relating to open and flexible learning systems. Specific reactions included the following observations: "Across all industries and academia there is a tremendous concern for standards and for finding just the right instructional methodologies and metaphors" (Plagis-Tsitsikaos, 1999, p. 134). In addition to pedagogical issues, Khan (1999b) noted, "Major challenges in designing distributed courseware are management, user interface, resource support, and cultural issues" (p. 134). "Area of specialty is understanding how people learn. Need for more dynamic, flexible, adaptive systems" (Sonwalker, 1999, p. 134).

Dabbagh, Bannan-Ritland, and Silc (2001) used the WBL Framework to review courses developed by several of the more popular Web-based authoring tools. They found that the WBL Framework provides a competent guiding mechanism for the development of the Web-based courses. According to Dabbagh, Bannan-Ritland, and Silc (2001):

> In order for WBI to be effective, it must be pedagogically driven, dynamically designed, interaction oriented, and content specific. Focus should be placed on designing a pedagogical approach appropriate for the content, inclusion of organization and interaction strategies that enhance the student's processing of the information, and integration of the medium's attributes to support the designated goals and objectives of the course. Developers of Web-based training and educational materials need to place emphasis on these tasks and view the technology in relation to its capacity to deliver the planned design.

There is a tremendous need to develop an authoring "system" which will address all WBT-related issues discussed above. After reflecting on the various factors critical to open and flexible learning environments, Khan (1997b, 2001) developed the Web-Based Learning Framework (see Figure 1). Various WBT factors are clustered into the following eight dimensions:

- Pedagogical
- Technological
- Interface Design
- Evaluation
- Management
- Resource Support
- Ethical
- Institutional

Figure 1. The WBL Framework.

Each dimension has several sub-dimensions, consisting of items that address a specific aspect of a Web-based learning environment. To find more detailed information about the WBL Framework, please read Chapter 8. Khan (1999a) strongly believes that the WBL Framework should provide the architecture for a comprehensive authoring system for an open and flexible learning environment. As previously noted, Dabbagh, Bannan-Ritland, and Silc (2001) found that the WBL Framework provides a competent guiding mechanism for the development of the Web-based courses. In addition, after reviewing the framework, Reeves (personal communication, 2000) indicated that it provides a useful approach to clarifying the complexities of Web-based learning environments.

AuthorWeb

The suitability of the WBL Framework is so comprehensive that it was significantly instrumental in developing AuthorWeb, a Web-based authoring system for designing open learning environments (Khan, 1999a). At present, no other tool is available to adequately address the issues concerning all eight dimensions of Web-based learning environments. In 1997, Khan developed the conceptual model for AuthorWeb (for a view of course creation with AuthorWeb, see Figure 2) and presented it at the 1999 Association for Educational Communications and Technology (AECT) convention. The response toward the development of AuthorWeb was overwhelmingly positive. The inception of AuthorWeb's development began with a vision of providing a tool that would assist educators, trainers, and course developers to create meaningful online courses without prior skills or knowledge in instructional design, computer programming, and issues critical to distance learning environments (AuthorWeb.net).

As discussed earlier, AuthorWeb's Framework is rooted in the WBL Framework (Khan, 2001). Each dimension of the framework has several sub-dimensions (see Figure 3), each consisting of items focused on specific aspects of the WBT learning environment. These items are represented as simple queries in the AuthorWeb system. AuthorWeb can be used in two ways: (1) By providing the designer with the flexibility to create a course using its various features and tools like any other comprehensive authoring software, or (2) by providing the designer with five easy-to-follow stages of development for course creation (see Figure 2).

As previously stated, creating effective WBT can be an overwhelming process, and the WBL Framework with its eight dimensions addresses the comprehensive nature of the WBT learning environment. The five-stage course creation process outlined by AuthorWeb adequately involves the designer in creating comprehensive WBT. At each stage, the WBL Framework helps the designer to identify and clarify the critical issues and complexities in the WBT environment, and provides guidance on addressing these issues appropriately. The following section outlines the course creation process.

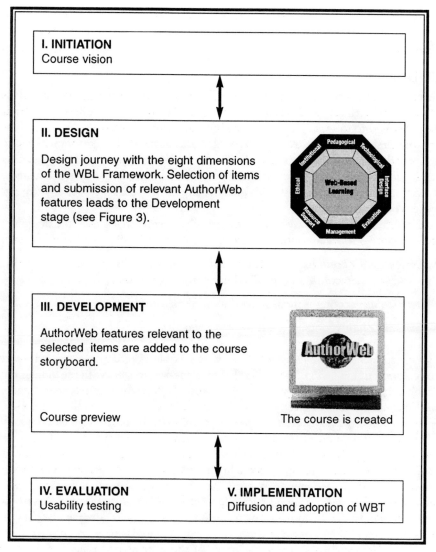

Figure 2. Course creation process by AuthorWeb.

Stage I. Initiation

In its opening screen, AuthorWeb provides the designer the opportunity to express the vision of the overall instruction. This vision will eventually be translated into a course. At this level, the designer can include any information he or she feels is necessary to convey into a vision of the course. AuthorWeb will provide guidance in this process through a series of basic questions aimed at refining the designer's vision to a more concrete and discrete level. These questions may include, for example: "What would you like your students/trainees to be able to do at course completion?" For conceptual support, the designer will have access to examples of other vision narratives in the AuthorWeb database as well. The goal for this vision creation step is to encourage the designer to articulate what he or she actually wants developed, without the perceived limitation of an instructional model traditionally imposed by a given software package. AuthorWeb includes functionality to allow the user the revisit and/or rewrite their initial vision and save it in a searchable database—or a designer can opt to skip this vision creation step all together.

Stage II. Design

Once the vision is created, AuthorWeb will retain and abide by the scope of the designer's original vision throughout the development process. The steps that follow will introduce the WBL Framework into the vision to create a truly meaningful Web-based learning environment. In effect, the designer will be asked to consider and address all eight dimensions and sub-dimensions of the framework (see Figure 3). The designer starts at the pedagogy dimension, but will then be able to determine the sequence in which to address the seven remaining dimensions. Note that the designer can also leave and visit another dimension at any time in the development process.

AuthorWeb provides an easy-to-use *Design Table* format that guides the designer through the process. Figure 3 is a snapshot of the *Design Table* which includes scrollable columns:

- *Dimension Column* lists all eight dimensions and sub-dimensions of the WBL Framework, which encompasses the WBT learning environment.
- *Item Column* contains items related to all dimensions.
- *Feature Column* contains the AuthorWeb features.

The functionality of the *Design Table* is very flexible. The designer can start with any of the three columns of the *Design Table*. If a designer chooses to start with the *dimension column* by selecting a specific dimension, which will prompt relative items and features to appear in the *item and feature columns,* respectively. For example, the selection of the 5.2 *sub-dimension* prompts items 5.200 through 5.299 to appear chronologically in the *item column* and the feature will appear in the *feature column* that is most related to item 5.200.

The naming convention of AuthorWeb's features was selected in a way to allow designers to immediately recognize its basic functionality. In addition, each feature will be supplemented with a description. If the designer encounters content-specific items that are not in the list (i.e., *item column*), the designer can simply locate the AuthorWeb feature that most closely addresses that content-specific issue. In addition, by using AuthorWeb, a designer may be able to identify more items relevant to their course content. As new technology and research surrounding WBT emerges, AuthorWeb will make sure that more of these items and their relative features are available to designers and learners. Because all issues surrounding WBT can be placed in AuthorWeb's WBL Framework, the inclusion of such new items will be facilitated by the AuthorWeb's adaptive software.

Within the scope of this chapter we will only be able to highlight and briefly discuss a few of AuthorWeb's features. The following paragraphs list some of AuthorWeb's features:

Breaking News. If a designer would like to use multiple methods for announcing changes in the course schedule, course assignments, etc., AuthorWeb can afford the designer a high degree of latitude with the *Breaking News* feature (originating from the management dimension of the framework). This feature provides the learner with multiple options for receiving key communication pertaining to course announcements (see Figure 3).

Instructional Design. AuthorWeb's *Instructional Design* feature (originating in the *pedagogical* dimension) will provide designers with just-in-time guidance on instructional theories, models, methods and strategies for both well-defined and ill-defined domains of learning as it

WBL Dimensions	Items/ Queries	AuthorWeb Features
1. Pedagogical 1.1 Goals/Objectives 1.2 Design approach 1.3 Organization 1.4 Methods and strategies 1.5 Medium **2. Technological** 2.1 Infrastructure planning 2.2 Hardware 2.3 Software **3. Interface Design** 3.1 Page and site design 3.2 Content design 3.3 Navigation 3.4 Usability testing **4. Evaluation** 4.1 Assessment of learners 4.2 Evaluation of the instruction and learning environment **5. Management** 5.1 Maintenance of learning environment 5.2 Distribution of information **6. Resource Support** 6.1 Online support 6.2 Resources **7. Ethical** 7.1 Social and cultural diversity 7.2 Geographical diversity 7.3 Learner diversity 7.4 Information accessibility 7.5 Etiquette 7.6 Legal issues **8. Institutional** 8.1 Academic affairs 8.2 Student services	5.200 How would you like to notify students about any changes in the course? 5.201 ... 5.202 ... 5.203 ... and so on ...	*Breaking News* feature provides the learner with multiple communication options as it relates to important course announcements. If the designer would like to select multiple methods of announcing changes, it will afford them a great deal of latitude.

Breaking News

	E-mail	Announcement Page	Alert Box	Running Footer	Phone	Mail
Due dates						
Instructor sick						
Exam cancelled						
Server down						
Technical problem						
Inclement weather						
Other						

Submit

Figure 3. An AuthorWeb feature for an item relevant to a WBL dimension.

relates to course content. Whatever the pedagogical philosophy (instructivist or constructivist) espoused by the designer, this feature will give the flexibility to choose the best method, given their course vision and course attributes.

Status Check. AuthorWeb's *Status Check* feature (originating in the *management* dimension) will keep track of the options used as well as options that were skipped. Please note that various options within AuthorWeb are systemically interrelated, meaning that a missed issue may require thorough revisitation. To prevent such arduous revisitations, AuthorWeb includes a *Status Check* feature that serves multiple purposes including:

- a bird's-eye view of the design process (Banathy, 1991);

- evaluating the compatabilty of the designer's original vision of the course to its current direction.

Culture Shock. The *Culture Shock* feature (originating in the *ethical and interface design* dimensions) provides the designer with sensitivity guidance regarding cross-cultural communication issues. For example, if a designer is developing training materials for an Arabic target population, which reads and writes from right to left, the screen location of the forward and backward navigation buttons will not be the same as it would be for an audience of other languages that do not read and write from left. The *Culture Shock* feature also provides the designer with a cross-culture navigation library, which houses all language/cultural-related issues relating to navigation conventions.

E-services. The *E-services* feature of AuthorWeb originates in the *management and the institutional* dimensions of the WBL Framework, since its functionality encompasses the most common applications to e-commerce and other services. The most commonly used application as it relates to e-commerce and training is the ability to provide online course registration and payment. *E-services* feature will let the user register, track, create corporate or personal accounts and create user profiles (if approved by user), all in real time. In effect, AuthorWeb's *E-service* feature gives the designer "one stop shopping" ability for all related e-functions.

Multilingual. The *Multilingual* feature (originating in the *interface and ethical* dimension) allows the designer to:

- Address a target audience that may speak several different languages.

- Convert WBT materials into any of the following languages (Spanish, French, etc.)

- Choose words and terms in different languages.

Since AuthorWeb has already guided the designer through the page, course, and content design process to a level of global acceptance, the language conversion process becomes simply a task of translating course materials as needed to the desired language. For example, a U.S. company used AuthorWeb to develop a Camera Repair course in English for its multinational workforce. The translation in the course occurs by using the same file and simply changing the language via the AuthorWeb language menu.

Testing. The *Testing* feature (originating in the *evaluation* dimension) will support designers in creating and modifying adaptive, multimedial, and randomized tests. This functionality includes multiple evaluation capabilities, like advanced grading mechanisms that can be used to redesign training to address learner-specific needs.

Simulation. The *Simulation* feature (originating in the *pedagogy* dimension) includes dynamic 3D modeling, virtual reality capabilities, and simple conversion tools that aid the designer in creating basic and complex designs.
In addition, some other AuthorWeb features include:

- *Reusable Instructional Objects* feature

- *Syllabus* feature

- *Multimedia* feature

- *Search* feature
- *Gradebook* feature
- *Discussion Forum* feature, etc.

Stage III. Development

AuthorWeb's flexible design and development environment makes creating meaningful WBT courses/classes relatively easy. A designer should not be limited to one instructional design model and should be able to choose the most effective strategy, given the course vision, goals, and specified objectives. AuthorWeb provides a competent vehicle for accommodating such flexible course development. AuthorWeb's innovative WBL Framework will allow the designer to address all issues relevant to WBT, while still providing numerous options for course content manipulation.

Stage IV. Evaluation

AuthorWeb's *usability* feature allows the designer to systematically perform usability testing. The highly interactive nature of the WBT now requires a course designer to constantly seek new ways to evaluate and test their course prior to the implementation.

Stage V. Implementation

AuthorWeb will guide the designer through the implementation process. Depending on course structure and content, target audience, in addition to other related factors, distributing a geographically dispersed WBT course can prove to be a difficult task. By identifying the critical issues that must be considered when implementing WBT, AuthorWeb provides a comprehensive, adaptable implementation process that will facilitate the successful distribution of course materials over the World Wide Web. Critical issues for WBT implementation include:

- Connectivity (access, systems, bandwidth, etc.).
- Communication (learner-related, instructor-related, etc.).
- Security (registration, access, accountability, etc.).
- Troubleshooting (hardware-related issues [systems], support-related issues [helpline], etc.).

Summary

AuthorWeb is a flexible and comprehensive authoring system with a simple vision of helping designers create meaningful online courses without having a background in instructional design, computer programming, and critical issues related to WBT. At present, there is not a single tool which adequately address all of the issues concerning the eight dimensions of the Web-based learning environment. With the increased focus on the use of the Web as a delivery medium within the last several years and given the rapid pace of change in the type of hardware and software needed to employ WBT, having a powerful and flexible system will be paramount to the success of any training/education effort. AuthorWeb will continue to expand its features and functionality by focusing on research and development. A significant amount of the research and development will focus on creating advanced designer and learner applications and will continue to explore implementation and integration issues with a global perspective. AuthorWeb is seeking collaboration and strategic partnerships to progress further with the development of AuthorWeb.

References

Banathy, B. H. (1991). *Systems designs of education: A journey to create the future.* Englewood Cliffs: Educational Technology Publications.

Dabbagh, N. H., Bannan-Ritland, B., & Silc, K. (2001). Pedagogy and Web-based course authoring tools: Issues and implications. In B. H. Khan (Ed.), *Web-based training.* Englewood Cliffs: Educational Technology Publications.

Gibbons, A. S., Lawless, K., Anderson, T. A., & Duffin, J. (2001). The Web and model-centered instruction. In B. H. Khan (Ed.), *Web-based training.* Englewood Cliffs: Educational Technology Publications.

Jones, M. G., & Farquhar, J. D. (1997). User interface design for Web-based instruction. In B. H. Khan (Ed.), *Web-based instruction.* Englewood Cliffs: Educational Technology Publications.

Khan, B. H. (1997a). Web-based instruction: What is it and why is it? In B. H. Khan (Ed.), *Web-based instruction.* Englewood Cliffs: Educational Technology Publications.

Khan, B. H. (1997b). A framework for Web-based learning. Paper presented at the Instructional Technology Department, Utah State University, Logan, UT.

Khan, B. H. (1999a). AuthorWeb: A conceptual framework for a Web-based course authoring system. Paper presented at the Annual Meeting of the Association for Educational Communications and Technology (AECT), Houston, TX.

Khan, B. H. (1999b). Interviewed by Debra Donston for an article entitled "From the trenches: Distributed learning is high priority," *PCWEEK, 16*(46), p. 134.

Khan, B. H. (2000, July–August). How do you train for B2B Success? "Ask the Experts" Column. *The New Corporate University Review, 8*(4), p. 19.

Khan, B. H. (2001). A framework for Web-based learning. In B. H. Khan (Ed.), *Web-based training.* Englewood Cliffs: Educational Technology Publications.

Khan, B. H. (in press). Web-based training: A discussion. In M. Marquardt (Ed.), *UNESCO encyclopedia on human development.* London: EOLSS Publishers.

McGee, M. K. (1999, Jan.). Train on the Web. *InformationWeek,* Issue 718, 101–105.

Phillips, V. (1998, April). Selecting an online authoring system: Corporate markets. *Training Magazine.*

Plagis-Tsitsikaos, K. (1999). Interviewed by Debra Donston for an article entitled "From the trenches: Distributed learning is high priority," *PCWEEK, 16*(46), p. 134.

Sonwalker, N. (1999). Interviewed by Debra Donston for an article entitled "From the trenches: Distributed learning is high priority," *PCWEEK, 16*(46), p. 134.

Welsh, T. M. (1997). An event-oriented design model for Web-based instruction. In B. H. Khan (Ed.), *Web-based instruction.* Englewood Cliffs: Educational Technology Publications.

The Authors

Badrul H. Khan (e-mail: khanb@gwu.edu, or khanb@BooksToRead.com; Web homepage: **Author Web.net**) is Associate Professor and Director, Educational Technology Leadership cohort graduate program, George Washington University, Washington, D.C. He is the founder of BooksToRead.com, a recommended readings site on the Internet. **David A. Ealy** (e-mail: DavidEaly@BadrulKhan.com) is with BadrulKhan.com—a hub for excellence in e-Learning.

SECTION III
Web-Based Training: Implementation and Evaluation Perspectives

40

Case Studies of Web-Based Training Sites

Badrul H. Khan, Deborah D. Waddill,
and Jane A. McDonald

Introduction

Web-based training sites have increased exponentially over the past several years, and the number continues to grow at an unprecedented pace as more organizations discover the benefits of using the Web to deliver training for employees. Participants, whether new or experienced workers, can log on at all times of day or night to a self-paced, interactive environment and access all relevant resources from any geographical location in the world. The aim of Web-based training (WBT) is to increase the performance levels of employees. Thus, the challenge of this delivery mode is to design meaningful learning environments in which the main thrust of the training is to assist users in developing and mastering specific workplace skills.

Courseware development for the mastery of skills is no easy task, for it places quality control at the core of WBT design. Because most architects of WBT are not learning specialists, numerous pitfalls abound. Until the recent introduction of Khan's Web-based Learning Framework (Khan, 2001), guidelines for constructing effective performance-based training sites were unavailable to a broad audience.

This chapter highlights case studies of WBT that illustrate one or more examples of the dimensions included in Khan's WBL Framework. An overview of the Framework presents the criteria on which the WBT sites were selected. Next, the process used to select the sites is explained. Then, mini-case studies of site courseware offer practical examples of the main dimensions of the Framework.

An Overview of Khan's WBL Framework

Khan's comprehensive Framework categorizes the criteria for Web-based learning into eight major dimensions: pedagogical, technological, interface design, evaluation, management, resource support, ethical, and institutional (Khan, 2001). Each dimension is punctuated with various subdimensions. A detailed explanation of the Framework is found in A Framework for Web-Based Learning (see Chapter 8).

Table 1 provides an overview of Khan's WBL Framework. Readers may refer to this abbreviated format, as needed, when viewing the case studies presented later in the chapter.

Table 1. Overview of Khan's Web-Based Learning Framework.*

Dimension	Function and Focus of Dimension
Pedagogical	The pedagogical dimension of Web-based learning refers to issues of teaching and learning. This dimension addresses: • Goals/objectives • Design approach • Organization • Methods and strategies • Medium
Technological	The technological dimension examines issues related to technology. This dimension addresses: • Infrastructure planning • Hardware • Software
Interface Design	The interface design dimension relates to the physical appearance of the site and the ease of maneuverability through the program. This dimension addresses: • Page and site design • Content design • Navigation • Usability testing
Evaluation	The evaluation dimension deals with: • Assessment of learners • Evaluation of the instruction and learning environment
Management	The management dimension includes the administration, maintenance, and operation aspects of Web-based courses. This dimension addresses: • Maintenance of learning environment • Distribution of information
Resource Support	The resource support dimension refers to the availability of various on- and off-line learning support and resources. This dimension addresses: • Archives • Bibliographies of related books/journals • Links to other sources • Glossary • End of unit/course summaries • Examples of other learners' work • Electronic performance support systems (EPSS) • Information facilitation of unanticipated technical problems or questions on course content
Ethical	The ethical dimension relates to ethical issues for consideration in the design of WBL. This dimension addresses: • Social and cultural diversity • Geographical diversity • Learner diversity • Information accessibility • Etiquette • Legal issues
Institutional	The institutional dimension includes issues of institutional concern. This dimension addresses: • Academic affairs • Student services

*Detailed information for each dimension is found in Chapter 8.

Selection of WBT Sites

A systematic approach was used to select training sites that represented practical applications of the dimensions in Khan's WBL Framework. The selection was limited to sites whose purpose was the development or mastery of workplace skills. In other words, examples of Web-based training, not instruction, were chosen.

Requests for WBT sites were submitted to four listservs: WWW Courseware Development (WWWDEV), Distance Education Online Symposium (DEOS-L), Web Based Training Online Learning Discussion (WBTOLL-L), and Instructional Technology Forum (ITForum). Letters also were sent to a number of leaders in the field of WBT, inviting them to submit or recommend courseware for consideration.

Over a period of three months, more than forty responses were received. Each course was thoroughly analyzed for its appropriateness as an example of one or more major dimensions of the Framework. Permission to publish the URLs was obtained from the WBT coordinators, and those training sites accessible to public viewing were selected for this chapter. Within the scope of this chapter, it was not possible to include all of the reviewed sites.

Case Studies of WBT Sites

The cases listed below represent business, industry, government, and military training sites that illustrate portions of Khan's WBL Framework. In all examples, specific dimensions of the Framework are highlighted as focal points of discussion. Also, the purpose of each training unit is identified to provide a context for decisions about site design and development.

It is important to note that site developers did not have access to Khan's WBL Framework when designing the training. Therefore, selected sites are *not* evaluated or judged on courseware quality. They simply represent practical examples of the Framework's major dimensions.

1. *Introducing Microsoft Office (gglearning.com).* The purpose of the course is to provide training on how to use Microsoft Office features and the features and functions shared across Office applications. This site demonstrates the *pedagogical* dimension of the Framework.

- **Pedagogical.** This course deals with a well-defined domain of knowledge. Prerequisite skills are clearly stated. The course's online environment looks and feels exactly like Microsoft Office because it simulates the actual environment and procedures used in Office. The course includes authentic activities, which are motivational (e.g., "Customize the Short Bar"). Information is chunked into manageable learning pieces, and the sequence of tasks moves from simple to complex, giving the learner a gradual feeling of accomplishment and satisfaction.

2. *Video Streaming Demo (liveware5.com).* The purpose of this course is to train participants in how to implement stored or live video streaming in the form of desktop video-conferencing. This demo is an example of Liveware5's series of management courses and demonstrates the *technological* dimension of the Framework.

- **Technological.** In this course, well-known authors and educators are used to provide training in live conferencing (synchronous communication) or stored video conferencing (asynchronous communication). Participants submit questions via their computers and simultaneously view the experts on their PCs. If the WBT is a live course, an expert/trainer replies directly and immediately to the questions asked. If it is a stored course, participants e-mail their questions to the expert/trainer and receive responses within the week. Because courses are offered in both stored and live formats, participants can select the presentation style that best fits their need. Under the Tech Support feature, hardware and software requirements are listed, along with minimum capabilities for an adequate Internet service provider. Tech Support posts the answers to Frequently Asked Questions, and a Problem Report function enables participants to e-mail the vendor's customer service representative for individualized assistance with technology. Specific plug-ins and players are required for the course, but there are links to resources where participants can download these items. The course also configures the learners' browsers to accommodate the video streaming feature.

3. *NASA's Kennedy Space Center's Nondestructive Evaluation (NDE) (pointcast.ksc. nasa.gov/wit/nde/body_intro.cfm).* The purpose of this training is to provide basic skills in the methods and procedures for nondestructive evaluation (NDE), a means of diagnosing potential problems in hardware and ground support equipment before a shuttle launch. This site demonstrates the *pedagogical* dimension of the Framework.

- **Pedagogical/Evaluation.** The course provides simulated environments in which learners use nondestructive evaluation techniques to identify and diagnose potential equipment problems. The learning environment is enriched by the use of multimedia such as audio, video, and graphics. Participants interact with online resources and select their own paths to navigate through the training. Simulations are used to give immediate feedback to participants and to evaluate their course knowledge. Quizzes (multiple choice, fill-in-the-blank, and true/false items) are given and graded.

4. *Microsoft Message Que Web-Based Training Demo (integritytraining.com).* The purpose of this course is to train participants to use Microsoft's Message Que Server software. This site demonstrates the *interface design* of the Framework.

- **Interface Design.** The course follows good design principles for attention, perception, comprehension, retention, and retrieval. Complementing colors used on background and foreground screens help to make this course attractive and appealing. The text is legible and a standard placement of titles is used. Although the course is graphic intensive, the graphics load quickly and enhance a learner's understanding of the software. Navigational markers consistently appear in the upper right of the screen, and organizational markers throughout the text contribute to the ease and speed of use. At the bottom of each page is a graph and page count feature that indicates progress made in the course. Also, every page links to the site's main page. A useful feature allows participants to search by key terms. Results of the search display the term, context, and page where it appears.

5. *E-Mail Pro (e-techknowledge.com).* The purpose of this WBT is to help participants write effective e-mail. Course designers offer this skill-building course for free in return for evaluation feedback from participants. This site demonstrates the *pedagogical* dimension of the Framework.

- **Pedagogical/Evaluation.** The learning outcomes and performance objectives for E-Mail Pro are clearly specified. A discussion database for e-mail users and course participants provides the opportunity for participants to air pet peeves. The course employs peer review of e-mails. For the final project, participants send an e-mail message to the course tutor and receive personal coaching. All participants are encouraged to use the learner assessment test to evaluate their performances. Upon completion of the training, participants are able to use e-mail for business communications without inadvertently violating e-mail conventions.

6. *Marketing Technical Services—Market Research (trainingplace.com/demo/demo. html)*. The purpose of this training is for participants to develop and apply basic communication skills in marketing. The Market Research module is part of The Training Place's Marketing Technical Services curriculum and demonstrates the *online support* and *management* dimensions of the Framework.

- **Resource Support (online support).** Technical resources and troubleshooting assistance are offered to participants as they collaboratively research, plan, and create thematic Web sites and electronic presentations. Trainees receive orientation support and can register for the training over a secure server. Asynchronous discussion groups are available, and audio lectures (available through RealPlayer) are used to supplement texts. The instructor, who can be reached by e-mail or phone, provides just-in-time responses to queries. Online Instructor Bios are available.

- **Management.** Participants in the Market Research module are provided with course descriptions, goals/objectives, and required texts. The Web pages are maintained and up-to-date. Public messages for the group can be left in the Caucus room, and a notebook feature allows trainees to mark and save discussion points in their personal notebooks. All links to outside resources are active and relevant (e.g., the Market Survey). The registration process has security measures, and the course is password protected for enrolled participants.

7. *World Links: Wired Communications (georcoll.on.ca/courses)*. The purpose of this project-based course is to help participants develop electronic media skills to communicate effectively. This site demonstrates the *interface design* and *management* dimensions of the Framework.

- **Interface Design.** A GANTT Chart, called a Syllabus Interface, is used to provide a recommended sequence for course content. The Syllabus Interface enhances participants' understandings of the course organization, sequence, readings, and projects. A subset of the course calendar appears at the top of every page, and each page links to the introduction. Group Conferencing Software, FirstClass Gold, allows participants to leave messages for the group and provides trainees and instructors with an easy and clear mechanism for electronic publishing.

- **Management.** Participants in this training collaborate to research, plan, and create thematic Web sites and electronic presentations. Course goals and objectives appear in the Introduction (About This Course), along with due dates for assignments, grading information, and required texts. Participants track their own interactions. E-mail addresses of the instructor and technician appear on the Course Faculty Web Page, where personal resumes also are available. Hands-on experiences help trainees relate the characteristics of computer-mediated communication, its role in society, and its use in the workplace.

8. *Authoring Systems II (dl.miramichi.nbcc.nb.ca/index.html)*. The purpose of this course is to use the Authoring Systems II Director 5 WBT to develop an interactive multimedia-

based training product that effectively incorporates digital sound, graphics and video. This site demonstrates the *institutional* dimension of the Framework.

- **Institutional.** The format for this course is all Web-based. Required texts include a Learning Guide (for progress tracking), a Survival Guide (generic document about distance learning), a Quickstart Guide, and a supplemental text. Most texts are available on line. The course is part of a degree program for Multimedia Authoring Certification, but participants are not required to be in the degree program to enroll in the course. Participants build an end-of-course portfolio as an evaluation tool rather than take tests or quizzes. Upon registration, a courier delivers course materials to participants. At the same time, the course URL, password, and user account are communicated to participants by e-mail. Registered participants have the option of selecting the start date for their course. Two months are allowed for completion of the thirty-hour course and four months for the sixty-hour course. Participants may apply to take the Prior Learning Assessment Recognition (PLAR) to receive formal credit for a course in a certificate program if they already have acquired the knowledge and skills for the course through previous education, work, or life experiences.

9. *Environmental Safety Occupational Health (ESOH) (esoh.com).* The purpose of the ESOH courseware is to provide basic training in the major federal regulations pertaining to environmental safety and occupational health. This site demonstrates the *resource support* dimension of the Framework.

- **Resource Support.** This course includes a comprehensive online searchable glossary with over 1,500 terms. Also provided are links to other online reference aids such as relevant papers, Web sites, and lectures. Participants can purchase required books through an online bookstore. Other readings can be accessed through links embedded in the course materials. By using an electronic performance support system, participants can access the complete text for each of the laws and regulations cited and bookmark relevant passages for future reference. Course summaries are provided, and an end-of-course quiz assesses the comprehension of participants. The external links are highly appropriate to course content.

10. *Development Education Program (worldbank.org/html/schools/depweb.htm).* The purpose of this course is to train participants to think creatively and critically when making decisions about how to balance social, economic, and environmental objectives. The target audience is current secondary education students who live in developing nations around the world and are considered leaders of tomorrow. This is a leader-led course with a WBT component and demonstrates the *ethical* dimension of the Framework.

- **Ethical.** This course is offered in English, Spanish, and French. Graphics are simple, such as the puzzle representing three factors that contribute to sustainable development. Primary and secondary colors make the site bright and attractive. Because the course relies on asynchronous communication, it sidesteps the need to adjust for different time zones. Cross-cultural interaction among students and instructors is encouraged. However, participation rules and guidelines that promote cross-cultural sensitivity are clearly delineated. Students can submit journalistic contributions to the Sustainable Development Post, an international electronic newspaper for students. The training encourages collaboration and creative problem solving among students from different schools and countries. Consequently, it promotes mutual respect, tolerance, and trust. Other cross-cultural related sites are available in the online resource room.

11. *Contracting Officer Representative (COR) Mentor Training (gsa.gov/fai).* The purpose of this Web site is to provide Contract Officer Representatives with self-paced training for their specific duties and the elements of each duty. This course is part of an entire curriculum designed for the Federal Acquisition Institute of the Defense Acquisition University and demonstrates the *interface design* and *institutional* dimensions of the Framework.

- **Interface Design.** The interface design includes a lot of white space for easy reading and uses standard placement of titles and content. Screens load relatively quickly with an option of text or images. There is a suggested linear pathway through the course, but a non-linear approach using a search function is also provided. This feature offers structural flexibility for trainees by allowing a choice of multiple pathways through the training. Specific pieces of content can be found by using the ad hoc query function. This site provides a progress map for participants.

- **Institutional.** The course is entirely Web-based and part of a degree program for certification as a COR Mentor. Learners are not required to be in the degree program to take the course. Registration information is submitted online to the registrar's office where it is kept secure and confidential. There are no prerequisite courses, and the institution provides an online record of course completions. Participants are kept aware of their achievement through feedback on pre-tests, scenarios, and post-tests. Information is provided about the accreditation of the Federal Acquisition Institute, although the course is transferable only to those agencies that participate in the training. Participants complete a learner profile prior to taking the course, and then the courseware adapts to each trainee's profile.

Quick Reference to WBT Sites

Table 2 provides a quick reference to the WBT sites examined in this chapter. Courseware for each site is listed next to the Framework dimension it best represents. To access these training courses, use the URLs and follow the log-in, password, and procedures specific to each site.

Summary

The World Wide Web is the fastest growing communication system in history (Crossman, 1997). Since its release onto the Internet in 1991, it has become a major vehicle to augment and replace many tasks that traditionally were performed in a face-to-face format. Web-based training is a prime example. To maintain quality control within this popular, yet complex delivery system, WBT must be carefully crafted as an effective tool for obtaining knowledge and mastering skills. Khan's WBL Framework provides the scaffolding on which to construct this important work. Its comprehensive set of dimensions and subdimensions stimulates critical discussions about a wide variety of learning issues and serves as a guide to address the intricacies involved when training via the Web. Although none of the sites reviewed for this chapter represents the full expression of Khan's Framework, each case study illustrates a relevant example of what is needed to create effective WBT training environments.

References

Crossman, D. M. (1997). The evolution of the World Wide Web as an emerging instructional technology tool (pp. 19–23). In B. H. Khan (Ed.), *Web-based instruction.* Englewood Cliffs: Educational Technology Publications.

Khan, B. H. (2001). A framework for Web-based learning. In B. H. Khan (Ed.), *Web-based training.* Englewood Cliffs: Educational Technology Publications.

Table 2. Quick reference to WBT sites.

References to Web-Based Training Sites of Case Studies by Framework Dimension, Course Name, and URL		
Framework Dimension	**Course Name**	**URL**
Pedagogical	*Introducing Microsoft Office NASA NDE Training*	gglearning.com pointcast.ksc.nasa.gov/wit/nde/body_intro.cfm
	E-Mail Pro	e-techknowledge.com
Technological	*Video Streaming Demo*	liveware5.com
Interface Design	*MSMQ Web BT Demo*	integritytraining.com
	World Links: Wired Communications	georcoll.on.ca/courses
	Contracting Officer Representative (COR) Mentor Training	gsa.gov/fai
Evaluation	*Introducing Microsoft Office NASA NDE Training*	gglearning.com pointcast.ksc.nasa.gov/wit/nde/body_intro.cfm
	E-Mail Pro	e-techknowledge.com
Management	*Marketing Technical Services—Market Research*	trainingplace.com/demo/demo.html
	World Links: Wired Communications	georcoll.on.ca/courses
Resource Support	*Environmental Safety Occupational Health (ESOH)*	esoh.com
	Marketing Technical Services—Market Research	trainingplace.com/demo/demo.html
Ethical	*Development Education Program*	worldbank.org/html/schools/depweb.htm
Institutional	*Authoring Systems II*	dl.miramichi.nbcc.nb.ca/index.html
	Contracting Officer Representative (COR) Mentor Training	gsa.gov/fai

The Authors

Badrul H. Khan (e-mail: khanb@gwu.edu, or khanb@BooksToRead.com; Web homepage: BooksTo Read.com/khan) is Associate Professor and Director, Educational Technology Leadership cohort graduate program, George Washington University, Washington, D.C. He is the founder of BooksToRead.com, a recommended readings site on the Internet. **Deborah D. Waddill** (e-mail: deb.waddill@erols.com; Web homepage: erols.com/deb.waddill) is an independent consultant in instructional technology. **Jane A. McDonald** (e-mail: jmcdonald@wdn.com) is an Associate Professor and Coordinator of Educational Leadership at George Mason University, Fairfax, Virginia. Updates to the WBL Framework may be found on the Web (BooksToRead.com/framework). For a comprehensive review of online courses based on the WBL Framework, please visit: **WebCourseReview.com**

41

Implementation Issues in Web-Based Training

Kinshuk and Ashok Patel

Web-based training systems (WBTS) can relatively easily be designed as multi-sensory systems, offering flexible navigation through different parts and types of information. They allow relative ease of modification and extension, facilitating incremental design and improvement strategies for creating instructional resources. A further advantage is that both the training resources as well as the tasks of their creation can be shared across geographically distant regions. For vocational and workplace training, it is possible to provide rich contextual information for situating what is learned and thus enable rapid and relevant knowledge construction by the trainees.

The multimedia and hypermedia technologies enable addition of a richer context to the primary information and are similar to the well-received "case study" methodology of traditional training. However, the flexibility and ease of integrating multiple media, particularly across heterogeneous populations, is not an unmixed blessing, and there are certain critical issues based on the context of design and implementation (Patel, Russell, Kinshuk, Oppermann, & Rashev, in press) of WBTS that need careful consideration (see Figure 1). While it is beyond the scope of this chapter to systematically examine each context, particularly the issues of trainee motivation and learning styles, which have received a lot of attention, the figure serves to highlight the relative importance of all the factors affecting the success of WBTS and helps in identifying the critical implementation issues. The chapter discusses the issues that are more closely connected with the "Web" and the "workplace."

Constraining the Learning Process

It is critical to recognize two important factors at this point (Clark, in press): (i) it is the instructional methods and not the media that cause learning, as demonstrated in hundreds of media comparison studies; and (ii) the human brain, the product of millions of years of evolution, is not changing rapidly and can be overloaded by the sensory output that technology is capable of delivering. To prevent such overloading and to curtail possibilities of distraction, the amount of information and especially the richness of the contextual information may need to be constrained in early stages of training.

The situation, however, is not straightforward. It is the novice trainees who are likely to benefit from richer representations as these provide multiple stimuli. It is also the same group

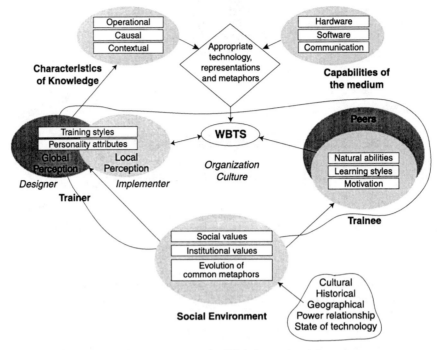

Figure 1. The contexts of a Web-based training system.

of learners who are most likely to get distracted in the absence of directed training, since they may still be developing adequate meta-cognitive skills of setting learning goals, selecting effective learning techniques, monitoring progress towards the goals, and adjusting strategies as needed (Clark, in press). Different trainers would therefore direct the learning process by constraining it in different ways, including defining an appropriate grain size of learning, learning in a situational context, or abstract learning that is applied to problems of varied context. The WBTS can be of great help if some mechanism is provided for controlling the amount of information to suit the level of training and the training style of an implementer.

Characteristics of Knowledge and Appropriate Representations

While creating training resources, it is useful to keep in mind that computers, in their currently not-so-advanced state of natural language processing, are better at providing learning in the action oriented *know-how* and *know-how-not* components (Patel & Kinshuk, 1996) of domain competence where the learning is based on "doing" and "observing." While the "observing" action enables simple acquisition of explanatory representations, there is no mechanism for freely conversing with the system to argue a viewpoint, exchange different perspectives, and get the misconceptions pointed out and corrected. These are essential steps to obtaining a deep learning of the reflection oriented *know-why* and *know-why-not* components. However, as the learners are intelligent beings, they can process the acquired explanatory representations more fruitfully if these are multi-sensory, offer flexible navigation between different parts of the information, and are rich in contextual information. Multimedia and hypermedia representations facilitate the way to exploit the benefits of multi-sensory and more realistic domain representation by relying on multi-sensory input.

The representations selected for WBTS need to support efficient acquisition of both conceptual and procedural knowledge. Depending on the nature of the subject matter and the level at which it is learned, there will be a different mix of such knowledge. For example, the Elaboration theory (Reigeluth, 1992; Reigeluth & Stein, 1983; for a critical review see Wilson & Cole, 1992) identified four types of relationships that are important in the design of training resources: conceptual, procedural, theoretical, and learning prerequisites. The first two respectively map onto the *know-why* and *know-how* discussed above, while the third relates to a level of abstraction. The fourth may be viewed as procedural (in a meta-learning sense) within an overall learning sequence and relates to the different stages of training. It should be noted, however, that different theories highlight different aspects of learning, and practitioners have been unable to determine a single best method of implementing the theories.

Representations for Supporting Skills Acquisition

It appears that the problem may gainfully be addressed in the context of the nature of the subject matter and the level at which it is learned. These are the determinants of the mix of conceptual, procedural, and theoretical knowledge to be acquired by a trainee and therefore determine the suitability of representations that may be employed. For example, dentistry students learning diagnosis of a malformed jaw may benefit conceptually from a video sequence depicting the progress of the malformation over a period of time, but they need to learn to evaluate static x-ray pictures, as diagnosis relates to evaluating a given state at a given time. Similarly, an accountant needs to learn to evaluate a balance sheet in its entirety to make judgments about a business, though it might be easier to learn about how each item in a balance sheet changes through an episodic representation using a suitable medium. While certain representations might be useful at the initial stage of training, it should be borne in mind that a representation that is efficient from the learning point of view may be inefficient for a performance task, and the optimization of efficiency and expressiveness is often mutually exclusive, requiring a trade-off, possibly per domain (Dutton & Conroy, 1996).

While there may be many domains of specialization within a functional discipline, these may be very similar in nature and require identical sets of cognitive processes. For instance, all engineering tasks emphasize problem-solving, reasoning, creativity, and team playing, while requiring a good grasp of mathematics. WBTS for engineering domains should, therefore, go beyond the declarative knowledge and address the acquisition of the functional cognitive skills. They also need to address the procedural skills for employing precise and concise mathematical representations of the concepts and need a suitable representation to practice the skills. As Salomon (1977) observed, ". . . when the task calls for some act of analytic comparison and the coded message activates imagery instead, the learning may be debilitated."

Integrated WBTS and Peer Supported Learning

In the case of workplace training, even the concept of a "domain" is very much situated in the "communities of practice" and evolves as a result of group learning. As Sumner and Stolze (1996) observed, ". . . for communities of practice, what constitutes their *domain* is not a given static entity. Instead *domains* are dynamic entities that reflect a workgroup's ongoing learning and knowledge construction processes." The dynamics of the modern workplace demand continual extension of existing knowledge to changing situations and construction of new knowledge to compensate for any shortfalls. WBTS in such environments need to recognize the importance of the peer group and encourage group learning, preferably in an open-ended manner and integrated with the actual work.

McCalla, Greer, Kumar, Meagher, Collins, Tkatch, and Parkinson (1997) have described the success of PHelpS (a Peer Help System for workplace training) as based on its knowledge representation scheme that captured authentic tasks at many levels of detail. They observed that such task hierarchies could become the basis for performance support on the job, for structuring training activities in the training center, for allowing workers to learn more as and when they saw the necessity, for modeling knowledge states of workers and peer helpers, and for structuring the communication during peer help interactions. While PHelpS may be seen as an embedded performance support system with some intelligent help facilities, it can also be used explicitly for training. Workers learning a new task are guided through the simulated cases by the system and can request help from fellow learners or from the trainer through the peer help interface. With "minimalist" artificial intelligence techniques and collaborative communication facility, PHelpS has been successful in task-oriented training focused on procedural skills (McCalla *et al.*, 1997). This suggests that WBTS can benefit from the traditional approaches to intelligent tutoring system design. The availability of considerably platform independent programming languages, such as Java, has enabled interactive procedures for adding "intelligence" to WBTS.

Culturally Diverse Users

Since the Web can offer a potentially world-wide scope for WBTS, problems arising from the heterogeneity of target population have to be considered. As Bourges-Waldegg and Scrivner (1998) note, "Designing interfaces for culturally diverse users is fundamentally a problem of communicating the intended meaning of representations . . . in every culturally determined usability problem a divergence between the target meaning and the interpreted meaning of representations was present." Their study found, however, that intercultural communications between users are less problematic since the users jointly develop a communication space in order to succeed in their task, despite differences in culture and language.

These observations suggest two important considerations: (a) the selection of representations needs great care, and multiple representations are necessary, and (b) synchronous or asynchronous communications based on video conferencing, Web meetings, electronic white boards, or discussion forums enable the explanation and negotiation of *meaning*. Such communications should be systematically integrated in the training environments. If there is a mechanism for capturing, generalizing, and storing communications among the trainees, peer helpers, and trainers, the WBTS can incrementally add the amount of support provided and remain relevant to current conditions. For example, in the PHelpS referred to earlier, the dialogue exchanged through the collaborative communication facility is trapped for each case, examined by a moderator, edited to remove personal information, indexed to sub-tasks where applicable, incremented for inclusion of other useful information, and finally committed to the Help Case repository (McCalla *et al.*, 1997).

Social Environment and Sub-Cultures

It should be remembered, however, that communication breakdowns do not require wide "cultural" differences. The differences in backgrounds, goals, or outlooks can be as problematic in communication between two people as their not speaking the same language (Devlin, 1997). The possibility of such communication failure needs to be recognized by WBTS designers in both the educational and workplace sectors. For educational institutions, the different social environments in the catchment area can affect the usability of a training system differently between a suburban school and an inner city school. Such differences may also affect cognitive styles; unfortunately, little attention has been given in research literature to the effect of class or socio-economic differences upon variations in learning style (Anderson, 1995). The entertainment industry has created a sub-culture so that the "MTV generation" may share common metaphors, but to what extent this commonality transfers to educational processes is a matter of further study. In the case of workplace based WBTS, the typical background of employees in different organizational functions may render, say, a WBTS for shop floor workers unsuitable for office workers or one for salespersons unsuitable for accountants. The entertainment industry induced new sub-cultures which may also create diversity in workplace trainees due to dominant sub-cultures of different age groups.

Organizational Culture

While limited purpose and localized WBTS for training in procedural skills can be employed productively within a workplace with relative ease, this seems to be a limited use of the power and flexibility offered by the information technology and its enabling role for re-engineering the business processes (Hammer & Champy, 1994). For example, an embedded performance support system that can also function as a training system offers opportunities for continuous learning. WBTS built along this model enable an organization to become a "learning organization." However, it appears that in spite of the rhetoric, many organizations are unwilling to face the harsh realities of increased competition and their senior management lacks the will to risk radical change (Grint, 1997). An ambitious WBTS will not be successful in the absence of supportive organizational culture.

Conclusion

In conclusion, while the critical issues discussed above might appear to be insurmountable, the purpose of the discussion is to draw attention to the complexity involved in designing and implementing any substantial WBTS. The awareness of these issues not only helps in creating more realistic expectations from the WBTS, but also helps in designing more flexible systems so that alternative sets of representations may be used to suit the requirement of diverse groups of trainees. It highlights the role of peers and group learning and focuses on the importance of systematic communications between trainees, peers, and trainers, while acknowledging that communication breakdowns may occur due to differences in backgrounds and outlooks. It recognizes that powerful WBTS can and should be created to integrate performance enhancement support and help in creating learning organizations, but the task of fostering appropriate organizational culture rightly belongs to senior management, as a WBTS can achieve its potential only to the extent its aims are supported by the organization culture (supplementary information on the contexts of Intelligent Tutoring Systems and other works by the authors is available on the Web at: dmu.ac.uk/~apatel/wbt/).

References

Anderson, J. A. (1995). Towards a framework for matching teaching and learning styles for diverse populations. In R. R. Sims & S. J. Sims (Eds.), *The importance of learning styles* (pp. 68–78). Westport, CT: Greenwood.

Bourges-Waldegg, P., & Scrivener, S. A. R. (1998). Meaning, the central issue in cross-cultural HCI design. *Interacting with Computers, 9*, 287–309.

Clark, R. (in press). Chapter 2. In H. Stolovitch & E. Keeps (Eds.), *Handbook of performance technology* (2nd ed.). San Francisco: Jossey-Bass.

Devlin, K. (1997). *Goodbye Descartes: The end of logic and the search for a new cosmology of mind.* New York: John Wiley.

Dutton, D. M., & Conroy, G. V. (1996). A review of machine learning. *The Knowledge Engineering Review, 12*(4), 341–367.

Grint, K. (1997). *Fuzzy management: Contemporary ideas and practices at work.* Oxford: Oxford University Press.

Hammer, M., & Champy, J. (1994). *Reengineering the corporation: A manifesto for business revolution.* London: Nicholas Brealey.

McCalla, G. I., Greer, J. E., Kumar, V. S., Meagher, P., Collins, J. A., Tkatch, R., & Parkinson, B. (1997). A peer help system for workplace training. In B. du Boulay & R. Mizoguchi (Eds.), *Artificial intelligence in education* (pp. 183–190). Amsterdam: IOS.

Patel, A., & Kinshuk. (1996). Knowledge characteristics: Reconsidering the design of intelligent tutoring systems. In A. Behrooz (Ed.), *Knowledge transfer* (pp. 190–197). London: Pace.

Patel, A., Russell, D., Kinshuk, Oppermann, R., & Rashev, R. (in press). An initial framework of contexts for designing usable intelligent tutoring system. Chapter in *Information services and use.* Amsterdam: IOS.

Reigeluth, C. (1992). Elaborating the Elaboration Theory. *Educational Technology Research & Development, 40*(3), 80–86.

Reigeluth, C., & Stein, F. (1983). The Elaboration Theory of instruction. In C. Reigeluth (Ed.), *Instructional-design theories and models.* Hillsdale, NJ: Lawrence Erlbaum Associates.

Salomon, G. (1977). *Interaction of media, cognition, and learning.* San Francisco: Jossey-Bass.

Sumner, T., & Stolze, M. (1996). Integrating working and learning: Two models of computer support. *AI & Society, 10,* 70–78.

Wilson, B., & Cole, P. (1992). A critical review of Elaboration Theory. *Educational Technology Research and Development, 40*(3), 63–79.

The Authors

Kinshuk (e-mail: kinshuk@ieee.org; Web homepage: fims-www.massey.ac.nz/~kinshuk/) is a Senior Lecturer, Information Systems Department, Massey University, Palmerston North, New Zealand. **Ashok Patel** (e-mail: apatel@dmu.ac.uk; Web homepage: dmu.ac.uk/~apatel/) is Director, CAL Research and Software Engineering Centre, DeMontfort University, Leicester, United Kingdom.

42

Copyright Issues in Web-Based Training

David Throne

Background

Many company and corporate trainers and educators in the United States are creating Websites to deliver their training or courses at a distance. They are spending countless hours creating new materials or revising old materials for distance delivery. Sometimes they retain the rights from their employers for the design and development of these materials; other times they do not. Intellectual property has become an extremely sensitive issue with wide-ranging opinions by all. When independent training contractors (as well as leased workers) and work made for hire are added, it becomes confusing, and litigation is occasionally necessary.

The Internet or corporate intranets, as used for Web-based training and delivery of courses, provide a unique situation and medium wherein complex copyright issues arise. Many authors have written about this, but few have addressed trainers developing Web-based materials for companies and corporations and retaining the copyright of their materials when dismissed or moving to another work situation. This chapter is directed toward company and corporate trainers, as well as independent training contractors (referred to hereafter as contractors, who are usually hired for the short-term), who develop Web-based materials and Websites for employers; it offers suggestions to help them avoid problems associated with copyright and intellectual property. However, all trainers, educators, administrators, and managers may find the chapter useful.

The Problem

In general, issues of *who* owns *what* are not brought up, as many trainers and Web developers assume they own what they have created. On the other hand, administrators and managers, citing company and corporate policies, assume that *they* own what their employees created, including creations by trainers who were hired for the short-term. Independent contractors are particularly affected because they are not afforded the same rights as regular employees at many companies and corporations.

Professional organizations are urging their members to help one another understand these sensitive issues. For instance, the Association for Educational Communications and Technology (AECT) states in its Code of Ethics: "In fulfilling obligations to the profession, members

381

shall inform users of the stipulations and the interpretations of the copyright law and other laws affecting the profession and encourage compliance" (AECT, 1998).

Suggestion One: Carefully Read and Understand Contracts

Trainers should read their contracts and understand their legal rights on signed documents before giving companies and corporations Web-based materials or Websites they have created outside the scope of their contract. They should look for ownership policies in particular and know what they want to retain. Kurtz, a copyright attorney, believes that it is deceiving to employees for the company or corporation to not specify up front who will own the finished product (1998b). He states that the company or corporation has "usually been advised by legal counsel and is intentionally ambiguous in contracts because absent a specific written assignment to the creator (employee), the law grants ownership to the employer." It should be noted, however, that most large corporations usually have corporate compliance plans in place that stipulate copyright and intellectual property policies succinctly.

Consequently, trainers should understand their contracts and employment status before they allow their time, work, words, and ideas to be taken from them:

- First, they should understand their legal position and the term "work made for hire," if they are contractors.

- Second, they should understand their rights as owners of words and ideas, which falls under copyright, intellectual property, and fair use.

- Third, they should understand the difference between creating under contract and bringing in developed material prior to contract. If they have developed material prior to contract, they should note it in the contract as their work and stipulate how the employer can use it.

- Fourth, they should know what can happen if they don't protect themselves, and should understand certain court cases that may be relevant to their situation.

- Finally, they should be aware of sensible remedies in situations in which infringements have taken place in relation to their work on Websites.

Suggestion Two: Know Policies of Companies/Corporations Concerning Contractors

Trainers, if they are contractors, should know their position at companies and corporations, that is, understand their legal rights as contract employees. Contractors and leased workers are individuals who are not on the corporation payroll, but are providing services to the corporation and are classified as such under Federal law. This basically means that contractors:

- have been hired on an as-needed basis;

- are subject to terms of employment written in their contract at the time of hire; and

- have no company or corporate benefits except those provided by law.

Smaller companies are sometimes not as clear in their employment policies as larger corporations; thus, all contractors should request these policies before commencing work.

Contract employees are considered temporary workers and not regular employees. They have *fewer rights* compared to regular employees, which may include appeal processes if terminated. Also, many companies and corporations are not legally required to give contractors reasons for ending employment. Different employers have different policies concerning contractors' status, so contractors should check with their personnel departments. In other words, trainers who are contractors should understand their rights and responsibilities before they sign company or corporate contracts, and should be aware that they are expendable and that their contracts can be terminated without reason at any time.

Suggestion Three: Know Policies Concerning Work Produced

Before trainers agree to sign contracts to design or develop online courses and supporting materials, they should understand company and corporate policies concerning work produced. Smedinghoff (1996) states, "Copyright [ownership] is an issue that is frequently not even discussed between the parties" (p. 147). Trainers and their company or corporate administrators should agree on:

- who owns the course and its contents;

- how much the owners will be paid;

- what percentage of royalties, if any, the owners will be afforded for future sales.

In most cases, since trainers who are contractors are temporary employees, companies and corporations will have them sign a contract, which most likely will be a "work made for hire" document and falls under the Copyright Act of 1976 (17 U.S.C.A., Section 101):

> (1) A work prepared by an employee within the scope of his or her employment; or (2) a work specifically ordered or commissioned for use as a contribution to a collective work, as a part of a motion picture or other audiovisual work, as a translation, as a supplementary work, as a compilation, as an instructional text, as a test, as answer material for a test, or as an atlas, if the parties expressly agree in a written instrument signed by them that the work shall be considered a work made for hire. (Electronic Frontier Foundation, 1997)

Companies and corporations should provide information on copyright procedures. These policies concerning copyright and intellectual property vary greatly from employer to employer. For instance, some policies may state that work or products that are copyrightable, patentable, or of commercial value generated by an employee shall remain the exclusive property of that employee and that the employee shall have the sole right of its ownership and disposition.

Other companies and corporations policies may state something totally the opposite, such as the following *hypothetical* position:

> Any inventions, discoveries, creations (including software, writings, drawings, and audiovisual and other works) improvements, confidential information or other intellectual property that employees develop or create, or assist in developing or creating, during employment shall remain the property of this company. Further, employees are required to disclose such intellectual property and execute legal documents and assist in other ways to secure and enforce rights to that intellectual property for the company.

There is quite a contrast between these policies. The point here is that many companies and corporations do not have their copyright and intellectual property policies stated within contracts when trainers sign them. *Employers should be encouraged to do so.* If trainers want to retain the rights to their work, they should request ownership clause inclusions in all contractual agreements with employers before beginning work. However, if this has not been done, a fairly recent Federal court decision favors trainers who are contractors.

Court Cases Related to Work Made
for Hire and Property Rights

Kaplan and Lee (1995) state that the Act's work made for hire doctrine seldom has been applied in training and education, but a recent Supreme Court decision has clarified this further. Since the work made for hire doctrine is an exception to the Act's presumption that authors of works hold the copyright and that copyrights are owned by employers because of this doctrine, it is necessary for both parties to enter an agreement for authors to retain their copyright. In *Community for Creative Non-Violence (CCNV) v. Reid,* 490 U.S. 104 (1989), the Court was asked to decide who owned a statue commissioned by CCNV, since both parties (the sculptor and the employer) had competing copyright registrations. The court ruled that the work made for hire doctrine did not apply to Reid because he was an independent contractor, not an employee of CCNV.

This case is considered quite significant because it rejected approaches to the Act's interpretation used by Federal appellate courts, which ruled that a work was made for hire if an employer exercised production control, with the controlling issue being whether the author is an employee, listing factors relevant to such a determination (Maggs, Soma, & Sprowl, 1992). The court ruled that Reid was an independent contractor, but it did not further define the phrase "within the scope of employment." The court felt that it was not clear whether the company could, if it wished to, assert copyright ownership of books, articles, and so forth (Maggs, Soma, & Sprowl, 1992). However, the court did rule that the company could be a co-author, but remanded that decision and argument to a lower court for a retrial.

Kurz (1996), an intellectual property litigation expert, states:

> This traditional employer/employee relationship is to be distinguished from the relationship which arises when a party hires another as an independent contractor. The independent contractor may be specifically hired, paid, and directed to perform a particular task, e.g., write computer software or create artwork. However, under the copyright laws, this situation does not necessarily give rise to a work being considered a "work made for hire." Instead (unless very specific conditions can be met), the independent contractor who created the software or artwork will be the copyright owner, rather than the party who hires the independent contractor. (p. 9)

Kurz (1996) explains what conditions are to be considered or met that seem to favor independent contractors who do supplemental work for their companies. He states that "there are many companies who . . . are not the copyright owners in various computer programs and other works which were created by independent contractors" and believes this could have "dire consequences should the independent contractor seek to enforce his or her copyright" (p. 9).

Several cases have upheld plaintiffs' ownership of their published work: *Williams v. Weisser* (1969), *Hays v. Sony* (1988) and *Weinstein v. University of Illinois* (1987). Other cases, such as *Colorado Foundation v. American Cyanamid* (1995), have not (Sinofsky, 1995, p. 13). But a copyright owner's first goal is to stop the infringement (Smedinghoff, 1996). To recover monetary losses, a damage suit must be brought, incurring greater expenditure in time and money. Smedinghoff (1996) describes the remedies available to copyright owners concerning infringers.

Copyright Protection for Original Works

Copyright protection vests automatically to original works that are fixed in a tangible medium. Can a company or corporation own the copyright of work that trainers created prior to the signing of a contract? Is this fair use? Carter says (1996): "Work you do while moonlighting, or that is not part of your duties, is not work made for hire" (p. 175). For example, trainers who create work during their spare time, and put this work on Websites where they are contract employees, own the copyright of the work. Such situations are now covered in the latest revision of the Act, the Digital Millennium Copyright Act, H.R. 2281, which was enacted into law on October 28, 1998. It covers property rights over written material, audio recordings, and software in cyberspace. Smedinghoff (1996) states: "Only works created by the employees within the scope of their employment will be governed by the 'work made for hire' doctrine. Work done outside the normal scope of employment will not be normally covered" (p. 147).

Realistically, all trainers should look at their company's or corporation's policies *first* concerning copyrightable material and intellectual property, understand them, and take appropriate action to protect their work. Otherwise, the old adage of "ownership is 99 percent possession" becomes reality.

Suggestion Four: Thoroughly Read and Understand the Copyright Act of 1976 and Its Revisions

Since copyright is a form of protection provided by the laws of the United States to the authors of original materials, including literary, dramatic, musical, and other intellectual works, trainers should understand the Act and its revisions. Cavazos and Morin (1994) state:

> Few computer communication issues have received more attention and caused more confusion than those dealing with questions of intellectual property. Copyright law . . . can seem especially difficult. Some legal issues in cyberspace require a great deal of attention because of the novel problems they present. With copyright law, however, the issues raised in cyberspace are readily addressed by well-established principles. (p. 47)

These principles come from the Act itself. Usually, the policy as passed by our lawmakers and the policy of companies and corporations are similar, but trainers should read the Act or synopses of it. Excellent places to start are:

- past issues of *Tech Trends'* copyright columns;

- Electronic Frontier Foundation (1997) Intellectual Property Archive on the Web at eff.org/pub/Intellectual_property/cni_copyright_act_1976;

- Copyright Basics on the Web at lcweb.loc.gov/copyright/circs/circ1.html.

Trainers should read Title 17, United States Code, Chapters 1 through 8, to fully understand the stipulations/limitations of Federal copyright law and its applicability. Trainers who are contractors should be aware that laws may not always favor them implicitly, especially since employers will point out that they are contract employees and declare they signed "work made for hire" contracts. These trainers can fight this, but this should be their first warning that if they end up in litigation concerning ownership, it is going to cost an exorbitant amount of money to retain lawyers to argue their copyright case although monetary compensation is written within the law.

Fair use, a privilege that permits one other than the copyright owner to reproduce, distribute, adapt, perform or display a work, is a much-contested issue also. Dalziel (1995) states: "Due to the confusing nature of the Act with regard to distance education, many colleges and universities [including companies and corporations] have very different notions of what constitutes fair use" (p. 7). For an easy-to-understand report on fair use and recent legislative actions, see James (1997). For an overview of fair use online, see Dalziel (1998) at: libraries.psu.edu/avs/fairuse/default.html

Suggestion Five: Understand and Use the Copyright Symbol (©)

Most Website creators think that the copyright symbol (©), if properly placed, will protect their sites and related materials per Federal law. Since the U.S. became a member of the Berne Convention, and Berne signatories do not require the copyright notice, "[this] formal copyright notice is no longer required in the U.S. This means works copyrighted before March 1, 1989 require a copyright notice; those after, don't" (Sinofsky, 1997, p. 10). See this document on the Web (eff.org/pub/Intellectual_property/bern_convention.treaty).

Although the misconceptions begin here, there are fundamentals to the "copyright notice" that all Website creators should follow, as it is still *customary* to attach a copyright notice on copyrighted works to be eligible for damages and to strengthen copyright claims in the event of litigation. There are four parts to a copyright notice (O'Mahoney, 1998):

- the copyright symbol and word copyright—use both the numeric entity and the full word "Copyright" with your notice to help in case of litigation;

- year of publication—when a copyright notice is given, the year of publication should be included in the notice;

- name of the copyright owner;

- reservation of rights (optional).

Suggestion Six: Register Work with the U.S. Copyright Office

"To secure copyright protection . . . an original work must be registered with the Copyright Office" (Botterbusch, 1996, p. 8). If trainers want to register their work, it is fairly simple and currently costs $20. An excellent self-help book is *How to Register a U. S. Copyright* by Warda (1995), but other guides are available to walk trainers through the process. The fastest and easiest way is to go directly to the U.S. Copyright Office's Website and download the forms (lcweb.loc.gov/copyright/). There are two reasons why trainers should pay this money and spend time filing a copyright: ability to sue and statutory damages:

> Although copyright attaches upon fixation, you cannot actually sue someone for infringing your copyright until you have registered your work with the Copyright Office. And if you register your work within three months from the date of first publication, or at least prior to the date of infringement, you can collect statutory damages from the infringer. Otherwise, you are stuck with actual damages, which depending upon the situation, may be only nominal. (O'Mahoney, 1998)

Suggestion Seven: Understand Monetary Damages

In Chapter 5 of the Act, legal actions are spelled out succinctly to infringers of owners' creative works. Statutory damages can range from $500 to $20,000 per work infringed, plus attorney's fees, actual damages, and so forth. Fees can run higher. If the plaintiff can prove that the infringement was committed willfully, the presiding judge may award damages up to $100,000 per infringement (Cavazos & Morin, 1994). Although Chapter 5 stipulates that employees of nonprofit educational companies may not be liable for statutory damages if they believed that they were acting within the scope of their employment per fair use guidelines, the leadership of the company and its governing body can be held responsible at least monetarily.

Infringement evidence must be collected for comparison if trainers copy their Websites with dates shown. This precedent was set in *Williams Electronic, Inc. v. Artic International, Inc.,* 685 F 2d 870, 876 (3rd Cir. 1982) when the Third Circuit court noted:

> There is overwhelming evidence in the present case that the [plaintiff's] computer program has been copied in some form. The following facts, among others, manifest the similarities between the [plaintiff's] program and that stored in the [defendant's] memory devices . . . other, miscellaneous evidence of copying abounds. (Maggs, Soma, & Sprowl, 1992, p. 147)

Trainers are advised to gather Website snapshots weekly to show that the company or corporation was guilty of copying and using their work for profit. They may try to sue the company or corporation for damages within the ethical section of the Act as it provides for compensable damages (lost profits). Where the infringement is blatant, punitive damages are set to the limits in the statute. Again, Congress has shown that it is willing to become even tougher on infringers with the recent passage of the Digital Millennium Copyright Act. The questions raised are noteworthy:

- Does a company or corporation want to put its employees at risk with criminal charges for violating this revision?

- What is the employer's education plan for its employees concerning copyright and the Web?

- Is it ethical for employees who follow directives from managers to use copyrighted material?

- Are the copyright policies made by companies and corporations current with Congress' recent revisions of copyright laws, especially the Digital Millennium Copyright Act?

Attitudes About Ownership of Web-Based Materials and Websites

Let us take an example from higher education to understand the attitudes about ownership of Web-based training materials and Websites in today's marketplace as it could possibly pertain to the company or corporate trainer.

> Traditionally, universities cared very little about copyrights as faculty mostly wrote and published in academic journals read primarily by other faculty and students conducting research, and there was little or no market value. Even the occasional textbook which generated some royalties was not significant enough for the university to claim ownership. Those attitudes have drastically changed with the copyright of computer software and distance education. . . . Universities now see a new potential source of revenue. The course that will be presented over the Web, for credit, will bear the university's name and the university will have the final decision over whether the course is of sufficient quality to be placed on the Web. The university has a significant investment in its resources and a legitimate claim to ownership. . . . The faculty member has an equally strong claim for ownership as he/she has essentially created the content of the course and how it will be delivered, with little or no direct supervision from the university administration. (Kurtz, March 10, 1998)

Copyright and intellectual property questions that trainers who use the Web are facing today elude the existing legal provisions. What do trainers do if their Web-based materials or Websites are taken illegally?

Suggestion Eight: Work with the Company and Appeal to Leadership

Carter (1996) believes that there is a "disturbing poverty of ethics in the digital age" (p. 163). To intelligently remedy copyright and intellectual property problems, go directly to the leadership of the company or corporation and explain the facts. Sometimes these leaders are not fully attuned to the situation. Badaracco and Ellsworth (1989) state: "A leader must be an exemplar to the organization, demanding the highest standards of integrity, and be doggedly consistent in word and deed in all matters affecting the company's values (p. 174)." If leaders are not aware of unethical conduct, such as copyright violations on Websites and the materials created within, who is to blame for companies and corporations that take trainers' copyrighted works? Can it be the chief executive officer (CEO), administrator of training, or trainer? In a study done by Grace (1995), the results clearly indicate that the majority of media directors across the United States do not have sufficient knowledge of copyright law and related guidelines.

Leaders at companies and corporations should want to avoid litigation. Mills and Paul (1995) state: "A total quality programme [sic] must start at the top. It must be more than the latest device to motivate staff to provide better service, but a fundamental value which is both espoused and exemplified by senior management" (p. 117). Trainers should talk with the highest authorities where they are employed and relate their concerns before starting litigation. Show these leaders the problems.

Final Thoughts

Ely (1996) states: "Advocacy for the use of educational technology has increased among policy groups" (p. 25). He points out that "training should be provided for educating employees in the use of technologies and their applications," including an understanding of copyright laws (p. 28). Other authors have advocated these same thoughts and carried them to logical fruition. Talab (1995) says: "In a capitalistic society, it is necessary to maintain the concept of individual intellectual property" (p. 9). She believes that ways should be explored to make sure that individuals could retain the rights to their work if they want.

Professional trainers may be declared independent contractors in the courts (although this depends, of course, on the nature of the contract they sign). What they have creatively produced for any company or corporation may be owned by them, including the copyright, wholly or partially, as long as such ownership was noted in the contract they sign. Consequently, employers should seek a trainer's permission to use these materials if the trainer leaves or is terminated. Company and corporate leaders should take responsibility to see that copyright concerns are current, proper, and follow Federal law. They should make sure training and distance education policies are thoroughly intact before giving employees permission to develop Web-based materials and Websites and make sure ownership policies are included in all contracts. They should provide educational opportunities such as in-service meetings for their community of trainers, educators, administrators, and managers to help them understand the copyright policies.

Essential administrative personnel in distance education programs should also maintain high ethical standards concerning original authors' ownership and keep current with the Act and its revisions. Willis (1993) states:

> Effective distance education administrators are more than idea people. They are consensus builders, decision-makers, and facilitators. They maintain control of technical managers, ensuring that technological resources are effectively deployed to further the institution's acad-

emic mission. At the same time, they lead and inspire . . . staff in overcoming obstacles that arise. (p. 34)

Barlow emphasizes the importance of Website and online ethics and points out that communities (such as companies and corporations) with solid ethical standards work better and shouldn't have to lean on legal standards (Carter, 1996). Why would training personnel and other employees want to sue the firm at which they grew as professionals? Why would company or corporate leadership risk litigation? Administration or management should provide the modeling behavior that demonstrates integrity and trust (Chase, 1989).

Stansbury (1996) states: "The future of distance learning is in the balance—the copyright balance. With distance learning guidelines, we can: balance an author's rights; provide access for teaching and learning; establish clarity for financial ambiguities; institute multiple use options; instill trust; and acknowledge ethical concerns" (p. 11). However, if copyrights are to work in the era of digitization, Carter (1996) believes that ethical consideration will have to be woven into the Internet or intranet. Company or corporate leaders will have to make ethical choices. Quality training and distance learning programs start at the top.

References

Association for Educational Communications and Technology. (1998). Code of ethics; aect.org

Badaracco, J. L., & Ellsworth, R. R. (1989). *Leadership and the quest for integrity.* Boston: Harvard Business School Press.

Botterbusch, H. R. (1996, March). More copyright Q&A. *Tech Trends, 41*(2), p. 8.

Carter, M. E. (1996). *Electronic highway robbery: An artist's guide to copyrights in the digital era.* Berkeley, CA: Peachpit Press.

Cavazos, E. A., & Morin, G. (1994). *Cyberspace and the law: Your rights and duties in the online world.* Cambridge, MA: The MIT Press.

Chase, M. E. (1989). *An evaluation of the interpretation of the fair-use doctrine with respect to the videotaping in Pennsylvania state system of higher education and selected state related schools.* Unpublished master's thesis, Slippery Rock University, Slippery Rock, PA.

Cyrs, T. E. (1996). *Teaching at a distance with the merging technologies: An instructional systems approach.* New Mexico State University, Center for Educational Development.

Dalziel, C. (1995, October). Fair use guidelines for distance education. *Tech Trends, 40*(5), 6–8.

Dalziel, C. (1998). Fair use guidelines for educational multimedia; libraries.psu.edu/avs/fairuse/default.html

Electronic Frontier Foundation (1997). EFF "Intellectual Property Online: Patent, Trademark, Copyright" Archive; eff.org/pub/Intellectual_property/cni_copyright_act_1976

Ely, D. P. (1996). *Trends in educational technology.* Syracuse University, Informational Resources Publications.

Grace, M. (1995). An analysis of the knowledge of media directors concerning relevant copyright issues in education (ERIC Document Reproduction Service No. ED 383 290).

James, A. F. (1997, Nov./Dec.). Understanding fair use and fair use guidelines. *Tech Trends, 42*(6), 11–13.

Kaplan, W. A., & Lee, B. A. (1995). *The law of higher education.* San Francisco: Jossey-Bass.

Kurtz, C. (1998a, March 10). Course Ownership; DEOS-L@lists.psu.edu

Kurtz, C. (1998b, April 17). Intellectual rights; DEOS-L@lists.psu.edu

Kurz, R. A. (1996). *Internet and the law: Legal fundamentals for the Internet user.* Rockville, MD: Government Institutes.

Maggs, P. B., Soma, J. T., & Sprowl, J. A. (1992). *Computer law: Cases, comments, questions.* St. Paul, MN: West Publishing.

Mills, R., & Paul, R. (1995). Putting the student first: Management for quality in distance education. In T. Evans & D. Nation (Eds.), *Reforming open and distance education: Critical reflections from practice* (pp. 113–129). New York: St. Martin's Press.

O'Mahoney, B. (1998). The Copyright Website; benedict.com/

Sinofsky, E. R. (1995, Nov./Dec.). Copyright: The water's not safe yet. *Tech Trends, 40*(6), 12–14.

Sinofsky, E. R. (1997, Sept.). Copyright and you. *Tech Trends, 42*(4), 9–10.

Smedinghoff, T. J. (Ed.). (1996). *Online law: The SPA's legal guide to doing business on the Internet.* Reading, MA: Addison-Wesley.

Stansbury, R. (1996, Nov./Dec.). Copyright and distance learning: A balancing act. *Tech Trends, 41*(6), 9–11.

Talab, R. (1995, Jan./Feb.). Copyright and multimedia, part two: Higher education. *Tech Trends, 40*(1), 8–10.

Warda, M. (1995). *How to register a U. S. copyright.* Clearwater, FL: Sphinx Publishing.

Willis, B. (1993). *Distance education: A practical guide.* Englewood Cliffs: Educational Technology Publications.

The Author

David Throne (e-mail: cd_david@cccs.cccoes.edu; Web homepage: etech.unco.edu/gradstudents/throne/default.html) is an instructor and doctoral candidate in Educational Technology at the University of Northern Colorado, Greeley, and teaches online for e.college.

43

Needed: Digital Libraries for Web-Based Training

John Schmitz

Introduction

Usage patterns of Web search engines suggests that people conceive of these tools as access points to a world digital library. This is not surprising, since search engines return information on any topic, wherever the information may be stored. In our research on search engine usage, we find evidence that some people think that search engines are intelligent. Science fiction work by H. G. Wells, Arthur Clarke, and others seems to have prepared people to understand and access the growing global brain that the Web is becoming. There seems to be little need to teach the concept of a global digital library; users have it. The problem is that while the concept may be there, the library is not.

In reality, we are far from realizing a highly searchable digital library on the Web. It is clear that, for now, users' expectations of Web searching exceeds present capability by a large margin. For example, recent estimates indicate that less than a quarter of available Web resources is searchable by any particular engine. Furthermore, the results returned by searches are often massive in number and of low quality, requiring careful checking of myriad links to find desired resources. Some users adopt advanced search strategies to cope, but the usage of these strategies seems rare. Even if the strategies are used, the same problems often arise. A related limitation is that searches do not pinpoint the correct point in a resource. The limitations of search in light of its explosive popularity teach the lesson that the Web is not yet a true digital library, though users expect it to be.

There are other reasons the Web does not offer users a true digital library. Full text documents are the basis of any library, yet they are relatively rare on the Web. Even when full text documents can be located, the formatting of the document falls far short of the quality offered by print publications.

By these three criteria just introduced—high searchability, full text content, and rich formatting—only a fraction of publicly available content on the Web constitutes a true digital library. This is a serious problem to the degree that effective education and training depends on widespread availability of true digital library content.

Digital libraries are integral to Web-based education and training, for both producers and consumers of education and training. Teachers, instructional designers, and trainers must be able to easily locate and assemble content for their online materials. Students and trainees must be able to easily search and locate content needed for the completion of training exercises and for their overall development (Romiszowski, 1997, p. 32).

The education and training community, like the broader community of Web users, is beginning to expect such capability. For example, it is becoming common on home pages and in distance learning environments to see a "Library" listed as a link or on a toolbar. What is found in these libraries will often fall short of the designation, but their presence indicates an obvious need and expectation: If education and training are to be online rather than in person, there must be an online library, too.

Digital Library Technologies

Emerging technologies for marking up documents, for attaching metadata to documents, and for building universal tool suites are extremely important for the future of distance education and virtual training. It is these technologies that will enable the Web to become a true platform-independent, distributed digital library that will serve the millions of students and trainees who are online. In particular, it is extremely important that common, open standards be adhered to when creating documents and tools.

The state of mark-up technologies is promising but dynamic. It is generally agreed that we are on the cusp of an entirely new scheme for marking up documents for posting on the Web, but that we do not know which scheme will win the day and become widely adopted and supported. Nonetheless, emerging and evolving standards are gaining momentum and deserve close attention by anyone planning to enter the distance learning and virtual training arena. It is particularly important that those who plan to create digital library-type sites monitor these technologies closely.

Metadata standards are important and in flux. These standards will enable allow future search engines to better pinpoint needed content. For example, EduCom's Instructional Management System is a possible metadata scheme for tagging any kind of educational "object," such as a tutorial or module, with descriptive categories as well ownership and copyright information. It would enable students and trainees, for example, to locate courses they wish to take, modules they need to use, articles they need to read, videos they need to view, and even enable course registration. Other prominent metadata standards under development include the Dublin Core project, an effort that intends to bring global interoperability and transparent resource discovery to the Web. Adherence to emerging metadata standards would truly enable a worldwide digital library.

In such a library, each "object" contributed would be directly searchable and accessible from any browser. Even "parts" of an object could be searchable to allow pinpoint linking to needed content. For example, where previously we would have to go to a library, then a book-stack, a shelf, a source, and finally to a particular page in the source, we will be able to locate any point in a resource on demand, whether the source is text, audio, video, or spatial data. Indeed, the entire library becomes a hypertext, so trainers and trainees can select relevant portions from a variety of sources into custom hypertexts. Libraries will become more like flexible databases rather than collections of separate resources. Resources will be easily be pieced together to meet particular instructional needs. Students and trainees will easily draw together disparate materials to create a paper or project. Such flexibility and modularity is another benefit of a true digital library, and underscores the need to follow common standards for metadata and mark-up.

Digital libraries can also offer tool suites to work the knowledge they house. Here, too, this projection assumes that standards can be negotiated; in this case, standards for the creation and support of tools. Will the language used to create the tools be Java or some other alternative? Many labs that create tools and many users who need them no doubt wish that some standard be selected and supported by the browsers so that we can all get on with our business.

Assuming a "tool standard" is agreed upon, there are exciting things that lie ahead of us in providing a universal tool suite for the digital library. For example, tools will enable visualization of library holdings, greatly aiding search and navigation and addressing the problems of being "lost in cyberspace" and information overload. For example, some digital library projects are experimenting with online landscapes and concepts maps of holdings to support patron visualization of large, complex information holdings. Schatz (1997) calls such capability "information space flight."

Other tools will be available, allowing users to calculate, manipulate, and model based on digital library resources. One exciting area is Web-based GIS (Geographical Information System) tools, a powerful tool category previously restricted to use with proprietary software packages. Yet another class of tools can be classified as meta-cognitive tools, or "knoware." These tools range from routine mnemonic aids to sophisticated aids for critical and creative thinking and collaborative problem solving, all Web-based. Especially important are potential problem-solving environments that guide trainees through problem-solving steps with supporting library resources available.

Tool functionality can be provided to patrons through separate control panels or be embedded in texts and tutorials. The range of tools possible is unlimited. The potential for coupling tool suites with a true digital library is unlimited. There is also great potential for merging tool suites and digital library content with Web-based personal information systems.

Digital Libraries and Web-Based Training

Hundreds of billions of dollars are devoted to training. The scale of this investment indicates that technological challenges in providing digital libraries for Web-based training (WBT) can be met and advanced capabilities realized. The value of the digital training library for the bottom line is that uses and re-uses of training resources will be increased many-fold and that synergies of integration will add value as well. For example, Clark (1994) argues that one objective in the evaluation of distance learning is to assess the degree that existing instructional resources are integrated into a distance learning system. The upshot for WBT is that the more integration of existing training resources, the more efficient and powerful the system. A digital training library aims for precisely that: Optimal access to online resources for WBT. It is likely that the administrators will reward integrative approaches to building standardized online archives. Training programs can enjoy greatly heightened efficiency by exploiting re-uses of information and resulting economies of scale.

Interactive digital libraries support recent trends in WBT, such as an emphasis on active and collaborative learning. An especially strong example is the promise of online case studies and repositories of cases. Traditional case studies can be transformed into hypercases that are richly informed by related digital library resources.

Another instructional trend supported by a digital library approach is to ensure that what is learned in WBT is as similar as possible to the situation in which the training is applied, shortening transfer distance. A digital library approach makes available the same tutorials, case studies, and tools on the floor as in the classroom. Potentially, the same system could support both training and work, representing a convergence of WBT systems with EPSS, as anticipated by Romiszowski (1997). In a related vein, the same WBT system can also support both formal and informal training. Training resources in the digital library can be used in formal training, but also at home, allowing trainees to review and practice or to develop new knowledge and skills.

Digital libraries are one key component of the knowledge bases being designed by many organizations. Arguably, the methods used to create digital libraries should be applied across the knowledge base. For example, one goal of the knowledge base is to capture and make accessible informal documents that contain organizational knowledge. A digital library can encompass these more transitory sources of information, although a library traditionally houses formal publications. There is much promise and value in treating selected informal sources of information in the same way that formal sources are treated. After informal sources are mined from workflow environments, they can be made as accessible, standardized, and searchable as formal documents.

Another consideration for the designers of digital libraries for WBT is the accessibility of resources *outside* the organization. This step is controversial. Why should proprietary training resources be made publicly available? Aren't resources too specific to be of general interest? It is argued that when resources *are* of general value, they should be shared with the worldwide community of trainers and trainees. The Web allows us to collaborate on a distributed digital training library, freely available to all. Such an approach follows in the tradition that grew the Internet, a tradition many fear is being lost as the Internet becomes commercialized. A key incentive is that one's own organization will have the advantage of drawing on outside resources.

Conclusion

Ordinary problems add credence to the view that digital libraries should be built to support WBT. As the Web continues to scale in size, such problems will only get worse; at the same time, many more users will be online, expecting a digital library at their fingertips. The viewpoint of this chapter is that online resources for WBT should built as a library—a true digital library—to ensure that available resources are complete, highly searchable, and richly formatted. In the short history of the Web, Webmasters have been programmers; now they will also become librarians.

References

Clark, R. (1994). Evaluation of distance learning programs. In E. L. Baker & H. F. O'Neil (Eds.), *Technology assessment in education and training* (pp. 63–79). Hillsdale, NJ: Lawrence Erlbaum Associates.

Romiszowski, A. J. (1997). Web-based distance learning and teaching: Revolutionary invention or reaction to necessity? In B. H. Khan (Ed.), *Web-based instruction* (pp. 25–40). Englewood Cliffs: Educational Technology Publications.

Schatz, B. R. (1997). Information retrieval in digital libraries: Bringing search to the Net. *Science, 275,* 327–334.

The Author

John Schmitz (e-mail: jschmitz@uiuc.edu; Web homepage: web.aces.uiuc.edu/aim/john) is Director of the Advanced Instructional Media Lab and Assistant Professor in the Department of Human Resource Education, University of Illinois at Urbana-Champaign.

44

Positioning for Effectiveness: Applying Marketing Concepts to Web-Based Training

Nancy M. Levenburg

Introduction

As providers of education and training look to the future, most face challenging prospects. New competitors have emerged as telecommunications and distance education technology have torn down traditional boundaries, resulting in new spheres of influence. New competitors have emerged as private firms and professional organizations have created their own training and certification programs, and have thereby served learning needs that were previously provided in-house or by colleges and universities. Many organizations as well have entered into strategic alliances with colleges and universities, thereby creating new sponsoring organizations that are making available a wider array of learning/training opportunities than ever before. In short, new players and new telecommunications and distance learning technologies have resulted in a complex and rapidly changing environment for providers of Web-based training. As a result, how can Web-based training be used by business, industry, government, military, hospitals, law enforcement, and other organizations (profit and not-for-profit) to position their offerings most effectively to attract and retain a "critical mass" of learners?

The critical issue to be addressed in determining a business-level strategy is how the Web-based training-provider organization should compete within its industry to achieve a sustainable competitive advantage. Literature on competitive strategy (Day, 1984; Lele, 1992; Porter, 1980, 1985; Treacy & Wiersma, 1995) provide many useful insights. Porter's works (1980, 1985) articulated that a business unit must distinguish itself from its competitors in order to attain a unique position relative to its competitors in the industry. Essentially, Porter felt that this could be achieved along one of two broad dimensions: either attempting to be the low-cost producer for a given target market, or through differentiating itself from other competitors through market offerings (product/service combinations, promotional and pricing programs, etc.). More recently, the work of Treacy and Wiersma (1995) expands the bases, or disciplines, for achieving competitive advantage to operational excellence, product leadership, and customer intimacy. *Operationally excellent organizations* are those that strive to deliver good value to the customer with popular-quality products and low prices. *Product leader organizations* achieve distinction through innovation, providing cutting-edge products to the market year after year. Organizations achieving unique market positioning through *customer intimacy* maintain intimate relationships with their customers; they do not serve "markets" per se, but rather focus on the individual customers comprising them.

Literature from the field of marketing (Cravens, 1994; Jain, 1993; Perreault & McCarthy, 1996; Slater & Narver, 1994; Slywotzky & Shapiro, 1993) also provides many useful insights. The marketing discipline delves into concepts relating to how the market should be divided into customer—or learner—segments, which segments to target, what products and service enhancements to offer and where, how to promote those products and services, and what prices to charge. Market segmentation and market targeting are of critical importance, since the question of how to best position Web-based training alternatives cannot be adequately determined until market segments have been identified, described, evaluated for their attractiveness, and matched against business strengths.

As such, insights from strategic planning and competitive strategy, and marketing, can be applied to evaluating Web-based training opportunities in order to suggest alternative ways for viewing market opportunities, and to help organizations assess their internal capabilities, as well as those of their competitors, and possible bases for determining which avenues to pursue. Most important, it outlines specific implications that can furnish providers with the leverage to be more effective in designing, developing, and delivering Web-based training programs.

Understanding Marketing Opportunities

Market segments in Web-based training can be defined in a number of ways, and they are constantly evolving, creating new marketing opportunities. The goal in market segmentation is to uncover breakthrough opportunities—opportunities that help innovative organizations create sustainable competitive advantages. Breakthrough opportunities emerge only when providers deeply understand target markets.

Four descriptors may be used to define a market (Perreault & McCarthy, 1996): product type (type of good and type of service); customer (user) needs; customer types; and geographic area. Once identified, markets can be segmented into groups possessing similar needs and seeking similar ways of satisfying those needs—for example, whether the offering is targeted towards computer users or non-computer users.

In assessing internal capabilities, the various publics served by an organization will have an important impact on its mission and values. To be most meaningful, missions should be based on a thorough analysis of all stakeholders, or publics served, as well as available resources, including internal capabilities, technology, culture, and the ability to interact with the external environment. Additionally, Web-based training programs should clearly articulate their training/educational mission, since the way the mission is defined can profoundly affect program design, as well as resource allocation, decisions.

Following the above assessment, some institutions leverage for effectiveness through operational excellence. The institution pursuing a product leadership position strives to place the best possible products or services on the market. As such, it requires an internal spirit of constant innovation and creativity, and a continual quest to be the best—especially if that means bettering its own creations. The product leader organizational structure is more loosely-knit than that of the operationally excellent firm, and is composed of imaginative risk-takers. The product leader firm is results-driven; experimentation is encouraged and successes are rewarded.

The customer-intimate organization seeks to establish long-term relationships with its clientele; this means that it seeks to provide satisfaction, or exceed the customer's expectations, with each and every transaction. Customer-intimate firms are willing to customize their product and service offerings to meet their customers' needs, since they place a strong value on retaining the customer for the long-term. Employee empowerment characterizes customer-intimate organizations, since front-line employees often play a crucial role in problem-solving with customers. Above all else, a premium is placed on creating deep and lasting relationships with clients through using the organization's expertise to design "custom solutions" to customer's problems. As a by-product, customer-intimate organizations typically charge more for their products.

Leveraging for Effectiveness

Four possibilities exist for positioning Web-based training programs: market penetration, market development, product development, and diversification.

Market penetration means that an organization is attempting to increase sales of current products (or programs) in current markets. Applied to Web-based training, a market penetration strategy might involve the training provider, through its distance education offerings, concentrating on: (1) attempting to increase the number of training sessions delivered to current learners over a given time period; (2) trying to attract learners from competing organizations; or (3) trying to re-attract former learners. In fact, distance education, since it makes programs available in more locations, is ideally suited for market penetration strategies, since it may enable learners to conveniently partake of more training sessions.

Market development strategies involve courting new learners for current programs. Again, Web-based training programs may allow the organization to expand into new or more remote geographic areas, since it provides service to areas with relatively small populations of learners economically (geographical expansion). Too, Web-based training options provide people who, for geographic or temporal reasons, were previously unable to participate in an organization's offerings, the opportunity to do so now. In a similar vein, a market development strategy might also suggest finding new applications for current programs; for example, translating Web-based training programs into other languages to provide wider global reach.

Product development strategies involve presenting new or improved products (or programs) to current learners. With this strategy, Web-based training offerings might be "improved" to incorporate new technological features in order to better satisfy students. Similarly, thoughtful and carefully constructed trainer development programs which are designed to hone trainers' core Web-based training competencies (e.g., planning and organizing; session/program delivery; assessment/evaluation of learner achievement; training session/program assessment, and continuous improvement) might also enhance current training environments.

Diversification strategies are the riskiest of all, since the organization would pursue both new programs and new learners simultaneously, moving into totally different lines of business (Perreault & McCarthy, 1996). Since diversification strategies involve moving away from familiar programs and learner groups, such an option may appear both immensely attractive and immensely risky.

Whichever types of opportunities the training provider chooses to pursue, next steps include determining what objectives might be attainable, given both the risks and returns present in the market, and what internal resources, or competencies, would be required to fully exploit identified opportunities.

Conclusion

Attractive market opportunities exist nearly anywhere the potential for new programs or new markets exists. The essential question providers of corporate training need to address is which opportunity is the most viable, with respect to not only fit with the mission and goals of the organization, but also the organization's internal capabilities. Strategies must be carefully deliberated, considering the array of factors described above, and how they can be used to achieve sustainable competitive advantage. This requires both an intimate knowledge of the markets—or learner segments—and their characteristics and an in-depth understanding of competitors and their program offerings/markets served. Web-based training options, in short, provide organizations with innovative and creative avenues to achieve institutional goals. How these options may be employed, however, and the resulting effectiveness will vary depending on the business strategies that are selected.

References

Cravens, D. W. (1994). *Strategic marketing*. Homewood, IL: Richard D. Irwin.

Day, G. S. (1984). *Strategic market planning: The pursuit of competitive advantage*. St. Paul, MN: West Publishing Co.

Jain, S. C. (1993). *Marketing planning & strategy*. Cincinnati: South-Western Publishing Co.

Lele, M. M. (1992). *Creating strategic leverage: Matching company strengths with market opportunities*. New York: John Wiley & Sons.

Perreault, Jr., W. D., & McCarthy, E. J. (1996). *Basic marketing: A global-managerial approach*. Chicago: Times Mirror Higher Education Group.

Porter, M. E. (1980). *Competitive strategy*. New York: Free Press.

Porter, M. E. (1985). *Competitive advantage: Creating and sustaining superior performance*. New York: Free Press.

Slater, S.F., & Narver, J. C. (1994). Does competitive environment moderate the market orientation-performance relationship? *Journal of Marketing, 58,* 46–55.

Slywotzky, A. J., & Shapiro, B. P. (1993, Sept.–Oct.). Leveraging to beat the odds: The new marketing mind-set. *Harvard Business Review,* 97–107.

Treacy, M., & Wiersma, F. (1995). *The discipline of market leaders*. Reading, MA: Addison-Wesley Publishing Co.

The Author

Nancy M. Levenburg (e-mail: levenbun@gvsu.edu; Web homepage: www.4.gvsu.edu/levenbun/) is Visiting Professor of Marketing, Seidman School of Business, at Grand Valley State University, Grand Rapids, Michigan. (This chapter is based on an article published in the *Michigan Community College Journal,* Volume 3, Number 2.)

45

Benchmarking Educational Technology for Military Planners

R . T h o m a s G o o d d e n

Introduction

In the Summer of 1998, the Chairman of the Joint Chiefs of Staff asked for a review of Joint Professional Military Education (JPME) in terms of insuring that the system will adequately support the needs of U.S. forces in the year 2010. A team composed of educators from each of the Armed Services (Army, Navy, Air Force, and Marines) was established to benchmark current leading-edge educational technology policies and practices in academia, business, and government outside of the Department of Defense (DoD). "Benchmarking" is used here to mean fixing in the time domain the relative use of a range of educational technologies in a sample of institutions of higher (or specialized) learning. Besides benchmarking current practice, the "EdTech" Team was asked to identify potential trends. Over a short period, the Team interviewed over 40 practitioners in various places in the U.S., using telephone conferences, the Internet, and direct contact. The final report on which this chapter is based presents the Team's findings.

The reason for the Chairman's request for a review stemmed from the fact that the year 2010 has become the focus of DoD military planning. Doctrine, procedures, and acquisition of military hardware are being driven by a vision of the potential military environment in the year 2010. It is an environment of broad, global military commitments in support of the United Nations, precision operations designed to apply military force where necessary without collateral damage to civilian non-combatants, with a compression of time due largely to the high mobility most adversary targets will likely possess. In this environment, education and training of military personnel will need to be just-in-time, unit-based, and of uniformly high quality. The traditional school-house approach used today will not suffice in the highly complex, time-compressed world of 2010.

What the Team found could, in general terms, be likened to the stories of the Oklahoma land-rush at the close of the last century. Like the old land-rush, the global introduction of the Internet in 1993 spawned a "shotgun start" on a wide front to secure a place in a new territory before the opportunity was gone. The new territory is the cyber-classroom, a virtual location for learning to which potentially anyone in the world has immediate and simultaneous access. The rush to harness a broad menu of proven and promising technologies for the new cyber-classroom is today closing the book on the limitations of traditional classroom education and training as surely as the final land rushes of a bygone era closed a frontier. This report will have value if readers use it to reach out to the innovators and partner in ways to perfect invention and regularize discovery. For those who are looking for a comprehensive catalogue of conveniently documented templates for easy application, the Team found that such a catalogue, if even possible with a lot more time, would be obsolete before printing. Educational technology is moving too fast for handbooks.

Before delving into the particulars of the study, it may be useful to define a few terms. *Distance Learning* was defined for our study as learning which takes place when the instructor and the students are in different places, beyond touch and sight, during the instructional period. Distance learning is a general term which includes correspondence courses, telephone or other audio instruction, CD-ROMs, video tapes, and synchronous video-teleconferencing. *Distributed Learning,* as defined for our study, is a newer term for network or Web-based learning which not only takes place between teachers and remote students, but is multimedia, asynchronous, "anytime and anywhere" instruction.

In 1993, staffers at the University Continuing Education Association (UCEA) found that there were 40 institutions offering distributed learning via electronic means, largely synchronous television. The Stanford (University) Instructional Television Network (SITN), which began in 1969, is an outstanding example. As a former Program Manager at GTE in 1973, I approved several requests for engineers on my projects to finish degree programs via SITN. Staffers reported that the program has graduated thousands of engineers in its distinguished tenure. By 1996, UCEA staffers told us, there were over 700 such programs, many now using the Web, as opposed to cable TV. There was not time to benchmark or even conduct a rigorous sample of all of these programs for this study effort. What was possible in 45 days was to reach out to a number of proven programs, those with successful graduates, in order to document policies, procedures, and issues relevant to the DoD. Those fact-based impressions were the basis and the value of the final EdTech report.

The EdTech Report

The Team found great breadth and depth to the innovations in educational technology that could be relevant to defense needs in the year 2010. By way of continuing with the SITN example just raised, today's electrical engineering program at Stanford has an Internet option. Not only are classes carried asynchronously, but also library resources are offered to facilitate research from the terminal. Databases are established to aid students in answering questions. Enrollments, course selection, book buying, lab experiments, testing, and grade reporting are available at the Website.

Elsewhere, at George Washington University, Dr. Badrul Khan assembles Web-based research aids to assist students in learning how to efficiently use the Web to do research. At MIT, Dr. Georgiana Davenport conveys multi-disciplinary topics in a computer-based matrix of the life of a giant in American science and education, Jerome Weisner. These and many more examples were recounted in the chapters of the EdTech report.

The format of the report was a series of chapters, authored by members of the Team, to focus attention on major themes found in our observations of over 30 programs. The chapter presentations were backed up by unpublished raw notes and data reports from interviews made in person, by telephone, and via e-mail with people actually managing distributed learning programs in academia, industry, and government. Interviews were built based on a set of assumptions the Team compiled in the first days of its existence. It was a significant finding of this research that the assumptions have been validated by those the Team interviewed. It may be useful to review them here.

The study assumptions were: Technology will support our requirements, the cost of distributed learning technologies will decline over time, object-oriented standards for reuse of modules will evolve, open (platform independent) architectures will become the rule, the focus will be toward learning (not education versus training), learning will become an accepted part of the duty (business) day, and learning will move from the classroom to the unit (home/job) environment. These assumptions allowed the Team to concentrate on benchmarking. Nevertheless, implicit in these assumptions are societal changes in work ethic and environment which must be made to realize the full potential of distributed learning.

From the study assumptions, a list of interview questions was devised for the purpose of insuring uniformity in data gathering. While not every question was wholly relevant to every interview, the Team was able to use the questionnaire as a point of departure for developing and exploring cogent themes. Notes from the interviews were used by the Team to construct interview reports from which it based its chapters.

The sample size of distributed learning programs was very small in proportion to the number of programs in being, largely due to the compressed timeframe of this study and funds available for research. The sample size was not judged to be representative of the total population of distributed learning programs because it was developed "on the fly," using Delphic methods of referrals. For both of these reasons, no attempt is made to statistically quantify study results nor to suggest that it is truly representative of all that is ongoing in distributed learning. It is, as was suggested, a collection of anecdotal observations of what appears to be a rising tide. The value of the report is that it provides documentation of some things that are known to work and some that need further development.

In the seven chapters of the EdTech Report, Team members discuss themes that emerged from the benchmarking and trends effort. These themes proceeded from the goals of the study, the assumptions initially made, and directions provided by the data. Despite the lack of hard, quantifiable data in many areas, researchers were driven by the tangible success and the confidence expressed by distributed learning operators who were "betting the farm" on their programs.

MAJ Chris Sharp, USMC, an instructor with the Marine Corps University, Quantico, Virginia, led off with a discussion of requirements analysis as practiced by program operators. In his monograph, Chris discussed a range of programs from the well planned to the "on-the-fly." It was apparent that time and financial resources could be wasted by taking a "here is the technology solution, now find the problem" approach. He argued that educational program managers need to thoroughly study the needs of their students, the community they serve, their institution, and the resources available for carrying out a distributed learning program. Realistic cost estimates must be made for curriculum development. Full broadband, multimedia instruction can be wasteful if area telecommunications cannot support it. Few benefits are gained if the full curriculum cannot be developed to the same standards as the lead courses. Enrollment management and faculty development are as important as curriculum development and delivery.

Learner-centric focus and planning were addressed by Professor Tom Hazard, a retired U.S. Marine officer now employed at the Institute for Defense Education Analysis (IDEA) at the Naval Postgraduate School in Monterey, California. He looked at the challenge of matching the many technology products and procedures available to the needs of the student, the faculty, and the school system. Development of a full range of tools to reach the total population of learners was key to the successful programs studied. For example, a school system which serves both urban and rural areas may be able to push full multimedia net-based instruction to the urban dwellers, but the rural telecommunications infrastructure may require narrow bandwidth solutions, perhaps even audio-teleconferencing or paper-based correspondence systems. The University of Wisconsin has found this in building their program. There is no single solution that reaches all learners and all different learning styles. Overall, the range of experience between what works in similar circumstances and what does not appear to work well offers planners ample bounds within which to craft alternative strategies.

LTC Don Gelosh, PhD, USAF, of the National Defense University in Washington, DC, discussed the technology toolbox available to distributed learning planners. Drawing from a variety of sources found during the Team's research, he provided planners with topics, points of contact, and reasons to explore selected ideas further. He found that a balanced approach to curriculum building and delivery, as well as student management, faculty development, and learner support systems, produced the most successful programs. Faculty and learner support systems like Frequently Asked Question (FAQ) data bases with intelligent search engines were key to getting students timely answers while reducing faculty overload. Analysis programs that could track student involvement, span of attention, and preferences for colors, segues, types of avatars, and other devices contributed significantly to successful learning.

Next, LTC Fred Vornbrock, USAF, of the Air University at Montgomery, Alabama, explored how distributed learning managers are evaluating their programs. Methods and tools that show great promise were discussed. LTC Vornbrock used his considerable experience at coordinating a large Air Force synchronous learning network to look at conventional and leading-edge ways to evaluate whether learning is taking place. Adaptive measures of performance were found to be crucial to successful distributed learning programs. The uniquely singular environment of the Web-based learner requires diligent observation and continuous evaluation to insure that interest and discipline remain strong through a long-term program. Measures capable of discerning lapses in interest or patterns of sloughing off are necessary to permit timely faculty intervention to determine and correct system failures or inadequacies. Learning systems must promote, but cannot always count on accurate and timely student feedback when things are going wrong for the learner.

Then, Mr. Ken Pisel, Chief, Distance Learning Division at the Armed Forces Staff College at Norfolk, Virginia, looked at the affective learning domains being touched by distributed learning today. Mindful of the crumbling distinctions between education and training, he focused on learning and looked at the important affective education in ethics, traditions, and mores, as well as motor skills, that takes place informally in a group and at an institution. Successful distributed learning programs have found ways to build "campus pride," pride and confidence in the program, and "cohort" bonding between learners who may never meet. Remote learners must have means to assimilate the culture and ethics of a profession like engineering or accounting even when there is no opportunity to join a professional fraternity or other campus organization to promote the values of a profession.

Next, this author looked at faculty issues that are so closely coupled with educational technology that they must be treated with it. Intellectual property rights, time demands on faculty, and incentives for distributed courseware development were viewed from the perspective of this former faculty member at the Army War College in Carlisle, Pennsylvania. The chapter examined some of the ways technology freed the faculty from burdens that have been roadblocks to establishing distributed learning programs in some institutions. Software systems to cope with the greatly accelerated interaction between a teacher and multiple students via e-mail were found to be key to keeping the faculty engaged and meeting student needs. The use of video archives was an attribute of most successful distributed learning programs. These programs placed high emphasis on the enduring worth of lectures by Nobel Prize winners and other leading practitioners, creating a rich institutional archive for succeeding generations. Some institutions have rewarded faculty entrepreneurs with personally held copyrights which generate revenue streams to fund additional work. Some tenure systems treat the development of a module of distributed learning as equivalent to publishing in a professional journal. The Hypermedia Teaching Facility at MIT and IDEA at the Naval Postgraduate School were both developed to teach, reinforce, and support faculty in the development of distributed learning courseware and programs.

Finally, Mr. John Shulson from the U.S. Army Transportation School at Fort Eustace, Virginia, closed the report with a look at some trends that can be discerned from the research conducted for this study. While only a few institutions, like the Western Governors University, are fully virtual, distributed learning, especially via the Internet, exists at most top-echelon schools. The trend toward distributed learning is growing. As distributed learning moves to the leading edge of mainstream education and training, faculty must become more than subject matter experts. They must also become experts in the process of bringing appropriate tools to bear on different learning styles and measures of performance. Competence-based testing is replacing standard end-of-course examinations in order to create for the student a more realistic and comprehensive simulation of the actual work environment. Management concerns with assuring the integrity of courseware delivery systems and testing are being met with promising new security systems to insure quality and surety.

Findings of the Study

The report serves to invest the reader with people to contact and places to go for assistance in determining requirements, specifying approaches, selecting tools and methods, and gaining both institutional resources and commitment. In the end, the Team demonstrated convincingly to DoD planners that theirs is not a unique system, nor challenged by unusual circumstances, but amenable to proven and cutting-edge educational technology. The findings and conclusions that the Team drew from its research data illustrate the point.

The first significant study finding was that study assumptions appear valid, at least from this sample. While no one has perfected forecasting the environment in the year 2010, it appears that our assumptions fit well with those developed outside the study via independent means. Technology declines in cost as others like rent, travel, and wages increase. Time compresses for all. Student pressure to deliver education to a time and place convenient to lifestyles was a common demand seen by civilian educators.

The second significant study finding was that issues thought to be unique to the DoD system are in fact common to a variety of other educators. Costs must be weighed against benefits. Quality must be maintained. Progress appears to be a way of life among those interviewed because they are all in commercially competitive environments that assign the complacent to anachronistic obsolescence. Concepts such as socialization, mores, and traditions of professional service, cohort building, professional network building, and competence testing are common to most education programs, especially at the graduate level. Fears of failure to maintain standards by shifting in whole or part to asynchronous, remote instruction appear ill-founded.

The third significant study finding was that educational technology can probably support any direction that DoD or other education and training managers want to go. Technology is often said to be neutral to development. When co-evolved with organization and policy, technology is not seen to be neutral; it is a multiplier of progress. It was reassuring to the Team to find that industry, academia, and some places in government have successfully brought together a variety of resources to achieve excellence and efficiency.

It was exciting to see the possibilities for future enhancements to learning being crafted at places like the Sarnoff Labs, Northwestern University, and Universal Studios. More than virtual environments, three-dimensional perspectives like that from Sarnoff seem ready made for giving students a macro view of problem solving, competence testing, or incidental learning. Co-evolution of these technologies with organization and policy will multiply their value.

Related to the co-evolution going on in the civilian world is what may be considered an unintended consequence of this study. An entrepreneurial spirit permeated the people and places the Team interviewed. There was general surprise that the DoD system is so late in harnessing the possibilities of distributed learning.

By formally asking for comparisons, DoD has now informally opened its mainline education and training process to external comment. The Team is confident from the responses we've gotten that the study has awakened outside of DoD a view that there is profit to be made by exporting success and experience to so large an education system. Renovating DoD education and training may not much longer be solely an internal initiative; it may come from concerted external pressure in the form of a mandate.

It was significant that all experienced course operators found higher drop-out rates for distributed learners. It takes a special discipline to carry through a distributed learning program of study. DoD has seen this for years in its numerous correspondence programs. Civilian education in America has always been defined by its numerous "second chances" for the casual student to "get serious." It is apparent that some graduate schools are using the superior discipline necessary to complete distributed learning to cull the "apt but unmotivated."

It was also significant for trends analysis that IBM, Arthur Andersen, Lotus, and other major software vendors indicate on their Web pages that they are opening distributed learning business areas.

The final significant study finding was that the DoD system today lags behind comparable education programs in academia, industry, and government for the provision of satisfactory education and training. By "satisfactory," it is meant that fully accredited education, even at the graduate level, and fully certifiable training, even at the technical level, is being carried out in a wide variety of places and programs. The civilian education and training community has embraced distributed learning in its most modern Web-based forms and is successfully using it to a degree not now contemplated in the DoD system. It is apparent that there are efficiencies and savings from distributed learning that have been proven to be possible elsewhere without sacrificing quality.

As a result of the report, DoD is revamping its Joint Professional Military Education program to move more instruction to the Internet. Additionally, we have provided Congress with a Strategic Plan for Advanced Distributed Learning. It shows major reinvestments by the Services into distributed learning.

The Author

R. Thomas Goodden (e-mail: goodden@worldnet.att.net; Web homepage: adlnet.org) is Director of Institutional Learning, Office of the Undersecretary of Defense for Personnel and Readiness, Washington, DC.

46

Designing Web-Based Learning Environments at the Department of Defense: New Solutions

Sharon G. Fisher and

Will S. Peratino

Introduction

A Web-based learning environment opens many new doors to instructional designers. At the same time, instructional designers must expand their design considerations to harness the power of a Web-based learning environment. This chapter presents the authors' experience in designing and implementing a Web-based learning environment at the U.S. Department of Defense's Defense Acquisition University (DAU).

DAU provides education and training to more than 400,000 DoD employees worldwide. Increasing work demands coupled with decreasing staff resources and travel funds led DAU to explore the use of Web-based training as an alternative to classroom delivery. For the majority of the University's 70 courses, Web-based training is becoming the preferred mode of training delivery. Web delivery allows DAU to rapidly update content due to changes in policies while offering a collaborative learning environment for students and faculty at different locations. In addition, a database has been created to automate routine tasks so that faculty members can spend their time providing individualized instruction at a distance. Creating this learning environment required the design team to overcome both technical and instructional design challenges. This chapter summarizes lessons learned from this effort beginning with a brief look at the technical approach.

The Technical Environment

The first challenge was to create a highly interactive environment within limited bandwidth and across various platforms/browsers. The technical solution was to use an environment that included HTML pages, Middleware script, Authorware lessons, and an Oracle database. Table 1 summarizes the functions accomplished by each component.

Table 1. DAU Learning environment: Technical components.

Technical Component	Description
HTML Pages	*HTML pages are used to:* • Create the homepage environment. • Provide a graphical interface for registering. • Present long-term performance support tools/links. • Introduce and summarize each Authorware lesson. • Link to asynchronous and synchronous discussion forums with students and faculty members. • Post new or changing information.
Middleware Script	*Middleware script is used to:* • Transfer information to and from the Authorware lessons to the database (e.g., the student's name appears in the lesson, lessons resume where the student left off, and performance data are collected). • Randomly generate test items from pools and record test scores into the database. • Send automatic e-mail messages from faculty members to students that are generated based on certain events (e.g., registration, completion of a lesson, time remaining before the course deadline, etc.).
Authorware Lessons	*Authorware lessons are used to:* • Deliver the main content. • Provide a simulated task environment that would be difficult to do using other Web-based technologies given the bandwidth limitations.
Oracle Database	*The Oracle database is used to:* • Store student profile information. • Collect lesson and test performance data. • Generate more than 20 standardized reports. • Create custom reports.

When accessing the lessons for the first time, the student proceeds through an automated installation process. This process helps the student install the Authorware plug-in and a graphics library. This common library allows for the use of graphically rich lessons to be displayed using low bandwidth connections. A de-install function allows the students to erase the graphics library after course completion.

When the student selects "begin the lesson," the Shockwave-processed Authorware lesson begins to download. At the same time, the database provides information about the student's status. This feature returns the student to the last screen accessed and ensures credit for past performance on exercises.

Figure 1 shows screen captures that represent the different technical components used in the DAU learning environment.

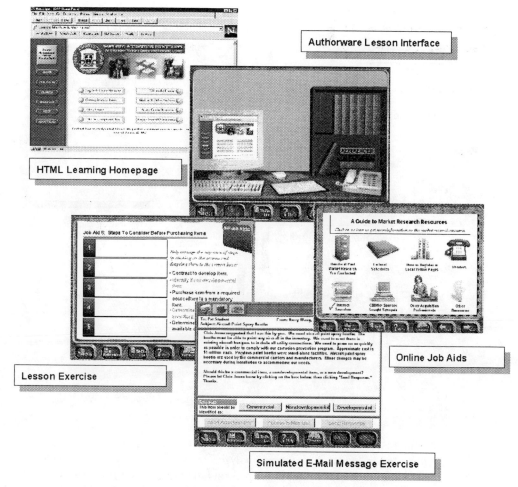

Figure 1. DAU learning environment sample screens.

Instructional Design Factors

In today's environment of rapid change, there is a need for instructional system design (ISD) processes that are quick and efficient while still maintaining effectiveness of traditional ISD approaches. In the commercial arena, software developers have turned to rapid prototyping models to balance the challenges of maintaining high quality while decreasing cycle time. According to Tripp and Bichelmeyer (1990), rapid prototyping is a viable model for instructional design, especially computer-based forms of instruction. DAU is developing courses using a rapid prototype approach to course development.

In addition to working in a rapid prototype environment, designers have learned to expand their focus to consider both student and faculty requirements. Most designers focused their attention on what the student needs to learn and how best to teach these new knowledge and skills. Often, faculty support needs are overlooked. Because DAU was creating a total learn-

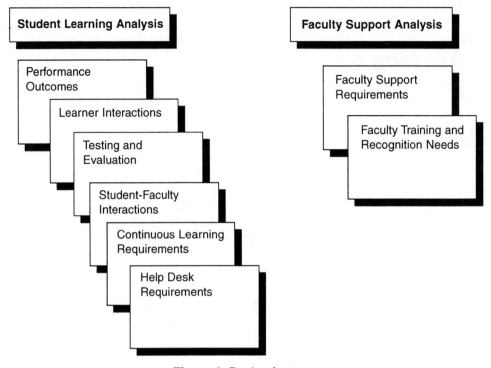

Figure 2. Design factors.

ing environment, the team felt it was equally important to focus attention on the faculty support needs. As illustrated in Figure 2, the team analyzed both student and faculty needs:

Table 2, beginning on the following page, presents the types of student learning analysis questions that designers considered and the lessons learned in creating the DAU Web-based learning environment.

Studies of distance education programs report that instructors more readily adapt to technology-based instruction if effective training and support are provided. (See Dillion & Walsh, 1992; Gehlauf, Shatz, & Frye, 1991; Schaeffer, Kipper, Farr, & Muscarella, 1990.) Table 3 presents the types of faculty support analysis questions that designers considered and the lessons learned in creating the DAU Web-based learning environment.

Conclusion

The key to a successful Web-based learning environment is a comprehensive design that considers technical, instructional, and faculty support requirements. All three elements are critical and interact with one another. For example, instructional outcomes may dictate the type of faculty interaction desired. However, the organizational and technical environments must be able to support that desired level of faculty interaction. Integrating the technical and faculty support aspects into Web-based course design requires that instructional designers become creative problem solvers who can work in a team environment to help find new solutions (see Moore & Kearsley, 1996.)

Table 2. Student learning design considerations.

Consideration: Performance Outcomes	
Analysis Questions	**Lessons Learned**
• What are the primary tasks to be trained? • What are the characteristics (i.e., procedural, cognitive) of the desired task performance? • What are the current and desired performance levels?	• *Have Task Performance Drive Technical Aspects:* The DAU Web-based learning environment is designed to support both procedural training and more complex cognitive training related to decision making and problem solving. Simple HTML-based lessons are used when presenting basic procedural information. In other courses, students must be able to practice responding to complex cognitive stimuli encountered on the job. For these courses, Authorware lessons, video teletraining, Webconferencing, or other methods are combined with the HTML environment to address these more complex learning outcomes. One size does not fit all!

Consideration: Learner Interactions	
Analysis Questions	**Lessons Learned**
• Do the target students have strong learning style preferences? • How diverse are the target students? • What types of collaborative learning are desired? • How motivated are the students?	• *Layer Information:* DAU students have diverse backgrounds and prior training experiences. Therefore, it is essential to allow students access to layered or "pop-up information" for additional explanations of terms and concepts. By layering information, students who knew the information could bypass it. • *Maximize Student Control:* Students are given learner control for the majority of the pathways through the lessons. A recommended sequence is provided, but students are allowed to select their own pathways after completing the first lesson. • *Manage Web Surfing:* In conducting trials, the team discovered that Web links within lessons needed to be managed carefully. Some students who were unfamiliar with the Web environment were unable to find their way back to the lesson. The design solution was to offer the student selected Web links after completing the core lesson materials. The Authorware lesson brings the student to a unique HTML lesson exit page. After completing the core learning, the student may surf the Web. • *Encourage Collaboration:* Both synchronous and asynchronous forums are offered to students. Because most students are taking courses while on the job, asynchronous communication modes are preferred. • *Motivate:* Motivation is addressed by creating simulated characters that reappear throughout the lessons, using appropriate humor, and by sending personalized e-mail messages from an assigned faculty member when milestones are reached.

Table 2. Student learning design considerations (*continued*).

Consideration: Test and Evaluation Requirements	
Analysis Questions	**Lessons Learned**
• What types of testing will be administered? • What types of test security will be required? • What if students fail to demonstrate mastery? • Will follow-up data be collected?	• *Address Test Security Issues:* DAU students are required to complete courses as part of job certification requirements. Therefore, testing is critical. At the present time, DAU is addressing test security using the following strategies: — Random generation of test items from item pools so that students get unique combinations of test items. — Random placement of distractors within test items. — E-mail notification to the student's supervisor informing him or her when a test is being administered to the student and requesting oversight. — Comparison of performance within lesson quizzes to final test performance. — Inclusion of items that are difficult enough to be valid if the student uses references. (Assume all tests are open book.) — Password protection of the subWeb where the test is located. • *View Testing as a Learning Activity:* At the present time, DAU students are allowed three trials on each test. If a student fails to demonstrate mastery, the student is told to contact his or her assigned faculty member. The faculty member also receives a notice that the student has failed to reach mastery. The faculty member reviews the questions missed on each trial. Based on this item analysis, the faculty member develops an individualized plan for helping the student to improve his or her performance. When the faculty member is satisfied that the student is ready for a retest, he or she allows access to the test Web. • *Plan Follow-Up Evaluation Activities Early:* DAU plans to use the profile information collected in the database to do follow-up evaluations. The profile information includes e-mail addresses for the individual's supervisor. Follow-up surveys will be sent automatically to the student and to his or her supervisor after a set time period from course completion. Completed surveys will be returned and tracked using the database. The key is to identify all the different uses of the student profile and database when designing the system.

Table 2. Student learning design considerations *(continued)*.

Consideration: Test and Evaluation Requirements *(continued)*	
Analysis Questions	**Lessons Learned**
• What types of interaction are required between students and faculty? • What is the anticipated faculty-to-student ratio? • Will students be assigned to faculty in cohorts?	• *Assign an Individual Faculty:* Each DAU student is assigned to a faculty member. After registering for the course, the student receives an e-mail message with a greeting from the assigned faculty member. Subsequent communications with faculty are based on the course being presented and the student's needs. The environment provides for: — Synchronous and asynchronous private conferences between faculty and students. — Customized and automatic e-mail messages. — Instant feedback button present on most screens. — Teleconferences and netconferencing. • *Decide Between Cohorts and Rolling Admissions:* The DAU environment allows designers to set up courses in cohorts (all students within a section that start at the same time) or rolling enrollment (students are enrolled in a section as long as the faculty has an opening). Cohorts are used when it is critical to keep students progressing through lessons at the same pace. For example, cohorts are used when Web-based training is combined with video teletraining. Using a cohort approach ensures that all students will be ready for the scheduled video teletraining broadcast. Rolling admissions are used when quick access to course materials is more important than keeping students moving at an assigned pace. • *Set Faculty-to-Student Ratios Based on Course Design:* The first step is to identify the critical types of faculty interactions to be offered and then to determine the demands those interactions will place on the assigned faculty. For example, if you set a standard requiring a 24-hour response to student inquiries, then you need to anticipate faculty resources required to meet this standard. DAU estimates the faculty-to-student ratio during the course design. During the operational trial of a course, the ratio may be adjusted based on the actual demands on faculty time. If an instructor needs additional support, a second instructor and section can be established. DAU found it was critical to designate backup instructors so that assigned instructors can take a day off without impacting the progress of the course.

Table 2. Student learning design considerations (*continued*).

Consideration: Continuous Learning Requirements	
Analysis Questions	**Lessons Learned**
• What types of new information may need to be posted? • What types of contact will there be with course graduates? • What performance support tools should be provided for use after graduation?	• *Allow Easy Posting and Broadcasting of Information:* Much of the content presented in DAU courses is based on DoD policies and Federal Acquisition Regulations. The Web-based learning environment must allow for rapid posting and distribution of new information. The DAU design solution is to incorporate an update section where faculty can post changing information. The second solution is to use the profile information in the database to broadcast information to both current and previous students who need the new information. • *Distinguish Public Areas from Student Only Areas:* DAU allows course graduates and DoD employees access to the portions of the Web-based learning environment that support job performance but do not require direct faculty support. These "public areas" include text-based lesson summaries, frequently asked questions, posting of new information, glossary, links, and other resources. Current students have complete access to all areas of the Web-based learning environment. The database is used to set these different permission levels.
Consideration: Helpdesk Requirements	
Analysis Questions	**Lessons Learned**
• What type of technical support will target students need? • What types of data will be collected?	• *Plan for Helpdesk Support:* During operational trials it became clear that a well-trained helpdesk was essential to help students address technical issues. The DAU environment must work on a variety of student platforms and communicate through hundreds of different servers. Operational trials showed that some network administrators had blocked the downloading of needed plugins or restricted packet sizes. Having a well-trained helpdesk was critical to address these issues and to help first-time Web users. • *Track Helpdesk Inquiries:* The second lesson learned was the importance of establishing a database to collect helpdesk questions. Capturing helpdesk questions allows designers to: — Fix any recurring technical problems. — Rewrite online help to address recurring problems. — Train helpdesk staff and faculty members in how to diagnose and address common technical problems encountered by students.

Table 3. Faculty support design considerations.

Consideration: Faculty Support Requirements	
Analysis Questions	**Lessons Learned**
• What faculty activities can be automated? • What type of collaboration is needed among faculty? • What types of data do faculty need to monitor students and assess course effectiveness?	• *Decrease Faculty Workload Through Automation:* Web-based learning can increase faculty workload. The DAU learning environment is designed to support faculty by automating tasks such as routine e-mail messages to students and reporting of student performance events (e.g., completing lessons, passing tests, failing to pass a test after a set number of trials, failing to meet established course deadlines, etc.).
• What role will faculty have in keeping the Web-based learning materials updated and dynamic?	• *Involve Faculty in Report Design:* Initially, DAU faculty members were provided with a menu option allowing access to more than 20 standardized reports. During the operational trial, feedback was collected from faculty members on reducing the numbers of reports and ensuring that the most pertinent data were being reported. • *Allow for Ad Hoc Reports:* The DAU system includes a series of pull-down menus that allow faculty to design custom reports. • *Create Templates for Site Updating:* Another lesson learned is the importance of using templates that allow faculty to keep the site current. The faculty's role in maintenance of the Website should be considered in the initial design process. If a Webmaster is required to make simple changes, faculty may be discouraged from updating the environment. Web-based learning environments should be dynamic and allow faculty to make easy updates. To that end, DAU is now developing databases that faculty can use to add, modify, or remove items that are displayed within each course Website.
Consideration: Faculty Training and Recognition Needs	
Analysis Questions	**Lessons Learned**
• What are the faculty's current competencies and experience in offering Web-based training? • What training do faculty need? • How should that training be delivered?	• *Provide Faculty Training:* DAU faculty members receive training sessions before instructing via the Web. The sessions introduce faculty members to: — The role of faculty member in the new environment. — The technical aspects of operating in the Web-based learning environment. — The techniques used for encouraging, monitoring, and reinforcing collaborative learning through synchronous and asynchronous communication tools. — The trends to look for when identifying students who may need additional assistance.

Table 3. Faculty support design considerations *(continued)*.

Consideration: Faculty Training and Recognition Needs *(continued)*	
Analysis Questions	**Lessons Learned**
• What type of change management is needed to gain organizational support for Web-based faculty members? • What type of recognition should be provided to faculty?	— The most effective ways for responding to inquiries. — The uses of other communication technologies to augment Web-based delivery. • *Use Web-Based Technology to Support Faculty:* After the initial training, new DAU faculty members receive continued support using Web-based technologies. • *Ensure Organizational Support:* Another important lesson learned is that Web-based faculty need to have the support of their organization and their co-workers. DAU learned that it is important to educate the entire organization to the role of the Web-based instructor. Faculty who spend their day on the Web may be perceived as contributing less than those who spend the day in front of a class. Education and change management must be considered as part of the design process. • *Recognize Faculty:* Finally, faculty members who embark on new ways of teaching should receive recognition for their willingness to embrace new technologies.

References

Dillion, C., & Walsh, S. (1992). Faculty: The neglected resource in distance education. *The American Journal of Distance Education, 6*(3), 5–21.

Gehlauf, D., Shatz, M., & Frye, T. (1991). Faculty perception of interactive instructional strategies: Implications for training. *The American Journal of Distance Education, 5*(3), 20–28.

Moore, M., & Kearsley, G. (1996). *Distance education: A systems view.* Belmont, CA: Wadsworth Publishing.

Schaeffer, J., Kipper, P., Farr, C., & Muscarella, D. (1990, Spring). Preparing faculty and designing courses for delivery via audio teleconferencing. *MPAEA Journal,* Spring, 11–18.

Tripp, S. D., & Bichelmeyer, B. (1990). Rapid prototyping: An alternative instructional design strategy. *Educational Technology Research and Development, 38*(1), 31–43.

The Authors

Sharon G. Fisher (e-mail: humtec@aol.com; Web homepage: humtech.com) is Vice President, Technology-Based Learning Systems, Human Technology, Inc. Will S. Peratino (e-mail: peratiws@acq.osd.mil; Web homepage: acq.osd.mil/dau) is Director of Distance Learning, Defense Acquisition University, U.S. Department of Defense.

47

Repurposing Instructor-Led Training into Web-Based Training: A Case Study and Lessons Learned

Kenneth G. Brown,
Karen R. Milner, J. Kevin Ford,
and Wendy Golden

Recent changes in the nature of work and workers challenge traditional training and development methods. Aging workers increase the number of retirements, and the need for replacements raises training demand. A shrinking pool of skilled workers further increases training demand because replacements are often under-trained and under-educated (Carnevale, 1995). In addition to rising demand, globalization of industry results in dispersed locations of workers (Adler, 1990). Because travel costs can consume major portions of a training budget (Hall, 1997), traditional classroom instruction may be an inefficient method to handle increased demand in today's global marketplace.

Computer-based training delivered via Internet and intranet technologies, or Web-based training (WBT), is a promising alternative to traditional classroom instruction. WBT has the potential to increase training access and throughput by providing a centralized program that can be used by anyone with a computer, Internet connection, and Web browser. Furthermore, after initial expenditures for the technology, Web-based training is likely to have lower maintenance costs than face-to-face, instructor-led training (Hall, 1997). Unfortunately, training via the Internet involves relatively new technology, and many practical questions have yet to be answered, including how to develop and administer WBT effectively. Many companies have an additional challenge—how to transition existing training content from the classroom to the Web.

Recent literature has focused on how to design hypertext learning environments (e.g., Kommers, Grabinger, & Dunlap, 1996) and how to use the Web to teach college and K–12 students (e.g., Brooks, 1997; Cotton, 1997). There is very little literature that specifically deals with how to transition or "repurpose" traditional classroom instruction for the Web. In addition, the focus of most computer-based design literature has been on designing for schoolchildren rather than adult learners (Bates, Holton, & Syler, 1996) and for textbook (verbal) rather than practical (skill-based) knowledge (e.g., Cotton, 1997). As a result, there is a considerable need for research on the challenges of creating workplace training in a Web-based format.

This chapter is a case study of a Web-based training (WBT) project that was completed by an outside vendor for a Fortune 500 company. The project involved the creation of stand-alone Web-based instruction from an existing instructor-led class. Observations of the development process and results of a computer laboratory pilot are presented. To summarize the data and draw implications for the design and development of WBT, the chapter ends with a discussion of lessons learned. Suggestions derived from these lessons come directly from this particular experience and from trainees' suggestions and recommendations. As a result, these suggestions are inductively-derived principles that can guide future design but may require future research.

Background

The course examined in this chapter provides instruction on the basic knowledge and skill necessary to perform a team-based, problem-solving process. The course had been taught for over two years as a three-day instructor-led course. At the request of the company, the course was repurposed into a Web-based format by an outside vendor. The course was selected for practical reasons alone; this problem-solving course is popular and always has a waiting list.

The vendor that completed the project is a growing company that has worked with a number of Fortune 500 firms to develop, implement, and support Web-based business solutions. The vendor assigned a lead instructional designer to manage the project and make design decisions. The vendor's project manager was responsible for communicating with the company's oversight team. Additional team members were added to the vendor team as necessary to assist with such tasks as designing graphics and text layout, creating Web pages, programming active server pages, developing an evaluation plan, and proofreading. Total number of active members varied from one to six at any given time.

Course Design and Development

The course was designed to be sequential in order to follow the subject matter, which teaches a step-by-step process. Each step in the process was organized into a module with an overview, text, and graphic presentations, with embedded questions and practice, a final case practice activity, knowledge quiz, and summary. Supplemental examples and exercises were provided to allow for some customization of the learning experience. To ensure that the practice activities, exercises, and quizzes were informative, feedback for each was developed.

To begin development of the course, the instructional designer attended the instructor-led course and obtained all materials used by the instructors. As development progressed, company and vendor design teams held a series of joint meetings to ensure that the content matched the instructor-led course, and that interface characteristics were acceptable. In addition, a preliminary pilot was run in which subject matter experts completed portions of the course.

Overall, the development process worked well. The vendor's lead designer was provided direct access to the company's subject matter experts. Experts were essential for determining the appropriateness of suggested content and presentation modifications and supplemental examples, activities, and feedback. An early pilot was also useful as a means to ground suggestions from the company's subject matter experts within the context of a specific interface. The project itself was too large and complex for a single individual to handle successfully, so team members with diverse skills were another essential component to project success.

There were some difficulties encountered during the development process. First, although the team initially envisioned simply repurposing the instructor-led course for the Web, a number of important instructional design decisions had to be made. These decisions included how to shorten and reorganize content, what exercises/activities to add in order to keep trainees active during long periods of reading, and what feedback to provide for existing and new exercises. Second, a couple of delays caused the design process to take longer than planned. Subject matter experts often took considerable amounts of time to review the new activities and the feedback messages, and this added to the original timeline. Also, after the preliminary pilot, content, and interface changes were suggested. Implementing the content changes required additional work by subject matter experts, and the interface changes required time-consuming modifications to computer programs that control the course.

Formative Evaluation Pilot Method

A second pilot was run with trainees taken from the waitlist of the instructor-led course. The purpose of the pilot was to bring trainees from the target audience to a controlled environment where they could be observed and questioned face-to-face about their experience. This information was targeted toward improving the course prior to its full release.

In groups ranging in size from eight to 15, a total of 80 trainees were brought into a corporate training laboratory. Trainees were given two days to complete the course, but the vast majority finished in a day and a half or less. One trainee did not complete the course in the allotted time and one trainee chose to withdraw from the pilot to attend to work-related responsibilities.

Trainees worked independently at networked PC stations. Trainees were told to pace themselves and take breaks as needed. Two of the authors served as facilitators, walking around the room answering interface questions and resolving technical problems. Trainees were told to ask content questions, so they could be recorded, but that facilitators were not subject matter experts and could only provide information already contained in the program.

The facilitators kept a log of all questions and problems encountered during the session. At the end of training, a series of open-ended questions were asked including: What was most useful to you about the program? What was least useful to you? How could the course be improved? If the choice was entirely yours, where would you choose to take the course—home, work, or a corporate training center? Is this course better or worse than instructor-led training? The data obtained from these two methods form the substance of the lessons learned and implications presented in this chapter. These methods were expected to be complementary in that both would provide formative evaluation information that could be used to improve the course.

Results

Results of the pilot evaluation indicated that trainees generally reacted very positively. Trainees noted that they liked the interface and felt the course was effective. Two forms of data were the focus of the formative evaluation: Questions/problems and question responses.

Question/Problem Log

The vendor organized the list of questions and problems according to the scope and difficulty of potential corrections. This helped the company to prioritize changes in the course. Changes that could be made without review or consultation were noted as "easy." Changes that would require review or testing were labeled "possible." Finally, changes that would require considerable resources were labeled "difficult."

Table 1 presents the categories developed and the two most common question/problems in each category. "Easy" and "possible" changes included suggestions related to content simplification (e.g., add summaries, shorten cases), feedback changes (e.g., improve explanations),

Table 1. Question/problem log selected solution categories.

Solution Type	Selected Questions (Q), Problems (P), and Proposed Solutions (S)

Easy	**Q:** "Can I get a completed worksheet on the example in module four?"
	P: Trainees seemed overwhelmed by the amount of information in the case.
	    S: *Add concise content summary for certain examples.*
	
	Q: "How come this answer does not go in this column?"
	P: Trainees appeared frustrated by the brevity of some feedback.
	    S: *Improve explanations contained in feedback.*

Possible	**Q:** "For this exercise, do I rate all three examples or only one?"
	P: Trainees appeared disoriented moving from example 1 to example 2.
	    S: *Improve directions, make next step more apparent.*
	
	Q: "This example is too long, it causes overload. Is all of it necessary?"
	P: A few trainees gave up on this exercise and moved on.
	    S: *Have experts review possibility of removing unnecessary information.*

Difficult	**Q:** "What happened? The computer is not responding!"
	P: Program freezes when trying to print to a network printer that is busy.
	    S: *Reprogram (difficult) or provide trouble-shooting guide.*
	
	Q: "I just got logged out. How do I get back to where I was?"
	P: A few trainees had some difficulty starting the programming and navigating.
	    S: *Reprogram (difficult) or provide tips for operating the program.*

and interface revisions (e.g., modify directions, provide visual cues). The easy changes were almost all completed with little interaction between vendor and client company. The majority of the possible changes were done, but only after discussion and review by the company's design team. "Difficult" changes included suggestions that required structural revisions (e.g., reprogramming to include error-catching routines for hardware and network printing problems). As these changes were difficult to incorporate directly into the program, alternative solutions for the problems were also suggested. These included a trouble-shooting guide and tips on how to take Web-based training. Following the course pilot, these alternative solutions were adopted in the form of Frequently Asked Question (FAQ) documents.

Responses to Open-Ended Questions

Trainee responses to open-ended questions were organized according to their content. Table 2 presents the two or three most endorsed content themes for each question, along with one or two examples. To be considered a theme, at least five (6%) of the trainees had to comment on the issue.

The open-ended comments were generally positive. In fact, the most frequent response to a question about the least useful aspect of the program was that all aspects of the course were useful. Another notable positive theme was that a large percentage of trainees liked the self-pacing and review capabilities that the program emphasized.

Table 2. Open-ended evaluation questions and response themes.

Question	Selected Responses (R) and Themes (T)

What did you find most useful about the program?	**R:** I liked being able to proceed at my own pace.
	   T: *Self-paced learning*
	R: The ability to browse forward and backward is very useful.
	   T: *Review capability*
	R: [I liked] the immediate and specific feedback to errors I made.
	T: *Feedback*

What did you find least useful about the program?	**R:** It was all very useful. **T: *Nothing*** **R:** The answers provided by the computer were unclear. **T: *Feedback*** **R:** No success stories, no mention of what works on the "real" shop floor. **T: *Examples***

How could the course be made more effective for you?	**R:** By making it simple . . . examples were too complicated and lengthy.
	   T: *Simplify examples and cases*
	R: Go into more detail on quiz problem explanations.
	   T: *Provide more detailed feedback*
	R: Hard copy materials.
	   T: *Add hard copy materials*

How does this compare to instructor-led training?	**R:** Better for people with experience, worse for people [with] lots of questions.
	   T: *It depends*
	R: I'd say it's better than face-to-face. It keeps me more involved and alert.
	   T: *Web-based is better*
	R: Face-to-face has certain advantages, like getting questions answered more easily.
	T: *Instructor-led is better*

Where would you choose to take the course?	**R:** You cannot take training in the office because of the distractions. **T: *Away from desk*** **R:** I like the flexibility, the software should be available at work, home, and . . . a facility. **T: *Multiple places***

Many trainees offered constructive comments regarding feedback and content. Feedback was a common theme in three of the five open-ended questions. Although feedback had been a central focus of the course development process, trainees indicated that they would prefer even more detailed feedback than what was included. They also suggested simplifying content and examples. In particular, a number of trainees noted that the examples should be more "real." An additional suggestion for improvement was to provide hard copy materials. Apparently, a number of trainees, while comfortable with computers, prefer to work with paper.

With regard to the Web-based delivery of the course, trainee comments were mixed. The majority of trainees said that their preference for Web-based or instructor-led training depends on their experience with the subject or on the course materials. Of the remaining trainees who indicated a preference, more preferred the Web to instructor-led courses. In explaining this preference, trainees typically referred to the flexibility provided by the Web in terms of timing (i.e., when to take it and for how long each sitting) and pacing (i.e., time on each topic).

Finally, trainees offered opinions regarding course administration. Most trainees indicated a preference for a training facility away from their desk, noting that there are too many potential distractions in their offices. Taking the course at their desk is not listed as theme for this question because fewer than six percent of trainees indicated that this would be their first preference.

Lessons Learned

There are a number of lessons regarding the design and development of WBT that can be drawn from this experience. A few of these lessons are presented below.

These lessons are organized into four categories: content, interface, administration, and development.

Content. Nearly all trainees felt the course was useful. However, many trainees noted they were dissatisfied with the length and complexity of the examples. The most common comment was that cases and examples were too long. In addition, trainees asked a number of questions about the necessity of all provided information. Because the same materials were appropriate for the classroom, material presented as Web-based text may need to be shortened or simplified. **Lesson #1: Content should be clear, concise, and easy to read.**

A number of trainees noted that they would have preferred examples to be directly relevant to their work. These trainees noted that some realism was missing because there were no "success" stories about how this process can actually be completed in their organization. **Lesson #2: Content should clearly indicate how trainees use knowledge and skills conveyed in the course back on the job.**

Interface. The vendor invested a lot of time developing feedback but results indicate that trainees often want even more information. In particular, trainees noted that they wanted explanatory feedback for all activities. **Lesson #3: Detailed feedback should be provided for all activities and exercises.**

The program received many compliments on ease of use, yet trainees had difficulty learning the interface at the beginning of training. This difficulty was indicated by the number of questions and navigation errors early in training, all committed despite the fact that explicit directions were provided. Apparently trainees did not understand or remember the instructions. **Lesson #4: Multiple indications (text and visual cues) should be provided about what a trainee can do next at every point.**

Administration. Many trainees commented that they were comfortable working on computers, but they still wanted some material in print. These trainees argued that spreading paper over a desk makes complex material easier to understand. The course program did contain an option to print, but this option was apparently not emphasized sufficiently. **Lesson #5: Paper versions of important information should be made easily available.**

Nearly all trainees mentioned that distractions would make it difficult to learn at their desk. According to them, a learning laboratory or other computer away from their desk would be necessary. Even though the extent of these distractions is unclear, the volume of trainees that noted this concern suggests that this is an important issue to consider. **Lesson #6: Trainees should have access to an environment free of distractions while working through the course.**

Development. Supplemental activities required creating feedback that an instructor could ordinarily provide. Development of these activities and associated feedback added time to the design process, and required review by instructors. **Lesson #7: Repurposing from instructor-led to Web-based training requires revisions and additions to course materials.**

Once the interface was designed and the content was embedded into an established navigation framework, requested changes required significant revisions. What would have been small changes early in the process took substantial amounts of development time, and risked creating other problems because of the structure of the computer programming. In this project, changes suggested by the preliminary pilot slowed development because they were difficult to implement. A few of these changes were not as effective as they could have been had they been implemented earlier in development. **Lesson #8: Interface and navigation decisions made after the early development stages are difficult to implement and may not work as well as desired.**

Implications

Lessons learned provide summaries of data. Often these summaries fall short of indicating clear directions for future efforts because of the complexity of design decisions. In particular, training designers must often balance competing demands and make trade-offs between equally important alternatives. Some of the lessons noted above suggest trade-offs while repurposing training. While it is beyond the scope of this chapter to address how any one project would address these trade-offs, they are discussed here with regard to revising this course.

Content. Repurposing training is a design challenge because the content is established but the media must change. A balance must be maintained between preserving content so it is consistent with existing materials and modifying the content so it is appropriate for the medium. The findings in the pilot suggest that content that is appropriate for instructor-led training may be too lengthy and complicated for the computer screen. This course may have benefited from greater simplicity, but doing so would have required even greater efforts by subject matter experts to determine how to simplify without compromising learning objectives.

Interface. In WBT, the interface is a critical because it determines how the trainee interacts with all of the information presented. The temptation is to provide an attractive interface that provides many options and alternatives, anticipating all users' needs. This temptation must be balanced with a need to provide navigation methods obvious to naïve trainees. For this course, a balance was attempted by providing instructions for complex interface actions. The problems encountered by users early in the pilot suggest that a more appropriate balance would be to provide a graduated interface where, early in training, navigation decisions require little or no instruction. After trainees are comfortable, more complex options may be made available.

Administration. One of the most interesting findings of the pilot was the concern trainees indicated about learning at their desks. In essence, each trainee was saying, "desktop learning is a great idea, just don't make me do it at MY desk." The trade-off that arises with this concern is how to balance the benefits of flexibility and increased access offered by the Web with problems from providing learner control in potentially disruptive learning environments. Access to decentralized learning laboratories may be one way to handle this trade-off effectively.

Development. Development nearly always requires meeting tight deadlines. The need to finish on schedule must be balanced with a need to address content and interface challenges that arise during development. Some challenges are not easy to predict without significant content and medium experience. The lessons learned here suggest that particular attention should be paid to considering content simplification and feedback additions that may be necessary to adequately maintain learner interest. In addition, interface decisions should be settled early to avoid programming difficulties. With these potential problems in mind, designers may more effectively anticipate delays or avoid them altogether.

Conclusion

The lessons presented here have already been used to modify the course, design supplemental documents for trainees, and change the development process for future courses. By using multiple evaluative methods in a controlled environment, a wealth of data was collected and dramatic improvements to the course were implemented. Hopefully, the lessons learned and implications noted here may assist others in the process of moving instructor-led materials to the Web. Furthermore, these lessons are offered to help ensure that companies employ WBT in a way that effectively addresses the challenges provided by recent human resource trends. Only through effective design and development can the advantages of WBT be realized.

References

Adler, N. J. (1990). *International dimensions of organizational behavior.* Boston, MA: Kent Publishing Company.

Bates, R. A., Holton, E. F., & Syler, D. L. (1996). Principles of CBI design and the adult learner: The need for further research. *Performance Improvement Quarterly, 9,* 3–24.

Brooks, D. W. (1997). *Web-teaching: A guide to designing interactive teaching for the World Wide Web.* New York: Plenum.

Carnevale, A. P. (1995). Enhancing skills in the new economy. In A. Howard (Ed.), *The changing of work* (pp. 238–251). San Francisco: Jossey-Bass.

Cotton, E. G. (1997). *The online classroom* (2nd ed.). Bloomington, IN: EDINFO Press.

Hall, B. (1997). *Web-based training cookbook.* New York: John Wiley & Sons.

Kommers, P. A. M., Grabinger, S., & Dunlap, J. C. (1996). *Hypermedia learning environments: Instructional design and integration.* Mahwah, NJ: Lawrence Erlbaum Associates.

The Authors

Kenneth G. Brown (e-mail: kenneth-g-brown@uiowa.edu; Web homepage: biz.uiowa.edu/faculty/ kbrown) is Assistant Professor in the Department of Management and Organizations at the University of Iowa, Iowa City. **Karen R. Milner** (e-mail: milnerka@pilot.msu.edu; Web homepage: io.psy.msu.edu) is Graduate Assistant in the Department of Psychology at Michigan State University, East Lansing. **J. Kevin Ford** (e-mail: fordjk@pilot.msu.edu; Web homepage: io.psy.msu.edu/fsa/faculty.htm) is Professor, Department of Psychology, Michigan State University, East Lansing. **Wendy Golden** (e-mail: wgolden@ siweb.com; Web homepage: siweb.com) is a Performance Technologist with Strategic Interactive, Lansing, Michigan.

48

A Corporate/College Partnership for Web-Based Training

Sharon Gray, Suzanne McCann, Earl Robinson, and Sean Warner

Higher Education's Challenge

Finding the right "market" for Web-based learning is a challenge for institutions of higher education. Many are looking to the Web in hopes it will be an antidote to flagging traditional student enrollments. They are hoping that the near-ubiquitous nature of the World Wide Web will result in non-traditional students flocking to their particular course offerings. While optimistic, this "shotgun approach," as it might be called, lacks strategic vision. There are educational and training needs existing in the "real world" that institutions of higher education can target, but targeting is crucial. Higher education revolves around individuals who, as experts in their fields, have a true interest in and love of teaching, but it requires "paying customers."

Corporations' Challenge

Today's corporate culture requires well-trained and multi-skilled employees. If those employees don't happen to come fully equipped with all the necessary knowledge and skills, they must quickly acquire them. Corporations, competitively attempting to attract highly motivated individuals, have found educational opportunities to be a well-appreciated human resource benefit.

A Mutually Beneficial Solution

Given the challenges facing higher education and corporations, a sensible approach to meeting those challenges might be to carefully assess one's own institution's strengths, resources, and *existing* relationships and capitalize upon those. The product higher education has to sell—education—is the product corporations are in need of buying. Enter a serendipitous solution: Higher education partnering with corporations to provide educational opportunities for employees.

Briar Cliff College and MCI have embarked on just such a partnership.

MCI, one of the many corporations utilizing distance learning, has implemented the **Virtual Education Center** (VEC) to cost-efficiently educate employees in the fast-paced field of telecommunications—a field where remaining abreast of changing technology can mean the difference between meeting or failing to meet customers' needs.

Through the VEC, MCI employees are able to "attend" class taught by a variety of educational and training institutions on whatever schedule is convenient for them, and without the need to commute to a geographically-bound classroom at a specific time. Favorable feedback from the pilot program, a certificate of management from the University of Dallas, prompted MCI to consider expanding the VEC program. The pilot had been targeted at the manager level; it was not geared toward the first level supervisor. MCI began researching curriculums of Internet education providers throughout the United States, trying to find courses of study which would meet the needs of employees at a variety of levels within MCI.

In 1996, there were already well over 6,000 different types of Internet education and training providers listed on the Internet. MCI looked at three criteria to determine which institutions to approach for inclusion in the VEC program. Since one of the largest concerns for MCI was quality, the first criterion was that an institution be accredited. The second criterion was whether or not MCI had a successful past relationship with the institution delivering educational content. The third, and crucial, criterion was whether or not the institution could provide education via the Internet. One of the colleges which met all three criteria was Briar Cliff College, Sioux City, Iowa.

Briar Cliff College had been offering courses to MCI employees at MCI's Sergeant Bluff, Iowa, center for three years. The college had developed a Certificate of Management program offered on site there, first to MCI's supervisors only, and later to all their employees. The program had been very successful. Faculty enjoyed teaching on-site in an environment very different from a college setting, and students appreciated the convenience of taking courses on-site. Indeed, the original idea for expanding the partnership further came from the *students* rather than the college. The students, in their routine teleconferencing with their colleagues across the country, had told them about the on-site program at Sergeant Bluff. Their colleagues began requesting that the corporation provide similar opportunities for them at their centers, and suggested the possibility of Briar Cliff College using MCI's existing teleconferencing technology (a PictureTel system) to broadcast the Certificate of Management program regionally or maybe even nationally. The idea made sense to both MCI and Briar Cliff College, since the College was developing expertise in using teleconferencing through the Iowa Communication Network, and was contemplating implementing a faculty development program to teach its faculty how to use this technology with its off-campus sites in Northwest Iowa.

MCI's VEC seemed the perfect vehicle for distributing access to Briar Cliff's Certificate of Management to MCI employees beyond the geographical confinement of Iowa.

Negotiation between the two parties was difficult (not due to any obstreperousness on either entity's part, but rather due to the difficulty inherent in the interfacing of corporate culture with higher education culture), and was spread out over a long period of time. It took eighteen months to get from the original idea to offering the first online course. The partnership would enable Briar Cliff College to extend its student body, which would in turn enhance its revenue, and it would enable MCI to provide accredited training to its employees regardless of where they lived or what shifts they worked.

MCI needed the courses and programs of study to be flexible and tailored to the needs of MCI employees. Further, employees would likely be required in the scope of their jobs to travel to different cities—and in some cases, different countries—while enrolled in the course of study. MCI needed Briar Cliff to be flexible and responsive to those needs. In essence, MCI was calling on Briar Cliff to be "customer-driven."

Briar Cliff developed its existing Certificate of Management program to be delivered completely via the World Wide Web, rather than through PictureTel, as was originally planned.

The program consists of nine undergraduate three-credit courses. Each course was **webized**™ (transferred from traditional delivery format to Web delivery format) using a template Briar Cliff had designed, which incorporated instructional design principles and assured a consistent form and function for the courses. It was Briar Cliff's intention that individual instructors would design and manage their own versions of the courses. The template facilitated this process. It was designed to be very flexible and responsive to individual instructors' needs. That flexibility is evidenced by the fact that each course, though based upon the same template, has taken on its own distinct form and character, incorporating unique collaborative elements.

One challenge quickly became apparent: acclimating the students to the experience of taking a course via the Web. In response to this challenge, Briar Cliff developed its **Online Orientation** on the Web (webized.com/orientation) to help students ease through the paradigm shift from traditional learning to Web-based distance learning. The orientation is offered free of charge to anyone interested in becoming familiar with Web-based instruction. The orientation has three major objectives:

- To enable students to successfully navigate and access information on the Web.

- To enable students to determine for themselves whether they have the necessary character to be successful taking a Web-based course. (Are they self-motivated? Did they do well in high school? Do they prefer working by themselves or with others?) To that end, the orientation includes a self-assessment tool.

- To enable the college to determine important technical information about the students, including the students' browser and e-mail software, the students' level of Internet expertise, and whether access to the course will be over a LAN or phone lines.

One of the major advantages for a college or university to partner with a corporation is that the corporation will usually advertise the programs through its corporate intranet. Each course that is implemented through MCI's Virtual Education Center is advertised throughout all sales and service centers to notify employees who may be interested in "attending." In addition, the directors of each division are provided with a course description and a list of which jobs in their organizations would benefit most from the distance learning. Management buy-in is essential for any corporate training program to be a success at any level. Without their buy-in and support the program is almost guaranteed to fail.

While it is true that an employee has access to non-corporate sponsored coursework through the World Wide Web, corporate sponsored coursework has the advantage of being linked to the specific needs of the corporation (even if the coursework in any given course is not altered to reflect this). To design programs which meet the corporation's and the employees' needs, the VEC program manager analyzes current job position competencies within the operation's support organization. The position competencies and typical employee career path for the position are then communicated to the institution of higher education partners for review. In turn, the institution provides curriculums that serve to develop and enhance the needed competencies.

MCI measures the success of the Virtual Education Center from several different angles. It is requested of the participants of the Virtual Education Center that they complete an internal evaluation on the course curriculum, format, facilitator, length, medium, college, and objectives. Each college also requests a survey or an evaluation typically focusing on the curriculum and the facilitator. In addition, MCI desires to solidify the return on investment in the form of cost savings, company time and equipment. This is measured by:

- How quickly an employee completes a given task before and after taking the course.

- The ability to successfully train another employee for his or her position.

- An improved global understanding of the telecommunications industry.

- Demonstrated improvement and understanding of managing projects and people.

- Employee evaluations.

- Career advancement.

Conclusion

MCI is planning on continually expanding the Virtual Education Center to eventually meet the training and educational needs of every employee throughout the corporation. The Virtual Education Center is in its primary growing years not only in size, but also in perfecting the right mix.

Briar Cliff College intends to be a long-term partner with MCI for the delivery of Web-based instruction, expanding its online programs and course offerings to meet the needs of MCI and its individual employees.

The Authors

Sharon Gray (e-mail: gray@briar_cliff.edu; **Web homepage:** briar-cliff.edu/sharongray/gray.htm) is Director of Instructional Technology at Briar Cliff College, Sioux City, Iowa. **Suzanne McCann** (e-mail: suzanne.mccann@mci.com) is Program Manager of MCI's Virtual Education Center, Colorado Springs, Colorado. **Earl Robinson** (e-mail: robinson@lmc.edu; **Web homepage:** lmc.edu) is President of Lees-McRae College, Banner Elk, North Carolina, and former Executive Vice President and Academic Dean of Briar Cliff College. **Sean Warner** (e-mail: swarner@nordec.monmouth.edu) is a Virtual Education Consultant with Virtual Design Associates in Elberon, New Jersey, and former Dean of Continuing Education of Briar Cliff College.

49

The Future of Continuing Medical Education on the Web

Henry L. Shapiro

A Bedtime Story

Jacqueline Innes, age 4, had an earache. Again. Dr. Sanders hesitated before going in to see her. She looked at her Physician's Digital Assistant (PDA) and noticed that Jacqueline had been in six times this year with earaches. There was a new message from the audiologist about her hearing. She was still showing a mild hearing loss in both ears. The PDA showed a list of Jacqueline's medications. Dr. Sanders vaguely remembered an otitis media update at Grand Rounds last year. They mentioned something about reading disabilities. She wanted to review that. Dr. Sanders put the PDA in her pocket and went in to see Jacqueline.

Just as she suspected, Dr. Sanders discovered that Jacqueline had severe ear infections. Jacqueline's mother burst into tears.

"I read an article on the Internet that said that Jacqueline might develop learning disabilities because of her ear infections. I think she needs to see a specialist. How come we can't prevent these ear infections? Isn't there some kind of new treatment we can try?"

Dr. Sanders touched Jacqueline's mother on the shoulder, and looked over at Jacqueline, who looked on, worried and confused. "It's all right. We will get Jacqueline back on this new medication. Send me an e-mail if she's not much better in two days." Dr. Sanders touched an icon and sent the prescription to the pharmacy. A message popped up, alerting Dr. Sanders that there was a new review of antibiotics in otitis media available. She clicked to have it faxed to the office.

Dr. Sanders paused before going on to the next patient to complete Jacqueline's record. The PDA glowed at her. She instructed the PDA to search and retrieve some relevant articles on ear infections and learning disabilities, which was on her list of learning goals for this year anyway. And out of curiosity, she asked the PDA to print out a list of all of her patients who failed antibiotic treatment in the last 12 months to study later. Maybe she could bring this up at the next teleconference.

That evening, Dr. Sanders got on the Web, looked through several of the articles, and found that the connection between ear infections was still unresolved, but there were three multicenter studies going on around the country. She reviewed the grand rounds lecture notes from last year, which had been updated last week, and reviewed her own results and was alarmed at the number of treatment failures in the last year. She dictated an addendum into the PDA, and sent a message to the receptionist to schedule a teleconference with Jacqueline's mother to discuss enrolling Jacqueline into a new study at the medical school. The PDA showed that Dr. Sanders had earned 1.5 hours of Continuing Medical Education credit, and then flashed a message:

"Time for bed."

D r. Sanders' PDA has not yet been invented. Perhaps Dr. Sanders has not yet even been born. Just like physicians today, though, Dr. Sanders is in the information business. Diagnosis and treatment management is an information game. Many physicians carry what they call an "auxiliary brain" in their pocket, with information about medication, tests, treatment algorithms, and diagnostic criteria. Medical mythology states that the mark of a brilliant clinician is his or her ability to make the snap diagnosis of a rare condition. Yet we know that failure to look things up, a rote or cursory style of practice, may result in outdated or even incorrect diagnosis or treatment.

In this chapter, we are going to consider continuing medical education, universally referred to as CME, how it relates to medical practice, and how Web-based technology may revolutionize it. While the author's point of reference is allopathic medicine in the United States, the same principles apply to western medicine in general.

Traditional CME

Trains, planes, and automobiles transport physicians to locations around the globe for traditional CME, a billion-dollar industry. Physicians use many channels to maintain and improve their knowledge, skills, and competence. About 30 states require continuing medical education for licensure, and many hospitals require evidence of continuing medical education for maintaining hospital privileges (Joint Commission on the Accreditation of Healthcare Organizations, 1997). Specialty and subspecialty boards may also require CME for re-certification. For example, the American Board of Pediatrics requires recertification every seven years. The American Academy of Pediatrics works closely with the board to provide comprehensive CME materials on a multi-year cycle designed to meet recertification needs (Sahler, 1992). Several organizations set standards and accredit organizations that provide CME, including the American Medical Association (1998) and the Accreditation Council on Continuing Medical Education (1998). State medical societies also sponsor CME. Internationally, few other countries formally require CME but most encourage it in different ways.

Is traditional CME effective? The literature does not support the effectiveness of most of short, lecture-based CME courses. Traditional lectures are passive, with little opportunity for evaluation, even immediate recall. Knowledge gained from lectures has a short half-life, and is often difficult to retrieve at the critical moment in the clinic or at the bedside. Both trainees and established physicians seem refractory to traditional CME (Seelig, 1993).

Some CME strategies do positively affect outcome (Davis, Thomson, Oxman, & Haynes, 1992, 1995; Holm, 1998). Physicians probably learn the most from preparing educational material for presentation to others (Abernethy, 1994). Feedback based on physician behavior (practice) may also be particularly effective (Manning, 1990). Intensive CME campaigns have also been effective at changing health outcomes, for example, suicide rate (Davis, 1998). Problem-based learning and small discussion groups may be effective. Opinion leaders, reminders, and academic detailing by pharmacists can be effective.

The "Sage on the Stage" model still dominates CME. In contrast, workshops at professional meetings may offer "hands-on" activities such as suturing, casting, and other procedural skills. Less often, workshops afford opportunities to hone cognitive skills. Because they draw more motivated learners, workshops may be more effective than lectures. Breakfast and lunch roundtable discussions "with the professor" are very popular at medical meetings, because they promote interaction. None of these approaches can claim to develop mastery or certify competency, which requires time and ongoing supervision and mentorship.

Forms of Web-based CME

The current form of Web-based CME is largely a "port" from print and lectures. Long, online articles followed by multiple choice questions, or slide shows on the Web, are the typical formats for current Web-based CME. New formats, such as RealAudio and RealVideo do a better job of simulating a lecture online. Online Chat currently serves only a small niche for physicians in spite of its popularity in some online communities. We will consider approaches to Web-based CME that hold a potential for improving on traditional CME.

Many factors are driving the interest in Web-based CME. Not surprisingly, they are divided into cost and revenue issues, and educational issues. There is competition to be first in a national market. Individual organizations see Web-based CME as a marketing tool. Though a sound economic model has not yet emerged, some see this as a viable commercial market, perhaps to replace revenue lost through managed care discounts and decreased funding for graduate medical education. Advertising, in the form of "unrestricted educational grants" which has driven traditional CME, has not yet had a strong impact in the online world. Finally, among educators, there is a genuine hope that Web-based CME might just be a better way to influence practice and outcomes. The advantages of Web-based CME over traditional CME include:

- Elimination of travel and lodging costs.
- Convenience (learn on demand).
- Automated record keeping.
- Potentially richer educational experience.
- Closer interaction with teacher.
- Potentially better learning outcomes.

MacKenzie and Greene (1997) describe several affordances of Web-based CME. Options include:

- Distance Learning.
- Interactive communication.
- Collaborative development of learning and reference materials.
- Drill and practice programs.
- Tutorials.
- Models of physiological processes.
- Interactive simulations which are case-based or represent artificial environments.

Of these approaches, we will put special emphasis on simulation, serial instruction, performance support systems, and self-directed learning.

Simulation

The *Interactive Patient* is a well-publicized example of forms-based simulation (Lehmann & Hayes, 1995). Users respond to prompts by asking questions about medical history, and the program responds to their questions, allowing users to work their way through common complaints, such as abdominal pain. By requiring the user to formulate questions, the learning situation is a better model of real medical decision making than multiple choice tests. The designer still has to predict the range of possible questions and develop appropriate algorithms, but this could be done empirically. Universal "engines" have to be invented to make this type of simulation updateable and affordable.

Immersive multimedia simulations can provide compelling experiences, and allow detailed exploration of complex material. Three-dimensional models, in which the user interaction includes complex virtual object manipulation, are very costly to produce. Physiologic simulations which allow multiple "what if" scenarios have been successfully used in learning lab situations (Lehmann, Lehmann, & Freedman, 1997). We are still a long way from "virtual patients," but simulations have great potential for mastery learning.

Serial Instruction

Interactive multimedia often relies on linear tutorial models. The strength of serial instruction is in rapidly bringing beginners up to speed in terms of prerequisite knowledge. It is a model familiar to most physicians, and its short-term effectiveness is easy to measure using automated multiple-choice questions. Redundancy can be made more entertaining, and can help lead to mastery of information. Rapid development approaches are feasible. Use of multimedia in the form of video, audio, animation, figures, tables, and other illustrations can improve the experience for the user, but increases the development cost correspondingly. One negative side of serial instruction is its unproven effectiveness in changing behavior, and the short half-life of the knowledge obtained this way. Because of its relatively low cost and conceptual simplicity, serial instruction is likely to remain the dominant modality in Web-based CME.

Electronic Performance Support Systems: Just-in-time Learning

As with many innovations in education (Postman, 1993), industrial processes provide a metaphor. The notion of "just-in-time" shipping of parts and supplies has allowed industry to decrease inventory costs. In medical education, providing information just in time allows educators to capitalize on the teachable moment. Manning (1990) reported that physicians have a mean of six unanswered questions at the end of clinical encounters. The advantages of immediate feedback are obvious.

This is the basis of many proposed electronic performance support systems or integrated academic information management systems, such as the Virtual Hospital Project at the University of Iowa (D'Alessandro, Galvin, Erkonen, Curry, Flanagan, D'Alessandro, Lacey, & Wagner, 1996). Physicians would be able to get immediate answers to questions, send electronic mail to a peer or subspecialist, request print materials, or schedule an individually tailored online tutorial adjusted to the physician's profile. Challenges include developing a substantial information infrastructure informed by usability data, suitable content development, information architecture (see Rosenfeld & Morville, 1998), user profiling, quality management, and an ongoing training system. Users could gain incremental CME based on their use of the system, paid for by subscription or membership in a network.

Self-Directed Learning

The Web can facilitate educational self-management. Through database transactions, the individual's interests can be fed back into the CME provider's database, allowing continuous needs-assessment. External expectations (such as recertification requirements) from professional organizations can be incorporated into the individual's CME plan. For example, the physician may want to participate in a quality assurance plan for an office laboratory, improve his or her skills in office dermatology, or prepare for recertification exams. By documenting this ongoing self-assessment and learning program, expensive formal recertification examinations could be eliminated (Bashook & Parboosingh, 1998).

If more formal learning is desired, the learner would have an opportunity to discuss issues with a mentor, who would provide supervision and encouragement as needed, as well as certifying the effort of the learner. The Web lends itself to such mentor networks sponsored by medical centers, professional organizations, and third party payers. Learning circles could involve individuals, and members of local, regional, or global groups who share goals and objectives rather than physical proximity. Since many physicians work on geographical and temporally dispersed teams, it is important that Web-based CME address the needs of team learning (Headrick, Wilcock, & Batalden, 1998).

The Future of CME

Current CME activities are extremely expensive in terms of physician time, not to mention costs of travel, meals, registration, and record keeping. Much CME is ineffective. Multi-modal approaches, including lecture, serial instruction, written handouts, simulations, projects and activities, and self-directed learning could improve the effectiveness of CME. The Web as a medium is perfectly situated to providing customized reminders as well as updates and corrections. *Just-in-time* approaches may be still more effective, though this has yet to be proven. Still, innovative systems such as integrated academic information management systems hold great promise.

Progress Towards Web-Based CME

Gray-haired academic physicians and country doctors alike have Web sites. According to the 1997 Periodic Survey of Fellows of the American Academy of Pediatrics, 46 percent of pediatricians had access to the Internet in their offices, and another 7 percent intended to have Internet access within 12 months. A previous survey in 1996 indicated that about 50 percent of pediatricians could access the Internet either at home or at work; 57 percent of the pediatricians who used the Internet, according to this 1996 survey, used it for "general medical learning;" 21 percent reported using it for CME (L. Olson, personal communication, June 29, 1998). Many medical schools now require students to own laptop computers. It seems only a matter of time for physicians to develop the habit of using the Web for learning, treating patients, and self-growth. Younger physicians will see the Web as a normal part of their professional life. Older physicians will come on board quickly when they see the advantages of the Web. The history of innovations such as X-rays, antibiotics, and coronary artery bypass surgery demonstrates the potential for rapid diffusion of innovation in medicine.

Major medical journals are increasingly co-published on the Web. Organizations such as the American Medical Informatics Association, the Association of American Medical Colleges (AAMC), and the American Medical Association actively promote the Internet to physicians. The AAMC sponsors a listserv, Med-Ed, where there are active discussions on the use of technology for medical education. A recent discussion on Med-Ed turned up many sites that archive RealAudio versions of lectures synchronized with slides. Funded faculty positions in medical informatics are increasingly common, and many grant making agencies are supporting online resources.

If the Internet is at the toddler stage, then the medical information infrastructure is in its infancy. While medical librarians have kept up, the promised natural language systems, intelligent agents, and expert systems remain vaporware. We are just beginning to encode medical knowledge in ways that it can be processed by automated systems, and there is a huge amount of legacy material that will probably never been converted. In the short term, there will probably be a proliferation of proprietary systems and prototypes, some intentionally isolated from each other in order to protect intellectual capital. Before Dr. Sanders' PDA can be a true gateway to information, education, and management tools, the electronic infrastructure and databases will have to be built, populated, and supported. The Web offers the promise of a common standard of interoperability, but the real work will be in the back end.

Conclusion

We have looked at ways in which the Web might be used to help physicians and other health care providers continue their education and maintain their competence. Continuing Medical Education and Continuous Performance Support will coalesce. The Web will serve as a medium and front end to an information infrastructure that has not yet been built. The real power of the Web is its potential to stimulate and enhance communication among peers and to provide access to information and data management resources. It will be critical that all of the stakeholders participate in the design process, including practicing physicians and the public. We will all benefit if Web-based CME achieves its promise.

References

Abernethy, D. (1994). Britain leads continuing medical education—whither America? *Postgraduate Medical Journal, 70,* 643–645.

Accreditation Council on Continuing Medical Education. (1998). ACCME essentials; accme.org/essent/essent.htm

American Medical Association. (1998). *Physicians recognition award booklet;* ama-assn.org/med-sci/pra2/contents.htm

Bashook, P. G., & Parboosingh, J. (1998). Continuing medical education: Recertification and maintenance of competence. *British Medical Journal, 316,* 545–548.

D'Alessandro, M. P., Galvin, J. R., Erkonen, W. E., Curry D. S., Flanagan J. R., D'Alessandro, D. M., Lacey, D. L., & Wagner, J. R. (1996). The virtual hospital, an IAIMS integrating continuing education into the work flow. *M.D. Computing, 13,* 323–329.

Davis, D. (1998). Continuing medical education: Global health, global learning. *British Medical Journal, 316,* 385–389.

Davis, D. A., Thomson, M. A., Oxman, A. D., & Haynes, R. B. (1992). Evidence for the effectiveness of CME. A review of 50 randomized controlled trials. *Journal of the American Medical Association, 268,* 1111–7.

Davis, D. A., Thomson, M. A., Oxman, A. D., & Haynes, R. B. (1995). A systematic review of the effect of continuing medical education strategies. *Journal of the American Medical Association, 274,* 700–705.

Fox, R. D., & Bennett, N. L. (1998). Continuing medical education: Learning and change: Implications for continuing medical education. *British Medical Journal, 316,* 466–468.

Headrick, L. A., Wilcock, P. M., & Batalden, P. B. (1998). Interprofessional working and continuing medical education. *British Medical Journal, 316,* 771–774.

Holm, A. H. (1998). Quality issues in continuing medical education. *British Medical Journal, 316,* 621–624.

Joint Commission on the Accreditation of Healthcare Organizations. (1997). *JCAHO Comprehensive Manual for Hospitals.* Oakbrook Terrace, IL: JCAHO.

Lehmann, C. U., & Hayes, K. A. (1995). The interactive patient. Marshall University School of Medicine, West Virginia; medicus.marshall.edu/medicus.htm

Lehmann, H. P., Lehmann, C. U., & Freedman, J. A. (1997). The use of simulations in computer-aided learning over the World Wide Web. *Journal of the American Medical Association, 278,* 1788.

MacKenzie, J. D., & Greene, R. A. (1997). The World Wide Web: Redefining medical education. *Journal of the American Medical Association, 278,* 1785–1786.

Manning, P. R. (1990). Continuing education needs of health care professionals. *Bulletin of the Medical Librarian Association, 78,* 161–164.

Postman, N. (1993). *Technopoly.* New York: Vintage Books.

Rosenfeld, L., & Morville, P. (1998). *Information architecture for the World Wide Web.* Cambridge, MA: O'Reilly.

Sahler, O. J. (1992). Pizza, pickles, and PREP. *Pediatrics in Review, 13,* 3–4.

Seelig, C. B. (1993). Changes over time in the knowledge acquisition practices of internists. *Southern Medical Journal, 86,* 780–783.

Sherman, C. D., & Lambiase, P. (1993). Continuing medical education in the United States: A critique. *European Journal of Cancer, 29A,* 784–787.

Towle, A. (1998). Continuing medical education: Changes in health care and continuing medical education for the 21st century. *British Medical Journal, 316,* 301–304.

Acknowledgments

The author acknowledges Dan Coury, M.D., and James Blackman, M.D., for their ideas contributed in the development of the Web project, and the All Children's Hospital Library for helping get journal articles "just-in-time." Camille T. Fine, Ph.D., reviewed and commented on the manuscript. This work was supported in part by project grant MCJ399617 from the Maternal and Child Health Bureau (Title V, Social Security Act), Health Resources and Services Administration, Department of Health and Human Services. Supporting materials, including hyperlinks to sites mentioned in the chapter and other Web-based CME sites, may be found at: dbpeds.org/webcme/

The Author

Henry L. Shapiro, M.D., FAAP (e-mail: hshapiro@hsc.usf.edu; Web homepage: dbpeds.org), is an Assistant Professor of Pediatrics at the University of South Florida, and Medical Director of Developmental and Behavioral Pediatrics at All Children's Hospital. He is also the Web Editor and Co-Director of the *Developmental and Behavioral Pediatrics Homepage.*

50

Long Distance Collaborative Authentic Learning (CAL): Recommendations for Problem-Based Training on the Web

Alison A. Carr-Chellman

Introduction

Using the Web to its best advantage has been seen as an effective way to communicate large amounts of information to training audiences. But extending the Web beyond its natural information dispensation mode stretches its limits. Recent learning theory strongly suggests that effective higher-level learning, such as the development of problem-solving skills, needs to involve collaboration and authenticity. Informed by a comparison of traditional residential instruction and distance education experiences, this chapter addresses recommendations for effective training of higher-order problem-solving skills through the collaborative use of Web resources for authentic problem solving. Differences between the instructional and learning models for problem-solving collaboration at a distance versus face-to-face, as well as limitations of the current technologies for Web-based training, are also addressed.

Fueled by recent shifts in Web-based design tools, the economies of scale for distance education have become *very* attractive. Travel costs and employee time costs are dramatically slashed by using the Web for training employees. But does the distance education model support and surpass old models of on-site training? Can we create Web-based learning environments which effectively employ current advances in learning theory? Situated cognition, collaborative/cooperative learning, problem-based learning, and constructivist learning models are increasingly recognized in human learning theory as more effective methods for higher-level learning than direct instruction. Training via authentic problems and cases can contribute new thinking to corporate performance challenges. But can we bring these models to bear on Web-based training efforts? What happens when we ask groups of employees to collaborate with one another over long distances to solve real problems?

Web-based instruction is a popular form of education being adopted at all levels of schooling and it is generating a great deal of interest in the instructional technology R&D community (Hackbarth, 1997; Khan, 1997). Encouraging a student-centered, learning-focused approach to distance education, however, has been difficult in the face of increasing pressures to get courses online quickly. Heeding the calls of constructivism (Jonassen, 1991), situated cognition (Brown

& Duguid, 1994), cooperative learning (Johnson, Johnson, & Holubec, 1984) and problem-based learning (Barrows, 1986; Septien & Gallagher, 1993) in the context of distance education may seem impossible, or at best improbable.

Based on an extensive study which examined the potential for collaborative, authentic problem-based learning and solving at a distance, this chapter begins by describing the differences in instruction and learning between a modified distance education and face-to-face instruction. The chapter then turns to a brief description of the informing study and its findings. The implications of this study translate into recommendations for Web-based training design where problem-solving and collaboration/team building are goals. As educators, we have begun the task of learning about and understanding what Web-based training is and isn't capable of, and in particular the ways in which Web-based education, perhaps the least expensive form of distance education, can be employed to the best advantage (Khan, 1997). The chapter ends with words of caution by discussing the potential limitations of Web-based training.

What Is CAL?

Collaborative Authentic Learning (CAL) combines the strength of group work collaboration with authentic problems to build strong teams and increase problem-solving skills. While this concept is certainly not new, it has many advantages for organizations as they build their workforce for the changing needs of business and industry. Specifically, organizations are increasingly in need of creative problem-solvers and employees who can work effectively together to think deeply about organizational goals. Training activities such as ropes courses and group dynamics activities have long been used with management training to encourage team-building skills. Case-based or problem-based learning has been around for nearly three decades now, primarily utilized in medical and business education (Barrows, 1986). Waldhalm (1995) identifies the following advantages of the problem-based learning approach: (1) demands active student participation in learning; (2) focuses on problem-solving; (3) encourages reflective self-assessment; (4) builds strong communication skills; (5) hones information access and utilization skills. In CAL, these advantages are accomplished in the context of real problems posed for the students to collaboratively solve through discussion and inquiry processes in small groups. CAL combines these two relatively recent advances in learning theory to the best advantage of both.

The important point here is that while none of these ideas is new, their combined use on the Web for distance training is. Pennell and Deane (1995) describe the use of Web resources in undergraduate biology courses, and there is even a resource from NASA for teachers wishing to use the Web for PBL (Problem-Based Learning) (cotf.edu/ete/). These exemplars of the intersection of Web-education and PBL typically do include a collaborative component, but the students are usually co-located (in the same geographical space). So a "Long Distance" CAL, in this case, is a particularly new and innovative application of the Web to instruction because it asks the learners to meet the challenge of collaborating on a real-world problem while scattered across time zones and even across potential language barriers.

Differences in Problem-Solving Training on the Web

Understanding the differences between Web-based problem-solving and traditional face-to-face instruction for problem-solving is an important cornerstone upon which effective long distance CAL's are built. Instruction *and* learning of problem-solving varies substantially when employed in traditional versus distance education. Today there is a blurring between traditional and distance education. Many traditional residential programs employ some form of distance contact (e.g., virtual office hours, e-mail communication among group members, and phone conference

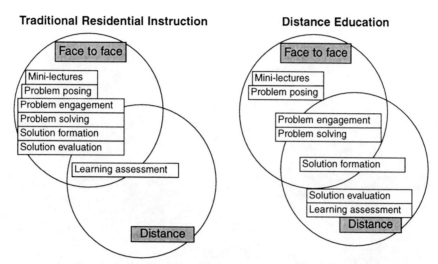

Figure 1. Instructional models: Distance versus face-to-face.

calls for group meetings). Meanwhile, many distance programs are requiring some level of face-to-face contact (e.g., mini-seminars, initial orientation on campus, individual meetings with the instructor).

If we examine the **instructional** models and the **learning** models employed in the study (described below), this blurring becomes more apparent. The instructional model can be seen graphically by displaying the uses of instructional methods (e.g., lecture, problem posing, evaluation) in face-to-face versus distance education (see Figure 1).

The instructional model, which represents the instructional activities, can be contrasted with the learning model, which represents the ways in which people *learn*. Learning modalities such as problem conceptualization, an activity constructed in the learners' head, are quite different from problem posing, in which authentic problems are provided to learners in a class activity. However, since the communication channels are not assumed to be unidimensional (instructor to student and back), the learning models are arrayed by various interactions (instructor → learner, learner → learner, etc.). In this case, arraying the various learning models against the communication sites in which they occur illustrates their relationships across distance and traditional learning modalities (see Figure 2).

These descriptions are used here to illustrate the ways in which instruction and learning *change* from traditional to distance education. Because of these substantial shifts, and even larger ones when a course is delivered *exclusively* on the Web, training design must be aligned with the instruction and learning models employed more heavily in distance education. Such alignments will prevent us from simply putting what is traditionally done in a classroom directly onto the Web without careful consideration of the differences between the two media. These diagrams may be used as templates to identify the primary processes involved in different instruction and learning models. Then these processes can be aligned with the understood site of the activity in traditional instruction. Finally, critically anticipating the shifts that will take place when moving to distance media will ensure a more systematic approach to Web-based training design. Once you have a clearer understanding of the ways in which CAL will differ from the traditional manner in which you have taught these skills face-to-face, you will be able to begin to change your training design to meet these differences and possibly any limitations these differences pose.

Traditional Residential Instruction   **Distance Education**

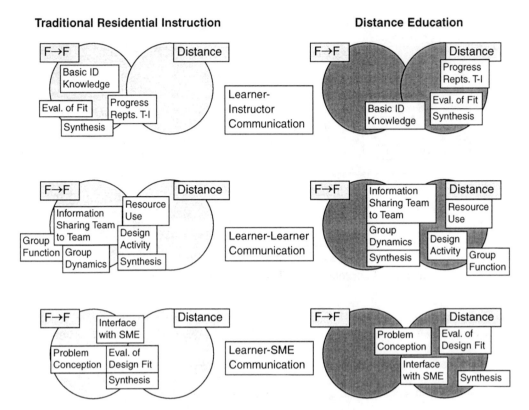

Figure 2. Learning/interaction modes in distance versus face-to-face.

The Informing Study

Along with two of my graduate students,[1] I recently undertook a large-scale research project to investigate the possibilities of CAL at a distance. This study was done to explore the differences between traditional residential learning of instructional design through problem-based collaboration in student groups of 4–5 learners and those same experiences among similar groups of learners enrolled in a distance curriculum requiring collaboration at a distance. This study was based on qualitative research paradigms (Lincoln & Guba, 1985) as well as recent developments in student-centered learning theories (Savery & Duffy, 1996; Wilson, 1996) and systemic approaches to Web-based distance education (Collis, 1996; Moore & Kearsley, 1996).

Settings

This study took place in two rather diverse settings. The first is a traditional residential instructional systems program with well over a hundred graduate students at the masters and doctoral level. Many students travel from remote parts of the state to take classes at night, and almost all courses are offered during the evening hours to facilitate working schedules. Along with the faculty, several full-time students with assistantships make up a primary core of scholarly and social community. The second, a distance-education institution, takes the form of a

---

[1]Thanks and acknowledgments for all their hard work in the conduct of this study to Mr. Dean Dyer and Mr. Jeroen Breman.

low-slung office building in an office park approximately a mile from the main campus buildings. In this study, the students enrolled in the traditional program attended class once per week, on campus, for three hours, while the distance education students attended a three-day face-to-face seminar in a hotel conference room, and the remainder of the coursework was conducted via the Web and telephone.

The Course and Course Projects

The course, an introduction to instructional design, is founded on the basic premise that authentic learning of instructional design principles is inherently advantageous to the learners as well as to the outside community. Real-world projects were the centerpiece of the course, and all learning of basic concepts, such as needs assessment, instructional strategies, learning objectives, test items, and evaluation tasks, was conducted within the context of the real-world ID problem. These problems were posed by Subject Matter Experts (SMEs) from three contexts reflecting the settings of most students' eventual employment: higher education, K–12 education, and business/industry.

SMEs were invited by the instructor to pose their instructional problem to the class after first meeting with the instructor and being briefed on the appropriate problem type, learning approach, and anticipated learning/project outcomes. SMEs were advised regarding the ways in which the problems should be posed to the class, team requirements, and approximate time commitments on their part. Very early in the course, SMEs presented their problems. In the traditional course, all SME's were present to describe their instructional problem face-to-face. In the case of the distance education course, one SME happened to be in the area and was present in person, while the rest were all contacted and made their presentations by phone via audio conference call. As many as seven different problems were posed to each class and learners were tasked with creating their own groups of three or four colleagues. Problems included firefighting training in Colorado, FAA training in Washington DC, course design for university faculty in libraries, mathematics, and fuel sciences, and professional development for teachers learning to use new technologies in two school districts. As a result of this project, more than 14 real-world external agencies were served free of charge, and the students worked together on a collaborative project in which no one student had any more information or stake in the outcome than any other student.

Study Process

This study employed a naturalistic inquiry orientation and used case study and interview methodologies (Lincoln & Guba, 1985; Merriam, 1988; Stake, 1986). Two sections of the same course, basic instructional design, were followed for one semester to examine their experiences with regard to the solution of authentic instructional design problems. The students' challenge was to create a complete instructional design project from analysis through evaluation (analysis and design sections were completed, while development, implementation and evaluation portions were to be partially developed and described as a plan for the future due to time limitations). The study examined results of surveys, pre- and post-interviews,[2] and classroom observations. The study also conducted artifact analysis on class projects, problem solutions, e-mails, Web board discussion records, and promotional materials from both institutions. These documents were analyzed along with interview transcripts, student journals, surveys, audioconference transcripts, and observational field notes.

---

[2]Pre-interviews were conducted face-to-face with both groups, and post-interviews were conducted by e-mail with both groups.

Results

Data analysis showed several important concerns with authentic problem-based collaboration at a distance. First, the students in both groups exhibited a certain amount of resistance to the problem-based curriculum; however, the students working at a distance exhibited more frustration over the problem-based approach because of the added difficulties of truly collaborating at a distance in a consistent fashion. They were concerned about their ability to truly perform all tasks involved in instructional design because they felt they had learned only the part their team assigned them rather than the whole process. This feeling was more prevalent among the distance students than the residential students. This heightened level of concern may be the result of increased division of labor among distance students (and corresponding decreases in collaborative behaviors), or possibly because they saw more direct applications of their learning to their current work situations, since more of them were employed full-time in related work contexts.

In addition, the survey results confirmed that the distance students were farther along in their program, generally a little older, employed full-time in a related position, and had a good deal more experience with education and instructional design than did the residential students. The products that both groups created in response to the authentic problem were of approximately equivalent quality and evidenced similar levels of understanding of the instructional design process. While the distance students showed a bit more depth of understanding, this may have had more to do with their ability to articulate as a function of their maturity.

The students in the distance group consistently pointed to the importance of the audio-bridges (phone) contact with the group, where all members could work together on the problem and speak to one another. Many felt the project would have been impossible without the audio-bridges and felt that relying solely on the Web or e-mail (less expensive options) would have been extremely frustrating, if not impossible. In addition, they listed a plethora of technical difficulties that emerged from their attempts to transfer documents, graphics, information, and pieces of their projects back and forth between multi-platform users. These technical difficulties were their biggest frustration and one which was not mentioned at all by the residential students. Perhaps the biggest surprise of the study was the lack of group dynamics problems among the distance students as compared with the residential students. Possibly because of a feeling of access to the instructor or because of the ease of face-to-face contact with the instructor, more problems were shared from the residential students in terms of interpersonal problems, difficulties with group dynamics, and lack of collaboration or members' non-compliance than was shared from the distance students. The other possible explanation for this is the deep relationships that had formed among students in the distance section. These students were part of a cohesive cadre that had been together in several courses prior to this experience and appeared more committed to one another as a result.

Suggestions for Designing
Web-Based Training for CAL

Based on our experiences with Web-based CAL and with traditional instruction aimed at problem-solving through authentic learning, there are several specific recommendations for those engaged in Web-based training design. Obviously, these general considerations may not hold true in all cases, and, more importantly, one's own context is likely to need specific consideration of additional changes from traditional face-to-face training to Web-based training. But these guidelines are a good place to start. Informed by research and experience, they are currently our best set of recommendations for higher-order Web-based training for CAL.

• *Attempt Web-based CAL in stages.* Collaboration is a skill to be learned; Web-based collaboration requires even more finely honed group dynamics abilities than does face-to-face collaboration. In addition, problem-solving is a difficult skill that needs to be built up slowly. In both cases, embedding these experiences as a whole set of routinized skills in the context of an authentic problem should be an ultimate goal, not a starting point. It is important that these skills are built slowly, with prerequisite skills taught first and carefully assessed to be certain that students are capable of collaboration and problem-solving sub-steps prior to attempting to fulfill the needs of an authentic problem. The distance students in our study were very clear that they were successful at distance CAL because they had had similar prior experience with smaller projects that led to this capstone CAL experience.

• *Provide audio support.* Although this may put a dent in the efficiency arguments for Web-based training, it seems clear from our experiences and findings that students relied very heavily on the audio support for conference calls for team meetings, discussions of team progress with instructors, and working through stages of collaboration, group dynamics, and problem-solving techniques, such as trying out potential solutions. They did NOT find that the Web discussion boards or e-mails fulfilled these needs, although they did use them for routine tasks and communication. The audio support seems to be a vital link for problem-based, group-based, authentic learning at a distance. As Web tools increase our abilities to provide audio support on the Web, these technologies will become increasingly seamless and more cost-effective. Such audio support needs to be exploited to its best advantage whenever possible.

• *Provide technical support.* This probably goes without saying, but when students are engaged in high-level problem solving, working through group problems at a distance, and try-ing to apply their ideas to real-world contexts, they are easily frustrated by technological prob-lems. Providing adequate support for their learning and seeing that the technology functions for them in a seamless fashion are important first steps in effective Web-based training for CAL. Here again is the value of having had smaller experiences with the technologies prior to un-dertaking a large CAL project. In addition, wizards, guides, and online assistance can help to fill this gap. As the technologies become more advanced, problems of translation from group member A working with machine A and software B to group member B working with machine B and software C will become less and less frustrating for learners. However, at this point, there are still many potholes along the road to smooth Web-based training for CAL, and it is our job to be certain that these are filled—at least for the moment.

• *Ensure that the learners have appropriate prior experiences.* Learners should have prior experiences with the content before attempting collaborative, high-level problem solving in authentic contexts at a distance. Again, small steps are the best advice here. Be certain to de-sign small experiences with the content and information (effectively distributed via Web-based training) prior to Web-based CAL. In addition, it is very important that this learning is effec-tively assessed in order to be certain that learners have not only read Web screens, but also are able to *apply* this information to some fictional or contrived context prior to being able to apply it to a real-world context. It is also useful for learners to have early experiences with group work and even collaboration at a distance on smaller projects before engaging in Web-based CAL.

• *Allow groups to select their own members.* One of the keys, in our experience, to ef-fective collaboration was allowing students to choose their own group membership. Although this means that the instructor may not be able to evenly distribute talents across groups, it does put the responsibility for group functioning on the members themselves, facilitating effective distance collaboration.

Potential Limitations of Web-Based Training for CAL

While the efficiencies of Web-based training cannot be overlooked, neither can its limitations. It is important to offer a balanced perspective on the potentialities and limitations of Web-based training, particularly for higher-order learning such as CAL. Technology is certainly not without its critics (Postman, 1995), and technology, when applied to education, draws fire from many critical camps (Noble, 1998). Many of these critiques offer important messages to those of us engaged in Web-based training development. We need to heed the limitations of our own and our technology's abilities.

Galusha (1998) points out that distance education can create downwardly spiraling motivation levels for adult learners primarily because of the lack of face-to-face contact with peers and instructors. She also suggests that instructors, or in our case, trainers, may withhold support from the effort. This is possible given the radical shifts in the labor demands and the roles that trainers will take in a new Web-based delivery system. Finally, Galusha's literature review suggests that learners may be less secure about their own learning, their ability to evaluate their learning, and the absence of supports such as tutors.

Many researchers are concerned about the isolation issues associated with Web-based educational solutions (Iandoli & Norris, 1997; Taha & Callwell, 1993). Sleek (1998) writes, "A computer monitor can't give you a hug or laugh at your jokes. . . . In fact, in a study to be released this month in *American Psychologist,* [researchers] report that greater use of the Internet leads to shrinking social support and happiness, and increases in depression and loneliness" (p. 1). Drucker (1995) suggests that the nature of school as a public place is significantly compromised by the socially isolating aspects of distance education.

The fundamental assumption that Web-based distance education is essentially the same experience as traditional face-to-face instruction is currently being strongly questioned (Sigurjon, 1994; Thurber & Pope, 1998). It is important to recognize these differences and understand the limitations of training via the Web based on the drawbacks of electronically mediated communication. As an example, Thurber and Pope (1998) remain highly suspicious of the application of Web-based courses in the humanities:

> What should we do when students from a virtual course (or university) ask for equivalent credit at our own, presumably real institutions? . . . our response would be cautious to say the least; and as regards the last, given that access to information is only one aspect of what the humanities do, given that hypertextual (or e-mail- or listserv-based) responses are like writing but not exactly like it, and like conversation but not exactly like it, in ways we do not yet fathom, our response would be—no. Not until we know whether—or if—a virtual education is an education. (p. 5)

Conclusion

It is extremely important that combining current learning theories and technologies be approached with pragmatic eyes toward not only efficiencies to be discovered, but also implications for better learning. Extending the Web's utility beyond information access and transmission toward more interactive, collaborative, authentic modes of learning is one of the most promising avenues for Web-based training efforts of the future. Understanding the differences between CAL at a distance versus traditional face-to-face CAL is an important first step in effective implementation of advanced Web-based training techniques. Listening carefully to what students who have endured our early attempts at Long Distance CAL have to share about their experiences and using those reflections to inform our future attempts at utilizing the Web for CAL is good instructional design practice. Finally, balancing our enthusiasm for the promise of long distance CAL with the inherent limitations of the technology itself—and being prepared to respond to advances in the technology as they become realistically available to our learners—will allow us to truly take best advantage of the potentials of Web-based training.

References

Barrows, H. S. (1986). A taxonomy of problem-based learning methods. *Medical Education, 20*(6), 481–486.

Brown, J., & Duguid, P. (1994). Practice at the periphery: A reply to Steven Tripp. *Educational Technology, 34*(8), 9–11.

Collis, B. (1996). *Tele-learning in a digital world.* London: International Thomas Computer Press.

Drucker, S. J. (1995). Distance learning and education as place. *Telematics and Informatics, 12*(2), 69–73.

Galusha, J. M. (1998). *Barriers to distance education* (ERIC Document Reproduction Service No. ED 416 377).

Hackbarth, S. (Ed.). (1997). Web-based learning [special issue]. *Educational Technology, 37*(3).

Iandoli, C. C., & Norris, W. (1997). Contradictions and asides: A social critique of the Internet. *Journal of Technology Studies, 23*(2), 35–41.

Johnson, D. W., Johnson, R. T., & Holubec, E. J. (1984). *Circles of learning: Cooperation in the classroom.* Alexandria, VA: Association of Supervision and Curriculum Development.

Jonassen, D. (1991). Objectivism versus constructivism: Do we need a new philosophical paradigm? *Educational Technology Research and Development, 39*(3) 5–14.

Khan, B. (Ed.). (1997). *Web-based instruction* Englewood Cliffs: Educational Technology Publications.

Lincoln, Y. S., & Guba, E. G. (1985). *Naturalistic inquiry.* Beverly Hills, CA: Sage Publications.

Merriam, S. B. (1988). *Case study research in education: A qualitative approach.* San Francisco: Jossey-Bass.

Moore, D., & Kearsley, G. (1996). *Distance education: A systems view.* Belmont, CA: Wadsworth.

Noble, D. F. (1998). *The religion of technology: The divinity of man and the spirit of invention.* New York: Knopf.

Pennell, R., & Dean, E. M. (1995). *Web browser support for problem-based learning.* Paper presented at ASCILITE Conference, Melbourne, Australia.

Postman, N. (1995). *The end of education: Redefining the value of school.* New York: Random House.

Savery, J., & Duffy, T. (1996). Problem-based learning: An instructional model and its constructivist framework. In B. Wilson (Ed.), *Constructivist learning environments: Case studies in instructional design.* Englewood Cliffs: Educational Technology Publications.

Septien, W., & Gallagher, S. (1993). Problem-based learning: As authentic as it gets. *Educational Leadership, 50*(7), 25–28.

Sigurjon, M. (1994). Teacher education online: What gets lost in electronic communication? *Educational Media International, 31*(1), 46–52.

Sleek, S. (1998). Isolation increases with Internet use. *American Psychological Monitor, 29*(9), 1, 30–31.

Stake, B. (1986). *Quieting reform.* Urbana, Illinois: University of Illinois Press.

Taha, L. H., & Callwell, B. S. (1993). Social isolation and integration in electronic environments. *Behaviour & Information Technology, 12*(5), 276–283.

Thurber, B. D., & Pope, J. W. (1998). *Electronic communication and the humanities.* Paper presented at INET '98: The Internet Summit, Geneva, Switzerland.

Waldhalm, S. (1995). pegasus.cvm.msstate.edu/pbl/pblintro.html

Wilson, B. (Ed.). (1996). *Constructivist learning environments: Case studies in instructional design.* Englewood Cliffs: Educational Technology Publications.

The Author

Alison A. Carr-Chellman (e-mail: aac3@psu.edu; Web homepage: ed.psu.edu/insys/who/carr/default. htm) is Assistant Professor, Instructional Systems, at Pennsylvania State University, University Park, Pennsylvania.

51

Supporting Adult Learners in Web-Based Training

Larry R. Hudson, Linda Greer, and Teresa Buhler

with

Beverly Buck
Laura Decker
Rosemarie T. Florio
DeeAnn Hennighan
Roberta Hennessy
Linda A. Moseley

Lewis Parker
Marlene Rogers
Janet D. Skipper
Don E Starner
Dianna Zometsky

What Support Is Needed?

In industry, trainees often return to class for required re-certification or mandated training. Many of them come to Web-based learning with great trepidation, but they are willing to try anything to get out of traveling, spending weekends away, and using up income to go to class far from home. One student quipped, "Instead of having a hard drive *to* school, I use my hard drive *for* school." Another student said, "Support, to be a successful Web student, comes from family, friends, co-workers, and other Web students. Web courses are time-consuming." These are among the comments received in our survey of students who have taken Web-based training courses offered by the University of Central Florida in Orlando.

Novices to Technology

First-time Web students are amazed at the support offered by the experienced Web students within their classes. They get a great deal of encouragement and instruction from peers and are thus motivated to overcome the hurdles of learning new technology. For novices, it is not so much the assignment that may be in question as the mechanics of doing the assignment and then putting it into a legible format through the computer. For instance, new Web students often need instruction on sending attachments by e-mail, posting comments into a bulletin board or forum, managing time, using the copy and paste functions in the text editor, and so on.

Support By Instructors

Web-based training must be supportive of the learners. An orientation with hands-on instruction on the course pages and an opportunity for students to ask questions is advisable. It makes it easier on everyone if the information is first offered by the instructor at the beginning of a course in the form of a mandatory orientation. Specific introductions of key personnel involved in supporting the course and smaller course groups for practicing navigation and log-on are both beneficial. One new student commented on the orientation by saying, ". . . I was overwhelmed and questioned my sanity for even being there and taking these Web courses. I stayed because the course was required and I had no other choice." Sound familiar to industry trainees?

Some adults start with absolutely no experience on the Internet and little or no experience in word processing. There may be an initial period of "total frustration and tears." One student who was experiencing a steep learning curve with the technology said, "I got wonderful encouragement from the teacher by telephone until I worked out my server problems. I'd call in virtual tears; virtual flowers of encouragement would be sent in return."

According to the consensus of students, the best approach is to just do it and get online with the course. Support is available for each student through faculty, support staff, or seasoned students. One student voiced his appreciation for the instructional support by saying, "We only have to ask, and the answers are given."

There may be incompatibility with the course's server, or one may be unable to log-on due to some "glitch." Thus, it is necessary to "talk" to the teachers with some means other than the computer. One student realistically summarized this aspect and said, "Any time I have had a problem, I have received assistance immediately with satisfying results. Yes, I love the computer, but when it's down or something isn't working, there has to be an old fashioned back-up system."

Peer Support

Students are great at helping other students, and the use of Web PALs, or Peer-Assisted Learners, is a good idea. Trainees work in teams; why not assist as teams also? Support systems need to be in place in order to provide the encouragement and guidance needed by Web-based adult learners. When adults feel they are the only ones with technology troubles and become isolated, then they are likely to withdraw from a Web-based course. Peer support is an essential ingredient to building a learning community and team onsite in industry.

Because of improvements in software programs for Web courses, items available to students may change during the term of the course, eliciting the following reaction: "Often, when I log on to the class, new and easier things have happened to the Forum. It used to take a half-day to get through class discussion in what now I can cover in an hour. I learned quickly that I must dedicate that time everyday, double up the next day, or be lost."

As with most adult learners, life's responsibilities and pressures are many. Time management is essential in order to complete a Web-based course. One student summarized it well when she said, "I had days of 'Oh! This is awful, I'll never get through this,' to days of 'I love this, it is too cool. Yeah! I can handle this.' It was a constant and daily see-saw. I still have occasional days of frustration when I can't find a Website that fits the activity at hand. I no longer have to go to the beach to go 'surfing,' I can throw a log on the fire while I log onto the forums and I can do this in pajamas with a cup of coffee and no makeup or hairdo while making dinner. While my husband is in the driveway searching his engine for a problem, I am in the house using a search engine to answer my problem. I can start class, be interrupted to attend my daughter's open house at school, and come home to finish the discussion."

Organization in Web-Based Courses

The Course

Organization is essential both for the student and the instructor. Instructors should post tips to follow when using the forum, mail, and other course functions at the very beginning of class in order to save time and frustration. Changes within the course during the course term should also be minimized. Not all students can be online daily or even every other day. There should be announcements of any changes that occur which stay in place over several days in order to accommodate the different schedules of learners.

Due dates for class projects must be posted well ahead of time. Instructors and students need to be aware that for instructors this is a job—usually Monday through Friday—while for students this is a requirement for their job. This means that the adult learners must fit the course demands into any available remaining time outside of usual working hours. Much of the student's work may be done on weekends. The student may be restricted as to input or access if he/she is logged on to the computer only in the evening or on the weekend. Thus, students need to learn to adjust to questions that may go unanswered until the following instructor workday.

Instructors using the Web provide the opportunity for people to take classes who normally would not have been able to "attend" due to career obligations, distance for commuting, or other factors. One appreciative student commented, "They [instructional support personnel] treat us as equals and maintain that we are a team, each member an integral part, and what happens to one affects us all." Technology equalizes training access and flattens communication—be ready for it.

Time Management

Consensus from the Web students was that one must be able to schedule the time needed to do the assignments and correspond with fellow classmates. It is the student's responsibility to keep track of important dates. A coping mechanism was suggested by one student as follows: "Time management skills and a really big calendar with different colored pens to keep track of assignments are recommended."

Basically, the essentials for survival are organizational skills that are learned earlier in life; these can be used to complete the task at hand. One student said, "To insure learning and enjoyment of the course, each one of us needs some semblance of thought and ideas as to how to tackle the program with as much aplomb as possible. Am I cognizant of the avenues that are available to me for this assignment? If I am not, then some advisement needs to be attempted."

Another student commented, "Enrolling in Web courses lets you manage the time you spend on learning along with your everyday schedule, and therefore gives you a flexibility that isn't there with most classes. It could, however, be a problem for those that don't manage their time wisely. I wish this type of course delivery was available in more areas."

Self-motivation

If you are not a self-motivated person, you might not be successful in Web-based courses.

Despite the demands, one student appreciatively remarked, "Web-based learning is a wonderful opportunity. Education at your convenience. Who would have thought? I can work on my class any time I want without being tied down to a certain time period. I can have career, family, and an education at the same time. Without Web-based delivery, this wouldn't be possible."

Interaction

Most Web-based courses have some sort of interaction among students, or at least should have, because interaction is the "glue" that bonds Web-based trainees together. CMC (computer mediated communication) techniques for promoting learning communities may include: electronic mail, synchronous chat rooms, or asynchronous forums or bulletin boards.

One student warned, "If you fall behind in the class, you can become electronically 'buried.'" Most students agreed that it was essential to sign on to the class course page several times each week. According to one student, "If I check on a daily basis for the course forum messages, I can respond to classmates when the information is needed and keep on top of the class." Signing on daily and reading messages takes much less time than waiting to do it once a week. If comments are made only once each week, a student is responding to old messages, and "old news is cold news."

The more a person communicates on the class forums, the more involved he/she becomes in the class, and the more dynamic the learning experience. "I have received many tips from others in the course which have assisted me with my own classroom" was the summative comment for one learner.

Success in Web-Based Training

Web-based training is a means of furthering education for those who otherwise could not attend in-person courses. In addition to the training benefits, being forced to learn to operate within a technology-rich environment also has spin-off benefits.

Some adults come to Web-based courses with no computer skills. One student said, "In the period of time for my first course, I went from being essentially computer illiterate to being computer knowledgeable. I am proof that one can succeed in Web-based education because there are others that are more computer literate that have helped me. Now I have started helping others that are just beginning their Web-based education."

Other students come with ample computer skills, as one student noted: "When I came to the first course, I was not afraid of the computer, but now I am much more willing to strike out and investigate. If an error or hung script message pops up, then I try another tactic. I have learned to love the computer and spend hours looking around. These courses have given me the know-how and freedom to accomplish this. I have been exposed to the multiple search engines available and the numerous research areas to explore. Besides, I have learned the content of the specific courses as well. I am glad that I took these courses and will certainly consider taking some more—after I rest up."

One of the best advantages of distance learning is increased access and communication with classmates. When taking a class in a traditional classroom, there usually isn't enough time to share information. There is more student interaction in Web-based courses than in a traditional classroom. The positive aspects of CMC and increased student interaction were summarized by one student: "I know I am less apprehensive in making comments to questions that are posted on the Web. On the course forums, all you have to do is ask for information or place an idea to debate with others. The posted question then ends up with many more comments than the same question posted in a traditional classroom. I have received great tips that I have put to use in my classroom and they have made me a better teacher. It is also nice to hear that everyone else is having the same concerns or problems as you; you're not out there alone. One of our best teaching tools is the knowledge of other teachers. We all need to share and do what's best for the students; the forums provide an opportunity to do this."

In fact, communication increases dramatically over traditional classroom teaching. The democracy of Web-based collaboration was expressed by one student in the following way: "In the classroom environment, we gather in groups by who we like or fit in with. On the Internet, that opportunity is not available because you have to talk to everyone." Another student said, "What a great way to learn what is going on in other students' lives."

In several of the projects, students were assessed on degree and quality of communication with one another. To demonstrate that there is more interaction among students in a Web-based class than in the conventional classroom, well over 2,000 entries were made in the discussion forums for the classes which were surveyed. This number is far more than what would occur in a traditional course, and still does not take into account the thousands of Internet e-mail and course mail communications during the course. A student commented on the forum discussions this way: "These interchanges are thoughtful, meaningful entries posted in an online forum from the privacy of the students' homes."

The convenience of "getting to class" when you have time is important for adult Web students. The comments of one student were very revealing when he said: "I spend more time doing homework now than when I was in a classroom. I probably would not have gone back to school with my children so young if this type of class was not offered. I chose Web-based education because of the convenience. Between job, family life, and taking courses, time organization is also critical. I set aside a specific time, generally late at night, to work on my Web assignments."

The information received from fellow classmates about Websites assists peers in their work. A student summarized it as follows: "I have learned so much in a short time, not only about how to teach, but about myself and my fellow professionals. We have gone through a virtual bonding and give each other support, (and) encouragement and we share levity to spice up the class. By sitting right here at home, I am able to improve myself intellectually, learn information that benefits my work activities, and satisfy job requirements."

Web-based training is highly challenging and very fulfilling, but unless a person has first-hand experience, an accurate judgment on this learning environment is not easily made. One of the most interesting things is that some uninformed people believe that Web-based learning is similar to a poorly designed correspondence course. A student commented on the reaction that he got when discussing his Web course with an associate: "One person even asked if I was going to a 'qualified' college." Would the same question be asked about industry training that was not via the Web?

Experiences that students have are very positive. For example, one student commented: "For one who had thought that learning had to be in the old context of formal learning, i.e., being in a classroom, attending certain days and hours and having the teacher lecture each time—was I ever wrong! The success that you earn comes from the desire to succeed. This new endeavor has proven to be the easiest. Meaning that as long as I discipline myself to at least two hours a day/evening at the computer doing the assignments and answering other students in this class on the forums and posting my replies—then my time is my own."

"The first success for me was searching the Web and finding the needed information to complete the assignment. My next personal success was sending an attachment." Success is validated from the instructor in the form of points, with an idea as to why full points were not earned and guidance on earning the full point value. Applicability was the focus of one student's comments when he said, "I feel that I have learned more in one Web class than I have in all my years in school. The information I have learned will really help me out in the real world, right from the start."

Summary

The pleasure of succeeding in Web-based training was expressed by one adult learner as follows: "In all honesty, the idea of returning to college via the Web is phenomenal! In this day and age, I realize that very little is impossible, but to bring the classroom home and not have to run to class is a miracle and very much appreciated. I do not feel that anything has been eliminated taking this course or any future course over the Web. What I have been able to accomplish and learn absolutely astounds me. New friends have been made. I hope they will be there to completion; they are beautiful people. I hope that we maintain contact!"

Another student put it succinctly when he said: "In my opinion, Web-based learning is the best thing that ever happened; without it, I wouldn't be able to continue my education. Without Web-based technology, most students would not be able to complete their education, as they are working full-time and raising a family, which limits their opportunity to travel for classes. I am looking forward to continuing taking my classes via the Web. It gives one a feeling of accomplishment and well-being."

Suggested Readings

Ellsworth, J. (1994). *Education on the Internet: A hands-on book of ideas, resources, projects, and advice.* Indianapolis: Sams Publishing.

Evans, T., & Nation, D. (Eds.). (1996). *Opening education: Policies and practices from open and distance education.* New York: Routledge.

Harasim, L. (Ed.). (1990). *Online education: Perspectives on a new environment.* New York: Praeger.

Heldman, R. (1993). *Future telecommunications information applications, services, and infrastructure.* New York: McGraw-Hill.

Knott, T. (1994). *Planning and evaluating distance education: A guide to collaboration.* Memphis: Diphara Publications.

Khan, B. (Ed.). (1997). *Web-based instruction.* Englewood Cliffs: Educational Technology Publications.

Jager, R., & Ortiz, R. (1997). *In the company of giants: Candid conversations with visionaries of the digital world.* New York: McGraw-Hill.

Mason, R., & Kaye, A. (Eds.). (1989). *Mindweave: Communication, computers, and distance education.* New York: Pergamon Press.

Moore, M. (Ed.). (1990). *Contemporary issues in American distance learning.* New York: Pergamon Press.

Porter, L. (1999). *Creating the virtual classroom: Distance learning with the Internet.* New York, John Wiley & Sons.

Sullivan-Trainor, M. (Ed.). (1994). *Detour: The truth about the information superhighway.* Indianapolis: IDG.

Tapscott, D. (1995). *The digital economy.* New York: McGraw-Hill.

The Authors

The authors are at the University of Central Florida in Orlando (Web homepage: reach.ucf.edu/~voced).

Primary authors' e-mail addresses:
Larry Hudson (lhudson@cfl.rr.com)
Linda Greer (tutor@gdi.net)
Teresa Buhler (tmb66184@pegasus.cc.ucf.edu)

52

Web-Based Case Studies: A Multipurpose Tool for the Training Toolkit

M. Elizabeth Hrabe,

Mable B. Kinzie, and

Marti F. Julian

Introduction

To encourage development of the higher order thinking skills and professional expertise demanded of today's workers, instructional designers and performance technologists are turning to theories and models that focus on *active, situated* learning. Such active learning environments require authentic problems, a collaborative setting, and guidance from experts (Grabinger, 1996; Kass, Burke, Blevis, & Williamson, 1993/1994; Wilson & Cole, 1996).

At the Curry School of Education, University of Virginia, we have been designing and delivering multimedia cases via the Web for the professional development of our primary clientele—emerging instructional designers. We have found case methods to be a particularly valuable active learning tool:

- Cases place learners in a realistic setting with an authentic problem.

- Cases can encourage team-based problem solving or can be used for individual exploration.

- Cases draw on existing knowledge and call for the development of new knowledge.

- Cases can provide expert guidance and feedback in a variety of ways.

We believe that cases can be a powerful strategy for achieving performance improvement goals across a wide range of training venues.

In this chapter, we present the theory on which case methods are based, describe case methods, and offer examples of case materials. We also discuss how cases can be used: for training, performance support, and authentic evaluation.

Theoretical Background

Active learning. Active learning theory stresses the importance of the learner's built-in capacity to assimilate new information into his or her existing knowledge network, and in the process construct new and modified understandings. These new meanings are made in relationships with others (Bruner, 1966; Vygotsky, 1978). Research indicates that learning is often situation specific, as is its transfer to new settings (Brown, Collins, & Duguid, 1989; Lave & Wenger, 1991). Learning environments, then, must be *situated* in real or realistic settings, forcing the student to consider his or her learning in a specific place, time, culture, and situation.

Active learning provides students with rich experiences—a professional practice setting, authentic problems, opportunities for collaboration with others, and expert guidance (Grabinger, 1996; Kass, Burke, Blevis, & Williamson, 1993/1994; Wilson & Cole, 1996). "The idea is to let learners experience the intellectual changes that experts feel when modifying their own understandings from working with realistic situations" (Grabinger, 1996, p. 671).

Apprenticeships and other forms of actual professional practice are highly effective settings for learners to acquire depth of expertise (Brown *et al.,* 1989; Lave & Wenger, 1991).

Case method. The case study method is another approach to the provision of active, situated learning environments. In our own work, we have found that cases are a useful way of expanding the *breadth* of professional experiences for novices. (Our beginning designers may not have time in their educational programs to undertake instructional design projects for training across and within health care, financial, military, and museum settings, for example, but they do have time to explore case-based problems in a host of them.)

Long used in business and medical training, cases have recently received wide attention in such fields as engineering, education, nursing, counseling, social work, and increasingly, instructional design (Ertmer & Russell, 1995; Graf, 1991; Rowland, Parra, & Basnet, 1994). The *case study method* is ". . . a teaching method which requires students to actively participate in real or hypothetical problem situations, reflecting the kind of experiences naturally encountered in the discipline under study" (Ertmer & Russell, 1995). An important distinction between the case method and the general problem-based learning models to which it is related (Duffy & Cunningham, 1996) is noted by Grabinger (1996): "in case-based learning, teachers first teach students what they need to know to become interested in the case that will be examined . . ." (p. 677). It is at this point in the instructional process, following initial skills introduction, where we believe case methodology can have its greatest impact for most kinds of training.

Emerging technologies. As active learning models evolve, so, too, do new instructional technologies, with interactive multimedia technologies and the Web emerging as particularly appropriate for stimulating active learning. Non-linear hypertext, animated graphics, audio, and video can help to significantly increase the richness and realism of simulated settings in multimedia case presentations over their text-based precursors. Mounting cases on the Web provides the advantages of online delivery and communication. Students can access the materials when and where they like, with or without an actual instructor present. Learners can work alone, or collaborate virtually with others. The significant resources of the Internet are also available to students for use in their case analyses.

Case Design

What is a case? How does it work? We define a *case* as a narrative based on fact (though the account may be fictionalized) describing a problematic situation in a given professional arena. Varying in length from short scenarios to novelette-length accounts, the goal of a case study is to inform the learner of various elements of practice in the pertinent field. Thus, the case narrative may reveal instances of good practice, flawed practice, or practice in an ambiguous situation. The case "story" is supported by *case materials* or artifacts: interviews, memos, letters, video and clips, charts, graphs, photographs, and any other relevant data which serve to enhance the details of the case (Shulman, 1992).

Although learners can interact with cases in many ways, they generally address a case by analyzing the case materials to create a written (or oral) *case response* which suggests methods for resolving problems presented in the narrative. In the process, they identify the professional knowledge they have that applies; they focus on what additional knowledge they need and set about getting it; they propose, debate, and select solutions; and they hypothesize as to possible outcomes. Case-based instruction assumes that students who demonstrate the ability to perform these actions in a case analysis have the *potential* to do so in such a situation in the real world (McNergney, 1994; McNergney, Herbert, & Ford, 1994).

Well-written, compelling narratives are intrinsically motivating (Shulman, 1992). What will happen? How will it all turn out? Students have an interest in finding out, in changing the ending, in practicing the professional strategies they are learning in a realistic environment.

Guidance and Feedback. In our online cases, we provide guidance and feedback for students through the use of guiding questions, provocateur questions, expert perspectives, and peer responses.

Guiding questions. Guiding questions provide a problem-solving framework for the case analysis. Divided into four components, they direct the learner to consider the perspectives of important characters in the case, define the key issues, propose possible solutions, and consider the consequences for each proposed solution.

Provocateur questions. The case study method makes meaningful use of *novice-expert collaboration* in developing practical ways to understand and deal with problematic professional situations. In our own use of cases, we employ a twofold role for experts: experts as "coaches" and experts as "experience-relaters." Successful practitioners in the field themselves, expert-coaches furnish guidance, support, and feedback. They act as "provocateurs," asking probing questions that prompt novice learners to extend their consideration of other issues and perspectives.

Experts can also present possible case solutions—not as a model for students to follow—but as a method of engaging students with their own authentic experience and accumulated professional knowledge: "Here's what happened when I was faced with a similar issue." When Roger Schank and colleagues at the Institute for the Learning Sciences (ILS) develop goal-based scenarios for problem-based learning, they include coaching in the form of stories and advice that come directly from experts. Experts "help evaluate what's been done, put it in perspective, or relate it to the real world " (Riesbeck, 1996, p. 59).

Expert perspectives. For our own cases, we often seek expert opinions from *content* professionals. These experts, chosen to represent interested stakeholders portrayed in a case (a school administrator in a case involving a public school system, a rural extension agent in a case in which farm issues are important), give authentic voices to the characters and problems depicted and, thus, provide heightened realism for the case and breadth of perspective for the student.

Peer responses. Following a case analysis, participant responses are posted online, affording learners an opportunity to view multiple solutions for the case and analyze the strengths and weaknesses of the various approaches. Having access to peer responses can serve to ratify student perceptions, reveal personal biases, and deepen understanding. Such capability becomes even more powerful a learning opportunity when combined with local or online discussions in which students share their thinking, challenge each other's positions, and negotiate consensus.

An Online "Casebook"

Beginning in 1996, the Curry School has hosted yearly instructional design case competitions. (See Kinzie, Hrabe, & Larsen, 1998, for a description of one of the competitions.) The Instructional Design Case Event Web site is available (curry.edschool.virginia.edu/go/ITcases).

For these events, multimedia cases were created and presented online to competing teams of instructional design graduate students from universities across the United States. The case materials and accompanying expert opinions, competition guidelines, and posted analyses from student teams have been retained on the site to create an online "casebook" for instructional design students and professionals. These case materials continue to be used by instructor-led classes and by teams or individuals working on their own.

The cases present situations and design requirements an instructional designer might encounter in the real world, and exemplify the wide variety of experiences and contexts in which professional designers must operate. A public school system, a university/community agency partnership, a hospital, and a national electronics chain are the diverse settings, each presenting a series of challenges and unexpected difficulties for an instructional designer. By working through the series of cases, novice instructional designers can gain experience making the translation from design principle to design practice.

A Case Example—Prescription: Instructional Design

The Case

In one competition case, "Prescription: Instructional Design" (Hrabe, Julian, Kinzie, & Kovalchick, 1997), an instructional designer in a hospital setting is asked to develop staff training on the use of a new robotic blood analyzer. As the designer begins a needs assessment, it soon becomes apparent that there is significant "background noise" which could impede the implementation of any design for training: organizational turmoil, impending lawsuits, a managerial agenda out of sync with staff agendas, morale problems, and public misunderstanding.

The presentation of the case is largely non-linear. The student views the hospital environment and staff through the eyes of the designer, Will Brubaker. A floor plan of the hospital serves as the organizing feature with "rooms" (hypertext links) which may be visited for observation descriptions, personnel interviews, documents, and other artifacts (see Figure 1). By clicking on the rooms and collecting information, the student gradually discovers the important issues and the politically complex background of the case. Through interviews with various players in the case, students are exposed to differing perspectives on how these issues impact the interested parties. Eventually the case's instructional designer (and the learner analyzing the case) is faced with creating a needs assessment that accurately, and diplomatically, reflects the competing agendas and requirements of everyone involved.

Analysis, Scaffolding, and Feedback

Case analysis. In "Prescription: Instructional Design," students consider the guiding questions from the problem-solving heuristic (perspectives, issues, professional knowledge, possible

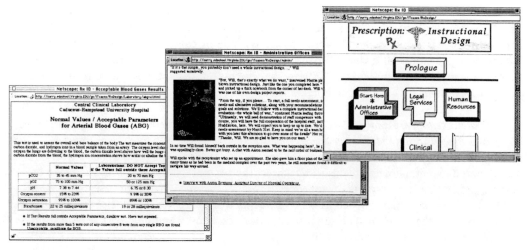

Figure 1. Floor plan and ancillary documents from "Prescription: Instructional Design."

action, and consequences of that action) as they define a solution for the case—a needs assessment for the client. They can add their written responses to the Website by means of an online form provided for that purpose.

Expert scaffolding and feedback. To act as "provocateurs" for the event, we invited three experts, who both practice and teach instructional design, to review student responses and provide feedback to students. Assuming character roles within the context of the case, our experts asked questions intended to force students to justify their positions and to expand their perspectives and consideration of pertinent issues presented by the case. An additional panel of experts evaluated teams' case and questions responses and provided insightful critiques for each. These critiques, together with the provocateurs' questions and the students' answers, are also posted to the Website.

We solicited an expert perspective for the case from a practicing instructional designer who provided her own case analysis and design solutions. When consulted following completion of students' own case analyses, this expert's response allowed students to benefit from the views of an experienced designer.

A Multipurpose Tool

Cases can be used in a variety of ways, for a number of different purposes. They can be used as a stand-alone activity or can be bundled with other types of online or on-site training. Groups and teams can simultaneously explore a case; individuals can pursue case issues and points of personal interest when analyzing cases on their own. Cases can be used to support the performance of professionals on the job. And cases can be used to evaluate skills and abilities in an authentic setting.

Cases for Training

Cases can be used as stand-alone skill-building experiences or employed as part of a training module. In the latter instance, the learner goes through some form of direct instruction, such as a tutorial, and then moves on to a case analysis as a way to practice and expand the new skills in realistic setting.

Instructor-led case analysis. "Instructor-*led* training" becomes a misnomer when cases are used. Commonly, instructors and students work through the analysis of cases together. At times, the instructor will proceed slightly ahead to act as guide or coach, providing alternative possibilities or suggestions for a direction the analysis might take. At other times, the instructor moves in step with the students and serves as a discussant and mentor, building meaning together with students (Duffy & Cunningham, 1996).

Student team case analysis. In another application of case methods, teams of learners are formed (either within a location or across locations) and assigned to analyze an online case together. An instructor can participate a great deal in the case analysis process (as above) or to a more limited extent, allowing teams to self-direct their inquiry and analysis and to make use of case materials and case experts at appropriate points in time. Our own research has documented the benefits which can accrue when students work together to collaborate in analyzing a case: collegial dialogue, interpersonal negotiation, consensus building, and appreciation for multiple perspectives (Kinzie *et al.*, 1998).

Individual case analysis. A single student can work independently to analyze the case as teams might. Missing, of course, are the advantages of collaboration during case analysis, but gained is ease in implementation and freedom to explore issues of personal interest. Even if individuals analyze and respond to the cases on their own, sharing of perspectives can always be encouraged by examination of and response to the analyses of others.

Cases for Knowledge Management and Performance Support

There are moves afoot in a number of organizations to record the experience-based knowledge of its members and make it available within the organization as a performance support and learning resource (Raybould, 1995). To this end, Roger Schank recommends: "Gather stories. Why stories? Because that's where golden nuggets of organizational knowledge reside" (1997, p. 20). These are the stories that have historically been passed from old hands to new recruits at the water cooler (Ruggles, 1997). Every organization has thousands of them; the problem in today's organizations is in getting them told (Schank, 1997), in part because of the organizations' large scope, geographic distribution, and workforce mobility (Ruggles, 1997).

An excellent example of the use of cases for performance support is the *NNAble* system developed by Jim Laffey and others at Apple Computer (Laffey, 1995). Among a number of other valuable support functions, this system distributes relevant cases to technical consultants as they assist clients in solving problems. At the same time, the system automatically captures the particulars of the current problem (observations, procedures, notes, and final diagnosis) which serve as the bones of a new case. The system forwards this information to an editor, who prepares the case for submission into the library knowledge base.

Cases for Evaluation

Because competent performance and professional expertise require both context and judgment, they are virtually impossible to measure with objective tests. Tests must be linked to the tasks, contexts, and "feel" of the real situations (Wiggins, 1993). The use of cases for assessment in the professions is not new. Case scenarios form a part of the medical boards, the United States Medical Licensure Examination (USMLE), and most state bar examinations, while full cases have been used as Ph.D. comps in education at Eastern Michigan University (Geltner, 1995). Although it is possible to objectify scoring of case analyses—the USMLE is scored on a "best choice" basis determined by a panel of experts (USMLE, 1997)—scoring rubrics based on model responses and descriptive narratives can be more useful descriptors of a learner's abilities than inflexible right/wrong numerical ratings. We suggest that cases provide authentic contexts in which instructors can look at student responses to more accurately assess the degree of professional understanding acquired. They are appropriate for many types of training.

Conclusions

We have found multimedia case studies to be effective and flexible learning tools. We believe that such cases presented online are suitable for performance improvement goals across a wide range of training venues: on-site, facilitator-led training or online training modules, for student teams or for single learners. Cases can also be a valuable format for recording and making organizational knowledge accessible for performance support. Finally, we recommend cases as an authentic way to evaluate higher order skills in a variety of professional practice settings.

References

Brown, J. S., Collins, A., & Duguid, P. (1989). Situated cognition and the culture of learning. *Educational Researcher, 18*(1), 32–42.

Bruner, J. (1966). *Toward a theory of instruction.* Cambridge, MA: Harvard University Press.

Duffy, T. M., & Cunningham, D. J. (1996). Constructivism: Implications for the design and delivery of instruction. In D. H. Jonassen (Ed.), *Handbook of research for educational communications and technology* (pp. 170–198). New York: Simon & Schuster Macmillan.

Ertmer, P. A., & Russell, J. D. (1995). Using case studies to enhance instructional design education. *Educational Technology, 35*(4).

Geltner, B. B. (1995). Shaping new leaders for new schools: Using the case method for innovative teaching and learning. Paper presented at the International Conference on Case Method Research and Application.

Grabinger, R. S. (1996). Rich environments for active learning. In D. Jonassen (Ed.), *Handbook of research for educational communications and technology* (pp. 665–692). New York: Simon & Schuster Macmillan.

Graf, D. (1991). A model for instructional design case materials. *Educational Technology Research and Development, 39*(2), 81–88.

Hrabe, M. E., Julian, M. F., Kinzie, M. B. , & Kovalchick, A. E. (1997). *Prescription: Instructional design.* University of Virginia, Curry School of Education; teach.virginia.edu/go/ITcases.

Kass, A., Burke, R., Blevis, E., & Williamson, M. (1993/1994). Constructing learning environments for complex social skills. *The Journal of the Learning Sciences, 8*(4), 387–427.

Kinzie, M. B., Hrabe, M. E., & Larsen, V. A. (1998). Exploring professional practice through an instructional design team case competition. *Education Technology Research and Development, 46*(1).

Laffey, J. (1995). Dynamism in electronic performance support systems. *Performance Improvement Quarterly, 8*(1).

Lave, J., & Wenger, E. (1991). *Situated learning: Legitimate peripheral participation.* Cambridge, UK: Cambridge University Press.

McNergney, R. F. (1994). Videocases: A way to foster a global perspective on multicultural education. *Phi Delta Kappan, 76*(4), 50–53.

McNergney, R. F., Herbert, J. M., & Ford, R. E. (1994). Cooperation and competition in case-based teacher education. *Journal of Teacher Education, 45*(5).

Raybould, B. (1995). Performance support engineering: An emerging development methodology for enabling organizational learning. *Performance Improvement Quarterly, 8*(1), 7–22.

Riesbeck, C. K. (1996). Case-based teaching and constructivism: Carpenters and tools. In B. G. Wilson (Ed.), *Constructivist learning environments: Case studies in instructional design* (pp. 49–61). Englewood Cliffs: Educational Technology Publications.

Rowland, G., Parra, M. L., & Basnet, K. (1994). Educating instructional designers: Different methods for different outcomes. *Educational Technology, 34*(6), 5–11.

Ruggles, R. (1997). Why knowledge? Why now? *Perspectives on business innovation,* Issue 1, online journal; businessinnovation.ey.com/journal/issue1/features/whykno/loader.html

Schank, R. (1997). *Virtual learning: A revolutionary approach to building a highly skilled workforce.* New York: McGraw-Hill.

Shulman, L. S. (1992). Toward a pedagogy of cases. In J. Shulman (Ed.), *Case methods in teacher education* (pp. 1–30). New York: Teachers College Press.

United States Medical Licensure Examination (1997); usmle.org

Vygotsky, L. S. (1978). *Mind in society.* Cambridge, MA: Harvard University Press.

Wiggins, G. (1993). Authenticity, context, and validity. *Phi Delta Kappan, 75*(3), 200–214.

Wilson, B., & Cole, P. (1996). Cognitive teaching models. In D. Jonassen (Ed.), *Handbook of research for educational communications and technology.* New York: Simon & Schuster Macmillan.

The Authors

M. Elizabeth Hrabe (e-mail: hrabe@virginia.edu; Web homepage: teach.virginia.edu/go/ITcases) is a Doctoral Student and Instructor, Instructional Technology Program, Department of Leadership, Foundations, and Policy, Curry School of Education, University of Virginia, Charlottesville. **Mable B. Kinzie (e-mail: kinzie@virginia.edu; Web homepage: kinzie.edschool.virginia.edu)** is Associate Professor, Instructional Technology Program, University of Virginia. **Marti F. Julian (e-mail: mfj3a@virginia.edu)** is a Doctoral Student, Instructional Technology Program, University of Virginia.

53

Web-Based Rapid Prototyping as a Strategy for Training University Faculty to Teach Web-Based Courses

Betty A. Collis

Introduction

At the Faculty of Educational Science and Technology of the University of Twente, a major initiative is taking place, involving the re-design of our courses for more flexible delivery, in particular to prepare for the simultaneous participation in our courses of three different groups of students: regular students attending locally, full-time students attending at a satellite campus on the other side of the country, and part-time students who work during the day and will participate in the majority of the course activities at times convenient to themselves, without having to leave their homes and workplaces. The key to this re-design process is our use of the World Wide Web, not only to support the new form of courses, but also to support the training of our own faculty to prepare for this new way of teaching. Staff development and engagement is our central challenge. In this chapter, I describe the approach we use to train and engage our own faculty members in the re-design of their teaching for Web-based delivery, and the way that different Web-based tools are a major component of this approach. We call the approach "Web-based rapid prototyping as a training strategy."

An Integrated Approach to Institutional Change

Integrating information and communication technology into institutional practice throughout a faculty requires an implementation strategy. A successful implementation strategy, in turn, requires many components: administrative vision and courage; the momentum and insight that comes from previous experience; a sound research-based educational framework to motivate educational change; extensive experience with the design, development, and use of computer-related and networked educational tools and environments; a design and development method utilizing powerful and locally-attuned tools and database technology; a robust technical infrastructure with high availability to all instructors and students; a culture that rewards innovation and quality in teaching; and at its core, a strategy for instructor engagement and commitment for change (Collis, 1998). In addition to all this, there needs to be creative energy, and skilled persons to translate creative ideas into usable forms.

Given these requirements, it is not surprising that implementation success regarding the sustained and integrated use of information and communication technologies to support teaching and learning across a faculty is difficult to achieve. In a recent inventory (Boon, Janssen, & Cox, 1997) of higher-educational institutions in The Netherlands, only a handful of departments and faculties were found to have made substantial progress in terms of this sort of institutional integration of technologies into the teaching and learning process. The Faculty of Educational Science and Technology at the University of Twente was acknowledged as being in a leadership position with regard to implementation depth and breadth.

But we have now moved even further. We have moved from the pioneering phase, through what can be called the "1,000 flowers blooming" phase (Collis, 1997a), into a phase of managed change. Through an implementation method (the "TeLeTOP Method," Tele-Learning at T.O., the initials of the Dutch name of our faculty) based on rapid prototyping as a key method for staff engagement and training, all of the ingredients necessary for successful institutional change, accompanied by the use of advanced technologies, are present in our situation. The first step in this rapid-prototyping method, an analysis strategy to guide faculty in considering Web-supported options for the re-design of their courses, has been developed and used as the basis of over 30 course re-designs. Table 1 summarizes the major aspects of this strategy.

Table 1. Suggestions to guide instructor decision-making in the re-design of courses for more-flexible delivery.
(De Boer & Hamel, 1998; De Boer, Strijker, & Collis, 1997)

Course aspect	Current practice, strengths	How to extend, make more flexible?
1. General course organization	—Faculty bureau makes ongoing information available to students via display boards, personnel available for questions, bulletins in the student newspaper, telephone availability, putting messages in students' individual mailboxes, sending e-mail. —Instructors provide course outline with all details of course organization; give updates and changes during lecture sessions, put messages on student notice board or in student postboxes (physical and e-mail).	—All courses are supported by an integrated Website; the courses themselves are integrated in larger Websites with faculty-wide information. —"Newsflash" areas on the Websites present announcements, changes, updates. —Administrative information (names of students, e-mail addresses, scores to date, etc.) are available through the Website. —Faculty bureau maintains channels of personal contact and availability, printed material still available on courses, timetable, etc.; e-mail and the Web used for student contact, updates in information, sign-ups for elective courses, etc. —Instructor still provides course outline but also has it on the Web; all updates and announcements are on the Web or via e-mail.

Table 1. Suggestions to guide instructor decision-making in the re-design of courses for more-flexible delivery *(continued)*.

Course aspect	Current practice, strengths	How to extend, make more flexible?
2. Communication	—Between instructor and students: Takes place during lectures, informally in the canteen and hallways, via personal visits to the instructor in his office, via notes between the instructor and students via their physical mailboxes or e-mail. —Among students, organized or informal, in the hallways and other locations around campus, in the computer laboratories, via their mailboxes or e-mail.	—Maintain all of these, but add: —Convenient communication through an e-mail center in the Websites, where not only individuals can be messaged, but also groups within the course (via aliases). Group members can have their own private communication areas within shared workspaces. —The opportunity for guided reflective discussions via a Web board (a form of computer conferencing within a Website). —Tools for scheduling and carrying out real-time communication at a distance, including chat, Internet telephony, and desktop meeting tools (such as *Netmeeting*).
3. Lectures, instructor presentations	—Instructors have long experience in lecturing; many use PowerPoint and other media. Students and instructors value good presentations to clarify and expand study materials.	—Each course will maintain at least two lectures in which all students are present; these will take place during the 18 Fridays in which part-time and satellite-site students come to the local campus. —Local and satellite-site students will have several additional presentation sessions, but with less instructor presentation and more student interactivity via the shared workspaces and communication possibilities in the networked interactive classrooms. —Highlights of these interactive classroom sessions will be available on the Web, synchronized with notes, for students not physically present. —More teaching done by guiding of self-study of interactive study materials on the Web page, and ongoing feedback during self-study between instructor and students, via various Web-based forms and communication tools.

Table 1. Suggestions to guide instructor decision-making in the
re-design of courses for more-flexible delivery (continued).

Course aspect	Current practice, strengths	How to extend, make more flexible?
4. Self-study and practice	—All courses have books, readers, and assigned readings. —Many courses have practical sessions for statistics practice and for computer-based activities.	—Expand existing study materials by adding interactive tools for self-study via the Web (see #3 above). —Expand and update study materials by using links to additional resources via the Web. —Provide the same or more support for exercises and small assignments, by having them submitted via the Web and by being able to offer direct (automatic) feedback (for exercises with a pre-determined correct answer), making a model answer available via the Web after the student has submitted his work, or via general feedback from the instructor or by the students to each other (possible when student responses are available via the Website). —Carry out certain computer-based and practical sessions when all students are on campus on the 18 Fridays; provide all students with convenient access to the network and all computer tools and resources so that physical presence for computer activities is not necessary.
5. Collaborative projects	—Emphasis on group work in many courses, carrying out a design project with many steps of analysis and leading to a group product of some sort (written, media based, etc.).	—Offer tools to support group activities such as a shared workspace. —Emphasize group interactions during the "interactive classroom" sessions (in place of instructor presentations). —Offer some choice in projects and in the way projects can be carried out, group or more individually based. —Require continual posting on the Website of work relating to the on-going process of projects, such as design decisions, task allocation agreements, draft versions; use the Website for students to give each other feedback on work-in-progress and for instructor comments. —Link final products to the Website and include student reflection on each other's work as part of the course requirements.

Table 1. Suggestions to guide instructor decision-making in the re-design of courses for more-flexible delivery *(continued)*.

Course aspect	Current practice, strengths	How to extend, make more flexible?
6. Testing	—Most courses have scheduled, monitored examinations. Students can repeat unsuccessful examinations.	—Look for ways to base assessment on a wider variety of inputs than mainly the traditional examination. —Maintain some examinations during the times when all students are present. —Present some forms of examination such as reflective comments via the Web, where questions are posted at a certain time and responses must be submitted within a specified time limit.
7. Other	—Students go to the library, they relax informally in the canteens and on the campus, they participate in sports and student associations, they meet students outside their courses, they evolve into close relationships with certain instructors, they take advantage of guest lecturers, colloquia, etc.	—Access to the library is fully available via the Web. —Campus events are supported via the Web so students have at least a way of being informed and asking questions. —E-mail and personal Web pages help people to know each other better. —Coming to the campus in person remains important. The experience of being part of an academic community is more than just the sum of taking courses!

Principles Underlying Staff Engagement

We know as researchers as well as practitioners that staff engagement is the critical component of the initiative. Not only must the teaching staff accept the innovations involved, but also, it is the instructors involved who must teach in the new ways and handle the new technologies. Their competency and commitment are the key factors. Also, our support staff, such as those who work with the student administration and handle student questions, complaints, and mentoring, must be equally well informed and committed. Our technical support personnel will face substantial new problems and calls for their services. Our administration must respond to the new issues and challenges that will occur, such as funding for laptop computers for all part-time students so that they do not suffer a technical-access disadvantage compared to our local and satellite-site and masters program students. The culture must be ready, in terms of staff who have adequate experience and confidence (McCartan & Hare, 1996). Thus, staff engagement is critical, involving commitment, skills, and willingness to change. The following principles are among those that underlie our staff-engagement strategy:

- Higher education faculties do not respond well to top-down steering. Decision making and the change process need to have the characteristics of a learning process in which participation is voluntary and everyone feels himself or herself represented (Mintzberg, 1990). Although the overall decision to change to more flexible teaching means that the instructor will not have a voluntary choice in terms of dealing with the different cohorts of students, the many different staff-development sessions and meetings which we offer are on a voluntary basis, and those who wish to adapt their courses without help from TeLeTOP are free to do so.

- Parallel to this, some administrative stimulants are valuable for a change process to move forward (Kluytmans, 1994). Each department is receiving financial compensation for each course being re-designed in cooperation with the TeLeTOP team. Also, other forms of recognition (for the instructor individually as well as his or her group) can result from participation; the administration has created the impression that being involved with this initiative is valuable and valued.

- Coordination within the faculty is valuable, so that cooperation can increase ("from individually inventing the wheel to being able to make use of available solutions"; Boon, Janssen, & Cox, 1997, p. 43).

- The incentive to invest time in re-designing one's teaching is not only for pragmatic reasons, but also coupled to the opportunity to make one's own teaching better in terms of enrichment, and of being able to try out some new possibilities to deal with previous problems in particular courses. The instructor's efforts are not to the disadvantage of his or her research productivity, as a number of research opportunities are available in association with the fact that the chair of the project is also the chair of a research area in tele-learning in the faculty. This confronts the familiar difficulty in higher education of not having enough time for research if one invests time in teaching improvement (Seminoff & Wepner, 1997).

- As much as possible, the instructor is being sheltered from technical problems, and scaffolded in his or her familiarization process with the aspects of technical competency that will need to be acquired (Juge, Hartman, Sorg, & Truman, 1997).

- We are fortunate in our good instructors; we want to build on their strengths, not ask them to abandon them. New ways of teaching more flexibly do not mean that the instructor needs to lose the social and communicative contact that he or she now enjoys with students (Collis, 1997b; Langlois, 1997).

How Web-Based Rapid Prototyping Works

To make this staff engagement and training happen, the TeLeTOP rapid-protyping method includes the following aspects:

- During the first two months of TeLeTOP (September and October 1997), seven different open training sessions were offered to staff, led by the TeLeTOP chair, in which a variety of examples of new teaching strategies and Web-based tools were introduced. Participation was voluntary, and good. Between 20 and 40 staff members came to each session. Some time was spent in giving staff some introductory lessons in how to change a word-processed file into a HTML file and how to change a PowerPoint file into a set of HTML files. Meanwhile, different informational meetings were held, and formal visits were made to the administration of each department in the faculty to discuss issues involving staff involvement.

- The actual instrument used for rapid prototyping and concurrent staff training is innovative and based on the above principles of staff engagement. A **decision-support tool** *(DST)* was built which is Web-based and integrated with a database environment (De Boer & Hamel, 1998; De Boer, Strijker, & Collis, 1997; Fisser, De Boer, Peters,

Strijker, Verheij, & Collis, 1998). The *DST* is designed as a tool for support of a structured interview involving the TeLeTOP chair, at least one of the design team, and each instructor whose course is being re-designed. The tool and procedure were pilot-tested in December 1997, after which some intensive revisions were made. During December 1997 and January 1998, the tool and procedure were used with the instructors of all the 30 courses being adapted. During this one-hour interview, the instructor is asked a series of questions about what he or she would like to see added or changed in his or her course, following the pedagogical re-engineering framework shown in Table 1. For each possibility, a link is provided via the *DST* to a Web-based example of what the possibility looks like in current practice in the courses in our faculty which already make use of the Web for course support. The members of the TeLeTOP team interact intensively with the instructor, trying to identify which ideas and approaches are most likely to be acceptable and interesting to him or her and to respond with ideas and suggestions, as well as to skip suggestions which do not seem like they will be comfortable for the instructor. When the instructor indicates that he or she has found a feature interesting, it is selected via the decision-support tool *(DST)*. When the interview is completed, the *DST* automatically generates a Web page for the instructor via which he or she can further examine the choices that were made, via any Web browser or by studying the printout. Figure 1 shows the (password-protected) homepage of the Web-based environment that not only offers instructors entry to the *DST,* but also to the automatically generated first prototypes of Websites, generated on the fly in response to the functionalities selected by the instructor during the *DST*-supported interview. This

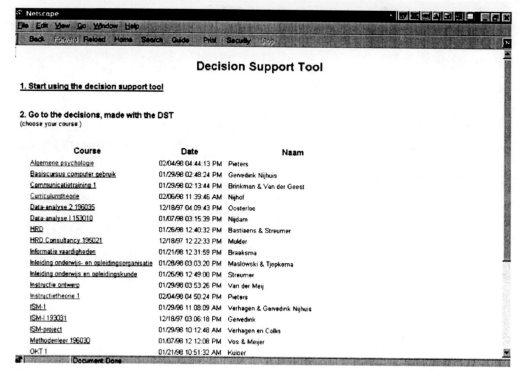

Figure 1. Homepage giving access to Web-based decision-support tool and to the automatically generated first prototypes of Web environments (course names are shown here in their native Dutch). "Naam" is Dutch for name (of instructor).

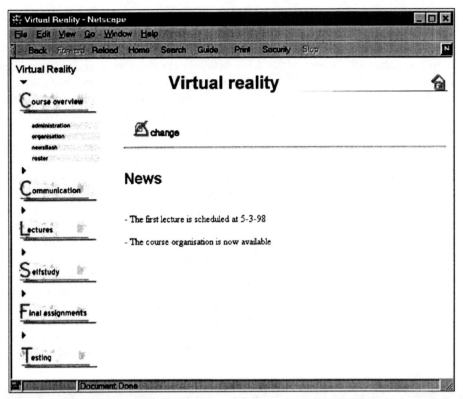

Figure 2. An example of a second prototype of a course Web environment, based on the decisions made with the *DST* and on weekly staff sessions, using rapid prototyping as a training strategy.

approach to rapid prototyping not only involves the instructor in a critical phase of the decision making about the functionalities to include in his or her Web environment, but also serves the purpose of giving the instructor a closer look at many different types of functionalities. This is a key form of staff training, done "on the fly" during the rapid prototyping.

- Within a few days, the TeLeTOP team members visited the instructor in his or her office, and walked through the first prototype of his or her course Website. This fast turnaround was possible because of the way that the *DST* is linked to an underlying database integrated with our method of rapid prototyping. The instructor's first prototype represents all the structure and functionalities that could be available in his or her eventual course site, but without any content other than minimal example material, and with only minimal attention to the visual aspects of the user interface. The TeLeTOP team members and the instructor walked through this site, and discussed possible additions or deletions, another way in which staff training is concurrently strengthened via the rapid-prototyping process. (Changes can continue to be made for a number of months.)

- The second phase of the TeLeTOP Method, from February through April 1998, consisted of three parallel activities. One of these is continual staff involvement and professional development based on weekly hands-on sessions for instructors only, in which the instructors learn to work with their own sites and handle the amount of content-entering and minor site modifications (i.e., editing the wording of an HTML page, adding some notes to a HTML page, etc.) that we have found to be necessary in practice when using Web-based environments in support of instruction. Parallel to this is the ongoing development of the course Websites, evolving from the first to second prototypes. Linking these first two activities is the device of using the instructors' own evolving sites as the media for their hands-on activities. Based on what options the instructors were most interested in, we tailored each week's session to focus on those options and how the instructors could be comfortable with using them within a Website and for teaching. Figure 2 shows a typical second-prototype course site evolving during the weekly staff-development sessions.

- The third of the parallel activities is also important: To demonstrate these new pedagogical approaches and the use of the technology involved, the author has structured the weekly staff sessions as an example of using a Web environment to support "course" activities by asking the instructors to think of the sessions as a simulated class (called the Wednesday Course, because this is the regular meeting day). Instructors were to take the roles of students using the sites, and the author modeled the role of an instructor, filling the site and using it to support the sorts of activities identified in Table 1. Figure 3 shows the interface of the "Wednesday Course," generated via the same rapid-prototyping method.

- As yet another aspect of the use of the Web to support staff training, the author also has evolved her own prototype into a fully functioning course-support environment. All instructors not only are invited to visit the course and the course environment to see it "in action," but also have been integrated into the course as contact persons and evaluators of the students' work.

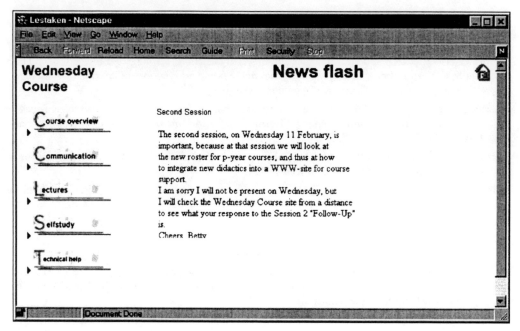

Figure 3. The "Wednesday Course" for the instructors to learn to work with the Web-based environment while continuing the evolution of their own environments.

Thus, staff engagement through training, established on the basis of Web-based rapid prototyping using our Web-based decision-support tool, is a major aspect of our strategy for systemic change in our faculty.

References

Boon, J., Janssen, J., & Cox, F. (1997). *ICT in de onderwijsorganisatie: Drie cases in het hoger onderwijs* (ICT in the educational organization: Three cases in higher education), Onderwijstechnologisch expertisecentrum OTEC, Open universiteit, Heerlen.

Collis, B. A. (1997a). Implementing ICT in the faculty: Letting 1000 flowers bloom or managing change? In M. Mirande, J. Riemersma, & W. Veen (Eds.), *De digitale leeromgeving* (pp. 121–136). Groningen: Walters-Noordhoff.

Collis, B. A. (1997b). Pedagogical reengineering: A pedagogical approach to course enrichment and redesign with the WWW. *Educational Technology Review, 8*(3), 11–15.

Collis, B. A. (1998, March). *Putting vision into institutional practice: The TeLeTOP Method at the University of Twente.* Paper presented at BITE '98 (Bringing Information Technology into Education), Maastricht.

De Boer, W. F., & Hamel, Q. (1998). *Designing courses for the WWW.* Masters thesis, Faculty of Educational Science and Technology, University of Twente.

De Boer, W. F., Strijker, A., & Collis, B. (1997). *The TeLeTOP Decision Support Tool,* Faculty of Educational Science and Technology, University of Twente.

Fisser, P., De Boer, W. F., Peters, O., Strijker, A., Verheij, G. J., & Collis, B. A. (1998). *Implementing telelearning: Decision support for instructors in the TeLeTOP Project.* Paper presented at the Networked Lifelong Learning Conference, Sheffield, UK.

Juge, F., Hartman, J., Sorg, S., & Truman, B. (1997). Asynchronous learning networks for distributed learning. In J. Hlavicka & K. Kveton (Eds.). *Proceedings: Role of the university in the future information society* (pp. 29–41). Prague: UNESCO International Centre for Scientific Computing.

Kluytmans, F. (1994). Verandering: Organisatorische en machtspolitieke vraagstukken. In J. Gerrichhausen, A. Kamperman, & F. Kluytmans (Eds.), *Interventies bij organisatieverandering.* Heerlen: Kluwer/Open universiteit.

Langlois, C. (1997). Information technologies and university teaching, learning, and research. In J. Hlavicka & K. Kveton (Eds.), *Role of the university in the future information society* (pp. 7–17). Prague: UNESCO International Centre for Scientific Computing.

McCartan, A., & Hare, C. (1996). Effecting institutional change: The impact of some strategic issues on the integrative use of IT in teaching and learning. *ALT-J (Advanced Learning Technology-Journal), 4*(3), 21–28.

Mintzberg, H. (1990). Strategy formation: Schools of thought. In J. W. Frederickson (Ed.), *Perspectives on strategic management.* New York: McGraw-Hill.

Seminoff, N. E., & Wepner, S. B. (1997). What should we know about technology-based projects for tenure and promotion? *Journal of Research on Computing in Education, 30*(1), 67–82.

The Author

Betty A. Collis (e-mail: collis@edte.utwente.nl; Web homepage: users.edte.utwente.ne/collis/) is Professor, Tele-Learning, Faculty of Science and Technology, at the University of Twente in the Netherlands, Web homepage for TeLeTOP: teletop.edte.utwente.ne).

54

Support for Teachers Enhancing Performance in Schools (STEPS): An EPSS Professional Development Tool

Pamela Taylor Northrup,

Karen L. Rasmussen, and

Janet K. Pilcher

Introduction

Support for Teachers Enhancing Performance in Schools (STEPS) is an electronic performance support system available on the World Wide Web, designed to assist educators in instructional planning using guidelines and standards for school reform and accountability. In Florida, the Sunshine State Standards have been implemented with the mandate for all educators, both preservice and inservice, to begin implementing them in the classroom. The ultimate accountability is a new test, the Florida Comprehensive Achievement Test (FCAT), that will measure the benchmarks established within the Sunshine State Standards.

In order to train educators across the state of Florida, a virtual professional development model, STEPS, was designed to provide training and continuous, just-in-time support to educators tasked with implementing Florida's Sunshine State Standards. The concept of day-one performance with a focus on four areas of school reform, including (1) integrated curriculum; (2) integrating technology; (3) alternative assessment; and (4) diverse learning environments, was the overall goal of the Web-based training tool development effort.

EPSS Defined

An electronic performance support system (EPSS) is a tool that provides "integrated access to information, advice, learning experiences, and tools to help someone perform a task with the minimum of support from other people" (Gery, 1991). More recent definitions include a more systems-oriented view with organizational workplace performance being the focus rather than the outcome of an individual learner (Raybould, 1995; Stevens & Stevens, 1995). Gery (1995) and Raybould (1995) refer to this concept as Performance-Centered Design (PCD). The design interface and the integrated knowledge within an EPSS are built based on a solid performance goal and an organizing design framework. Overall, EPSS approaches promote the concept of learning by doing, situated in real-world environments, rather than being taught in a training classroom (Northrup & Pilcher, 1997). The support for everyday performance is a primary goal of EPSS technology (Sherry & Wilson, 1996). Embedded within the context of an EPSS system is scaffolding that will provide users with cognitive training wheels to assist users in achieving task performances (Sherry & Wilson, 1996). These cognitive training wheels can be ignored once users are confident in their abilities to perform tasks. According to the Knowledge Integration Environment model (Bell, Linn, & Davis, 1997), the scaffolds, or cognitive training wheels, may answer the questions of: (1) What do I do? (2) How do I do it? and (3) What is the big picture?

Components within STEPS

STEPS, designed for PreK–12 educators and preservice teachers, has themes that correspond to each grade level cluster identified within Florida's Sunshine State Standards and Curriculum Frameworks including: (1) PreK–2 Cluster, Communities; (2) Grades 3–5 Cluster, Nautical Archaeology; (3) Grades 6–8 Cluster, Native Florida Habitats; and (4) Grades 9–12 Cluster, Terrestrial Archaeology. STEPS includes eight major components to assist educators in planning using Florida's Sunshine State Standards. Corresponding to the themes, model units and Web links are different for each grade level cluster. STEPS includes: (1) Lesson Architect; (2) Best Practices Database; (3) Model Units; (4) Instructional Web Links; (5) Tutorial Library; (6) Sunshine State Standards; (7) links to other planning tools; and (8) a series of scaffolds for assistance and guidance. Access STEPS at scholar.coe.uwf.edu/pacee/steps/. See Figure 1.

Figure 1. The STEPS tool.

Lesson Architect. The Lesson Architect is the centerpiece of STEPS and includes a model for instructional planning. The model follows the Events of Instruction (Gagné, Briggs, & Wager, 1992) along with elements of integrated curriculum models, including project-based learning, problem-based learning, and thematic learning. Educators can begin planning using the forms embedded within the Lesson Architect to design lessons. Scaffolds are built into the Lesson Architect to link educators to the coach and to the Guided Tour to provide the *"What do I do?"* assistance; to the Instructional Tutorials and the Model Units to gain information on *"How do I do it?"*; and to an InfoMAP to get the *"Big Picture"* of planning using STEPS and the Sunshine State Standards. Educators can save the lesson, exit the Internet, and return later to continue working on the lesson or to begin planning a new lesson. The Lesson Architect is designed to download lessons to an individual workstation in much the same way that e-mail is downloaded. The process is transparent to the user. Once a lesson is complete, the user can e-mail the lesson directly to the school principal, to a colleague, to a teacher education faculty member, or to a supervising teacher in a student practicum setting.

The user of the Lesson Architect may want to submit individual lessons to STEPS as a model unit or to become part of a new component, the Unit Digest. Users can submit lessons and units at any time to the Quality Assurance Contact (QAC) for STEPS. The QAC then reviews the unit for quality based on several criteria established for Instructional Planning. Or, users may want to self-evaluate the quality of their instructional lessons and units by using a checklist provided within the STEPS Lesson Architect. The criteria used for determining the quality of an individual lesson or unit includes items such as: (1) Do the objectives align to the Sunshine State Standards benchmarks? (2) Do the activities, when completed by students, achieve the goals of instruction? (3) Is technology being integrated meaningfully into the instruction? (4) Do the assessments reflect the outcomes trying to be achieved? (5) Is the content within the instruction accurate? Complete? Free of bias? (6) Are a variety of diverse learning environments addressed to include multicultural, multiple intelligences, and inclusion? (7) Is the unit designed to be integrated across more than one subject area?

Best Practices Database. The Best Practices Database is an InfoBase of ideas that work successfully in the classroom. The Best Practices Database was designed by hundreds of teachers from several school districts in Florida. The contributions included ideas for classroom assessment, cooperative learning, technology integration, and specific subject area ideas. The Best Practices Database includes ideas specific to grade level cluster as well as general strategies that may work at all grade levels. Users of the Best Practices Database can search by keyword, by Sunshine State Standards, or request to view all best practices within a specific area. All best practices are keyed to Florida's Sunshine State Standards. It is intended that best practices will be used to gather information and ideas for instructional planning within the Lesson Architect.

Educators can submit best practices by using the online "Submit" feature or may be solicited through training sessions and preservice education courses. Once best practices are received, they undergo a three-tier quality assurance process. Tier I is a review for accuracy and alignment to Florida's Sunshine State Standards. The Tier I reviewers are classroom teachers who have subject matter expertise and extensive training on the Sunshine State Standards. Tier II is a review for accuracy in grammar and spelling. Tier II reviewers are Language Arts and English educators. Tier III reviews are a final Quality Assurance check for overall accuracy, alignment to the Sunshine State Standards, and grammar. The Tier III review is conducted once each best practice has been placed on the Web site. The Tier III reviewer maintains a database of how many best practices by benchmark are submitted and by whom to ensure coverage of all benchmarks.

Model Units. Ten-day model units were designed by educators in each of the four grade level clusters as a model for how to plan using the four primary areas of school reform and accountability. The units parallel the themes for each grade level cluster. The model units were designed using the Lesson Architect, therefore, modeling exactly what should be included in an instructional plan. Model units include hyperlinks to Web sites that would strengthen the unit within a classroom or to provide additional resources for teachers and students. The model units also relate to a series of online Internet expeditions that are being developed to support the themes and the Sunshine State Standards. The Internet Expeditions will provide the student with resources and materials educators would need to fully implement the model unit in the classroom. Resources included may be PowerPoint presentations, HyperStudio stacks, graphics libraries, databases of relevant information, worksheets, letters to parents, and more. The model units have two main purposes. First, it is intended that educators will use the model units as an example of how to plan instructional units in conjunction with Florida's school reform and accountability initiatives. Secondly, model units can be implemented in whole or in part by classroom or preservice teachers.

Based on the Model Unit concept, several sample units have been designed for a new area of STEPS, the Unit Digest. Over time, the Unit Digest will contain hundreds of complete lesson plans including resources required for implementation in the classroom.

Model Units, once created, were reviewed critically using another three-tier system. Tier I review included faculty members with expertise in instructional systems design, instructional technology, and classroom assessment. The Quality Checklist mentioned above was used as a baseline for the review. Units not meeting the criteria were either returned to the developers of the unit or passed on to a revision team for modification. The Tier II review was conducted by educators with expertise in the subject area and the grade level cluster. Tier II reviewers looked at content accuracy as well as the reality of implementing the lesson in the classroom. Within the review, issues such as access to specific types of technology, timeframes provided, and learning styles of individual learners were considered. The Tier III review is a field test of the instructional unit in a classroom setting. The teacher team developing the unit is asked to implement the unit in its entirety while other team members videotape and take digital pictures of the unit. Teachers are interviewed after the unit is complete and final modifications are made to the unit based on the formative evaluation process.

Instructional Web Links. Over 400 Web links have been identified for this component within STEPS. The Web links were selected based on the following criteria: (1) quality; (2) alignment with Florida's Sunshine State Standards; (3) supplements to themes and model units; and (4) high interest to teachers. All Web links have a paragraph description to generally describe what is included in the Web site. Included also are the Sunshine State Standards that are addressed within the Web link itself. Educators can select the individual standard to view or can move into the instructional Web link to peruse for classroom use. This is a popular resource for teachers to use in instructional planning. Teachers report that having this resource saves a great deal of time in Internet surfing. The intent of the instructional Web links is to provide another resource to educators as they plan instruction for the classroom.

Tutorial Library. The Tutorial Library contains over 40 instructional tutorials designed to provide 10–15 minute overviews of specific concepts related to instructional planning. The tutorials are clustered into four categories: (1) integrated curriculum; (2) integrated technology; (3) alternative assessment; and (4) learning environments. The four categories are the primary areas of school reform addressed within STEPS. Additionally, the four categories parallel the Lesson Architect. As users encounter elements within the Lesson Architect that are unfamiliar, it is designed to link users to specific tutorials to provide assistance. The tutorials are designed to be "just-in-time" instruction for users at the point of need. The cognitive training wheels concept discussed above is evidenced here very clearly. Users can simply choose to ignore the tutorial links if already familiar with the concept, or may choose to study the tutorials in depth to assist further in instructional planning. A pretest and a posttest within each tutorial will provide district staff development coordinators with accountability measures for teachers choosing to use instructional tutorials for professional development. Districts are suggesting that tutorials alone can serve as staff development for teachers. One district links all teachers to the tutorials in assisting them to gain basic instructional technology skills as mandated by the district school board.

Quality assurance is also a factor for the Tutorial Library. The Quality Assurance Contact reviews each tutorial for: (a) updated references; (b) relevant graphics and videos; (c) content accuracy; (d) clarity; (e) alignment with school reform and accountability initiatives; (f) alignment with Florida's Accomplished Practices; and (g) overall design consistent with the established standard for tutorials.

Sunshine State Standards. This link is critical to the success of STEPS. Teachers obviously must have ready-access to the standards for which they are being held accountable. Many educators do not have paper copies of the standards and rely on this Web link to provide the knowledge base required for instructional planning. Linked to the Sunshine State Standards is a tutorial that describes why they exist and how they are being used in Florida. This scaffold serves as our awareness training on Florida's Sunshine State Standards. The intent of this component is for teachers to access, copy, and paste specific benchmarks into the Lesson Architect as they plan.

Links to ECPT and FIRN. These resources are additional sites for teachers to visit on the Web while planning. The Electronic Curriculum Planning Tool (ECPT) is a series of databases that provide instructional resources by subject area for teachers. Teachers can select resources from the ECPT and incorporate them into the total lesson planning process within the Lesson Architect. FIRN, or Florida Information Resources Network, is Florida's primary collection of resources maintained by the Florida Department of Education. This valuable resource provides educators with links to educational resources, FIRNmail, and more.

Scaffolding Resources. The scaffolds within STEPS are embedded throughout all of the components. Included are: (1) a guided tour; (2) the coach; (3) an InfoMAP; and (4) links to model units and the tutorial library. The scaffolds respond to the questions *What do I do? How do I do it? What is the Big Picture?* Each scaffolding element is intended to assist educators as they work through the EPSS, STEPS, at a time and place convenient to their schedules.

Conclusion

STEPS is an EPSS tool available on the World Wide Web to assist teachers in planning using Florida's Sunshine State Standards. The just-in-time concept is the driving force behind the tool. Teachers can receive professional development at times and places convenient to them. Districts are embracing the idea of teachers not having to attend workshops and seminars during the school day. Using STEPS, staff development can be accomplished at times more convenient to the teacher, with necessary skills being delivered in a state-of-the-art approach, EPSS.

Currently, educators across the state are using STEPS for instructional planning. Many colleges and schools of teacher education are using STEPS as required assignments in methods and practical experiences. STEPS, although designed around Florida's school reform and accountability initiatives, can be used by anyone with Internet access. The resources and the Lesson Architect are relevant to preservice and practicing educators across the country. Given that most states are undergoing school reform and accountability based on Goals 2000 and other national initiatives, plans are underway to link Florida's Sunshine State Standards to the Goals 2000 standards and to other state standards that parallel Goals 2000. This effort should provide educators nationally with a clear picture of how STEPS can be used in other states. Hudzina, Rowles, and Wager (1997) indicate that EPSS is "a mile wide and only a few inches deep, yet EPSS have all of the ingredients of a Renaissance Technology." We believe that STEPS is an effective Web-based training tool for educators to achieve knowledge, skill, and abilities in instructional planning in a virtual environment.

References

Bell, P., Linn, M., & Davis, B. (1997). Knowledge integration environments. KIE Research Group, University of California-Berkeley; kie.berkeley.edu/KIE.html

Gagné, R. M., Briggs, L. J., & Wager, W. W. (1992). *Principles of instructional design.* Orlando, FL: Harcourt Brace Jovanovich College Publishers.

Gery, G. (1991). *Electronic performance support systems.* Boston, MA: Weingarten Publications.

Gery, G. (1995). Attributes and behaviors of performance-centered systems. *Performance Improvement Quarterly, 8*(1), 47–93.

Hudzina, M., Rowles, K., & Wager, W. (1997). Electronic performance support technology. Defining the domain. *Performance Improvement Quarterly, 10*(1), 199–211.

Northrup, P. T., & Pilcher, J. K. (1997). STEPS: An EPSS tool for instructional planning. Proceedings of the annual conference of the Association for Educational Communications and Technology, St. Louis, MO.

Raybould, B. (1995). Performance support engineering: An emerging development methodology for enabling organizational learning. *Innovations in Education and Training International, 32*(1), 65–69.

Sherry, L., & Wilson, B. (1996). Supporting human performance across disciplines. A converging of roles and tools. *Performance Improvement Quarterly, 9*(4), 19–36.

Stevens, G. H., & Stevens, E. F. (1995). *Designing electronic performance support tools: Improving workplace performance with hypertext, hypermedia, and multimedia.* Englewood Cliffs: Educational Technology Publications.

The Authors

Pamela Taylor Northrup (e-mail: pnorthru@uwf.edu; Web homepage: scholar.coe.uwf.edu/coe2/faculty/pnorthru.htm) is Division Chair, Professional Studies and Technology, at the University of West Florida, Pensacola, Florida. Karen L. Rasmussen (e-mail: krasmuss@uwf.edu; Web homepage: coe.uwf.edu/coe2/faculty/krass.htm) is Coordinator of Instructional Technology at UWF. Janet K. Pilcher (e-mail: jpilcher@uwf.edu; Web homepage: coe.uwf.edu/coe2/faculty/jpilcher.htm) is Assistant Dean of the College of Education at UWF.

55

Integrating Web-Based Technology into Teacher-Preparation Training Programs

Nella B. Anderson, LeAnn McKinzie, Don C. Johnson, Jarvis W. Hampton, and Trey McCallie

Introduction

Teacher training programs should begin to integrate the use of technology into all methods courses in order to provide students with information about computer applications of interest to them and with real application to future teaching assignments (Johnson, 1996; Larson & Clift, 1996; Topp, Thompson, & Schmidt, 1994). The integration and modeling of technology in teacher training programs will increase the likelihood that these preservice teachers will incorporate the use of technology into their teaching in the future (Handler, 1993; Johnson, 1996). Modeling by instructors requires many changes from the traditional role of the university professor (Topp, 1996). Teacher educators must use technology as a tool themselves, modeling (Copley, 1992; Johnson, 1996; Knapp & Glenn, 1996; Reeves, 1996) for their students the many ways that technology can enhance teaching, learning, and scholarly activity.

The effective use of technology includes rethinking active learner exploration, cooperative groups, and new instructional delivery systems (Johnson & Harlow, 1993; Thompson, Schmidt, & Hadjiyianni, 1995). This focus moves away from teacher-centered, single-discipline, and product-oriented instruction to student-centered, cross-disciplinary, process-oriented learning (Ennis & Ennis, 1995–96; Reeves, 1996).

Teaching Online

U. S. Secretary of Education Richard Riley stated in October of 1996 that "Today's students still need to know the three Rs, the old basics. But they also need to understand how to use the three Ws—the World Wide Web—and take advantage of the unsurpassed learning opportunities available on the Internet" (U. S. Department of Education, *Community Update*, 1996). Teaching in an online setting challenges teachers to shift paradigms and use a constructivist model of learning (Peterson & Facemyer, 1996). In the dynamic learning environment available on the Internet, faculty members will be expert guides, helping students navigate new territories (Gates, 1996).

The Virtual Learning Environment

WTOnline is the virtual university at West Texas A&M University. It is composed of students and instructors who come together and fill spaces we know as classrooms—classrooms where real teaching and learning take place. The virtual classroom is mediated through information technologies that promote learning at a distance, specifically, Web-based instruction. It is important to note that in every case, technology is secondary to course content and should only be utilized to support the instructional environment. Two salient features, structure and support, have driven the development of the virtual university and will be discussed as they relate to its ability to support instruction.

Online Structure and Support

Structural concerns of the virtual university include organizational and technological issues. Organizational issues focus on the people aspect of the university, while technological issues focus on the creation of the virtual environment.

Organization. The salient feature of WTOnline is its people. Each contributes in a unique way, providing support for the student who enters the virtual classroom and the faculty member who teaches there. The following contributions are made as shown in Figure 1.

1. The faculty members are the content experts, instructional designers, and in some cases, HTML authors.

2. The student-based Web Team creates and maintains the virtual learning environment and provides Web programming, as well as HTML authoring expertise for faculty.

3. The Director of the Instructional Innovation and Technology Lab (IITL) provides oversight for the diverse groups involved in the virtual university, administration of the site, and training and instructional design assistance for faculty.

It must be pointed out that a team mentality further supports the organizational aspect of the online university and that the participants share many tasks. The team members work together

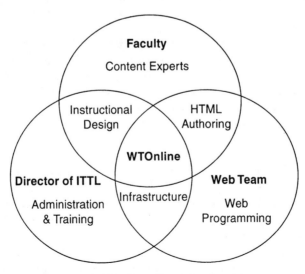

Figure 1. WTOnline: Organizational issues.

during the semesters prior to and during the delivery of instruction. In addition to the support of the Web team and the director, each faculty member is assigned a part-time graduate student to facilitate the process.

Support structures are also available for students taking the online courses. Content questions are directed to faculty via e-mail and chat sessions. Technology related problems are handled through the student-based dial-up help line and the employees of the IITL.

Technology. The flexibility of the Web-based interface used in the development of the virtual learning environment is natural and instinctive in the platform-independent delivery of instruction. More importantly, the Web's ability to support a multiprotocol environment has put the tools of teaching and learning into the hands of faculty and students. The user-friendly interface provides access to the hardware and software which supports WTOnline, including the Web server, mail server, chat server, and news server, as shown in Figures 2 and 3. This access flexibility is apparent in the internal and external navigation set up for the virtual classroom.

Internal navigation provides access to the resources inside of the classroom. Clicking on the indicated buttons on the navigation bar accesses the following resources (see Figures 2 and 3):

1. Go to Unit—provides access to the weekly unit of study.

2. Calendar—provides access to the upcoming events in the class.

3. Chat—a Java-based chat is used to support synchronous communication in the classroom. Each class is allotted one chat room, which can only be used by class members.

4. E-mail—provides access to an interactive form where instructors, classmates, and/or technical support personnel names can be checked off a list, submitted, and a new message page spawned that is correctly addressed.

5. Newsgroup—each class has a newsgroup set up in support of asynchronous discussion.

6. Peer Expertise—Web pages set up for the sharing of group projects. These pages are automatically posted via interactive forms.

7. Student Homepages—biographical information and a picture is provided in this area. Further links to the student's portfolio of work. These pages are automatically posted via interactive forms.

8. Syllabus—traditional classroom information is always accessible.

9. Help—general help provided for the resources, which support the classroom.

External navigation or the ability to "change channels" is provided in another navigation bar and includes a link to the virtual university homepage, the university homepage, and the university library, as shown in Figures 2 and 3.

Modeling Usage

The effective use of technology includes rethinking traditional forms of instruction. Instructors teaching online need to maintain the perspective that we learn best "with" technology rather than "from" it (Johnson, 1996). This perspective allows instructors to engage students in active (Copley, 1992; Reeves, 1996; Yakimovicz & Murphy, 1995), authentic (Copley, 1992), challenging tasks (Copley, 1992; Reeves, 1996), and collaborative efforts (Reeves, 1996).

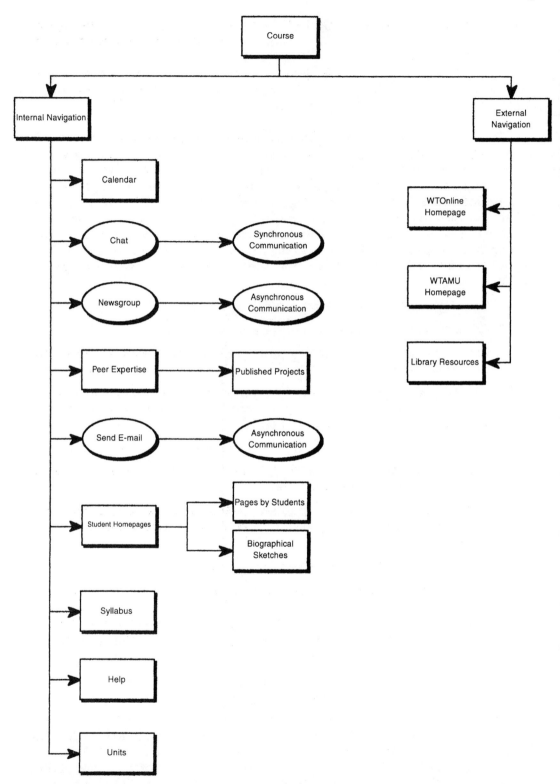

Figure 2. The user-friendly interface provides access to the hardware and software that supports WTOnline.

Figure 3. Internal navigation provides access to the resources inside the classroom.

A computer-specific introductory course is usually insufficient in modeling for preservice teachers the use of technology as a tool for teaching and learning (Topp *et al.*, 1994). Education professors from various disciplines must begin to use technology as a cognitive tool to mediate and transform the training experiences of teacher education students (Larson & Clift, 1996).

Instructional Design

Training preservice education students on the Internet requires the course to be more structured than would be required to teach the same course without an electronic component (Gillette, 1996). The structure that is embedded and remains consistent throughout each unit of study is shown in Figure 4. The structure of an introductory special education course taught online will be elaborated on in this section by clustering the components into categories and providing a brief description of each.

1. Instructional Design Framework (see Figure 4):

    (a) Each unit of study is divided into six instructional steps, as shown in the far-left column of Figure 4.

    (b) Each of the six steps is divided into instructional components, as shown in the horizontal rows in Figure 4.

    (c) Reference numbers are assigned to each of the instructional components. The reference numbers are depicted using three digits separated by decimals (e.g., 2.3.4

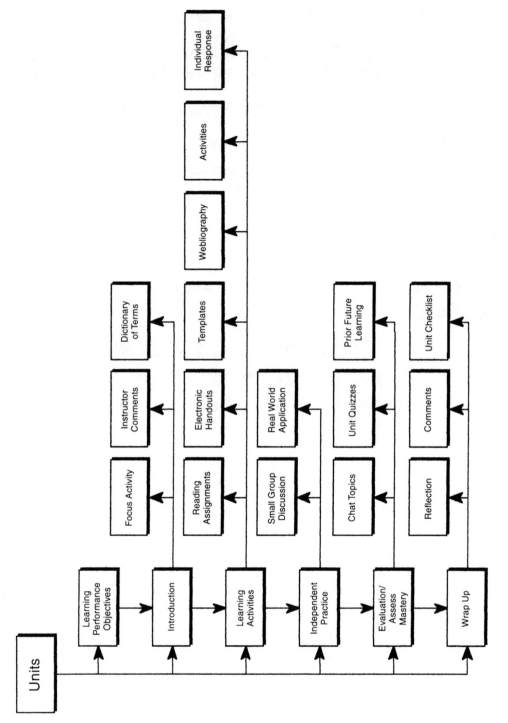

Figure 4. The Web-based organizational structure embedded within each unit of study.

represents Unit2.Step3.Activity4). The reference numbers are used when discussing activities via e-mail, newsgroup, and/or chat.

(d) Buttons are located at the bottom of each of the six instructional step pages so that students can go to the "next step" or return to the "unit index," which provides links to all six steps.

2. Curriculum Development (see Table 1):

(a) The curriculum is built upon the principles of active learning, cooperative groups, peer-mediated instruction, and content experts.

(i) Active learning is integrated into the course through the use of interactive forms and case studies found on the Internet.

(ii) The class is divided into cooperative groups of two, based on where students live and their educational major.

(iii) Peer-mediated instruction is used through the creation of student homepages and peer expertise pages. These pages allow students to share their work and ideas with each other.

(iv) Content experts are utilized by incorporating parents of students with disabilities and personnel in the special education field in local public schools into the class discussions (e.g., e-mail, chat, and newsgroup).

(b) All activities taught in the traditional course on campus are incorporated into this online course through the use of e-mail, chat, newsgroup, electronic handouts, forms, and Websites (see Table 1).

Teaching in this virtual classroom in comparison with teaching in the traditional classroom requires much more self-learning and much less teaching (Peterson & Facemyer, 1996). The dynamic learning environment available online, which is expanding at exponential rates, provides opportunities for students to become explorers and discoverers (Gates, 1996).

Education students have consistently expressed the need to see technology used by their university instructors if they are to use these tools effectively in their own teaching (Larson & Clift, 1996). All students enrolled in this online course had completed at least one required computer-specific course prior to the beginning of this online course. The development of a survey of instructional effectiveness was developed by the authors to measure the effects of learning educational content through the use of Web-based technology.

Web-Based Survey of Instructional Effectiveness

Due to both a lack of suitable instruments and the importance of being able to assess Web-course effectiveness, the authors developed the Web-Based Survey of Instructional Effectiveness (WebSIE) to meet this need. Expert opinion from individuals with both academic credentials (Ed.D. or Ph.D.) and Web-based course experience were sought to develop an original pool of 58 items. This pool of items was subjected to factor analysis. A five-factor model was adopted retaining 30 items: *Use* of the Internet (8 items); Integration of the Internet into *Instruction* (8 items); General *Computer Use/Attitude* (4 items); Using a Computer for *Communication* (5 items); and Web-based *Course Effectiveness* (5 items).

Pretest to posttest comparisons showed students improved in their self-reported Web-based skills and attitudes in the use of the Internet, integration of the Internet into instruction, general computer use/attitude, and using a computer for communication. These statistically sig-

Table 1. Traditional classroom instructional components
incorporated into Web-based instruction.

Traditional	Web-Based
Learning performance objectives for chapter given at beginning of class	— Learning performance objectives for unit given in first step of each unit
Instructor comments (lecture)	— Instructor comments page — Chat — E-mail — Newsgroup postings
Textbook to look up chapter definitions of educational terms	— Definitions of educational terms for units — Webliography of Websites with definitions of educational terms — Textbook
Handouts	— Electronic handouts — Webliography of Websites related to unit topics
Flash cards of educational acronyms	— Interactive form (exact name)
Matching card game of educational laws	— Interactive form (multiple choice)
Large group discussion with other students in the class and instructor	— Chat (attendance required weekly) — Newsgroup postings
Small group discussion with other students in the class	— E-mail with class partner — Chat — Newsgroup postings
Sharing of specific ideas with other students in the class and instructor	— Student homepages — Peer expertise pages — E-mail sent to other students — E-mail sent to instructor — E-mail sent to parents of children with disabilities — E-mail sent to personnel in special education field in local public schools — Chat — Newsgroup postings
Application of concepts to real-life situations (educational documents with specific questions to answer)	— Web case study of students in special education with specific questions answered using an interactive form (open-ended response) — Posted to students' homepages — Posted to peer expertise pages
None	— Unit concepts related to prior and future learning given in the fifth step of the unit
None	— Unit quiz using an interactive form (multiple choice)
None	— Reflection on unit using an interactive form (open-ended response)

nificant gains in Web-based skills and attitudes were noted after one education methods course that modeled the use of the Internet in instruction. Future studies need to replicate these findings and investigate the effects of the integration of technology into more and varied teacher training courses. Additional effects of the integration of technology into teacher training programs needs be studied after these preservice teachers become practicing teachers, focusing on how often and in what ways they integrate technology into their own teaching.

Conclusion

Teacher education students who have had experience using telecommunications while in college will be more likely to use the available technology in their classrooms, in comparison to those who have not had the experience (Russett, 1995). University instructors must model the best uses of telecommunications (Russett, 1995), because it has tremendous potential for teaching (Johnson, 1996). The Internet will help move more of the focus of education from the institution to the individual, making lifelong learning a reality for more people (Gates, 1996). Time has come for educators to master the new tools of the profession when training preservice education students (Tomei, 1996).

Additional supplementary materials and resources about courses taught through WTOnline is available on the Web (online.wtamu.edu/courses).

References

Copley, J. (1992). The integration of teacher education and technology: A constructivist model. In D. Carey, R. Carey, D. Willis, & J. Willis (Eds.), *Technology and teacher education annual* (pp. 381–385). Charlottesville, VA: Association for the Advancement of Computing in Education.

Ennis, W., III, & Ennis, D. (1995–96, Winter). One dozen ways to motivate teacher education faculty to use technology in instruction. *Journal of Computing in Teacher Education, 12*(2), 29–33.

Gates, B. (1996). Linked up for learning. *Educational Record, 66*(4), 34–41.

Gillette, D. (1996). Using electronic tools to promote active learning. *New Directions for Teaching and Learning, 59–70.*

Handler, M. (1993). Preparing new teachers to use computer technology: Perceptions and suggestions for teacher educators. *Computers and Education, 20*(2), 147–156.

Johnson, D. (1996). "We're helping them to be good teachers": Using electronic dialoguing to connect theory and practice in preservice teacher education. *Journal of Computing in Childhood Education, 7*(1–2), 3–11.

Johnson, D. L., & Harlow, S. D. (1993). Current research in technology and teacher education: Three phases of our mission. In H. C. Waxman & G. W. Bright (Eds.), *Approaches to research on teacher education and technology* (pp. 61–65). Charlottesville, VA: Association for the Advancement of Computing in Education.

Knapp, L. R., & Glenn, A. D. (1996). *Restructuring schools with technology.* Boston, MA: Allyn and Bacon.

Larson, A. E., & Clift, R. T. (1996). Technology education in teacher preparation: Perspectives from a year-long elementary teacher education program. *Educational Foundations, 10*(4), 33–50.

Peterson, N., & Facemyer, K. (1996). The impact of the Internet on learners and schools. *NASSP Bulletin, 80*(582), 53–58.

Reeves, T. C. (1996). Technology in teacher education: Electronic tutor to cognitive tool. *Action in Teacher Education, 17*(4), 74–78.

Russett, J. (1995). Using telecommunications with preservice teachers. *The Journal of Computers in Mathematics and Science Teaching, 14*(1–2), 65–75.

Thompson, A., Schmidt, D., & Hadjiyianni, E. (1995). A three-year program to infuse technology throughout a teacher education program. *Journal of Technology and Teacher Education, 3*(1), 13–24.

Tomei, L. (1996, April/May). Time for action: Talking about classroom technology is replaced by doing in this faculty development program. *Momentum, 27*(2), 53–55.

Topp, N. (1996). Preparation to use technology in the classroom: Opinions of recent graduates. *Journal of Computing in Teacher Education, 12*(4), 24–27.

Topp, N., Thompson, A., & Schmidt, D. (1994). Teacher preservice experiences and classroom computer use of recent college graduates. In J. Willis, B. Robin, & D. Willis (Eds.), *Technology and teacher education annual* (pp. 46–51). Charlottesville, VA: Association for the Advancement of Computing in Education.

U. S. Department of Education, Community Update. (1996). *Teachers volunteer to train colleagues in using technology* (p. 41). Washington, DC: U. S. Government Printing Office.

Yakimovicz, A., & Murphy, K. (1995). Constructivism and collaboration on the Internet: Case study of a graduate class experience. *Computers & Education, 24*(3), 203–209.

The Authors

Nella B. Anderson (e-mail: nanderson@western.edu; Web homepage: webct.western.edu.8900/) is an Assistant Professor with the Teacher Education Program at Western State College of Colorado, Gunnison, Colorado. **LeAnn McKinzie (e-mail: lmckinzie@mail.wtamu.edu; Web homepage: online.wtamu.edu/)** is Director of Academic Services in the Information Technology Department at West Texas A&M University, Canyon, Texas. **Don C. Johnson (e-mail: djohnson@mail.wtamu.edu)** is Assistant Professor in the Psychology Department at West Texas A&M University. **Jarvis W. Hampton (e-mail: jhampton@ mail.wtamu.edu)** is a Graduate Assistant in the Information Technology Department at West Texas A&M University. **Trey McCallie (e-mail: tmccallie@mail.wtamu.edu)** is a WTOnline Programmer in the Information Technology Department at West Texas A&M University.

56

The Teachers' Internet Use Guide: Web-Based Training for Educators

David Hoffman, Lorraine Sherry, Jonathan Lurie, and Jason McDaniel

History and Philosophy

Amid national and regional mandates for schools to "get wired," and generous corporate and government offers of "seed money," teachers of every philosophical persuasion are being urged (pushed) to adapt their curriculums to incorporate Web-based learning activities.
(Hackbarth, 1997, p. 191)

On October 20, 1994, Congress passed the Improving America's Schools Act (IASA). IASA's purpose was to help ensure that all children acquired the knowledge and skills needed to succeed in the 21st century as flexible workers and lifelong learners (U. S. Department of Education, 1997)—particularly at-risk children in traditionally underserved populations. From an institutional standpoint, the initiative makes perfect sense. However, as curriculum expert William Reid points out,

> . . . ideals are ideals and realities are realities. While the great ideas can define clear purposes, harness moral commitment, and energize administrative initiatives, their power to deal with the everyday vagaries of individuals and organizations is severely limited. (Reid, 1992, p. 51)

As we move from theory to practice, problems begin to surface. Budget limitations preclude frequent visits by trainers to conduct staff development workshops at individual schools. Some teachers have no training in educational technology and have never used a Web browser. More advanced teachers are in the process of adopting technology and using constructivist strategies to further engaged learning (Jonassen, 1995; Jones *et al.,* 1995). At the same time, they feel pressured to align their teaching with state and local content standards and to prepare their students for statewide assessments. To resolve this dilemma, teachers need training to develop lessons that use the Internet and its Web, that include an assessment component aligned with state standards, and that still honor their individual pedagogical styles.

Our Web-based training (WBT) product, the *Teachers' Internet Use Guide* (on the Web at: rmcdenver.com/useguide/), has proved to be a practical solution to this problem. It was developed under a federal grant through the Support for Texas Academic Renewal (STAR) Center as a free resource for educators to address the Texas Essential Knowledge and Skills content standards (TEKS). We also created a similar WBT module for the State of Arizona, through another federal grant. Then, we decided to add a new feature to the Web site—a page that includes sharable, teacher-created lessons that are aligned with state or local standards.

The Teacher's Dilemma

Let us shift our perspective from that of the IASA's "Great Idea" to that of a typical K–12 teacher who is trying to balance constructivist teaching strategies with standards-based instruction. In the following scenario, Ms. Jones is a fictional, composite character who shares many characteristics in common with teachers who participated in our initial training workshops in three different educational regions within the state of Texas in the late winter of 1998. However, in contrast with most of our workshop trainees, she already has had some experience in Internet use.

It is the beginning of the new school year. With Internet connectivity through the state or district network, and with funding from the district, local bond issues, and perhaps a small grant, Smith Elementary School now has access to the Web, four computers in the media center, and computers in several of the classrooms, all connected to the building's LAN. Ms. Jones, a first grade teacher, has just attended a staff development session in educational technology. Her training has given her the technical expertise to use e-mail and listservs, to navigate and search the Web, to find educational resources, and to troubleshoot her computer and printer. Now she must prepare to integrate telecommunications into her classroom teaching, and, at the same time, address the state and local standards. "By what means?" she asks. The district's technology plan has overcome three traditional barriers to technology integration (Duffield, 1997) by giving her the equipment, the training, and the time she needs to accomplish her task, but not the one thing she really needs—*a process she can use to incorporate standards, assessments, and the Web into her classroom instruction.*

Commercial publishing houses have been quick to spot this gap in staff development. Brightly colored ads in teacher-oriented magazines advertise CDs, saying, "We realize you are a busy teacher, and you don't have time to design lessons that use the Internet. We've done it for you—for our low, low price, we'll provide you with a dozen ready-made lessons that can help you to integrate the Internet into your curriculum." It sounds like the perfect solution, but wait . . . *is it really inexpensive? does it directly address the TEKS?*

Ms. Jones, an experienced teacher, favors the use of constructivist strategies in her classroom, and she now understands that technology can support her vision of engaged learning (Jones *et al.*, 1995). Her students work on relevant tasks, research real-world problems, and produce authentic products and performances. Moreover, she considers herself a facilitator and coach, not a didactic teacher. Ready-made lessons are not the answer for her. "How can a ready-made lesson address my particular group of students? How can it address the specific standards to which I am expected to align my teaching?" she asks.

She is not alone in this quandary. Teachers know how to teach. They understand the needs of their students. But they don't necessarily understand how the Web can support teaching and learning. Besides the commercial CDs and Web sites, there are many teacher-created Web sites that provide lists of education-related links that they may be able to retrofit to their learning objectives. But is retrofitting the answer? Is this how a good teacher—or a good instructional designer—would go about creating a lesson? Probably not.

The growing emphasis on state standards often tends to steer constructivist teachers away from their preferred style of teaching toward a more didactic model. Thus, teachers whose personal philosophy is at odds with a systematic approach to instruction now find themselves caught in a dilemma. On the one hand, they value their students' process of self-discovery; on the other hand, they are expected to align their teaching with a set of state standards which, in turn, are geared to state-mandated tests and, possibly, national tests as well.

Resolving the Dilemma

There are several issues here that need to be addressed. First, as W. Edwards Deming (1994) points out, tests only examine the results (or ends) of education; they have nothing to say about how those results are produced. When Ms. Jones focuses on a clear set of learning objectives and designs an assessment that is aligned with those objectives, she is focusing on the ends, not the means, of education. The process of designing instruction always includes an assessment component. The more explicitly the assessment component is linked to the learning objectives, the more coherent the instruction becomes (Alessi & Trollip, 1991, p. 246). However, *it is still the teacher's privilege and prerogative, as a professional, to create the means of instruction* that are most appropriate for her particular students, in her particular classroom, according to her own vision of learning.

Second, the Engaged Learning model (Jones *et al.,* 1995) makes an explicit connection between student-centered learning and technology. But *it does not suggest specific techniques or strategies* to support that connection. Here is where teaching becomes more of an art than a science—it is an ill-defined domain in which pedagogical matters are open to discussion, demand practical decisions, do not have single right answers, and are not amenable to theoretical or procedural analyses (Reid, 1992, p. 44).

Third, *learning how to use technologies is necessary but not sufficient* to restructure both a style of teaching and a classroom to accommodate the more open style of learning that the new technologies foster, especially since student-centered learning environments demand even more structure and feedback than traditional teacher-centered ones.

> Projects for projects' sake can just as easily be a waste of time if students' learning goals and the means to achieve them are not clearly structured, communicated, and assessed . . . Flexibility and structure are the yin and yang of effective use of technologies. (Foa, Johnson, & Schwab, 1997, p. 52)

This is the rationale for the creation of the *Teachers' Internet Use Guide:* alignment of ends and means throughout the lesson, with the ultimate decision left to the teacher as to what means may best result in the intended learning outcomes. Though our WBT module is geared toward the teacher-as-facilitator approach epitomized by Apple Classroom of Tomorrow (ACOT) teachers, it in no way mandates any specific instructional approach.

The Instructional Design Process

Translating instructional design theory into practice, the *Teachers' Internet Use Guide* walks a teacher through a standards-based ID process that involves:

(1) creating clear learning objectives;

(2) designing a lesson that addresses those objectives;

(3) implementing it with timely, relevant online resources; and

(4) evaluating the effectiveness of the lesson.

Though the *Teachers' Internet Use Guide* is specifically tailored to the TEKS, it can easily be generalized to align with any state's standards or curriculum framework. Since standards and assessment go hand-in-hand, the guide also contains a generic module that introduces teachers to the process of developing an aligned assessment:

(1) identifying and agreeing upon a set of performance standards and criteria;

(2) communicating those criteria to all students, teachers, and parents;

(3) designing an assessment strategy that measures the demonstration of learning; and

(4) evaluation and reflection.

The Training Process

Let us return to our fictitious teacher as she is first introduced to the *Teachers' Internet Use Guide*. Opening her Web browser, she looks at the opening screen of the Guide and sees two major sections: standards-based instruction and assessment. These sections are designed so they can be explored individually. Alternatively, the assessment section may be incorporated into the last step of the design process, depending on the teacher's familiarity with some of the newer concepts of performance assessment.

When Ms. Jones clicks on *Standards-Based Instruction,* she sees four modules. In the first module, she is introduced to a sequential, four-step ID process.

Module 1

Learn how to design, develop, implement, and evaluate an Internet-based lesson using a four-step instructional design process.

Step 1, *Creating Clear Learning Objectives,* asks the teacher to locate the content standards that she needs to address and either write them down or paste them into her word processor. A link to a page that describes how to use the Texas State Standards, with an embedded link to the TEKS, is included in the left banner. Using the reflective questions, she asks herself, What type of lesson might support those standards? How does this lesson address the learning styles and needs of my students?

Step 2, *Designing a Lesson,* invites her to explore some ideas, activities, and promising practices that address those standards. Granted, there is not, nor can there be, a "magic bullet" that tells her how to locate a specific resource that supports a specific state objective. However, invoking her art as a teacher and exploring the rich set of links provided by the *Teachers' Internet Use Guide,* she designs or finds a lesson created by another teacher, a commercial publishing house, a government agency, or a university that addresses the types of learning that she envisions for her students. She may print out sites that she feels are valuable, or she may simply paste the URLs into her word processor. She then asks herself: Will my students use their knowledge to solve problems in authentic performance settings? Do these activities promote higher level thinking? Do they provide some way for my students to demonstrate their learning?

Step 3, *Implementing a Lesson,* asks her to locate and explore some additional online resources that can support her lesson. As in Step 2, there is a list of carefully filtered sites with ideas, activities, projects, and links to online resources, organized by topic, that she and her students can use to enrich and enhance classroom activities.

Step 4, *Evaluating the Effectiveness of the Lesson,* asks her two questions: Did the lesson work? Did it teach? To answer those questions, she first needs to evaluate student proficiency in accessing and filtering information, and then assess student products and performances. Assessment activities should address the objectives of the lesson; honor individual learning styles; enable students to construct knowledge in a meaningful way; provide feedback to students so they can revise and improve their products and performances; and fit in with her self-concept as a coach and facilitator.

Module 2

Learn how to develop an assessment that is aligned with your lesson.

For convenience, there is a direct, but optional link from Step 4 of Module 1 to the second major section of the Guide, *Assessment*. In this major section of the Guide, teachers are introduced to the basic constructs of the assessment process, including student performances, portfolios, rubrics, and benchmarks. Teachers who are already familiar with performance assessment may skip this step and move on to Module 3.

Module 3

Explore some sample lessons that were developed using this process.

The third module of *Standards-Based Instruction*, namely, *Sample Lessons*, reviews the instructional design process and then applies it in four curriculum areas to develop a sample lesson in math, science, social studies, and language arts. Teachers who feel they have a good understanding of the ID process may skip this module and start designing their own lessons, using the information they have written down or stored in their word processor.

Module 4

Now use this form to design your own lesson.

The fourth module of this section, *Design Your Own Lesson*, consists of a form for documenting, printing, and submitting the finished lesson to the prototype database of teacher-created lessons. Each text area of the form contains explicit directions indicating what information should appear there. Lessons that are submitted to our design team are incorporated into a database of lessons that can be shared by all educators. Intellectual rights to the lessons remain the property of the teachers who created them.

Postscript

Ms. Jones, our fictional character, is experienced, comfortable with technology, and knows that technology can enhance learning. Most teachers in the first round of workshops did not have this type of training. Many of the paraprofessionals did not have any experience with instructional design, so they were not ready to start creating lessons during their initial training sessions. Thus, the sample lessons will be an excellent follow-up to the introduction to the instructional design process, since they apply the process directly to creating standards-based lessons. Most importantly of all, the Web sites in the resource lists emphasize the creation of authentic products by students, and the fact that there is no single right answer to an ill-defined problem. This is in the spirit of the IASA, which fosters lifelong learning and relevant learning activities.

References

Alessi, S. M., & Trollip, S. R. (1991). *Computer-based instruction: Methods and development*. Englewood Cliffs: Prentice-Hall.

Deming, W. E. (1994). *The new economics, second edition*. Cambridge, MA: MIT Center for Advanced Educational Services.

Duffield, J. A. (1997). Trials, tribulations, and minor successes: Integrating technology into a preservice teacher preparation program. *Tech Trends, 42*(4), 22–26.

Foa, L. J., Johnson, M. J., & Schwab, R. L. (1997, September 10). Connecting schools is only a start. *Education Week, 52–54.*

Hackbarth, S. (1997). Web-based learning activities for children. In B. H. Khan (Ed.), *Web-based instruction.* Englewood Cliffs: Educational Technology Publications.

Jonassen, D. H. (1995, July-August). Supporting communities of learners with technology: A vision for integrating technology with learning in schools. *Educational Technology,* 60–63.

Jones, B. F., Valdez, G., Nowakowski, J., & Rasmussen, C. (1995, April). *Plugging in: Choosing and using educational technology.* Oakbrook, IL: North Central Regional Educational Laboratory.

Reid, W. A. (1992). *The pursuit of curriculum.* Norwood, NJ: Ablex.

U. S. Department of Education. (1997). *Comprehensive centers network.* Available: STAR Center, 5835 Callaghan Rd., Suite 350, San Antonio, TX 78228-1190.

The Authors

David Hoffman (e-mail: dhoffman@dimensional.com; Web homepage: rmcdenver.com/useguide), Lorraine Sherry (e-mail: lsherry@carbon.cudenver.edu), Jonathan Lurie (e-mail: jlurie@rmi.net), and Jason McDaniel (e-mail: jmcdaniel@infotec.com) are with RMC Research Corporation, Denver, Colorado.

57

Virtual U: A Hub for Excellence in Education, Training, and Learning Resources

Badrul H. Khan

Introduction

In the information society, we are blessed with the emergence of the World Wide Web, commonly known as the Web, as one of the most important economic and democratic mediums of learning and teaching at a distance. As the Internet is emerging, the Web has become an increasingly powerful, global, interactive, and dynamic medium for sharing information (Khan, 1997a). The Web provides an opportunity to develop new learning experiences for students not possible previously (Alexander, 1995). As a result, individuals from around the globe can enjoy equal access to the many learning resources available on the Web. The Web has the ability to provide rich learning environments in a global, democratic, and interactive manner. Various attributes and resources of the Web make it possible for institutions to offer instruction, training, and learning resources without the time and place constraints of traditional face-to-face instructional and training programs.

Now, more and more educational institutions, corporations, and government agencies worldwide are increasingly using the Web to deliver instruction and training. At present, there are online courses on almost all subject areas. At all levels of these institutions, students and employees are being encouraged to participate in online learning activities. The increasing number of these online educational and training providers is creating a new paradigm for education, training, and learning resources. Learners now expect on-demand, anytime/anywhere, high-quality instruction with good support services. To stay viable in this global, competitive market, providers of education, training, and learning resources must develop efficient and effective learning systems to meet society's needs (Raymond Oglethorpe, AOL Technologies; Carl Kelly, Oracle Corporation; personal communication, May 8, 2000). Therefore, there is a tremendous demand for *affordable, efficient, easily accessible, open, flexible, well-designed, learner-centered, distributed, and facilitated learning environments.*

In this chapter, I discuss various aspects of organizing society's resources for learning, professional development, and continuing education by establishing virtual universities in order to meet the needs of open, flexible, and distributed learning. Various online universities and virtual universities are established worldwide to provide educational services for new educational needs. According to Krauth (1999), "An online university offers all its courses and programs via

491

the Internet or World Wide Web" (p. 4); for example, the New School for Social Research's distance learning program and the Online Campus of the University of Phoenix. Krauth (1999) continues, "A virtual university has no campus and no faculty of its own. Instead, a virtual university makes available programs and courses offered by other colleges and universities using technology. The Western Governors University and the California Virtual University are two examples of Virtual Universities" (p.4). However, in this chapter, I use the term "virtual university" in a broader scope by including the functions of both the online university and the virtual university as described above by Krauth. Therefore, in addition to its own courses and programs, a VU also provides offerings from other participating institutions. With this broader scope, a "virtual university" serves *as a hub for excellence in education, training, and learning resources.*

The availability of an increasing number of online courses and learning resources offered by various education, training, and resource providers from around the globe will have implications for individuals who live at a distance from college campuses and also for working adults who cannot attend regular face-to-face classes. Moreover, availability of quality online courses and programs from accredited institutions will attract regular on-campus students. All of this will have implications for traditional degree-granting institutions. In this regard, Bill W. Burgess, Chairman, State Regents of Oklahoma, stated:

> In 1997–98 alone, Oklahoma colleges and universities had more than 23,500 enrollments in electronically-delivered courses, and we expect that number to grow. . . . Higher education must continue to find ways to conveniently deliver courses and programs to the thousands of Oklahomans looking for alternative ways to achieve their educational goals. Changing student needs and lifestyles now make it necessary to take education to the community, home or workplace of students via technology, and the Online College of Oklahoma can do this in an accessible and economical way (okcollegeonline.org/news/oco1.html).

Many communities throughout the world can find common grounds with the above statement. As a result, traditional institutions may have to change the way they offer their courses, certificates, diplomas, and degrees (Khan, 2000). If traditional degree-granting institutions continue to have a policy of requiring students to take only their own courses to complete degree programs, then it seems that students who do not mind getting a degree with courses from multiple accredited institutions will look for accredited education/training brokers who can provide them with courses/programs bestfitting their individual needs. Western Governors University is an example of an education broker (it has applied for accreditation from the Inter-Regional Accrediting Committee). To help learners with an opportunity to review online courses before registration, *WebCourseReview.com* (or *BooksToRead.com/WCR*) is trying to build an online course review database.*

Considering the advancement of distributed technologies, learners now have access to the best educational and training services from around the globe. Our communities should organize these learning resources and make them meaningfully available to learners. "I know of very few states that don't have some kind of planning in the works," says Sally Johnstone, director of the Western Cooperative for Educational Telecommunications, at the Western Interstate Commission for Higher Education. Not all states, however, are calling their efforts virtual universities. "What we're seeing developing is new ways for institutions to work together" (cited

---

WebCourseReview.com will review online courses based on factors encompassing various online learning issues, including: pedagogical, technological, interface design, evaluation, management, resource support, ethical, and institutional. Once the Course Review Database is complete, one can search for a course based on course profiles and review criteria.

in Young, 2000). As the demand for open and flexible learning continues, the demand for both online universities and virtual universities will continue to grow.

The Virtual University

We are currently living in a fascinating time in history. New developments in learning science and technology provide opportunities to create engaging, interactive, and meaningful course content in almost all subject areas. Now we are able to create affordable, efficient, easily accessible, open, flexible, well-designed, learner-centered, distributed, and facilitated learning environments. We are blessed with the advancement of learning technologies that allow us to create exciting learning environments. Various educational institutions, corporations, government agencies, and individuals in the community are creating online learning materials and resources for their target audience. We should integrate this large reservoir of resources, opportunities, and situations available in all systems and domains of community to support learning and development of children and youth, and the continuous learning and development of adults through life (Banathy, 1991). With the blessing of distributed learning technologies, communities throughout the world can establish virtual universities by organizing society's best resources for learning, professional development, and continuing education. Therefore, virtual universities become hubs for excellence in education, training, and learning resources in their respective communities.

Understanding societal needs, communities seeking to establish comprehensive systems of learning and human development, such as virtual universities, must understand that they are purpose-seeking systems guided by their vision of the future (Banathy, 1992). In describing purpose-seeking systems, Banathy (1992) notes, "They are open and able to coevolve with the environment. They are complex and systemic. Being pluralistic, they define their own policies/purposes and constantly seek new purposes and new niches in their environments" (p. 13). Banathy recommends that a *purpose-functions-components* sequence is obligatory for establishing purpose-seeking systems.

In order to establish a VU, we must identify its *purpose*. Once the purpose is determined, the issue becomes: What are the *functions* that we have to attend to in order to achieve the purpose? What *components/parts* have to be involved, and in what arrangements that have the capability to attend to the functions (Banathy, 1992)? In establishing a VU, each community has to identify its purpose, functions, and components. The *purpose-functions-components* of a VU can depend on the type of community it encompasses and the scope of its operation (i.e., local, state, multistate, national, multinational or international level VU). For the purpose of discussing the establishment of a VU, I would like to follow a *purpose-functions-components* sequence in this chapter.

Purpose

The purpose of a virtual university is to serve as a hub for excellence in education, training and learning resources by integrating its community's best services and resources for learning, professional development and continuing education.

To achieve the above-mentioned purpose, primary functions of VU might include the following (but not limited to these):

Functions

- Maintain continuous interactions with all the stakeholders groups of VU.

- Identify VU-relevant programs, resources, and arrangements in the community.

- Establish and maintain programs, resources, and arrangements required to operate VU and attain desired outcomes.

- Use VU programs, resources, and arrangements.

Each of the primary functions defined above has set of sub-functions. As examples, following are some of the sub-functions for primary function "Use VU programs, resources, and arrangements" listed above.

- Provide easy and quick access to a 24-hours-a-day, seven-days-a-week, high-quality, interactive learning environment.

- Provide easy and quick access to the program and course catalog.

- Provide easy and quick access to individuals affiliated with VU programs, resources, and arrangements.

- Offer online courses (non-credit or for credit) based on individuals' needs.

- Offer certificates programs based on individuals' needs.

- Offer degree programs based on individuals' needs.

- Provide accreditation information.

- Provide information on how programs and courses are delivered.

- Provide orientation on self-learning and continuing education.

- Conduct continuous evaluation of quality control of course and resource delivery.

- Provide faculty with adequate hardware, software, and communications devices for interaction with students and other involved with the course.

- Provide faculty support services specifically related to teaching online courses.

- Provide appropriate training for faculty who teach online courses.

- Provide brief biographical information about faculty.

- Provide an environment for collaboration with individual(s) in other institutions.

- Maintain a system of appropriate interaction between faculty and students and among students in all online courses.

- Provide program information that clearly and accurately represents the program and the services available.

- Provide information about course delivery methods.

- Provide clear, complete, and timely information on the curriculum, course, and degree requirements.

- Provide information about prerequisites for courses/programs.

- Provide information about prerequisite technology competencies and skills.

- Provide information about technology hardware and software requirements for students.

- Provide information about availability of academic support services.

- Provide online applications for admissions.

- Provide information about credit transfer.

- Provide online registration and payment services.
- Provide information about tuition and fees, payment, and refund policies.
- Provide financial aid resources (forms, consultations, etc.).
- Provide a qualified mentor who can help learners to create a program plan and calendar for completing their degrees.
- Monitor learners' progress.
- Provide access 24-hours-a-day, seven-days-a-week to the library.
- Provide access 24-hours-a-day, seven-days-a-week to an online bookstore.
- Provide online counseling.
- Provide career development and placement advice.
- Provide job information.
- Provide internship information.
- Provide access to experts online.

To carry out the functions, we need to identify components that have to be involved (Khan, 1997b). Components of a VU must be selected and employed on the basis of their potential to carry out the above-mentioned functions that are necessary to attain the purpose of the VU (Banathy, 1992).

Components

Considering the VU as a hub for excellence in education, training, and learning resources, the systemic and integrated services of three major components: (1) education providers, (2) training providers, and (3) resource providers (see Figure 1) have the potential and ability to carry out the functions of the VU. Please note that, in addition to providing services via its own major components, the VU also provides services from its affiliates (participating institutions). Therefore, through the VU, one can take courses and earn a degree or certificate in a host of different participating institutions. By allowing students to be served by multiple providers, the VU fosters a seamless educational experience for learners.

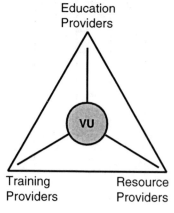

Figure 1. Components of a Virtual University.

The VU is a complex system, and it must create a coordinated inter-organizational linkage (Banathy, 1991) of all participating components in order to offer integrated arrangements and resources for learning and continuing education programs that are coherent, easily accessible, affordable, efficient, flexible, well-designed, and learner-centered. The VU must maintain continuous and intensive interactions with the providers of education, training, and resources to provide high-quality education and training with the best learning resources and support services. It should develop "Principles of Good Practice" for all its providers so that students are assured about the quality of courses and programs. For examples, Ohio Learning Network, a virtual university (but not degree-granting) developed "Principles of Good Practice" for its participating Ohio colleges and universities' online courses and programs (oln.org/pogp.htm).

Education Providers. Education providers are accredited educational institutions which must be approved by the VU to offer online courses and/or degrees/certificates through the VU. A VU should come up with its common standards for all participating institutions' courses and programs. Table 1 lists examples of education providers with their online offerings and accreditation information. Please note that online offerings and accreditation status of education providers listed in Table 1 may change based on their scope of operation and quality of services.

Table 1. Some education providers.

Education Providers	Types of Online Offerings					Accreditation
	Course Type		Certificate Program			
	Partial online	Full online	Non-credit	Leading to credit	Degree	
CyberSchool (cyberschool.k12.or.us) is an official program within the Eugene Public School District, USA. Provides high school credit courses.		✓				Northwest Association of Schools and Colleges, the Commission on International and Trans-Regional Accreditation, Accreditation Commission for International Internet Education.
University of Phoenix (phoenix.edu) provides degree programs and certificate programs in the United States and in dozens of foreign countries.		✓	✓	✓	✓	North Central Association of Colleges and Schools, National League for Nursing Accrediting Commission, American Counseling Association Council for Accreditation of Counseling and Related Educational Programs.
The Open University (open.ac.uk) offers courses throughout Europe and, by means of partnership agreements, with other institutions in the world.		✓	✓	✓	✓	The Open University was ranked 11th out of 98 United Kingdom universities in both 1998 and 1999 for the quality of its teaching.

Training Providers. Training providers include corporations, government agencies, educational institutions, nonprofit organization, or other entities which must be approved by the VU to offer online training and professional development courses and/or certificates/programs through the VU. Table 2 lists several training providers and their online offerings. Please note that training providers' online offerings may change over the period of time.

Resource Providers. Resource providers include both education and training providers, communities, individuals, etc. These resources can come from anywhere from the world. The VU will not have control over these resources. However, providers of education and training should utilize these resources meaningfully in designing their courses and programs. Table 3 lists several resource providers and their online offerings. Please note that resource providers' online offerings may change over the period of time.

Once the VU components are identified, the next step involves the process of carrying out the functions that are necessary to attain the purpose of the VU. All three components of the VU—education, training, and resource providers—are responsible for the design, development, and delivery of all programs and arrangements required for the functions identified for the VU. At this stage, the major activities of VU components include (but are not limited to) design and delivery of online courses, support services, and resources.

Design of online courses, programs, and resources requires a comprehensive understanding of open, flexible, and distributed learning environments, issues important to remote learners and how to use the Web's potential in concert with instructional design principles.

Table 2. Some training providers.

Training Providers	Types of Online Offerings							
	Tutorials	Presentation	Workshop	Conference/Seminar	Lesson	Course	Certification	Other
Teachers' Internet Use Guide (rmcdenver.com/useguide) provides Internet-based lessons that are aligned with theTexas Essential Knowledge and Skills (TEKS) exam.					✓			
Learn2.com provides online tutorials in many subjects.	✓							
Asynchronous Learning Networks (ALN) Center (netlearning.org) provides asynchronous workshops, courses, etc.			✓	✓	✓	✓		
Oracle University (education.oracle.com) provides e-business education and training to IT professionals worldwide.			✓	✓	✓	✓	✓	
Motorola University (mu.motorola.com) provides customized and licensed training services to Motorola associates worldwide.				✓	✓	✓		

Table 3. Some resource providers.

Resource Providers	Types of Online Resources																		
	Libraries	Webliographies	Books	Journals	Magazines	Newsletters	Newspapers	Listservs	Newsgroups	Archives	Documents	Dictionaries	Thesaurus	Tools/Software	Experts Online	TV	Radio	Conferences	Other
ipl.org The Internet public library	✓														✓				
cast.org/bobby Analyzes Web pages for their accessibility to people with disabilities																			
BooksToRead.com Recommended readings site on the Internet		✓																	
DEOS-L The Distance Education Online Symposium								✓											
bbc.co.uk BBC TV and Radio																✓	✓		
m-w.com Instant access to dictionary and thesaurus												✓							

Bothun (1997) discusses seven points to overcome to make the virtual university viable: pricing, mentoring, marketing, evaluation, curriculum development, accreditation, and access. Carnevale (2000) discusses some of the obstacles that virtual universities encounter, including winning accreditation, providing student services, setting tuition, figuring out finances, transferring course credits, etc. I have been researching the question, "What does it take to provide the best and most meaningful flexible learning environments for learners worldwide?" I have learned that there are numerous factors that help to create a meaningful learning environment (see Chapter 8), many of which are systemically interrelated and interdependent. A systemic understanding of these factors can help designers create meaningful distributed learning environments. After reflecting on the different grounds of open, flexible, and distributed learning environments, I developed a framework for Web-based learning (or a framework for e-learning) encompassing the eight dimensions of an online learning environment: pedagogical, technological, interface design, evaluation, management, resource support, ethical, and institutional. Each dimension has several subdimensions (see Table 1 in Chapter 8), consisting of items focused on a specific aspect of an online learning environment.

    The framework can be used to identify and clarify critical issues and the complexities of an open, flexible, and distributed learning environment. The VU and its affiliates can use the WBL Framework to design, develop, evaluate, and implement online courses, programs, and learning resources. By following design guidance discussed in the WBL Framework and employing the agreed upon "Principles of Good Practice," the VU and it affiliates can provide courses and programs with common format, quality, and services.

Virtual University: Scope of Operation

Each community can form its own VU based on its needs. The scope of operation of a VU can encompass any defined geographical region or level: local, state, multistate, national, multinational, and international. Of course, a VU with larger scope of operation would have more responsibilities, including accreditation, curriculum, management, etc. At each level of a VU, three components or entities (education, training, and resource providers) work collaboratively to meet the needs of communities that they serve. The Internet is a reservoir of information on almost all topics and issues. Each community is unique; therefore, each VU should organize information and learning resources in a manner appropriate for its own community's needs and values. In addition to organizing resources and services from its own community, a VU can also use resources and services from the outside of its community. Each VU should employ a system for continuous screening and monitoring of information on its site. Table 4 discusses the VU's scope of operation at the various geographical levels.

Table 4. Virtual universities: Six levels of scope of operation.

Local	A VU at the local level can be established by organizing the best educational and training resources from providers within a local community. For example, a local level VU in a school district in the United States (e.g., Eugene Public School District, Oregon) can offer high school credit courses and diplomas by organizing its own offerings plus offerings from both public and private schools.
State (or Province)	A VU at the state (or province) level can be established by organizing statewide educational and training resources from providers within the state. For example, a state level VU in a state in the United States (e.g., Texas) can offer courses, certificates, and degree programs by organizing its own offerings plus offerings from both public and private colleges, universities, and other institutions in the state.
Multistate (or Multiprovince)	A VU at the multistate (or multiprovince) level can be established by organizing educational and training resources from the providers of education, training, and resources from multiple states. For example, a group of states in the United States can establish a multistate VU by organizing its own offerings plus offerings from both public and private colleges, universities, and other institutions in the multistate regions.
National	A VU at the national level can be established by organizing nationwide educational and training resources from providers in the country. For example, a country such as the United Arab Emirates can establish a national level VU (United Arab Emirates Virtual University—UAEVU or UAEVirtual) by organizing its nationwide educational and training resources (discussed later in the chapter).
Multinational	A VU at the multinational level can be established by organizing educational and training resources from the providers of education, training, and resources in group of countries. For example, a group of countries such as the Arab Gulf nations (i.e., the United Arab Emirates, Kuwait, Saudi Arabia, Bahrain, Qatar, and Oman) can collaborate on the establishment of Arab Gulf Virtual University (AGVU or AGVirtual) by organizing six countries' educational and training resources (discussed later in the chapter).
International	A VU at the international level can be established by organizing educational and training resources from providers from around the globe. For example, colleges and universities from around the globe can establish an international VU.

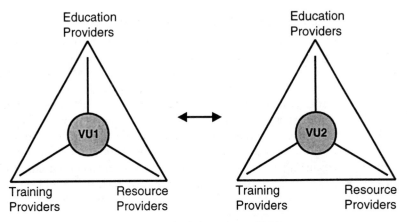

Figure 2. Collaboration of VUs.

Since VUs can be established at the various levels (i.e., local, state, multistate, national, multinational, and international) to serve as hubs for excellence in education, training, and learning resources in their respective communities, it is important to have strong support and commitment from all stakeholders. Each VU should be established based on the needs of the community it serves. Each VU should involve all stakeholder groups to establish principles of good practice as guidelines for delivering quality services and resources for learning. Based on their needs, VUs at any level can collaborate with other VUs to share courses, resources, and experts (see Figure 2).

Virtual Universities at the National and Multinational Levels

Within the scope of this chapter, VUs are now described at the national and multinational levels.

National Level

To establish the VU at the national level, strong leadership and support from the national department (or ministry) of education and commitment from all stakeholders groups, including providers of education, training, and learning resources in the country (and abroad, if necessary) are critical. Leadership and support from the national department (or ministry) of education may vary depending on the type of educational systems. Many countries have centralized education systems in which decisions are made at the central government level. Other countries have non-centralized educational systems, in which decisions are made at the local level. For example, in the U.S., local control and stakeholders' input weigh more, and many would resist a strong federal role. After reflecting on different aspects of national educational systems, I feel that countries with centralized educational systems would be more successful in establishing VUs at the national level. Each national VU should organize its nation's best resources for excellence in learning, training, and resources for its citizens and beyond.

Multinational Level

A VU can be established at the multinational level with a group of countries sharing some common factors. These factors may include (but are not limited to) geographical proximity, common interest, similar socio-economic-cultural-lingual status, long-lasting friendship, existing alliances, etc. A VU at the multinational level would improve communication and collaboration among member countries. A multinational level VU can organize resources produced by VUs of member countries. Existing alliances or consortia among groups of countries may accelerate the process of developing an international level VU. For example, the British Commonwealth countries have an existing alliance through the Commonwealth of Learning (COL). Therefore, a Commonwealth VU might easily be formed by the member countries. The Arab Gulf Cooperation Council (AGCC) was formed by the United Arab Emirates (UAE), Kuwait, Saudi Arabia, Bahrain, Qatar, and Oman (*United Arab Emirates Yearbook,* 1999, p. 17). An international level VU in the Arab Gulf region could thus be formed.

In this chapter, for discussion, the United Arab Emirates (UAE) and Arab Gulf (AG) countries are selected as examples to discuss VUs at the national and multinational levels, respectively. The rationale for selecting UAEVU and AGVU is influenced by an extraordinary speech supporting the distributed learning by His Excellency Sheikh Nahayan bin Mabarak Al Nahayan, the patron of TEND conference described below, the existence of highly respected and effective Arab Gulf Cooperation Council (AGCC), and enthusiastic support for distributed learning by several distinguished individuals from the Gulf region. Throughout the chapter, **UAEVU** (or **VirtualUAE, UAEVirtual**) is used for the United Arab Emirates Virtual University (national level), and **AGVU** (or **VirtualAG, AGVirtual**) is used for Arab Gulf Virtual University (multinational level). Please note that neither UAEVU nor AGVU exists at the present time.

I attended the TEND 2000 (Technological Education and National Development) conference in Abu Dhabi, UAE. At the TEND opening ceremony, His Excellency (HE) Sheikh Nahayan bin Mabarak Al Nahayan, the Minister of Higher Education and Scientific Research and Chancellor Higher Colleges of Technology of UAE emphasized the meaningful utilization of distributed educational technologies in education and training as the important national development criteria in the Information society. HE Sheikh Nahayan's interest and support for distributed learning initiatives were highly appreciated by the conference attendees from all over the world. At the conference, I discussed the concept of VU with HE Ahmad Al Ghazali, Former Education Minister of Oman; HE Mohammed Ali Al Abbar, Director General of Dubai Department of Economic Development, UAE; Dr. Abdulrazzak Al-Nafisi, Deputy Director General for Applied Education and Research, Kuwait; Dr. Sulaiman Al Jassim, Chairman TEND 2000 Organizing Committee, and other TEND2000 attendees from Arab Gulf countries, who were highly supportive.

United Arab Emirates Virtual University (National Level)

In this section, purpose, functions, and components for UAEVU are briefly discussed. Considering the purpose of UAEVU, a number of courses, certificates, and programs have to be organized and developed. Within the scope of this chapter, the development of a certificate program is proposed here as an example for discussion.

Purpose

The purpose of UAEVU is to serve as the national hub for excellence in education, training, and learning resources in the UAE by integrating the nation's best resources for learning, professional development, and continuing education in a format that is accessible by anyone, anytime, and anywhere. UAEVU can make restrictions on who can or can not have access to its resources. Some resources may be password protected and some may be open to the world.

Functions

UAEVU should take the leadership role in organizing educational, training, and learning resources from all levels of public and private education institutions, government, business, in-

Table 5. Examples of UAE online offerings.

Providers	Provider Type	Description
Centre of Excellence for Applied Research and Training (CERT) *cert.hct.ac.ae*	• Education • Training • Resources	CERT is the training arm of the UAE Higher Colleges of Technology (HCT), and is involved in creating programs to develop a national workforce with information technology skills. CERT has cooperative training programs with variety of multi-national partners. In 2000, the Harvard Institute at CERT held a series of training courses for leading educators in the Arab Gulf Cooperation Council (AGCC) states as a means of developing educational services.
Internet University at Dubai Internet City *dubaiinternetcity.com*	• Training	"To meet the increasing industry requirement for a skilled IT workforce, the world's first Internet University is being set up at Dubai Internet City. The University will offer a curriculum that covers all areas relevant to e-business, like e-finance, e-marketing, multi-media, e-design, e-management etc. It will be affiliated with world class academia and research institutions and will boast an international faculty to ensure cutting-edge training, education and involvement." Source: dubaiinternetcity.com/faqs.htm
Ras Al Khaimah Women's College Independent Learning Center *rkw.hct.ac.ae/ilc/main.html*	• Resources	Provides students with a wide variety of resources for independent study (e.g., resources for ESL students, resources for teachers, etc.)

dustry, health and other sectors of the UAE society (and outside of the UAE) in order to provide affordable, efficient, easily accessible, flexible, well-designed, learner-centered, distributed and facilitated learning environments. Many of the functions listed above for the VU can also be applicable to UAEVU.

Components

Education providers include accredited public and private educational institutions in the UAE that provide courses, certificates and/or degrees online. UAE universities, colleges, and schools are listed at *application.emirates.net.ae:80/messages/main/uaedirectory_t.html* under the Education category. *Training providers* include corporations, government agencies, educational and other institutions, and professional organizations in the UAE that provide online training and professional development programs. Table 5 provides examples of education, training, and resource providers in the UAE and their online offerings. *Resource providers* for UAEVU may come from the government, education, business, industry, health sectors, organizations, and individuals within the UAE (and outside of the UAE). Based on needs, UAEVU can offer courses, certificates and/or programs on various disciplines. However, within the scope of this chapter, a proposed certificate program is discussed as an example of UAEVU's offerings.

A Proposed Professional Certificate Program
Need: Professionals in the UAE want to expand their skill-set by taking online courses from their desktops, homes, or on the road.

In response to workforce needs, UAEVU can offer a certificate program to help busy professionals remain current and develop important new skills. The proposed program can create a 24-hours-a-day, seven-days-a-week learning environment that can deliver engaging, interactive, and meaningful courses and resources to anyone, anytime, anywhere. UAEVU will provide these courses from its affiliates (accredited colleges and universities and corporations) in the UAE or abroad. UAEVU and its affiliates can use the WBL Framework (see Chapter 8) to create interactive and meaningful online courses.

All courses in the program will be self-paced, allowing learners to progress at their own speed. Learning environments will be supported with an online bookstore, UAEVU central library, and other learner support services. UAEVU's flexible delivery formats allow learners to earn certificates from the convenience of their home or workplace. They can select the courses that best suit their needs and their learning styles. I believe professionals are better off completing such a program via UAEVU because it brings all required courses together in one place (meaning that learners may take courses from several institutions, but they deal with only one administration; that is, UAEVU). By these means, UAEVU will make high-quality, interactive learning more accessible and affordable to learners. That means an individual from Fujairah (one of the seven emirates of UAE) will be able to take these specialized courses and earn a certificate from his/her desktop, home, or the road without traveling to other parts of the country from which some of these courses may come.

Arab Gulf Virtual University (Multinational Level)
In this section, a brief description of AGVU is offered, and its purpose, functions, and components are discussed. Considering the purpose of AGVU, a number of courses, certificates, and programs need to be organized and developed by the six AG countries' national VUs. Within the scope of this paper, the development of an academic degree program is proposed here as an example for discussion.

Arab Gulf Virtual University (AGVU) can be established by the collaboration of national VUs of the United Arab Emirates (UAE), Kuwait, Saudi Arabia, Bahrain, Qatar and Oman (see Figure 3). Considering existing collaboration on various aspects, geographical proximity, strong alliance, common language, culture, religion, and other common interests among the six Arab Gulf countries, the creation of the Arab Gulf Virtual University (AGVU) as the hub of excellence in education, training, and learning resources would greatly benefit the region and beyond. AGVU will promote the quality and standards of the development of lifelong learning in the region. AGVU can provide opportunities for individuals to share ideas and experiences with their colleagues/counterparts in other Arab Gulf (AG) countries. AGVU would allow colleges and universities and educational and training institutions in the gulf region to share resources, knowledge, course content and expertise.

According to the *United Arab Emirates Yearbook* (1999), "The Arab Gulf Cooperation Council (AGCC), grouping the United Arab Emirates (UAE), Kuwait, Saudi Arabia, Bahrain, Qatar, and Oman, was founded at a summit conference held in Abu Dhabi in 1981, and has since become, with strong UAE support, an effective and widely respected grouping" (p. 17). I hope that education ministers from Arab Gulf countries would take leadership roles in establishing their national level VUs and collaboratively establish AGVU. I proposed the idea of establishing UAEVU and AGVU to HE Sheikh Nahayan bin Mabarak Al Nahayan, the UAE Minister of Higher Education and Scientific Research, during my visit to the UAE in 2000.

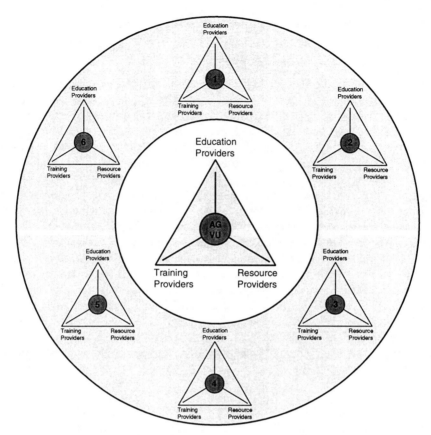

Figure 3. Hypothetical Arab Gulf Virtual University (AGVU) and its Affiliates' National VUs. (United Arab Emirates = 1, Kuwait = 2, Saudi Arabia = 3, Bahrain = 4, Qatar = 5, Oman = 6.)

Purpose

The purpose of AGVU is to serve as the multinational hub for excellence in education, training and learning resources in the Arab Gulf region by integrating the region's best resources for learning, professional development, and continuing education so that they can be accessed by anyone, anytime and anywhere.

Functions

AGVU should take the leadership role in organizing educational, training and learning resources from its affiliates (AG countries' national VUs) in order to provide affordable, efficient, easily accessible, flexible, well-designed, learner-centered, distributed and facilitated learning environments for learners in the Arab Gulf (AG) countries. Many of the functions listed above for the VU can also be applicable to AGVU.

Components

Education providers include accredited public and private educational institutions in the Arab Gulf region that provide courses, certificates, and/or degrees online. *Training providers* include corporations, government agencies, educational, and other institutions, and professional organizations in the AG region that provide online training and professional development programs. *Resource providers* for AGVU may come from government, education, business, industry, health sectors, and organizations within AG countries (and outside of the AG).

A Proposed Master's Degree Program

Need: Advances in information technology, coupled with the changes in society, are creating new paradigms for education. These massive changes have tremendous impact on educational systems in Arab Gulf countries. Today's students require affordable, efficient, easily accessible, open, flexible, well-designed, learner-centered, distributed, and facilitated learning environments. There is a tremendous need for professionals who can design technology-based flexible learning environments to satisfy the needs of learners in Arab Gulf regions.

AGVU can offer an innovative Master's degree program in *Distributed Learning Systems Technology* (DLST), which can provide individuals with an integrated array of specialized information and skills, ranging from software and learning systems design to distance-learning delivery and evaluation strategies. Six Gulf countries can collaboratively develop this exemplary master's degree program. The distributed nature of the proposed DLST program, coupled with existing collaboration among Arab Gulf countries, is the impetus for AGVU to create a collaborative, cost effective, and efficient DLST program with a multinational initiative. Colleges and universities in AG countries will save both money and time by not creating the whole DLST program on their own. They can benefit from being able to offer the DLST program via AGVU to their own student population without duplicating courses that are already offered by other institutions in the region.

The proposed program can be delivered completely online. A variety of information and telecommunication technologies can be used to support the delivery of content and academic interaction. In this highly interactive learning environment, learners can interact with peers, instructor, online databases, CD-ROM programs, and interactive links on the Web. In DLST courses, learners will be using a wide variety of distance learning technologies, including electronic mail, various conferencing software, bulletin boards, databases, slide presentations, CD-ROMs, etc.

AGVU can develop the DLST curriculum with recommendation from experts in the field of distributed learning. Once AGVU provides six national VUs with the DLST curriculum, then each national VU can identify appropriate institutions from its education/training/resource list that can best develop particular courses. This democratic process of letting national VUs select and develop courses for a particular program under the standard policies of AGVU will contribute to the establishment of a great DLST program in the region. I believe that selecting and developing courses will attract leading authorities from the most respected universities in each country of the AG. Course developers can use the WBL Framework (see Chapter 8) to create meaningful learning environments for the DLST students.

Conclusion

In response to increased demand for anytime, anywhere learning, every society in the world will try to establish virtual universities. Some may not call their efforts virtual universities, but their purposes are aligned with those of virtual universities. Regardless of what name a virtual university uses, the quality of services to the learners is the key to its success. In emphasizing the quality of services, Fadia M. Alvic noted, "The plan is to create an online university that is a one-stop shop that a student can enroll in and get everything—not just the courses, but the services as well. Exactly what services the institution offers will depend on the amount of support it receives" (cited in Young, 2000). I believe that a VU should be established with the purpose of serving as the hub for excellence in education, training, and learning resources by providing a high-quality learning environment supported by well-designed resources and the best all-around services for learning.

As indicated earlier, the WBL Framework (see Chapter 8) can provide guidance in the design and delivery of a meaningful distributed learning environment supported by well-designed resources and services for virtual universities and their affiliates (providers of education, training, and resources). Please note that based on the WBL Framework, AuthorWeb (AuthorWeb.net), an authoring system, is under development with a vision of helping subject matter experts to design meaningful online courses/virtual universities without having backgrounds in instructional design, computer programming, and critical distance learning issues (see Chapter 40). The potential is exciting for the creation of distributed learning technologies to support the creation of affordable, efficient, easily accessible, open, flexible, well-designed, learner-centered, distributed, and facilitated learning environments.

References

Alexander, S. (1995). Teaching and learning on the World Wide Web; scu.edu.au/sponsored/ausweb/ausweb95/papers/education2/alexander/

Banathy, B. H. (1991). *Systems designs of education: A journey to create the future.* Englewood Cliffs: Educational Technology Publications.

Banathy, B. H. (1992). *A systems view of education: Concepts and principles for effective practice.* Englewood Cliffs: Educational Technology Publications.

Bothun, G. (1997). Seven points to overcome to make the virtual university viable. CAUSE/EFFECT, Volume 20, Number 2, Summer 1997, pp. 55–57, 65; educause.edu/ir/library/html/cem972a.html

Carnevale, D. (2000, May 19). Western Governors U. is behind projections while Southern effort exceeds expectations. *The Chronicle of Higher Education;* chronicle.com/free/v46/i37/37a05301.htm

Khan, B. H. (1997a). Web-based instruction: What is it and why is it? In B. H. Khan (Ed.), *Web-based instruction.* Englewood Cliffs: Educational Technology Publications.

Khan, B. H. (1997b, February). Designing matrix: A tool for understanding the visions and images of new educational systems. *Performance Improvement, 36*(2), 32–36.

Khan, B. H. (2000, April). A framework for Web-based learning. Invited keynote presentation at the business meeting of American Educational Research Association (AERA) Special Interest Group, "Education and the World Wide Web," New Orleans.

Krauth, B. (1999). Distance learning: The instructional strategy of the decade. In G. P. Connick (Ed.), *The distance learner's guide.* Upper Saddler River, NJ: Prentice-Hall.

*United Arab Emirates Yearbook. (*1999). London: Trident Press Ltd.

Young, J. R. (2000, May 26). South Dakota and Tennessee join the ranks of states building virtual universities. *The Chronicle of Higher Education;* chronicle.com/free/v46/i38/38a05101.htm

For additional readings in Web-based learning and distance education, please visit the Recommended Books Site for this area (BooksToRead.com/de).

About the Author

Badrul H. Khan (e-mail: khanb@gwu.edu, or khanb@BooksToRead.com; Web homepage: BooksTo Read.com/khan, or BooksToRead.com/VU) is Associate Professor and Director, Educational Technology Leadership cohort graduate program, George Washington University, Washington, D.C. He is the founder of BooksToRead.com, a recommended readings site on the Internet.

58

Evaluating Web-Based Training: The Quest for the Information-Age Employee

Joanne P. Hall and

Conrad A. Gottfredson

Why We Need Information-Age Employees

As more organizations "rightsize," the focus in training has shifted to providing more training with fewer resources. Organizations now strive to create teams of information-age employees with a training budget that has been hit hard in the rightsizing reshuffle. Hill Associates (1998) surveyed 104 Fortune 500 companies and found that 73% expected to increase the amount of computer-based and other self-paced technology training for their employees, and 41% expected to increase their use of intranets in the immediate future for in-house training.

In 1990, Mary Jane Gill, a former manager of training services with Bell Atlantic, saw the potential of new training methods using computer-aided, learner-oriented technology. Dryden and Vos (1993) quote her as saying:

> What you really get is an "information-age" employee. You (need) somebody who can work independent of supervision, a better problem-solver, a person who can work by himself or herself but also works well in a team. I can't over-emphasize the importance of this . . . So the information-age employee has to be a skilled self-manager. And that's what the new training techniques are achieving. (p. 467)

Since 1990, technology's potential to deliver self-paced training has expanded exponentially with the development of the Internet. "Students born in 1980 and growing up in the Nintendo generation . . . are flood(ing) the workforce. These students bring an increased sophistication of computer competency and experience with online learning" (Rice, McBride, & Ruttan, 1998). These students are leaders in the management of information. As the amount of information available to the world rapidly increases, our challenge is to train the rest of the workforce in information management skills.

Our ability to conceive of new ways for using technology for information management expands far beyond the current training systems limitations. Hall (1997) suggests that it is "technology [itself which] is significantly limiting the growth of the [Web-based training] market because of the difficulty of delivering multimedia over the Internet and intranets." In the meantime, we struggle to design appropriate Web-based training materials to meet the expanding needs of training departments in organizations as they seek to create environments conducive to the development of information-age employees.

Training Environments for Information-Age Employees

The role of evaluation in developing training programs has been defined as the means to "determine their quality and gain direction for improving them" (Sanders *et al.,* 1994, p. 1). Applications of evaluation techniques vary almost as widely as the evaluators themselves. These applications "employ a variety of techniques during the development of any new instruction. When we understand the conceptual underpinnings of evaluation, we can use these underpinnings as guides in the development process whether we are skilled or novice Web developers" (Rice, McBride, & Ruttan, 1998).

There are several ways to approach the evaluation of Web-based training (WBT). Kovacs (1995) recommends "subject-expert evaluation, one-on-one evaluation, and small-group evaluation [as] the most easily employed." Companies are most likely have subject experts who can help with short evaluations. It is easy to organize one-on-one evaluations or small-group evaluations with potential end users when planned for in advance. These groups, which are superb resources for user testing, can also help in choosing appropriate training content, in designing structure, and in defining actual performance.

Formative evaluation provides guidance through the development process and summative evaluation assigns a final judgment of worth. If formative evaluation is eliminated, the summative evaluation conducted at the end of the development process to evaluate overall effectiveness and "goodness" will not lead to the development of a quality training product (Worthen & Sanders, 1987).

Trainers need to address five fundamental questions when evaluating WBT:

1. Is Self-Paced Web-Based Training (WBT) Justifiable? Before rushing into WBT, it is important to be confident the training needs justify the development of a large Web-based training environment. The need must warrant the investment of both time and money. Designers need to address several issues to justify such an immense investment.

How large is the training audience? How much does prior knowledge vary among users? Consider the opportunity cost of pulling groups of workers into large group instruction and whether traditional methods can deliver timely and specific training. When a company's training is frequent or ongoing for a sizable community of workers dispersed over a large area, the cost associated with WBT pale in comparison to its potential benefits. A checklist to determine if self-paced Web-based training is justifiable can be found in Figure 1.

As Rice (1998) points out, "in order for Web-based instruction (WBI) to be a true alternative to traditional instruction, it must be perceived by both students and [trainers] as a viable alternative and must produce learning results at least as good as those obtained in the classroom" (p. 1). In comparison to classroom learning, Web-based training allows for the learner to have significantly more control over how much he/she learns at a given point in time. Measurable performance improvements suggest the most cost-effective performance-support training takes place when learners are in charge of their learning because they get what they need just when they need it. This assumes that organizations know what training their workers need, what types of learners they are, and how to best meet those needs.

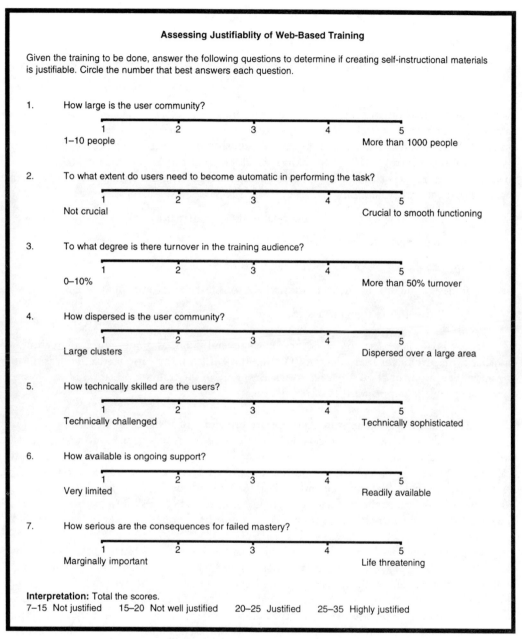

Figure 1. Assessing justifiability.

2. **Does the WBT Have an Iterative Development Life Cycle?** Evaluating early and throughout the development process is the key both to performing good formative evaluation and to creating an effective training tool. Flagg (1990) states that "formative evaluation refers to the process of gathering information to advise design, production, and implementation decisions" (p. 14). During the "ramping-up" stages of training development, formative evaluation requires identification of three areas:

1. **Task Analysis:** Detailed needs of those to be trained.

2. **Strengths:** Aspects that work in the training design.

3. **Weaknesses:** Parts in the interface, content structure, or design that require improvement.

At first glance, steps one through three may seem more like design issues, but they are so intertwined with formative evaluation and user testing that they are hard to separate, and from a practical viewpoint, they should be done simultaneously. Once the first iteration of a task analysis is completed, Horton's (1994) formative developmental process can be initiated. The following five-step process builds upon Horton's work in describing the formative stages of training development and evaluation:

1. **Build** a prototype of one instructional unit, no matter how crude.

2. **Test** that unit with several real users.

3. **Analyze** the results of the test to understand the weaknesses of the design.

4. **Redesign** the unit by incorporating the lessons learned into the new design.

5. **Get "buy-off"** on the unit design.

It may prove necessary to repeat these steps several times, as money and resources allow, in order to resolve major user concerns. Getting buy-off from the various stakeholders during the initial development allows for shared responsibility in the training process and emphasizes to management the important role of evaluation.

3. Does the WBT Incorporate Appropriate Principles of Instruction into a Complete Instructional System? Advance organizers, like a table of contents or side menu bar, structure the training experience and provide a meaningful way to navigate and interpret the training material. Having material that is hard to find due to poor organization and inadequate navigation cues prevents optimal performance and undermines the instructional integrity of the training. For example, Web pages that indiscriminately use frames add confusion to the novice user, as the URL for a given page within the frames is not immediately obvious and is difficult to bookmark correctly.

Objectives for each instructional unit need to be precise and clearly broken down into what the learner has to know (essential concepts) and what the learner has to be able to do (optimal performance). With the use of guided and unguided practice examples, the instructional unit can result in the mastery of essential concepts. Trainers can assess simple computer performance tasks to a limited degree via the computer, depending both on the type of performance being evaluated and on the simulation software used. Figure 2 reviews these general areas of consideration while evaluating Web-based training sites and consolidates them in an easy-to-use rating scale.

Criteria for each question in Figure 2 are subjective. Gagné, Briggs, and Wager (1992) outline broad and encompassing standards for instructional design; however, criteria for what success would look like are best solidified in collaboration with the client. Further discussion and a short list of sample criteria are available on the Web (mse.byu.edu/ipt/students/ruttan/wbteval.html).

4. Does the WBT Learner Management Strategy Address the Learner Control Requirements of the Audience? In the real world, training developers typically have limited time and

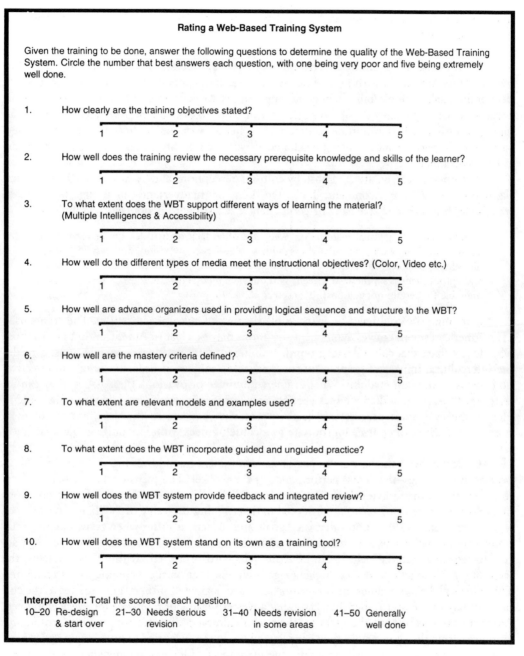

Figure 2. Rating a system.

money for each development cycle. It is tempting to skip over much of the formative evaluation and user testing necessary to meet the needs of different types of learners. Generally, every hour of early formative evaluation saves two or more hours of frustrating reworking. WBT is easier to evaluate and improve during the design process.

Motivated learners with efficient, intentional learning strategies do not need a highly structured learning environment (Martinez, 1998). Unsophisticated learners need structure to be productive. The nature of the content and the critical requirements of mastery also determine the best instructional design. We need to support and design for content adaptation for different learning styles.

5. Does the WBT Address Performance Barriers? Accessibility is important to performance. "The Americans with Disabilities Act has set our sights on removing the barriers that deny individuals with disabilities an equal opportunity to share in and contribute to . . . all aspects of society" (Dunne, 1996). Too often the attempt to evaluate performance is really evaluating accessibility. It is important to determine whether workers' ability to overcome barriers to acceptable performance is being evaluated versus their ability to learn and perform in the WBT environment.

Performance can be affected both by cultural perceptions and by disability when interacting within the WBT environment. Too often designers inadvertently or thoughtlessly create training Websites that are partially or completely inaccessible to people with disabilities.

> Graphics and other visual material on Web sites often lack textual descriptions that could allow individuals with print-related disabilities (blindness, low vision, and certain learning disabilities) to access the content. Speech output software can take the textual descriptions and output them as synthesized speech. Without such textual descriptions . . . the site may be unusable [to certain populations]. (Hansen *et al.,* 1998, p. 6)

A training site could also be inaccessible because of cultural association. The colors used in an American site to convey symbolic associations may be clear to Americans but not to those who do not share that cultural background. Training for multinational companies must consider the intercultural impact of graphics, icons, and color choices in order to design an effective, non-offensive training medium. When trainers minimize or overlook these issues, they can interfere with learning and create messages at cross purposes with the intended training content. Hence, the evaluation process is crucial in removing barriers to the development of user-friendly WBT. It is, of course, appropriate to include trainees with disabilities in our evaluation samples.

By dealing with the barriers to performance, trainers can address the more traditional aspect of the training—the actual performance of the worker. The focus of the evaluation shifts to judgments of the individual performance in a WBT environment. The answers to questions in Table 1 (Gottfredson, 1998) are essential in determining the value of WBT materials.

Darrell Sano (1996) notes that the "goals and objectives differ when providing information to an internal versus external audience." An intranet allows for increased control over access to sensitive material, which can be easily password protected. Within these systems, the technology is available to detect the language preference set on the incoming user's computer. This allows global companies the opportunity to specifically tailor their training sites to the cultural affinity of the user rather than assuming a western frame of reference for every employee. Another option is to have the users set their own cultural preference for language, color, and graphics within the system once they have logged on. Preferences tied to users' login codes need only be specified once for each user. Imagine the impact of logging on anywhere in the world and receiving individualized training to meet a company's needs globally, from Luxembourg to Australia.

Training Information-Age Employees
Will Affect a Company's Bottom Line

The summative or final evaluation of any training is its effect on the business bottom line. Poor quality training may cost a company in lost productivity if the "go-live" date of a new system is fraught with stress, including numerous calls to the help desk. Without the necessary evalua-

Table 1. What is the value of WBT?

1. Can learners actually perform the skills or tasks outlined in the objectives of the WBT?
2. Does WBT provide an understanding of the critical concepts necessary for competent performance?
3. Is WBT a positive learning experience that encourages on the job performance?
4. Does WBT provide learners the support they need after initial training?
5. To what extent has the WBT reduced the support burden typically carried by more expensive support resources: for example, the hotline or help desk?

tion, Web-based training will be hampered by virtual user-interface speed bumps that slow the learning process and frustrate the user.

A carefully designed and evaluated training process avoids many of the problems associated with self-paced Web-based training and does much toward creating productive information-age employees. When Web-based training is incorporated into a larger instructional system for performance support, it enables information-age users to quickly sift through a plethora of information and training materials to get exactly the training they need, just when they need it (for detailed examples and how-to resources, see the Website at: mse.byu.edu/ipt/students/ ruttan/wbteval.html).

References

Dryden, G., & Vos, J. (1993). *The learning revolution.* New Zealand: Profile Books.

Dunne, J. R. (1996). *Title II of the Americans with Disabilities Act technical assistance manual;* janweb.icdi.wvu.edu./kinder/pages/tam2.htm

Flagg, B. (1990). *Formative evaluation for educational technologies.* Hillsdale, NJ: Lawrence Erlbaum Associates.

Gagné, R. M., Briggs, L. J., & Wager, W. W. (1992). *Principles of instructional design.* New York: Harcourt Brace Jovanovich.

Gottfredson, C. A. (1998). *Writing onestop documentation.* Alpine, UT: Gottfredson Group.

Hall, B. (1997). Web-based training: Market trends, risks, and opportunities; multimediatraining.com/ report.html

Hansen, E. G., Forer, D. C., Jacquemin, D. H., & Katz, I. R. (1998, April). *A process for improving the accessibility of Websites for people with disabilities.* Paper presented at the meeting of the American Educational Research Association, San Diego.

Hill Associates. (1998). Fortune 500 companies increase and expand technology training; hill.com/ press_releases/fortune_500.html

Horton, W. (1994). *The icon book: Visual symbols for computer systems and documentation.* New York: John Wiley & Sons.

Kovacs, D. K. (1995). *The Internet trainers' guide.* New York: Van Nostrand Reinhold.

Martinez, M. (1998). Intentional learning projects; mse.byu.edu/projects/elc/ilprojects.html

Rice, J. C. (1998). Evaluating Web-based instruction; byu.edu/ipt/workshops/evalwbi/

Rice, J. C., McBride, R. H., & Ruttan, J. P. (1998). *Formative evaluation instruments for designing Web-based instruction,* unpublished manuscript.

Sanders, J. R., & the Joint Committee on Standards for Educational Evaluation. (1994). *The program evaluation standards* (2nd ed.). Los Angeles: Sage Publications.

Sano, D. (1996). *Designing large-scale Websites: A visual design methodology.* New York: Wiley Computer Publishing.

Trochim, W. M. K. (1996). Evaluating Websites; trochim.cornell.edu/webeval/webintro/webintro.htm

Worthen, B. R., & Sanders, J. R. (1987). *Educational evaluation: Alternative approaches and practical guidelines.* New York: Longman.

The Authors

Joanne P. Hall (formerly Ruttan) (e-mail: ruttanj@ed.byu.edu; Web homepage: mse.byu.edu/ipt/students/ ruttan/wb) is with Instructional Psychology and Testing at Brigham Young University, Provo, Utah. **Conrad A. Gottfredson (e-mail: cgottfredson@compuserve.com)** heads the Gottfredson Group in Alpine, Utah.

59

Evaluating Web-Based Training Programs

Zane L. Berge

E ssentially, *evaluation* is a process of assigning value. In this chapter, I focus on the value of training or educational programs in the context of a Web-based environment. A training or educational program is a set of organized learning activities that are systematically and intentionally designed to achieve planned learning outcomes, usually within a set timeframe.

Program planners design specific learning outcomes. They often have additional professional responsibilities, such as analyzing the needs and characteristics of the trainees, developing instructional materials, implementing the instruction, and evaluating and managing the program leading to successful learning (see Rothwell & Cookson, 1997, for a complete description of their Lifelong Education Program Planning Model). While there are many models useful to program planning, all share the overarching principle that, without determining the desired results in advance of the learning activities, it may be impossible to gather the necessary data to determine how successfully the learning program has been implemented.

The roles and functions of program planning can be performed by various people in an organization with titles such as trainer, program director, professor, instructional development professional, human resource development professional, training and development specialist, conference planner, or team facilitator. For the purposes of this chapter, a "program" can be as small in scope and size as a single, short workshop or as extensive as a university degree program—systematic evaluation is an important component in each. That the programmatic context here is the Web is important to parts of the evaluation plan and will be discussed below.

What Questions Does Program Evaluation Answer?

Basically, there are two reasons for program evaluation (also known as course evaluation or curriculum evaluation). One reason is for *decision-making* in helping to improve the program, and the other is for *accountability*. Program evaluators are interested in finding out through systematic methods about the learning they have designed: What happened, what do stakeholders believe about what happened, and how can improvements be made in the system (Freddolino, 1997). Some of the questions often asked in these categories follow (Boyle, 1981; Gery, 1991; Knowles, 1980; Rothwell & Cookson, 1997):

What happened during the learning event?

- Does the selection of participants comply with equal opportunity regulations?
- What are the characteristics of the learners? (e.g., occupation, age, gender)
- What were the expected and unexpected outcomes of the program?
- Could it have been more cost-effective (e.g., reduced support costs; reduced implementation costs)?
- Was there decreased time to performance?
- Did the training decrease the gap between less experienced and star performers?
- Was increased performer confidence realized?
- Are instructors capable of using the chosen method of instruction?
- Was the program well received by those for whom it was intended and in the intended way?
- Do learners have adequate opportunity to address their practical concerns?
- Was there evidence that learners' morale was raised?

What do stakeholders think about what happened?

- Which agencies are interested in program collaboration?
- Is it probable that the proposed procedures will produce the desired consequences?
- Are program planners overlooking some potential program goals?
- Can the intended outcomes be obtained efficiently?
- Is there justification for increasing the size of the program?
- Is there reason for program planners and stakeholders to have pride in their accomplishments?
- What was the return on investment (ROI)?
- What are worthwhile program goals?
- Can what happened in this program serve as the foundation for promotion, marketing, and public relations for the future?

What can be done next time to make it better?

- What procedures could be changed to improve instructional delivery?
- How could the content of the program be strengthened?
- How might greater impact on the learners' institutional setting be attained?
- Are there alternative topics that would better facilitate achieving stated program goals?
- Is the format of the program consistent with the setting of the instruction?
- Would it be useful to go into greater topic depth?

- Would the proposed method of instruction be compatible with the learning styles of the target group?

- How could the planning activities be improved to enhance participation?

- How can program goals more realistically correspond to learner goals?

- What technological equipment, trained staff, and ongoing infrastructure development are needed for improvement to future implementation of the Web-based training?

Framework for Program Evaluation of Web-Based Training

There are many approaches to program planning (e.g., Phillips, 1991; Workforce Development Staff Skills and Training Project, n.d.). Program evaluation is done to help with decision-making and accountability regarding stakeholder outcomes and the instructional development. While both the reasons for decision-making and accountability are important, the perspective taken in this chapter is that evaluation is done with a focus on *planning*. Formative evaluation leads to planning for continuous improvement of learning in the workplace or educational environment. Once program goals are established, program evaluators are fairly adept at formulating plans to evaluate stakeholder outcomes and instructional design elements. What is not usually emphasized is the need for evaluating the program with regard to political and technological factors (Freddolino, 1997; Wilson & Cervero, 1996).

Stakeholder Outcomes

Stakeholders vary greatly among learning systems, and, depending on what is being evaluated, the identity of the primary, secondary, and tertiary stakeholders will vary greatly. The complexity of the identification process cannot be given justice here, but this step is critical to evaluation in program planning, and the reader is directed to the references at the end of the chapter as a starting point for further details. Certainly the trainees, instructor, trainees' supervisor, and the business unit to which the trainees belong are key stakeholders. Others often include customers, vendors, trainees' family members, and funding agencies. The techniques used in evaluating whether stakeholder outcomes are being met are similar in Web-based training to those used in any other learning environment. But it should be noted that when planning for Web-based evaluation, there could be additional members of the team, such as Web-based designers/developers and information management staff, who would not be directly involved in the instructional environment if it were not Web-based.

Instructional Development and Content

Web-based training involves the analysis, design, development, implementation, evaluation, and management of instruction within an online learning and teaching environment. Quality of instruction (i.e., effectiveness) is mainly determined by the *instructional design* of the educational interventions, not the technology or delivery system. The design sets the parameters for quality and *limits* quality—as the effectiveness of the design decreases, so does the upper limit of quality in instruction. While the development of materials and the delivery can be detractors to learning, a ceiling for the effectiveness of learning is created at a height which depends on the instructional design (Berge, 1997).

The plan for evaluation of Web-based training follows the same principles as any delivery system with regard to questions such as how well did the participants learn, apply, or change their performance because of the instruction received (Asao, n.d.; Morita, 1996; Sweeney, Roop, & Lazzarotto, 1997). It is the change in scores between a pre- and posttest that is used for evaluation of the effectiveness of instruction. Surveys can be completed by students prior to the program's beginning to measure student characteristics and expectations (Hiltz, 1994). Generally, the intent is to make sure that the content, practice the trainees receive, examination of trainees, and the instructional objectives all match one another (Yelon & Berge, 1988). Nichols (1995) points out that compared to evaluation of face-to-face instruction, especially in the prototype stage, it is critical that evaluation of Web-based programs match the actual conditions the learner will face in a real-world environment. Often the shortcuts provided in evaluation of the training program (i.e., the assistance from instructor or developer that provide small insights to the try-out to keep the pace moving) that are useful and relatively harmless for face-to-face instruction can be fatal to the success of the Web-based training if real-world conditions are not met.

Tools used to help evaluate stakeholder outcomes and the instructional design, content, and quality of the program include learning contracts, team follow-ups, document reviews, tests, work samples, role plays, observations, class evaluations, conducting cost-benefit analyses, calculating break-even, committee reviews, critical incidents, meetings, focus groups, success stories, interviews, and surveys.

Levels of Evaluation

There are several frameworks for classifying areas of evaluation (Phillips, 1991). Kirkpatrick's (1983, 1996) model is perhaps the most well-known (Gordon, 1991) and consists of four levels of evaluation: reaction, learning, behavior, and results. With Level 1, data is most often gathered using questionnaires at the beginning, middle, or most likely at the end of the program. The evaluator is measuring the trainee's perceived satisfaction with the program, delivery implementation, and other factors involved with the training program. In Level 2 evaluation, the goal is to measure whether learning took place. Often a pre- and posttest design can be used for gathering evidence at Level 2 evaluation. At Level 3, the evaluation is geared to finding out if the trainee can perform in a real-world situation. Suppose the data from the Level 2 evaluation shows that the trainee can fly the airplane using a simulator. But can that person fly a real plane to Chicago from New York City? On the first flight after simulator training, would you crawl into the passenger seat of a plane flown by a pilot who just passed the Web-based training course you conducted and make first-hand observations? (Or, you could conduct exit surveys of the passengers getting off that plane in Chicago.)

At Level 4, the goal is to measure business results. Given Level 3 evaluation indicating that the trainees are performing on-the-job to the standards they have been trained, what does it matter to the organization? The efforts at this level are seeking to give summative evaluation about such things as reduced employee turnover, reduced costs, improved quality of products or services, increased sales, fewer grievances filed, or increased profitability (see, for example, Chabrow, 1995; Hassett, 1992, Robinson & Robinson, 1989).* There are almost always several confounding variables when trying to determine if Web-based training causes significant growth in the organization. Gathering data to measure return on investment and other evaluations at Level 4 is expensive and time-consuming, and therefore rarely attempted, even in the corporate sector. In 1996, the percent of courses evaluated at Kirkpatrick Levels 1 and 2 were reported by ASTD's Benchmark (American Society for Training and Development) companies as 92% and 34%, respectively. Only 11% of courses were evaluated at Kirkpatrick Level 3, and

---

*Some authors (see, for example, Phillips, 1996), would say that return on investment (ROI) should be a separate and higher Level 5 than the original four Kirkpatrick described. For the purposes of this discussion, Kirkpatrick's levels suffice.

a mere 2% were reported as being evaluated at Level 4 (ASTD Benchmark Forum, 1996). While these statistics are not broken out by delivery method, I would not expect Web-based training to differ from other program delivery methods.

Political and Technological Infrastructure

While the above framework is useful at various levels for designing evaluation for stakeholder outcomes and the instructional design used for the program, the context in which the program operates is critical, too. Creating a powerful learning environment means designing learning experiences that teach skills central to business issues, and make people central to an organization's success (Forum Corporation, 1996). A key element is linking training to business results, and that is done in a political arena with negotiated interests (Wilson & Cervero, 1996).

Freddolino (1997) speaks of the "interconnected mass of intra- and inter-organizational relationships and interactions among governing, advisory, user, and other interested stakeholder groups in addressing such issues as financing, staffing, usage, networks, and sustainability" (p. 82). Political factors often have significant impact upon the success of a program. A major change in the funding source or a change in the mission of the company, for instance, can have more of an impact on the success of a program than its quality.

For example, it does not make sense from a learning and teaching sense to conduct a comparison between Web-based training and "traditional" face-to-face training, given the same instructional design. This type of media comparison study, when well done, produces no significant differences (Clark, 1983). For the most part, I believe the field is moving past this type of comparison to the more relevant questions in need of evaluation, examples of which are listed throughout this chapter. Still, if the CEO asks for such a comparison, it may make political sense to do it.

It matters, too, at what stage or level of technological maturity the organization is. While data collection may not change, the way the data is interpreted probably will. For instance, the criteria for "success" may vary depending on whether this is the business unit's first Web-based course, or its twentieth. The bar is probably somewhat higher for an instructional development team used to working with sophisticated computer/telecommunication systems for several years than for a team with minimal experience and knowledge of these systems.

Tools used to help evaluate the political and technological infrastructure of Web-based training include social participation scales based on recorded observations of attendance, analysis of persons holding of leadership positions, Delphi, nominal group, committee review, team follow-ups, document reviews, critical incidents, meetings, work samples, observations, class evaluations, stories, interviews, and surveys. In my experience, evaluation along the dimensions of political impact are perhaps no different in a Web-based training environment than in any other learning environment (Khan & Vega, 1997). However, when planning for evaluation, let me again remind the reader that there could be additional members of the team, such as Web-based designers/developers and information management staff, who would not be directly involved in the instructional environment if it were not Web-based. Evaluation of the technological impact directly involves the hardware, software, and warmware used in the technological infrastructure on the Web.

Formulating a Program Evaluation Plan

Caffarella (1994) states that there are many acceptable systematic processes for conducting program evaluation. The composite model has 12 steps:

1. Secure support for the evaluation from those who have a stake in the results of the evaluation.

2. Identify the individuals to be involved in planning and overseeing the evaluation.

3. Define precisely the purpose of the evaluation and how the results will be used.

4. Specify what will be judged and formulate the evaluation questions.

5. Determine who will supply the needed evidence.

6. Specify the evaluation approach to be used.

7. Determine the data collection techniques to be used and when the data will be collected.

8. Specify the analysis procedure to be used.

9. Specify what criteria will be used to make judgments about the program or what process will be used to determine the criteria.

10. Determine the specific timeline and the budget needed to conduct the evaluation.

11. Complete the evaluation, formulate recommendations, and prepare and present an evaluation report.

12. Respond to the recommendations for changes in the overall program, specific learning activities, and/or the educational unit or function.

Again, in most if not all of these steps, especially in the early ones, the major challenge to the program evaluator/planner is in negotiating power and interests among the stakeholders (Wilson & Cervero, 1996).

Conclusions

Persons charged with program evaluation of Web-based training are often asked to explain the worth of a program in a *formative* manner. This is signified by terms such as improving organizational operations, recruitment and training, public relations, and administrative management. They are asked to improve such program aspects as objectives, selection of methods and materials, and the quality of learning outcomes. Sometimes they must supply *summative* evaluation to defend against cutbacks, justify expansion, raise morale, and speak to personnel evaluation or promotion of persons within the organization. In each of these cases, systematic program evaluation can be critical to decision-making and issues of accountability within the organization. The value-added focus occurs when evaluation is seen as a management tool for program planning. This may be especially true when the learning program is Web-based, given that this technology is quite new and much program evaluation still needs to be completed.

Often, evaluation is centered on stakeholder outcomes. While it is an essential component, an over-emphasis on outcomes may mean missing opportunities in other important areas, such as the likelihood of a program being replicated under somewhat different conditions, how administration of the program can be improved, what alternative technological systems may improve trainee satisfaction, or what characteristics of the current students would help in recruiting new students. Each of these factors is among those forming a Web-based training *system.*

The political and technological infrastructure present in any Web-based course may not change the level of the evaluation, nor change the data gathered. Still, it may have a great impact upon the interpretation and evaluation given to a particular program in *context*. In order to appropriately evaluate Web-based training, the person coordinating the evaluation must first consider the political situation in which that training will take place, the state of the organizational infrastructure, the organization's state of technological sophistication, the stakeholders and their interests, the content of the course, and the desired outcomes for the training. Program evaluation for a Web-based system involves the process of assessing, for the purposes of decision making and accountability, stakeholder outcomes and instructional development and content, all within a technological infrastructure and political environment.

References

Asao, K. (n.d.). Evaluating evaluation: Online instruction of EFL/ESL; leahi.kcc.hawaii.edu/org/tcc-conf/pres/asao.html

ASTD Benchmark Forum (1996). 1995 training statistics; astd.org/who/research/benchmar/96stats/graph14.gif

Berge, Z. L. (1997). The instructional technology train: Why use technology in education? In Z. L. Berge & M. P. Collins (Eds.), *Wired together: The online classroom in K–12. Volume 1: Perspectives and instructional design* (pp. 17–27). Cresskill, NJ: Hampton Press.

Boyle, P. G. (1981). Planning better programs. New York: McGraw-Hill.

Caffarella, R. S. (1994). *Planning programs for adult learners: A practical guide for educators, trainers, and staff developers.* San Francisco: Jossey-Bass.

Chabrow, E. R. (1995, July 10). The training payoff. *InformationWeek, 535,* p. 36.

Clark, R. E. (1983). Reconsidering research on learning from media. *Review of Educational Research, 53*(4), 445–459.

Forum Corporation (1996). Evaluations: Obstacles and opportunities; forum.com/forissue/eval.htm

Freddolino, P. P. (1997). A general model for evaluating distance education programs. *Proceedings of the Conference on Distance Teaching and Learning* (pp. 81–85), Madison, Wisconsin.

Gery, G. J. (1991). *Electronic performance support systems.* Boston: Gery Performance Press.

Gordon, J. (1991, August). Measuring the "goodness" of training. *Training, 28*(8), 19–25.

Hassett, J. (1992, Sept.). Simplifying ROI. *Training, 29*(9), 53–57.

Hiltz, S. R. (1994). *The virtual classroom: Learning without limits via computer networks.* Norwood, NJ: Ablex Publishing Corporation.

Kirkpatrick, D. L. (1983, Nov.). Four steps to measuring training effectiveness. *Personnel Administrator,* 19–25.

Kirkpatrick, D. L. (1996). Evaluation. In R. L. Craig (Ed.), *The ASTD training and development handbook: A guide to human resource development* (2nd ed.) (pp. 294–312). New York: McGraw-Hill.

Khan, B. H., & Vega, R. (1997). Factors to consider when evaluating a Web-based instruction course: A survey. In B. H. Khan (Ed.), *Web-based instruction* (pp. 375–378). Englewood Cliffs: Educational Technology Publications.

Knowles, M. (1980). *The modern practice of adult education: From pedagogy to andragogy.* River Grove, IL: Follett.

Morita, M. (1996). How to evaluate learning activities through the Internet in English language classes; graduate.edu.ibaraki.ac.jp/paper/evaluate.html

Nichols, G. (1995). Formative evaluation of Web-based training; ucalgary.ca/~gwnichol/formeval/formeval.html

Phillips, J. J. (1991). *Handbook of training evaluation and measurement methods* (2nd ed.). Houston, TX: Gulf Publishing Co.

Phillips, J. J. (1996). Measuring the results of training. In R. L. Craig (Ed.), *The ASTD training and development handbook: A guide to human resource development* (4th ed.) (pp. 313–341). New York: McGraw-Hill.

Robinson, D., & Robinson, J. (1989). *Training for impact.* San Francisco: Jossey-Bass Publishers.

Rothwell, W. J., & Cookson, P. S. (1997). *Beyond instruction: Comprehensive program planning for business and education.* San Francisco: Jossey-Bass Publishers.

Sweeney, J., Roop, C., & Lazzarotto, S. (1997). Teaching soft skills using distance education: A comprehensive evaluation of a BTV/TO program. *Proceedings of the Conference on Distance Teaching and Learning* (pp. 323–329), Madison, Wisconsin.

Workforce Development Staff Skills and Training Project (n.d.). A six-step training process prepared as a companion to "The Workforce Development Staff Skills and Training Challenge" report; icesa.org/national/update/sixsteps.htm

Wilson, A. L., & Cervero, R. M. (1996). Paying attention to the people work when planning educational programs for adults. In R. M. Cervero & A. L. Wilson (Eds.), *What really matters in adult education program planning: Lessons in negotiating power and interests.* Number 69 in "New Directions for Adult and Continuing Education." San Francisco: Jossey-Bass Publishers.

Yelon, S., & Berge, Z. L. (1988, January). The secret of instructional design. *Performance and Instruction,* 11–13.

The Author

Zane L. Berge (e-mail: berge@umbc.edu; Web homepage: jan.ucc.nau.edu/~mpc3/berge/zane.html) is Director of the Graduate Program in Training Systems at the University of Maryland, Baltimore County.

60

Online Implementation of Kirkpatrick's Four Levels of Evaluation Using Web Databases

Harvi Singh

Introduction

In 1959, Donald Kirkpatrick developed a four-level model for evaluating training programs. The "Kirkpatrick Model" has since become the most widely used approach to evaluating training.

With the rapid expansion and acceptance of Internet and intranet technology and Web-based training, the World Wide Web serves as a fertile ground for implementing comprehensive training evaluation programs. The Web offers several benefits for implementing training evaluation:

- **Accessibility:** In a training environment, evaluation data is seldom available in a dynamic, meaningful format for the stakeholders of the training programs. In an online environment, the evaluation data can be made available anywhere, anytime.

- **Ease of collecting input:** The user (learners, facilitators, or administrators) input can be gathered easily through a Web browser-based application and stored in Web databases for instant queries, statistics, and reports.

- **Time and cost saving:** The time and cost of implementing evaluation at each level is often described as the main reason for omitting evaluation. Seamlessly embedding online evaluation features in an online learning infrastructure can save tremendous amounts of time and cost of implementing training evaluations.

- **Opportunity for immediate follow-up:** Linking evaluation data and events with learning resources and online notification, for example, via e-mail, creates the scope for timely follow-up activities, such as remediation, correction of errors in training content or its delivery, or management intervention.

The illustrations provided in this chapter are from a Web-based performance and knowledge management system called KaleidoScope Enterprise, created by Empower Corporation (see Figure 1).

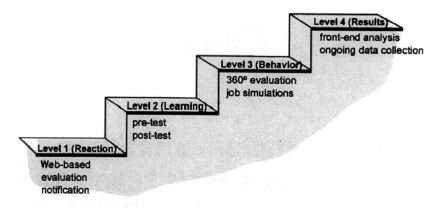

Figure 1. The four levels of evaluation in Kaleidoscope (after Kirkpatrick).

Overview of the Four-Level Evaluation Model

The four-level evaluation provides a comprehensive system for evaluating effectiveness of training programs. Each level has its own importance and influence over other levels, and therefore, skipping levels is highly discouraged. The four levels of evaluation are:

1. **Reaction:** The first level gauges the learners' reaction or satisfaction with the training program.

2. **Learning:** The second level verifies improvement in skill, acquisition of knowledge, or positive change in attitude.

3. **Behavior:** The third level determines the impact of training on behavior, on-the-job performance, and application of learned skill, knowledge, or attitude.

4. **Results:** The fourth level ascertains whether the training program achieved or impacted desired end-results such as increased revenue, productivity, return on investment, or reduction in errors.

Indeed, evaluation needs to be part and parcel of the overall training process, as opposed to an afterthought, and the evaluation concern therefore spreads from front-end analysis and instructional design to delivery and management of training.

Architectural Overview of Web-Based Learning and Online Learning Infrastructure

Implementation of a comprehensive and ongoing online evaluation program requires an enterprise-wide online learning infrastructure. This infrastructure can be deployed within an intranet or Internet environment.

The infrastructure captures the complete process of analysis, design, development delivery, and management of training. The evaluation process weaves through all aspects of the training process. Multiple stakeholders, including performance consultants, instructional designers, learning content developers, learners, facilitators, and management staff, need to be able to access, input, and query the system from various points of view, using a Web browser.

The online learning infrastructure is supported by a Web database system which can be implemented as central (single server) or distributed (distributed data on multiple Web servers) configuration.

The types of applications and inter-linked data managed in the Web database include:

- Organization information, including organizational performance goals and progress indicators and metrics

- Jobs, competencies, work practices, and tasks linked with related organizational performance goals

- Repository of learning goals and objectives

- A data bank of online (Web-based instructional content chunks, threaded discussion groups, or chats) or offline (classes, seminars, books, etc.) learning interventions. The learning interventions may either be facilitated or non-facilitated.

- Topic related assessment (pre-test and post-test)

- Individual participant profiles and performance and progress history

- Individual action plans and learning contracts

- Survey forms and associated data

- 360 degree feedback (in which feedback is collected from participant, peers, management, and customers) and statistics

- Notification (e-mail, etc.) based on triggers and rules

Level 1—Reaction

Learners' reaction to the learning programs can be sought through Web-based surveys. The survey forms may include simple yes or no answers, rating scales, and free-text questionnaire responses. The survey data is immediately collected in the Web database without requiring additional manual data entry. See Figure 2. A Web-based survey can also prompt or remind non-responders to enter their responses into the system.

Surveys can include questions about the effectiveness of the:

- overall learning Website

- learning content

- training facilitators

- training facilities

Survey results may also be used to inform new learners about the past success of certain programs.

In a more sophisticated environment, the surveys may be dynamically generated based on certain attributes of the learning intervention. For example, a facilitated program may automatically include certain questions about the facilitator's contribution to the success of the program.

Automated tracking of learners' progress and progression through a learning program may be yet another indication of involvement and engagement of the learners. Automated tracking includes online content visitation, completion, time spent, and interactive responses.

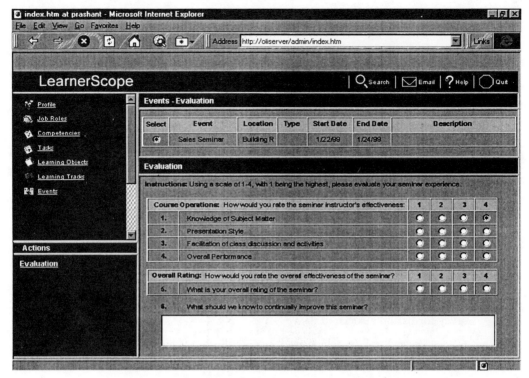

Figure 2. Level 1 Evaluation—surveying learner's reaction.

Aggregated reports constructed via Web database queries are presented to the training facilitators or administrators. This data can be saved and queried by management to determine continuity of existing programs and future offerings.

Level 2—Learning

Online pre-tests and post-tests provide an indication of success of learning and extent of skill and knowledge transfer or change in certain attitudes. Figure 3 illustrates an example of pre-test and post-test comparison data. An inventory of learning goals and supporting learning objectives and related test or question items can be stored in the Web database.

The test items may include simple multiple choice, match the columns, or fill in the blank questions, but may also include more complex computer job-related simulations or scenarios.

The test item responses are stored in the database during the test delivery. The facilitators or training administrators can query the data and generate reports to evaluate learning.

The pre-test results may also be queried by instructional designers and developers to focus on learning objectives for test items with the most erroneous responses. The test item analysis report may also be used to replace incorrect test items from the database.

Linking learning objectives with test items and learning content topics in the database provides the additional benefit of allowing individualized learning paths to be created. The learner can focus on topics related to incorrect test item responses. Remediation may be offered during immediate feedback in certain cases to provide links from within test items to topics. Adaptive testing algorithms may also be applied to the questions in a test, including randomized item selection based on learner performance.

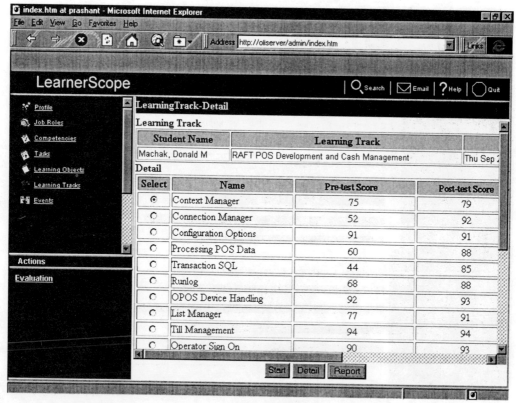

Figure 3. Level 2 Evaluation—comparison of pre- and post-test results.

Level 3—Behavior

Successful learning does not guarantee a successful application of learning on the job. Online 360-degree surveys provide a vehicle for conducting evaluation of behavior change and its application. Figure 4 shows a graphical view of 360 degree evaluation results.

An online 360-degree evaluation allows each employee to be evaluated by a group of individuals ranging from supervisors to peers to customers. The survey questions can be based on the job role and competency requirements and behavior change expected in the training program. A before and after 360-degree evaluation provides a better way to gauge transfer of skills, knowledge, or attitude to the job because it provides concrete comparison data.

An online 360-degree survey simplifies the bookkeeping, administration, and management of the evaluation process. Like an individual's survey data, reviewer lists are again managed through a Web database. Reviewers and supervisors may be notified via e-mail about successful completion of evaluation or any discrepancies. In addition, learning contracts and action plans can be set up for subsequent improvement and remediation.

Level 4—Results

An online front-end analysis before the design and deployment of training is a critical element to results evaluation. In order to measure results, the organizational goals and performance gaps must be analyzed and captured in the Web database for further tracking and eval-

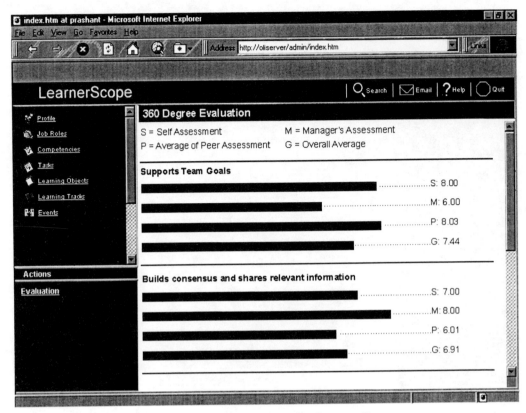

Figure 4. 360-degree evaluation results.

uation. See Figure 5 to see a database form showing relationship between performance indicators and related gaps, probable causes, and potential solutions.

The front-end analysis includes determining key business issues, business goals, performance indicators and associated gaps. For example, number of products sold may be a performance indicator for a business goal involving increased revenue. Each performance indicator's value is updated from time to time using spreadsheet-like function. Causal factors, such as lack of skill and knowledge, are linked to the performance gaps. If training is deemed a potential solution to the performance gap, then each associated performance indicator could be tracked at multiple intervals before and after the training to judge the impact of training. Furthermore, results from Level 1, 2, and 3 could be correlated with the results from Level 4 evaluation.

A Web-based system provides a decision support system to the senior management about how training investment is linked to business objectives and whether training is making any measurable impact to bottom line results.

Conclusion

The World Wide Web and other Internet technologies are expected to create a huge impact on delivery of learning by bringing learning to the workplace anytime, anywhere. Online learning, therefore, offers the benefits of fusion of learning with work through on-demand access to learning interventions. The scope and process of evaluation must also change and take advantage of enabling Web and Internet technologies.

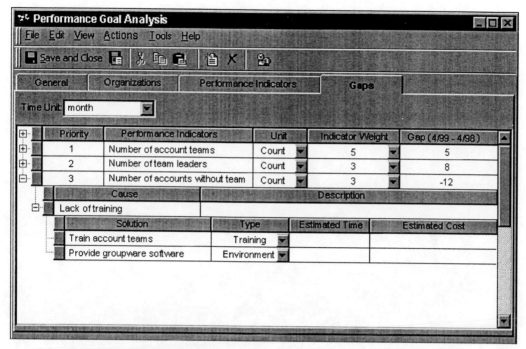

Figure 5. Level 4 Evaluation—front-end analysis and ongoing tracking.

Just like the learning content, the evaluation data become instantaneously accessible and updatable to provide dynamic rapid decision making opportunities.

Most importantly, a Web-based system provides a vehicle for tightly incorporating evaluation in the overall (analysis, design, development, delivery, and management) process of building effective and sustainable performance and knowledge management systems.

References

Dubois, D. (1993). *Competency based performance improvement.* Reading, MA: HRD Press.

Edwards, R. M., & Ewen, J. A. (1996). 360-degree feedback. New York: AMACOM.

Hannum, W., & Hansen, C. (1989). *Instructional systems development in large organizations.* Englewood Cliffs: Educational Technology Publications.

Khan, B. H. (Ed.). (1997). *Web-based instruction.* Englewood Clifffs: Educational Technology Publications.

Kirkpatrick, D. (1996). *Evaluating training programs: The four levels.* San Francisco: Berrett-Koehler Publishers.

Knowles, M. (1984). *Andragogy in action.* San Francisco: Jossey-Bass.

Phillips, J. (1997). *Handbook of training evaluation and measurement methods.* Houston: Gulf Publishing Company.

The Author

Harvi Singh (e-mail: **harvis@empower-co.com**; Web homepage: **empower-co.com**) is the President of Empower Corporation, Raleigh, North Carolina.

61

Usability Testing of Web-Based Training

M i c h a e l   H u g h e s   a n d
L o r e n   B u r k e

The student kept scrolling, trying unsuccessfully to find the course's supplemental readings, never clicking on the hypertext heading labeled "Supplemental Readings," underlined and highlighted in blue. Fortunately, this mistake was being made in a usability lab with the developer watching through a one-way mirror, and not being made all over the world by the hundreds of students meant to take this training. When the test facilitator asked the participant why he didn't use this link, the answer was, "Oh, is that a link? I thought it was just a heading."

The test had detected an important navigation problem: When a heading was used as a hypertext link, the student did not interpret it as a link. He assumed it was a different color and underlined merely because it was a heading. Most important, however, the developer had found the problem before the course had been launched and before this problem and dozens like it had created support or performance issues.

This example is typical of the kinds of problems that can detract from the success of Web-based training materials—problems not related to course content or its instructional model, rather, problems associated with the usability of the online materials or the interfaces themselves. "One reason that computer applications fail, particularly with respect to usability and usefulness, is that a system well-crafted with respect to function-level requirements . . . may nonetheless be completely unsuited to the real situated practices of the people who will use the system" (Carroll, 1994, p. 68).

This chapter focuses on how usability testing can be used to evaluate Web-based training in order to improve how effectively students can use the online interface and course materials. As such, its principles and precepts can be applied to any learning model that relies on students accessing instructional materials or interacting in any way through the Internet.

What Is Usability Testing?

Usability testing is the observation of typical users performing tasks with a product and is conducted for the purpose of determining what changes need to be made to the content presentation or user-interface for that product. "User testing with real users is the most fundamental usability method and is in some sense irreplaceable, since it provides direct information about

531

how people use computers and what their exact problems are with the concrete interface being tested" (Nielsen, 1993, p. 165).

Usability testing is one method of conducting formative evaluation of an educational product when that product is Web-based or computer-based. *Formative evaluation* is "the systematic collection of information for the purpose of informing decisions to design and improve the product" (Flagg, 1990, pp. 1–2). As such, usability testing can be done very early in the development of the product, using prototypes, in order to gather user requirements and shape presentation concepts, or it can be done toward the end of the development process to detect problems that have been inadvertently built into the design. An important limitation to remember, however, is that usability testing does not evaluate transfer or efficacy of instruction. Its focus is on determining how easily the materials are accessed and understood during instructional use. For this reason, developers should conduct additional evaluation procedures to assess how well the product meets instructional goals.

Usability testing, as we present it in this chapter, is a form of qualitative, action research. It is interpretive and directed at problem-solving. More directly, it is a tool by which the developers and stakeholders can view the product through the user's eyes and make improvements based on that perspective. As such, usability testing follows a different set of rules than quantitative, experimental methods. Carroll (1990, p. 92) notes, "[A] typical mistake at [early testing] is to lapse into quantitative methods of experimental psychology (counting error frequencies, timing performance on tiny tasks). . . . The information they produce is often not the kind that helps to shape and reshape a design."

The Usability Team

Since the ultimate goal of the usability test is to implement necessary changes, the test needs to be designed and observed by a team composed of the stakeholders and the change makers, representing a cross-section of different organizational and functional units. This approach also enhances both the validity and the reliability of the test through the qualitative research technique of *triangulation* (Creswell, 1998). Problems with human-computer systems tend to be complex and are best evaluated and solved by the combined perspectives of people bringing different expertise and perspectives to the process. These generally include the following:

- *Targeted trainees (clients).* If possible, include someone who is representative of the group to be trained.

- *Instructional designers.* The person(s) responsible for the integrity of the instruction.

- *Web developers/programmers.* The person(s) responsible for the technical delivery of the instruction.

- *Training/development managers.* Those responsible for the design and development resources and schedules.

- *Risk manager.* The person whose success depends on the clients being trained. This could be the manager of the targeted trainees, as is often the case for internal training, or a product manager who feels that his or her product cannot achieve its market goals without trained personnel, e.g., customers, sales persons, technical support personnel, etc. The risk manager is the most important person to identify and have on the team.

The Process

A usability test has a user perform a set of tasks in a controlled environment where the user's actions and comments can be observed. Formal tests use a lab that allows the test to be

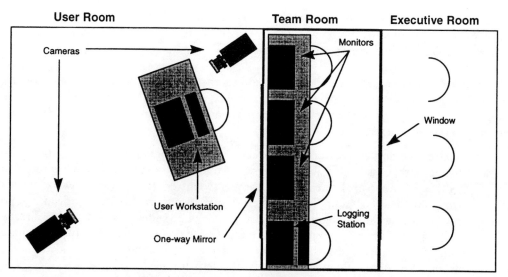

Figure 1. Layout of a typical usability lab.

videotaped and observed through monitors and a one-way mirror. Some labs allow additional viewing rooms for executives and other interested parties who are not directly associated with the current test. Figure 1 shows the layout of a typical usability lab.

For usability testing to achieve its two-fold goal of gathering data and facilitating solutions based on that data, it must be implemented as a process composed of the following events: Planning Meeting; Scenario Generation; Walk-through; Rehearsal; Assessment; and Action Meeting.

Planning meeting. The purpose of the planning meeting is to define the users and select the tasks for the usability test. All members of the team must attend the planning meeting. The main outcomes are:

- user profiles that can be used to recruit the appropriate users;

- descriptions of the tasks to use in the usability test; and

- concurrence among the team members concerning user profiles and the tasks to be tested.

The user profiles describe the types of people who will use the training. These profiles should include key attributes, demographics, and questions that can be used to recruit potential users for the tests. Most importantly, the profiles should include the level of Internet experience and expertise as well as the entry-level content knowledge and skills for which the training has been designed.

One rarely has the opportunity to test every aspect of a training package; therefore, it is important to choose carefully the tasks one does test. Tasks should be identified based on their risk and their impact on user perception of the training. The following tasks should be included: installation (if done by the user); first tasks with the product (including registration); and highly interactive tasks in the instruction (such as exercises and tests).

A typical usability test lasts an hour and a half (after which the amount of new data collected drops drastically), so only about seven to ten tasks need to be identified. Tasks take much longer when done by users who are new to the product than developers think they will. If someone who knows the product can do a task in five minutes, that same task typically will take fifteen minutes when an inexperienced user does it.

Scenarios Generation. After the team identifies the tasks to be included in the usability test, someone from the team must write scenarios, i.e., short, high level descriptions that are given to the user during the test to situate each task in a context. In general, scenarios should have the following characteristics:

- **Goal orientation (vs. feature orientation).** Scenarios should be centered around authentic learner tasks. By "authentic tasks" we mean tasks that are stated in terms of high-level learner goals, i.e., things learners would do and for the reasons learners would do them. For example, in one test of a Web-supported course, students had no trouble finding the bibliography the instructor had provided when they were directly told to do so. When the scenario was restated as "Find out what textbook(s) you have to buy," it became evident that this information had not been made explicit within the bibliography. Above all, avoid "procedural" scenarios, e.g., "Click on File, then print the current Web page." An important datum that might be missed is would a learner want to have a hard copy of that page. A second datum that would be missed is would the learner know to go to File to print.

- **Minimum use of user interface terminology.** An important objective of usability testing is to determine what terminology on the user interface is intuitive and what terminology is not. For example, if lecture notes are located under a menu called "Activities," this word should not appear in a scenario that asks the user to find the notes from a particular lecture. Part of the important data to be gathered would be if a trainee would think of an online lecture as an "activity."

- **Clear ending points.** A task should never be considered to be complete until the user thinks it is complete. There needs to be a definite ending step, such as calling the test facilitator, to signify that the user feels the task is complete. For example, the user may successfully complete a training module but not realize it. Developers observing the test may want to stop the task at that point and consider it a success, but the user may go on and get frustrated by lack of feedback, or worse, commit a functional error that has a negative impact on system or product operation.

Walk-through. The walk-through is a session where the person who will facilitate the test (work with the user) goes through the scenarios using the product to see if the scenarios work. Usually the person who is responsible for writing the scenarios works with the facilitator, although it may be useful to have the designers and developers there as well. This event also lets the facilitator get familiar enough with the product to facilitate the test itself. When an independent consultant is used as the facilitator, valuable evaluation data can come out of the walk-through.

Rehearsal. The rehearsal is an actual test with a real user, the product, the scenarios, and the full team. It has the following objectives: ensure that the equipment works; reconfirm the scenarios; and train the usability team to run a test.

Only one user is used and is usually told there may be problems. The rehearsal is normally the day or evening before the assessment so that there is time to correct any problems that occur. Even though the rehearsal is to "shake out the test setup," it gathers useful data.

Assessment. The assessment is a sequence of users (typically three) and the associated findings meetings after each user is done. The facilitator gives the user the scenarios one at a time and leaves the user alone in the room to accomplish the task. Users are encouraged to think out loud about what they are doing, why they are doing it, and what results they expect from each action they take. We find that this combination of direct observation and "think aloud protocol" reveals problems otherwise not uncovered by interviews and surveys.

Quantitative researchers sometimes ask how data taken from such a small sample can be reliable. In a usability test, the user is there mostly to help the team see the product through a user's eyes (to see the product for the first time, again). For example, if a download screen tells the user to enter an "access code" from a document and two of the users get confused because it is called the "student ID" in the document, the team knows this needs to be changed without having to see it happen twenty-seven out of thirty times. In cases of obvious problems such as this, the scenario may even be dropped or changed for the next user. Our experience is that after three or four users, no significant additional data are collected. If we think sufficient data have been gathered after two users on a particular task, we may drop that scenario and add additional ones for the next users. This practice is consistent with the emergent nature of qualitative research.

After each user, the team holds a findings meeting in which it reviews logs and individual notes kept during the tasks. Items that represent possible usability problems are noted on flip-chart sheets that are taped to the meeting room wall. This information is color-coded according to each user. As the same item is encountered by different users, the new notation is added below the original notation for the first user who encountered that problem. In this way, problems encountered by several users stand out due to the multi-colored entries. This type of data analysis is consistent with methods used in qualitative research.

Action meeting. After all the tests have been conducted, the data are summarized into categories, such as navigation, response time, browser issues, etc., and the team meets to decide what to do. Problems are usually prioritized by their severity using a three-tiered system such as the following: (1) product will not work if this problem is not fixed; (2) serious usability problem, fix before shipping; (3) OK to ship product if this is not fixed.

Solutions are decided for each problem. This is where the multi-discipline team is beneficial. Members from one function can see innovative solutions that others, who were too close to the problem, could not see.

Finally, specific persons are assigned the responsibility for implementing each solution. What makes this approach to usability testing so effective is that by having the same members of the usability team involved throughout the whole process, changes do get made.

Conclusion

Use this checklist to verify that you have a rigorous (valid and reliable) test design:

- ❑ Is the usability team composed of stakeholders and fixers?
- ❑ Is the usability team multi-disciplined or cross-organizational?
- ❑ Does the test rely on observations of actual or typical users (versus opinions of "usability experts")?
- ❑ Are the scenarios written in a user, goal-centered context?
- ❑ Are direct observation and think aloud protocol the primary sources of data, versus interviews and surveys?

❑ Are the observations discussed and key usability issues noted after each user?

❑ Do the findings rely on descriptions of user actions and perceptions, versus numerical findings such as average time to complete tasks or error rates? (If not, does the sample size support statistical inferences?)

❑ Is the final outcome a list of solutions (versus merely a list of the usability problems)?

For further information on usability testing, see the Usability Center's Website (ulabs.com). For handbooks on usability testing, readers may wish to refer to works by Dumas and Reddish (1993) and by Rubin (1994), in addition to Nielsen's (1993) work cited in this chapter.

References

Carroll, J. M. (1990). *The Nurnberg Funnel.* Cambridge, MA: The MIT Press.

Carroll, J. M. (1994). Designing scenarios for human action. *Performance Improvement Quarterly, 7*(3), 64–75.

Creswell, J. W. (1998). *Qualitative inquiry and design: Choosing among five traditions.* Thousand Oaks, CA: Sage Publications.

Dumas, J. S., & Reddish, J. C. (1993). *A practical guide to usability testing.* Norwood, NJ: Ablex.

Flagg, B. N. (1990). *Formative evaluation for educational technologies.* Hillsdale, NJ: Lawrence Erlbaum Associates.

Nielsen, J. (1993). *Usability engineering.* Boston: Academic Press.

Rubin, J. (1994). *Handbook of usability testing: How to plan, design, and conduct effective tests.* New York: John Wiley and Sons.

The Authors

Michael Hughes (e-mail: mikehughes@mindspring.com; **Web homepage:** mindspring.com/~mikehughes/ **home/index.htm**) is an Instructor in the Humanities and Technical Communication Department at Southern Polytechnic State University, Marietta, Georgia. **Loren Burke** (e-mail: loren@ulabs.atlanta.com; **Web homepage:** ulabs.com) is President and CEO, the Usability Center of Atlanta.

62

Cost Analysis and Return on Investment (ROI) for Distance Education

Kent L. Gustafson and

Lynne Schrum

Introduction

D istance education (DE) has been implemented in one form or another, including Web-based training, in every state and province in the US and Canada and in countries around the world. Reasons for implementing DE range widely, including:

- meeting the needs of learners who otherwise might be underserved (e.g., Australian DE programs for school-age children in remote locations);

- creating new markets (e.g., advanced degree programs via Web-based courses in higher education);

- reaching large numbers of learners with varying interests, backgrounds, and needs (e.g., computer training for teachers via the Internet);

- quickly distributing time-sensitive business information (e.g., new product training via teleconferencing for sales personnel in the computer industry);

- creating a sense of community for geographically dispersed learners (e.g., discussion listservs to support university courses serving commuter populations);

- addressing the scarcity of qualified instructors (e.g., environmental monitoring and re-mediation training by a single expert to a national and ever-changing audience);

- increased consistency and quality of instruction (e.g., short course by a department of human services on interpreting state regulations for new social workers); and

- providing "just-right," "just-in-time" company training (e.g., systematically designed and tested course on changing tax regulations).

While each of these reasons may have its own social, moral, or legal justification, several of the above examples (and many others) would lend themselves to some form of cost and benefit analysis. An analysis can take different forms and might be limited to costing alone or might involve more complete analysis, possibly including calculating Return on Investment (ROI). It is generally advisable to do costing and ROI analysis before a project is started, while it is underway, and at its conclusion (or at least after it has been fully implemented).

Consider the example of a DE project that will be looking at ROI at all three of these times that is designed to provide executives a way in which to complete an advanced degree while maintaining their workload and travel schedules.

Today many business organizations face a difficult and costly situation: retaining competent workers while encouraging them to pursue MBA degrees so as to successfully compete for higher positions in the company. Currently, many companies sponsor a valuable employee to return to school; however, they typically lose the services of that employee for the two years of schooling. To address this challenge a large financial corporation recently joined with a large southeastern university College of Business's MBA program to use distance learning technologies to create a combined model uniquely suited to their high level workers' needs.

This corporation was prepared to invest significant resources in the design and development of this tailored program, with the understanding that it would become a model to assist many of their current and future executives. Once the concepts and coursework had been designed, the corporation assumed it could be replicated for others. Faculty were invited to participate in the creation of this integrated, multiple-technology, combined-format, online MBA program. The project was designed for a cohort of 54 successful executives to complete the MBA in an intense two-year format. Substantial resources were devoted to a technological support team to assist faculty, design materials, and support students. These costs, although substantial, were considered to be "start-up," with the pay-off coming from retention of quality employees.

A plan has been developed to look carefully at all costs at the end of the first year, in order to gauge the true costs. For example,

- Were participants able to continue their full job responsibilities as intended?

- Were estimates of incidentals (phone, fax, materials) too high or too low?

- Were peripheral costs (to family or health, for example) too costly?

At the end of the first cohort's two years, an extensive evaluation of all costs is planned. Similarly, the costs to the department and faculty will be calculated. The determination of the continuation of this experiment will be based on many factors, but accurate financial data will be a significant consideration. When thinking about doing cost and benefit analysis of distance education programs, it is generally easier to examine costs than benefits. However, even the relative lack of solid cost data for many DE efforts is disturbing. If the promised rosy scenarios of a future overflowing with individually tailored, high quality, widely available DE are to become a reality, better cost and benefit analyses will have to take place. Society simply will not continue to increase its expenditures on DE unless at least some meaningful data become available to justify the costs. This is particularly true in industry, where the very existence of training departments may well depend on their ability to demonstrate their contribution to critical business objectives and corporate bottom line (Mager, 1996; Phillips, 1998). We believe educators also would be well served by carefully analyzing the estimated and actual costs and (to the degree possible) benefits of DE initiatives (Gustafson & Watkins, 1998).

Fortunately, some forms of analysis are relatively easy to do, while others require a bit more expertise and effort. This chapter describes a number of common approaches to cost and benefit analysis and describes how they might be used in specific settings.

Types of Cost and Benefit Analysis

Although there are many different ways to conduct cost and benefit analysis, we will discuss only five that are particularly useful when planning distance education programs. Keep in mind that the specific terms we use are sometimes used in different ways by other authors. Therefore, it is necessary to understand the underlying concept being described and not assume, for example, that all writers on ROI mean exactly the same thing. Five analytic methods are described below, including: full costing, cash flow per unit of time, break-even analysis, cost/benefit ratio (benefit/cost), and return on investment.

Full Costing

Full costing by itself does not attempt to directly relate cost to benefits, but is advised for all DE projects to determine their feasibility *over their lifespan* and is essential if more complete analysis is planned. At a minimum, full costing in education should take into account:

- instructor compensation (salaries and benefits);
- travel and per diem for instructors;
- support staff compensation (salaries and benefits);
- initial program development;
- program revision;
- equipment and software acquisition;
- maintenance and upgrade of equipment and software;
- consumable program materials;
- delivery (e.g., satellite or Internet charges);
- other operating costs (telephone, postage, supplies, publicity, etc.); and
- facilities (optional).

In business settings, one also needs to add what is likely to be the largest single costs: compensation for those receiving training. Additional costs might include: trainee travel and per diem; lost productivity; and need for replacements workers while some are in training, and training for those who will supervise the trainees if new policies or procedures are being implemented in the workplace.

When calculating full costs, it is necessary to project the useful life of the DE program before major changes are likely to occur due to changes in the nature of the instruction, new technology, or changed business conditions. Thus, for example, a university might project the full cost of a DE program over five years on the basis that beyond that time, conditions are likely to be so different that any projections are meaningless. If this is done, the residual value of any hardware, software, and materials can be subtracted when determining the full cost over five years. The case study presented later in which we describe the statewide DE network for training teachers illustrates the importance of calculating the full cost of equipment upgrades and program revisions to determine whether a program can remain viable.

Cash Flow per Unit of Time

Calculating estimated cash flow per unit of time can be useful for multi-year planning as well as for monitoring and managing a DE program once implemented. This involves projecting on a month-to-month or quarterly basis what expenditures will occur during that time. Any revenues can also be projected on the same timeline to determine how much money will be required to support the program, particularly in its early stages when there are likely to be no revenues. A typical DE program will show very heavy expenditures during start-up as the instruction is developed and infrastructure created. Only after it is implemented will revenues begin to flow and it may take some time for them to meet or exceed continuing expenditures on a monthly basis.

The results of cash flow analysis may be reported in various forms including tables, graphs, and charts. Spreadsheet software often has available several options for how to display results so they may be tailored to the preferences of specific audiences. A typical summary graph might look like Figure 1. It indicates there will be a negative cash flow until month eight of the project, after which there is a positive cash flow. However, even when the positive cash flow point is reached, the project has not reached the break-even point. (Break-even analysis is discussed below.) One of the important uses of cash flow analysis is to determine whether the organization can fund the project until it reaches the positive cash flow point.

Break-even Analysis

Break-even analysis (sometimes called payback period) takes data analysis one step beyond cash flow to determine when *cumulative revenues* from a project match or exceed *cumulative costs*. Unless one desires to include the time-value of money (essentially this is the interest on the money invested and the effects of inflation), break-even analysis is relatively simple to calculate. The break-even point is when the sum of all the monthly costs is equal to the sum of all revenues to that date. Different organizations may have different criteria for judging how long is too long before the break-even date occurs, but projects that exceed 30 to 36

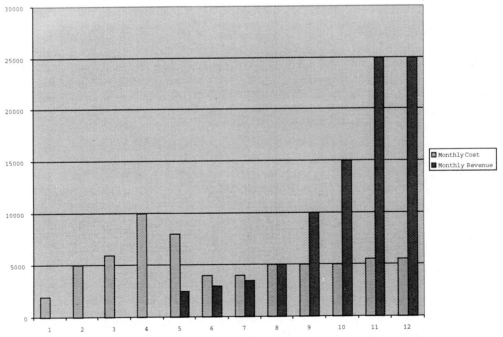

Figure 1. Example of a monthly cost/revenue cash flow graph.

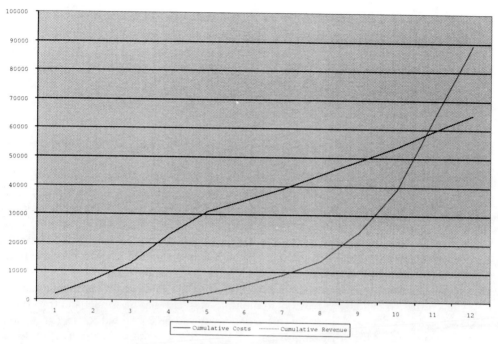

Figure 2. Example of a break-even curve.

months deserve extra scrutiny before deciding to proceed. The results of break-even analysis can be displayed in various ways, with cumulative cost/revenue curves being one easily understood format (see Figure 2). In Figure 2, the break-even point is reached at about 11 months.

From a risk perspective, the further away the break-even point, the greater the risk the project has of failing to reach that point. This is partially because unanticipated events can invalidate the assumptions upon which projects are made (Murphy's Law is alive and well in DE projects) and also because even small upward deviations in costs or downward deviations in revenues from projections often will dramatically extend the break-even date.

None of the three analytic methods described above directly takes into account any monetary benefits of the DE program other than revenues. Of course, to an educational institution, revenues may be the only monetary benefit that can be determined. However, businesses and, in some cases, educational institutions may be able to determine other financial benefits to be derived from a DE program. Benefits can be thought of by considering delivering training via DE versus by some other method (e.g., DE versus flying trainees to a central site for training), or by comparing DE to no intervention. In either situation, benefits to which dollar amounts can be attached must be identified in order to calculate a cost-benefit ratio. Among the more common monetary benefits to consider are:

- saved wages of trainees due to shortened and/or flexible training times;
- reduced number of replacement workers for those in training;
- saved instructor time;
- saved travel and per diem for trainees and/or instructors;

- reduction in lost productivity;

- increased productivity (e.g., sales or services);

- increased quality or less defects;

- reduced operational costs;

- increased safety or less worker's compensation costs;

- lower absenteeism; and

- increased worker flexibility (e.g., ease of reassignment).

When comparing corporate training via DE to more traditional methods such as "stand-up" lectures, there is some evidence to suggest that DE is at least as effective while reducing trainee's learning time (Charron & Obbink, 1993; Garrison & Shale, 1990; Mason & Kaye, 1990; Moore & Thompson, 1990). The resulting cost savings can be substantial, especially when large numbers of trainees are involved. When trainees travel to a central site for traditional training, costs are incurred for compensation for both training and travel days and per diem expenses. These can be substantial when there are many individuals traveling great distances. The alternative, sending instructors to multiple sites, also has personnel and travel costs that likewise can be calculated. Lost days of productivity can be converted to costs in various ways: lost sales; overtime for other employees, and the·need for additional employees to do the work of those in training.

Increases in productivity can usually be converted to dollar amounts when tied to increased products or sales or reduced numbers of employees to provide a given amount of services. Reduction in the amount of rejected products, or those requiring rework, can be converted to dollar amounts as can reductions in the amount of product or service recalls or customer support required. Similarly, the value of less waste of resources, less loss of employee time off the job due to accidents, and lower absenteeism can often be estimated with some degree of confidence. The last item on the list, increased learner flexibility, is more difficult to quantify. However, in some situations the value of having employees who can fill in temporarily on other jobs during vacations or illness, or who can readily take on new positions due to company growth or personnel turn over can be estimated by upper management and included in a cost benefit and ROI analysis. (For example, lab technicians might also be trained to draw blood or assist on an EKG to expand the flexibility of staff assignments.) For specific examples of how to attach dollar amounts to various types of data, see the two books of case studies by Phillips (1994, 1997) and the sample data included in the instructional module by Decker and Campbell (1996).

Cost/Benefit Ratio (Benefit/Cost)

Cost/Benefit Ratio (CBR) is often calculated as Benefit/Cost Ratio (BCR), with the latter being similar to ROI. Both use exactly the same values with the only difference being which figures are placed in the numerator and which in the denominator of the ratio. As one might expect, the cost/benefit ratio is calculated by dividing the full cost of the initiative by its total monetary benefits.

The cost/benefit formula is:

$$CBR = \frac{\text{Total Costs}}{\text{Total Benefits}}$$

Alternatively, the formula for benefit/cost ratio is:

$$BCR = \frac{\text{Total Benefits}}{\text{Total Costs}}$$

The size of the resulting value indicates the size of any monetary benefit to the organization. When examining the BCR ratio, unless the value is equal to or greater than 1, the benefit is worth less than it costs. The larger the value above 1, the greater the benefit, with a value of 2 or more generally being desired by managers who are looking for ways to rapidly increase productivity or profitability. From a risk analysis standpoint, the closer the BCR value is to 1 and the longer the project takes, the greater the risk. For example, a BCR of 1.5 over three years is much less attractive than the same BCR over 18 months since the opportunity for things to go wrong, or external events to overtake the project, is greater for a longer project.

Return on Investment (ROI)

Calculating ROI is identical to BCR except that costs are subtracted from benefits before dividing by total costs to obtain the rate of return. This subtraction of costs from benefits is necessary so that only *additional* (net) benefits beyond costs are considered since they represent the growth in value beyond the original money invested. Thus, net benefits equal total benefits minus total costs.

Thus, the formula for ROI is:

$$ROI = \frac{\text{Benefits} - \text{Total Costs}}{\text{Total Costs}}$$

If this seems confusing, think about putting $100 in the bank. If after one year you took out all the money and it amounted to $105, then your rate of return was 5%. To obtain this value, you had to subtract your initial investment from the amount withdrawn before calculating your rate of return. The same logic applies to calculating ROI.

Return on investment is often calculated on a yearly basis, even though the expected benefits may occur over several years. There are many different ways to treat multiple year projects, with the simplest (and least accurate) being to calculate the overall ROI and divide it by the number of years to obtain the yearly rate of return. For more detailed information on conducting sophisticated ROIs, see Carnevale and Schultz (1990).

What constitutes a reasonable rate of return varies for different organizations, just as it does for individuals. Corporations commonly seek an annual return rate of 20% or more before launching new projects. However, the importance of non-tangible benefits or how a project fits long-term strategic plans can have a major impact on the decision. Certainly, not every proposed DE project will require an ROI of 20% or larger to be initiated, since there are many other important reasons for DE.

Intangible Benefits

Intangible benefits (sometimes called soft data) may be far more important for some DE projects than their monetary benefits. When planning an analysis, a variety of potential benefits which either cannot be easily measured or to which monetary value cannot be easily or objectively assigned should be identified and considered during the decision-making process. Among the more common intangibles are:

- employee morale;
- student satisfaction with the program;
- instructor ratings;
- widely held belief that "something must be done";
- "political" pressure can be responded to;
- sense that it is the "right thing to do";
- desire to test out a new technology before committing to it;
- "experiments" to test the feasibility of strategic plans; and
- development of more "sophisticated" learners who are able to use new technologies and ways of learning in the future.

Although some may try to assign dollar values to some of these intangibles, Phillips (1994) recommends that often this is undesirable, since it may taint the credibility of the more objective benefits data. He recommends dividing the data into "hard" and "soft" categories and simply reporting the soft items as factors to keep in mind during any discussion of the results of the analysis.

Intangible benefits analysis might be particularly appropriate for an institution as it considers the creation of a distance learning program. This example involves a small community college in the northeast—where congestion impacts travel and learners struggle to make it to classes. Serving a wider audience is not the immediate goal, but staying current and meeting the needs of the enrolled learners is. The plan was to begin with a pilot program by providing developmental support for three classes taught by interested faculty. A consultant was brought in to raise the issues for all the faculty, and provided a modest amount of time for planning.

The financial commitment included a quarter time effort for three development individuals, and money for hardware and software. Since this initial small DE project will not expand the number of students served, the financial investment may never be returned, nor will more money likely come into the institution. To understand this institution's actions, we have to look beyond financial remuneration to the intangible benefits resulting from the project. This institution is looking for enhanced professional development for its faculty, greater satisfaction of its learners by offering some of its classes electronically, and the potential to be on the cutting edge if it is suddenly faced with reduced state funding and the resulting need to expand its student population.

"What If" Scenarios

Although an ROI calculation might be done for only one set of values and their accompanying assumptions, it may be desirable to experiment with a variety of "what if" scenarios based on different assumptions to determine their impact on the results. For example, if one of the assumptions is that the cost of developing Web-based modules will be $5,000 each, what would be the effect of that cost increasing to $6,000? Or, if the assumed rate of student retention across courses is projected to be 80%, what is the impact if it turns out to be only 60%? Sometimes what appears to be a small difference in a variable can have a major impact on the results. Understanding the interaction of the cost and benefit variables at this deeper level adds considerably to one's understanding of what is necessary to make a DE project financially successful.

Using a variety of "what ifs" to test the impact of each cost variable may promote better project planning and management. For example, using a piece of commercial software rather than something in the public domain may have little impact on total costs but have substantial benefits to learners and module developers. Similarly, if the relative weight of each benefits variable is known, as the project is implemented, the actual numbers can be compared to those projected to see if the project might need to be expanded, contracted, or perhaps even terminated before its completion.

Presenting decision-makers with a variety of analyses based on different values may be an excellent way to insure that they carefully consider their options. It also draws them into "owning" the project, since they played a role in determining the assumptions upon which the decision was made to proceed. Spreadsheet programs are ideal for calculating results based on different assumptions and can display the results in easily read charts, graphs, and tables.

Before, During, and After Analysis

Although most of the discussion so far has talked about performing cost and benefit analysis before commencing a project, as the title of this chapter implies, it is also desirable to do analysis during and after the project. As actual cost figures begin to become available, they can be compared to those from the original estimate, and if they differ widely, a new cost and benefits analysis can be conducted. In some cases, cost overruns (there never seem to be underruns) may be able to be accommodated if the benefits, too, are more than anticipated. In other situations, increased costs may call for terminating a project early. Enroute benefits data may become available if, for example, a series of DE courses is to be developed and implemented one at a time. Initial enrollment numbers and the retention rates of those completing each course and signing up for subsequent courses might be of particular importance to an educational institution. Or, a corporation might examine the impact of training received to date on sales or other benefits measures for those who have received the training to determine whether to continue to train others, modify the design, or perhaps even abort the effort.

Analysis after a project is complete, or at a previously agreed upon date after implementation (e.g., one or two years), can confirm the benefits are in fact being obtained, or perhaps that they are not. In either event, the organization should want to know periodically what the results have been. As reported in the two books of case studies of training interventions by Phillips (1994, 1997) the results can be very positive. However, there are no doubt many cases with the opposite results that will likely never see the light of day.

This leads us back to a point we made earlier but which bears repeating. The lack of almost any cost and benefit data from DE efforts is most disappointing, and if those in the field fail to address this shortcoming, the long-term prospects for its continued expansion are seriously diminished. We further believe that a critical first step in planning any DE project should be for all stakeholders to agree on all costs and benefits, and how to measure them, as part of the overall project plan.

Consider the ways in which examining ROI before, during, and after the implementation of a statewide distance learning project might have saved the project, or at least provided more feedback to stakeholders. This statewide distance learning system was unique, in that it included state sponsorship and start-up funding, creation of an independent office and board of directors, and the integration of three types of networks within one office. The goal was to provide ongoing educational opportunities for both rural and urban citizens. For seven years, the system struggled. Prior to the beginning of the system a quasi-needs assessment was conducted; however, a significant demand for the programming was not established. No effort was made to evaluate the consumers' satisfaction or willingness to pay real costs of delivering courses to remote corners of the state. Because the state was losing money throughout the seven years, no funding was committed to upgrades of technology as the years passed.

Had those involved planned for and conducted some form of ROI before they began, they might have been able to give a more accurate estimation of true costs of establishing and operating the system. Given a realization that the break-even point might never be reached, perhaps state funders would have been able to identify important non-financial reasons for supporting the system, or perhaps made a determination to scrape the entire project. Instead, this project became a political football, limping along until it was barely serving the rural and underserved populations. In this instance, lack of planning and failing to collect and analyze any cost and benefit data have cast doubt on the whole concept of learning at a distance.

References

Carnevale, A., & Schultz, E. (1990). Return on investment: Accounting for training. Supplement to the July issue of *Training and Development Journal,* S1–S32.

Charron, E., & Obbink, K. (1993). Long-distance learning: Continuing your education through telecommunications. *The Science Teacher, 60*(3), 56–60.

Decker, C., & Campbell, C. (1996). *Determining the cost effectiveness of training (A self-contained instructional module).* ERIC Clearinghouse, ED 394 045.

Garrison, D. R., & Shale, D. (Eds.). (1990). *Education at a distance: From issues to practice.* Malabar, FL: Robert E. Krieger Publishing Company.

Gustafson, K., & Watkins, K. (1998). Return on investment (ROI): An idea whose time has come—again. *Educational Technology, 38*(4), 5–6.

Mager, R. F. (1996). Morphing into a 21st century trainer. *Training, 33*(6), 47–54.

Mason, R., & Kaye, T. (1990). Toward a new paradigm for distance education. In L. Harasim (Ed.), *Online education: Perspectives on a new environment* (pp. 15–38). New York: Praeger.

Moore, M. G., & Thompson, M. M. (1990). *The effects of distance learning: A summary of the literature.* (Vol. 2). University Park, PA: American Center for the Study of Distance Education.

Phillips, J. (1994). *In Action: Measuring return on investment.* Alexandria, VA: American Society for Training and Development.

Phillips, J. (1997). *Measuring return on investment: Volume 2.* Alexandria, VA: American Society for Training and Development.

Phillips, J. (1998). The return on investment (ROI) process: Trends and Issues. *Educational Technology, 38*(4), 7–14.

The Authors

Kent L. Gustafson (e-mail: kgustafs@coe.uga.edu; Web homepage: itech1.coe.uga.edu/gustafson.html) is Professor and Chair, Instructional Technology Department, the University of Georgia, Athens, Georgia. **Lynne Schrum** (e-mail: Lschrum@coe.uga.edu; Web homepage: itech1.coe.uga.edu/schrum.html) is Associate Professor, Instructional Technology Department, the University of Georgia.

63

Usability Testing and Return-on-Investment Studies: Key Evaluation Strategies for Web-Based Training

Thomas C. Reeves and

Bryan J. Carter

Introduction

The evaluation of training has long been the subject of more academic discussion than actual practice. The classic "four level" model of training evaluation was first proposed by Kirkpatrick (1959, 1994) more than 40 years ago. Although Phillips (1994) added the conception of Level V evaluation as "Return On Investment" (see Figure 1), the Kirkpatrick/Phillips model continues to be the dominant conception of how training evaluation ought to be done. However, according to Moller and Mallin (1996) and other critics of training development practices, there is little evidence that instructional designers or others involved in the training enterprise actually conduct "adequate evaluations" at any level.

Is this criticism justified? It must be acknowledged that what is considered "adequate" in terms of evaluation is different from organization to organization and time to time. Every organization develops its own norms for acceptable levels of evaluation as well as expectations for the influence of evaluation on decision-making. For example, when times are good and budgets are generous, a training group may conduct level one evaluation activities simply to find out whether employees like training, and as long as satisfaction levels are high, management is happy. The same group may be compelled to provide level three, four, or even five evidence when budget cuts are imminent and down-sizing is in the wind. Further, although low level evaluations are clearly inadequate in many contexts, higher levels of evaluation often appear to cost more than many organizations are prepared to pay.

The reluctance of organizations to invest in evaluation is short-sighted, given that more and more dollars are being spent on training on all kinds, representing annual expenditures in the billions of dollars on the part of corporations, governments, and other agencies around the globe. The need for training and retraining workers has never been greater than at the dawn of the 21st century. A relatively new technology-based approach is Web-based training (WBT), the subject of this book. Just as training programs in general have not been subjected to in-depth evaluation, the history of technological innovations in training is no better with respect to the

Level V—ROI	Did the benefits of the training exceed its costs?
Level IV—Results	Did the training have any benefits, e.g., improve profits?
Level III—Behavior	Did participants change their on-the-job behavior?
Level II—Learning	Did participants' knowledge, skills, and attributes improve?
Level I—Reaction	Did participants like the training?

Figure 1. Five levels of training evaluation (Kirkpatrick, 1994; Phillips, 1994).

application of reliable and valid evaluation strategies. We would like to propose that things could and should be different with respect to WBT! Therefore, our goal in this chapter is to describe two different strategies, usability testing and return-on-investment studies, that have the potential to improve the state of practice of WBT, and in the process, build more support for evaluation. But first, we wish to clarify our rationale for evaluating WBT.

A Decision-Oriented Rationale for Evaluation

When selecting a site for a new business, it is commonplace to say that the three most important criteria are "Location, Location, Location." Similarly, in the process of evaluating WBT, the three most important criteria are "Decisions, Decisions, Decisions." In other words, your primary focus should be on the decisions your evaluation must influence. Whether your WBT role is development, implementation, or management, you must make decisions. Should content be organized using a hierarchical or conceptual model? Should your WBT training be accessible via all browsers or should you rely upon the features of one specific browser? Should WBT navigation be under trainee or program control? Should the training budget be cut because WBT has decreased the need for classroom space? Or should the budget be increased to hire more Java programmers? These and other decisions will be made, regardless of whether evaluations are done or not. Such decisions are often made on the basis of experience, habit, politics, guessing, or in many cases, just plain ignorance.

Another, and arguably better, basis for making these kinds of decisions is the information provided by evaluation. For example, in the process of developing, implementing, or managing WBT, you may interview subject matter experts about ways of presenting complex content, submit prototype versions of the WBT to usability testing, or even conduct a ROI study of your WBT program. None of these activities (interviewing, usability testing, or ROI) is especially complicated in and of itself, and there are a few useful guides to help you (e.g., Brown & Seidner, 1997; Flagg, 1990; Kirkpatrick, 1994; Newby, 1992; Phillips, 1994). In practice, most evaluations involve activities that are relatively simple in concept. However, all of these procedures require skillful application at appropriate times. Most of all, they require a willingness to make evaluation an integral part of development, implementation, and management processes because of the belief that evidence-based decision-making is better than the aforementioned alternatives.

It is beyond the scope of this chapter to present complete guidelines for evaluating WBT throughout the development, implementation, and management processes. There is only space to highlight two strategies that we believe have great potential for enhancing evaluations of WBT. These are usability testing and return-on-investment (ROI) studies.

Usability Testing

According to Shneiderman (1987), usability of any type of computer program is a combination of the following user-oriented characteristics: (1) ease of learning, (2) high speed of user task performance, (3) low user error rate, (4) subjective user satisfaction, and (5) user retention over time. Hix and Hartson (1993) and Nielsen (1993) provide expert guidance to evaluating user interface issues, a process known as usability testing.

Three major usability classifications are efficiency, user satisfaction, and effectiveness. Characteristics such as cost savings, time savings (via low user error rate or efficient design), or minimizing training time fall under the classification of efficiency and are obvious concerns for any organization making the investment in WBT. Ease of use, perceived benefit vs. time invested, intuitiveness, and visual appeal are generally classified ás user satisfaction. User satisfaction is often measured using level one evaluation strategies, e.g., a satisfaction survey (Kirkpatrick, 1994). Immediate retention, retention over time, and transfer to actual job performance are categorized as effectiveness. Effectiveness encompasses both benefits to the learner and to the organization. Ironically, effectiveness is the least likely classification to be measured, even though it is the primary intent of training in most cases.

In evaluating the usability of Web-based training environments, it is important to recognize that any given evaluation can become dated quickly. This is related to the swiftly changing technical environment that has been persistent since the Web's conception. Ever-increasing technical innovation has occurred despite the most commonly cited problem with the Web, that of bandwidth. Although the bandwidth problem has not significantly improved, technology wizards and electronic entrepreneurs have adapted by finding ways to squeeze more into the same space rather than waiting for the technology to accommodate the increasing demand for bandwidth. The experience of using the Web, once a painfully slow experience characterized as the "World Wide Wait," is increasingly efficient. At the same time, new media features and interactions are also evolving, many of which push the existing bandwidth to its limits. Given this context, it seems doubtful that the need for usability testing will decrease, and we argue that it becomes more important for training developers and their clients as the dependence on innovations such as WBT increase.

Some trainers are drawn to WBT because the nature of the Web lends itself to quick updates, making the Web a perfect habitat for volatile training content that can be developed via a rapid prototyping approach. Although this is a great advantage in some respects, it also means that the shelf-life of any given usability evaluation is severely limited as content, user interface, and interactivity evolve. Whatever degree of usability testing you undertake, you must take into account the ever-changing nature of the Web. Usability testing must be able to happen quickly. It must allow for quick modifications, which means that the process must be flexible and easily modified—a real concern for any formal usability testing process.

We will describe two methods of testing that seem to work best when used together. The first addresses usability testing with a small local audience and the second approach addresses a larger, often dispersed audience via a form of rapid prototyping. Neither method is sufficient in and of itself, although they can be (and often are) used separately.

When the user audience available for usability testing is small and personally accessible, a formative, one-on-one approach can be very effective in gathering in-depth, detailed feedback. Figure 2 outlines one approach to this type of usability testing. (The chapter in this volume by Michael Hughes and Loren Burke provides much more detail about a more formal approach to this type of usability testing.)

Our experience has shown that one- to two-hour sessions where a single user is observed, then personally interviewed, can provide more accurate feedback than many group studies. Just four or five participants can provide sufficient information to complete a study of a WBT prod-

1. Pretest	A very short pretest, five minutes at most, that captures the participant's basic personal information, preconceptions of the medium being used, and possibly a survey of methods available to the individual to access the training.
2. Observation	Quietly observing the individual in a hands-on environment with the software. During this time the observer carefully notes the actions, frustrations, and levity of the participant as designated tasks are completed, only speaking when absolutely critical to the participant's progress (and making note of the intervention).
3. Post-test	A short post-test to gather level one feedback along with comparison data to measure changes in preconceptions captured on the pretest.
4. Candid Interview	Finally, a very open and candid interview in which the interviewer uses techniques to draw out design suggestions and concerns as well as praise. In this session, the interviewer may represent the vision of the product, whereas, previously, the interviewer was required to maintain secrecy and let the product speak for itself.

Figure 2. A one-on-one session may consist of four simple steps.

uct. Because of the small number of participants, this approach is more easily arranged than those with larger groups, and can be completed in one to three days, depending on the facility and availability of facilitators and participants.

When conducting one-on-one usability studies, it is very helpful to maintain a relaxed and informal atmosphere to encourage participant feedback, both negative and positive. Without proper rapport, the participant will likely be less open and may even undermine the study through uptight indifference. With experience, you can develop the skills to conduct usability testing at the minimum level of formality required to obtain strong evidence.

If there is sufficient funding, WBT designers should utilize the services of an outside, un-biased party, or better, a professional usability testing service (see Hughes and Burke chapter in this volume). If funding is modest, designers may choose to conduct their own usability testing, possibly using portable usability lab equipment.

Once usability testing has been conducted, a modification of a rapid prototyping strategy can be used to improve the WBT product based upon user feedback. If the audience for WBT is dispersed and/or large, special "pop-up questions" incorporated in the Web-based training can gather feedback in real time. Suppose the components of a WBT module are designed with the expectation that learners will interact with them within a limited range of sequences. If a learner diverges from one of the expected paths in the WBT program, a pop-up window can appear that requests feedback (as illustrated in Figure 3). This rapid prototyping approach usu-ally involves having an instructional designer and a programmer review the feedback as soon as it arrives so that they can resolve design issues or fix bugs on the fly as quickly as possible. In-formation about other issues, such as navigation errors and content misunderstandings, can also be captured via tracking and pop-up questions. Problems can be resolved, possibly within min-utes or hours of discovery. This method of "rapid prototyping" promotes the evolution of a WBT prototype into a robust instructional product. The issues that are raised become fewer and fewer as revisions are implemented. Web-based delivery allows training to be deployed in real time. Thus, the training product being reviewed is always current, a clear advantage over other software based approaches where delivery is static.

When you completed the last section of the module, we expected you to choose at least one practice exam, but you have selected to go to the final exam. Please indicate your reason for this choice:

- I don't need a practice exam because I am ready to take the final.
- I forgot there were practice exams, and I'd like to go back and try one now.
- Other (Please explain in the space below):

Figure 3. Pop-up question to be used in WBT.

In our experience, using the above usability testing and rapid prototyping methods in tandem is extremely effective. Ideally, beginning with personal one-on-one usability testing flushes out larger, deeper design issues early. Following up with a Web-based remote evaluation on the tested design enables bugs in the software and in the content to be quickly worked out of the WBT product.

As in most forms of evaluation, an important consideration in usability testing is that of expense. Since WBT development tools and resulting products are changing so rapidly, deciding how much should be invested in evaluation is a constant challenge. At the highest levels of management, where the cost savings to be realized from Web-based training (compared to more traditional approaches) are of maximum importance, the business case for evaluation must be made concerning the overall benefits of evaluation rather than by looking at the specifics of an individual usability test. Determining the usability of a particular type of animation may not be worth the expense, especially considering that the technology may change overnight or the impact of the animation may be negligible, whereas testing the usability of the primary navigation options or the interactions involved in critical skill assessment is essential. It is important to target stable aspects of WBT when justifying the expense of a usability study.

An interesting aspect of WBT design is the reoccurrence of interface speed issues that have been present in the beginnings of all computer delivery trends, including floppy drives, and more recently, CD-ROM-based software. Speed issues have all but disappeared when evaluating CD-ROM based or hard disk based software. However, the issue of speed remains a big issue on the Web, perhaps bigger than it ever was for CD-ROM based or hard-disk based software. (Isn't it strange that just as we get used to quicker speeds with one technology, e.g., CD-ROM, a new one comes along that requires us to go back to waiting . . . and the new one still catches on?)

Inevitably, in addition to financial concerns, every design team will be forced to deal with the issue of download time versus production quality and media choice. Graphics, video and audio are costly in terms of required bandwidth and, depending upon the weakest link in the delivery chain, may be unattainable as a group or individually. On the other hand, the technology is improving almost daily, and what is not available today will probably be available in

Technology Issues	User Issues
What is the delivery platform of the user?	What is the experience of the WBT as
What support issues exist?	seen through the eyes of the user?
What's the user's access?	**Most common complaints**
	Too slow
Speed?	Too difficult to find the information being
T1, ISDN, 14.4K–56K, Cable Modems	sought
	Too many levels
Browsing?	Meaningless or improper categorization
Internet Explorer, Netscape Communicator,	Redundant titles for different links
WebTV, etc.	Can't see past "the look"
	Meaningless screens and graphics are
Physical location?	not as endurable when you have to
Local, intranet, Internet, hybrid	wait
Servers	
Server speed and connections	
The use of server-based software such as Java,	
PERL, etc.	
Versions, plug-ins, etc.	
Installations, updates, legacy software, configuration,	
browser compatibility, cookies, etc.	

Figure 4. Typical criteria for evaluating the usability of WBT.

the near future. Of course, the brief history of the Web has shown that whatever is available is rarely enough. Therefore, setting expectations for bandwidth, delivery methods, and where concessions will be made are all very important decisions for the design team, decisions that can and should be informed by usability testing.

It is beyond the scope of this chapter to describe all the criteria for evaluating usability, but we believe that when designing usability tests for WBT, it is important to consider both technology and user aspects, as listed in Figure 4. Technology issues require that the usability testing occur using systems and connectivity exactly like that to be experienced by the intended users. User issues require that the people in the testing be as much like the real users as possible.

Return-on-Investment (ROI) Evaluation

Another approach to evaluating training, increasingly popular in corporate settings, is called "return on investment" (ROI) evaluation. More and more training personnel are being called upon to conduct ROI studies to demonstrate that the resources expended on training programs have yielded profits or benefits that exceed their costs. This is a difficult task, but not an impossible one. Unfortunately, there may well be more theoretical models for conducting ROI studies than there are practical examples of their application.

Medsker and Roberts (1992) describe a return on investment (ROI) study conducted by a large company whose business is delivering packages overnight. This company relies upon an accurate, highly motivated workforce. Before sending them out into the field, new delivery personnel are subjected to an intensive and expensive two-week training course. To demonstrate the value of the training, the training department conducted a risky experiment. They allowed 20 new employees who had only been given a brief safety-training program to start delivering packages without the two week training program. They compared their performance with that of 20 new employees who had completed the training and with 20 veteran delivery personnel. They found that the trained new employees made far fewer mistakes than the untrained workers, and that the savings resulting from their lack of errors more than made up for the costs of the training program. Ironically, they also found that the veteran employees made almost as many mistakes as the novices, indicating a serious need for retraining. (Perhaps WBT could remedy this problem!)

Essentially, ROI involves comparing the costs of training to its effectiveness and benefits (Kearsley, 1993; Phillips, 1994). In some contexts, cost-effectiveness and cost-benefit studies will involve complex and controversial methodologies. These studies are difficult to conduct and defend because whenever you begin to put actual monetary figures on various effects and benefits, others who have a stake in a different set of values will challenge your calculations. It is also difficult in many contexts to calculate the actual costs of developing and implementing WBT. In the business world, some training departments are included as an overhead cost charged to all departments, whereas in others there is an internal charging system whereby various units pay for training within the company. This is complicated further when development and delivery budgets are divided, as the sponsors may only be interested in the piece of the project they are funding and will base decisions on their interests rather than considering the holistic impact on their company or organization. Increasingly, large and small corporations are contracting outside vendors for training and development, but there are still costs within the corporations for those responsible for managing these outside contracts.

If the costs of developing and implementing WBT are hard to track, the monetary values that can be attached to various effects and benefits are even more difficult to calculate. If sales go up in a retail organization, that type of effect is relatively easy to detect (although often difficult to attribute directly to a particular training program). However, what monetary value should be attached to improved morale on the assembly line? What is the life worth that may have been saved as a result of the new interactive multimedia WBT about safety in the workplace? What are the financial costs of the "mindshare" or brand loyalty that might be lost when customers and/or employees suffer through poorly designed WBT? Despite these and other difficulties, there is great interest in investigating ROI of WBT. Initial investments in the infrastructure for WBT may be driven by a desire to be on the "cutting edge" or by the persuasive powers of dynamic individuals within an organization, but over the long haul, the cost effectiveness of interactive training on the Web will have to be supported through rigorous evaluation.

ROI studies are sometimes confused with simple cost comparison studies. Figure 5 presents a hypothetical cost comparison between two alternative methods of training flight attendants for an airline. Although such a cost analysis might be useful when trying to promote WBT within a corporation, it is not the same as a ROI evaluation.

ROI studies involve calculating the percentage of return for a dollar invested in training or another intervention. Phillips (1997) provides a simple formula for calculating ROI as:

$$\text{ROI (\%)} = \frac{\text{net program benefits}}{\text{program costs}} \times 100$$

Phillips (1994) provides eighteen case studies of ROI studies in corporate training contexts, although none utilize WBT per se.

How can Phillips' ROI formula be applied to WBT? Figure 6 illustrates an ROI study for WBT. The Ajax Steel Company is confronting an absentee problem such that employees are averaging 2.7 days away from work per month at a cost of $200 per day per employee. There

Problem: Alpha Airlines must provide 10,000 flight attendants with training every year to maintain certification by the Federal Aviation Administration (FAA)

Traditional Training Program: Flight attendants (10,000) are flown to the corporate base in Dallas twice a year for FAA mandated safety training. Training sessions are leader-led with heavy use of airplane mock-ups. Costs per attendant per training session are listed below.

Travel Costs	$300
Hotel Costs	$100
Per Diem	$50
Average Training Costs	$50
Salary Paid to Attendant During Training	$150
Total	$650
Total Training Program Costs Per Year Based on Two Yearly Training Sessions for 10,000 Flight Attendants	**$13,000,000**

New Training Program: Flight attendants (10,000) are flown to corporate base in Dallas once a year for FAA mandated safety training. Training sessions are leader-led with heavy use of airplane mock-ups. Costs per attendant per training session remain at $650. The *other day of training* is accomplished using WBT distributed to all 25 Alpha Airlines bases around the country. Flight attendants accomplish the training objectives while waiting between flights. Travel, hotel, per diem, and salary costs are eliminated. WBT development and implementation costs are listed below.

WBT Development Costs	$1,800,000
WBT Delivery Systems Costs	$ 500,000
WBT Maintenance Costs	$ 200,000
Total	$2,500,000
Total Training Program Costs Per Year Based on One Yearly Training Session Plus WBT for 10,000 Flight Attendants	**$9,000,000**

First Year Savings = $4,000,000

Figure 5. Hypothetical cost analysis of WBT.

are 5,000 employees in the company, so the annual costs of absenteeism exceed 32 million dollars. The training department produces a WBT program for all employees that clarifies the effects of absenteeism on corporate profits and worker profit sharing rates. The primary goal of the program is to motivate employees and lower absenteeism. The cost of the WBT and the infrastructure to provide Web access to employees are 3 million dollars, and after three months of usage, the absenteeism rate has fallen to 1.8 days per month. Using Phillips' formula, the ROI for the first year would be 260% or for every dollar spent on training, $2.60 in benefits are realized. Although this may seem high, the eighteen case studies in Phillips' (1994) book report ROI values ranging from 150% to 2,000 % for training investments.

Although the benefits of conducting ROI studies may appear obvious, there are reasons why they are not carried out more often. It has been our experience that a ROI is high on the list of casualties of a reduced evaluation budget. Or, in many cases, the perception exists that the primary purpose for a ROI is to do a cost comparison of the new solution (e.g., WBT) with the method or solution being replaced (e.g., face-to-face training) (as illustrated in Figure 5).

When an organization is considering whether to invest in WBT, management will likely have an interest in seeing how other companies are (or are not) saving money with WBT—especially the competition. This same interest in ROI may not carry over once the decision to develop WBT has been made within an organization. If management has decided that WBT is

---

Problem: Ajax Steel workers are averaging 2.7 days per month absenteeism rates. At an average cost of $200 per day and 5000 workers, company losses exceed 32 million dollars per year.

Solution: WBT is provided to all employees to motivate them and lower absenteeism. Absentee rates fall to 1.8 days per month.

ROI Calculation: The first year savings are projected at 10.8 million. The ROI formula requires calculation of net program benefits (10.8 million minus 3 million equals 7.8 million) and dividing by the program costs as illustrated below.

$$\text{ROI (\%)} = \frac{7,800,000}{3,000,000} \times 100$$

$$\text{ROI (\%)} = 260\%$$

First Year Results = For each dollar spent on WBT, $2.60 in benefits are realized.

Figure 6. Hypothetical ROI study of WBT.

the appropriate solution to training needs, poor ROI results could embarrass the decision-makers, and therefore management may avoid the risk of finding anything other than positive results.

In other situations, ROI studies may be regarded as analogous to buying a service contract for new hardware. If a company has a fixed budget and can buy 20 multimedia worksta-tions for a training lab or 15 stations plus an extended service contract, a decision can be made either way. A company may opt for more computers without the service contract because if one or two stations should die in the next couple of years, the company may still break even or be ahead. On the other hand, the decision may be made to buy fewer workstations and purchase a strong service contract to avoid the risk of loss or repair expenses. A third scenario describes something in between, a few more computers but with lesser support. The decision of whether or not to do an ROI will be biased based on the perceived value and criticality of a ROI study.

In many cases, the existing perception and requirement set forth for ROI is simply to compare the cost of a newly implemented intervention to the one previously used; thus, as-suming equal and sufficient validity for both solutions. Although this is a valid point of view from someone managing a budget and trying to fill a curriculum on paper, it completely dis-regards impact of different training approaches on the audience. To someone unfamiliar with the evaluation of educational products, a cost comparison may appear to fall in the same cate-gory as Level V ROI evaluation. It is clear that a cost comparison is useful for those with their eye on the budget; however, a simple cost comparison which disregards educational benefits completely misses the point of ROI, which is designed to measure the benefit of the program first and compare it to the cost of implementation. Otherwise, comparing educational solutions is like comparing securities based on price alone.

It is common that interest in ROI is rekindled once a project has reached completion and is being deployed. Not surprisingly, given human nature to support a "winner," products that appear most successful attract the greatest interest for ROI results. Generally speaking, no one wants to invest money in a ROI for a product that has clearly failed. It would only highlight mistakes that may have been made in design, production, or implementation. If a product simply meets expectations, again, little interest in ROI exists. Sponsors generally feel confident enough that assumed results are achieved, since the product performed as expected.

Certainly a ROI study won't shed any more glory on the project. However, when a product appears wildly successful, suddenly a great interest in measuring the success of the product emerges. Those who feel threatened by the success of the project grow suspicious and would like to see a ROI in order to ferret out information that can support their suspicions. Likewise, those who would like to be empowered to create similar products seek the knowledge a ROI provides to be able to build a case for their own attempts at such works. It is our experience that successful products are a good basis to begin growing a ROI practice within an agency, since they generate the most interest and acceptance from all parties.

In cases where a ROI study is approved, there are some important considerations. A good ROI study will demand much more effort and expertise than the routine level one "smilometer" evaluation that usually suffices for training evaluation in many companies. In addition, support for ROI evaluation may shift depending upon the stage of WBT development. Clearly, the freedom to conduct a ROI evaluation is often limited. However, there are times when the nature of the knowledge, skills, attitudes, cost, and strategic value inherent in the objectives of a WBT program may be so important that nothing less than a full-scale ROI is required.

The Realities of WBT Evaluation

Organizationally, an alternative delivery system such as WBT most often becomes adopted for its perceived effectiveness at a lower cost. Among training developers and their clients, this perception derives largely from industry news of how other companies, particularly competing companies, are saving money by using the new technology. Such industry news inevitably involves more hype than real evidence for greater or equal effectiveness at lower costs. Nonetheless, within any given organization, there is usually a grass-roots campaign to try a new approach such as WBT, often strongest in the developer community and low-level management. There may also be a contingent in the ranks that is diametrically opposed to the new approach because of job security issues or the unwillingness to do something new. In any event, once there is support from upper management within the organization, the game changes and the challenge of implementing an alternative delivery approach such as WBT cascades down the ranks.

At this point, perhaps the most important decision-makers are those in middle management positions. They are usually not experts in training development, let alone alternative delivery systems. Those in middle management are, however, quick to identify with cost and time issues. They may still be resistant to change, as managers tend to be once they establish a working system. Uncertainty does not sit well with most middle managers. Ideally, what will win this group over is evidence that the new approach works, that it is relatively easy to manage, that it results in time and money savings, and that it is at least as effective as the company's current solution. This kind of evidence only comes from good evaluation. Other common influences on middle managers are corporate push, perceived value/hype (from trade magazines, conferences, documented success stories and word of mouth), and/or the political persuasiveness of a few dynamic individuals from the design/development side or upper management that can sell the idea and make them a bit more confident in the success of such an endeavor.

Given the lack of strong belief in or support for evaluation among middle managers and other decision-makers, we believe that it is important to make careful, strategic investments in evaluation. Most managers only want the results of evaluations when it is convenient and inexpensive. Fortunately, evaluations do not have to be difficult, expensive, or risky. For example, we have outlined relatively inexpensive strategies for informal usability testing. ROI studies are inherently more costly (and involve more inference) than usability testing, and therefore, ROI evaluations are only recommended when the stakes are sufficiently high. As an important first step, we recommend moving beyond the ubiquitous level one (Did the learners like it?)

evaluations to usability testing as a form of formative evaluation. In doing so, the support for more substantive summative evaluation, perhaps even ROI, will be nurtured within the organization. The bottom line is that evaluation is not an inherently attractive practice for most people, and therefore, like physical exercise, it must be introduced slowly and carefully monitored. The good news is that, done with care, evaluation inevitably will prove its worth.

References

Bennett, G. J., & Clasper, T. D. (1993). Training evaluation. In G. M. Piskurich (Ed.), *The ASTD handbook of instructional technology* (pp. 29.1–29.26). New York: McGraw-Hill.

Brown, S. M., & Seidner, C. J. (1997). *Evaluating corporate training: Models and issues.* Norwell, MA: Kluwer Academic Publications.

Flagg, B. N. (1990). *Formative evaluation for educational technologies.* Hillsdale, NJ: Lawrence Erlbaum Associates.

Hix, D., & Hartson, H. R. (1993). *Developing user interfaces: Ensuring usability through product & process.* New York: John Wiley & Sons.

Kearsley, G. (1993). Costs and benefits of technology-based instruction. In G. M. Piskurich (Ed.), *The ASTD handbook of instructional technology* (pp. 16.1–16.19). New York: McGraw-Hill.

Kirkpatrick, D. L. (1994). *Evaluating training programs: The four levels.* San Francisco: Berrett-Koehler Publishers. (First published in 1959.)

Lewis, T. (1996). A model of thinking about the evaluation of training. *Performance Improvement Quarterly, 9*(1), 3–22.

Mark, M. M., & Shotland, R. L. (Eds.). (1987). *Multiple methods in program evaluation.* San Francisco: Jossey-Bass.

Medsker, K. L., & Roberts, D. G. (Eds.). (1992). *ASTD trainer's toolkit: Evaluating the results of training.* American Society for Training and Development.

Moller, L., & Mallin, P. (1996). Evaluation practices of instructional designers and organizational supports and barriers. *Performance Improvement Quarterly, 9*(4), 82–92.

Newby, A. C. (1992). *Training evaluation handbook.* San Diego: Pfeiffer & Company.

Nielsen, J. (1993). *Usability engineering.* Boston: Academic Press.

Phillips, J. J. (1994). *In action: Measuring return on investment.* Alexandria, VA: American Society for Training and Development.

Phillips, J. J. (1997). *Return on investment in training and performance improvement programs.* Houston: Gulf Publishing Company.

Reeves, T. C. (1993). Evaluating technology-based learning. In G. M. Piskurich (Ed.), *The ASTD handbook of instructional technology* (pp. 15.1–15.32). New York: McGraw-Hill.

Shneiderman, B. (1987). *Designing the user interface: Strategies for effective human-computer interaction.* Reading, MA: Addison-Wesley.

Shadish, W. R., Cook, T. D., & Leviton, L. C. (1991). *Foundations of program evaluation: Theories of practice.* Newbury Park, CA: Sage Publications.

The Authors

Thomas C. Reeves (e-mail: treeves@coe.uga.edu; Web homepage: itech1.coe.uga.edu/Reeves.html) is Professor of Instructional Technology at the University of Georgia, Athens, Georgia. **Bryan J. Carter** (e-mail: bryancarter@learningatplay.com; Web homepage: learningatplay.com), formerly with NCR Corporation, is now an interactive learning systems consultant, specializing in immersive gaming environments.

Author Index

Subject Index

A

About the Editor

While growing up in Chittagong, Bangladesh during the 1970s, Badrul H. Khan used to dream about having access to well-designed learning resources available only to students in industrialized countries. In the '70s, it was unthinkable to have equal access to those resources. In the '90s, with the emergence of the World Wide Web, Khan's dream of equal access to quality learning resources became a reality. His desire for broadly available distributed learning systems and his scholarly grounding in the field of educational systems design and technology have enabled him to present a total vision for educational and training possibilities of the new worldwide communications technologies.

Through his teaching and publishing, Dr. Khan has been instrumental in creating a coherent framework for Web-based instruction, training, and learning. In his first book, *Web-Based Instruction* (1997), he took a leadership role in defining the critical dimensions of this new field of inquiry and practice at all levels of education. Researchers and practitioners in distributed learning from all over the world supported his vision for Web-based instruction (WBI) by contributing to the book. Reflecting its enormous acceptance, *Web-Based Instruction* has become a bestseller and has been adopted by colleges and universities worldwide. In this new book, *Web-Based Training,* Khan explores the role of the Web in training. He continues to advance the discourse in the field of distributed learning.

He is currently working on a new book, *Web-Based Learning,* which will include case studies, design models and strategies, and critical issues encompassing the multiple dimensions of his Web-Based Learning Framework. He is also hard at work on a book devoted to online learning strategies entitled *E-Learning Strategies,* and he is helping to establish virtual universities in communities around the world.

The most sought-after keynote speaker in Web-based learning, Khan is past President of the International Division of the Association for Educational Communications and Technology (AECT). He is a contributing editor of *Educational Technology,* a consulting editor of *The International Review of Research in Open and Distance Learning,* and a member of the editorial board of *Distance Education.* He is founder of *BooksToRead.com* (a recommended readings site), *AuthorWeb.net* (a comprehensive authoring system), and *WebCourseReview.com* (a course review site).

Dr. Khan is currently associate professor and Director of the Educational Technology Leadership graduate cohort program at the George Washington University. Previously, he served as assistant professor of education and the founding Director of the Educational Technology graduate program at the University of Texas, Brownsville. He served as instructional developer and evaluation specialist in the School of Medicine at Indiana University, Indianapolis. He received a B.A. in Chemistry and a Ph.D. in Instructional Systems Technology from Indiana University, Bloomington. His personal Website is: **BadrulKhan.com/profile/khan**